THROUGH OUR ENEMIES' EYES

Also by Michael Scheuer

Imperial Hubris: Why the West Is Losing the War on Terror

THROUGH OUR ENEMIES' EYES

Osama bin Laden, Radical Islam, and the Future of America

Revised Edition

Michael Scheuer

Potomac Books, Inc.
Washington, D.C.

*For the brilliant officers of Alec who gave America opportunities not taken.
They now know, with Lieutenant General Daniel Harvey Hill (C.S.A.), that
"it is unfortunate to have different views from the rest of mankind.
It secures abuse."*

and

*For the Bay, past and present; the Class of '52; the Inchon-Chongju Duo;
Ranch Hands Beth and Bernice; and, as always, "So long, Chiefy."*

and

*For America's clandestine service and the U.S. Marine Corps — bringers
of victory, if unleashed.*

Library of Congress Cataloging-in-Publication Data
Scheuer, Michael.
Through our enemies' eyes : Osama bin Laden, radical Islam, and the future of America / Michael Scheuer. — 2nd ed.
    p. cm.
First edition published: Washington, D.C.: Brassey's, c2002, and entered under title.
Includes bibliographical references and index.
ISBN 1-57488-967-2 (pbk.: alk. paper)
1. Bin Laden, Osama, 1957- 2. Terrorists — Saudi Arabia — Biography. 3. Jihad.
4. Violence — Religious aspects — Islam. 5. Qaida (Organization) 6. Terrorism —
Government policy — United States. I. Title.
HV6430.B55.S34 2006
958.104'6'092 — dc22

2005024233

Printed in the United States of America on acid-free paper that meets the American National Standards Institute Z39-48 Standard.

Potomac Books, Inc.
22841 Quicksilver Drive
Dulles, Virginia 20166

Second Edition

10 9 8 7 6 5 4 3 2 1

Contents

Foreword by Bruce Hoffman   vii

Preface to Revised Edition   ix

Preface   xv

Acknowledgments   xix

Introduction   xxi

Part 1: Context

1. Context for Understanding bin Laden's Aims   3

Part 2: Arrogance, Money, and Ideas

2. Obstacles to Understanding bin Laden   17

3. Chasing bin Laden's Money   31

4. Getting to Know bin Laden: Substantive Themes
of the Jihad   45

5. Getting to Know bin Laden: Character Traits   75

Part 3: Years of Preparation, 1957–1996

6. The Young bin Laden, 1957–1979: Family, Education,
and Religion   85

7. Bin Laden and the Afghan War, 1979–1989: Facilitator,
Engineer, Fighter, and Visionary   97

8. Bin Laden and the Saudis, 1989–1991: From Favorite
Son to Black Sheep   119

9. Bin Laden in Exile: Afghanistan and Sudan, 1991–1996   129

10. Bin Laden Begins: Inciting and Waging Jihad from
     Sudan, 1992–1996   145

Part 4: War Years, 1996–2001

11. Bin Laden Returns to Afghanistan: Getting Settled
     and Politicking   163

12. Bin Laden in Afghanistan: Targeting America and
     Expanding al Qaeda   181

13. Bin Laden Stands at Armageddon and Battles for
     His Lord   205

Part 5: No End in Sight

14. What to Expect from al Qaeda   257

15. Spring 2002: Where Are We? Where Are We Going?   275

*Epilogue: "That They May Go in and Look Their Redeemer
     in the Face with Joy"*   287

Epilogue to the Revised Edition   291

*Appendix: "We Are Not Ashamed of Our Jihad": Bin Laden's
     Growth as an Islamic Leader and Hero After 1996*   299

Note on Sources   315

Notes   323

Glossary   385

Bibliography   395

Index   439

About the Author   443

Foreword

Through Our Enemies' Eyes is among the most important books published on terrorism since September 11, 2001. At a time when it has become fashionable to blame the U.S. intelligence community for the failures that led to those tragic events, *Through Our Enemies' Eyes* provocatively challenges such broad-brush indictments, clearly showing that not everyone was asleep at the wheel. Written during 1998 and completed the following year, it not only "connected the dots," but did so in a uniquely authoritative and compelling manner that would eventually establish its reputation as a classic in the field.

First published in 2002, *Through Our Enemies' Eyes* was arguably a most unlikely candidate to attain that stature. Written by a long-serving Central Intelligence Agency officer, it initially attracted scant attention. The nature and importance of its author's national security work required that he remain anonymous. This meant that there was no intriguing photograph of a suitably contemplative figure available for publicity purposes. There was no one to invite onto television and radio talk shows for interviews or to profile in the features sections of newspapers. There could also be no public book launches, signings, or opportunities to field interested readers' questions. That the author also had the temerity to compare Osama bin Laden to some of America's most hallowed statesmen and political figures in order for readers to better understand our enemy and comprehend his magnetism and standing within the Muslim world, doubtless rendered *Through Our Enemies' Eyes* a publishers' and publicists' nightmare.

Yet *Through Our Enemies' Eyes* slowly but inexorably began to gather a loyal readership and increasingly enthusiastic following. Among the "war on terrorism cognoscenti" in and around Washington, D.C., mere word-of-mouth established the book as required reading for anyone seeking to understand bin Laden, the movement that he cofounded and led, and the profound threat that it posed (and continues to pose) to the United States and to international peace. Accordingly, the book's reputation spread as a thoroughly reliable, trenchant, and commendably clear exegesis of al Qaeda's ideology, goals, and alarming ambitions.

Through Our Enemies' Eyes is especially noteworthy for another reason: it was based entirely on open source literature — that is, nonclassified information. This is particularly significant at a time when America's national security architecture and intelligence community have undergone the most extensive reorganization and reorientation since their creation following World War II. *Through Our Enemies' Eyes* incontrovertibly demonstrates that probing analysis, deductive reasoning, and accurate conclusions can be drawn about even highly secretive movements and reclusive leaders independently of classified and other highly restricted government information.

As a result of a second book published in 2004 titled *Imperial Hubris* — which also challenged the conventional wisdom, this time in the context of America's conduct of the war on terrorism — we now know the identity of the anonymous author of both works. He is Michael Scheuer, a twenty-two-year CIA veteran who headed its bin Laden unit from 1996 to 1999 and was at the vortex of the intra- and interagency disputes and disagreements since laid bare by the 9/11 Commission, congressional investigations, and other inquiries into the events leading up to the attacks that fateful day. Scheuer's academic training as a historian — and his longstanding personal interest in the American Civil War — explains his command of primary sources, his identification and interpretation of seminal events, and most importantly, his profound understanding of the role of leadership and ideology in shaping world events and affecting the course of history.

Publication of this second edition of *Through Our Enemies' Eyes* is timely. Four years into the war on terrorism, the United States seems at a crossroads in this monumental struggle. The sustained successes of the war's early phases appear to have been stymied by the protracted insurgency in Iraq, the inability to kill or capture bin Laden and his chief lieutenant, Ayman al-Zawahiri, and most critically by an inability to break the cycle of recruitment and regeneration that has sustained a terrorism campaign that, as *Through Our Enemies' Eyes* persuasively argues, commenced long before 9/11. The recent bombings in Bali and London, no less those in Madrid, Istanbul, Jakarta, Casablanca, Riyadh, and elsewhere, demonstrate the continued resonance and appeal of a movement and an ideology that Scheuer magisterially charts and describes in these pages. The key to success in warfare, the Chinese strategist Sun Tzu wrote, is to "know your enemy and you will know yourself." In *Through Our Enemies' Eyes*, Scheuer answers the first part of that irrefutable formulation. It is up to the book's readers to answer the second. Thanks to Mike Scheuer they have a very solid foundation from which to begin.

Bruce Hoffman
Washington, D.C.

Preface to the Revised Edition

The future always comes as a surprise, but political wisdom consists at least in some partial judgement of what may surprise us. And for my part I cannot but believe that a main unexpected thing of the future is the return of Islam. Since religion is at the root of all political movements and changes and since we have here a very great religion physically paralyzed but morally intensely alive, we are in the presence of an unstable equilibrium which cannot remain permanently unstable.

Hilaire Belloc, 1938

The great Catholic apologist and historian Hilaire Belloc believed Islam a heresy and a permanent enemy of Christianity, but he recognized and respected its mobilizing power, vitality, and durability. Belloc, in 1938, marveled that over Islam's history, "No fragment of Islam ever abandons its sacred book, its code of morals, its organized system of prayer, its simple doctrine. . . . [it] has always possessed a reservoir of men, newcomers pouring in to revivify its energies." Lost in the confusion and feverish politics and intrigues of the final prewar years, Belloc's 1938 warning to the West never received the attention it deserved. "It has always seemed to me," he wrote in *The Great Heresies*,

> possible, and even probable that there would be a resurrection of Islam and that our sons or our grandsons would see the renewal of that tremendous struggle between the Christian culture and for what has been for more than a thousand years its greatest opponent. . . . I say the suggestion that Islam may re-arise sounds fantastic — but this is only because men are always powerfully affected by the immediate past: — one might say they are blinded by it!"[1]

One does not need to be a Catholic, or a believer of any sort, to appreciate Belloc's warnings about Islam's latent power, mobilizing force, perserverance, and theological indestructibility. America's leaders, however, seem never to have read Belloc. And so, America's war against Osama bin Laden, al Qaeda, and their allies continues, and, unfortunately, the elected leaders of America and its allies continue to choose to lose the war. Ten years after the CIA began to analyze, track, and attack bin Laden and his organization, U.S. leaders of both parties continue to tell the citizenry that bin Laden and Sunni militants are attacking America for who we are, what we think, how we live, and not for what we do in the Muslim world. A decade ago, our leaders might have been given the benefit of the doubt for failing to understand the motivation of our enemy. Today, they merit no such indulgence from American citizens. They merit only scorn and contempt. President George W. Bush, Senator John Kerry, Vice President Dick Cheney, Senator John McCain, Congresswoman Nancy Pelosi, Senator Hillary Clinton, Secretary Donald Rumsfeld, former President Bill Clinton, and their print and electronic media acolytes are, quite simply, lying to Americans. The motivation of these leaders to lie is not for me to say; I cannot see into their hearts or minds. On the basis of easily accessible evidence, however, that they are lying is irrefutable.

This edition of *Through Our Enemies' Eyes* is meant, as was the first edition, to explain bin Laden, his motivation, and his appeal in the Muslim world to Americans. In many ways, this expanded edition of the book may be of more value to Americans now, four years into a war about which their leaders have intentionally misled them and in which most of the media have not had the wit to ask the obvious questions that would puncture the penumbra of bipartisan fairy-tale telling. If people of other countries can profit from this book, so much the better. But the book is meant for Americans, because it is their country and children — and those of their English-speaking allies — that are most at risk from al Qaeda, and it is their leaders who have been the most resolute liars about the threat they face.

When drafting the book in 1999, I envisioned it, in the pedantic way of a historian, as a sort of nineteenth-century "life and times" biography, one of those in which the author and publisher allow the book's subject to speak in his own words to the greatest extent possible. Bin Laden's words are plentiful, thoughtful, historically aware, and brutally direct. They are the indispensable key to understanding the religious motivation driving him and his allies. Most important, his words leave no room to doubt that Americans are being attacked for what they do in the Islamic world, not for how they think, live, or govern themselves.

Sadly, bin Laden's words are available to Americans only in snippets, and those usually taken out of context. Several U.S. publishers have raised the idea of publishing bin Laden's "works" but have been pilloried by the media for even suggesting a project that would "support" terrorism. Nonsense, and nonsense that will kill Americans. The decision to publish the works of Karl Marx and V. I. Lenin in English did not make the publishers "communists," but it did help Americans understand and eventually defeat the communists. From another angle, reading and understanding bin Laden's words might save today's Americans from the fate of the generation of Americans and Europeans who failed to read and heed the words that explained the thinking, motivation, and plans of the author of the book entitled *Mein Kampf.*

In preparing this expanded edition of the book, I defined my job not as revision or update but as reconstitution; readers interested in the updating of this book can find it in *Imperial Hubris: Why the West is Losing the War on Terrorism,* where I devoted a good deal of space to updating the nuts and bolts of the U.S.-al Qaeda war through January 2004. In *Imperial Hubris,* I also covered what bin Laden had said in the period since *Through Our Enemies' Eyes* was published in 2002. Thankfully, bin Laden is a man who, in U.S. political parlance, stays on message, and so the bin Laden of *Imperial Hubris* remains the man I encountered and presented in my first book—calm, eloquent, persuasive, supremely confident, experienced, patient, and immensely dangerous to America. He has added detail and sharpened his message's clarity—as always, he is eager to ensure Americans understand what he is up to and why—but the crux of the message is the same.

Restoration, therefore, is what the second edition of this book is about; about 35,000 new words have been added. When I gave the original manuscript to Potomac Books (then Brassey's, Inc.) in October 2001, the firm—to its credit—kept a good deal of the draft intact. That said, the manuscript was substantially reduced. The reduction was the result of two considerations, both of which I thought at the time were legitimate. First, because of my status not only as a first-time author, but also as one who was obligated by his employer to remain anonymous, the publisher was taking an economic risk. Without a readily identifiable author, significant advertisement and promotion were nearly impossible.

Second, the book was going to be controversial; indeed, it clearly was going to offend some people. In writing the book for Americans, I had compared bin Laden's words and justifications for fighting the United States with those written and uttered by several figures from the Anglo-American pantheon, including men who had instigated and led America's revolution against Britain. Americans, that is, who used ideas and words to deliberately incite violence against a country they deemed irredeemably repressive. My goal was not to suggest moral equivalence, but rather to provide context and points of comparison for Americans reading about a leader—Osama bin Laden—evolving and acting in a culture far different from their own. The folks at Potomac Books expected some rancor over this approach and were not disappointed. They sent the book, for example, to one eminent Washington wise man—the holder of top defense and intelligence posts in several administrations—and he damned the comparisons; said they made him "gag," and refused to be associated with the book. This wise man would later greet the book, and later *Imperial Hubris*, with the favored tool of the bipartisan league of the they-hate-us for-our-freedoms liars—he labeled me an anti-Semite in a cowardly effort to foreclose debate on the topics the books raised. In this edition, I have restored several additional comparisons between the founders' justifications for inciting violence and destruction and those of bin Laden. May that wise man's gagging be horrific.

Because of these circumstances, my publisher cut more than 40 percent of the original manuscript, including several full chapters. The cutting, I believe, was masterfully done, and the central message of the book remained clear and pointed. The book was published, reviewed sparsely but favorably, and sold moderately well. So far, in terms of accuracy and forecasts, it has stood the tests of time and subsequent events.

In preparing this restoration of the original, I have been guided by my original intent: to allow bin Laden to speak for himself and thereby afford American readers the chance to absorb, evaluate, and decide what this war is about for himself or herself. Thus, I have added a good deal of bin Laden's words, all of which were in the original manuscript, and none of which were spoken after the publication of the book. Indeed, none of the material in this book—with few exceptions, such as the issue of operational ties between al Qaeda and Saddam's Iraq ties—is based on research materials that became available after the original date of publication. New material or analysis within the main text of the revised edition has been italicized.

As noted above, I did not focus on incidents of warfare in reconstituting the book, although we have included a comprehensive chronology of the bin Laden versus Crusaders war through 1 October 2005. Indeed, such incidents are increasingly difficult to disaggregate because in places like Iraq, Saudi Arabia, southern Thailand, Mindanao, and Afghanistan the steady day-to-day pace of combat makes few individual incidents stand out. This reality also, I believe, will make it more difficult in the future to assess who is winning in a military sense—insurgencies are notorious for a certain opaqueness.

Therefore, I focused in this book on restoring materials that pertained to issues that have been particularly misunderstood or ignored in America: bin Laden's personality; his early years as a nonviolent Saudi dissident and reformer; the substantive issues motivating al Qaeda and its allies, especially their perception that U.S. foreign policy threatens Islam's survival; the role the Islamic religion plays in that motivation; the relationship among bin Laden, his family, and the rulers in Riyadh, the al-Saud family; and the profound impact the Afghan-Soviet war had and continues to have on bin Laden, al Qaeda, and worldwide Sunni Islamic militancy.

I also restored material showing that bin Laden is following the path of earlier Islamic soldiers, theologians, revolutionaries, and folk heroes and legends. This to demonstrate that bin Laden, to be understood, must be placed in the continuum of Islamic history, and that he is perceived by Muslims as speaking and acting in a specific historical context and tradition. Also restored is analysis—based on and citing the work of Muslim and Western experts on Islamic law and traditions—showing that bin Laden's call for a "defensive jihad" is within the purview of an individual who is not a Muslim cleric or scholar and is, for many of these experts, an appropriate response to U.S. activities in the Islamic world.

Beyond the foregoing, I have restored passages from the original manuscript that address issues about which there has been either confusion or outright ignorance. Among these are bin Laden's long history of interest in and support for the Palestinian cause against Israel and the West's pathetic misperception of the brilliant Afghan insurgent commander Ahmed Shah Masood as the sword capable of slaying the Taliban and bin Laden. In addition, I have added as an appendix a chapter that was cut in its entirety from the first edition. The chapter deals with bin Laden's evolutionary growth as an Islamic hero and leader between 1996 and 2001.

Finally, and as noted above, I have added a section refuting the analysis in the first edition of this book in which I concluded that there likely was a working relationship between Iraq and al Qaeda, especially in regard to cooperation in the field of chemical, biological, radiological, and nuclear (CBRN) weapons. This is the only part of the book's main text based on research materials that became available since the date of publication. I have kept the original, incorrect analysis in the text, because the data on which it is based is quoted accurately, but have followed it with several italicized paragraphs explaining the new research and the conclusions I have drawn from it. A professional intelligence officer learns early on never to say never, but I now conclude that, unless and until new data come to light, it is extremely unlikely that there ever was CBRN-related cooperation—or substantive, ongoing cooperation of any kind—between al Qaeda and Saddam Hussein's regime.

While I believe the foregoing discussions will be helpful, it is, at day's end, bin Laden's words that matter most. Hearing and understanding them, Americans can see the world as it is, appreciate the dire threat facing their country, and prepare a strategy to defeat it. Without bin Laden's words, Americans are left with their leaders' lies, the media's superficiality, and little chance of preventing their country's ultimate defeat. That the safety and survival of Americans lies in understanding their enemies' words, and disbelieving their leaders', speaks directly to the corrupt, dissolute state of America's political culture. I suppose the best we Americans can do, for now, is to read what bin Laden says, think for ourselves, and pray our society soon produces another Thomas Paine, Patrick Henry, Thomas Jefferson, John Bunyan, or William T. Sherman—or perhaps even our own Osama bin Laden.

Preface

God Almighty hit the United States at its most vulnerable point. He destroyed its greatest buildings. . . . I swear by Almighty God who raised the heavens without pillars that neither the United States nor he who lives in the United States will enjoy security before we can see it as a reality in Palestine and before all the infidel armies leave the land of Muhammad, may God's peace and blessing be upon him.

Osama bin Laden, 7 October 2001

The will of God prevails. In great contests each party claims to act in accordance with the will of God. Both *may* be, but one *must* be wrong. God cannot be *for* and *against* the same thing at the same time.

Abraham Lincoln, September 1862

On 11 September 2001, forces led and incited by Osama bin Laden attacked and utterly demolished the twin towers of the World Trade Center in New York City and heavily damaged the center of U.S. military power at the Pentagon. The human cost exceeded that of Pearl Harbor by nearly a factor of two, the economic cost by an as yet undetermined multiple, and a cost in national confidence and equanimity that dwarfs that inflicted by the Japanese Imperial Navy six decades previously.

In 1941 U.S. president Franklin D. Roosevelt described 7 December as a "date that will live in infamy." The infamy the president described belonged to the Japanese attackers. In the midst of peace talks, Japan had staged a brilliantly executed, stunningly successful, and, as Roosevelt said, "dastardly" surprise attack on the United States. FDR and many Americans believed war was coming to the Pacific, but the cunning and brutality of the attack while negotiations were proceeding shocked the American mind. We were shocked because our own naivete and insularity led us to underestimate the complexity and determination of our adversaries.

For the decade preceding the attacks in September 2001, we similarly naively assumed that we knew the world, and we were confident that the effective use of the tools and weapons of modernity was impossible for those grounded in twelfth-century Islamic theology. But we have now seen that there is no absolute incompatibility between medieval theology and the use of modern tools, weapons, and technological concepts.

Tuesday, 11 September, will assume its place on the short roster of dates that live in infamy in U.S. history. But before this occurs, we as a nation must accept the fact that the day was, in many ways, a day of infamy for Americans, the leaders and the led. Bin Laden's attacks were indeed brutal and stealthy; they were designed to inflict massive civilian casualties; they in every way deserve to be described with Roosevelt's evocative word — "dastardly." And, like the Japanese attack on the at-anchor U.S. Navy, they were expertly planned and executed, and by bin Laden's own admission, they produced even more death and destruction than had been anticipated. "I was the most optismitic of all," bin Laden said, but the results exceeded "all we had hoped for."[1]

Where the two events part company, however, is that unlike that sunny Sunday morning in 1941, there was far less reason for Americans to have been surprised by the sanguinary events that occurred on the sunny Tuesday morning in 2001. Osama bin Laden publicly declared war on the United States on 2 September 1996; for good measure, he did so again on 23 February 1998. Since 1996, bin Laden has repeatedly warned Americans — again, always in public — that he would incrementally increase the lethality of his attacks on U.S. interests until we stopped supporting Israel, withdrew our military forces from Saudi Arabia, and ended the embargo on Iraq. During this period, he was true to his word; his forces and those he incited attacked us with steadily increasing skill, lethality, and audacity in Somalia, Saudi Arabia, Kenya, Tanzania, and Yemen. He warned that if the United States did not yield to his demands, he would bring the war he was waging into the continental United States.

When issuing these warnings, bin Laden invariably described his intent as identical to that manifested by Ramzi Ahmed Yousef when Yousef attacked the World Trade Center in New York City in February 1993. Again, promise made, promise kept.

Without justifying, excusing, or defending bin Laden's 11 September 2001 attacks, Americans need to recognize that we underestimated bin Laden's motivation, complexity, and determination. The United States has never had an enemy who has more clearly, calmly, and articulately expressed his hatred for America and his intention to destroy our country by war or die trying. For five years in media interviews, public statements, and letters to the press, bin Laden told us that he meant to defeat the United States and that he would attack — and urge others to attack — U.S. military and civilian targets both in the United States and abroad. In response, the United States never seemed to take bin Laden too seriously, let alone accept the fact that our nation was in the path of real danger.

Unfortunately, much of this misunderstanding appears to have survived 11 September. In a statement worthy of Lewis Carroll's consideration for an updated edition of Alice's adventures, a senior U.S. official said in early 2002 that bin Laden had underestimated America's readiness to attack al Qaeda on the ground in Afghanistan. As will be shown later in this book, bin Laden has long sought to prompt such an attack, and the following statement — if the phrase "the Taleban and al Qaida" is replaced by the phrase "the United States" — more accurately could have been made by al Qaeda's chief about his foes. Bin Laden, the U.S. official said,

> did not believe we would invade his sanctuary. He did not know about the collection and operational initiatives that would allow us to strike with great accuracy at the heart of the Taleban and al Qaida. He underestimated our capabilities, our readiness and our resolve.[2]

This book is an effort to acquaint Americans with a deadly foe — the forces that have been unleashed by Osama bin Laden and his al Qaeda terrorist network. The draft of this book was completed in mid-June 2001, but the vagaries of the manuscript-to-book process found it unpublished on 11 September 2001. My initial thought after the attacks was to revise the entire work, but while the events of 11 September and after have been dramatic, bloody, and varied, they have not fundamentally altered the story I intended to tell; that is, the activities of the forces bin Laden has led, incited, and inspired — with or without his continued physical presence — are a mortal threat to the United States. Americans need to understand the historical and religious context in which bin Laden and his supporters have acted as well as why these forces emerged. The manuscript I completed last June, I think, still performs this task. Those looking for details about the ordnance, modus operandi, and forged documents used in the September 2001 attacks need to look elsewhere; the purpose of this book is to help awaken the United States to its need to listen to and take heed of explicit warnings both that the bin Laden style of warfare is here for the long term and that the United States can no longer rely on its continental breadth, friendly neighbors, and broad oceanic shores to insulate it from dastardly acts of those Islamists who mean us harm.

A final word needs to be said about words. The reader who proceeds through this book will notice that I have used some analogies drawn from

Anglo-American history. Periodically, the words of the English Protestant preacher John Bunyan and members of the pantheon of American's founders will appear in the text as epigraphs. Let me hasten to say that I am not in any way inferring a moral equivalence between Osama bin Laden and these heroes of Anglo-American history. The analogies are meant to remind the American reader that the formation of our republic was based on the founders' theological, political, and philosophical beliefs. Men of honesty, bravery, piety, and integrity, the words of the founders nonetheless unleashed — indeed, they deliberately encouraged — passions, domestic confrontations, and war. In our war of independence, as *Wall Street Journal* columnist Mark Helprin recently reminded Americans, "we broke free in a long and taxing struggle that affords a better picture of our kith and kin than any the world may have today of who we are and of what we are capable."[3] Recalling Helprin's analysis and the undeniable power of the founders' words will stand the reader in good stead. For the threat posed to the United States by the forces unleashed by bin Laden lies not only in his actions, but also in his words and character, and in those of his followers. Like our founders, bin Laden has been viewed by his many followers as a man of faith, intellectual honesty, courage, and integrity, and for that reason the movement he established is a foe that must be understood before his movement can be, as it must be, defeated and eliminated.

Acknowledgments

Recognizing assistance for a book published anonymously is tricky, but here goes. First, the support and enthusiasm for this project from the editor and his associates at Sub Rosa Press in Virginia kept me on track and productive. While this book's subject is far from Sub Rosa's field, the firm's editor and his associates steadily aided in the manuscript's completion and helped place it at Brassey's in the hands of the firm's exceptional academic publisher, Mr. Stephen M. Wrinn, and his equally excellent deputy, Ms. Christina Davidson. To Sub Rosa, Mr. Wrinn, and Ms. Davidson, my sincere thanks.

Next, readers will recognize in this volume's endnotes the debt I owe to the work, thoughtfulness, and passion of numerous scholars, journalists, and commentators. These individuals — men and women, Muslim and Western — devote their efforts to covering Islam, the Middle East, South Asia, and the interaction of each with the United States. While, as the reader will come to know, I disagree with much that has been written about Osama bin Laden, the variety of these writings and analyses provide a tremendous body of research material. With this work and my own, I have tried to present a portrait of Osama bin Laden that will prompt better understanding of the man — and understanding does not connote sympathy — and a debate about how best to identify, confront, and defeat the threat he poses and personifies. In his review of William J. Cooper's excellent book *Jefferson Davis, American*, the historian Peter J. Parish wrote, "Cooper seeks not to defend Davis but to understand him, not to excuse him but to explain him." I have taken those words as a guide; only the reader can judge my success.

I also would like to thank several fellow senior civil servants for trying to first prevent and then delay the publication of this book. The manuscript began as a much-shorter primer for civil servants newly assigned to work the issues of Islamism and Osama bin Laden. In that form, my senior colleagues used and praised the work. On broaching my intention to publish, however, their politically correct antennae deployed and their efforts to suppress the work ran a gamut from damning the book because it would offend Muslims to an ominous suggestion that my personal views might well disqualify me from further performance of official duties. After a year of delay over 2000–2001, my request to publish was approved. At day's end, I would like to thank those who granted my request and those who opposed publication. Indeed, the latter steeled me to press the issue to a conclusion and not yield to men who, in Mark Helprin's 1998 words, "knowing very little or next to nothing, take pride in telling everyone else what to do."[1]

I too must thank God for the opportunity I have had over twenty years to work with dozens of young U.S. civil servants at home and abroad. The U.S. Civil Service is splendidly stocked with young men and women—particularly women—who take seriously their oath to preserve, protect, and defend the Republic, and whose work ethic, intellectual honesty, and personal courage inspire awe and—if unleashed—are more than match for America's foes, foreign or domestic. Too often, however, their work is stymied by senior officers of my own generation. Mostly men, these senior officers have made careers by keeping silent in the face of unfairness, avoiding risk, and refusing to make decisions. As a result, they have, again in Helprin's words, allowed America's power, wealth, and decency to flow "promiscuously" through their hands "like blood onto sand, squandered and laid waste by a generation that imagines history to have been but a prelude for what it would accomplish." Fortunately, most of the Republic's younger civil servants recognize with Helprin that this behavior is "more than a pity, more than a disgrace, it is despicable."[2] Often throttled by my generation, these young professionals are coming into their own and soon they no longer will be lions led by donkeys. Again, I thank these lions for what they taught me and pray that I was not too much in their way. And, as God wisely accelerates the pace at which he is culling my generation, I am sure my children and grandchildren, as well as our Republic, will be secure and free because of the talent and devotion of these fine civil servants.

Finally, I alone am responsible for any errors in this manuscript.

Introduction

"It has been nine years since we have been struggling against the United States," Osama bin Laden told the media in May 1998, "and I am alive in front of you despite all the attempts to kill me. In these nine years we have inflicted considerable damage on the United States and will continue to do the same in the future."[1] Because of such statements, and because the forces of Osama bin Laden destroyed two U.S. embassies in East Africa two months after making the one just noted and eventually brought their attacks to U.S. soil, this study will review and analyze what bin Laden was saying, planning, and doing in those nine years and since — and, indeed, since he emerged as an Islamist leader during the Afghan jihad — and will estimate what those things mean for U.S. interests specifically, and for the West generally. This study emphatically is not a detailed examination of specific terrorist attacks, modus operandi, explosives, and weapons.

After reviewing what bin Laden has said since first speaking to the Western media in late 1993, there appeared inescapably, for me, a stark contrast between what I considered to be bin Laden's clear, calm, and carefully chosen words and the media's portrait of him as a more-or-less blood-crazed "terrorist." This is true of the U.S. press in particular, presumably because, as Ronald Steel wrote in 1996 in the *New Republic,* "We [Americans] do not consider ourselves threatening. Puzzled when vilified, we assume our accusers must be demented."[2] It was clear bin Laden automatically was placed by the West's journalists and terrorism experts in the traditional terrorist category, where the only important issues are who or what bin Laden attacked, the method of attack, and how future attacks could be prevented. What bin Laden had been saying about why he and his al Qaeda forces were attacking was given short shrift. British journalist Robert Fisk hit the mark in this regard in an article in the *Independent* on 22 August 1998 in which he argued,

> The use of the word "terrorist" — where Arabs who murder innocents are always called "terrorists" whereas Israeli killers who

slaughter 29 Palestinians in a Hebron Mosque or assassinate their prime minister, Yitzhak Rabin, are called extremists — is only part of the problem. "Terrorist" is a word that avoids all meaning. The who and the how are of essential importance. But the "why" is usually something the West prefers to avoid. Not once yesterday [21 August 1998, the day after U.S. cruise missile attacks on bin Laden-related targets in Afghanistan and Sudan] — not in a single press statement, press conference or interview — did a U.S. leader or diplomat explain why the enemies of America hate America. Why is bin Laden so angry with the United States? Why — just not who and how — but why did anyone commit the atrocities in East Africa?[3]

One wonders if Americans would understand what Osama bin Laden meant, or believe he meant it, if the media presented the material of what he actually said to them. Many Americans and other Westerners appear to be nearing the point where few will attach much importance to what public persons say because the mass audience cynically believes everything is said for personal advantage, shock value, or to prolong a photo opportunity, not because the speaker is sincere and therefore has something worth considering. Even our public persons at times seem unable to hear, let alone understand, what foreign public persons are saying. When asked if the anti-U.S. anger of the Muslim world toward the United States was mistaken, for example, a senior U.S. State Department official said, "I believe it is. I don't think we consider it unimportant, but we believe it is misplaced, misdirected, it misperceives American policy." After reflecting, the official blithely disclosed he did not understand what bin Laden and other Islamists are saying. "Maybe it [Muslim anger] means," the official said, "that we need to continue to do a better job with our public diplomacy, in getting the story over to the [Muslim] people."[4] In other words, the world's unsophisticated and uninformed Muslims neither understand the altruism of U.S. foreign policy nor that the policy is designed for their own good.

This sort of deafness, arrogance, and cynicism does not much matter when Americans listen to entertainment-world celebrities; after all, often little wisdom or common sense can be had from athletes, movie stars, and media personalities. When the same factors are consistently applied to domestic and foreign political, religious, social, or intellectual leaders, however, the issue becomes more troubling, because threats to our society and nation remain unresolved, even unrecognized. In this scenario, problems are left to fester and, more dangerous, are not understood, because people assume their leaders are either crying wolf or seeking personal advantage. In essence, people turn inward, stop listening, and go about their business: making a buck, paying the mortgage, and putting the kids through college.

This auditory cynicism is most dangerous for Americans when they are listening to foreigners who are America's implacable enemies. This cynicism, combined with traditional American insularity and the post-1990 absence of a single, steady, and credible nation-state threat, makes it likely we will miss the importance of what our foes are saying. This seems to have been the case with Osama bin Laden. While we all have seen and viscerally felt the damage bin Laden has unleashed on the United States, most do not have a coherent understanding of what motivates the threat his movement poses. Or, if some have heard what he has said — such phrases as, "If we cut off the head of America, the kingdoms in the Arab world will cease to exist"[5] — they have dismissed it as hyperbolic rhetoric meant to win notoriety and thereby have missed the substantial kernel of truth at the statement's core.

This is the road to disaster, for the positions and forces bin Laden has presented are a far more lethal and varied threat than that posed by any of those we have labeled as "terrorists" over the past quarter century. The strength of his personality and message is likely to lead to an enduring legacy that will long survive his own departure from the scene. Muntasir al-Zayyat, a prominent Islamist lawyer and longtime friend of bin Laden's Egyptian deputy, Ayman al-Zawahiri, warned the West not to try to fit bin Laden and other Islamist leaders into the traditional definition of terrorists. In a 1999 interview with the London-based journal *Al-Wasat*, al-Zayyat said that,

> they [the Americans] deal with Usama Bin Ladin, [Gam'at al-Islamiyah spiritual leader] Shaykh Umar Abd-al-Rahman, and [Egytian Islamic Jihad chief] Ayman al-Zawahiri, as if they were carbon copies of [the] international terrorist Carlos, and that reflects their inability to understand the facts of the matter. Carlos was a terrorist whose activities stopped when he was arrested. The fundamentalist movement's leaders are ideas, a heritage, a stature, and principles that do not disappear when they disappear.[6]

For present purposes, debating the legitimacy of bin Laden's theological justifications is not necessary. This study is narrowly focused to outline what bin Laden has said and done and to estimate the impact of those things in the Muslim world; to assess bin Laden as a person — his leadership capabilities, organization, and future intentions, and the historical and religious contexts in which he is acting; and to assess what all this means for U.S. interests. At day's end, this study will suggest that the threat America faces from bin Laden is not the episodic terrorist campaign typical of those perpetrated by traditional terrorist groups. It is rather a worldwide, religiously inspired, and professionally guided Islamist insurgency against "Christian Crusaders and Jews," which is being waged by groups bin Laden has controlled, directed, and inspired.

Bin Laden has claimed that the United States has waged "a war against Muslims" since 1945, and that he and his allies "are only striving to give it a fitting reply."[7] A senior Egyptian Islamist has said that bin Laden intends to incite "guerrilla warfare against Israeli and American interests not only in Arab and Muslim countries but everywhere in the world."[8] And the literature suggests the al Qaeda forces he has created will continue to attack U.S. interests at home and abroad and will use the weapons they have at hand or can acquire, be they daggers, Kalashnikovs, car bombs, or chemical/biological weapons.

The forces of bin Laden, then, are waging war on America in God's name; they have made it clear that their goal is not the tactical one of inflicting pain, but the strategic one of defeating the United States "in the same way in which the USSR suffered humiliation at the hands of the Afghan and Arab mujahedin in Afghanistan."[9]

In the United States before the events of 11 September 2001, however, there was almost no recognition that bin Laden's war is well under way. The first step in countering the forces that bin Laden has established is to listen more patiently to what he said in the past and to understand the personal, historical, and geopolitical contexts in which he thought, spoke, and acted. Americans also need to answer a question asked by the attorney for one of the attackers of the U.S. embassy in Kenya. "Why [are] many young people . . . willing to kill themselves to strike America," defense attorney David P. Baugh asked during the trial of the East Africa bombers. "Why does bin Laden and al Qaeda have more young people willing to die than projects they can do?" For starters, perhaps it is best to let bin Laden describe his intentions. In late 1998, ABC's John Miller reported that bin Laden used a soft, grandfatherly voice to warn the United States of his plans:

> So we tell the Americans as people, and we tell the mothers of American soldiers and American mothers in general, that if they value their lives and the lives of their children, to find a nationalistic government that will look after their interests and not the interests of the Jews. The continuation of tyranny will bring the fight to America, as [convicted World Trade Center bomber] Ramzi Yousef and others did. This is my message to the American people: to look for a serious government that looks out for their interests and does not attack others, their lands, or their honor. And my word to American journalists is not to ask why we did that [attack U.S. targets] but ask what their government has done that forced us to defend ourselves.[10]

Having kept bin Laden's promise to bring the war to U.S. soil, al Qaeda forces are now absorbing the U.S. military response, which, to date, has been the usual post–cold war application of overwhelming air power, this time seasoned with small numbers of ground troops mostly anchored to static positions. Notwithstanding the damage al Qaeda and the Taliban have suffered — which, as will be seen, is of consequence — bin Laden's forces now have the United States where they have wanted it, on the ground in Afghanistan where Islamist insurgents can seek to reprise their 1980s' victory over the Red Army. Al Qaeda now has the chance to prove bin Laden's thesis that the United States cannot maintain long-term, casualty-producing military engagements, and bin Laden's forces are surely praising God for the opportunity. In this regard, *Al-Quds Al-Arabi* editor Abd-al-Bari Atwan has written, "We, who know Shaykh Osama bin Laden, can say definitely that he is now living his happiest days because he has been waiting for the day when Americans get embroiled in Afghanistan."[11] With Washington also committed on the ground in the Philippines, and seemingly set for similar commitments in Yemen and Somalia, al Qaeda is getting the multifront war with U.S. forces it has long wanted. Time will tell if its "happiest days" will last, but for now, bin Laden's forces are eager to lead Muslims to victory in what bin Laden has called "the most dangerous, fiercest, and most savage Crusade war launched against Islam."

> God willing, the end of America is imminent. Its end is not dependent on the survival of this slave of God. Regardless if Osama is killed or survives, the awakening has started, praise be to God. This was the point of these [11 September 2001] operations. . . . In a previous interview with ABC television, I warned that if it [the United States] enters into a conflict with the sons of the two holy mosques, America will forget the horrors of Vietnam. This, indeed, was the case; praised be God. What is to come is even greater, God willing.[12]

The names and terms and documentary and media sources associated with bin Laden's world are complex, sometimes confusing, and ever changing. To aid the reader's navigation of the material in this book, a glossary of names and terms and a section of notes on sources are included following the epilogue.

Middle East

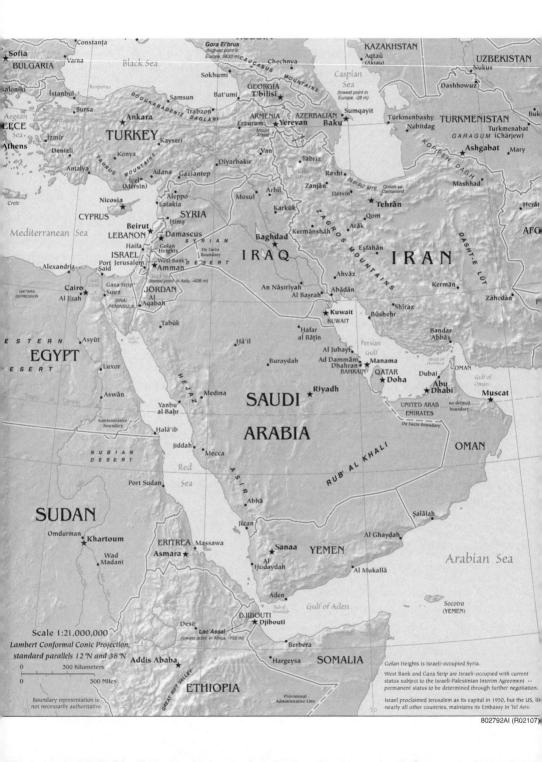

Scale 1:21,000,000
Lambert Conformal Conic Projection,
standard parallels 12°N and 38°N

Boundary representation is
not necessarily authoritative.

Golan Heights is Israeli-occupied Syria.

West Bank and Gaza Strip are Israeli-occupied with current
status subject to the Israeli-Palestinian Interim Agreement --
permanent status to be determined through further negotiation.

Israel proclaimed Jerusalem as its capital in 1950, but the US, like
nearly all other countries, maintains its Embassy in Tel Aviv.

802792AI (R02107)

Central and Southeast Asia

CONTEXT

1

CONTEXT FOR UNDERSTANDING BIN LADEN'S AIMS

To shape policy and actions to nullify the threat posed by Osama bin Laden's al Qaeda network, we, in the West, must first understand the man and the underlying circumstances that brought him to the forefront of a movement that has effectively learned how to take advantage of the functioning of a free society to do us harm. I think we in the United States can best come to grips with this phenomena by realizing that bin Laden's philosophy and actions have embodied many of the same sentiments that permeate the underpinnings of concepts on which the United States itself is established. This can be illustrated, I think, with reference to the writings or actions of such seminal figures in our history as John Brown, John Bunyan, Thomas Jefferson, Patrick Henry, and Thomas Paine.

According to his closest Muslim associates and many of the Westerners who have interviewed him, Osama bin Laden appears to be a genuinely pious Muslim; a devoted family man; a talented, focused, and patient insurgent commander; a frank and eloquent speaker; a successful businessman; and an individual of conviction, intellectual honesty, compassion, humility, and physical bravery. It is ironic that this man today leads an ideological and military force with more lethal potential than any other nonstate threat faced by the United States. Although U.S. leaders have rightly decided to confront bin Laden with military means, their recognition of the motivation and destructive power of the bin Laden phenomenon remains superficial. Witness the eagerness of the United States to move on to fight Iraq even before a war against bin Laden had begun. To gauge the seriousness and likely extended length of this war, our leaders can do no better than to accept at face value bin Laden's belief that the United States is intent on destroying Muslims, their religion, and the Islamic world; he has said that U.S. leaders have the same respect for Muslims and their God as Europe's Catholic Crusaders had for his coreligionists nine centuries ago.

Armed and inspired with these beliefs, bin Laden has focused on rallying the world's Muslims and inciting them to wage a defensive jihad against what he has described as the onslaught of the United States and its Western and Arab allies. The goals of this jihad continue to be to annihilate what is seen as the brutal U.S.-led enemies of Islam—the Crusaders, as bin Laden has called them—to restore to Muslims their dignity, holy places, and lost territory; and to reestablish what they see as the purity of God's rule across the Islamic world. In essence, bin Laden has called for a worldwide version of the successful defensive jihad Muslims waged for more than a decade against Soviet forces in Afghanistan.

Bin Laden has publicly outlined his military plans and intentions with precision. Despite the warfare that has now reached U.S. soil, most Americans still have paid little heed to his words. They regard him as a terrorist with above-average skills, but still an isolated lethal nuisance. As Professor James T. Johnson has written in his insightful book, *The Holy War Concept in Christian and Islamic Traditions,* "the contemporary [Western] perception [of jihad] tends to reduce it to terrorism—uses of violence whose forms and targets make it deeply repugnant to Western sensibilities."[1] That this could be a fatal misconception is argued fully below. For now it suffices to say that the dominance of the secular fundamentalists in American and Western elites, along with the pacifism and fear of defending moral absolutes in much of Christendom's religious establishments, leave Americans singularly unprepared to understand what bin Laden is saying, the historical context and religious tradition in which he is acting, and the danger posed by the forces he inspires. Professor Johnson goes on to warn that the West does not comprehend the "contemporary phenomenon of holy war," which has "become an object of suspicion from both the secular and Christian perspectives."

> As a result of the fundamental cultural rejection of war for religion by the West in the early modern period, it has been especially difficult for Western culture to accept and make sense of the ongoing presence of the phenomenon of war for the faith in modern Muslim societies. . . .
>
> We mistake it for an anachronism from the past, an expression of more primitive, less developed minds and societies. We consider it something that has no place in modern secular society, and so by definition alien and threatening. We confuse it with something that we ourselves know very little about, the nature of holy

war and its role in Western culture and history. And finally, we grasp it only dimly because it is rooted in a close connection between religion and politics, a connection we in the West either do not make or find uncomfortable.[2]

Simply put, the United States and the West have little useful context in which to try to understand Osama bin Laden. The aim of this study is to provide some of this missing context from the works of historians, Western and Muslim journalists, expert commentators, and, most especially, the words of Osama bin Laden himself. I also will use several analogies from Anglo-American history that are meant to show that bin Laden's character, religious certainty, moral absolutism, military ferocity, integrity, and all-or-nothing goals are not much different from those of individuals whom we in the United States have long identified and honored as religious, political, or military heroes; men such as John Brown, John Bunyan, Thomas Jefferson, Patrick Henry, and Thomas Paine. I do not argue that these are exact analogies, but only that they are analogies that seemed pertinent as I researched bin Laden. In the case of John Bunyan, in fact, there is a wide divergence between his goals and those sought by the other individuals noted. Brown, Jefferson, Henry, and Paine were eager to overthrow the existing political order. Bin Laden's philosophy shares this aim and means to change the world. In contrast, Bunyan "kept his mind on 'that world which is to come'" and "was expressly loyal . . . publicly condemning apparent rebellion as loudly as possible."[3]

Moving the Issue to Center Stage: John Brown

"Was John Brown a bad man, Dad?" That question came from my son a decade ago as we watched a 1940 Warner Brothers' movie called *Santa Fe Trail*. The movie featured Raymond Massey as the incendiary pre–Civil War figure John Brown. While the film has only a few contact points with American reality in the decade before the Civil War, Massey's portrayal of John Brown was a marvel, mirroring the historical record of Brown as a man who looked, sounded, and acted like the violent prophet of a vengeful God. "Brown had a great yearning for justice for all men, yet a rage for bloody revenge," historian Ken Chowder has written. "These qualities may seem paradoxical to us, but they were ones that John Brown had in common with his deity. The angry God of the Old Testament punished evil: An eye cost exactly an eye."[4] So frightening was Massey's sterling performance that it took several years before my son did not shield his eyes or hide behind the chair when Massey was on screen.

Less scared but, with age, more curious, my son continued to ask if John Brown was a bad man. After ducking the question a few times, I did some research and found that scholars have shown that Brown was a multi-faceted character who combined virtues and vices, probably more of the latter. He combined iron resolve, religious zeal, and physical courage with a single-minded devotion to the goal of doing what he saw as God's work by annihilating the institution of slavery. As David W. Blight has written, the Bible was the only "moral and legal compass" Brown acknowledged. Brown appeared to be a "high-minded, unselfish, belated Covenanter," as was said at the time, and a "Cromwellian Ironside introduced in the nineteenth century for a special purpose.[5] Even the pro-slavery firebrand Edmund Ruffin grudgingly credited Brown with "animal courage . . . [and] complete fear-lessness of and insensibility to danger and death."[6]

At the same time, Brown was overwhelmingly self-righteous, excelled at cold-blooded murder, seldom repaid debts, and cultivated a self-centeredness so great that he often left his large family without support. In contemporary America, it would be easy to dismiss Brown as a fraud and a fanatic because of his substantial character flaws and willingness, even eagerness, to sacrifice his life and those of several of his sons to instigate a war he believed was ordained by God. What today could be more unintelligible, after all, than a man eager for martyrdom and who said, "I have been whipped, as the saying is, but I am sure that I can recover all the lost capital occasioned by the disaster [at Harper's Ferry]; by only hanging a few moments by the neck. . . . I am worth infinitely more to die than to live."[7] It is little wonder that many in the United States cannot begin to fathom Osama bin Laden's calm, Brown-like assertion, "I am not afraid of death. Rather, martyrdom is my passion because my martyrdom would lead to the birth of thousands of Osamas."[8]

I eventually answered my son to his satisfaction by saying that some of Brown's actions were bad — fraud, murder, and treason for starters — but that there have been few causes in American history as vital as the abolition of slavery. I tried to explain to him the paradox that Frederick Douglass caught in his 1860 observation about John Brown. "Men consented to his death," Douglass said, "and then went home and taught their children to honor his memory." The bad man/good cause summation is the historical consensus on Brown, and I had this fact in my mind as I began trying to write a study to explain bin Laden to Americans. Although the dissimilarities between Brown and bin Laden as individuals are greater than their similarities — the latter is, by far, the better man — the two men share a passionate, uncompromising devotion to ridding their nations, the United States and the Muslim community of believers, or the ummah, of what they perceived to be a dominating evil.

In his exacting biography of the abolitionist editor William Lloyd Garrison, *All on Fire,* the late Henry Mayer wrote that Brown's actions, and especially his raid on Harper's Ferry in October 1859, "shocked the entire country and produced an emotional fervor without precedence in the nation's experience." Then, when Brown was hanged, the fervor intensified. "In the free states church bells tolled morning, noon, and night from Cape Cod to Kansas," Mayer noted, and even the eminent American Ralph Waldo Emerson saw Brown as "the new Saint . . . whose martyrdom if it shall be perfected, will make the gallows as glorious as the cross." Most important, Mayer argues, Brown's raid "irrevocably moved the slave controversy from the sphere of constitutional and moral abstraction to the visceral realm of feelings intensified beyond measure and reason."[9]

Bin Laden's al Qaeda movement, it seems to me, is traveling a path parallel to Brown's, a path that led America to a civil war that yielded a harvest of more than 600,000 dead. Bin Laden's philosophy has not completely moved Muslim perceptions of America's lethal intentions toward the Islamic world "irrevocably" from abstract discourse and deepening resentment to hatred and widespread violence. His movement seems to be moving it in that direction, however, and after the October 2000 attack on the U.S. destroyer *Cole* in Aden, Yemen, the prominent Egyptian Islamist lawyer Muntasir al-Zayyat said such attacks are becoming "acceptable to the Arab and Islamic peoples, and even a subject for praise and pride." In addition, the threat and use of violence by bin Laden, as they did for Brown, has kept his cause in the eye of the world, among both men in the street and members of the Muslim elites. And just as some educated, wealthy, and religious Americans thriving in the antebellum United States applauded the Harper's Ferry raid and committed treason by providing Brown the means to stage it—thereby supporting a man out to destroy the union in which they prospered—so too are some educated, prosperous, and devout Muslims, who are thriving in the Islamic world's status quo, supporting the al Qaeda network's efforts to destroy that status quo, apparently forgiving bin Laden's "errors of judgment" because of "the nobleness of his aims," as the historian James McPherson has described the attitude of many Americans toward John Brown. Both Brown and bin Laden present their respective societies with the difficult task of reconciling what Professor Blight called the contrast of high ideals and ruthless deeds. Blight's estimate of John Brown as "one of the avengers of history who does the work the rest of us won't, can't, or shouldn't" seems equally applicable, at least in the eyes of his followers, to Osama bin Laden.[10]

Staying the Course in God's Name: John Bunyan

Again, historical analogies—especially cross-cultural analogies—are double-edged tools, equally capable of producing invalid comparisons as valid ones. Still, they are useful for putting events or patterns of thought foreign to a society's experience into a context from which a measure of understanding can be drawn. The analogy between John Brown and Osama bin Laden is useful in this regard. Another that occurred to me as I studied bin Laden is a comparison between bin Laden and the English Puritan preacher John Bunyan's heroic-but-very-human protagonist Christian, the pivot of Bunyan's brilliant allegory *The Pilgrim's Progress.*[11] Though now largely untaught in American schools, Bunyan's book historically has been among the most influential in English, after the Bible and Shakespeare's works. Bunyan's readers come to know Christian's strengths and weaknesses and learn that Christian's ultimate success in overcoming the world's material seductions and the physical attacks of the ungodly is due to the fact that, in the face of obstacles and threats, he persevered, "believed steadfastly concerning things that are invisible," and, like Moses, "was rather for dying where he stood, than to go one step without his God."[12]

Like John Brown's journey, Christian's pilgrimage produced personal salvation and demarcated a road toward salvation for others to follow. Christian believed traveling in God's path was a personal responsibility because "what God says, is best, though all men in the world are against it"; because it would win him everlasting life in the "Celestial City"; and because it would shield him from temptation with the knowledge that "[t]he Glory of the next World will never wear out." Bunyan wrote that Christian must match his words with actions if he was to win salvation — praising God was necessary but insufficient. In *The Pilgrim's Progress,* Christian dismisses the faith of a man named "Talkative" because his faith is a matter of words.

> They [saying and doing] are two things indeed, and are as diverse, as are the Soul and Body; for as the Body without the Soul is but a dead carcass, so saying, if it be alone, is but a dead carcass also. The Soul of religion is the Pracktick part: *Pure religion and undefiled, before God and the Father is this, to visit the fatherless and widows in their affliction, and to keep himself unspotted from the World.* This *Talkative* is not aware of; he thinks that hearing and saying will make a good Christian; and thus he deceiveth his own soul. Hearing is but as the sowing of seed; Talking is not sufficient to prove that fruit is indeed in the Heart and life; and let us assure ourselves, at the day of Doom, men will be judged according to their Fruit: It will not be said then, *Did you believe?* But were you *Doers or Talkers* only? And accordingly shall they be judged. The end of world is compared to the harvest; and you know men at harvest regard nothing but fruit.[13]

Bunyan's hero Christian, like John Brown, also deliberately was setting an example that would encourage — bin Laden would say to "incite" —

others to follow. Christian and Brown succeeded. Christian's initially unbelieving wife and sons decided to follow his example and undertook what Bunyan calls "the most dangerous way in the world . . . that which Pilgrims go."[14] Brown, after his hopeless attack on the federal arsenal at Harper's Ferry, was captured and hanged, but within two years a civil war ensued that achieved his and, as he believed, God's goal of ending slavery, allowing the "crimes of a guilty land" to be "purged away in blood."[15]

As will be seen, bin Laden's goals in traveling his God's path mirror Christian's, to assure his entry to paradise by performing his religious duty to defend Islam against attack and by instigating all Muslims to do likewise, thereby redeeming themselves and doing God's work by restoring the Islamic nation's honor and dignity. "My marks and scars I carry with me," Christian said in words that easily could have come from John Brown or Osama bin Laden, "to be witness for me, that I have fought His battles, who will now be my redeemer."[16]

A Time for War: Thomas Jefferson, Patrick Henry, and Thomas Paine

A final analogy I found useful in thinking about Osama bin Laden in a context pertinent to Americans is drawn from Thomas Jefferson's Declaration of Independence and the political debate in the years before its adoption. Professor John L. Esposito drew me to this analogy in his fine book *The Islamic Threat. Myth or Reality?*, as did the editors of the respected Pakistani newspaper *Nawa-i-Waqt*. In his book, Esposito warned that when Americans automatically identify Islamist individuals and groups as terrorists, they forget the "heroes of the American Revolution were rebels and terrorists for the British Crown," while the editors of *Nawa-i-Waqt* lamented that "it is unfortunate that the United States, which obtained its independence through a [revolutionary] movement is calling Muslim freedom fighters [a] terrorist organization."[17]

When Thomas Jefferson wrote America's most important state paper, his argument was not drafted in a fit of pique and neither did it pivot off a single grievance against the British Crown. Rather, Jefferson's clarity, logic, dispassion, and historical precision captured the perception of many Americans — although not most — that by 1775 a lengthy and mostly peaceful journey had ended, a line had been crossed, and inaction was no longer tolerable. Jefferson, in essence, wrote that enough was enough and that further discussion was pointless, a conclusion later also reached by John Brown when, after years spent speaking, writing, and working against slavery, he declared: "Talk, talk, talk. That will never free the slaves. What is needed is action — action."[18] In asserting that the time for "talk" was over, Jefferson reminded his readers that "In every stage of these oppressions, we have petitioned for redress in the most humble terms: our repeated petitions have been answered only by repeated injuries. A prince whose character is thus marked by every act which may define a tyrant is unfit to be a ruler of a free people." Despite what he called the "patient sufferance" of Americans, Jefferson concluded that the Crown's unresponsiveness and continued abuses had yielded a situation for Americans where "necessity constrains them to alter their form of government."[19]

While he wrote a clear indictment of America's oppressor and a precise justification for war, Jefferson did not catch the exact heat of America's pre-Declaration political debate. His references to God and religion were, in particular, the calm language of the Deist he was and not the voice of the Old Testament that then thundered through American political discourse. Jefferson's war against Britain would be a just but reluctant necessity. In the spring of 1775, Patrick Henry better captured the more heated, Biblical tone of the debate. Henry spoke as God's zealous champion, leading a long-suffering people in a struggle to regain usurped rights. "It is in vain, Sir, to extenuate the matter," Henry said. "Gentlemen may cry peace, peace — but there is no peace. The war is actually begun."

> We have petitioned — we have remonstrated — we have supplicated — we have prostrated ourselves before the throne, and have implored its interposition to arrest the tyrannical hands of the ministry and parliament. Our petitions have been slighted; our remonstrances have produced additional violence and insult; our supplications have been disregarded; and we have been spurned, with contempt, from the foot of the throne. In vain, after these things, may we indulge in fond hope of peace and reconciliation? There is no longer any room for hope. If we wish to be free — if we mean to preserve inviolate those inestimable privileges for which we have been for so long contending — if we mean not basely to abandon the noble struggle in which we have so long been engaged, and which we have pledged ourselves never to abandon, until the glorious object of our contest shall be obtained — we must fight! — I repeat, Sir, we must fight! An appeal to arms and to the God of hosts is all that is left to us.[20]

Osama bin Laden: Like America's Heroes—Fighting Not Submitting

Common among these Anglo-American leaders was the journey from remonstrance to war, from pen to sword. Common also was sincerity, dedication, and an absolute refusal to compromise after the line between tolerable and intolerable was crossed. Osama bin Laden has traversed a nearly identical journey and shares the grim determination to prevail or die trying. Bin Laden's words and deeds are slowly changing the nature of Islamic political discourse, because, as Professor Esposito has said, his "message and cause resonates with many in the Arab and Muslim worlds."[21]

Like John Brown, bin Laden has framed his argument in the context of God's words and has acted on those words, mirroring Bunyan's assertion that the genuinely faithful must do God's work with deeds as well as words. Indeed, bin Laden seems to be moving the Islamic world toward violence in the manner of Brown, altering the nature and intensity of the Muslim debate over U.S. foreign policy. "[A]s a result of John Brown," Professor G. A. Fine has written in his study of the abolitionist crusader's impact, "more people committed themselves to abolition and committed themselves more strongly. If Brown did not cause a revolution in thinking, he increased the number who accepted militant action. Brown made militant verbal abolition seem moderate in comparison."[22]

The Muslim media are making a similar judgment about bin Laden, and correctly so. By his deeds, bin Laden "has earned the respect of men hardened in battle,"[23] and by his words he is inciting Muslims "who will stand against the evil force [the United States] and will continue their struggle seeking the liberation of our Islamic land from the forces of evil, sins, and darkness."[24] Also like Bunyan's heroic pilgrim Christian, bin Laden is described as having "the courage to turn the tide of the times. . . . Such a Muslim revolutionary is hard to find in this age."[25]

And the tie to Jefferson and the founders? Well, almost exactly 200 years after the signing of Jefferson's exposition of America's profoundly conservative and religious mind, bin Laden published a declaration of his own, which, like Jefferson's, displayed a deeply conservative and religious mind. Bin Laden's "Declaration of Jihad against the United States"[26] deserves quotation at length because it details, as did Jefferson's declaration, the "patient sufferance" of Saudi nationals under the misdeeds of their own king and his family; the "long train of abuses and usurpations" to which they have been subjected; and their duty to destroy a government that is ignoring the rights that Muslims "were endowed by their Creator."

As had Jefferson, bin Laden drafted a detailed indictment of the al-Saud family's transgressions, a list that includes harassment, persecution, and incarceration of reformers; media censorship and manipulation; official corruption in the financial and economic sectors; perversion of the Islamic legal system with man-made laws; use of foreign mercenaries against Muslims; failure to defend the country; and material support to the enemies of Islam. The Muslim media paid close attention to this indictment and told its readers that bin Laden was turning to armed resistance because the al-Sauds had rejected all efforts at peaceful reform. "Shaykh Usama also concentrates on the reasons that justified his recourse to this [warlike] attitude," *Al-Islaah*'s editors commented in words reminiscent of Patrick Henry's, "[i]n this context he reviewed the past peaceful attempts and all means to deal with the [al-Saud] regime in this regard had been exhausted, with the regime countering them with ferocity, roughness, and defiance." *Al-Islaah* likewise noted that bin Laden and his brother Saudi reformers had not acted impetuously. "Those who are fully familiar with the Shaykh's [bin Laden's] personality," *Al-Islaah* explained, "were surprised at his delay in taking this attitude and his failure to take this attitude long before." The editors also said that bin Laden had long controlled forces capable of military action against the al-Sauds and their allies.[27]

While the ideological, political, and theological foundations of the two declarations are worlds apart, each comes to the same conclusion: arms must be used against the established rulers and their supporters, because, as Patrick Henry said, "There is no retreat but in submission and slavery."[28] After describing the patient attempts to persuade the al-Sauds to reform, bin Laden wrote in the crossing-the-Rubicon tone of Brown, Henry, and Jefferson. Armed action was mandatory, bin Laden wrote, because "all peaceful means to expel foreign occupation and reverse the process of de-Islamization in Saudi Arabia have been exhausted by opposition groups," implicitly echoing John Brown's realization that he had "vainly flattered myself that without very much bloodshed it [the end of legal slavery] might be done."[29]

Because the al-Sauds had "violated legitimate rights" of their subjects, bin Laden wrote that he and his fellow reformers had

> offered advice secretly and openly, in verse and in prose, singly and in groups, and they sent petition after petition, and memorandum after memorandum. They left no stone unturned and there was no influential person they did not include in the reformist moves. In their writings they applied the gentle and lenient method of wisdom and good advice calling for reform and penance for the major wrongdoings and corruption that transgressed the categorical religious limits and the public's legitimate rights.
>
> More regrettably, however, the only response they got from the regime was rejection, disregard, and ridicule. The matter did not stop at the point of just humiliating them [the reformers] but that was followed by greater and greater misdeeds throughout the land of the two holy mosques. Therefore silence was no longer appropriate and overlooking the facts was no longer acceptable.
>
> When excesses intensified and went beyond the limits of simple wrongdoings and misdeeds to violation of the clear basis of Islam, a group of ulema and religious scholars grew tired of the deafening sound of misguidance and injustice and the suffocating smell of corruption. . . . The submitted petitions and memoranda to the King urging reform . . . but he ignored the advice and ridiculed those who offered it, and the situation got worse.

Those who offered advice then send more memoranda and petitions, the most important being the advice memorandum handed to the King in the month of Muharram 1413 Hegira [corresponding to 1992] which diagnosed the disease and prescribed the medicine with a sound Shari'ah approach and in a sound and scientific way. It dwelt on the main gaps in the regime's philosophy and the main anomalies in the regime's foundations. . . . It also dwelt on the country's laws and regulations and what they allowed and disallowed against God's will.

Although the memorandum submitted all that leniently and gently, as a reminder of God and as good advice in a gentle, objective, and sincere way, [and] despite the importance and necessity of advice for rulers in Islam, and despite the number and positions of the signatories of the memorandum, it was to no avail. Its contents were rejected and its signatories and sympathizers were humiliated, punished, and imprisoned.

The preachers' and reformers' eagerness to pursue peaceful reform methods in the interest of the country's unity and to prevent bloodshed was clearly demonstrated. So why should the regime block all means of peaceful reform and drive the people toward armed action? That was the only door left open for the public for ending injustice and upholding right and justice.[30]

Thus, bin Laden and his reformer colleagues laid claim to the right asserted by Jefferson, Henry, Paine, and their colleagues after they had exhausted all avenues of peaceful remonstrance; "it is their Right, it is their Duty to throw off such a government, and to provide new Guards for their future Security."

I believe that the decision to move from petition to arms deserves no less respectful consideration — if America is to be protected — than that of the American patriots we rightly revere. Unfortunately, America and the West today hear bin Laden and his colleagues with a predisposition identical to that with which the British Crown heard the founders; that is, in Professor Esposito's words, "by the tendency in the international system to regard those in power as legitimate rulers or governments, regardless of how they came to power or whether they are autocratic or repressive."[31]

This is not to say that bin Laden and his colleagues are correct and merit sympathy; as I have said, the United States will eventually have to use military force to confront and defeat bin Laden and the forces he is inciting. It is to say, however, that bin Laden is an honorable man and a worthy enemy, one who turned his energies to war only after years of peaceful, law-abiding agitation. Reflecting on the events before our revolution, Thomas Paine concluded that no honest man could condemn Americans for acting in haste. "I have as little superstition in me as any living man," Paine wrote in *The American Crisis,*

> but my secret opinion has and still is that God Almighty will not give up a people to military destruction or leave them unsupported to perish who have so earnestly and so repeatedly sought to avoid the calamities of war by every decent method that wisdom could invent. Neither have I so much of the infidel in me as to suppose that He has relinquished the government of the world and given us up to the care of devils, and as I do not, and can not, see on what grounds the King of Britain can look up to heaven for help against us; a common murderer, a highwayman, or a housebreaker has as good a pretense as he.[32]

As matters turned out, Paine's "secret opinion" was validated and the American incendiaries prevailed. Across centuries and cultures, who is to say with confidence that another well-led group of formerly patient and peaceful incendiaries could not again prevail?

ARROGANCE, MONEY, AND IDEAS

2

OBSTACLES TO UNDERSTANDING BIN LADEN

Now, Faithful, play the man, speak for thy God;
Fear not the Wicked's malice, nor their rod;
Speak boldly man, the truth is on thy side;
Die for it, and to life in triumph ride.

The Pilgrim's Progress, 1678

It is commonplace to say each of us brings to the understanding of people, events, and ideas the biases formed by our upbringing, family, and education; our personal, religious, professional, and political experiences; and the degree to which we have accepted or rejected society's norms and conventions. Each of us, therefore, views any particular person, idea, or event from a slightly different angle. In general, however, Americans currently seem to share several basic beliefs that differ markedly from those that have historically shaped American life, to wit: there are few if any absolutes; most people think as we do, share our values, admire us, and want to emulate us; wars can be fought and won with few or no casualties; foreigners benefit from U.S. foreign policy and should be grateful for our efforts; and there are issues about which it is wise not to talk for fear of being labeled as prejudice. Contemporary Americans also are impatient, quickly frustrated, and have short attention spans; they accept being told how and what to think by the media; often form views on first appearances; are deeply cynical about their own and foreign leaders; have marginal knowledge of their history and almost none of others; and have an aversion to risk, and a love of ease. Finally, a few historic American characteristics still factor into our national life: a focus on making a buck; an insular eagerness to get on with life and pursue personal and local interests; and a perfect willingness to let the world go its own way if the world will leave us alone.

These attributes leave Americans singularly unprepared to really hear what Osama bin Laden has been saying; to understand why he said it; to recognize the sincerity and seriousness of purpose with which he spoke when declaring war on the United States; or, at least until the events of 11 September 2001, to appreciate the extent of the damage he intended to do to U.S. interests. Journalist John Miller caught this point exactly. "In modern day America," he wrote in *Esquire* in February 1999, "we no longer have the stomach for endeavors that don't seem like sure bets, which can make things tricky when you are up against someone who doesn't give a damn, someone who is willing to risk everything. and gladly." More troubling, U.S. leaders fear to remind citizens of the eternal truth that, as Professor Robin Fox has written, "war has been a constant in human history . . . [and] may very well have intrinsic self-rewarding qualities, and that these are easily appealed to, and the emotions associated with them easily aroused."[1] Since the cold war's end, U.S. and Western leaders have said that war is obsolete, and that the world is now — under the rubric "Globalization" — marching toward an inevitable and worldwide liberal-democratic society.

The pervasive belief in the inevitable triumph of Western liberalism is one of the main reasons for the self-righteous fury liberals focused on Samuel Huntington's clash-of-civilization thesis. Having rejected Huntington, Western elites are now going through what Professor Fox has described as "one of those 'war is dead' periods that occasionally try to brighten up the otherwise uninterrupted march of human conflict." The danger of such ahistorical thinking lies in the fact that it becomes "wishful thinking, which in turn becomes a refusal to admit that the basic premise may just be plain wrong." And the premise is clearly wrong. War is here to stay as long as human beings walk the earth, notwithstanding what Mark Helprin has called the American elites' "insatiable mania to dissemble." "No one will state that the lion has not lain down with the lamb," Helprin has argued. "No one will state that, if we do not take care, perhaps those now playing in our schoolyards or resting in their mothers' laps will die in enormous numbers in a war that will seem to have no end."[2]

Let us now look at how the foregoing characteristics are not shared by Osama bin Laden and his associates, and how that fact gives them a decided advantage over their American enemies.

Suppressed Debate

Osama bin Laden is not constrained by America's tenets of political correctness, which have had the impact of "outlawing generalizations about peoples and regions [and thereby] immobilizes meaningful discussions about them."[3] He has asserted without doubt, vagueness, or qualification the superiority of Islam and Islamic life and has described in detail his hatred for Jews and Christians because of their occupation of Islamic lands and sanctities, heretical beliefs or lack of religious belief, focus on money, and relentless persecution of Muslims. Because many Americans are silent on such touchy issues as race, religion, and sexual mores, so as not to offend, be labeled a bigot, or risk legal entanglements for violating the "hate speech" laws the Federal government uses to protect its policies from criticism, they tend to consign to the lunatic fringe those who publicly and forcefully articulate nonmainstream beliefs. In bin Laden's case, this behavior could be fatal; bin Laden has been far from the lunatic fringe in the Muslim world, and his views and actions have an increasing following.

What must be understood is that what bin Laden has said and done has everything to do with religion and that we will neither understand him nor the threat he has unleashed until we recognize and articulate that there are tens and perhaps hundreds of millions of Muslims who, like bin Laden, hate the United States for what they believe is its consistently anti-Islamic behavior. "Bin Laden has become a pan-Arab hero," Egyptian Islamist lawyer Muntasir al-Zayyat has said, "because the Arab and Muslim peoples are yearning to [*sic*—for?] any voice that says no to the United States." Bin Laden is attempting to repel what he views as Christian aggression, to end what he considers the West's deliberate "humiliation" of the Islamic world, and to restore to Muslims their dignity and control over their destinies. In doing so, bin Laden's supporters will kill, in God's name, those they deem enemies of Islam, and will kill them with whatever means and in whatever numbers are necessary to achieve their goals.[4]

When U.S. and other Western leaders describe bin Laden as a terrorist problem, not a religious issue, they mislead their publics. By doing so, they fail to teach their listeners that bin Laden is far more than a run-of-the-mill terrorist, that he is, rather, a multitalented Muslim leader who claims to be motivated by his love for God and his fellow Muslims and has acted in a manner he believes is prescribed by laws given by that God and explained and amplified by God's messenger, the Prophet Muhammed. "This war is fundamentally religious," bin Laden said in November 2001. "Under no circumstances should we forget this enmity between us and the infidels. For, the enmity is based on creed."[5]

These leaders are also misleading when they fail to explain that policies pursued by the United States and the West for decades in the Middle East and Muslim world generally are seen by many Muslims as anti-Islamic. For the little they pay attention to international affairs, Americans tend to believe U.S. foreign policy is benign and characterized by generosity, altruism, support for the underdog, concern for human rights, and advocacy of democracy. Americans are surprised when ungrateful foreigners try to knock down our airliners, blow up our skyscrapers, sink our ships, and kill our servicemen and drag their nude and mutilated bodies through the streets. To understand the perspective of the supporters of bin Laden, we must accept that there are many Muslims in the world who believe that U.S. foreign policy is irretrievably biased in favor of Israel; trigger happy in attacking the poor and ill-defended Muslim countries, Sudan, Iraq, Afghanistan, Somalia, and so forth; rapacious in controlling and consuming the Islamic world's energy resources; blasphemous in allowing Israel to occupy Jerusalem and U.S. troops to be based in Saudi Arabia; and hypocritical and cruel in its denial of Palestinian rights, use of economic sanctions against the Muslim people of Iraq, and support for the Muslim world's absolutist kings and dictators. It matters not a lick if these perceptions hold water; they have been dogma for bin Laden, his followers, and tens of millions of Muslims around the world. Until that fact is accepted, America will not be able to defend itself. As the strategist Williamson Murray has written, America's defense is not optimal, because its leaders are "wholly disconnected from what others, think, want, and can do" and refuse to accept that "[w]hat matters most in war is what is in the mind of one's enemies, from command post to battlefield points-of-contact."[6]

Obsolete Experts

Another problem for Americans as they try to comprehend what bin Laden is about is their tendency to accept the views of those the media term "experts." These experts are usually of two types: retired government and military officials or "informed" commentators, the latter mostly journalists and academics. In many cases, this stable of experts is working from a database of experience and knowledge that was relevant in the 1970s or 1980s, when they were professionals working against "international terrorism." The relatively small number of retired U.S. government officials among the experts the media roll out after a terrorist attack is composed mostly of individuals who labored against Lebanese Hizballah, the Abu Nidal Organization (ANO), the Popular Front for the Liberation of Palestine-General Command, and the phalanx of leftist groups that once bedeviled Western Europe. None of these groups ever posed a direct national security threat to America — with the possible exception of Hizballah, which last attacked a U.S. target in 1991 — and none was more than a sporadically lethal nuisance to the United States. Today most of these groups have either ceased to exist, are internationally inactive, or have meandered into a geriatric limbo where neither their bark nor their bite is a particularly large worry.

In any event, the experts' detailed knowledge of these groups — as valuable as it was when they were in government service — is not transferable to the bin Laden problem. Bin Laden's organization is larger, more ethnically diverse, more geographically dispersed, younger, richer, better educated, better led, and more militarily trained and combat experienced than the groups the experts faced. Most important, it also has more growth potential and is more religiously motivated than any organization mentioned above. Only Hizballah has remotely approached the religious intensity that is the signal characteristic of al Qaeda. The central motivating role of Islam in al Qaeda activities, then, is a factor largely absent from the milieu in which most media experts worked.

The media experts are hamstrung in another way by their professional experience. When they were working, the experts confronted the peak years of activity by what the U.S. government identifies as the "State Sponsors of Terrorism," a group now consisting of Iran, Iraq, Cuba, Syria, North Korea, Libya, and Sudan. Many of the above-mentioned terrorist groups were, in the lingo of the day, "surrogates" for state sponsors. The two brands of terrorist entities existed in a symbiotic relationship believed to benefit both. The terrorist groups, for example, benefited from their state sponsor's provision of money, training, explosives, weapons, logistical assistance, and identity and travel documents. At the same time, the state sponsor gained by having a terrorist group to do its lethal bidding. This arrangement gave the state sponsor what was called "plausible deniability" by allowing it to attack without using its intelligence service or special forces.

This line of analysis was the standard and largely accurate assessment for the structure of Middle Eastern terrorism for most of the 1970s and 1980s, although the goofy concept of plausible deniability was operable only because of America's obsession with securing court-quality evidence of culpability before retaliating, and the Europeans' always-desperate eagerness to cling to any speck of doubt that might allow them to sidestep militarily retaliation against attacks on their interests. Overall, the importance of the state sponsors in the 1970s and 1980s gave the media experts a frame of reference in which the threat posed by a terrorist group was determined by its state sponsor's strength and audacity. Certainly the groups never posed a meaningful threat to U.S. national security. Ergo, groups without state sponsors were thought not to pose much of a threat. The Hizballah-Iran pairing, of course, was the colossus that dominated the experts' professional lives and today still dominates much of their analysis.

In the context of their professional experience, therefore, the media experts look at bin Laden through a lens yellowed with age and focused on a more easily understood time when state sponsors and their surrogates were the main terrorist threats to U.S. interests. That scenario is now invalid; as Anatol Lieven has written in the *National Interest*, "to deter a state . . . you have to be fighting against a state."[7] The experts, however, have tried to wedge bin Laden into that analytical framework. Regarding bin

Laden's al Qaeda organization, for example, the U.S. Secret Service's former counterterrorism chief told *U.S. News & World Report* in October 1998 that "the tradecraft is just not there because they don't have the support of a patron state's intelligence service."[8] This analysis came eight weeks after bin Laden blew up two U.S. embassies, in two different countries, within minutes of each other, something even Hizballah has never done. In the same month, Dr. M. C. Dunn wrote in *Middle East Policy* that the West should not treat bin Laden as "the devil incarnate" and reminded his readers that bin Laden "lacks the protection and support of a major power."[9] As frequently seems the case, former U.S. State Department counterterrorism officials take the cake in underestimating bin Laden. "If he [bin Laden] had the where-withal to kill Americans," one such official told *Frontline* in April 1999,

> and attack U.S. targets he would do so, but he doesn't. He is not in the position; he's not an army. He doesn't have an arsenal of nuclear weapons; he doesn't have an arsenal of chemical/biological weapons. He doesn't have military forces in place ready to launch, because he'd then also need transportation to move them from point A to point B and once they get to point B, then he's got to figure out how to get them back to point A. . . . He's serious about wanting to kill Americans, but as long as he's in Afghanistan, as long as he doesn't have access to a cell phone, . . . his ability to plan and conduct terrorist operations is extremely limited.[10]

Perhaps it is more obvious in the post–11 September atmosphere that the dominance of the state-sponsor mind-set must be ended and replaced by the realization that organizations such as that led by bin Laden are a threat to U.S. national security precisely because, as Professor A. E. Wisgerhof argues, they are not "supported by or beholden to the good graces of one government, have their own financial and logistical resources, and are often immune to the need for traditional foreign relations."[11]

The few hints of analytic hope on the horizon come mostly from working journalists, although they too largely ignore the motivating power of theology and look to helpful but incomplete analogies found in the world of modern business. "The new terrorist chiefs are more like international businessmen," London's *Sunday Times* wrote in August 1998. "All the resources of modern technology are at their disposal — and they are ruthless. Bin Laden surfs the internet and talks to his henchmen and investment managers by satellite phone from a cave . . . he depends on no state sponsor."[12] Almost simultaneously, the *Financial Times* made this crucial point more directly. "Until the advent of the Afghan Arabs," the daily explained, "terror networks had generally depended on the patronage of 'rogue' states, upon which retribution could be visited. But the extensive international network built by Mr. Bin Laden, a wealthy Saudi exile who has developed an operational capability equivalent to what state sponsorship can furnish, has tended to base itself in countries which barely qualify as states, overwhelmed by factional and tribal strife and which cannot easily be held to account."[13]

Impatience

A simple, unalterable fact is that bin Laden and his compatriots are patient and Americans are not. To illustrate this point with a tale that may be apocryphal, in the 1980s a junior American diplomat attended a meeting in Peshawar, Pakistan, of the military coordinators of the seven main Afghan resistance parties. Arriving a bit before the appointed time of 1:00 p.m., this officer and his associates took seats near the stage, across which a wall-to-wall drape was drawn. Within an hour after the meeting was to start — a good hint of the Afghans' non-Western sense of time — the mujahedin began to seat themselves at tables on the stage. The meeting began at 2:10, and just before it did, the drapes were opened to reveal a wall-to-wall map. All of Afghanistan and bits of Iran and Pakistan were on the map; all three countries were labeled appropriately. Across the top of the map ran a swath of what was then Soviet Central Asia and China's Xinjiang Province. Neither was labeled that way, however. Instead, the area was boldly labeled "TEMPORARILY OCCUPIED MUSLIM TERRITORY." The junior American diplomat chuckled on reading the label, chalking it up to wartime bravado. Chatting with English-speaking mujahedin after the meeting, the diplomat asked about the labeling of Central Asia and was told, in perfect seriousness, "Yes, *Inshallah* [God willing], the region will be won back for Islam one day." The diplomat came away, it is said, believing his interlocutors' sincerity, but convinced that if the Soviets left Afghanistan, the jihad's fervor would wane and Moscow's gates would never be darkened by the insurgents' scruffy shadows.

These days one wonders if that junior diplomat was not too cynical. While the gates of Moscow are secure — though creaky after car-bomb attacks in 1999 left three hundred Russians dead — Islamist insurgencies are under way in Tajikistan, Uzbekistan, Chechnya, and Dagestan, and portents of similar insurgencies are rumbling in Kyrgyzstan and western China. If the Afghan mujahedin had not fallen out with each other after the Soviets' departure, it might be that the world would have several Islamist states aborning in Central Asia.

The foregoing is to stress that bin Laden's movement and the Muslim world possess, from the Western perspective, superhuman and maddening amounts of patience. The Afghans who spoke of the map spanning that Peshawar stage did not say they would reclaim Central Asia for Allah, only that they were confident that through jihad it would be reclaimed, if not by them, then by their sons, grandsons, or great-grandsons. For bin Laden and those supported or inspired by him, the mind-set is identical; indeed, it appears bin Laden and the Arab Afghans not only acquired combat experience in Afghanistan but also acquired the patience, stoicism, and long-term approach to life that typify the Afghan character.

Bin Laden has never urged haste on his followers, although near-term victory is preferable to end Muslim suffering and liberate Islam's sanctities. He has built his organization methodically, caring most about security, resilience, and lethality, and least about speed. In developing his organization, the Jordanian daily *Sawt al-Ma'rah* has said, bin Laden has displayed patience. "His favorite method," the Amman daily explained, "is to gather full personal information on the members of security organs working in customs, port, airports, heads of sections in interior ministries; [and] in penetrating import and export companies operating in Arab countries."[14] Bin Laden's success is seen in reports that his operatives have penetrated the military, security, and police services in Kuwait, Egypt, Yemen, Pakistan, Qatar, and Jordan. Bin Laden also asked God to give Muslims "patience and steadfastness" as they fight what he terms the Crusaders — the U.S.-led primarily Christian Western nations,[15] and has sought to steel Muslim hearts for the long haul by reminding them that "he who abandons resoluteness is humiliated" and using in his fatwa the following passage from the Koran: "So lose no heart, nor fall into despair. For yea must gain mastery if yea are true in faith."[16] In addition, bin Laden's public grooming of his eldest son as his successor is another sign that he suspects his goals may not be accomplished in his lifetime.[17]

Most eloquent, the communiqué claiming responsibility for the August 1998 East Africa bombings testified to the long-range endeavor on which bin Laden is embarked. "The days to come," the message concluded,

> are sufficient for the U.S., God willing, to see a black fate like the one that befell the Soviet Union. Blows will come down on the U.S. one after another from everywhere and new Islamic groups will emerge one after another to fight U.S. interests that are still based on stealth and usurpation. Islamic armies will set off one following the other to fight the U.S. criminal forces. And you will see: As for the unbelievers, never will disaster cease to seize them for their ill deeds or to settle close to their homes until the promise of God has come to pass, for verily, God will not fail in his promise.[18]

That bin Laden is not alone in possessing a level of patience far exceeding the West's chronically low norm is underscored by his colleagues' words. They and bin Laden share the belief that their struggle is an integral part of Islam's more than 1,400-year historical continuum in which the central feature is the defense of Islam against Christian aggression. They see themselves as part of this long defensive historical struggle — which Allah has not only blessed, but has also directed to be waged as part of the price of entering paradise — and are prepared, as President Ronald Reagan used to say, to stay the course. "The Americans should know," Zawahiri wrote in late 1998, "that we have resolved to fight them fiercely in a long battle. . . . Generations will pass on the torch to the following ones so that the Prophet's flag remains raised in victory till eternity."[19]

In this context, the ingrained impatience and short attention span of the United States — its people, media, and government — are major obstacles to understanding the long-term nature of the al Qaeda movement's threat and the intensifying confrontation between the Western and Muslim worlds, between Christianity and Islam. After five years of interviewing bin Laden about his motivation and intentions, for example, most Western journalists continue to treat him as a transient terrorist phenomenon. "The exiled Saudi millionaire," the *Economist* wrote in the summer of 1998, "is fast becoming a cult figure to many of his more devout countrymen."[20] Cult figures are, of course, a dime a dozen in Western popular culture and generally have limited shelf life. Cults also generally consist of small groups of people who lean toward the wacky if not fanatical side, like those who committed suicide en masse only after ensuring they had a pocket full of quarters for car fare in the next life. The knee-jerk tendency to classify bin Laden as a cult hero is absurd and probably says more about the West's impatience with things that require puzzling out or take more than ninety seconds of video to summarize.

Bin Laden made quite clear following the 1998 East Africa embassy bombings that he was patiently planning future attacks on U.S. targets. "The people involved in these explosions," he said in January 1999, "have just given a slight warning to the United States. A full-fledged reply is still to come forth."[21]

There it is, laid out by leaders and fighters in clear, precise language. And yet we still failed to appreciate the resolute patience of America's Islamist foes. "Too often we forget," the *Washington Post* said in 1998, "that if the terrorist has any outstanding quality besides vengefulness and cunning, it is patience; he may strike back next week, next month, or next year."[22] If true for a terrorist, how much truer must it be for a man dedicated to waging a worldwide insurgency on what he sees as God's behalf?

Imperial Hubris

How can hubris be measured in its effect on an individual's or a nation's ability to understand foreign events, personalities, ideas, threats, and ideologies? Because science has yet to build such a device, any measuring must be more or less impressionistic. Regarding Osama bin Laden, Americans, and especially politicians, opinion leaders, academics, the "experts," and most of the media, seem afflicted by a severe case of imperial hubris, an attitude that attributes the emergence of bin Laden to one or another U.S. action. Thus, Mary Anne Weaver writes in the *New Yorker* that bin Laden was produced by the Afghan jihad, which, in turn, was part of that "Pan Islamic effort whose fighters were funded, armed, and trained by the C.I.A., [and which] eventually brought twenty-five thousand Islamic militants, from more than 50 countries, to combat the Soviet occupation of Afghanistan. The United States, intentionally or not, had launched Pan-Islam's first jihad, or holy war, in eight centuries."[23] The often-acute Ms. Weaver seems here to be suffering from imperial hubris. For her, neither the Soviet invasion of Afghanistan and the Red Army's barbarity, nor the tenets of Islam that compel believers to defend their religion and territory against attack and assist those who are so doing, can account for the emergence of bin Laden and his colleagues and followers. The Islamic world, for Weaver, supported the Afghan jihad primarily because the U.S. president made the CIA available to arm, train, and fund non-Afghan Muslim volunteers who wanted to assist the Afghan mujahedin. Other prominent foreign policy commentators, such as the *Washington Post's* Jim Hoagland, former senior CIA officer Milt Bearden, and terrorism expert Brian M. Jenkins, also have followed Ms. Weaver's analytic line.

In many discussions of the Afghan jihad's residual problems, the U.S. media seemed determined to establish U.S. aid to the mujahedin as the main cause of today's growing Islamist militancy. The fact that there would have been no mujahedin — Afghan, Arab, or otherwise — if the Bolsheviks had not invaded and brutalized Afghanistan seems to escape their ken completely. Only recently, Walter T. Vollman, in one of the few balanced assessments of Afghanistan's Taliban regime, found it necessary to remind readers that Soviet actions gave birth to the mujahedin. "The deeds of the Soviets were unspeakable," Vollman wrote. "They raped women in the name of emancipating them. In defense of national security, they machine-gunned illiterate peasants who couldn't have found Moscow on a map. They burned people alive and drowned them in excrement. They razed villages, slaughtered livestock, and destroyed harvests. They even scattered mines disguised as toys to lure people to their maiming."[24] Beyond Vollman's words, American journalists can do no better to appreciate Sovietized Afghanistan than by examining Moscow's grizzly handiwork — which Eric Margolis describes as "the combined merciless destructiveness of Genghis Khan with the calculated terrorism of Stalin — in the photographs in Radek Sikorski's *Dust of the Saints* and Robert Kaplan's account of his travels with the mujahedin in *Soldiers of God*.[25]

All of the explanations offered by the U.S. media for the rise and influence of Osama bin Laden basically come down to the same idea, to the same universalist ideology: The United States is the center of the world; it is, in one way or another, responsible for what happens in the world; and anti-American international actors like bin Laden are violent, medieval, and un-enlightened anachronisms because the overwhelming percentage of the world's population shares our values and wants to be like Americans. This distorted America-centric vision of reality is leading to a clash of civilizations, as outlined by Professor Samuel P. Huntington in his book *The Clash of Civilizations and the Remaking of World Order.*[26] Some of Huntington's critics, however, have concluded that the non-Western world is suffering not from too much American universalism but from too little. Thus, in *Foreign Policy,* Richard E. Rubenstein and Jarle Crocker argue that the civilizational conflicts predicted by Huntington — Christendom vs. Islam, China vs. the West, and so forth — "can be averted and can be resolved if they do occur." More likely, according to the authors, is a "violent clash of civilizations [that] could well result from our continuing failure to transform the systems of inequality that make social life around the globe a struggle for individual and group survival — systems that feed the illusion that either one civilization or another must be dominant. . . . Satisfying basic human needs on a global scale will require a powerful movement for social change — a movement waiting to be born."[27] Surely the phrase "our continuing failure to transform the systems of inequality" means nothing more than that we have so far failed to remake the whole world on the American pattern and must try harder.

Though the delusion-producing nature of this ideological approach to international affairs is apparent — it can be argued that bin Laden and other Islamists similarly suffer from their ideological lens — the number of informed and learned people advocating it is astonishing, perhaps validating Gertrude Himmelfarb's definition of cognitive dissonance as "the discrepancy between reality and ideology that only truly learned and clever people can achieve."[28] It is precisely because Huntington dared to challenge the dominance and indict the arrogance of the universalists that his essay and book on "the clash of civilizations" earned a torrent of condescending scorn from Western academics, journalists, and foreign policy analysts. Huntington was damned for using "simple visions or catch phrases," for focusing on "the supposed revival of religion in the late twentieth century," for suggesting a "Muslim cavalry" rode to the rescue of its Bosnian brethren, and for "his lack of political common sense and responsibility" that led him to "excessive simplification" and arguments that are "often incredibly one-sided and inflammatory."[29]

Most strikingly, but most in character for Huntington's critics, was Mark Huband's denunciation of Huntington's suggestion that there is a "Muslim conflict propensity." On this issue, Huband claims, via the use of scientific-sounding percentages, Huntington's work is "an obvious slur against perhaps the 75 or 80 percent of Muslims who do not consider themselves Islamists, and the far greater proportion who, Islamist or not, have never engaged in violence and have no intention of doing so."[30]

Perhaps tellingly, non-Western scholars have paid more respect to Huntington's ideas. In an essay in the *Journal of Church and State,* for example, Professor Mahmood Monshipouri wrote that even though Huntington over-estimates the role of religion in international affairs and undervalues the impact of "the global resurgence of democratization and interdependence," Huntington's view that Western values are not universally applicable is on target. "The West must realize," Monshipouri argues, "that its political and cultural experiences do not serve as a universal model and that other forms of political and cultural organizations may be just as valid and functional."[31] Similarly, Wang Gungwu, a former vice chancellor of the University of Hong Kong, wrote in the *National Interest* that Huntington was "admirably frank about the relative decline of the West." "In doing so," Professor Wang argued,

> he offers a major corrective to the complacency and arrogance that have dominated Western self-perception for the past century and a half. If his calculations are widely accepted by Western scholars and commentators, a new language and vocabulary will have to be de-veloped for future generations, for to depict the values that the West has stood for in the past two centuries as less than universal will call for a revolution of attitudes. This is courageous talk, not only in terms of what it means for Westerners themselves, but also for those from other civilizations who have been educated — and possibly converted, if not misled — to accept the supposed universalism of Western civilization.[32]

For his part, bin Laden did not, it is clear, accept the universalist ideol-ogy that he believes treats Muslims in a humiliating, discriminatory, and capriciously lethal manner. Neither did he accept the denigration of Islam that is inherent and often smugly explicit in the West's aggressive secular-ism. Again, this is not to say that bin Laden is correct, but it adamantly is to say that the West's road to hell lies in approaching the bin Laden problem with the presumption that only the lunatic fringe could oppose what the United States is trying to accomplish through its foreign policy toward the Muslim world. Bin Laden's philosophy is slowly harnessing the two most powerful motivating forces in contemporary international affairs: religion and nationalism. In this effort, bin Laden's movement has an advantage, because the tenets of Islam strictly guide all aspects of Muslim life, personal, political, and sacred. "If Christianity says, give Caesar what is [due] to Cae-sar," eminent Sunni scholar Shakh Yusuf al-Qaradawi recently explained, "our religion says, Caesar and what is due him belongs to God Almighty."[33] As a consequence, the legitimacy of the Muslim leader — be he president, king, prime minister, or military dictator—depends on his steadfastness in hewing to the Sharia in governing at home and conducting relations abroad. So strong is this tradition in Islam, Professor John Kelsay argues in *Islam and War: A Study in Comparative Ethics,* that "Any Muslim ruler who omits to impose the regimen specified by the traditional judgments of the classical jurists of the [Sharia] law is an apostate and must be fought."[34]

Realistically, bin Laden has stolen a march on his American and Western enemies because he recognizes the power of these forces and is acting to mobilize and exploit it. In the post–World War II West, in contrast, the elites have long railed against and ridiculed the possibility of nationalism and religion playing a telling role in personal, societal, or international affairs. Although the foes of bin Laden's philosophy believe his appeal is limited to those few sorry and anachronistic fools who do not accept the universality of Western values, bin Laden has spoken to a broadening spectrum of Muslim society for which U.S. foreign policy, secularism, materialism, and unchecked individualism are anathema.

Until Americans begin to see that some of their values and goals are neither accepted nor acceptable to all races, nations, and creeds, they will not begin to understand the appeal of a person like bin Laden or be able to defend their interests against him. Indeed, they will need to go another step and recognize that, for many Muslims, U.S. foreign policy is seen as an attack on Islam. Until this realization sinks in, American experts will mislead their audience by claiming that religion has emerged as the predominant impetus for terrorist attacks rather than acknowledging that U.S. foreign policy, from the perspective of millions of Muslims it directly affects, is interpreted as an attack on Islam and Muslims and is drawing an armed response as a matter of self-defense and scriptural requirement.

Perhaps bin Laden's words give Americans the context in which to recognize this point. This, again, is not to say bin Laden is correct, nor is it to say that his words reflect a universally held view in the Muslim world. It is possible, however, that bin Laden expresses a common Muslim view about the impact of U.S. policy and, if so, Americans must understand that reality—whether or not they concur. "The killing of innocent civilians, as America and some intellectuals claim, is really very strange talk," bin Laden said in October 2001.

> Who said that our civilians and children are not innocent and that shedding their blood is justified? The entire world from east to west screams at us, and America rallies agents, and sons of its agents. Who said our blood is not blood, but theirs is? Who made this pronouncement? Who has been getting killed in our countries for decades? More than one million children, more than one million children died in Iraq and others are still dying. Why do we not hear

someone screaming or condemning, or even someone's words of consolation or condolence. . . . How come millions of Muslims are being killed?[35]

3

CHASING BIN LADEN'S MONEY

That is, said the Shepherds, to show you, that he who has a heart to give his labor to the poor, shall never want wherewithal. He that watereth, shall be watered himself. And the cake the widow gave to the prophet, did not cause that she had ever the less in her barrel.

The Pilgrim's Progress, 1678

Shortly after Osama bin Laden's fighters destroyed the World Trade Center and damaged the Pentagon, the U.S. government launched yet another concerted effort to close down bin Laden's financial assets. I believe, however, that one of the most debilitating misperceptions about Osama bin Laden is the deeply held American and Western belief that the bin Laden phenomenon is overwhelmingly fueled by the power of his money and the money of others to which he has access. *Time* magazine correspondent Scott Macleod caught the essence of the Western view in 1996 when he wrote that bin Laden is "a big fish. Bin Laden is the kind of guy that can go to someone and say 'I need you to write a six-figure check,' and he gets it on the spot."[1] The widely held concept is simple: Bin Laden has a personal fortune of $300 million, derives profits from his own businesses, and his family is worth more than $5 billion. In addition, bin Laden receives funding from wealthy Muslims who share his beliefs, wealthy Muslim dilettantes who contribute lavishly to "Islamic causes" without caring how the money is spent, regular collections taken up at mosques across the Muslim world, Islamic nongovernmental organizations (NGOs), and some portion of the immense profits from the trafficking of heroin in South Asia.

For cynical Westerners, convinced money and not ideas have been the source of bin Laden's power and influence, this cornucopia of funding sources leads to another simple but simply wrong mantra: "Take bin Laden's money and bin Laden is defeated." Two comments by media experts on this theme are typical and emphasize the pervasiveness of the view. "Bin Laden's money is the key to his power," an unnamed U.S. official said in 1998, "He needs his fortune to pay his thousands of Muslim followers, bribe officials and plan terrorist activities."[2] More directly, a retired U.S. intelligence analyst lands in the heart of error by asserting, "Money is his main weapon without a doubt."[3]

Perhaps the foregoing is too harsh on Americans. It is not only, or even mainly, that many of us are cynically prone to believe money is power — although there is much of that abroad in the land — but more that Americans know about money, use it daily, and know that it is the necessary route to home ownership, educating the kids, acquiring transportation, and retiring to a warm locale. Americans, in short, are intimate with money, know it can be used for good and evil, and are comfortable in examining and solving problems through a financial lens. This is not a fault — although it is an analytic handicap — it is simply a fact of American life.

Contemporary Americans, however, are much less conversant and comfortable than contemporary Muslims with religious tenets that shape day-to-day individual and societal behavior and that establish well-defined and fairly inflexible rules for personal behavior, relationships within families and between individuals, and intercourse among nations and religions. Most Americans are especially unfamiliar with religion being life's core motivation and with religious rules that require an individual to willingly sacrifice wealth and life, if necessary, to defend God's word. Even when the United States was a more religious country, it was never comfortable with the idea that one should be eager to die for ideals, religion, God, and country. Throughout their history, Americans have been ready to risk death to defend each — and, I would hope, still are — but they have always looked for ways to render such service and still survive.

An old Marine's story seems appropriate here. This lance corporal's regiment was among the unit's occupying Japan at the end of 1945. As the unit settled in, the Marine recalls that he and his comrades engaged the local Japanese in conversation to the best of their limited linguistic abilities, this to put to rest Tokyo's presurrender propaganda that the Marines would kill all Japanese if they stopped fighting. As the Japanese became comfortable with the Americans, conversations often turned to Japanese fanaticism during the war. The lance corporal said that whenever a Marine asked a Japanese of either sex or any age why anyone would become a kamikaze pilot, the answer would invariably be that it was an honor and a duty to die for their divine emperor. A bit perplexed at the Marines having missed this obvious point, the Japanese would always ask "were you not eager to die for Roosevelt?" The question, of course, left the Americans scrambling to summon enough fractured Japanese to ask "Are you crazy?"

If those Marines felt that way, how much less likely is the current self-centered governing elite to understand that bin Laden and those he leads are ready to sacrifice their lives to perform a duty that comes from their God? When bin Laden says, "I am fighting so I can die a martyr and go to heaven and meet God. Our fight is now against the Americans. I regret having lived this long. I have nothing to lose,"[4] most Americans hear spectacular bravado or the ominous fanaticism of an irrational madman. Because the motivational force of religion in their lives is minimal, American leaders are largely incapable of hearing — let alone understanding — bin Laden's quiet, sincere, and rational voice. As a result, they slot bin Laden in the terrorist category and look to neutralize him by eliminating his funding sources; an event they know from personal experience can disastrously limit an individual's options, activities, and prospects. Because Americans are comfortable with the power of money, bin Laden becomes a more understandable and less dangerous enemy. If bin Laden's money was taken, many Americans believe that bin Laden would, like Major Strasser and the Nazis in *Casablanca* after Rick and Ilsa escape, become only a "minor annoyance." Unfortunately, bin Laden's ability to kill Americans is not based on money, and it will not end even if much of his money does. As the fine scholar Paul R. Pillar recently concluded, "Financial controls do have a modest part to play in counterterrorism, but the bolder claims for what can be accomplished by going after the terrorists' money are oversold."[5]

The Islamic media shake a collective head in wonder when they see the strength of America's conviction about the overwhelming importance of money to bin Laden. The editors of *Jang,* Pakistan's largest daily, wrote in December 1998, "The biggest tragedy of the Americans growing up in the vulgar culture is that they believe in the magic of money and incorrectly believe that money is the strongest and most decisive power in history." Because of their belief in money, *Jang*'s editors wrote, Americans are blind to the fact that "God . . . has produced saints in Afghanistan to defeat the international imperialist, who would soon put an end to the money-dominated culture. May God help Osama and the Taliban."[6] *Frontline*'s unattributed biography of bin Laden also made a key point often overlooked in the West; namely, "Bin Laden's activities are not very dependent on money. His followers are not mercenaries. Training does not cost a lot of money. Explosives and weapons are very cheap in some parts of the world."[7]

Overall, the Muslim media do not understand why the West views bin Laden as a combination of a demented Muslim Daddy Warbucks, a general of mercenaries, and the "Don Corleone of terror." Rather than money, the media argue that bin Laden's "real strength lies in his piety, unquestionable honesty, and courage of his conviction."[8] Fleshing out this position, the Islamic media focus on three factors to account for bin Laden's growing influence in the Muslim world: his personal reputation for bravery, piety, and support for the oppressed; his outspoken condemnation of U.S. policies and attacks on U.S. targets; and the dictates of Islam. The first factor, as *Al-Islah* said in 1996, is bin Laden's "long record in the jihad and his renowned piety and asceticism despite all the worldly goods God bestowed on him."[9] Second is the growing animosity among Muslims at all levels of society toward U.S. foreign policy. British journalist Robert Fisk noted the Muslim hatred of U.S. policies in the *Independent* in August 1998. Although he has a strong anti-American bias, Fisk is a veteran, internationally honored Middle East correspondent and his analysis rings true.

> For what really lies at the root of Arab reaction to the [20 August 1998] U.S. attacks on Sudan and Afghanistan is that they come when America's word has never been so low; when the Arab sense of betrayal has never been greater. America's continued military presence in Saudi Arabia, its refusal to bring Israel to heel as it continues to build Jewish settlements in violation of the Oslo agreement, its almost lip-smacking agreement to continue sanctions which are clearly culling the civilian population of Iraq — Arab fury at this catastrophe is one reason why a normally compassionate people responded with so little sympathy to the [7 August 1998] bombing of the U.S. embassies.[10]

Third, bin Laden, for increasing numbers of Muslims, does have God on his side. Since the year 641, Professor Bernard Lewis has written, "the holy land of the Hijaz [Saudi Arabia] has been forbidden territory for non-Muslims. According to the Hanbali school of Islamic jurisprudence, accepted by both the Saudis and the declaration signatories [i.e., those who signed bin Laden's 1998 fatwa], for a non-Muslim to set foot on the sacred soil is a major offense." Therefore, Lewis concluded, "Where the holy land is involved, many Muslims tend to define the struggle — and sometimes also the enemy — in religious terms, seeing the American troops sent to free Kuwait and even Saudi Arabia from Saddam Hussein as infidel invaders and occupiers. This perception is heightened by America's unquestioned primacy among the powers of the infidel world."[11]

To say these factors and not money have been the keys to bin Laden's power is not to say money does not make him a more sovereign, powerful, and flexible international player. Money clearly facilitates and speeds the growth and self-sufficiency of the jihad bin Laden has instigated. From this perspective, Professor M. C. Dunn's contention that "continuing efforts to trace, block, and seize his [bin Laden's] funds may do more to constrain his activities than air attacks could" is theoretically correct.[12]

However, multiple funding sources are the core of the West's problem in regard to the financial component of the bin Laden problem. As of 11 September 2001, bin Laden appeared to have at least four different funding channels that would have to be targeted by the West: his personal fortune and the profits of his businesses, funds he gets from his family and other wealthy Muslim families in Saudi Arabia and worldwide, witting and unwitting donations from wealthy Muslim governments and individuals via mosque collections and Islamic NGOs, and an undefined cut of the huge profits earned from trafficking heroin in South Asia. This diversity of funding channels provides bin Laden a financial network that is so redundant that, while it can be damaged, it will be almost impossible to destroy.

Personal Wealth

How big is bin Laden's personal fortune? This is a question that fascinates Americans and Westerners and one on which bin Laden has toyed with his interlocutors. Bin Laden has publicly asserted "that his wealth increased and his business grew with the amount of money he spent on the Jihad" and, in answering *Al-Quds Al-Arabi*'s question about the size of his wealth, he simply replied that God "has granted us money sufficient, God willing, to repulse the unjust attacks committed against our nation." Is he worth the $30 million to $40 million suggested by Sa'id Aburish? Is he worth the $300 million the U.S. State Department ascribed to him in summer 1996? What about the assertion by *Al-Watan Al-Arabi* in September 1998 that bin Laden's cut from his family's fortune was $600 million and its suggestion that his total personal worth was near $1 billion?[13]

If bin Laden has ascended the financial ladder, how do we deal with the data pointing the other way. In October 1998, for example, *U.S. News & World Report* quoted "experts" who "believe that bin Laden exhausted that [$300 million personal] fortune long ago." Then in April 1999, Sa'd al-Faqih told *Frontline* that bin Laden suffered three large financial losses in the 1990s, which, if Faqih is correct, would have wiped out even the largest estimates of his personal wealth. Faqih claims bin Laden has $250 million to $300 million in bank accounts frozen by the Saudis, that he lost $250 million to $300 million when he left Sudan in May 1996, and that he lost millions when his financial chief Maddani al-Tayyib ended up in Saudi hands and identified his businesses, many of which were shut or sold at a loss. UPI also has reported that bin Laden lost substantial amounts in the 1991 collapse of the Bank of Credit and Commerce International (BCCI).[14]

Wealthy desert prince or charismatic pauper? Financial wizard or Muslim spendthrift? One can conclude from the foregoing that bin Laden is either flush with cash or mortgaged to the hilt. The former conclusion is correct, but not only, or even primarily, because of bin Laden's personal wealth. There is every reason to believe members of bin Laden's extended family have ensured that he has gotten his share of family profits. In addition to funds from his family, bin Laden himself has been a successful entrepreneur and businessman. He built profitable construction, manufacturing, currency trading, import-export, and agricultural businesses in Sudan, which, at the same time, gave his operatives logistics and communications support, as well as providing cover. Since 1996, he also established nascent but apparently profitable agricultural concerns in eastern Afghanistan. In addition, besides having military bases in Yemen — bin Laden and the Egyptian Islamic Jihad (EIJ) have long had training camps at Lhaj, Sadah, Abyan, and Jabal al-Mariqishah, the latter hosted final planning for the 1998 East Africa bombings — bin Laden is economically active there, and a portion of his investment activities are with "businessmen from the Hadramut who have strong relations to the fundamentalist leader in view of historical family affiliations."[15] Bin Laden also is reported to run "a number of [unidentified] projects with the participation of high-ranking army officers and politicians."[16]

Beyond these businesses, bin Laden is reported to own or control up to eighty companies in Africa, the Far East, South Asia, Europe, and the Middle East from which,[17] according to *Al-Watan Al-Arabi*, "he harvests riches." In particular, bin Laden's businesses appear to be flourishing in Islamic countries.[18] *Al-Sharq Al-Awsat* reported in April 1999 that "bin Laden's business activities, which he conducts under various guises, extend from import-export activities to trading in arms and ammunition from the former Soviet Union markets and to construction and road surfacing for the Taliban and other Asian fundamentalist groups and movements, indeed for some governments."[19] *Al-Watan Al-Arabi* added to this list, noting that bin Laden also owns real estate and maritime transportation companies.[20]

In bin Laden's business and investment activity — especially since al-Tayyib's defection — "the name bin Laden does not necessarily figure prominently. . . . [The companies] are registered in the name of others or are administered by companies that are owned by holding companies registered in countries with poor financial monitoring." Each company, moreover, was designed to earn enough to cover its expenses and finance al Qaeda activities in the country or region where it is based. Instead of channeling profits to bin Laden's headquarters, the funds have been used locally, thereby substantially reducing the need for electronic or by-courier financial transfers that might be tracked or interdicted. Multiplying complications for the West in unraveling bin Laden's front company network is the fact that his associates have added another layer to the maze by establishing their own front companies. Bin Laden's top U.K.-based advocate Omar al-Bakri, for example, recently told the press that his Al-Muhajoroun organization owns twelve firms in the United Kingdom and frankly admitted that beyond business activities, the "companies are in fact useful as commercial fronts that allow the organization to collect funds and contributions and are political offices for the [Islamic] cell activities."[21]

Another unknown about bin Laden's personal finances is whether he has used Western banks and financial markets, and, if so, has he been successful? Reports on this aspect of bin Laden's finances are contradictory but suggest he has used the West's system. On the one hand, the author of *Frontline*'s biographical sketch of bin Laden said that early in life bin Laden decided to make sure his finances were always of an "Islamic nature." "For example," the author wrote, "he would never invest in [a] non-Islamic country. He would never use [non-Islamic] banks unless it was absolutely necessary. He does not believe in [the] stock market because he thought the investor could not escape interest since his money has to be in a bank and produce some interest. He also is preoccupied with the idea that Jews control banks and stock market[s]."[22] In support of this analysis, my own pre–11 September 2001 research found no data showing that any money tied directly to bin Laden had been located, blocked, or seized in the West's system. The only financial institutions publicly identified as used by bin Laden are all non-Western: the Khartoum-based al-Shimal bank; the Saudi Faisal Islamic Bank; the Islamic Bank in Tirana, Albania; the now-defunct BCCI; and the Dubai Islamic Bank. The latter is the world's oldest and largest Islamic bank, operates under Islamic law, and is, the Associated Press (AP) reports, "effectively controlled by the United Arab Emirates government."[23] In July 1999 the *New York Times* claimed bin Laden was funneling money through the Dubai Islamic Bank, a claim supported by "UAE banking sources" who denied knowing if the practice continued. A bit defensively, the sources said, "There is as yet no international resolution banning banks from dealing with bin Laden and that there is no legal reason not to conduct banking transactions for him as these involved legal activities and are not subject to money-laundering laws."[24]

On the other hand, a good deal of information exists suggesting bin Laden uses Western banking and financial systems; this information is backed by the commonsense conclusion that bin Laden — whom Saudi intelligence officials call a "skilled executive" — would not put all his financial eggs in the fragile and, in Western terms, unsophisticated Islamic banking basket.[25] The problem is that the data, while plentiful, lack checkable facts; the data are suggestive, not conclusive, and the secretiveness of Western banks offers little hope of comprehensive tracking by analysts of the issue. While it can be confidently assumed that bin Laden must have accounts and investments in Western banks, the statement is only a defensible conjecture.

Realizing the West's frustration over his well-hidden money, bin Laden has taunted his foes and even hinted at a cyber attack on those who seek to freeze his funds. "God opens ways for those who work for Him," bin Laden said in late September 2001. "Al Qaeda comprises of such modern and educated youths who are aware of the cracks inside the Western financial system, which are becoming a noose for it and this system could not recuperate in spite of the passage of so many days."[26]

Voluntary Donations

After such sensational items as a personal billion-dollar fortune, a family company worth many times that amount, and a multinational financial network as intricate as a nation-state's, the idea that private voluntary donations may be the key—and least detectable and interdictable—source of funding for bin Laden's organization is a rather dull concept. Still, a betting individual could do far worse than put his money on this horse; charitable contributions are one of the five pillars of Islam, and bin Laden himself has said: "Thank God, our financial situation is all right. The Muslim brothers who support us make us not need anything material."[27] Quoting unnamed U.S. officials, for example, the *Washington Post* reported in August 1998 that Washington was "trying to overcome bin Laden's continuing ties to wealthy individuals in Saudi Arabia and the Persian Gulf countries who have donated funds to Islamic social service organizations."[28] Try as Washington might in its new, concerted efforts to close down the financing of al Qaeda, it may well be impossible to "overcome" ties that are now twenty-plus years old and over time appear to have become dominated by bin Laden-like true believers.

When the ties first developed after the Soviet invasion of Afghanistan, the donors covered the spectrum of wealthy Muslims, from those who were committed Islamists, to those believing they were simply fulfilling a religious duty by helping Afghans defend themselves, to those super rich, often-royal ne'er-do-wells who donated to all "Islamic causes" and did not give a hoot about how the money was spent.

Who, then, are the donors. "Rich Arabs" or "Rich Muslims" are the standard but unhelpful catch phrases. The hard fact is that the donors are difficult to identify, but they surely represent a cross section of the wealthy in Muslim society worldwide: merchants, bankers, investors, and members of various royal families. "It is not only the bin Laden family that is supporting him," Sa'd al-Faqih told *Frontline*. "Bin Laden has never relied on his own money or his family's money to survive. Many rich Muslims believe that the best way to serve jihad is through him."[29] Adding credence to al-Faqih's contention is Ahmed Shah Masood's description of bin Laden as a master at securing funds from others. "When Bin Laden was not so widely known to the world, he did not have much money," the late leader of the anti-Taliban Northern Alliance told *Izvestiya* in December 2000.

He came to our country not as a terrorist or a military man but as a civilian to provide the mujahedin's Islamic movement with organizational and moral support. He did not have large savings. Even today when he is supplying the Taliban with everything they need, he does not have the flows of finance people ascribe to him. He knows where to find finance and how to persuade interested people to invest in him and his cause. You cannot take that away from bin Laden.[30]

Saudi Connection

As discussed above and will be addressed below, money flowed jihadward from the bin Laden family and other wealthy Saudi and Gulf merchant families. The sons of these families fought the Soviets alongside bin Laden and the Afghan mujahedin more than a decade ago and became influential members or managers of family businesses. They can be counted on to finance those fighting in God's name anywhere in the world. As Professor Khalid Duran has said, "In the nineties, sons began to step into the shoes of their mujahedin fathers."[31] In this vein, Sa'id Aburish told *Frontline* he believed that money for bin Laden "comes from inside Saudi Arabia, from other people who belong to merchant families."[32] Aburish's view was seconded by *U.S. News & World Report,* which explained that among bin Laden's "other benefactors" are "merchants in the Gulf states," as well as by the *New York Times,* which said funding for bin Laden comes "from powerful people and financial institutions in Kuwait and Qatar."[33] Like the "Secret Six" who funded John Brown, some members of the Gulf's economic elite appear to be funding efforts by bin Laden to destroy the status quo in which they have both ruled and prospered.

Tending to confirm these conclusions, the Saudi government in 1999 audited the kingdom's National Commercial Bank and found that "five of Saudi Arabia's top businessmen ordered the National Commercial Bank . . . to transfer personal funds, along with $3 million diverted from a Saudi pension fund, to New York and London banks." The money went to "the accounts of Islamic charities . . . that serve as fronts for bin Laden." According to the media, the five donors are collectively worth over $5 billion, and two prominent Saudi merchant and banking families were involved in the transfers, the al-Amoudis and the bin Mahfouz — the latter family owns a large share in the Saudi banking industry. Interestingly, the son of one of these families, Abdul Rahman Mahfouz, is a director of one of the charities that has fronted for bin Laden; the charity's assets were frozen by the British government after the 11 September 2001 attacks, and most of the trustees were identified as "members of the wealthy bin Mahfouz family of Saudi Arabia." Although *USA Today, U.S. News & World Report,* and Reuters all claimed that the businessmen were paying bin Laden "protection money" —

U.S. News said, "Two representatives of wealthy Saudis visited bin Laden in the early summer [of 1998] and paid him not to conduct terrorist operations in Saudi Arabia"—this analysis smacks of Western thinking and Saudi disinformation.[34] Closer to the mark is Sa'id Aburish's claim that "support for bin Laden comes from all levels of society in Saudi Arabia," including members of the al-Saud family, because there are people across society who believe bin Laden is performing a religious duty they are obligated to support.

Since the August 1998 U.S. missile raid on bin Laden's Afghan camps and bin Laden's November 1998 indictment by a U.S. grand jury, "donations from across the Muslim world have been pouring in [to bin Laden]."[35] In July 1999 the AP reported that Saudi authorities had found tens of millions of dollars were being donated to bin Laden until they "uncovered the donations and stopped the transfers. Without Saudi intervention, bin Laden may have received much more said one source." The AP said that "The sources, who included a Saudi businessman, said Saudi officials questioned several leading entrepreneurs after their names were discovered among those of other Saudi donors. One of those questioned is the Saudi owner of a major advertising firm. He was severely rebuked by Saudi authorities."[36]

Although the practice seems counterintuitive, money is provided to bin Laden by members of the Saudi royal family and by other royal families in the Gulf. "Mr. Bin Laden," the *New York Times* reported in early 1999, "receives funding and political support from princes of the Saudi royal family, whose king he has vowed to depose."[37] How to account for behavior that to the West appears shortsighted if not suicidal? At base, the al-Sauds themselves are to blame for creating a society in which their family members would voluntarily contribute to a man determined to eliminate the dynasty. Among members of the al-Saud family, and to a far greater extent in Saudi society as a whole, there is a strengthening belief—particularly as the basing of U.S. forces in the kingdom nears its tenth anniversary—that American pressure has "led King Fahd to act subserviently to U.S. interests and designs by arresting opposition [read religious] leaders and suspending Islamic law." Many others, including bin Laden, have argued that subservience to U.S. interests is manifest in Riyadh's production of oil at a rate that keeps world prices at levels the West can tolerate, but starves the kingdom's treasury and reduces its ability to care for citizens. In this context, Professor Magnus Ranstorp has written, "Bin Laden is part and parcel of a broader effort by a growing internal opposition since 1992 to challenge the Saudi regime's claim to sacred authority."[38]

Islamic NGOs

Islamic NGOs have been another source of funding, as well as a fairly easy and secure mechanism for invisibly transferring funds to bin Laden and other Islamist leaders. These organizations proliferated and matured during the Afghan war and are now found in virtually every location in the world where Muslims are at war, suffering, in refugee camps, or where there are populations susceptible for conversion to Islam. Bin Laden has been closely involved with several NGOs and has used his money to support their growth. Most Islamic NGOs are overwhelmingly occupied with humanitarian work; they most often practice the three forms of jihad not associated with the sword: the jihad of the heart, or moral reformation; the jihad of the tongue, or proclaiming God's word abroad; and the jihad of the hands, or good works in accord with God's will. "These foundations' official aims," *Le Figaro* explained in September 1998, are "to assist the underprivileged of a country regarded by them as a land of Islam. Present in working-class districts, they build schools, mosques, and water pipes; provide financial assistance for widows, orphans, and the elderly; take charge of the poorest children's education, and send the most receptive adolescents to Pakistan for 'religious training.'"[39] All are equipped, however, to knowingly or unwittingly assist bin Laden's movement and other Islamists because they can provide employment, move and distribute funds, and acquire legitimizing documentation, such as identity cards, residency documents, and work permits.

Disastrously for Western countries, Islamic NGOs are largely immune from Western police action, because they are almost always legally registered, certifiably involved in humanitarian and charitable activities, and affiliated with legitimate religious organizations. The use of Islamic NGOs as conduits for funds and contraband, and as curtains behind which to hide illicit activities, is an excellent example of how bin Laden and other Islamists have manipulated the West's legal system to their benefit. As Omar Bakri Mohammed, leader of the U.K.-based Al-Mujaharoun organization, recently told *Al-Sharq Al-Awsat*, "Having lived in the West for many years, we have realized that there are loopholes in the temporal laws that could be exploited in favor of Islam and Muslims." Bakri told of sending of well-educated Muslim youths from the United Kingdom to the United States for military training because, unlike British laws, "U.S. laws allow the purchase and possession of weapons and shooting practice. This enabled the fundamentalist movement's sons to learn practical military sciences in special camps in Missouri and Michigan." In turn, the British press has reported that hundreds of these Muslim youths subsequently travel to Kashmir for more training and combat experience "using holidays from good jobs to fight in what they regard as a holy war."[40]

Bin Laden got in on the ground floor of the development of Islamic NGOs for military-support activities when he joined with Shaykh Abdullah Azzam to found the Makhtab al-Khidimat (MAK) — or Services Office — in Peshawar in the mid-1980s. While the MAK provided relief to Afghan war victims, it also received, organized, and moved into Afghanistan the volunteers, arms, and money flowing to the mujahedin from the Muslim world. In the financial realm, *Al-Watan Al-Arabi* has said that between 1979 and 1989 about $600 million was sent to bin Laden's organization through charitable institutions in the Gulf, especially those in Saudi Arabia, Kuwait, Oman, the UAE, Bahrain, and Qatar. *Al-Watan Al-Arabi* noted that this is not the total amount that went to bin Laden, but "there are no statistics on the amount of money that used to come to him from other Muslim states." Since the end of the Afghan jihad, the MAK has supported embattled Muslims around the world.[41]

Beyond the MAK, the media report bin Laden also has been well connected to other Islamic NGOs that operated in Afghanistan or have been founded since that jihad. Among these NGOs are Human Concern International (HCI) — which bin Laden helped to found — the Third World Relief Agency (TWRA), the Kuwaiti Society for the Revival of the Islamic Heritage (KSRIH), Mercy International, the Muwaffaq Foundation, and the International Islamic Relief Organization (IIRO). In addition, several of bin Laden's close associates have worked for one or another of these NGOs. Mohammed Jamal Khalifah, bin Laden's brother-in-law, for example, once worked for the World Muslim League and then ran an IIRO branch in Manila in the early 1990s that Philippine military authorities have identified as a "conduit of Arab financiers for money to the Abu Sayyaf [terrorist group]." In June 2000, in fact, the chief of Philippine military intelligence said that Islamic NGOs are still being used to fund the Moro insurgency. He also claimed bin Laden had transferred $3 million to the Moro Islamic Liberation Front (MILF) to assist its fight for an independent Islamic state in Mindanao.[42]

Narcotics Trafficking

A final arena from which bin Laden presumably has derived funding, perhaps substantial funding, is the cultivation and trafficking of narcotics, primarily heroin, in South Asia. The information available on bin Laden's involvement in narcotics is of varying quality, some obviously true, some analysis by assertion, and some propaganda meant to defame bin Laden. Quoting unnamed sources in South Asia in late 1998, for example, the *Washington Times* and London's *Observer* claimed, "Osama bin Laden sees heroin as a powerful new weapon in his war against the West that is capable of wreaking social havoc while generating huge profits."[43] This utility of such a weapon is underscored by reports that 80 percent of the heroin consumed in Europe originates in Afghanistan, while the total in the United Kingdom is 95 percent. New Delhi's *Pioneer* also has claimed that bin Laden "sees heroin as a powerful weapon of religious 'jihad,'" and has used the money earned by his "opium syndicate" in western Afghanistan to fund Kashmiri insurgents. Russian officials also added to the story, telling *Al-Hayah* that bin Laden directed "the establishment of 'mobile plants' for producing narcotics in Chechen territory," and *Al-Sharq Al-Awsat* has reported that Chechen political leader Shamil Basayev — whose fighters bin Laden supports — controls "the Abkhaz heroin road" on which the Taliban transported heroin from Afghanistan to Europe.[44]

While these claims are possible — like any talented guerrilla commander, bin Laden will use any weapon that comes to hand — they provide little hard fact on which to hang a hat. Other reporting during the past several years, however, draws a stronger and more plausible link between bin Laden and the income his Taliban hosts purportedly derived from the heroin business. In August 1998, for example, the *Washington Post* said that the Taliban was taking advantage of bin Laden's talents as a financial adviser and manager by having him handle their "multi-billion dollar opium earnings." A month later, *Al-Watan Al-Arabi* followed the *Post*'s lead, reporting, "Bin Laden administers the funds of this movement [the Taliban], which are estimated at $8 billion," much of which is derived from the "narcotics trade." By 2001, moreover, this revenue base had increased; the United Nations claims that in 1999 Afghanistan's "poppy-based economy" accounted for nearly three-quarters of the world's opium and involved 200,000 farmers. In addition, Afghan traffickers also refined a large amount of their opium into heroin, thereby cutting out middleman refiners and keeping more of the profits. It also is interesting to note the *Financial Times* claim that between 1995 and 2000, Afghanistan's "normal agricultural economy" was transformed and became "80 percent . . . dependent on the drug industry."[45]

This period approximates that in which the Taliban had access to the business, financial, and management acumen of bin Laden's organization. It also may be that bin Laden contributed his talents as an agriculturist to the Taliban's goal of doubling the Afghan poppy crop. Bin Laden has told the media that farming is his first love, and other reports show he invested in genetically improved seed in Sudan and that his farms there produced record crops of sunflowers.[46]

The soundest conclusion on bin Laden and narcotics is that where there is smoke, there is fire. The Taliban controlled the world's most efficient heroin industry and it produced more than 70 percent of the world's opium; they, bin Laden, and the Islamic insurgents that each supported in Central Asia, the Balkans, Kashmir, the Caucasus, India, and Western China need money to run their wars; and it would be Pollyannaish to think they would have refused to exploit the cash cow that bestrode the Afghan poppy fields like a colossus.

Outside Afghanistan, the most dangerous tie between bin Laden and narcotics traffickers has been the one that appears to exist between him and the Indian Muslim narcoterrorists Dawood and Annis Ibrahim and their allies Iqbal and Tiger Memon. The Ibrahim brothers' criminal organization traffics in narcotics and smuggles gold, alcohol, silver, explosives, and electronic goods. It is based in Mumbai (formerly Bombay) — where the Ibrahims are known as Bombay "mafia dons" — and has an international network that includes other Indian cities, Pakistan, the UAE, Dubai, Nepal, Singapore, Thailand, and countries in eastern and southern Africa.[47]

Ibrahim and his senior lieutenant, Iqbal Memon, were responsible for twelve nearly simultaneous explosions in Mumbai on 12 March 1993. The attacks destroyed several buildings, killed more than three hundred people, and wounded about twelve hundred. The attackers are reported to have received small-arms training in Pakistan by "paramilitaries" and were processed through the country clandestinely so that their travel documents did not show a stay in Pakistan. Ibrahim's attack was one of the most ambitious and sophisticated terrorist operations — in terms of planning, logistics, and coordination — of the 1990s. The attack responded to the Indian government's decision to allow the demolition of the Barbri Masjid Mosque — a five-hundred-year-old Muslim holy site — and permit the construction of a Hindu temple, and was timed to occur on "the seventeenth day in the month of Ramadan. On this day, the Prophet won his first battle [in the Great Badr Raid]."[48]

Although New Delhi was quick to blame Pakistan's intelligence service for the bombings, *India Today* reported that Indian investigators believed that "the prime movers of the operation were pan-Islamic fundamentalist groups working outside state control." Recently, the Indian media reported that bin Laden may be using Ibrahim's international network to move fighters and explosives, as well as to acquire travel and identity documents. Ibrahim's smuggling network and those of the Afghan heroin traffickers afford al Qaeda multiple additional lines for nearly invisible communication and movement.[49]

4

GETTING TO KNOW BIN LADEN: SUBSTANTIVE THEMES OF THE JIHAD

Not all the treasures of the world, so far as I believe, could have induced me to support an offensive war, for I think it murder; but if a thief breaks into my house, burns and destroys my property, and kills or threatens to kill me, or those that are in it, and to "bind me in all cases whatever," to his absolute will, am I to suffer it? What signifies it to me, whether he does it as a king or a common man; my countryman or not my countryman: whether it be done by an individual villain or any army of them? If we reason to the root of things, we shall find no difference; neither can any just cause be assigned why we should punish in the one case and pardon in the other.

Thomas Paine, *The American Crisis*, 19 December 1776

In 1993 Osama bin Laden began speaking in detail to Muslim and Western journalists about his beliefs, goals, and intentions, and began publishing commentaries on these matters in the media. The best known of the latter is bin Laden's "Declaration of Jihad against the United States," first published in the Movement for Islamic Reform in Arabia's (MIRA) *Al-Islah* newsletter in September 1996. While bin Laden's words have not been a torrent, they are plentiful, carefully chosen, plainly spoken, and precise. He has set out the Muslim world's problems as he sees them; determined they are caused by the United States; explained why they must be remedied; and outlined how he will try to do so. Seldom in America's history has an enemy laid out so clearly the basis for the war he is waging against it.

What bin Laden has said is central to each chapter that follows. Before proceeding, however, some analysis of the main themes outlined by bin Laden is warranted. In this chapter, bin Laden's words are examined for substantive themes: who are Islam's enemies, why are they attacking Muslims, what have they done, how should Muslims defend Islam, and so forth. In chapter 5, bin Laden's statements are examined to show how they reflect character traits that play into his appeal and abilities as a leader.

The Main Enemy

For Osama bin Laden and, indeed, much of the Muslim world, the Christian West has been and still is Islam's main enemy; bin Laden clearly sees himself as playing a role in what Professor Bernard Lewis has described as "the struggle between these two rival systems [that] has now lasted for some fourteen centuries." Led by the United States and allied with Israel — and, more recently, with India, Russia, and China — bin Laden identifies the U.S.-led West as "the Crusaders," and as the primary and most vicious, aggressive, and rapacious enemy of the Islamic world. "America continues to claim that it is upholding the banner of freedom and humanity," bin Laden has said, "while these deeds [atomic bomb attacks on Japan and attacks and sanctions on Iraq] that they did, you would not find that the most ravenous of animals would descend to." For bin Laden, the United States is an inhuman and evil entity with a half-century record of humiliating Islam and devastating Muslims. "The thing that needs to be understood," bin Laden has written, "is that the United States is threatening to use its power to impose a solution of its choice. It considers others as inferior. It feels proud of its arms, resources, and technology. Pride is something that God Almighty greatly dislikes, as it arouses a man to feel superior." In his 1996 "Declaration of Jihad against the United States," bin Laden addressed to the world's Muslims — "his Muslim Brothers in the Whole World," as *Al-Islah* termed them — the following detailed indictment of what he called the Crusaders.[1]

> You are not unaware of the injustice, repression, and aggression that have befallen Muslims through the alliance of Jews, Christians, and their agents, so much so that Muslims' blood and their money and wealth are plundered by their enemies. Your blood has been spilled in Palestine and Iraq. The image of the dreadful massacre in Qana, Lebanon, is still vivid in one's mind, and so are the massacres in Tajikistan, Burma, Kashmir, Assam, the Philippines, Fatani [*sic* — perhaps Thailand's Muslim-dominated Pattani Province?], Ogaden, Somalia, Eritrea, Chechnya, and Bosnia-Herzegovina

where hair-raising and revolting massacres were committed before the eyes of the entire world clearly in accordance with a conspiracy by the United States and its allies who banned arms for the oppressed there under cover of the unfair United Nations. That alerted Muslims to the fact that they are the main target of the Jewish-crusade alliance aggression, and all the false claims [by the United States and the West] about human rights fell under the blows and massacres committed against Muslims everywhere.[2]

Bin Laden says proof of America's barbaric international behavior is found everywhere. In addition to repeatedly referring to Hiroshima and Nagasaki as examples, he cites as U.S.-led anti-Muslim attacks the U.S. role in the bombing and sanctioning of Iraq; Israel's occupation of Jerusalem; the stationing of U.S. "Christian" forces near Mecca and Medina; the prolonged UN sanctions on Libya, Syria, Iran, and Sudan; and America's countenancing of Israel's 1996 "massacre" of civilians at a UN refugee facility at Qana, Lebanon. In his rhetoric, bin Laden portrays Americans and their allies as inhuman creatures that thirst for Muslim blood, delight in gore, and aim to annihilate the Islamic world. This is particularly true when he cites the U.S.-orchestrated UN economic sanctions on Iraq, attributing to the sanctions casualties far greater than those caused by the atomic attacks.

In reviewing these U.S. actions, bin Laden has focused almost obsessively on the deaths of Muslim children. "Those [Westerners] who talk about the loss of innocent people didn't yet taste how it feels when you lose a child, don't know how it feels when you look in your child's eyes and all you see is fear," bin Laden ominously said in late 2001. "Are they not afraid that one day they [will] get the same treatment?"[3]

In this area, bin Laden's language resembles that used by Arab historians to describe actions of the eleventh-century Catholic Crusaders. In his book *The Crusades through Arab Eyes*, Amin Malouf quotes the Arab historian Osamah Ibn Munqidh, who wrote, after reviewing the Crusaders' behavior while sacking the Syrian city of Ma'arra in late 1098, that the consensus of "those who are well-informed about the Franj [the Crusaders] saw them as beasts superior in courage and fighting ardor but in nothing else, just as animals are superior in strength and aggression." Malouf reminds his readers that the record of Crusaders' depredations, such as the July 1099 sacking of Jerusalem and the attendant slaughter of Muslims, was "preserved and transmitted by local poets and oral tradition" and effectively "shaped an image of the Franj that would not easily fade."[4]

Bin Laden's public words demonstrate his deliberate stoking of the Islamic world's historical memory of the Crusades, reminding Muslims, as Professor Manstorp has written, that today, as it did a thousand years ago, the Islamic world "stands at a critical juncture in history, threatened by a phased plan by the Judaeo-Christian conspiracy . . . to gradually de-Islamicize and occupy the Muslim holy places in the Arabian Peninsula."

> Somalia: "Some 13,000 from among our brothers, women, and sons in Somalia were killed [by the Americans] under the banner of the United Nations. Reports, corroborated by photographs, said that our Somali brothers were grilled as if they were sheep."[5]
>
> Kosovo and Bosnia: "This condemnation [by Washington of the 1998 East Africa bombings] is meaningless because it comes at a time when Muslim blood is spilled abundantly in Kosovo at the hands of the Serbian butcher, just like it was in Bosnia under the supervision of the U.S. and its allies. Mass graves that accommodated thousands of victims were numerous, and concentration camps, slaughtering, and rape were widespread. . . . America every time makes a decision to support them [the Serbs] and prevent weapons from reaching Muslims, and allow Serbian butchers to slaughter Muslims. . . . The evidence overwhelmingly shows America and Israel killing the weaker men, women, and children in the Muslim world and elsewhere. . . . [For example] there withholding of arms from Muslims of Bosnia Herzegovina leaving them prey to the Christian Serbs who massacred and raped in a manner not seen in contemporary history."[6]
>
> Palestine: "The West's wolves, both Christians and Jews, have set upon them [the Palestinians], slaughtering them and massacring them, violating their honor basely and maliciously and expelling them from their country to be tossed around from country to country."[7]
>
> Lebanon: "The mention of the U.S. reminds us before anything else of those innocent children who were dismembered, their heads and arms cut off in the recent explosion that took place in Qana [referring to Israel's attack on UN refugee facilities, killing 106]. The U.S. Government abandoned even humanitarian feelings by these hideous crimes. It transgressed all bounds in a way not witnessed before by any power or any imperialist power in the world."[8]
>
> The American People: "You may have heard these days that almost three quarters of the U.S. people support Clinton's strikes on Iraq. The [Americans] are a people whose president becomes more popular when he kills innocent people. These are a people who increase support for their president when he commits one of the seven cardinal sins. They are a lowly people who do not understand the meaning of principles. . . . if the majority of the American people support their dissolute president, this means the American people are fighting us and we have a right to target them."[9]

Bin Laden's purpose in using Crusader-era imagery appears to have several possible explanations. First, of course, it is meant to describe Islam's Christian enemies in the worst possible terms to make them appear inhuman and immensely dangerous. In this case, bin Laden's rhetoric is a steeped-in-history siren call to make the Muslim world recognize that the threat from today's Crusaders is as bloody and barbarous as that which they have been taught was posed by the original Crusaders. Second, by stoking memories of the original Crusaders' barbarity, bin Laden is trying to deaden Muslim sensibilities to the killing of large numbers of what he has depicted as modern-day Crusaders—military and civilian, men, women, and children—with weapons of mass destruction. Again and again in public remarks, bin Laden returns to the atomic bombs dropped on Hiroshima and Nagasaki as examples of America's disregard for human life and as actions that justify Muslim responses of equal quality. "Did the U.S. forget today, while it is shedding crocodile tears over world security and peace," bin Laden's forces asked in the communiqués sent to *Al-Hayah* claiming responsibility for the August 1998 East Africa bombings, "what it did to the residents of Hiroshima and Nagasaki and how it exterminated them in seconds with its atomic bombs?"[10]

Third, and most important, these descriptions have focused the Muslim world on what bin Laden has wanted to be seen as the main enemy and a single target. Before bin Laden attained prominence and began speaking publicly, *Jane's Intelligence Review* noted, "the [Islamic] fundamentalist creed also believes that the secular Arab governments must be overthrown before the greater enemy, the West, can be tackled." Professor Emmanuel Sivan also made this point in his 1998 analysis of the central role jihad plays in classical and contemporary Islamic theology. "Islamic movements in opposition," Sivan wrote in the journal *Orbis*, "tend to concentrate upon its own state context, whose regime is the 'nearest enemy' in Muslim legal lingo. 'Further away enemies,' such as the state of Israel or the United States, are to be tackled later, after the seizure of power."[11] Bin Laden has labored in public and private to reverse the sequence and claims that "if the United States is beheaded, the Arab Kingdoms will whither away." Bin Laden has given priority to attacks on the United States and argues that "there must be concentration on hitting the main enemy who has thrust the [Islamic] nation into whirlpools and labyrinths for decades since dividing it into states and statelets."[12] After al Qaeda destroyed the U.S. embassies in East Africa in 1998, Abd-al-Bari Atwan, editor in chief of *Al-Quds Al-Arabi*, told his readers that the attacks "were the logical results of the unjust and demeaning policies which the United States has been pursuing in the Muslim world."

> Since World War II, the United States has pursued a policy of bolstering all dictatorial [Arab] regimes, encouraged corruption and the corrupt, prevented the democratic tide from spreading toward

the region and dedicated its intelligence apparatuses to safeguarding the rotten conditions in the Arab world, whereas in other countries it has speeded up the collapse of dictatorships, exposed corrupt and corrupting regimes, sided with reform forces, and bolstered the prospect of democratic change.[13]

The goal for Islamists, bin Laden told *Al-Hayah* in August 1998 and ABC News in December 1998, is to join together to create a situation where "Islamic groups will emerge and follow other groups, and all will be fighting U.S. interests which are still based on theft and pillage. . . . The main effort, at this phase, must target the Jews and Crusaders." Most recently, bin Laden told the daily *Pakistan* that Muslims must unite against America "because it is very difficult, if not impossible, to defeat anti-Islam forces without unity."[14]

Betrayal from Within

Another factor that has motivated bin Laden and permeated his statements is the idea that Islam has been betrayed from within by Muslim governments whose leaders are, per bin Laden, "criminal despots who betrayed God and his Prophet, and betrayed their trust and their nation." According to bin Laden, the premier betrayers have been Islamic governments that cooperate with the United States, regimes, he has said, that are "morally depraved" and that he has described as "hypocrites" that "champion falsehood, support the butcher against the victim, the oppressor against the innocent child."[15]

Bin Laden fairly dripped venom, for example, when he denounced the Muslim governments that, after several suicide attacks by HAMAS (Islamic Resistance Movement) in Israel in early 1996, "came to Sharm al-Shaykh, [Egypt,] submissive and servile, to embrace the Jews and Christians and to aid them . . . [and] to submit their condolences to the occupying Zionist thugs in Palestine." For bin Laden, the Saudi regime has been the first among equals in this regard, having let U.S. troops into the kingdom and by having previously given aid to the Yemeni Communists and PLO chief Yasir Arafat, both of whom, bin Laden has said, "are fighting against Muslims." "So the [al-Saud] regime has betrayed the nation and allied with and supported the infidels against Muslims," bin Laden wrote in *Al-Islah* in September 1996. "As is known, this is one of the contradictions in Islam. By opening the Arabian Peninsula to the Crusaders, the regime has violated the Prophet's will to his nation before his death: 'Move the atheists out of the Arabian Peninsula.'" He also said, "'If I live, I will move the Jews and the Christians out of the Arabian Peninsula.'"[16]

In addition, bin Laden has argued that these governments have betrayed the ummah — the worldwide community of Islamic believers — not only by permitting infidels into the holy land of Saudi Arabia, but also by gradually surrendering their sovereignty to them and allowing them to plunder the nation's energy resources. While stressing that the United States is the primary target, for example, bin Laden told ABC journalist Rahimullah Yusufzai in December 1998, "Some regimes in the Arab and Muslim worlds have joined the [Crusader-Jewish alliance in] preventing us Muslims from defending the holy Ka'aba [in Mecca]. Our hostility is in the first place, and to the greatest extent, leveled against these world infidels, and by necessity the regimes which have turned themselves into tools for this occupation of the greatest House in the Universe and the first House of Worship appointed by [*sic* — for?] men." The Gulf countries and the "criminal despots who betrayed God and his Prophet" who rule them, bin Laden told ABC, "have lost their sovereignty. Now, infidels walk everywhere on the land where Muhammad, God's peace and blessing be upon him, was born, and where the Koran was revealed to him through Gabriel, peace be upon him. This happens while our scholars and Ulemas, who are the heirs of prophets, are in jail. . . . These Ulemas are jailed while infidels, be they Jews or Christians, are free to go wherever they want in these countries."[17]

Bin Laden has also claimed that Saudi leaders — whom he derides as the Riyadh-based "branch or agent of the U.S." — and those of other Gulf states have allowed the United States to "devour its Gulf prey" by depriving Muslims of the full financial benefit from the exploitation of their natural resources. Bin Laden argued that these losses resulted from three factors: the fiscal and religious corruption of the al-Saud family; excessive Saudi spending on Western military equipment; and the calibration of oil production at levels that keep prices acceptable to Western consumers. In 1932, bin Laden has said, "The [al-Saud] regime started under the flag of applying Islamic law and under this banner all the people of Saudi Arabia came to help the Saudi family take power. Abd-al-Aziz [al-Saud] did not apply Islamic law; the country was set up for his family." This situation has caused "terror, repression, and corruption" in the kingdom, bin Laden argued, "[and] the rivalry of the princes overseeing their own personal interests has ruined the country." Worse than fiscal corruption is what bin Laden saw as the al-Sauds' willful flouting of Islamic law.[18]

"We firmly believe," bin Laden told *Al-Quds Al-Arabi* in 1996, "that the [al-Saud] regime has passed numerous laws without referring to God and appointed itself as a lawmaker and a co-lawmaker with God. This is unbelief as endorsed by the Ulema and the Book of Almighty God: 'He does not share His command with anyone.'" So far have the al-Sauds betrayed their duties to Islam and the ummah, bin Laden said in April 1997 after two thousand pilgrims died in a fire near Mecca, that they cannot even be relied on for the "preparation of suitable utilities and their maintenance in a manner for the needs of the pilgrims" during the annual Hajj.[19]

Bin Laden has also condemned the exorbitant amounts Riyadh has spent for U.S. and European weapons and for the basing of U.S. forces in the kingdom. The U.S. "aggressors" could be badly hurt, bin Laden has argued, if they were denied "the huge profits they make from [the arms] trade with us." What is the point of this spending, bin Laden asked, after the "small numbers, poor training, and inefficient command" of Saudi forces were "exposed by the Gulf crisis, despite the astronomical and unreasonable figures" spent on them.[20]

Bin Laden has also argued that the Saudi regime is squandering the Muslim world's energy resources by selling them at prices set by political considerations, not by market forces. Bin Laden has characterized Saudi oil policy as Islam's "economic hemorrhage," and has said that when Islamists take power in the kingdom, they will still sell oil to non-Muslim consumers, but at "the price of the market according to supply and demand." After all, bin Laden added, "We are not going to drink it." The results of Riyadh's oil policy, in tandem with the al-Sauds' excessive defense expenditures, are, according to bin Laden, increasing poverty, ill health, and illiteracy in Saudi Arabia. Bin Laden also claims that the al-Sauds' pro-Western energy policies are causing identical ills across the Muslim world, this based on his belief that Saudi energy resources are—like the Peninsula's holy places—held in trust for the benefit of the ummah. "The U.S. is increasing its presence in Arab countries in order to capture its [sic] oil reserves," bin Laden told the Islamabad daily *Pakistan* in November 1997, a point that resonates in the Muslim world, as Abd-al-Bari Atwan noted in August 1998 in *Al-Quds Al-Arabi*, when he wrote that Muslims have seen "successive American administrations" maintain a policy to "consolidate hegemony over Arab oil resources and oil derivatives and have controlled prices to ensure that Arab oil prices remained low so that Western economies would flourish while the Arab economies crumbled."[21] The controlled oil prices, bin Laden has said, have significantly hurt the Muslim world, and are the result of "the Saudi regime playing the role of a U.S. agent . . . [by] increas[ing] production and flooding the market [in a way] that caused a sharp decrease in oil prices."[22] Further, bin Laden told the daily *Pakistan,*

> After 1973 the increase in the price of oil was not significant when compared to the increases in almost every other commodity in the world. Since 1973, the increases in the price of oil have only been eight dollars per barrel, while the price of other commodities have gone up three fold. Oil should have gone up by the same rate, but that did not happen. U.S. wheat has become three times costlier, but not Arab oil. During the past twenty-four years the price of oil has not increased more than a few dollars, because the U.S. is holding a gun against the forehead of the Arab countries. We [the Is-

lamic world] are suffering a daily loss of one hundred and fifteen dollars per barrel. Every day, ten million barrels of oil are produced by Saudi Arabia alone. Therefore, the daily loss is more than one billion dollars, while the total loss [when other Arab producers are included] is two billion dollars. During the last 13 years, the U.S. has cost us a loss of eleven hundred billion dollars. It is important that we get this large amount of money back from the U.S. The total population of Muslims in the world is more than one billion. Thus, the eleven hundred billion dollars could be distributed amongst the Muslims at the rate of ten thousand dollars per family. Muslims around the world are dying from hunger and the U.S. is stealing our oil. The U.S. buys cheap oil from us and then sells us its own tanks and aircraft with the threat of Israel. This is how the U.S. takes its own money back from us.[23]

There is one other component of the theme of betrayal by the al-Sauds that has held a prominent place in bin Laden's thinking. This is what he has considered to be the betrayal of the Afghan jihad by its external supporters, led by Saudi Arabia and the United States. "After our victory in Afghanistan and defeating the Russians," bin Laden told ABC's John Miller in May 1998, "the world media, led by the American media, started a campaign against us that is still going on despite the fact that the Russians left in 1989, almost ten years ago. They have carried out this campaign accusing us of being terrorists."[24] Bin Laden argued that just as the Afghan and Arab-Afghan mujahedin were about to defeat the Afghan Communists and form a successor government, "America managed, through its agents and especially some Arab countries and Pakistan, to perpetuate the division of the strongest Islamic people in this region [the Afghans], a people that was able to turn the Soviet Union into a myth."[25] U.S. and Saudi actions in this regard were responsible for intensifying post-Soviet intra-mujahedin quarreling and hence for the still ongoing Afghan civil war. The "U.S. scheme" for an interim Afghan government, bin Laden told Qatar's Al-Jazirah television in late 1998, was meant to deny victory to the Islamists by supporting the Afghan Communist leader Najibullah and "pressuring the Mujahedin through Pakistan, to form a secular government. Fifty percent of its members would be former communists and some of those who had studied in the West, and the rest would be from the seven Afghan [mujahedin] parties."[26]

Quite simply, bin Laden argued, "The United States did not want to see an Islamic government in Afghanistan" and so when "[Soviet president Mikhail] Gorbachev announced the withdrawal of the Soviet Army from Afghanistan, the U.S. and Saudi Arabia suspended their aid to the Mujahedin." For bin Laden and other Islamist leaders, America's betrayal of the Afghan jihad also is evidence of immense ungratefulness. In 1999, Karachi's *Jasarat* wrote that after Moscow's defeat, the United States turned "against the Muslim countries whose sons made unprecedented sacrifices [in Afghanistan] and helped the United States to become the sole superpower in the world."[27]

The Islamic Duty of Self-Defense

Central to bin Laden's position, and key to understanding his actions and appeal, is his belief that Islam and the Muslim world are being attacked by a more modern, powerful, and predatory version of the medieval Catholic Crusaders: the United States, Britain, or the West generally, allied with Israel, India, and Russia, and supported by apostate Muslim regimes. Armed with this version of reality, bin Laden has said that Muslims are required by God to wage jihad to defend themselves, their creed, and their land against the new Crusaders. The West, bin Laden told *Al-Quds Al-Arabi* in 1994, wants to "keep Muslims weak and incapable of defending themselves."[28]

U.S. support for Israel, the continued sanctioning and bombing of Iraq, and the West's occupation of holy sites in Saudi Arabia are, according to bin Laden, "crimes and sins committed by the Americans," and these actions are a "clear declaration of war on God, his messenger, and Muslims." Therefore, bin Laden wrote in his August 1996 Declaration of Jihad, "It is no secret that warding off the American enemy is the top duty after faith and that nothing should take priority over it. . . . The main disease and cause of the affliction [in the Muslim world] is the occupying U.S. enemy. We should lie in wait for him until he is defeated, God willing."[29]

Establishing the U.S.-led Crusaders as aggressors is vital to bin Laden in religious terms because it enables him to ask all Muslims to participate in a defensive jihad, just as they joined the Afghans' anti-Soviet defensive jihad. "Let all [Muslims] know," bin Laden wrote in a letter the AP published in 1998, "that unless they take up the jihad, it will be an inescapable and inevitable catastrophe—a catastrophe in which faith and honor will be lost, as dignity and land have been lost. It will be a catastrophe with which we will turn [Muslims] into slaves in the hands of God's basest creatures, Jews and worshippers of the cross."[30]

The aura of an offensive war waged by Christians against Islam is powerful in emotive terms, in terms of theological requirements, and in terms of collective historical memory. "In the technical language of the ulema," Professor Bernard Lewis has written, "religious duties may be collective, to be discharged by the community as a whole, or personal, incumbent on every individual Muslim. In an offensive war conducted by Muslims, the religious duty of the jihad is collective and may be discharged by volunteers and professionals. When the Muslim community is defending itself, however, jihad becomes an individual responsibility."[31] Lewis's analysis was supported in April 2001 by the highly influential Egyptian Islamist scholar

Shaykh al-Qaradawi—now in exile in Qatar—when he explained the difference between the two types of armed jihad recognized by Islamic jurisprudence. "First of all, there are two types of jihad," Shaykh al-Qaradawi said.

> There is the call-up jihad and the defensive jihad. Muslim scholars call the call-up jihad collective duty. In other words, if some Muslims carry out this duty, the rest are absolved of it. This type of jihad calls for the recruitment of every rational, mature person who can fight. . . . As to the defensive jihad, it is when an enemy enters a country and occupies it. In this case everyone must carry out jihad, each according to his ability. This is called a state of public mobilization. In this case, all people resist. The woman goes to war without permission from her husband. The same applies to servant and master. The children also go to war without asking their father's permission, as the right of the entire society takes precedence over the private rights of individuals. So the children go out. Here the fathers do not force the children to go to war. The children themselves went to war acting on religious and national motivations. So they throw rocks at the enemy. As the saying goes, throw rocks rather than flee. The children throw stones and do what they can. This is different from the call-up jihad that some of our brethren talk about, when jihad becomes a collective duty and we select the persons needed and resist as much as we can.[32]

Concurring with al-Qaradawi, the American religious scholar John Kelsay has written that the call for a defensive jihad against non-Muslim aggressors "is intended to reflect increased urgency," which in turn speeds the mobilization of Islamic forces. In a defensive scenario, Kelsay maintains that "jihad becomes a duty for all conscientious Muslims, and one need not—cannot—wait for authorization other than that given by God: command good and forbid evil."[33] In the preamble to a fatwa issued on 23 February 1998, therefore, bin Laden closely follows the analysis of both al-Qaradawi and Kelsay, stressing that the individual Muslim's responsibility to engage in jihad against those attacking Islam. Self-defense is simply complying with "God's order," bin Laden wrote, and supported his argument by reminding Muslims that "ulema have throughout Islamic history unanimously agreed that the jihad is an individual duty if the enemy destroys the Muslim countries." Quoting Islamic authorities, bin Laden said that "nothing is more sacred than belief except repulsing an enemy who is attacking religion and life."[34]

Beyond religious interpretations, bin Laden's call for a defensive jihad harkens the Muslim world to the successful anti-Crusader exploits of two of its most famous soldiers—Nura al-Din and Saladin—who rallied the faithful on the basis of each Muslim's duty "to protect the territory and religion of Islam from attacks by [non-Muslim] aggressors." In his book *The Holy War Idea in Western and Islamic Traditions*, the American scholar J. T. Johnson accurately describes the valid historical and theological precedents to which bin Laden appeals.

> This conception [of defensive jihad] is associated historically with the heroic figures of Nur al-Din and Saladin, but actually the authority they possessed to wage jihad arose from the authority and responsibility of all Muslims, incumbent on every one as an individual duty, to defend the religion and territory of Islam against aggressors. The concept of such individual responsibility and the accompanying responsibility is defined in classical [Islamic] juristic thought. What was different in the conception of the leader's authority in the struggle against the Crusades, and particularly in Saladin's war against the Latin Kingdom of Jerusalem, was that this Muslim leader put himself at the head of a jihad legitimized not by the authority of the caliph or imam of the Muslim community, but by the individual responsibility and authority of Muslims to oppose Crusaders as aggressors against the dar-al-Islam. Their authority as the leaders of the jihad, that is, did not flow downward from the juridically correct authority of caliph or imam, but upward from the religious and moral authority implied by the individual obligation of every Muslim.
>
> Embedded in this reasoning is the concept of the authorization for jihad exemplified by the historic struggle of Saladin against the Crusaders — a coincidence magnified by the frequent pejorative references to "Crusaders" by contemporary radical Muslim advocates of revolutionary jihad, who, associate any kind of Western influence with the Crusades. Fundamentally, though, the rationale is that the duty to protect Islam and the territory of Islam is every Muslim's, and that this universal duty is what gives particular spokespersons for revolutionary action the right to call for jihad. In doing so they are not claiming the authority to declare offensive jihad, for this would be a usurpation of a right the classical tradition reserves to the imam of all the dar-al-Islam; rather, they are simply calling for all Muslims to do their duty to defend Islam from attack.[35]

That bin Laden's approach probably is the most effective available to him has largely gone unrecognized in the West, although the Muslim scholar Professor Khalid Abou El-Fadl has written in the journal *Ethics and International Affairs* that "it is important to note that the notion of defensive jihad is well-rooted in the classical [Islamic] juristic tradition and that contemporary Islam has not had a problem in adopting the idea of a defensive jihad."[36]

Indeed, the Islamic world accepted the concept of a defensive jihad without reserve when the Soviets invaded Afghanistan, and it has revalidated that acceptance by its unstinting support for Islamist fighters in Bosnia, Kashmir, and Chechnya.

Aside from El-Fadl and Professor Bernard Lewis, perhaps only Professor Magnus Ranstorp has recognized the potential impact of bin Laden's words. "In an effort to mobilize the masses to support this 'self-defense struggle,'" Ranstorp maintains, "bin Laden taps into the collective Muslim psyche by skillfully exploiting massacres of Muslims in Iraq, Bosnia, Chechnya, and even Qana (Lebanon), linking these to historical battles between Muslims and their enemies by then remolding them into a contemporary context. These themes naturally invoke broad Muslim grievances, especially as the phraseology refers to crusades and 'martyrdom.'"[37]

Dealing with the Devil

Bin Laden has a clear strategic goal—defeating the United States—and the most important issue for him is attaining that goal. He has not, however, scripted the tactical means for accomplishing the goal. On the road to success, bin Laden has made it clear that odd bedfellows will turn up and that religious purity and identical beliefs will not be required from all of the jihad's allies, associates, and contacts, noting that in more than fourteen centuries of Islamic history "there were many types of dealings between the Muslim nation and other nations in times of peace and war, including treaties and matters to do with commerce." British journalist Mark Huband has noted that bin Laden's approach is not unique; before World War II, for example, Algeria's senior association of ulema cooperated with Algerian Communists against the French.[38]

While bin Laden may not exactly be a proponent of an "ends justify the means" policy, he is within arm's length of it. As in all the issues he addresses, bin Laden finds religious justification for such an approach, saying that Islamist leaders should "be using every good as well as sinful person, for God supports this in the interest of the cause of religion." In his Declaration of Jihad, bin Laden wrote that throughout Islamic history, Islamic scholars have held that there are times when devout Muslims must work with the less devout, and even the sinful, if they are to repel the enemy attacking the Muslim world. For bin Laden, the top Muslim priority is to defeat the Crusaders, and he asserts that the medieval Islamic jurist Shaykh al-Islam Ibn-Tammiyah, as well as the Prophet Muhammad, sanctioned something akin to working with the devil. "If warding off the aggressive enemy," bin Laden wrote,

> becomes impossible without all Muslims of all walks and ranks
> getting together, then that is their duty and they should in that

case overlook some disputed issues. Overlooking such disputes at this stage is less harmful than the continuation of the great heresy afflicting the countries of the Muslims. That is why Shaykh al-Islam, explaining the matter, pointed out a main and great principle which should be taken into account, which is that work should concentrate on warding off the greater of two evils. Referring to the state of the mujahedin and the Muslims, he said that if among them there happened to be very sinful soldiers, that would not justify abandoning the jihad against the aggressive enemy. . . . That is why one of the principles of the Sunnah and the [Prophet's] group is to do conquest using every good as well as sinful person, for God supports this in the interest of the cause of religion because, as the Prophet, may God's prayers and blessings be upon him, said, if conquest can only be achieved with the help of sinful princes or very sinful soldiers, then one of two things must be done: Either abandon the conquest with their cooperation, which means the greater harm of others taking over, or proceed with the conquest along with the sinful princes, and that way the greater harm is avoided and most of the rules of Islam are established, if not all.[39]

Remembering bin Laden's just-cited words will stand the reader in good stead as he or she finds the forces of bin Laden cooperating, or at least in contact, with an eclectic assortment of nominal Muslims; heretics; infidels; atheists; European, Russian, and South Asian gangsters; gray-market arms dealers; and narcotraffickers — each of whom has potential for helping facilitate al Qaeda's anti-U.S. activities. As will be seen, bin Laden's version of Churchill's claim that he would speak well of Satan if Satan would attack Hitler will be echoed when al Qaeda is found working with Iraq's intelligence service; Lebanese and Iranian Shia of the deepest heretical hue; Italian criminal groups; China's 14K organized crime gang; and Chechen, Albanian, South Asian, and Russian mafia chiefs, among them former Red Army and KGB officers who once could be found cheerfully torturing and killing Afghan civilians and mujahedin when the Soviets occupied Afghanistan.[40] In terms of his finances, bin Laden's willingness to deal with the devil suggests that he has worked through Western banks when necessary and has been able to tolerate earning some interest for the good of the jihad.

Another facet of this theme deals with how bin Laden views the certainty that his forces will kill Muslims when attacking Crusaders and Jews. After the heavy casualties caused by the August 1998 attacks on the U.S. embassies in Nairobi and Dar es Salaam, some Western and Islamic media commentators speculated that bin Laden would be deterred from similar attacks because of the large number of non-U.S. citizens, including African Muslims, killed or wounded in the attacks. The media argued that bin Laden would be more careful next time so as not to risk his popularity among Muslims. This speculation, which certainly has been put to rest by the destruction of the World Trade Center, which housed firms that included Muslim-world employees, fell away as early as December 1998, when Pakistani journalist Rahimullah Yusufzai interviewed bin Laden for ABC News. In reviewing the East Africa attacks, Yusufzai asked bin Laden "if the targets of jihads are Americans, how can the death of so many Africans be justified?" In response, bin Laden basically said that deaths of this sort, though regrettable, were unavoidable and religiously permissible.

> Suppose that the Americans have attacked an Islamic country and kidnapped my children, the children of Osama bin Laden, to use as a shield, and then started to kill Muslims as is the case in Lebanon, Palestine, and these days in Iraq, and also when they supported the Serbs in massacring the Muslims in Bosnia. According to Islamic jurisprudence if we abstain from firing on the Americans lest we should kill these Muslims (used by them as shields), the harm that could befall Muslims at large, who are being attacked, outweighs the good of saving the lives of these Muslims used as shields.
>
> This means that in a case like this, when it becomes apparent that it would be impossible to repel these Americans without assaulting them, even if this involved the killing of Muslims, this is permissible under Islam.[41]

In terms of the historical application of Islamic law, it appears bin Laden is correct and the speculations of Western experts are ill-founded. Regarding the law covering the treatment of Islam's non-Muslim enemies, J. T. Johnson has held that "the fundamental principle was that after unbelievers in the dar-al-Harb [house of war] had been issued the call of Islam (the da'wa) and refused it, they might be killed combatants and non-combatants alike." Johnson's analysis is validated by the late HAMAS spiritual leader Shaykh Ahmad Yasin in precisely the terms bin Laden uses to call for attacks on civilians as well as military personnel. "Any Israeli," Yasin declared in December 2000, "who walks on the street will be considered a member of the Israeli army. . . . All the Israeli people are recruits [for military service]. Therefore the spilling of their blood is lawful."

Although Islamic history has documented cases where non-Muslim civilians were spared by Muslim warriors, the decision was not based on the idea that the individuals had "rights derived from nature or from considerations of fairness or justice, but rather that they are potentially of value to the Muslims [as slaves, hostages, servants, etc.]." J. T. Johnson has explained that the decision to spare a non-Muslim was made solely on the criteria of what would be of most benefit to Muslims; and that, further, even Muslim casualties caused by Muslims during a jihad were acceptable as long as they were not intended.

> The general principle that all enemies might nonetheless be killed provided the rationale that permitted the besieging of enemy cities, along with the use of inherently indiscriminate weapons like catapults and bows and arrows, even though this led to the harming of noncombatants. . . .
>
> In the siege or in the storming of an enemy city whatever measures are necessary to subdue the city may be taken: it would be [according to Islamic jurists] "permissible to inundate a city in the territory of war with water, to burn it with fire, or to attack [its people] with mangonels, even though there may be slaves, women, old men and children" or even Muslim merchants or, at the extreme, Muslim children in the city. . . . But while Muslims may carry on their warfare, they should not intend to harm those who should not be harmed. If such harms occurs, that is the result of war, and the Muslim soldiers do not incur guilt from it.[42]

Every Little Bit Helps

Bin Laden wants Islam's defensive jihad against the Crusaders to be waged by Islamist organizations and by individual Muslims, a position he believes God sanctions. The role of Islamist organizations — al Qaeda, the World Islamic Front, the Egyptian Islamic Jihad (EIJ), the Taliban, and so forth — to date has been the core element of the jihad. Quoting Islamic scholars and jurists, however, bin Laden has said that God is not content to see the struggle waged only by organizations and that the Koran calls for every Muslim to kill Americans and destroy or steal their property and money; the taking of booty — in terms of material assets and slaves — has long been an integral component of the conduct of jihad, according to Professor James Turner Johnson.[43] In several statements, bin Laden has highlighted Shaykh al-Islam Ibn-Tammiyah's dictum that the Islamic "duty of self defense . . . is unconditional and is done according to means. . . . The severest defensive war is the war to repel an invader threatening the sanctities and the faith. This war is the duty of all." In a do-what-you-can-where-you-can appeal to the Muslim world in his Declaration of Jihad, bin Laden echoed Ibn-Tammiyah's words. "Brother Muslims worldwide," bin Laden wrote, "your brothers in the land of the two holy mosques and Palestine seek your help and ask you to participate with them in their jihad against their enemies and yours, the Israelis and the Americans, with everything that would drive them out of the Islamic holy places, with each of you doing what he can."[44]

Bin Laden has said he does not expect Muslims to make conventional military attacks against the Crusaders in the jihad's initial phase. To the members of the Saudi military and security services, for example, he said in 1996 that he was certain they wanted to attack U.S. forces "to restore the nation's glory and liberate its occupied holy sites," but he warned that "due to the lack of parity between our regular Armed Forces and the enemy's forces . . . it is wise to spare the Armed Forces the task of engaging in traditional fighting with the Crusader enemy's forces." It is far better, bin Laden said, for the Saudi military to let "the people's sons other than the Armed Forces" confront the crusaders by "waging guerrilla warfare." In his do-what-you-can modus operandi, however, bin Laden made clear there was an important role for each Saudi serviceman. "What your mujahedin brothers and sons want from you at this stage," he explained, "is to provide every possible support: information and materials and arms needed for their work. And they want the security men — in particular — to turn a blind eye and deceive the enemy about their whereabouts, spread false rumors among its ranks, and do whatever is liable to help the mujahedin against the occupying enemy."[45]

Bin Laden also has spent much time urging Muslims to ready individual attacks on Westerners. "It is a great honor," bin Laden said in late 1996, "for every Muslim to defend his Qiblah [the direction Muslims face to pray] and liberate it from these aggressors who are plundering its riches."[46] Bin Laden has reminded Muslims that Allah has called them to "fight and slay the pagans wherever you find them, and lie in wait for them in every stratagem (of war)."[47] He also told them to ignore "Crusader" efforts to identify "the mujahedin as terrorists, [for] the following proverb applies to them: 'She found comfort in accusing me of her own illness.'"[48] Following his chief's lead, Aymen Zawahiri has stressed how easy it is for individual Muslims to attack Crusaders. "Tracking down Americans and Jews is not impossible," he wrote in his 2001 book *Knights under the Prophet's Banner*.

> Killing them with a single bullet, a stab, or device made up of a popular mix of explosives or hitting them with an iron rod is not impossible. Burning down their property with Molotov cocktails is not difficult. With the available means, small groups could prove to be a frightening horror for the Americans and the Jews.[49]

To all Muslims, bin Laden has said, "I confirm that all the youth, and the whole nation [ummah], should concentrate their [jihad] efforts on Americans and Zionists because they are the head of the spear that has been pointed at the nation and delivered into the nation's heart, and that every effort concentrated on the Americans and Zionists will bring good, direct and positive results. Therefore, if someone can kill an American soldier, it is better than wasting time on other matters."[50] On this point, bin Laden concluded in his February 1998 fatwa: "The ruling to kill Americans and their allies — civilians and military — is an individual duty for every Muslim who can do it in any country in which it is possible to do it. . . . We — with God's help — call on every Muslim who believes in God and wishes to be rewarded to comply with God's order to kill the Americans and plunder their money wherever and whenever you find them."[51]

The Obligation of the Young

Bin Laden has always made a special appeal to Muslim youths, instructing them on their religious duty to participate in jihad and urging Muslim scholars to "teach [young] Muslims that there is no honor except in jihad in the way of God." In March 1998, for example, he sent a letter to *Al-Quds Al-Arabi* asserting that this era requires "young men, ulema, notables, traders and tribal chiefs to move out of Muslim countries to work in God's cause, and run the jihad-for-God's-cause battalions in order to expel the occupying invaders." In August 1999, bin Laden added that, "young Muslim men . . . should devote their life to the religion and should opt for jihad." Sounding like a biblical prophet, bin Laden told the young "There are a lot of ways to earn this world, but there is only one to earn the life hereafter. Follow that way and the world will fall into your lap."[52]

Many Western and some Muslim commentators characterize bin Laden's appeal to the young as a cynical attempt to manipulate the misery and hopelessness of the most economically deprived segment of Muslim society. They argue that bin Laden's message does not elicit support from believers ready to defend their faith, but only from disenfranchised youths who have nowhere else to turn. "The difficulty in destroying this threat [from bin Laden and Sunni militancy]," then-director of Central Intelligence George Tenet said in early 2000, "lies in the fact that our efforts will not be enough to overcome the fundamental causes of the phenomenon — poverty, alienation, disaffection, and ethnic hatred deeply rooted in history." The director, it must be noted, avoided mentioning the possibility of Islam being part of the militants' motivation. Similarly, another commentator said that bin Laden's war "is a war of the disillusioned who blame their grievances on the West. . . . [F]undamentalism has given deprived youth a chance to escape the feelings of inferiority engendered by the hegemony of Western culture," while an "unnamed" U.S. official told the *Philadelphia Inquirer* in 1999 that "bin Laden preaches about a lost Golden Age of Islam, destroyed by the West and its culture. He offers them [young men] hope for a better life and someone to blame for their current predicament."[53]

Ascribing the motivation for lethal Sunni militancy to poverty and deprivation appeals to a Western mind used to believing that social problems are always remediable through material improvements. It also suits those in the West who identify people in the twenty-five- to thirty-year age bracket as "youths" and have forgotten that in their own history that it is always the eighteen- to twenty-five-year-olds who do the fighting and dying in war. The divide between Western and Islamic culture on this issue is very broad, but bin Laden's words—as always—provide a useful insight into the reason why fighting falls to the young in his cultural context.

> People between birth and age 10 constitute the largest segment of society, followed by people between 60 and 70. The section given to servicing the debt [religious obligations], particularly in jihad, has narrowed. As we know, a person between the birth age and 15 years has no obligations and is not aware of major events. From age 25, a person gets involved in family obligations, graduation from university, and professional obligations. He has a wife and children. He becomes mature, but his ability to contribute [to jihad] becomes very weak: With whom should I leave the children? Who would support them?
>
> Therefore people between the ages of 15 and 25 are the segment that can contribute and engage in jihad. This is what we noticed in the jihad in Afghanistan. Most mujahedin were of this age. . . . I say the crusader world has decided to devour the Islamic world. The nations have rallied against us, and we have no one else to turn to after Almighty God except the youths, who have not been burdened by the problems of the world.[54]

When talking to the young, bin Laden has stressed that he and his "brothers" who fought in the Afghan jihad "were near 20 years of age," and argues it always is the young who fight and die in wars. Bin Laden vigorously rejects the idea that young men join the jihad only because they are poor, unemployed, undereducated, or despairing. "We believe that this [jihad] is a form of worship we must follow despite our financial ability," bin Laden told ABC's John Miller. "This is a response to Westerners and secularists in the Arab world who claim the reasons for the [religious] awakening and the return of Islam is financial difficulties. This is untrue. In fact, the return of the people to Islam is a blessing from Allah, and their return is a [demonstration of their] need for Allah."[55]

Bin Laden's views were seconded by Palestinian journalist Sa'id Aburish. "[T]his is not a movement that is an offspring of poverty or anything of the sort. This is a political program. A political attitude." As an example of this "attitude" in practice, Mary Anne Weaver has reported that the Gama'at fighters responsible for the November 1997 massacre of more than fifty tourists at Luxor, Egypt, were not "driven by economic desperation or by a sense of being marginalized. They were not part of the floating population of university graduates [in Egypt] who were unemployed or underemployed. . . . [They] were still moving forward, not yet rejected by society." Weaver then quotes a Cairo-based Western diplomat whose conclusion alligns with those of Aburish and bin Laden. "What the Luxor massacre suggests to me," the diplomat told Weaver, "is that even people who are not known to be part of a militant group may be sufficiently impassioned to risk their lives to carry out a dramatic statement, and that is frightening."[56]

To the nonlistening West, bin Laden has repeatedly explained that the young men of the Muslim world always have been "sufficiently impassioned," and that they are the key to defeating the Crusaders and "the bright future of Muhammad's nation."

> There is nothing strange about this: Muhammad's companions were young men. And the young men of today are the successors of the early ones. It was the young men who killed the [Islamic] nation's tyrant, Abu Jahl. Abd-al-Rahman Bin-Awf, may God be pleased with him, said: A young man told me: I heard Abu Jahl insulted the Prophet, peace be upon him. A companion [of Muhammad] said: I swear by God that if I see him I will fight him until the strongest wins. . . . God is great. This is how the young companions [of Muhammad] behaved. Two young men asking one another about the most important target in the enemy's ranks, namely to kill the tyrant of the nation and the leader of the atheists in Badr, namely Abu Jahl. Abd-al-Rahman Bin-Awf's role was to tell them about Abu Jahl's whereabouts. This is the role that is required from those who have knowledge and experience about the enemy's vulnerable spots. They are required to guide their sons and brothers to these spots. Then the young men will say what their predecessors said: "By God, if I see him I will fight with him until the strongest wins."[57]

Among the Muslim world's young, bin Laden has emphasized the heavy moral and religious responsibility carried by those who have already borne arms in God's cause: the veteran mujahedin from Afghanistan, Yemen, Central Asia, Somalia, the Balkans, Kashmir, the Philippines, and the Caucasus. "We believe that those who participated in the jihad in Afghanistan bear the greatest responsibility in this regard," bin Laden told journalist Salah Najm, "because they realized that with insignificant capabilities, with a small number of RPG's [rocket-propelled grenades], with a small number of antitank mines, with a small number of Kalashnikov rifles, they managed to crush the greatest empire known to mankind. They crushed the greatest military machine. The so-called superpower vanished into thin air." Bin Laden says that these men must now "spearhead the Islamic rejection of

U.S. policy against the Islamic nation." It is these young men who must train and lead their generation and the next, as did the "four heroes who blew up the Americans in Riyadh [in November 1995]."[58] "I tell the young men of the Islamic world who fought in Afghanistan and Bosnia Herzegovina with their money, lives, tongues, and pens that the battle has not yet ended," bin Laden has written.

> I remind them of Gabriel's discussion with the messenger of God after the al-Ahzab battle: When the messenger of God arrived in Medina, he put his weapon aside. Gabriel came up to him and said: Have you laid down your weapon? By God, the angels have not laid down their weapons. So move with those who are with you to Bani Qurazah, as I will be moving in front of you, rocking their fortifications and striking terror in their hearts. So Gabriel joined a procession of angels with the Prophet behind them, joined by emigrants and supporters.[59]

Inspiring and Inciting Muslims

The substantial increase in bin Laden's stature as an Islamist leader following his return to Afghanistan in 1996 caused some journalists, policy makers, and terrorism experts to wonder if he was more a media creation than anything else. This is particularly true in the Western media. "Not since Che Guevara's face was a ubiquitous presence on the walls of American college dormitories has a revolutionary figure [bin Laden] been so blown out of proportion," according to a *New York Times* piece by a retired U.S. intelligence official. "One might argue that the following of Osama bin Laden that has been created by the romantic mythology has become more dangerous than the man himself" and that Islamists are "more often inspired by him than controlled by him."[60]

"Inspired by him" — exactly, that is exactly what makes bin Laden so dangerous to U.S. citizens and interests. Some commentators have begun to see that bin Laden's "strategy may be to create the leadership and motivation that might galvanize individual independent units into action." When discussing bin Laden's organization, *Al-Watan Al-Arabi* warned that the West should not think "bin Laden controls these organizations from an operational point of view. In other words, despite his relationship with these organizations, bin Laden may not be in a position to choose their operations or targets and is not in control in this regard. He extends such aid to these groups that have wide networks in a number of states but he does not always control their operations."[61] Bin Laden repeatedly has said he did not control all of the jihad's forces and instead claimed only that he and his lieutenants wanted to rouse, instigate, and incite Muslims, to drive them "to the ignition point not in a long time" and to support "anyone who carries out military action against the Americans."[62] "We seek to instigate the nation [the ummah]," bin Laden told *Al-Jazirah* in late 1998, "to get up and liberate its land, to fight for the sake of God, and to make the Islamic law the highest law, and the word of God the highest word of all."[63]

In this enterprise, bin Laden is following the lead of his earliest mentor, the Palestinian Islamist scholar Abdullah Azzam. U.S. terrorism expert Steven Emerson argues that Azzam contributed greatly to the jihad bin Laden is waging through his writings, speeches, and actions, all of which were aimed toward "reigniting the Islamic rage against those non-Islamic powers that had conspired against Islam since before the crusades."[64] Bin Laden concurs with Emerson. "The shaykh [Azzam] left the atmosphere that was familiar to Muslims, the atmosphere of the mosques and the narrow confines of the city, and launched a struggle to liberate the Islamic world," bin Laden told the journalist Jamal Ismail.

> He instigated the nation from the farthest east to the farthest west. During the blessed [Afghan] jihad, the activities of Shaykh Abdullah Azzam, may God bless his soul, as well as the activities of our brother mujahedin in Palestine, particularly HAMAS, increased. His books, particularly *The Verses of the Merciful*, began to enter Palestine and instigate the nation against the Jews. The Shaykh proceeded from the narrow, regional, and often city atmosphere, that was familiar to Islamists and shaykhs, to the larger Islamic world and began to instigate this Islamic world. We and the Shaykh are in one boat.[65]

Bin Laden has said that he believes instigation is his chief responsibility and is proud of this role and the success he has had thus far. "Come to me, O people of ours," he wrote in a letter published in March 1998. "I am your herald in this grievous catastrophe of the U.S. occupation of the Arabian Peninsula and the Americans' firm control of the wealth of Allah's land, of the Muslims' Ka'aba, of the cradle of the revelation, and of the resting place of the heroic prophet, may Allah's peace and prayers be upon him."[66] When the United States accused him of responsibility for the four bombings in Saudi Arabia and East Africa, bin Laden denied culpability, but he said that "if [the U.S. accusation] means that I have something to do with instigating them, [then] I would like to say that this is obvious. I have frequently admitted to having done so."[67] Driving home the point in late 1998, bin Laden told ABC's Rahimullah Yusufzai—with some heat—that "if the instigation for jihad against the Jews and Americans in order to liberate Al-Aqsa mosque, and the Holy Ka'aba, is considered a crime, then let history witness that I am a criminal."[68] In the final analysis, bin Laden told ABC's John Miller, "It is our duty to lead people to [the] light," and that he and other Islamists are essentially calling on Muslims to "abide by religious principles that are already deeply embedded in the consciousness of the great majority."[69]

After decades of covering Islamic insurgencies, journalist Eric Margolis has cogently summed up the reason why the Islamists' rhetoric of incitement attracts attention and support across the Islamic world. "Such earnest and pious professions may sound romantic, even theatrical to western ears," Margolis wrote. "In our world consumerism and movie-star worship long ago replaced religion. But among Muslims it is common to 'live by the book' and be guided by its commands." Margolis's judgment is on the mark. Shaykh Kamal Khatib, a senior Muslim cleric in Israel, for example, amplified Margolis's point in an article about bin Laden and the Chechen Islamist leader Shamil Basayev; the article also supports bin Laden's contention that his major duty is incitement, not direct command-and-control of a huge military organization. "We are certain," Shaykh Khatib wrote in late 1999 in response to U.S. and Russian animosity toward Islamist leaders,

> that the United States is not fighting bin Laden's person as much as it is fighting bin Laden's phenomena and model. It actually fears that bin Laden will become a hero to be imitated or an example to be followed by many Arab and Muslim youths.
>
> The United States which has invaded us in our very home, fed hamburgers to our youth, made them wear blue jeans, and had them listen to Michael Jackson and CNN reports, also fears a "renegade" move by Arab and Muslim youths. In this case, they would imitate the heroic deeds, positions, manliness, loftiness, and pride of bin Laden and Basayev instead of imitating John Travolta, Michael Jackson, and Superman.
>
> Moreover, the United States . . . has actually been prevented from sleep and shaken by the fact that someone from Saudi Arabia arose from the rubble to tell the Muslims to turn their faces again to the first Qiblah and not to the United States. He also told Muslims: "Close your ranks under the banner [of the] Prophet Muhammad, may peace be upon him. It is shameful to rally around Russia or the United States. . . .
>
> We know and expect that bin Laden and Basayev may fall as martyrs or may be held captive during this unequal war. But this is not a shame for them, nor is it a source of pride for their enemies. On the path of martyrdom, bin Laden and Basayev were preceded by those better than them, such as the companions of the Prophet and the elite Muslims throughout Islam's eventful and great history.
>
> However, we will tell the enemies of bin Laden and Basayev, as well as the drunken president and philanderer [Yeltsin and

Clinton]: If you capture or kill bin Laden or Basayev, this will not close a chapter on what you call terrorism. It will, rather, open chapters of pride and unleash further hostility to Russia, the United States, and other infidels.

We also tell them: Their martyrdom does not mean at all their death. Rather, it means instilling a spirit and breaths of life into thousands of youth who will follow the path and good example of bin Laden and Basayev. The blood of bin Laden and Basayev will draw the map of the future with bright letters that cannot be erased and their bones will be torches that will light the dark night.[70]

Participate or Be Damned

While bin Laden has championed the "natural right of all Muslims to defend themselves,"[71] he has been critical of some of his coreligionists for not yet emigrating from lands where Muslims are persecuted — as did the Prophet Muhammed and his companions — and from a foreign refuge waging a jihad to defeat attacks on Islam by Americans, other infidels, and apostate Muslim regimes. Many Muslims, bin Laden told the *Pakistan Observer*, "[have] displayed lethargy in fulfillment of this obligation," adding that "they would be held accountable and would have to face the anguish of [the] Almighty on the day of Judgment."[72] In a poem, bin Laden has asked, "How can I awaken the conscience of insensitive people who seek material benefits? Jews kill my brethren but the Arabs hold summit conferences and feel satisfied with passing resolutions."[73]

Bin Laden's position is supported by Islamic history, as well as by contemporary Islamic scholars. Historically, as Amin Malouf has written, in the first phases of the Crusades, the Catholic knights "commanded a weapon even more formidable than their fortresses, and that was the torpor of the Muslim world," a torpor that initially was so widespread and durable that Saladin attempted to shame Muslims into action. "Behold with what obstinacy they [the Crusaders] fight for their religion," Saladin said, "while we, the Muslims, show no enthusiasm for waging holy war." In 1986 Shaykh Abdullah Azzam followed suit, declaring emigration and jihad to be the duty of all Muslims. "Those who believe that Islam can flourish [and] be victorious without jihad, fighting, and blood," Azzam maintained, "are illusioned and do not understand the nature of this religion. The prestige of preachers, the influence and dignity of Muslims, cannot be attained without jihad." More recently, HAMAS's Shaykh Yasin urged Muslims not to despair if the cause of jihad required "deportation and exile from the homeland." Yasin said such events are necessities and should be seen as "tourism for the sake of God."[74]

In his 1996 Declaration of Jihad, bin Laden first focused his anger on his fellow Saudis, whom he said correctly fear "God is tormenting them because they kept quiet about the [al-Saud] regime's injustice and illegitimate actions, especially its failure to have recourse to the Sharia, its confiscation of people's legitimate rights, the opening of the land of the two holy mosques to the American occupiers, and the arbitrary jailing of the true Ulema, heirs of the Prophet."[75] In other statements, bin Laden has said that what is true of the Saudis is also true of other Muslims—witness the decades-old plight of the Palestinians, the suffering of Iraqi civilians, and the mass murder of Muslim Bosnians and Kosovars. "You should all shed tears," bin Laden told his brethren in early 2001, "[when] assessing the prevailing conditions in which the Ummah is going through now. Your hearts should bleed and bemoan the insensitivity the Ummah is reflecting now." Because of Muslim quiescence in the face of the modern Crusaders' aggression, bin Laden has said, Muslims must now stand up and attack, in the words of medieval Muslim jurist Shaykh Tammiyah, the "invader who corrupts the faith and the world." Urging Muslims to action, bin Laden wrote it is time that men "from all parts of the land of Islam must come forth and emigrate for the cause of Allah so they will make the decision and so they may arrange for jihad battalions to serve the cause of Allah and expel the occupying Christian invaders. Let the persevering young men of the Peninsula emigrate to the sacrifice arenas and join the vanguards preparing for jihad."[76]

Notwithstanding scripture's demands, bin Laden is not sanguine that all Muslims are ready to wage jihad against Christian aggression and fight to end the suffering, humiliation, and murder of Muslims. Even though it is clear to his followers that "since it abandoned the jihad the [Islamic] nation has been suffering the calamities of murder, dispossession, and plunder at the hands of the Crusaders and their allies, led by the United States and Israel," bin Laden has said that "people are paying no heed . . . and most of them have failed to obey Allah with jihad and emigration."[77]

At times, bin Laden has expressed exasperation with Muslims who are not participating in the jihad. "Where are you, O people of ours," he asked in a 1998 letter published by the AP. "Rather, where do all Muslims stand vis-à-vis this hard trial, horrid ordeal and atrocious calamity? How come Muslims have been absent, and you have been absent as witnesses against the treachery of the Romans [Christians] and against the raising of the cross on the land of the Two Holy Mosques. What more horrible catastrophe than has already afflicted the people of the Peninsula are you awaiting?"[78] He has argued that those who attacked the U.S.-Saudi military facility in Riyadh in November 1995 not only "showed the Americans what manliness is but taught the hordes of opulent and weak materialists [in Saudi Arabia] a lesson in the triviality of life without a creed and in the abjectness of life when dignity is stripped away and honor soiled. They did their utmost to wash away disgrace from the Muslim nation's face." Still, their efforts are not enough; all Muslims must participate. "What happened to the honor of Muslims?" bin Laden asked Pakistani journalist Hamid Mir in 1997. "Can we not defend the Ka'aba — the center of prayers. . . . We Muslims have to defend ourselves. We Muslims should now take care of the Ka'aba, instead of the White House." Again, in late 2000, bin Laden praised renewed Palestinian attacks on Israel, but expressed "surprise and astonishment" over the failure of other Islamists to aid the fighters. "The Arab and Islamic street have played its role," he told *Al-Hayah,* "but the ulema of the [Islamic] nation and the leaders of the Islamic movement have proven they are far below the level of events." In a clear call for God's punishment to fall not only on Crusaders, but also Muslims who do not support jihad, bin Laden has prayed

> Allah, the Exalted and the Almighty, we implore to send down His wrath, His aversion, and His force on the U.S. troops in the Gulf and on their Jewish allies in Palestine and on all hypocrites who support them. We implore Him to send upon them from His heaven a thunderbolt that rolls their heads, destroys them to the last man and keeps none. We implore Him to awaken the spirit of jihad in the Muslim nation so it will break away from the shackle of weakness and will meet for heroic sagas. We also implore Him to bless all Muslims with a righteous state in which those who obey Him are honored and those who disobey him are humiliated; in which virtue is promoted and vice prohibited — a state that supports the oppressed and the powerless in all parts of the world and exacts justice from every oppressor on earth, and this is not difficult for Allah.[79]

Beyond criticizing Muslims for standing aloof on the jihad's sidelines, bin Laden kept an eye peeled for any group whose ardor for fighting the good fight appears to be slackening. In summer 2000, for example, the Pakistan-based Kashmiri insurgent group Hezb-ul-Mujahedin (HUM) unexpectedly announced a unilateral cease-fire and readiness to talk to Indian officials about a negotiated settlement in Kashmir. The HUM's move immediately drew withering condemnation from other Kashmiri insurgents and the group abandoned the cease-fire after a single unpromising meeting with the Indians. After the HUM initiative failed, bin Laden wrote that Kashmiri groups must avoid even hinting at the possibility of a negotiated settlement in Kashmir. His warning was temperately addressed to all Kashmiri groups, but there is no doubt his ire was focused on the HUM.

> The mujahedin in Kashmir are engaged in a jihad to please God. We pray for them. They are part of us. All of us are like a body. If any part of the body has pain, the other parts also feel it. India's

enmity toward Islam and Muslims is growing. All Muslims are obligated to undertake jihad against India and to support the forces engaged in jihad. I am sure that the Kashmiri mujahedin would decide anything with deliberation. No mujahid can waste the 16-year-old jihad and the blood of 300,000 martyrs. All I want to say is that they should not trust the enemy's promises, unless the enemy proves its credibility with its actions. Jihad is a very precious thing and it should be treated very carefully. I am sure that [the] mujahedin would never let it be harmed. The entire Muslim world is with them and praying for them.[80]

Finally, bin Laden's readiness to call down God's wrath on fellow Muslims who are not participating in the jihad has implications for his attitude toward the death of innocent Muslims in the course of his military operations. While not explicitly stating such a position, there is a clear suggestion in bin Laden's statements that the prospect of casualties among Muslims choosing to live in — and not, as the Prophet has urged, emigrate from — Western countries or in Islamic countries "occupied" or "oppressed" by Crusaders and apostates, will not prominently figure in his calculations. In the expendable category, therefore, are Muslims living, working, or shopping near U.S. military, economic, or diplomatic facilities in places such as Saudi Arabia, Pakistan, Egypt, other countries in the Gulf, the Caucasus, Africa, and the Balkans. Bin Laden made this clear in al Qaeda's claim of responsibility for the East Africa bombings, telling Muslims "not to get near anything American in order to avoid a repeat of what happened in Nairobi and so that they are not unwittingly affected by the flames of God's army."[81]

All Weapons Are on the Table

Bin Laden is in an enviable position regarding the choice of weapons with which to attack those in the West, and he knows it. In March 1998 bin Laden quoted a passage from the Koran that emphasizes and justifies not only his personal inclination vis-à-vis weaponry, but also his belief that there is a binding religious duty to acquire and use all weapons against those he depicts as the Crusaders. "Against them," says the passage, "make ready your strength to the utmost of your power, including steeds of war, to strike terror into (the hearts of) the enemies of God and your enemy, and others besides them, whom ye may not know, but whom God doth know."[82] That bin Laden believes there now is a struggle to the death between Islam and the West, and hence Muslims must be armed as well as their foes, is clear in a March 1997 statement he sent to *Al-Islah*. "What we are interested in," bin Laden wrote, "is our people's awareness of the dimensions of the current battle and the need for them to join the mujahedin and get ready for the day of the decisive confrontation, with its heavy costs in terms of money and lives. Everything is of little importance when it comes to defending God's religion, Islamic holy places, and Muslim countries, for the sake of applying God's law."[83]

The weapons most sought by bin Laden, and those his foes most fear he will acquire, are either off-the-shelf chemical, biological, radiological, or nuclear (CBRN) weapons, or their components. Bin Laden wants to use CBRN weapons, as Gavin Cameron has written, "to achieve finite (although widespread) political objectives for religious reasons" — the removal of the Crusaders from Muslim lands and the subsequent destruction of Westernized Muslim regimes. Bin Laden is not interested in using a CBRN weapon to terrorize his foes; he is seeking a first-strike capability, a strategic not a tactical weapon. Bin Laden sees CBRN weapons as "war winners" and intends to use them to pin a strategic defeat on Islam's foes.[84] "I would say that acquiring [CBRN] weapons for the defense of Muslims is a religious duty," bin Laden told Rahimullah Yusufzai in late 1998.

> To seek to possess the weapons that could counter those of the infidels is a religious duty. If I have indeed acquired these weapons, then this is an obligation I carried out and I thank God for enabling us to do that. And if I seek to acquire these weapons I am carrying out a duty. It would be a sin for Muslims not to try to possess the weapons that would prevent the infidels from inflicting harm on Muslims. But how we would use these weapons if we possess them is up to us.[85]

Shortly after this statement, a query about CBRN weapons again was put to bin Laden, this time by Qatar's Al-Jazirah television. Unusually, bin Laden replied with heat, momentarily losing his imperturbable calm. Appending a lengthy excerpt here is worthwhile because it is a rare instance of bin Laden in high dudgeon and, more important, because bin Laden unambiguously pledges to use weapons of mass destruction. "We believe that the right to self-defense is enjoyed by all people," bin Laden said.

> Israel is stockpiling hundreds of nuclear warheads and bombs. The Christian West is largely in possession of such weapons. Hence, we do not regard this as a charge [i.e., seeking CBRN weapons], but rather as a right. We do not expect to see anybody level charges against us in this regard. It is as if you were accusing a man of being a courageous knight and fighter. It is as if you were denying him this. Only a man who is not in his right mind would level such accusations. We supported the Pakistani people and congratulated them when God was gracious enough to enable them to acquire

the nuclear weapon. We regard this as one of our rights, our Muslim rights. We disregard such worn-out U.S. charges.

Let us say that there are two parties to the conflict: The first party is world Christianity, which is allied with Zionist Jewry and led by the United States, Britain, and Israel; while the second party is the Muslim world. In such a conflict, it is unacceptable to see the first party mount attacks, desecrate my [sic] lands and holy shrines, and plunder the Muslims' oil. When it is met by any resistance on the part of the Muslims, this party brands the Muslims as terrorists. This is stupidity. People's intelligence is being belittled. We believe that it is our religious duty to resist this occupation with all the power that we have and to punish it using the same means it is pursuing us with.[86]

The use of CBRN weapons again raises the issue of causing Muslim casualties. As noted above, bin Laden has pronounced on the issue in the context of the conventional East Africa bombings, saying the losses there were religiously acceptable, and even blaming the Kenyans because "it is your government that has brought death and ruin to your country when it allowed the Americans to use its territory to kill the neighboring Islamic peoples [in Somalia] and besiege their ecomomy."[87] He has not yet commented on inflicting such casualties, perhaps on a massive scale, when he uses CBRN weapons on Crusader targets. Bin Laden's vociferous U.K.-based advocate, Omar Bakri Muhammed, however, has spoken of the civilian casualties likely to be attendant to an al Qaeda CBRN attack, and his words probably are a fair reflection of bin Laden's perspective. "Using any biological weapons in self-defense is, in Islam, permissible," Bakri wrote in a letter to bin Laden in September 1999, "and I believe that we [the ummah] are currently operating under a defensive jihad. Obviously, we regret what could happen to innocent people, but there are always people who are war casualties or, if you will, victims of war."[88]

No one should think that the prospect of Muslim casualties — even in large numbers — will prevent bin Laden from using a CBRN weapon on a target in the United States. As John Kelsay has written, "[C]onsiderations of proportionality are important [in Islamic law on war] since no one wants to shed more blood than necessary. But the necessities of the war effort motivated by religious considerations allow for considerable discretion." Intentions count regarding Muslim casualties, Kelsay notes, and in a Muslim attack on Islam's enemies, Muslims caught near or on the battlefield "are not considered legitimate targets for direct attacks by Muslims, though their deaths may be brought about indirectly." On this point, Kelsay quotes classical Islamic jurist Muhammad ibn al-Hussein al-Shaybai's answer when asked if Muslims were prohibited from attacking if noncombatants and

Muslims would be killed. "If Muslims stopped attacking the inhabitants of the territory of war [*dar-al-harb*] for any of the reasons you have stated," al-Shaybai responded, "they would be unable to go to war at all, for there is no city in the territory of war in which there is no one at all of these you have mentioned."[89]

Ominously, this judgment from classical Islamic jurisprudence was reaffirmed in April 2001 by Shaykh Yusuf al-Qaradawi, one of contemporary Islam's most respected scholars, and in words that also echo bin Laden's view. Speaking in Qatar, al-Qaradawi's statement show the enduring pertinence of al-Shaybai's judgement.

> The basic thing for Muslims is not to kill a child, woman, or an old man who has nothing to do with war. But there are necessities sometimes. When our brethren set off a car bomb, they do not mean to kill a child. But, he gets killed without any real intention. They did not mean to kill the child. But sometimes a child happens to be on the scene and he gets killed. This is not intentional killing of children. In the *Intifadah,* children receive direct hits [from the Israelis] in their heads and their chests. This is the deliberate killing of children. On the other hand, the operations carried out by HAMAS, Islamic Jihad, or Fatah, or others do not mean to kill children. The child is killed accidentally not intentionally.[90]

5

GETTING TO KNOW BIN LADEN: CHARACTER TRAITS

> Perhaps the strongest feature in his character was prudence, never acting until every circumstance, every consideration was maturely weighted; refraining if he saw a doubt, but, when once decided, going through with his purpose, whatever obstacles opposed.
>
> *Thomas Jefferson on George Washington,* 2 January 1814

As they would for any person, Osama bin Laden's statements, interviews, and writings allow a glimpse at his personality, values, and beliefs. Having examined substantive themes in this material, it is worth noting three personality traits that also emerge prominently. These characteristics — personal responsibility, piety, and professionalism — provide a powerful base from which bin Laden has been able to persevere in the face of setbacks and delay. In addition, the material clearly shows bin Laden has a substantial knowledge of Islamic history and a strong sense that he is playing a role in a historical process that has been under way for more than fourteen centuries.

Personal Responsibility

Bin Laden's actions and statements have shown that he believed that by inciting a defensive jihad he was doing no more than fulfilling his personal duty as a Muslim. "All ulema . . . are unanimous that it is an individual duty to fight an invading infidel enemy," bin Laden wrote in March 1998. "The son may take up arms without his father's permission and the indebted may do so without the debtor's permission. This duty must be given priority over other individual duties when conditions become difficult and concerns become severe."[1] In bin Laden's public statements there is not one hint that he is calling for jihad because he wants to be the Muslim world's leader, the next caliph. "I am one of Allah's worshippers," he told ABC's John Miller. "I worship Allah, which includes carrying out jihad to raise Allah's word and evict the Americans from all Muslim land."[2] Bin Laden believes he is simply performing a required religious duty in circumstances not of his own making, but that have conspired to put him at the center of affairs. "Our encouragement and call to Muslims to enter jihad against the Americans and the Israeli occupiers," bin Laden said in 1996, "are actions which we are engaging in as religious obligations. . . . We have given an oath to Allah to continue in the struggle as long as we have blood pumping in our veins or a seeing eye, and we beg of Allah to accept and to grant a good ending for us and for all the Muslims." In articulating this position, Azzam's influence is clear. In 1986 Shaykh Azzam wrote "that every Muslim bears responsibility of abandoning jihad, and the sin of abandoning the gun. Every Muslim who passes away without a gun in his hand faces Allah with the sin of abandoning fighting. . . . I strongly believe (God knows better) that there is no difference between who does not fight, and he who does not fast, pray, or pay zakat [tithes] . . . I believe that no Muslim is excused in abandoning jihad."[3]

Bin Laden will brook no dispute on this point. He adamantly defends using force to repel the Crusader offensive and stresses that each Muslim is personally responsible for participating in the effort. "Islam is a moderate religion. It is the religion of Muhammad, Peace Be Upon Him," bin Laden told *Al-Quds Al-Arabi.*

> Everything is just and right. Words and explanations are used to clarify the matters than can be explained. And Almighty God has sanctioned Al-Da'wah [preaching]. This is justice and moderation. In regard to the matters in which spearheads need be used, it is a just right. If some people confuse the two, Islam is not responsible, since the error is in the application. If anyone means by violence and renunciation of violence to prevent us from starting the jihad, [then] he has deviated from the path. The jihad is part of our Shariah and the nation cannot dispense with it against its enemies.[4]

Piety

One can be exasperated with the West's inability to hear what non-Westerners are saying. This frustration stems not from a naive belief that what is said is wise or accurate, but because what is said is often a threat to be taken seriously. In *Middle East Policy,* for example, Dr. M. C. Dunn noted in 1998 that "Bin Ladin relishes publicity. Rather than a reclusive mystery man, Bin Ladin is almost a media star. . . . [and] his claims to be a religious scholar are highly questionable."[5] In an otherwise excellent article, Dr. Manstorp hits the latter theme and suggests the bin Laden threat is limited because he is not a religious scholar. "Bin Ladin will inevitably fail to command a sizable following in the broader Islamic community, as he lacks any formal religious training or scholarship," Manstorp asserts, "[t]his means there is no binding requirements on Muslims to adhere to any fatwa issued by him. In particular, Bin Ladin's lack of religious stature is illustrated in the fatwa's call for killing civilians, an act strictly prohibited by Islamic law and reinforced by scholars."

As noted above, two of the most famous Muslim soldiers, Nur al-Din and Saladin, led victorious, religiously motivated jihads, even though they were merely pious believers and not Islamic scholars or jurists. "For some contemporary Islamic groups," Dr. Kelsay has explained, "the struggle of Saladin with the Crusaders serves as a lens through which to interpret their situation." In a passage that mirrors bin Laden's justification for his actions, Kelsay writes that "Muslims are said to struggle in the manner of Saladin" when "[t]heir goal is to rid themselves of the rule of non-Muslims and to recover a lost portion of Muslim territory."

Clearly, the lack of formal training in Islamic jurisprudence does not preclude the ability of an individual to call for and lead a jihad. In addition, the killing of civilians is not as open and shut as Dr. Manstorp suggests. The American scholar J. T. Johnson, for example, has written that Islamic jurists have long taught that if Islam's enemies refuse to convert to Islam "the war may be prosecuted as harshly as necessary as long as Muslims do not resort to treachery." The jurists have added that "the faithful participating in the military form of jihad were advised to refrain from shedding blood or the destruction of property unnecessary for the achievement of their objective."[6]

Most pertinent, bin Laden has never posed as a religious jurist or scholar and has repeatedly said that he is not the appropriate leader for the jihad. He describes himself as a simple Muslim who is ready and waiting to be directed by a rightful leader, one drawn from what he refers to as "the honest [Islamic] scholars . . . who hold the solution and have the ability to effect change."

> My personal life is always driven by my responsibilities as a Muslim. I am a humble man of God who only wants to please his God. I don't care what people say about me. It neither hurts nor gives satisfaction. Thousands of people like me are working at their place

for the glory of Islam. I do not consider myself superior to any of them. I always seek guidance from many religious scholars.[7]

Bin Laden claims that he has taken the lead because "our elite Ulema have put in the jails of the Islamic world, especially the Kingdom's jails."[8] He repeatedly has emphasized that it was only after "the Saudi Government harassed the Ulema, dismissed them from their jobs in the universities and the mosques, and prevented the distribution of their tapes, I decided that, if it [the Saudi regime] was going to prevent them from speaking, I would begin to promote virtue and repudiate vice, something which has been suspended." It also should be noted that bin Laden moved to the fore only after Shaykh Azzam was murdered in Pakistan. In this regard, a U.K.-based Islamist leader, Abu Hamzah al-Masri, has said that "Azzam would have been much more dangerous than Usama Bin Laden because he had more credibility as the founder of the jihad movement in Afghanistan."

There is no reason to think bin Laden would dispute al-Masri's conclusion, although bin Laden likely would add that Azzam's scholarly credentials also would have made him a more appropriate leader. Even now, almost a decade after bin Laden began rising to international prominence, *Jeune Afrique* has reported that he is keenly aware of his "theological limitations and he is surrounded by imams and ulemmas." Like Nur al-Din and Saladin, bin Laden stepped forward to assume the jihad's leadership because no more well-credentialed individual made himself available and because participating in a defensive jihad is a binding responsibility for every pious and devout Muslim.[9]

Professionalism

In the West, the word *jihad* evokes visions of wanton acts of violence, pillage, and rape. In this view, the jihad style of war is closely associated with the human-wave attacks of the Japanese on Guadalcanal, the Chinese in Korea, and the Iranians in their war with Iraq, and not the painstaking, well-planned, and casualty-limiting — at least for the attackers — operations executed by the Afghan commanders during their jihad against the Soviets. Bin Laden, of course, learned his military skills in Afghanistan, not on the Iran-Iraq border, and, as a result, his methodological approach to waging jihad is marked by a measured manner stressing patience, preparation, and professionalism, or, as author Khalid Asaad has termed it, the Afghan policy "of the long breath and good planning to lessen losses."[10] In his statements, as Professor Magnus Ranstorp notes, bin Laden's themes "demonstrate a sophisticated mixture of religious legitimization for the jihad (through selective retrieval of sacred passages from the Koran and the use of Muslim history) coupled with an astute political analysis of accumulated Muslim grievances within a Saudi Arabian context and the wide Middle East context."[11] Likewise, bin Laden's patient and thorough method of warmaking is apparent. In his Declaration of Jihad in August 1996, for example, he wrote:

> Today we begin to talk, work, and discuss ways of rectifying what has befallen the Islamic world in general, and the land of the two holy mosques in particular. We want to study the ways which could be used to rectify matters and restore rights to their owners as people have been subjected to grave danger and harm to their religion and their lives, people of all walks of life, civilians, military, security men, employees, merchants, people big and small, school and university students, and unemployed university graduates, in fact hundreds of thousands who constitute a broad sector of the society.[12]

Bin Laden always forgoes haste in favor of optimal operational planning and will not be hurried or hustled by others. Nearly a year after the Declaration of Jihad, for example, he told the London *Independent* that "[w]e are still at the beginning of our military action against American forces."[13] Bin Laden's strong suits as military commander appear to be patience, organizational excellence, and fatalism. Beyond his experience as a construction engineer and insurgent, these traits also flow from his belief that he exists at God's pleasure and is performing God's will. "Whatever God has ordained, He always in the past has given us the ability to be patient and accept whatever He has ordained for us," bin Laden told Pakistani journalist Rahimullah Yusufzai, adding that he needs to neither hurry nor fear.

> A true Muslim should thank God in prosperity and be patient in adversity. There is good for him in both cases.[14] . . . Life is only in the control of God and no human can do anything about it. God can give life or death to anybody He wants. It does not matter if you are a superpower or not. If God wants me to live, even ten countries like the United States cannot kill me. But when God wants me to die, even an ordinary person would have no difficulty in killing me. It is my faith that the United States cannot do anything to me and I am not afraid of it at all. My life and death are in the hands of God. We are fighting for the truth. The United States is plundering our resources and wandering about our sacred places. It may do anything it wants because it can never harm us because God is with us.[15]

Bin Laden's academic training, experience as a construction engineer, effectiveness as an insurgent, and success over twenty years in building a unique multiethnic organization have fostered his patience and precision.

In Professor Khalid Duran's estimate, bin Laden's "intelligence and inventiveness are considerable. Like many Afghan Arabs, the Saudi jihadist is a messianic zealot. And yet, in his own right he is a restrained person with a practical bent of mind."[16] Bin Laden has said that each Muslim's responsibility is to patiently prepare for jihad against the Crusaders.

> Muslims must prepare all the possible might to repel the enemy on the military economic, missionary, and all other areas. It is crucial for us to be patient and to cooperate in righteousness and piety. . . . We have urged all Muslims to study the case of each of their countries and to decide when they can start their jihad. If the time is not suitable this does not mean they should just sit. It means they must work hard in preparation. You have to do many things before waging jihad, and every Muslim should prepare himself very well for this.[17]

Bin Laden's professionalism extended to those he recruited as senior lieutenants and major operatives. The bond between bin Laden and these men has been brainpower as well as Islam. The West too often has been misled by the raggedy appearance of bin Laden and his subordinates—squatting in the dirt, clothed in robes and turbans, holding AK-47s, and sporting chest-length beards—and automatically assumes they are an antimodern, uneducated rabble. "Too many Westerners and staff officers in every age," Anatol Lieven has written, "have dismissed such adversaries as 'savages,' their sacrificial courage as mere 'fanaticism'—and have subsequently paid the price."[18]

Bin Laden has a university degree in economics, reads a great deal, has a "data management team" travel with him, and, according to the editor of *Al-Quds Al-Arabi,* maintains "computers, modern reception equipment, a huge database on computer disks, and other information kept in the usual way." The result of this education, reading, and tracking current events, Professor Ranstorp has noted, is a suppleness in bin Laden's statements that shows a "general political astuteness and awareness of local regional and global issues, especially how changes in each of these environments affects the situations of Muslims in diverse political, geographical, and operational contexts." In addition, since the early years of the Afghan jihad, bin Laden's senior cadre always has been staffed by well-educated men who are experienced in their professions; Atwan, for example, said he found bin Laden surrounded by men who "hold high scientific degrees: doctors, engineers, and teachers."[19]

Egyptian Islamic Jihad (EIJ) leader Ayman Zawahiri is a medical doctor; Mustafa Hamza is an agricultural engineer; the late Abu Ubaydah al-Banshiri, the captured Mamdouh Mahmoud Salim, and the late Mohammed

Atef were professional military or security officers; Salim also is an electrical engineer, as are Mohamedu Ould Slahi—who is linked to a thwarted 1999 bin Laden attack in the United States—and the jailed Ramzi Yousef; Khalid al-Fawwaz, awaiting extradition from the United Kingdom to the United States, is a graduate civil engineer; al Qaeda's explosives and CBW expert, Abu Khabab al-Masri, is a chemical engineer; Wadi El-Hage is a graduate urban planner; the jailed Yousef, Ahmed Salamah Mabruk, and the recently unjailed Khalil al-Deeq each studied computer sciences, and the latter teaches his skills to others; Chechnya-based Islamist Ibn Khattab is a propaganda master, broadcasting video on the Internet—often on the Abdullah Azzam Home Page—to show Muslims insurgent victories and Russian atrocities; and Wael Juleidan and Mohammed Jamal Khalifah are experienced, well-traveled, and successful businessmen and nongovernmental organization operators.[20]

Thus, overwhelmingly, bin Laden's senior leadership team is experienced, well educated, and drawn from the Islamic world's urban middle- and upper-middle classes. The ideological message of militant Islamists like bin Laden, therefore, may, as Professor Mahmood Monshipouri has written, "represent the most advanced international movement in formulating a broad and coherent set of grievances against the West and the 'Western-dominated' international system."[21]

YEARS OF PREPARATION,
1957–1996

6

THE YOUNG BIN LADEN, 1957–1979: FAMILY, EDUCATION, AND RELIGION

Few words will be necessary, with good disposition on your part. Adore God. Reverence and cherish your parents. Love your neighbors as yourself, and your country more than yourself. Be just. Be true. Murmur not at the ways of Providence.

Thomas Jefferson, February 1825

Like most matters pertaining to bin Laden, information about his youth, education, and family relations is not definitive and often is contradictory. What *Time*'s Internet service said about bin Laden is true in spades for his family and their businesses: they are "a fact-checker's migraine."[1] That said, there are enough data to sketch the family and the business and the effect of each on bin Laden.

The bin Laden family originally came from peasant origins in the village of al-Rubat in the Hadramut area of northwest Yemen. Muhammed bin Laden, Osama's father, appears to have left the Hadramut area for Saudi Arabia in the late 1920s. In 1931 Muhammed founded the company that is known today as the Saudi Bin Laden Group. Muhammed is said to have retained affection for Yemen and often brought Hadramis to settle in Saudi Arabia and work on his construction projects; this practice may have yielded benefits for Osama, because *Newsweek* has reported that 80 percent of the fighters involved in the October 2000 attack on the U.S. destroyer *Cole* were born in Mecca of transplanted Yemeni families, several of which still have ties to the Hadramut. Muhammed did not trumpet pride in his Yemeni origins, however, because he was striving to be accepted in the highest levels of Saudi society despite being a foreigner.[2]

Osama, however, retains a strong and unhidden residual pride in his Yemeni origins, saying in 1994 that Yemen is "one of the best Arab and Muslim countries in terms of its adherence to tradition and the faith . . . [its] topography is mountainous, and its people are tribal and armed, and allow one to breathe clean air unblemished by humiliation." Osama frequently notes Islam spread to Yemen soon after the religion's founding and argues that Saudi Arabia benefits from "the strategic depth and the extended manpower fighting for God in happy Yemen." He also stresses that the Prophet valued the strong faith of the Yemenis, saying that when Islam was attacked, there "would come 12,000 [from Yemen] who would support God and His Prophet, and they are among the best of us."[3] The Hadramut's Kindah tribes have returned Osama's affection. This favorite-son status was clear in the late 1990s when tribal chiefs told the United States to stop "the intensive terrorist campaign and the illegal pursuit waged against their son, Shaykh Osama Bin-Muhammed Bin Laden al-Kandi."[4]

Rise of Muhammed Bin Laden

Described as "a genius in many ways" with "a mind that was like a computer for figures,"[5] the reporting about Muhammed bin Laden suggests a rags-to-riches story in which he arrived in Saudi Arabia and took a job as either a hotel porter or a bricklayer. From that toehold, Muhammed saved money and slowly built a company specializing in commercial construction.[6] As Osama has said, his father's company "was one of the founders of the infrastructure of the Kingdom of Saudi Arabia," and in mid-1999 the Bin Laden Group's Web page proudly asserted that since the 1930s the company has "helped the Kingdom to develop its resources and infrastructure."[7]

Over the decades, the Bin Laden firm grew and diversified, so that by the 1990s it was involved in road building, housing construction, infrastructure projects — palaces, airports, tunnels, harbors, mosques, highways, and so forth — agriculture, petrochemicals, irrigation, and telecommunications. The family business also is extensively involved in light manufacturing and exports crystal tableware, foodstuffs, paint, and a variety of other products to at least eighteen countries in Europe, Asia, Africa, and North America. The company has offices in most Saudi cities, about one hundred offshore subsidiaries, and offices or representatives in Beirut, Cairo, Amman, Dubai, Geneva, London, and Washington, D.C. Another company speciality has been power plants; it has built plants in Riyadh, Mecca, Cyprus, Jordan, and Canada.[8] In recent years, the Bin Laden Group also has become the representative for some foreign firms in the kingdom, ranging from Porsche, Audi, and Volkswagen to Snapple fruit drinks. Overall, the group has a deserved reputation for "professional excellence and a 'can do' spirit in large projects."[9] By the late 1990s, the bin Ladens were "the richest non-royal family in Saudi Arabia." Estimates of its wealth are in the vicinity of $5 billion, and *Forbes* and *Fortune* count the bin Ladens among the wealthiest families in the world.[10]

Muhammed bin Laden consistently is described as a modest man, a strict disciplinarian, and a hardworking, ambitious, generous, and religious individual. The prominence of his Yemeni-origin family in Saudi society and the tremendous financial success of his company, however, have not derived solely from the sweat of his brow. Soon after arriving in the kingdom and establishing his company, Muhammed became—in ways that are not clear—a friend and then a confidant of King Abdul Aziz al-Saud. The PBS program *Frontline* reported that Muhammed bin Laden won the king's favor by submitting below-cost bids on palace construction projects and then producing a quality structure on time.[11] From this costly start, Muhammed's company became the al-Sauds' favorite contractor for infrastructure projects and palaces, and was later awarded "exclusive rights to all construction of a religious nature, whether in Mecca or Medina or—until 1967—the Holy Places in Jerusalem."[12]

The friendship between King Abdul al-Aziz and Muhammed bin Laden continued to strengthen and, in the 1960s, survived bin Laden's role in successfully persuading the king to step down in favor of his brother Faisal. Shortly after Faisal became king, according to *Frontline*, Muhammed bin Laden further cemented his relationship with the new monarch and his family by paying the Saudi civil service with his own funds for six months after it was found that the former king had emptied the country's treasury. Muhammed also later served for a time as Faisal's minister of public works. Muhammed's relationship with the two Saudi kings spawned broad and close relations between the two families. Many of Muhammed's twenty-five sons went to school with the sons of the two kings, and the bin Ladens often served as chaperones for the kings' sons. In these personal relations, as well as in joint economic projects, the al-Sauds found they could rely on the bin Ladens' discretion; the firm has a record of avoiding "any and all publicity."[13] Of the world-class Saudi companies, the Bin Laden corporation is one that "rarely if ever buys advertising space in industry publications," and *Dunn and Bradstreet* reported in 1999 that "all Bin Laden companies restrict information release." As *Frontline* noted in April 1999, the bin Laden–al-Saud relationship is not simply one of business ties; it is also a relationship of trust, of friendship, and of shared secrets."[14]

When family patriarch Muhammed died in a plane crash in 1968— Osama claims King Faisal reacted by saying that "his right arm had been broken"—his eldest son, Salem, became head of the family and its businesses.[15] Salem remained a royal confidant and one of King Fahd's two closest friends until 1988, when he too died in a plane crash. Currently, Bakr bin Laden is the family's chief, and he is personally and economically close to the al-Sauds. Bakr is "part of a small group of friends around the king," and his firm is still viewed in Saudi Arabia as "the King's private contractors."[16]

The status of Bakr and his family was most recently attested to by a senior member of the royal family. "The Bin Ladens are a noble family," Prince Turki al-Faisal told the *Arab News* in November 2001. "Its members, except Osama, are an example of fine patriotism, and allegiance, brotherhood, and friendship. . . . They are true followers of Islam and have strong family attachments."[17]

Muhammed's Influence on Osama

Muhammed appears to have played an important part in Osama's youth, and, according to John F. Burns, writing in the *New York Times*, those who knew Muhammed claim that his character is replicated in Osama, as the son shares "his [Muhammed's] shrewdness and singularity of purpose, his deeply conservative religious and political views, his profound distaste for non-Islamic influences, . . . [and] even the cunning tradecraft he has used in his meticulously planned attacks."[18]

Osama was born in Riyadh in July 1957, the last-born son of Muhammed's brood. Like other aspects of his life, the status of Osama's mother in the pecking order of Muhammed bin Laden's wives is a subject of controversy. *Newsweek,* for example, has claimed she "was one of the last and least regarded of the father's many wives," and *Time* has said that Osama's mother "is universally derided as the billionaire's tenth and least favored wife." In contrast, Mary Anne Weaver reported in the *New Yorker* that Osama's mother was a "Syrian beauty" who was "considered by the conservative bin Laden family to be far ahead of her time. (For instance, she refused to wear a burka over her Chanel suits when she traveled abroad)," and it has been said Muhammed bin Laden preferred "the tiny last one" to the other wives.[19]

Until he was seventeen, Osama is reported to have spent portions of each summer with his mother, visiting her family in Syria. Bin Laden is said to hold his mother in high regard, a sentiment she returns, saying that he is "a good son who is kind to" her. After the press reported that she was angry with her son for the 11 September 2001 attacks, she took up the cudgels in defense of herself and Osama. In a press statement — rare for any member of the bin Laden family, but especially so for a woman — bin Laden's mother adamantly set the record straight.

> I do not approve of the ambitions, ideas and actions attributed to
> him [by the press]. But I deny what was attributed to me that I am

angry with him. I, like all mothers, am satisfied and pleased with my son, and pray to God to guide him to the right path and save him.[20]

During his childhood, Osama absorbed a zeal for Islam from his father, who, Cherif Ouazon has written in *Jeune Afrique,* "was very conservative [and] raised his children in the Wahabite tradition, a demanding Islamic education that advocates a return to the Prophet's austere life." Muhammed bin Laden is said to have "developed a reputation for piety as well as wealth," and Movement for Islamic Reform in Arabia (MIRA) leader Sa'd al-Faqih has said Muhammed was a "fairly devoted Muslim, very humble and generous. The father had [a] dominating personality. . . . He had a tough discipline and observed all the children with strict religious and social code. . . . He dealt with his children as big men and demanded them to show confidence at a young age. He was very keen not to show any difference in the treatment of his children." Muhammed bin Laden was intent on maintaining a pious family that was closely knit; unusual for a wealthy and multiwived Saudi businessman, Muhammed "kept all of his children in one residence" so that he could preside over "their discipline and observance of religion and morals." All of Muhammed's sons participated in the family construction business from an early age, and he arranged managerial experience for each son on individual projects.[21]

Osama has said that he received a hands-on education in construction work during his school holidays. "I started working with my father when I was a child," bin Laden told journalist Hamid Mir in March 1997. "I worked on the expansion of the Al-Aqsa Mosque [in Jerusalem]. During the early years of my life, I received training in the use of explosives for construction work and [for the] demolition of mountains."[22]

Although some writers speculate Osama "turned to God" after being ignored by his father and siblings because of his mother's low status, there is little information to support this contention.[23] To the contrary, Osama speaks proudly of his father, consistently portraying him as a pious man who worked for the glory of God. In late 1998, for example, Osama told Qatar's Al-Jazirah television that "Allah blessed him [Muhammed bin Laden] and bestowed on him an honor that no other contractor had ever known. He built the holy Mecca Mosque . . . [and] the Prophet's Mosque in Medina." Osama also claims that his father submitted a below-cost bid for the contract to refurbish the al-Aqsa Mosque in Jerusalem. Osama said that his father did this "to guarantee that Allah's mosques, and this mosque [in Jerusalem] in particular are well served." Bin Laden's company won the contract, and Osama has said that his father was later able to "sometimes pray in all three mosques in a single day."[24] Bin Laden's long-standing support for the Palestinians against Israel also appears to have been learned at his father's knee. "My father . . . once contracted to restore a mosque in an area under the control of Israel," bin Laden told

Hamid Mir in 1997. "My father thought of converting the firm's 200 bulldozers into military tanks. He wanted to use them to attack Israel. However, his technicians told him that it would be impossible and he gave up the idea. But he was disappointed."[25]

Osama told Pakistani journalist Hamid Mir that, at his death, Muhammed bin Laden had set aside $12 million to contribute when the Hazrat Mahdi — the "Rightly Guided One" — returned at the end of time to "revive the glory of Islam," and Amman's *Al-Ra'y* explains that Osama's career reflects his father's success in ensuring he "was brought up in a religious environment, which says that jihad is a duty that must be fulfilled."[26] Osama also has said that his father would surely approve of his current line of work. "My father used to say," Osama told Hamid Mir in March 1997, "that he had fathered 25 sons for the jihad." He also added that he intends to follow his father's example. "It is my desire," Osama wrote in summer 2000, "that my children grow up in the atmosphere of jihad and absorb Islam in its true spirit."[27]

Osama's Family Relations

Beyond his father, Osama always has spoken well of his mother, brothers, and sisters, notwithstanding the spring 1994 letter Bakr bin Laden published in which he — in the family's name — expressed "regret, denunciation and condemnation" of Osama's activities.[28] Osama has never publicly objected to this statement or to a similar statement issued by the family four days after the September 2001 attacks. According to the Islamabad daily *The News*, "Bin Laden doesn't believe that his wealthy clan . . . has disavowed him. 'Blood is thicker than water,' he [Osama] remarked when asked whether the bin Laden family had declared him an outcast."[29]

MIRA leader al-Faqih concurs, noting "there is a very interesting thing in the structure of [the Islamic] family. You are obligated to support your family members. . . . Well, they [the bin Ladens] have to say that [they disowned Osama]. They have to pretend to be cutting off Bin Ladin. But in all actuality they admire him, they respect him. . . . I do not claim that all . . . the [bin Laden] brothers do that. But quite a significant number of them work hard to get [rid of what they see as] sinful money — which has to reach its rightful owner."[30] *Frontline*'s unattributed biography of bin Laden amplified this point, explaining that

> Most of the [bin Laden] brothers and sisters are observing Muslims and are very keen not to "spoil" their income with money that is not theirs. They believe that it is their duty to let the owner of any riyal to have it. The only way they guarantee [this] is by letting [Osama] Bin Ladin's share reach him. Some of the brothers and

sisters also believed it was their religious duty to support this distinguished brother from their own money. While many are very careful not to irritate the royal family, many more do not care and insist on letting the money reach Usama.[31]

Rather than being alienated from his family, Osama has praised their role in his life and has strongly implied that the family has supported his commitment to jihad. "I am immensely thankful to God that He enabled my family to understand this," Osama told Karachi's *Ghazi Magazine* in August 2000. "My family members are pray[ing] for me and no doubt have gone through a lot of difficulties. But God gave them the courage to face all that."[32]

Regarding these difficulties, bin Laden resents the al-Sauds for their treatment of his own and his extended family since he left the Kingdom in 1991. In January 1999, for example, he told *Newsweek* that the Saudis had kept his eldest son and other family members from visiting him in Afghanistan, and added that at various times "four of my sons have been imprisoned in Saudi jails."[33] He also explained that his brothers had been hurt. "Obviously, the family has been harmed . . . but relatively," he told *Al-Quds Al-Arabi*. "Great pressures have been exerted on them for the sake of my return." He said the pressure was most acute in the financial area as "a lot of our money is still in the hands of the Saudi royal family [which has accrued due] to the activities of our family and company."[34]

In the context of this close-knit family, Osama was raised and educated in a more religious and insular manner than his brothers. Of Muhammed's sons, only Osama received all of his education in Saudi Arabia; according to Sa'd al-Faqih, Osama received his primary, secondary, and university education in Jeddah, although Osama himself says he also received some schooling in Mecca and Medina. Osama claims to speak only Arabic, although other reporting disputes his contention. Journalists Rahimulah Yusufzai and Peter Bergen claim Osama understands English, and Edward Giradet, the journalist who brilliantly covered the Afghan jihad for the *Christian Science Monitor,* claims that in early 1989 he encountered Osama near Jalalabad and describes him as a "young, arrogant Saudi" who spoke "fluent English."[35]

Only recently, Giradet's recollection appears to have been confirmed by a man named Brian Fyfield-Shayler, who claims to have taught English to bin Laden and thirty other wealthy Saudi youths four times a week in Jeddah around 1970. Fyfield-Shayler's words offer the fullest view yet available of bin Laden as a student and sketch some of the unpretentious characteristics he has displayed in his adult life.

> He was very courteous — more so than many of the others in his class. . . . He also stood out because he was singularly gracious and

polite, and had a great deal of inner confidence. [In his work, bin Laden was] very neat, precise, and conscientious. He wasn't pushy at all. Many students wanted to show how clever they were. But if he knew the answer to something he wouldn't parade the fact. He would only reveal it if you asked him.[36]

In addition to a Saudi-only education, there is no solid evidence that Osama traveled to Europe or North America, although there are unconfirmed reports of trips to Britain and Turkey. His overseas trips appear limited to the Gulf, Syria, Pakistan, Sudan, the Philippines, Algeria, Yemen, and Afghanistan. The data on Osama's university education is conflicting. He himself claims he graduated in 1981 from Jeddah's King Abdul Aziz University with an economics degree; other reports claim he studied engineering or public administration and that he never graduated.[37] What is most important in Osama's university education is that he began his studies with a deep religious faith that he, according to al-Faqih, strengthened by adopting "the main trend of many educated Muslims at the time, [that of] the Muslim Brotherhood." The Brotherhood's goal was and is as stated in the late 1920s by its founder Hassan al-Banna: "[The] doctrine of reclaiming Islam's manifest destiny: an empire, founded in the seventh century, that stretched from Spain to Indonesia."[38]

University Years

Osama attended King Abdul Aziz University when its atmosphere was one "of freewheeling Islamic thought." While there, his faith was made more assertive by the influence of three Islamic scholars, one who was then teaching at the institution. The first two influences came from the writings of medieval Islamic scholar Taqi al-Din Ibn-Tammiyah and those of modern Egyptian Islamic scholar Mohammed Qutb. Tammiyah belonged to the Hanbali school of Sunni Islam and polemicized against the other Sunni schools. He also attacked Christians and Jews for refusing to recognize that Islam had displaced them. Most important for Osama, Tammiyah said jihad was the responsibility of each individual when Islam was attacked by non-Muslims, when Muslim rulers were ungodly, when they ruled by man-made law rather than Sharia, and when they oppressed their subjects. In short, as Professor Iftikar H. Malik has argued, "Tammiyah established jihad as an ideology for self-defense." Tammiyah's work inspired the Arabian Peninsula's eighteenth-century Wahabi sect, whose intolerant, puritanical, and martial interpretation of Sunni Islam still dominates Saudi Arabia.[39]

Mohammed Qutb, who is revered today by many Islamists, was a member of the Muslim Brotherhood, was its leading theoretician, and argued after a three-year stay in the United States that Western civilization had led humanity "to corruption and irreligion from which only Islam can save it." Qutb was imprisoned and then executed in 1966 for his role in "an ill-defined plot against Nasser's government." While in prison, Qutb wrote a book titled *Signposts along the Road* in which he argued "that jihad — or struggle — should be waged not only defensively in the protection of Muslim Lands, but offensively against the enemies of Islam."[40]

In addition to Tammiyah and Qutb, Shaykh Abdullah Azzam, who taught at the university when Osama attended, decisively influenced Osama. Shaykh Azzam would later play a pivotal role in the Afghan jihad and in Osama's personal Afghan experiences, and, as American terrorism analyst Steven Emerson has written, the Al-Azhar-educated Azzam "is more responsible than any Arab figure in modern history for galvanizing the Muslim masses to wage an international holy war against all infidels and non-believers until the enemies of Islam were defeated." More subtly, Osama's affinity for the teachings of Ibn-Tammiyah, Qutb, and Azzam may have been sharpened by the humiliation his generation of Muslims felt as what author Kahlid Khalil Ahmed has called "the young sons of that era of severe defeats" — Israel's defeat of the Arabs in 1948, 1967, and 1973.[41]

The steeling of Osama's faith at the university complemented his upbringing and work and social experiences. Together they gave Osama an enduring foundation for the views and cause he now espouses. Faqih says Osama grew up as a "religiously committed boy." Osama's brother, Abdul Aziz, remembers his youngest brother as "tall . . . thin and very religious," and Osama says he spent much of his childhood in Mecca and Medina and so was exposed early and for long periods to the atmosphere of Islam's two most holy cities.[42] Osama is said to have been "occupied with fundamentalist groups" as a youngster and there are reports his first contact with the groups was at age seven.[43]

While a teenager, Osama "struck those around him as an ordinary man. But he was more pious than his brothers and was deeply affected by the involvement of his family's company in rebuilding the holy mosques in Medina and Mecca."[44] Indeed, some argue that the "teen-aged Bin Laden" became "fired up with religious fervor while working on restoring the Islamic sites in Mecca and Medina."[45] Osama's personal circumstances in his teenage years also kept him focused on religion. He was a young man, Cherif Ouazon wrote, whose "status as the son of a rich man allowed him to rub elbows with the princes, but, starting in his teenage years, he preferred the company of the ulemas." *Frontline*'s unattributed biography says bin Laden was "married at the age of seventeen to a Syrian girl who was a relative. . . . The early marriage was another factor in protecting him from corruption." Osama's first wife was the daughter of his mother's brother, again suggesting his father and siblings did not ostracize his mother.[46] Conjugal activities appeared to be favored by Osama for the time he spent away from prayer, mosque, and jihad; in 1998, London's *Al-Majallah* reported he was then married to three wives and had ten sons and ten daughters from a total of four wives.[47]

During his youth, Osama also regularly met well-known Islamists in social and religious settings arranged by his father and elder brothers, and these events "started forming an Islamic responsibility [in him] at an early age." His father, for example, "financed *halaqat,* nighttime meetings that brought together the kingdom's greatest preachers over a theological topic. It was in this environment that Osama grew up." In addition, Osama's family hosted "hundreds of pilgrims" — prominent Muslim scholars, jurists, and leaders — from outside the kingdom whom Muhammed bin Laden, and later his eldest sons, would entertain at the family's many residences during the annual Hajj season. "Some of those [guests]," according to *Frontline,* "were senior Islamic scholars or leaders of Muslim movements. He [Osama] used to make good contacts and relations through those gatherings."[48]

Among those Osama met at his family's pre-1979 Hajj gatherings were the future Afghan jihad leaders Burnahuddin Rabbani and Abdur Rasul Sayyaf. Both men, according to *Frontline,* "became common faces to him." In 1980 Rabbani received one of Osama's first two jihad-related monetary donations; the other went to the virulently anti-U.S. leader of the Afghan Hisbi Islami party, Gulbuddin Hekmatyar. Overall, Osama's exposure to the Hajj visitors his family hosted introduced him to the variety of the Islamic world beyond Saudi Arabia and the Arabian Peninsula, and, in essence, prepared him to work in the 1980s and after with the ethnically diverse band of Muslims he would encounter in Afghanistan, fight alongside, and eventually lead and shape into an effective international insurgent organization.[49]

Militant Sentiments

On the eve of the Afghan jihad, then, Osama was a young adult who had been "pious since he was a small child" and who had been "brought up with very good manners. He matured as an extremely humble and very generous person" and was described as "quiet and unremarkable." According to the *Frontline* biography, "there was nothing extraordinary in his personality and the trend [of Osama's personality] was very non-confrontational." Not surprisingly, an exception to Osama's well-mannered, nonconfrontational demeanor was his support for the Palestinians and negative attitude toward the United States and Israel. "Since the late 1970s," *Frontline*'s unattributed biography noted, "he [Osama] had strong anti-American feelings. He committed himself and his family and advised all friends to avoid buying American goods unless necessary."[50] According to the Associated Press, Osama described the reasons for this economic boycott on an audiocassette recorded and distributed in the 1990s. "When we buy American goods," Osama said, "we are accomplices in the murder of Palestinians. American companies make millions in the Arab world with which they pay taxes to their government. The United States uses that money to send $3 billion a year to Israel, which it uses to kill Palestinians." In a late-1998 interview, Osama acknowledged his long-held anti-American sentiment, saying, "Since I became aware of things around me, I have been in a war, enmity, and hatred for the Americans."[51] Testifying to the depth of this hatred, bin Laden has said that he stuck to this boycott even as he was procuring much-needed materiel for the mujahedin fighting for Allah's cause in Afghanistan.[52]

Ironically, during Osama's youth, it was his brother Mahrous who was the son of Muhammed bin Laden most noted for fervent devotion to Islam. When more than one thousand armed anti-al-Saud Islamic extremists—led by a Wahhabi radical named Juheiman al-Utaiba—seized the Grand Mosque in Mecca in November 1979, for example, it was afterward discovered that Mahrous had allowed the rebels to use Bin Laden Company trucks to drive into the area of the mosque. Also found in the trucks were maps of the tunnels and passages under the Grand Mosque. The Bin Laden Company was rebuilding the mosque and had been given the maps by the government, and its trucks carried permits allowing them to enter and depart the Grand Mosque and Mecca at all hours without being inspected. According to *Frontline*, Mahrous had formed a friendship with several exiled members of the Syrian Muslim Brotherhood, and these individuals had duped him into providing Bin Laden Company trucks. Mahrous was arrested by Saudi authorities but was later freed and now manages the Bin Laden Company office in Medina. Osama bin Laden, according to *Frontline*, did not support either the raid or the ideology of the Juheiman al-Utaiba. Interestingly, Osama now echoes the claims that al-Utaiba made in 1979, namely, that "the House of Saud has sunk into decadence and immorality" and that al-Sauds have involved the kingdom in un-Islamic alliances with "Western powers."[53]

The al-Sauds' gentle treatment of Mahrous bin Laden in the midst of their otherwise savage response to the mosque takeover goes a long way toward explaining the elite social status and economic power of the bin Laden family in the kingdom, as well as toward understanding why Riyadh will do everything possible to avoid having to deal decisively with the Osama bin Laden issue. While a prominent Arab social scientist has argued that despite their wealth, the bin Ladens are a "marginal" family in Saudi society because they are from Yemen, it is impossible to believe that a marginal family could have survived—let alone continued to flourish—in the wake of Mahrous's activities, charges that Osama's brother Khalid sponsors Islamist groups, the Saudis' issuance of an arrest warrant for Osama, and Riyadh's subsequent revoking of his citizenship. *Frontline*'s biography of Osama amply captures the strength and durability of the al-Saud–bin Laden tie. "Had it been some other group [than the bin Ladens]," *Frontline* concluded, "there is no doubt that Mahrous — whether accomplice or patsy — would have been thrown in prison and the group banned from further economic activity in the kingdom, the sentencing serving as a warning to others. Such was not the case."[54] In November 2001, as if to confirm *Frontline*'s judgment, one of the most senior Saudi princes told the *Arab News* that the bin Ladens "are an exemplary family and a model for patriotism, good behavior and conduct. They did not face anything [negative because of Osama's activities], either from the state or from the citizens [of Saudi Arabia]."[55]

7

BIN LADEN AND THE AFGHAN WAR, 1979–1989: FACILITATOR, ENGINEER, FIGHTER, AND VISIONARY

> These mountains are the basis of my plan. God has given the strength of the hills to freedom; they were placed here for the emancipation of the Negro race; they are full of natural forts where one man for defense will be equal to one hundred for attack; they are full also of good hiding places, where large numbers of brave men could be concealed, and baffle and elude pursuit for a long time.
>
> John Brown to Frederick Douglass, 1847

Like an Islamic Maltese Falcon, the Afghans' victorious jihad against the Soviet Union was for the Muslim world "the stuff that dreams are made of." In discussing the Afghan war, the imprisoned spiritual leader of Egypt's Gama'at, Shaykh Omar Abdul Rahman, has said his "strongest emotion [about the Afghan jihad] was pride. I felt so proud of my religion, so proud of the power that Muslims had. And I knew that Allah would aid these people and that Islam would be victorious in the end."[1] For bin Laden, the Afghan jihad was a personal turning point and a historic moment for the Muslim world. Concurring with Shaykh Rahman, bin Laden has said that, in Afghanistan, "the largest heretic power on earth was destroyed and [it was] where the superpower myth vanished in the face of the mujahedin's outcry of Allah Akbar [God is great]."[2]

In addition, bin Laden's participation in the Afghan war was the indispensable stepping-stone toward the leadership role he has risen to in the

−97

Islamic world. "It is crucial to understand," Professor Magnus Ranstorp has written in *Studies in Conflict and Terrorism*, "that Bin Laden's constituency stems primarily from his legendary role in fighting alongside the [Afghan] Mujahedin and among those 7,000 to 9,000 Arabs he came in contact with during his ten-year guerrilla experience in Afghanistan."[3] On this point, John Miller wrote in *Esquire* that bin Laden believes "the United States, which was so heavily involved in supporting the Afghan rebels, misses the profound point of the exercise: Through sheer will, even superpowers can be defeated." Miller says bin Laden told him "there is a lesson to learn from this [the Afghans' victory] for he who wishes to learn. . . . The Soviet Union entered Afghanistan in the last week of 1979, and with Allah's help their flag was folded a few years later and thrown in the trash, and there was nothing left to call the Soviet Union. . . . It cleared from Muslim minds the myth of the superpowers."[4]

Bin Laden's activities during the Afghan jihad are the subject of debate, confusion, and distortion. In 1994 he told *Al-Quds Al-Arabi* that he went to Lahore, Pakistan, soon after the Soviet invasion and began "working with the Islamic Group [Pakistan's Jamaat Islami] there to support the mujahedin against the Soviet invasion."[5] Egyptian journalist Issam Darraz, in his 1991 book *Osama Bin Laden Recounts Arab Al-Ansar Lion's Lair Battles in Afghanistan*, says that his research shows "Osama bin Laden came to Pakistan just 17 days after the Soviet invasion of Afghanistan . . . and handed him [Jamaat chief Qazi Hussein Ahmad] a sum of money for a donation for the mujahedin." Given the Jamaat's close ties to Pakistani president Zia and his military and intelligence services, it must be assumed that at this time bin Laden met and began working with Pakistani officials, signaling, as Mary Anne Weaver wrote in the *New Yorker*, the start of a relationship in which bin Laden "dined regularly with President Zia ul-Haq . . . and cultivated generals in the Pakistani intelligence service."[6]

Soon after, bin Laden is said to have become involved in combat-support activities. According to a Pakistani who fought with bin Laden in the jihad — and later worked for him in Sudan — bin Laden "was a hero to us because he was always on the front line, always moving ahead of everyone else. He not only gave of his money, but he gave of himself."[7] *Al-Quds al-Arabi* editor Abd-al-Bari Atwan has noted the romance surrounding bin Laden's career in the Afghan jihad, saying, "he is a man that seeks the afterlife and who truly feels that he has lived more than enough. You feel there is a sadness in him — which he did not express — that he was not martyred when he was fighting the Soviet Army of the communists of the heathen. You feel like he is saying: Why am I alive?"[8] Bin Laden also has described the joy he derived from fighting in Afghanistan, saying "those were the prettiest days of our lives . . . what I lived in two years there, I could not have lived in a hundred years elsewhere."[9]

At the spectrum's other end are those who take satisfaction in questioning and denigrating bin Laden's activities in the Afghan jihad. The *New Republic* has said, "Bin Laden has cultivated a reputation as a courageous warrior, although his real contribution may have been simply to bank roll Afghan rebels and their families."[10] A former senior U.S. intelligence official — who is now a media "expert" — has told *Frontline* "the Afghan people did that [defeated the Soviets]. The Arab role in the combat situation on the ground was minimal to non-existent, period." The same official claims bin Laden and the Arab Afghans were "a rag tag bunch of Muslims who were taken from one jail or another, whether it's in Cairo or Algiers or any other country in the Gulf [sic] and put on an airplane to go to the jihad" and were "by and large a disrupting factor in the jihad." Bin Laden, he adds, "was not a valiant warrior on the battlefield . . . [but] his activities have taken on mythical proportions, when, in fact, he spent more time in Pakistan with refugees, fund-raising and establishing centers for widows and orphans of martyrs in the Afghan jihad."[11]

A retired U.S. congressman, who supported the mujahedin and is a self-proclaimed Afghan expert, cast more aspersions on bin Laden, claiming, "Whenever I see that picture of bin Laden with an AK-47, I think he probably doesn't even know how to chamber a round."[12] In an even more condescending tone, another retired U.S. government counterterrorism official has said that bin Laden's hatred for the United States — especially for U.S. troops in Saudi Arabia — can be attributed "to the passion of an idealist and someone who's relatively young and when you're young and full of passion and you really believe what you say you believe, you're going to do some things which, to the rest of the world, may not appear terribly rational."[13]

The data in the public domain suggest the truth about bin Laden's activities in Afghanistan is much closer to the picture of him as "the great Freedom fighter of the Islamic world" than to the Western experts' description of him as an Islamic do-gooder or an immature, irrational youth. Indeed, British journalist Mark Huband has written that the latter description of bin Laden and the Arab Afghans borders on self-delusion. "American officials who were on the ground in Afghanistan," Huband wrote, "portray the Arabs as lacking the fighting spirit of the Afghans themselves, and as having been deemed unreliable by the Afghan commanders, though this perception has not been borne out by the vitality of the Islamist groups that subsequently have emerged in the Arab world." Regarding bin Laden and the Afghan jihad, the vital points are that he fully committed to the Afghan cause; that his role in the jihad grew, changed, and increased in importance over time; that he engaged in combat activity as a construction engineer and as a fighter; that he provided financial aid to Afghan and non-Afghan fighters; and that his career in Afghanistan gave him the unassailable credentials that today anchor the leadership role he has grown into. The credentials also allowed bin Laden to return to Afghanistan in 1996 under the willing protection of all Afghan parties.[14] British journalist Robert Fisk may be on the mark in saying that when "the history of the Afghan resistance movement is written, Mr. Bin Ladin's own contribution to the mujahedin — and the indirect result of his training and assistance — might turn out to be the turning point in the recent history of militant fundamentalism; even if today, he tries to minimize his role."[15]

Bin Laden first visited Pakistan and Afghanistan in early 1980; Pakistani journalist Ahmed Rashid has said in his excellent book, *Taliban: Militant Islam, Oil and Fundamentalism in Central Asia,* that bin Laden went with his family's blessing, all of whom "responded enthusiastically" to his decision to support the Afghans. The initial visits were information-gathering endeavors to see what the insurgents needed and how he could help meet the requirements. They also were occasions for meeting leaders of established and nascent mujahedin groups and for donating funds to them.[16] At this point, bin Laden was on good terms with the al-Saud regime. He has said he was working with Saudi authorities in the first years of the Afghan war, and *Jeune Afrique* has reported that at this time bin Laden was the point man in Pakistan for Prince Turki al-Faisal, the Saudi intelligence chief.[17] During the early visits, bin Laden also renewed contact with Rabbani and Sayyaf and arranged to meet such other Afghan leaders as Ahmad Shah Masood, Gulbuddin Hekmatyar, Yunis Khalis, and Jalaluddin Haqqani.[18] In other visits, bin Laden may have seen his first combat with Sayyaf's Islamic Union party.[19]

In addition to expanding his Pakistani and Afghan contacts, bin Laden made a point of connecting with non-Afghan Muslims who, like himself, came to Pakistan to assist the mujahedin. Some of these men belonged to existing, or would later form, Islamist groups and political parties with which bin Laden would have enduring ties. Among these organizations are the Egyptian Gama'at al-Islamiyya (IG), the Egyptian Islamic Jihad (EIJ), the Moro Islamic Liberation Front (MILF), Yemen's al-Islah party, the Islamic Union of Kurdistan, the Filipino Abu Sayyaf Group (ASG), Burma's Rohinga Solidarity Organization, the Syrian Muslim Brotherhood, the Kashmiri Harakat-ul-Ansar, and the Algerian fighters who later founded Algeria's Armed Islamic Group (GIA).[20] This list continued expanding after the Soviets' 1989 withdrawal, and by November 1998 London's *Al-Hawadith* estimated "bin Laden had reached alliances with some thirty fundamentalist organizations in the world," an estimate that must be considered conservative.[21]

Bin Laden also provided funds for some groups to transport their fighters to Afghanistan[22] and personally established underground-railroad-type safe houses to assist the travel of Muslim volunteers. These facilities were in Jeddah and at a Bin Laden-owned business in Cairo; the latter was run by bin Laden's brother Khalid and operated under the cover of hiring laborers to work in the kingdom.[23] Bin Laden also provided training for large numbers of non-Afghan Muslims in the Afghan camps he built or funded in the 1980s.[24] In 1998, for example, the U.K.-based *Al-Wasat Magazine* reported that bin Laden funded "all the needs" of Gama'at fighters traveling from Egypt to Afghanistan, while *Al-Sharq al-Awsat* has claimed five hundred Filipino Islamists were trained in bin Laden's Pakistani and Afghan camps in the early 1980s.[25] Captured EIJ operative, and former Arab Afghan fighter, Shawqi Atiyah has told an Egyptian court that the EIJ's "main source of funding during the training period in Afghanistan depended on Osama bin Laden," and, more generally, *Al-Wasat Magazine* has analyzed the trial testimony of captured EIJ fighters and concluded that "all the Egyptian organizations that operated in Afghanistan relied to a large degree for their financing on bin Laden's financial support."[26]

Osama's Circle of Friends

Early in the Afghan jihad, bin Laden also befriended a number of men who would become important operatives and/or senior lieutenants in the al Qaeda organization. Among these individuals were:

- Wali Khan Amin Shah (aka Osama Azmiry) and Wa'il Julaidan: Both Saudi nationals, Wali Khan and Julaidan accompanied bin Laden to Afghanistan in 1980 and fought with him in the 1989 battles near Jalalabad. Julaidan ended his graduate studies in the United States before joining the Afghan jihad. He was bin Laden's logistics chief, as well as his voice in the community of Islamic nongovernmental organizations (NGOs) in the Peshawar area, serving for a period as president of the Islamic Coordination Council that represented thirteen NGOs. Bin Laden has described Wali Khan as one of the "cream of the Arab brethren" and "one of the best youths," and has said Julaidan's contribution to the Afghan jihad was close to Shaykh Azzam's. In 1998 bin Laden told Al-Jarzirah that "We and the Shaykh [Azzam] were in one boat, as is known to you, together with our brother Wa'il Jalaidan." Wali Khan later was involved in plots to assassinate President Bill Clinton and Pope John Paul II in Manila. In 1994 he was captured in Malaysia and is now in a U.S. prison. Julaidan still represents Islamic NGOs, surfacing in January 2000 as executive director of the Saudis' Joint Relief Committee for Kosovo, and most recently as the chief of the Pakistan-based Islamic charity, Rabita.[27]
- Mamdouh Mahmoud Salim (aka Abu Hajir al-Iraqi): Salim was born to Iraqi parents in Sudan. He later studied electrical engineering in Baghdad and was an Iraqi army communications officer from 1981 to 1983. He fought against Iran until 1983, when he

deserted and traveled through Iran to Pakistan. Salim met bin Laden in Peshawar in 1986, was weapons-trained at a bin Laden camp, and later became al Qaeda's chief buyer of communications gear and sophisticated weapons, including chemical, biological, radio-logical, and nuclear (CBRN) materials. In late 1998 bin Laden said Abu Hajir was "one of the best men I have ever met." Abu Hajir is now in U.S. custody.[28]

- Wadih El-Hage: El-Hage was born in Lebanon to a Christian fam-ily. He converted to Islam, studied urban planning in the United States, and became a U.S. citizen through marriage. In the mid-1980s, El-Hage went to Peshawar to join the jihad, but because of a crippled arm, he was limited to working in hospitals belonging to Islamic relief agencies. He was later bin Laden's personal secre-tary in Khartoum and, in 1994, was sent to Nairobi to run bin Laden's Kenyan operations. El-Hage returned to the United States in September 1997 and was arrested by the FBI in October 1998. He was convicted on terrorism charges in May 2001.[29]

- Ali-Amin al-Rashidi (aka Abu Ubaydah al-Banshiri): An Egyp-tian, al-Rashidi was a senior member of the Egyptian Islamic Jihad and supervised bin Laden's Afghan camps. He was a renowned combat commander and fought alongside bin Laden in the 1989 Jalalabad battles. Earlier, Rashidi served as a combat commander for Afghan Tajik leader Ahmed Shah Masood's forces in their battles against the Soviet Army in the Panjshir Valley, hence Rashidi's so-briquet "al-Banshiri." He later led bin Laden's fighters against U.S. forces in Somalia. Rashidi was bin Laden's point man in trying to unite the major Egyptian Islamist groups and was working to cre-ate a worldwide Islamic army when he drowned in Lake Victoria in Uganda in May 1996.[30]

- Mohammed Atef (aka Subhi Abu Sita; Shaykh Taseer Abdallah; Abu Hafs al-Masri): Atef was an agricultural engineer who served in Egypt's air defense forces and is a senior EIJ member. He went to Peshawar in 1983 to fight in the jihad, and, like al-Rashidi, be-came an excellent combat commander. Atef also is said to have been a close associate of Shaykh Azzam. Later, Atef was given re-sponsibility for all matters pertaining to bin Laden's security. Atef accompanied bin Laden to Sudan and helped to plan al Qaeda op-erations against U.S. forces in Somalia. On al-Rashidi's death, Atef became bin Laden's top military commander and right-hand man, almost always appearing with him at public occasions. In January 2001, Atef's daughter married one of bin Laden's sons. Atef appar-ently was killed in the U.S. bombing of Kabul in November 2001.[31]

- Tariq al-Fahdli: Al-Fahdli is a senior member a powerful south

Yemen tribe. He fought with bin Laden at Jalalabad in 1989 and was wounded. He led the failed late-1992 bin Laden-sponsored attack on U.S. troops transiting Aden for Somalia. Al-Fahdli lives in Sana, receives a government stipend, and is on President Salih's presidential council.[32]

- Mustafa Hamza: Hamza is an agricultural engineer, a former Egyptian military officer, and was jailed in Egypt from 1981 to 1988 for his part in the assassination of President Anwar al-Sadat. He arrived in Afghanistan in 1989 and was Gama'at operations chief until he was removed after the failed June 1995 assassination attempt on President Mubarak in Ethiopia. Hamza has been tied to bin Laden since the Afghan jihad and publicly said he planned the attack on Mubarak while he was managing a Bin Laden Group company in Sudan. Hamza is now the IG's senior outside-Egypt leader and most lately was based in Afghanistan.[33]

Construction Programs in Pakistan and Afghanistan

Until 1982, bin Laden made regular but relatively brief trips to Pakistan and Afghanistan to assess the fighters' material needs, donate personal funds to Afghan guerrilla chiefs, and carry money to them from wealthy Saudis and Gulf Arabs. He also presumably oversaw the dozen health centers in Peshawar sponsored by his family's business. In the first of a series of shifts in the focus of his efforts in Afghanistan—really a series of expansions—bin Laden in 1982 decided to enhance the aid he was providing by bringing to bear his own and his family's engineering and construction skills. According to ABC correspondent John Miller, bin Laden brought "his own bulldozers and dump trucks" to Afghanistan "to assist the mujahedin by building shelters, roads, trenches, tunnels, and underground bunkers." In May 1997, bin Laden told CNN's Peter Arnett that "When we saw the brutality of the Russians bombing mujahedin positions . . . we transported heavy equipment from the country of the two Holy Places estimated at hundreds of tons altogether that included bulldozers, loaders, dump trucks, and equipment for digging trenches. . . . We dug a good number of huge tunnels and built in them some storage places and in some others we built a hospital."[34]

Issam Darraz reported more fully on the decision that made bin Laden "contractor to the jihad," saying that bin Laden had been thinking "of how to develop his support for the Afghan jihad. Instead of [just] paying money and aid to the jihad, he decided to carry out projects helpful to the mujahedin by building mountain roads and building immense tunnels and shelters to protect Afghan mujahedin from air raids. These projects were carried out in coordination with his brothers in the mammoth Bin Laden Establishment who helped him effectively by sending him building equipment, gigantic bulldozers and power generators to Afghanistan." Tunneling is a specialty of the Saudi Bin Laden Group, and the tunnels built by the firm's youngest partner were formidable. Robert Fisk, for example, said he waited to interview bin Laden in one such tunnel and that it was "a 20 foot high air raid shelter — cut for hundreds of meters through the rock of the mountainside."[35]

A number of accounts, some by eyewitnesses, state that bin Laden trained and led the first construction operations of what can be described as a small unit of Arab combat engineers. "We were 11 brothers," bin Laden later recalled, "and we worked to build roads, tunnels in the belly of mountains, and shelters to protect the Afghan mujahedin." The initial construction work took place near the city of Khowst, capital of Paktia Province in eastern Afghanistan. The city was then held by a garrison of Afghan government troops, surrounded by the mujahedin, and supplied by air. The area's major insurgent commander was Jalaluddin Haqqani — from Yunis Khalis's Hisbi Islami party and a close associate of Shaykh Azzam — and bin Laden cooperated with him; in the early 1980s, Haqqani had built some military infrastructure at Khowst, primarily staging areas and training camps. These sites were picked for bin Laden to fortify because in April 1986 Afghan regime forces, including an elite commando brigade, and Soviet Special Forces (Spetznaz) fought their way into Haqqani's "complex of guerrilla base camps at Zhawar Khili, [which is] wedged hard against the Pakistan border, southwest of the Afghan town of Khowst. The battle lasted for three weeks and the [mujahedin] suffered hundreds of casualties." Although the Soviet and Afghan units eventually withdrew, the air support that effectively covered their attack and withdrawal convinced Haqqani and bin Laden to strengthen the insurgents' positions.[36] Bin Laden and his assistant, an Iraqi engineer named Mohammed Sa'd, led the engineers that managed the job. The new construction included a "huge tunnel" that "contained a number of hospitals, depots, and warehouses."[37] It is interesting to note that the Bin Laden company's Web site stresses the firm's unique experience in building tunnels. Since its inception, the company claims to have built 8,000 meters of tunnels, a total that presumably does not include the many meters built by its youngest partner in Afghanistan.[38]

Over time, bin Laden's engineering activities broadened to include other areas of eastern Afghanistan, particularly in the vicinity of Jalalabad, capital of Nangarhar Province. After initial activities at Khowst, however, bin Laden began in August 1986 to train more Arabs on construction equipment so he could focus on matters elsewhere. It also is possible that non-Arab Islamists were trained in construction given the Philippine military's spring 2000 discovery of extensive tunneling in an area controlled by the Moro Islamic Liberation Front, some of whom were trained by bin Laden's cadre or al Qaeda's Kashmiri associates.[39]

Two enduring themes emerge from bin Laden's formation and leadership of the engineering effort. The first is that the projects were professionally designed and built—per *Time* magazine and other sources—and gave the mujahedin stronger, better-protected base camps, storage facilities, and fighting positions. In April 1991, for example, Haqqani's fighters captured Khowst after their construction of successive trench lines brought them close enough to the town's airfield to shut down aerial resupply, and the Afghan air force was unable to neutralize the bunkers and revetments bin Laden had built for Haqqani's artillery, rocket launchers, and heavy mortars.[40]

Some of the same positions also weathered the August 1998 U.S. missile strike without irreparable damage, although it is not known how they stood up under the U.S. Air Force's drubbing in late 2001. In August 1998, retired Pakistani lieutenant general Hamid Gul summed up the value of bin Laden's construction work. General Gul has first-hand knowledge of bin Laden's activities, because he was chief of Pakistan's Interservices Intelligence Directorate (ISID) during the late 1980s and was responsible for managing Pakistan's support for the Afghan mujahedin. "Although Bin Laden was wounded on at least two occasions," Gul told the *Guardian*, "his main contribution to the war against Soviet forces was as an engineer. Osama is a gifted engineer who is an expert in building tunnels."[41]

The second theme that emerges is a vivid picture of bin Laden as a physically brave man. Bin Laden has recalled that at Khowst "our route was exposed and visible to the enemy, and so he shelled us. We would get out of the vehicles, spread out, and [then] move anew."[42] Other reports corroborate bin Laden's matter-of-fact description of his reaction to being shelled. A former Arab Afghan told *Time* magazine that bin Laden's style was always simple and unaffected. "He [bin Laden] came down from his palace," the fighter said, "to live with the Afghan peasants and Arab fighters. He cooked with them, he ate with them, he dug trenches with them. That was bin Laden's way." *Time* also reported that bin Laden was seen "driving a bulldozer and exposing himself to strafing by Soviet helicopter gunships," and *Reader's Digest* said when "Bin Laden could not find fighters willing to face the Soviet gunships, he drove the dozers himself. One time he was attacked by Soviet helicopters and wounded."[43] Even the always-skeptical John Miller wrote that he talked to "grizzled mujahedin fighters [who] recalled the young man who rode the bulldozers himself, digging trenches on the front lines."[44]

Funding of Combat Training Camps

Around 1984, bin Laden again expanded the scope of his activities after concluding "the mujahedin position was weak in both terms of numbers and equipment, especially in combat requirements." To fix these deficiencies, bin Laden began funding training camps in Afghanistan to train Afghans and non-Afghan volunteers. The first camps were built in a mountainous area near the village of Jaji in Paktia Province; British journalist Robert Fisk has reported that bin Laden also built tunnels at these facilities. The camps provided military training and lectures in Islamic theology and history; the latter because bin Laden believed "there wasn't enough awareness [among the mujahedin] of the importance of supporting this faith and of the need to fight the infidel so all religion will belong to God." To this end, bin Laden established a "huge library in Peshawar" to help educate "the Arabs arriving in a certain [theological] direction." Later, when bin Laden created al Qaeda, he expanded this educational effort by establishing "ideological institutes" in Pakistan, staffed by Islamist scholars from the EIJ and Gama'at, and through which new recruits were cycled before military training.[45]

Abu Mahmud, the war-name of a colleague of bin Laden who served with him on the Arab Afghans' coordination council in Peshawar, has said that at this time bin Laden's main goal was for the camps to "graduate the largest possible number of mujahedin who are enthusiastic for jihad." Abu Mahmud suggests that in this phase of bin Laden's activities there was a quality-versus-quantity problem, because bin Laden tended to "help any young man, regardless of his ideological orientation" as long as he wanted to fight. Bin Laden seems to concur, telling *Al-Quds Al-Arabi* in March 1994 that initially "We cooperated with everyone to help Muslims defend themselves and their religion."[46]

Also in 1984, bin Laden began a more formal working relationship with Shaykh Azzam, who was a major conduit for money and fighters flowing to the jihad from the Muslim world, and who, as noted, had been one of bin Laden's university instructors. Together the men opened an Islamic NGO called the Services Office, or Maktab al-Khidimat (MAK). The MAK was divided into training, military, logistics, and humanitarian committees, but was created "fundamentally to receive Arab brothers arriving from abroad and to train them and send them to Afghanistan." Shaykh Azzam officially was the MAK's chief, but others managed day-to-day affairs; among the managers was one of bin Laden's future senior lieutenants, Abu Hajir al-Iraqi.[47] The MAK immediately was well funded; Azaam was a magnet for money from the Muslim Brotherhood — he was a longtime, distinguished member — and bin Laden brought in money of his own, as well as from "the funds he received from rich Arabs in the Gulf and Muslims from across the Islamic world." At the time, journalist Jamal Ismail has said, "Osama bin Laden used to finance the largest part" of the MAK's budget. According to Issam Darraz, for example, bin Laden provided $25,000 per month to the MAK for "office expenses alone."[48]

Bin Laden said he opened the MAK and its guesthouses and camps because he saw "the Afghans loved the Arabs so much, [that] they treated them as guests. They did not assign them to any military or combat tasks." Bin Laden said, "The Arab youth felt offended by this because they wanted to operate as mujahedin. This is why I thought of establishing a place to receive the Arab brothers and to train them for combat. In 1404 of the Hegira [1984], I asked the leader of the Afghan mujahedin's Ittihad-e Islami [Abdur Rasul Sayyaf] for permission to set up an office to receive Arab brothers and to utilize their capabilities and to establish a camp in an area close to the border to train the brothers there." Sayyaf agreed, reflecting ties he established to bin Laden a decade before at bin Laden family Hajj events, and bin Laden's funding of the mujahedin generally and Sayyaf's fighters in particular.[49]

It is worth examining bin Laden's view that the Afghans "loved" the would-be Arab mujahedin. In his interviews with Darraz, bin Laden said he had "noticed the interest and joy the Afghans felt in the presence of the Arabs among them. The Arabs strengthened the Afghans, made them more faithful and enhanced their morale greatly."[50] While bin Laden was with the Afghans and the author was not, the literature pertinent to Afghan history and the Afghan-Soviet war makes it clear beyond doubt that Afghans never look to others for leadership or role models. Afghans, to put it mildly, are acutely aware and tremendously proud of their history. They see themselves as the heirs of 2,000 years of "glorious history," take enormous pride in being one of the few Muslim peoples the Europeans failed to colonize, and even regard the Persians as upstart, new kids on the block. The Afghans likewise believe they have nothing to learn about Islam, and there is strong anecdotal reporting about the resentful, angry, and at times violent reactions of Afghan fighters to unsolicited, often condescending theological tutorials from their Arab brethren.[51]

Beyond what might be called the Afghans "attitude" lies another key reason why Sayyaf and other Afghan commanders were pleased to see the creation of Arab-only camps and combat units — the Arabs wanted to die. For all the stereotypes portraying Afghan fighters as bloodthirsty wild men, the truth is that most Afghan commanders rose to and retained that status because they were pious, intelligent, and cautious men who maintained the loyalty of their fighters by supplying supplies and weapons, caring for their families, and keeping casualties as low as possible. While Afghans are genuinely ready to die for Allah, almost none wanted to reach paradise in any vehicle save a deathbed in extreme old age. There were no advocates of suicide attacks among the most effective Afghan commanders. Haqqani's forces, for example, besieged the city of Khowst for nearly a decade before reducing its defensive perimeter to the point where aerial resupply was untenable and victory could be had with tolerable casualties. For Afghans — today and historically — the path to victory that follows the slow, steady, and least-costly approach is always preferred to the faster but likely fatal tack.

The Arabs were a different story. The Afghans did not doubt the Arabs' courage and truly appreciated their willingness to "help us liberate our country, and many gave their lives for the glory of Islam."[52] The issue was one of too much courage, and that of a reckless variety whose major characteristic was an un-Afghan eagerness for death. On his arrival in Afghanistan, bin Laden seemed infected with this trait. "I felt that we would be failing our Afghan brothers," he said, "if we did not perform our full duty toward them and that the best atonement was to die fighting the holy war in the cause of God."[53] Most Afghan commanders sought to distance themselves from the Arabs because the latter were "crazy brave" and "racing to die." "Commander Saznur, from the Islamic Union Party [of Sayyaf], a famous commander," relates Issam Darraz, "used to refuse to allow the participation of Arab fighters with him. He used to say that the Arabs are disorganized, they only want to die as martyrs."[54]

Arab-Only Training and Combat Units

In the 1986–1987 period — by which time he was living full-time in Pakistan — bin Laden again reevaluated his activities and decided to build several Arab-only training camps in Afghanistan, as well as to form Arab-only combat units. Actually, these camps were for non-Afghan Muslims, and beyond Arabs included Sudanese, Kurds, Kashmiris, Turks, Filipinos, and so forth. To an extent, this decision created a parting-of-the ways for bin Laden and Shaykh Azzam. Earlier, at the MAK's 1984 formation, bin Laden said the MAK was needed because "the Arab presence had to be organized and it should have specific goals so the Arabs would play an effective role in the jihad and in combat training." At that time, Azzam agreed with bin Laden because bin Laden had not yet stated an intention to form Arab-only combat units. The Khowst battles in 1986, however, appear to have prompted bin Laden's decision to field such units; these battles were the first where a primarily Arab unit fought. "We must note," said Abu Mahmud al-Suri, a Syrian associate of bin Laden, "that the first battle the Arabs waged in a single group took place in Khowst in 1986. The Arabs gathered and formed a battalion they called al-Khasa, which Abu Hajer al-Iraqi called the battalion of the graceful. The battalion waged fierce battles in Khowst in which a large number of Arabs were wounded and others were martyred."[55]

As noted, bin Laden and his engineers were on hand for the 1986 Khowst battles — *Time* magazine claims bin Laden may have fought there — and watched the Arabs in action, seeing the large number of casualties they took.[56] Another Arab mujahedin, Ali al-Qazan, has said the high number of Arab casualties stemmed from the fact that "most of the Arab brothers were not well-trained. . . . The reason for poor training was the young men themselves, who came to Afghanistan seeking only a little training so they could go [to] the battle front as quickly as possible." Bin Laden appears to have shared this assessment and decided the best approach, for the good of the Arabs and the Afghan jihad, was to concentrate Arab and other non-Afghan

Muslims in their own training camps and units. It is on this point that bin Laden and Shaykh Azzam disagreed, with the latter continuing to favor the standard practice of dispersing Arab volunteers to Afghan mujahedin units and to Islamic NGOs.[57] There is little to show this was an acrimonious disagreement, aside from *Al-Hawadith*'s claim that bin Laden's initiative produced a divergence of approach with Azzam, and a report that Azzam was worried that the Egyptian Islamists might gain too much influence with bin Laden. To the contrary, *al-Hayat* has said, "Shaykh Azzam did not conceal his admiration for the young bin Laden," and Azzam was quoted just before his murder as saying "there is one person who has always stood by us—Osama bin Laden."[58] Later, Shaykh Azzam and Sayyaf were present as observers with bin Laden when the first Arab-only unit, formed and trained as a result of bin Laden's initiative, saw its initial combat near Jalalabad in April 1987.[59] In turn, bin Laden, who singles out few for praise or admiration, is always outspoken in regard to Shaykh Azzam. "Shaykh Abdallah Azzam, may God have mercy on his soul, is a man worth a nation," bin Laden told *Al-Jazirah* in June 1999.[60] "After his assassination, Muslim women proved unable to give birth to a man like him. The people of jihad who lived the epoch know the Islamic Jihad in Afghanistan had not benefitted from anyone as it has from Shaykh Abdullah Azzam."[61]

In October 1986, bin Laden established a base camp for non-Afghan Muslim fighters in the mountains southeast of Jalalabad; he and his colleagues called the site "Masadah," or the "Lions Lair." Even before the creation of the camp, bin Laden had attracted experienced "Arab ex-military men" to his organization. In particular, two former Egyptian servicemen and senior EIJ members, Abu Ubaydah al-Banshiri and Abu Hafs al-Masri, became training instructors at Masadah and led combat operations launched from the base. At Masadah in 1986–1987, bin Laden and his lieutenants had their hands full trying to control the ardor of the "brother young men." Abu Mahmud al-Suri has said the would-be mujahedin "persisted in their request to stage military operations. Osama bin Laden tried to pacify and persuade them of the need to construct the site and complete the fortifications first." Bin Laden, Ali-al Qazlan recalls, "preached patience to the brothers . . . [but it] was extremely difficult for the young men to keep on working and building shelters and fortifications for seven months without any operations. Therefore the brothers beseeched Osama to carry out operations even if only small ones." Bin Laden successfully "trained them [the brothers] to be patient," but his own words wearily testify to the energy spent in the effort. "Here [at Masadah]," bin Laden said, "many things collaborate against them [the Arab volunteers], including distaste for [the physical privations of] jihad, a foreign language, strange weather, and strange terrain. When one is with his brothers, one becomes patient." The real problem, according to bin Laden, was that "Arab youth have been raised in their countries in a life that is far from the true glory of jihad and of defending the faith."[62]

In mid-April 1987, a Soviet-Afghan force that included two hundred Soviet Special Forces soldiers attacked an Arab unit trained by bin Laden and his lieutenants at Masadah. Bin Laden told Darraz that he and Abu Ubaydah set a trap for the Soviets in which bin Laden led a group of fighters that engaged the Soviet troopers while Abu Ubaydah led a second group to "outflank the Russian force and attack it from the rear." Darraz reports the trap worked and the Soviets fell back. Bin Laden later recalled that "We were not military persons, we were civilians. No one hesitated, they all moved forward, God honor them. Each one of us ordered the brethren to carry their weapons and move forward. There were nine of them and myself. No one hesitated. . . . Each of us carried his weapon and moved forward. . . . While moving, I made sure there was a high hill separating us from the atheists."[63]

Formation of Al Qaeda

There is little information on whether the fighters of the Lions' Lair were active in combat between April 1987 and the April 1989 Jalalabad battles in which they played a prominent part. Given the penchant of the "young brothers" to push bin Laden to attack, it can be assumed that additional combat ensued. Whatever the fighting tempo, however, it was in 1988 that bin Laden, probably in cooperation with Abu Ubaydah al-Banshiri, began plans for a multinational insurgent organization that would survive the Afghan jihad and would come to be known as al Qaeda.[64] From the sparse data pertaining to al Qaeda, *al-Hayat* offers, courtesy of the memory of bin Laden associate Abu Mahmud, a concise, coherent picture of what that paper calls "the romantic idea" bin Laden presented in a speech to the "Arab Mujahedin's Shura Council in Peshawar." According to Abu Mahmud,

> The al Qaeda idea ran through Osama's mind for the first time in 1988, namely after the establishment of al-Masadah and after young Arabs began to join the jihad in large numbers with the emergence of the signs of victory in Afghanistan. Osama believed that he could set up an army of young men responding to the jihad call. When he presented the idea to us he did not speak of jihad against Arab regimes, but of helping Muslims against the infidel government oppressing them, as was the case in Palestine, the Philippines, and Kashmir, especially Central Asia, which was under Soviet rule then and no one dreamed that two years later it would be independent.[65]

As the insurgents' victory dawned, few thought about what that meant for the future. Amid the fawning kudos given Gorbachev for withdrawing from Afghanistan—something akin to presenting a medal, flowers, and a Mercedes to a raper when he concedes he is finished with his victim—three central facts were lost. First, in the words of a senior U.S. intelligence official, "[the] Afghans forced the Red Army to withdraw. And that's a great victory . . . they knocked off a superpower."[66] Second, in the words of Shaykh Rahman's adviser, Abdul Sattar, Muslims for the first time thought, "Yes, if I can defeat the evil empire, I can defeat anyone else."[67] Finally, RAND analyst Graham Fuller argued that Sattar's point was vital for bin Laden and the Saudis who fought in Afghanistan. "What was really important," he told CNN in April 1977, "was that the Saudis who went and fought became convinced that you simply don't have to accept regimes as they were, that as a Muslim you could take action against a ruling government."[68]

By 1988 Moscow had more or less accepted its defeat by Afghan "bandit gangs"—the term Moscow derisively used for the Afghan mujahedin and that it now uses for Chechen insurgents—and on 1 February 1989 the last commander of the "Limited Contingent of Soviet Forces in Afghanistan" theatrically walked solo across the Oxus River Bridge to Soviet territory. The world, then infatuated with new-look Bolshevik Mikhail Gorbachev, reacted by praising the Soviet leader for his altruistic and humanitarian efforts to end the Afghan war. Most were courteous and did not mention the Soviet military's abject but barbarous failure in the ten-year struggle; almost none were prescient enough to realize the Soviets were beaten by the Afghans' character, martial skills and aptitude, patience, valor, and religious faith, all of which inextricably intertwined. While external aid to the Afghan fighters was useful, it was not determinative. External aid simply helped the Afghans to kill Soviets and Afghan Communists more efficiently, using 1980s-vintage AK-47s instead of ancient British rifles left from Anglo-Afghan fracases a century and more ago.

With the Soviets gone, the Afghan Communist regime defended itself as best it could with a huge and steady supply of arms from its now fair-weather Soviet friends. In his well-informed book, *Bear Trap,* retired Pakistani brigadier Muhammed Yousef—who managed the nuts and bolts of the Pakistani intelligence service's support for the Afghans for much of the jihad—wrote that the Soviets gave the Afghan regime about $1.5 billion of military aid between January and June 1989, ensuring Kabul had a "tremendous superiority in the three A's—artillery, and aircraft, and armor."[69]

The regime did not do too badly. By concentrating forces in major cities—Kabul, Mazar-e Sharif, Jalalabad, and a few others—the regime held off the increasingly factionalized insurgents until spring 1992. For purposes of examining bin Laden's career, we need only look at the March–July 1989 battles near Jalalabad. These Pakistani-urged and Afghan-fought battles—which failed to capture the city—marked the high point of Arab participation in the jihad, and the actions are viewed by many Arabs, including bin Laden, as the point when Arab fighters began coming of age militarily. "The Arab brethren contributed greatly in these battles," Arab Afghan Abu Salman told Issam Darraz. "The Afghani commanders became dependent on them . . . [and the] Jalalabad battles proved the capability of Arab fighters, they participated in numerous liberation operations." Bin Laden has said that Jalalabad "was a long battle that continued forcefully for several months. During this battle the [Arab] brethren gained a lot of experience that was not possible in other previous battles." Bin Laden also said that at Jalalabad "more Arab fighters died than the number of [Arab] deaths during the [rest of the] war in Afghanistan."[70] *Al-Wasat* has said 187 Arabs were killed from bin Laden's unit alone.[71] Bin Laden's participation in the Jalalabad battles also strengthened his reputation for courage. During the fighting, Ali al-Jazlan has said, "Osama bin Laden was in continuous and direct contact with us. This has boosted our morale."[72]

In early July 1989 the insurgents almost took Jalalabad. Bin Laden and the Arab fighters reached the city airport's runway, where bin Laden was wounded, but were then soundly beaten by an unexpected counterattack.[73] Part of the regime's forces focused on bin Laden's Masadah stronghold, bombarding it before sending in mechanized infantry. During the artillery attack, according to Issam Darraz, bin Laden moved his fighters out of Masadah "in order to minimize losses." When the Afghan force failed to move into Masadah after the bombardment because night had fallen, "Osama bin Laden returned [to Masadah] with a group of youth after the morning prayer. He returned to the heart of the al-Masadah post, and decided to confront the commando force." Darraz says bin Laden ordered an ambush against the regime forces that was executed "in a perfect fashion under the command of Abu Ubaydah and Abu Hafas [Mohammed Atef]," thereby preventing the capture of the main Arab base.[74] Jalalabad also reinforced in bin Laden's mind the necessity of thorough training, strong organization, and combat experience for his fighters.

> Managing a long battle for several months was a difficult task. The forces will be in a state of continuous pressure. You are in need of continuous logistical support, you also need facilities to evacuate the injured and to carry the dead persons, we pray to God to accept them as martyrs. Also there is a need for someone to stay in the observatories [observation posts] to monitor enemy movements and to properly direct fire at them. The brethren's experience in using rockets, mortars and artillery has been broadened. Moreover, they used maps in order to determine the distance and direction of the target, so that it is fired on the basis of the [co]ordinates according to military terminology.[75]

Despite keeping Masadah, bin Laden recognized the mujahedin had let victory at Jalalabad slip away. He also had learned that his Arab fighters still needed to improve many aspects of their combat performance. After the Jalalabad battles, Abu Salman recalls that in the Afghan border town of Towr Kham, bin Laden "stood between the youth and lectured them, saying: 'It is possible that the enemy's success in attacking the Mujahedin is due to our mistakes, we must learn from these mistakes.'" Abu Salman says the fighters took bin Laden's words to heart and "started paying attention to matters they never paid attention to in the past, matters such as good hiding and camouflaging, and weapons and equipment hiding." Bin Laden also says that after the battles, he and other Arab leaders used the captured "heavy long-range field guns . . . tanks and armored vehicles" to train their fighters. Issam Darrraz makes the point that Jalalabad served as an "independent school" for the Arab Afghans and that they emerged from it better able to fight as, and against, conventional forces. The current strength and vitality of the Islamist insurgencies battling conventional forces in Kashmir, Central Asia, the Caucasus, the Balkans, and the Philippines — each of which is leavened with veteran Arab Afghans — seems to validate Darraz's judgment.[76]

"Lessons" Learned for bin Laden and Islamists

The last of the 1989 Jalalabad battles marked the end of bin Laden's first tour in Afghanistan. When it became clear that the city would not fall, bin Laden went to Saudi Arabia for what he intended to be a short visit. In his absence, the Afghan jihad continued, because the Afghan Communist regime proved much more durable than most in the West, including, alas, me, had anticipated. While for the rest of the world the nature of the Afghan conflict changed into a civil war after the Soviet withdrawal — with the West's new goal being not a mujahedin victory, but a UN-brokered "broad-based government" installed by elections — the Afghan Islamist guerrilla leaders simply shrugged and continued the war. They had started the jihad against the Afghan Communists before the Soviets invaded, and they intended to fight until the Afghan Communists were eliminated.

The Afghans' faith in this clear path to victory is plain in an anecdote related by a then-junior foreign service officer. In 1988 this officer sat in on a meeting in Pakistan between a senior pro-mujahedin Western ambassador and the Afghan resistance chief Yunis Khalis. The diplomat opened by telling Khalis that because Gorbachev was showing a willingness to withdrawal, the mujahedin should reduce combat operations to ease the Soviet exit. Khalis quietly responded, "No, we will kill them until they go." The diplomat then rephrased his argument, stressing that Moscow's withdrawal was produced by pressure from the West and that this pressure would be stronger if the Afghans slowed attacks on the Red Army. Khalis, as he walked away, simply repeated, "No, they will leave because we are killing them, and we will kill them until they leave. If we keep killing them, they will go." Bin Laden, it appears, took Khalis's lesson to heart. Asked by journalist John Miller how U.S. troops would be removed from Saudi Arabia and the Islamic world, bin Laden simply said, "You will leave when the [Islamic] youth send you in wooden boxes and coffins. And you will carry in them the bodies of American troops and children. This is when you will leave."[77]

The war-must-go-on mind-set was starkly apparent to the relatively few Westerners who followed the thought processes of the only Afghans who genuinely counted between 1979 and 1989 — those Islamist lads with the guns, the field commanders. To the rest of the West's "Afghan watchers," the idea that the jihad would be finished on the battlefield was anachronistic, unthinkable, and unfashionably barbaric. For these folks, the only solution was for the diplomats to take over and construct a popularly elected, all-party government — not unlike the attitude that prevails in 2005 among Western political leaders and diplomats. But the Afghan jihadists meant to finish with guns what they started with guns: establish God's rule in Afghanistan and then sort things out. In fact, it is vital to recall that, next to the Soviets, the biggest losers in Afghanistan were the Muslim world's Western-minded scholars, politicians, and intellectuals who had worked to build democracy and political pluralism in the Muslim world. These people had long ignored what Tarik Masoud has said is the basic political fact, that "there is no grassroots movement for democracy in the Arab world, largely because democracy does not resonate with the average Arab. It has no basis in the Arab past and is tainted by its association with the West." Concurring, bin Laden has argued — like his mentor Sayyid Qutb — that popular participation is incompatible with Islam. "Consultation is very important in Islam," bin Laden told the media in 1997, "but the consultation can be held only to appoint a pious and wise person as ruler." The Afghan jihad confronted the theoreticians of democratic Islam with a hard reality. The Red Army was not defeated by a democratic revolution, but by an Islamist revolution grounded, guided, and steeled by God's words as found in the Koran and explained by the Prophet. Driven by their faith, the mujahedin used bullets, not votes, to win one for Allah, and by so doing revalidated jihad as Islam's normative response to attack.[78] The experience and outcome of the Afghan jihad was of immense consequence to the future of Osama bin Laden and other Islamists. Bin Laden and many other non-Afghan mujahedin emerged from the jihad with some characteristics of the Afghan commanders — patience, stoicism, sound judgment, and unquestioning faith in Allah's ultimate victory — and having lost traits typical of non-Afghan Muslims who had joined the jihad and haphazardly raced for martyrdom. The major non-Afghan Islamist leaders of the jihad, moreover, recognized the unprecedented opportunity for the rejuvenation of armed jihad across the Islamic world. "The [Islamic] nation is asleep and Afghanistan is the route," Shaykh Azzam wrote. "It is the route of training and preparations and to build fighting cadres for this nation."

For Osama bin Laden and many Afghan and non-Afghan mujahedin, the jihad's success against the Soviets and Afghan Communists was first and most important a victory for Islam — for Allah, for his Prophet, and for all Muslims — that would, as journalist Eric Margolis has written, illuminate "a path that would lead the downtrodden Islamic world to renewal and dignity."[79] Religion and the desire to serve and sacrifice in God's name had been what motivated bin Laden and thousands of other Arabs and non-Afghan Muslims to come to Afghanistan.

While the Afghan fighters and the Arab Afghans were equally ready to give their lives in God's cause, the latter were much less confident that the jihad would end victoriously. There is a sense that the Afghan mujahedin always were completely confident that they would see the humiliating ouster of the Soviets, not only because Allah protects and ensures success for those battling infidels in his name but also simply because they were Afghans and therefore had long experience in defeating great powers, including a Macedonian named Alexander and the queen empress of the British Empire. The Arabs and non-Afghan Muslim fighters, in contrast, while confident in Allah's promise of paradise for martyred holy warriors, had not beaten anyone militarily for centuries. They learned in school about the glories won by Saladin's sword, but their most recent martial memories were of having seen Arabs whipped by Israelis on three occasions, and of likewise seeing Muslim Pakistan thrice whacked by infidel India. Like the young boy whose parents really do give him a BB gun for Christmas, the Afghan Arabs were surely delighted with the jihad's outcome, but also must have been slightly disoriented by the reality of victory.

Now, many Americans might find it counterintuitive for bin Laden and the Afghan Arabs to hate the United States after U.S. taxpayers provided several billion dollars to support the mujahedin — and they would be right. One senses bin Laden and his colleagues are troubled by the fact that America was on Allah's side from 1979 to 1992, and that bin Laden himself once said, "We are in alliance with them [the Americans] now because we have common interests, but they are the enemies of Islam." Since the mid-1990s, bin Laden has tried to make clear that the United States helped the mujahedin only to hurt the Soviets, and that Islamic history justified an "alliance" with Americans on the basis of cooperating with a lesser evil to defeat the greater threat to Islam.

> The Americans were not interested in our jihad. They were only concerned that the Soviets might gain access to warm water ports. . . .[80] I did not fight against the communist threat [in Afghanistan] while forgetting the peril from the West. For us, the idea was not to get involved more than necessary in the fight against the Russians, which was the business of the Americans, but rather to show our

solidarity with our Islamist brothers. I discovered that it was not enough to fight in Afghanistan, but that we had to fight on all fronts against communist or Western oppression. The urgent thing was communism, but the next target was America.[81]

We were doing our duty in support of Islam in Afghanistan, although this duty used to serve, against our desire, the U.S. interests. The situation was similar to the Muslims' fight against the Romans [in early Islamic history]. We know that fighting between the Romans and the Persians has always been strong. So, no wise man can say that when the Muslims fought the Romans first at Mu'tah battle they were agents to the Persians, but interests met at this point. In other words, your killing of the Romans, which is a duty for you, used to please the Persians. However, after they [the Muslims] finished with the Romans, they began to fight the Persians. So, conversion [*sic* – convergence?] of interests without agreement does not necessarily mean relations or agentry.[82]

In his 1994 article in the *Beirut Review,* Professor Anthony Hyman quotes an Arab Afghan fighter as saying that "the Afghan jihad does not need us [the Arabs]. We need the Afghan jihad." Hyman goes on to note "to many Arabs the Afghan cause appeared to be the only successful example of an Islamic struggle against communism and atheism in a world where failure and disappointment was, to the Arabs, all too common."[83] Bin Laden, moreover, always has gone another step by declaring the demise of the USSR was the result of Islam defeating the Red Army in Afghanistan. Bin Laden and his colleagues hold as an article of faith the belief that the Soviet Union died, like Kipling's Tommy Atkins, on "Afghanistan's plains" and that belief makes many of them eager to take on the remaining superpower, Islam's top enemy, the United States. "Having borne arms against the Russians in Afghanistan, we think our battle with America will be easy by comparison," *Readers' Digest* quotes bin Laden as saying. "We are now more determined to carry on until we see the face of God."[84] And the vivid prose of Issam Darraz again provides a good description of the importance of the Afghan experience to Sunni militancy worldwide.

The Afghan model was a great lesson. . . . When I talk about Masadah [bin Laden's activities in the Afghan jihad], I don't talk about the past, I don't talk about the place Afghanistan, [instead] I uncover the thread of hope in our lives. . . . I felt that I was in the cradle of a new historic movement and that those ardent young men were beginning to write a truly new page of Islamic history — a new and pure page written with the blood and lighted with the souls of the martyrs. . . . The youth [in Afghanistan] and similar Muslim youth will be this nation's [the ummah's] fortress and its defensive line against internal and external forces of destruction and devastation.[85]

Combat experience, self-confidence, increased religious faith, ambitions for a borderless Islamic world, leadership skills, hatred for the United States—bin Laden and the Afghan Arabs emerged from the Afghan war with all these attributes. There is, however, another element gained in the jihad that made this mix a lethal threat to America, the West, Israel, and pro-U.S. Arab states. This factor is the international ties and friendships—a "militant brotherhood without borders"—forged by bin Laden and his colleagues in the years 1979 to 1992. "The leading figures in the [Egyptian] Islamic movement," *Al-Watan Al-Arabi* said in 1998, "benefited enormously from the war in Afghanistan, because they were thus able to forge a wide network with Islamic movements throughout the world. A measure of the diversity of these contacts is that Palestinians and Syrians oversaw the training of the Egyptian Islamic groups." For bin Laden, the French weekly *VSD* captured the importance of this aspect of the Afghan war when it reported bin Laden returned home "with an address book containing the names of everybody who was anybody in Islamic activism and guerrilla warfare in his pocket."[86]

8

BIN LADEN AND THE SAUDIS, 1989-1991: FROM FAVORITE SON TO BLACK SHEEP

Let them call me rebel, and welcome, I feel no concern from it;
but I should suffer the misery of devils, were I to make a whore of
my soul by swearing allegiance to one whose character is that of a
sottish, stupid, stubborn, worthless, brutish man.

Thomas Paine, *The American Crisis*, 19 December 1776

Bin Laden left Afghanistan for home at the close of the spring 1989 Jalalabad battles. He meant his trip to the kingdom to be short, and it appears he fully intended to remain engaged in the Afghan jihad. Such was not to be the case—at least immediately—because on his return the Saudis marked his passport so that he could not reenter the kingdom if he departed. And therein lies a story.

Saudi Arabia led the Islamic world's hostile reaction to the 1979 Soviet invasion of Afghanistan and was the symbol of its determination to assist the Afghans as much as possible. "In a remarkable departure from their usual parochial self-absorption," Eric Margolis has written in *War at the Top of the World*, "Muslims in various parts of the world became inspired and gripped by the remote struggle in Afghanistan."[1] This response was prompted by several factors. The perception that the invasion was an infidel attack on Islam was widely held. In such a case, the Koran sanctions a defensive jihad, calling on each Muslim to defend the attacked and making this aid a religious duty and an individual responsibility. There also was anger over a superpower seeking to brutally impose its will on one of the poorest countries on the planet. Finally, leading Islamic governments—Egypt, Saudi Arabia, Pakistan, the Emirates, and so forth—could make political points by sending material aid and dispensing rhetorical support for the Afghan mujahedin. From the war's start, the mujahedin's cause was universally popular on the "Arab street"; the rulers of the Arab world quickly took note and saw it was in their domestic political interest, as well as in the interest of ensuring their admission to paradise, to support the Afghans. Stories abound about the popular, grassroots support for the Afghan mujahedin. A senior Saudi prince, for example, estimated in the late 1980s that donations for the mujahedin on Fridays from the kingdom's mosques amounted to nearly $80 million a year. For Muslims, the Afghan jihad was very much a people's war.

Another benefit accruing to these regimes was geopolitical in nature. The reaction of both the United States and the United Kingdom to the Soviet invasion was intensely negative. The usually dovish President Jimmy Carter demanded the Red Army's immediate withdrawal, canceled U.S. participation in the Moscow Olympics, and began the decade-long U.S. policy of arming the Afghan resistance. British prime minister Margaret Thatcher regarded the Soviet invasion as the return of Stalinist barbarism, and when Carter lost the 1980 election, she and newly elected U.S. president Ronald Reagan became an Anglo-American team that defied their own senior diplomats and brooked no thought of a negotiated settlement in Afghanistan that permitted a continued Soviet military presence. The rulers of the Arab and Muslim worlds therefore saw that the two preeminent Western powers were quite literally on "the side of the angels" and so found their own support for the resistance—which would have been forthcoming in any event—would win them big points in Washington. Western support for the mujahedin, in some ways, also probably caused the Arabs to ratchet up official and unofficial support for the resistance. The Muslim world's leaders, after all, could not be seen doing less to help Afghan Muslims than the "infidel" West.

In addition to reasons of religion and state, some Arab rulers cynically welcomed the Afghan jihad for the opportunity it afforded to buttress their internal stability by refocusing the discontent of domestic Islamists. These rulers found the Afghan battlefield an excellent venue to which to export a slowly festering element of the population, youthful Islamists, that seemed destined to cause domestic instability. The regimes wrapped themselves and their young would-be mujahedin in the Prophet's battle flag and sent them to war, while at home they taught the next generation, as Tariq Masud has written about Saudi Arabia, "that to take part in the just Afghan war—and to die in it—was a fate to which all Muslims should aspire." In the starkest terms, these "Islamicly committed youth were allowed, and sometimes helped, to go to Afghanistan in the hope that they would be killed there."[2] The Saudi government even threw in a "jihad ticket," its price reduced by 75 percent for Saudia Air flights from the kingdom to Pakistan, again validating the hoary truism that the al-Sauds are "always ready to fund Islamic militancy, provided it was as far away from the kingdom as possible." In their wildest dreams, Arab rulers had not imagined the Russians would be beaten or that "any of the Arab youth would come out alive."[3] Beyond sending young men to help the Afghans, then, there "was another, officially undeclared interest also. Saudi Arabia was attempting to remove from the Near East radical anti-Western groups that had become increasingly active there. The idea of sending them to the 'holy war' against the Soviet contingent in Afghanistan proved a success. For a whole decade . . . the Soviet Union became the main enemy of the radicals."[4]

As in most of life's actions, the decision of the rulers of Saudi Arabia, Egypt, Kuwait, and other Muslim states to encourage and help transport their young Islamists to fight in Afghanistan has encountered the iron and excruciatingly painful law of unintended consequences. Although Arabs and non-Afghan Muslims fought and died in the Afghan jihad, the Arab rulers, who, according to a retired U.S. intelligence official, had sent their young Islamists to Afghanistan "with the fondest hope that they would not come back . . . [found] that they didn't die in great numbers. They died in tiny numbers, and they did come back."[5] Moreover, bin Laden's formidable figure emerged as a leader of the non-Afghan Muslim fighters who did their Islamic duty by fighting the atheists but had failed to do their political duty by dying in the process.

Bin Laden returned to Saudi Arabia as a well-known and admired guerrilla commander, construction engineer, and logistician in the narrow milieu of Arab Afghans; he was neither the Arab Afghans' only leader nor an international figure. Bin Laden's first Western press interview, in fact, did not occur until December 1993, when Robert Fisk met him for the *Independent*.[6] So little did bin Laden regard himself as the Arab Afghans' chief that he was surprised by two realities he encountered when he arrived in Saudi Arabia—sometime in July or August 1989—both of which flowed from his war record. The first reality was that he could not leave again because the Saudis had restricted his passport. Apparently, however, bin Laden took this in stride and "was not hostile to the regime at this stage," and it seems that the government did not limit his activities or domestic travel. Bin Laden did not even mention the Saudis' action when he told Fisk that in 1989 he had simply "returned to road construction in Taif and Abha [in Saudi Arabia]. I brought back the equipment I used to build roads and tunnels for the mujahedin in Afghanistan."[7]

It appears that senior Saudi officials first began to worry about bin Laden's religious ardor, potential post-Afghan-jihad stature, and domestic popularity in the mid-1980s and tried at the time to deflect his focus from the Afghan war. Toward this end, King Fahd, according to an article posted on the *Abdullah Azzam* Internet site, offered bin Laden "the contract of expanding the Prophet's mosque in Medina. This deal would be worth a net profit of $90m[illion] to Bin Laden."[8] Bin Laden is reported to have refused the offer because of his commitment to Afghan jihad and because he suspected that the offer was made not to acquire his construction acumen but "to distract him from the Jihad in Afghanistan and content him with the building of a mosque."[9] In 1989 the trigger for the Saudis' decision to mark his passport was their fear that bin Laden wanted "to start a new front of 'jihad' in [Communist-ruled] South Yemen." The Saudis' suspicions were well founded, given that bin Laden is considered one of the founders of Yemeni Shaykh Abdel al-Zindani's powerful al-Islah party, had worked with Zindani to move thousands of Yemenis to Afghanistan to fight the Soviets, had been active "with the [Yemeni] mujahedin against the Communist party in South Yemen in the early 1980s,"[10] and had built strong ties to many of Yemen's senior Islamists during the Afghan jihad.[11]

Indeed, the Yemeni government later claimed that "Yemeni Afghan groups executed several socialist figures and mounted 158 operations . . . between 1990 and 1994 on the strength of fatwas issued by Osama bin Laden, who gave Friday sermons in Mosques in Sana, Abyan, and Shabwah [in] which he engaged in incitement against 'infidel communists.'" The Yemenis also claimed that bin Laden sponsored attacks on the country's "petroleum installations." Based on the Yemenis' claims and bin Laden's own words, the "eye" the Saudis kept on bin Laden after they banned his travel was far less than twenty-twenty, perhaps adding credence to Robert Fisk's estimate that the Saudi "intelligence service is one of the most unintelligent in the Arab world."[12] Bin Laden himself told *Al-Quds Al-Arabi* in 1996 that in Yemen after the Afghan jihad,

> we fought the communist socialist party before the union and the union plan because they are atheist, communist, and oppressive socialists. They oppressed the people, destroyed everything, destroyed God's religion and sanctified their party, saying nothing is louder than the party's voice. I delivered a number of lectures in mosques inciting Muslims to fight them, which prompted the Saudi government to prevent me from making any speeches. But with God's grace, the youths continued the jihad, and we continued to cooperate with them against the heads of atheism in the socialist party.[13]

The second surprise bin Laden faced in the kingdom was that he "had become a celebrity." French journalist Xavier Raufer, for example, has said bin Laden came home "trailing clouds of glory" from Afghanistan; the *Village Voice* has claimed "Bin Laden returned home as a celebrated hero and leader of the opposition movement to the House of Saud, claiming moral turpitude."[14] When he returned home, the Associated Press reported, bin

Laden "was showered with praise and donations, and was in demand as a speaker in mosques and homes. Over 250,000 cassettes of his fiery speeches were distributed, selling out as soon as they appeared." In the now-banned tapes, bin Laden flayed U.S. foreign policy and again called for a "boycott of American goods" to assist the Palestinians.[15] An unnamed "Saudi analyst" has told Reuters — with a bit of tongue in his cheek — "in the old days before he was an outlaw Osama was popular with all sorts of people here [in Saudi Arabia]. He was from a rich family and this [also] opened many doors."[16]

Bin Laden's popularity, his eloquent anti-American tongue, and the fact that the Saudis really did not know how many domestic followers he had — journalist Ahmed Rashid claims bin Laden resettled four thousand Arab Afghans in Mecca and Medina alone — also contributed to the authorities' desire to keep bin Laden under watch. Palestinian journalist Sa'id Aburish has said that bin Laden was a special problem for the Saudi regime. "Osama bin Laden," Aburish stresses, "is the prophet of these [fundamentalist] movements in Saudi Arabia. And Osama bin Laden is much more interesting than most of them because Osama bin Laden belongs to a family that is part of the ruling establishment and therefore it [bin Laden's popularity] is an indication of how bad things have got [in Saudi Arabia]."[17] The above-mentioned "Saudi analyst" concluded that "the Saudi government wants him to go away and be quiet,"[18] but, as shall be seen, even the al-Sauds do not always get what they want.

The uneasy modus vivendi between bin Laden and the al-Sauds grew tenuous in 1990 in the run-up to Iraq's invasion of Kuwait. Before the attack, bin Laden angered Saudi authorities by making a public "prophecy . . . [that] Saddam was going to invade Saudi Arabia." Sa'd al-Faqih claims bin Laden also sent "secret confidential letters to the King" about the Iraqi threat; according to al-Faqih, "he [bin Laden] was giving talks about it in the mosques. He was giving speeches in the mosques and talking about the dangers of the Ba'ath — which is a party of Saddam — having ambitions to invade Kuwait and Saudi Arabia. . . . And then his prophecy was correct. And he was never respected or rewarded for that. Instead he was advised to stay in Jeddah; he was put in sort of house arrest." Bin Laden's relations with the al-Sauds were ruptured beyond repair when King Fahd allowed U.S. and other Western troops into Saudi Arabia after convincing senior Saudi ulema that "Islam is in danger," infidel forces were needed to defend the kingdom, and, most important, "non-Muslim troops would respect the kingdom's Islamic traditions and leave as soon as they were not needed."[19]

While the world waited to see if Iraq would invade Kuwait, bin Laden tried to work with Saudi authorities. Before the invasion, bin Laden "presented a written advice in the form of a detailed, personal, private and confidential letter to the King." Sa'd al-Faqih has said even though at this point bin Laden was increasingly worried by what he saw as "America in alliance with the [al-Saud] family to loot the country's resources and suppress Islam in that part of the world . . . he [bin Laden] was still controlling his thoughts and words at this stage."[20] Before Iraq attacked Kuwait in August 1990, bin Laden, according to *Reader's Digest*, had met with Saudi defense minister Prince Sultan and offered to help protect the kingdom, "but only if the United States were not involved" in Saudi military operations.[21]

Bin Laden "presented a ten-page paper to Prince Sultan," the Associated Press reported "describing how he and his colleagues could train Saudis to defend themselves and how equipment from his family's large construction firm could be used to dig trenches on the border with Iraq and lay sand traps against potential invaders." Bin Laden told Prince Sultan he could "bring all his supporters and defend the country under his command. And he made all the [guarantees] that his supporters would not give you [the Saudi authorities] a hard time. They would defend the country against the invading Iraqi army. And he said 'You don't need Americans. You don't need any other non-Muslim troops. We will be enough. And I will even convince the Afghanis to come and join us instead of the Americans.'"[22]

For reasons unknown, bin Laden understood Prince Sultan to say that the regime was going to accept his offer. "While he [bin Laden] was expecting some call to mobilize his men and equipment," al-Faqih says, "he received news that transferred [*sic* — transformed?] his life completely." The news was that King Fahd and his ulema had approved entry of U.S. and other Western forces into the kingdom.[23]

Bin Laden's reaction to the arrival of U.S. troops was clear and frank. "The American government," he said, "has made the greatest mistake in entering a peninsula that no religion from among the non-Muslim states has entered for 14 centuries. . . . Never has Islam suffered a greater disaster than this invasion." He made it clear that he saw the arrival of U.S. forces as a Crusader attack on Islam, calling the event "a back-breaking calamity" marking "the ascendance of Christian Americans over us and the conquest of our lands."[24] While these words seem counterintuitive to Western readers, Professor Lewis has written that "bin Laden's view of the Gulf War as American aggression against Iraq may seem a little odd, but it is widely — though by no means universally — accepted in the Islamic world."[25] Lewis then notes another factor that played, and still plays, to bin Laden's advantage; namely, that for Muslims, Mecca and Medina rank ahead of Jerusalem in the hierarchy of Islamic holy places, notwithstanding the central place of the latter in the substance and rhetoric of the Arab-Israeli peace talks. In the modern era, the major European powers respected this reality. "During the period of Anglo-French domination of the Middle East," Lewis wrote, "they nibbled at the fringes of Arabia, in Aden and the trucial sheikdoms of the Gulf, but were wise enough to have no military and minimal political involvement in the affairs of the peninsula."[26]

For Muslims, as we in the West sometimes tend to forget but those familiar with Islamic history and literature know, the holy land par excellence is Arabia—Mecca, where the prophet was born; Medina, where he established the first Muslim state; and the Hijaz, whose people were the first to rally to the new faith and become its standard bearers. Muhammad lived and died in Arabia, as did the Rashidun caliphs, his immediate successors as the head of the Islamic community. Thereafter, except for a brief interlude in Syria, the center of the Islamic world and the scene of its major achievements was Iraq, the seat of the calpihate for half a millennium. For Muslims, no piece of land added to the realm of Islam can ever be finally renounced, but none compares in significance with Arabia and Iraq. . . . Of these two, Arabia is by far the most important.[27]

With U.S. troops on the ground, bin Laden "regarded the country from that moment as occupied," claiming "our country has become an American colony."[28] Because Riyadh sanctioned the basing of non-Muslim forces, "the ruling house of Saud lost the last remnant of legitimization [sic] for bin Laden."[29] Bin Laden said King Fahd had "sided with the Jews and Christians," and by doing so had committed an "unforgivable sin" and had desecrated the holy sites. Bin Laden also damned the kingdom's senior clerics, led then by Grand Mufti Shaykh Abd-al-Aziz Bin-Baz, for approving the entry of Christian troops, claiming that by doing so the clerics were playing "the most dangerous of roles in the entirety of the Arab countries."[30] "At stake is not a marginal issue or cause that may be compared to, say, a rise in the unemployment figures or crime rate," another of bin Laden's brother Saudi dissidents explained. "This is about the rape of our honor that no one of us must take lightly. . . . This is because the deployment of any non-Muslim military force in the Peninsula is a pivotal issue that admits of no compromise or tolerance. To remain reticent over an issue like this is equal to condoning murder, imprisonment, torture, and the embezzlement of public money; it is even tantamount to condoning blasphemy and enmity to Islam and the nation [ummah]."[31]

Bin Laden specifically focused on Shaykh Bin-Baz, characterizing the grand mufti's dealings with the al-Sauds as associating with "tyrannical idols who have declared war on God and his messenger." After Bin-Baz issued a mid-1994 fatwa authorizing reconciliation with Israel, bin Laden indicted the grand mufti for abandoning the word of God and urged him to again "join the faithful" by changing his course. "You were not content," bin Laden angrily wrote to Bin-Baz, "with opening the country of the two holy mosques to the Jewish and crusader occupation forces, so you included the third holy mosque [al-Aqsa in Jerusalem] in the disaster by granting legitimacy to the capitulationist deals that the Arabs are signing with the Jews." For these actions, bin Laden said, the al-Sauds and the clerics in their pay "would have to suffer the same fate as the Shah of Persia," that is, the family would have to "dissolve and disappear."[32]

In a final effort to stop the arrival of foreign troops, bin Laden turned not to the government or his family's royal intimates, but to lobbying religious scholars and Islamist activists. According to the *Frontline* biography, bin Laden "succeeded in extracting a fatwa from one of the senior scholars that [said] training and readiness is a religious duty. He immediately circulated the fatwa and convinced people to have their training in Afghanistan." The fatwa, issued by Shaykh Bin-Uthaymin, played no role in Iraq's defeat, but the four thousand Saudis who are said to have trained in Afghan camps as the result of the bin Laden-procured fatwa may yet be heard from.[33]

For bin Laden, the arrival of non-Muslim forces was the back-breaking straw. It is important to note, however, that many straws made up this lethal load and that bin Laden believed the al-Sauds' history was replete with examples of their support for "nations that were fighting against Muslims."[34] Bin Laden argued that while the al-Sauds never ceased "to cry in the open over matters affecting the Muslims," the historical reality was that they never made "any serious effort to serve the interests of the Muslim community apart from small efforts to confuse people and throw some dust in their eyes."[35] When bin Laden talks about the traitorous lineage of Saudi foreign policy, he is not referring to simple mistakes, disagreements over which Muslim issues to emphasize, or the compromises needed in diplomatic give-and-take. Rather, bin Laden argues that throughout the al-Sauds' rule—save for the reign of King Faisal, who engineered the 1973 oil embargo—Saudi foreign policy has been an expanding record of the un-Islamic aligning of the kingdom with Christians and Jews, a record ignominiously capped by the deployment of Western troops to fight Iraq.[36]

Bin Laden tackled this issue head-on in his "Declaration of Jihad," and the relevant passage from it is worth quoting at length, because it crisply communicates bin Laden's belief that the al-Sauds have consistently betrayed God. In 1996, bin Laden wrote that al-Sauds' claim that U.S. forces were needed to defend the kingdom,

> is another trick by the regime, but it will not fool Muslims as its first trick fooled the Palestinian mujahedin. The first trick resulted in al-Aqsa mosque being lost. When the Muslim people in Palestine rose up in their great jihad against the British occupation in 1354H, corresponding to 1936, Britain failed to stop the mujahedin or their jihad. Their devil inspired them that the armed jihad in Palestine can only be stopped by their agent, King Abd-al-Aziz, who they believed was capable of deceiving the mujahedin. And indeed King Abd-al-Aziz carried out his mission by sending his

two sons to meet with the mujahedin leaders in Palestine and inform him [*sic* – them?] of King Abd-al-Aziz's pledge to guarantee the British Government's promises that it would withdraw and meet their demands if they halted this jihad. So King Abd-al-Aziz was behind the loss of the Muslims' first Qiblah. He allied himself with the Christians against Muslims. And he abandoned the mujahedin, instead of espousing the al-Aqsa mosque issue and supporting those struggling for the sake of God's cause. And here is his son King Fahd, trying to fool Muslims with the second trick in order to squander our remaining holy sites. He lied to the ulema who sanctioned the Americans' entry and he lied to the Islamic world's ulema and leaders at the [World Muslim] League's conference in holy Mecca in the wake of the Islamic world's condemnation of the crusader forces' entry into the land of the two holy mosques on the pretext of defending it. He told them that the matter was simple and that the U.S. and coalition troops would leave in a few months. And here we are approaching the seventh year since their arrival and the regime is still unable to move them out.[37]

Because bin Laden was a popular figure when Iraq attacked, and because the arrival of U.S. troops "met with enormous domestic opposition," the Saudis decided to more closely control bin Laden. This determination was strengthened when bin Laden acquired the training fatwa and made vigorous "attempts to gather the ulema in an independent body" as an alternative to the government's Senior Ulema Commission, which, he believed, "had turned into a tool in the hand of the state." "The regime was not happy with his [bin Laden's] activities [regarding his attempt to organize dissident ulema] and so they limited his movements to Jeddah only," according to *Frontline*. "He was summoned for questioning twice for some of his speeches and activities and was given warnings. To intimidate him, the regime raided his farm in a suburb of Jeddah by the National Guard." Warnings and raids did not work and it has been reported that bin Laden was incensed by the raid – during which he was absent – and complained about it to Crown Prince Abdullah. The crown prince is said to have "apologized and claimed he [was not] aware and promised to punish whoever were [*sic*] responsible." Despite a polite response, bin Laden was placed under house arrest when U.S. forces arrived.[38]

Bin Laden's anger can be imagined as he watched the buildup of non-Muslim forces while under detention, comfortable though house arrest must have been in terms of creature comforts. There is no firsthand data about what bin Laden thought at the time, nor about with whom he talked. There may, in fact, have been few of either; bin Laden has said he and his colleagues "were shocked by the fatwas" allowing U.S. troops in the kingdom, and that "we had to wait until this shock disappeared before assessing the situation." Soon after Iraq's defeat, however, Sa'd al-Faqih said bin Laden began pressing his brothers to secure the regime's permission to take a short trip to Pakistan, telling them he had to "finish his little bit of business in Pakistan." The brothers secured travel documents for him, apparently pledging he would return. In April 1991 bin Laden left for Pakistan and does not appear to have returned since. He did have the decency, however, to write his brothers a "tender letter of apology" for abusing their good offices and embarrassing them with the al-Saud family.[39]

9

BIN LADEN IN EXILE: AFGHANISTAN AND SUDAN, 1991-1996

The Shepherds, I say, . . . took them by the hand, and had them
to their tents, and made them partake of that which was ready
at present. They said, moreover, We would that you should
stay here a while, to be acquainted with us, and yet more to
solace yourselves with the good of these Delectable Mountains.

The Pilgrim's Progress, 1678

From 1991 to 1992, Osama bin Laden lived in Afghanistan and then in 1992
went to Sudan, residing there until May 1996. In part of this period, he was
active in efforts to stop the bloody fighting among the Afghan mujahedin
factions that had increased after the Soviet withdrawal and the defeat at
Jalalabad. The precise reason for bin Laden's move to Sudan is unclear, but
it appears to have been motivated by his sense of the intractable nature of
the intra-mujahedin conflict and a belief that Saudi-backed agents were trying to kill him.

In Sudan, bin Laden renewed ties made in the Afghan jihad with Hasan
al-Turabi and other members of Sudan's ruling National Islamic Front (NIF).
From Khartoum, bin Laden built a series of Sudan-based businesses — some
in partnership with senior NIF members — that appear to have turned a profit.
He also moved fighters from Afghanistan to Sudan and employed them in
his businesses; made a connection to Iraq's intelligence service through its
Khartoum station; participated in the Yemeni civil war; survived at least
two assassination attempts; and moved Islamic fighters out of Bosnia after
the Dayton Accord. Bin Laden also was visited by prominent Saudis carry-

ing an olive branch from the al-Sauds; substantially expanded his organiza-tion in East Africa; and sponsored or supported attacks on U.S., Egyptian, and Christian targets outside Sudan.

In May 1996 bin Laden decided to leave Sudan in part as an effort to ease U.S. and UN pressure on the NIF regime. Bin Laden told journalist Robert Fisk that he entered Afghanistan for the third time on 16 May 1996, but other reports suggest he did so in late May or early June. The return to Afghanistan was paved by the friendships and personal reputation he had earned in the Afghan jihad.[1]

Bin Laden went to Afghanistan from Saudi Arabia in April 1991 just as the Afghan Communist regime collapsed. According to *Frontline's* unattributed biography of bin Laden, the regime's end gave birth to intensi-fied "dispute among the Afghan parties."[2] On arrival, bin Laden had access to all Afghan resistance factions through al Qaeda, which was functioning efficiently and, as the *Far Eastern Economic Review* reported, was "the most powerful and numerically the largest Arab group."[3] At the time, al Qaeda was operating "several camps on both sides of the Afghanistan-Pakistan bor-der." Bin Laden soon began acting as a "mediator" to "sort the differences in the [Afghan] factions," Sa'd al-Faqih and *Frontline* have reported. "He [bin Laden] spent a great effort [and presumably money] to arbitrate between them, but with no success."[4] Bin Laden was worried that an Afghan civil war would slow the advance of jihad elsewhere and has said he "was in grief during the dispute between these [Afghan] factions." He later argued that because of this strife "the results of the victory against the Soviet Union are being wasted." Bin Laden's mediation efforts were noted at the time in the media. "In 1991 and 1992," journalist Jamal Ismail told *Al-Jazirah,*

> I interviewed him [bin Laden] more than once. . . . At that time, . . .
> he was head of a reconciliation committee between the Afghan fac-
> tions that were at war in some states [*sic*—Afghan provinces?]. He
> was chosen by the factions as a neutral party that is supportive of
> the Afghan jihad in general. . . . After 1992, when the Afghan
> mujahedin entered the Afghan capital, and were at war with each
> other, which stunned all observers, Osama bin Laden—along with
> a number of Islamic activists who were in Peshawar and other Arab
> countries—exerted intensive mediation efforts between Hekmatyar,
> Masood, and Rabbani, but all these efforts failed.[5]

Bin Laden failed to stop the violent factionalism in the so-called Af-ghan cauldron, but he won high marks among the Afghans for impartiality and negotiating skills. He ordered his followers, for example, to avoid in-volvement in the intra-mujahedin struggle, telling them "it was a sin to side with any faction." In addition, Pakistan's *Nation* has said bin Laden "remained mostly neutral in the fray, building up strong relationships in the geographical areas adjacent to and or in the proximity of Pakistan." The *Nation* added that these relationships were in the area "roughly approximating the area of the origin of the Taliban."[6] Although bin Laden did not know it at the time, his even-handed attempts at peacemaking would stand him in good stead when he decided to leave Sudan in 1996.

While the Afghan leaders would try the patience of Job, were he a Muslim, bin Laden appears to have decamped from Afghanistan in late-1991 only in part because of their intractability. A number of reports suggest bin Laden left — some say in Hollywood style using a disguise and a private jet — because he had learned he was under threat of assassination, perhaps sponsored by the Saudi intelligence service. Sa'd al-Faqih has said that in addition to stubborn Afghans, bin Laden's mediation encountered obstacles strewn by Prince Turki al-Faisal, chief of the Saudi General Intelligence Directorate. In his book *Unholy Wars: Afghanistan, America and International Terrorism,* John K. Cooley has said Turki once admired bin Laden as "a young man who burned with a hard pure flame of devotion to religious principles" and who shared Turki's antipathy toward the corruption of the Arab world's leaders and his desire to reverse "the decline and decadence of Islam." Turki probably also respected bin Laden as the son of the man who helped Turki's father — King Faisal — gain the Saudi throne and who had funded the government during the new king's initial months in power. Faqih claims, however, that after the Soviets withdrew "Saudi intelligence [officers] were actually increasing the gap between Afghani factions to keep them fighting." In addition, the author of *Frontline*'s unattributed biography says bin Laden grew "suspicious of his [Turki's] role in Afghanistan, and once had an open confrontation with him in 1991 and accused him [Turki] of being the reason of [sic — for?] the fight between Afghan factions." This animosity apparently still lingers. In late 1998, bin Laden went out of his way to publicly deride Turki as nothing more than "an envoy for the American government."[7]

Admittedly, this is thin gruel to say the threat to bin Laden was from the Saudis. Still, as noted above, bin Laden had publicly condemned as un-Islamic King Fahd and the senior Saudi ulema during the Gulf War and had embarrassed the Saudis by not returning to the kingdom. In addition, bin Laden was willing to work with all of the Islamist Afghan factions that had fought in the war to find a workable political settlement, something to which the Saudis paid lip service but did their best to bedevil. Throughout the Afghan war, the Saudis favored the Al-Azhar-educated Afghan leader Abdur Rasul Sayyaf because of his staunch Wahabi views. Sayyaf also was the darling of wealthy nabobs in the Gulf, many of whom showered him with cash for his performance as a guest speaker whose rhetoric flowed in classical Arabic of a quality seldom heard. Beyond the Saudis' appreciation for Sayyaf's doctrinal rigor and his appeal as the boy orator of the Hindu Kush, however, lay Riyadh's eagerness to see a Wahabi-friendly Sunni Pastun regime in power in Kabul to act as a roadblock on the highway the Iranians would have to trod to reenter Central Asia, an old Persian stomping ground. After spending billions to beat the Soviets, Riyadh was determined to avoid seeing an Afghan sluiceway built through which Shi'ism could flow into the newly independent Sunni Muslim states of Central Asia.

Investment in Sudan

Bin Laden was among friends when he arrived in Khartoum. He had met many members of the Sudanese NIF who fought in Afghanistan during the anti-Communist jihad, and he also had trained NIF fighters in his Afghan camps. According to *Al-Watan Al-Arabi,* a Sudanese engineer named al-Tahir became a close colleague of bin Laden during the war and suggested he invest in Sudan. Bin Laden favored the idea and visited Khartoum in October 1990, the year after the NIF took power in a coup d'etat.[8] This appears to have been his first visit, although bin Laden told a reporter in 1994 that he "surveyed business and investment opportunities in Sudan as early as 1983."[9] During the 1990 visit, according to *Al-Watan Al-Arabi,* bin Laden rented a villa in the fashionable al-Riyadh section of Khartoum and made investments involving him in Sudan's agricultural, import-export, banking, construction, and leather tanning industries. After his arrival, bin Laden also is reported to have funded his always cash-strapped NIF hosts: $2 million to NIF leader Hasan al-Turabi for resettling Arab Afghans in Sudan; $10.5 million to upgrade Sudan's flour industry and build a modern airport at Port Sudan; and a $50 million share in a new Islamic bank called al-Shimal, the Bank of the North.[10]

When bin Laden became a resident of Sudan in late 1991 or early 1992 — again the data are not definitive — he expanded his business holdings and soon had a number of companies operating, including al-Hijra for Construction and Development; Wadi al-Aqiq Company, an international trading firm; an agricultural company named Al-Themar al-Mubaraka; Qudarat Transportation Company; and the Taba Investments Company, a currency trading firm. Bin Laden apparently designed his businesses to mesh with the economic advantages Turabi gave him, which included a full exemption from import and export duties and a huge tract of agricultural land in eastern Sudan.[11] Through these firms, bin Laden was involved in building the NIF regime's long-planned Khartoum-to-Port Sudan highway; growing and exporting maize, sesame, gum Arabic, cattle, palm oil, peanuts, and sunflower seeds; and producing leather for export to manufacturers in Italy and elsewhere in Europe.[12] The *New York Times* has reported bin Laden made some senior NIF members his partners in these endeavors, and Reuters said bin Laden employed "people linked to terrorist groups in his farms, companies, and construction businesses."[13] Whether the last contention is true, bin Laden did employ his own cadre and some Arab Afghans he paid Turabi to re-settle; "Yes, I helped some of my comrades to come here to Sudan after the [Afghan] war," bin Laden told Robert Fisk in late 1993.[14] Finally, bin Laden tried to help the NIF improve Sudan's economy by encouraging "Saudi busi-nessmen to invest in Sudan." In early 1999, *Frontline* reported bin Laden had "reasonable success" and "many of his brothers and Jeddah merchants had and still have investments [in Sudan] in [the] real estate, farming, and agri-cultural industry."[15]

Thus bin Laden methodically established substantial business inter-ests in Sudan that turned a profit and gave employment to his followers and their families. According to *Al-Wasat*, for example, former bin Laden em-ployee Sayyid Salamah—who is now jailed in Egypt—"use to manage $50 million worth of activities and enterprises belonging to Bin Laden in Sudan."[16] It also must be assumed that bin Laden built dual-use companies, designed to make a profit and, as the *Sunday Times* of London has said, "to support the increasingly sophisticated enterprise [bin Laden's international organization], and to provide cover for the procurement of explosives, weapons and chemi-cals and for the travel of the group's operatives."[17] In addition to these enter-prises, bin Laden was closely associated with al-Turabi and the NIF leadership in funding the construction and operation of the Sudan government-owned Military Industrial Corporation (MIC), which was intended to make Sudan self-sufficient in small arms, ammunition, and some other military equip-ment. The government-owned MIC, according to the *New York Times*, also has responsibility for "overseeing chemical weapons development."[18]

Search for CBRN Capability

In Sudan, bin Laden decided to acquire and, when possible, use chemi-cal, biological, radiological, and nuclear (CBRN) weapons against Islam's enemies. Bin Laden's first moves in this direction were made in cooperation with NIF leaders, Iraq's intelligence service, and Iraqi CBRN scientists and technicians. He made contact with Baghdad through its intelligence officers in Sudan, and by a Turabi-brokered June 1994 visit by Iraq's then-intelligence chief Faruq al-Hijazi; according to Milan's *Corriere della Sera*, Saddam, in 1994, made Hijazi responsible for "nurturing Iraq's ties to [Islamic] funda-mentalist warriors." Turabi had plans to formulate a "common strategy" with bin Laden and Iraq for subverting pro-U.S. Arab regimes, but the meet-ing was a get-acquainted session where Hijazi and bin Laden developed good rapport that would "flourish" in the late 1990s.[19]

Turabi's scheme for an overall strategy was not achieved, but there is information showing that in the 1993–1994 period bin Laden began work with Sudan and Iraq to acquire a CBRN capability for al Qaeda. Bin Laden lieutenant Abu Hajir al-Iraqi appears to have been his point man in this effort, and *Time* magazine reported that in 1993 al Qaeda tried to buy a "Russian nuclear warhead" on the black market. Bin Laden halted the effort when a warhead for sale could not be located, and instead, "his agents began scouring former Soviet republics for enriched uranium and weapons components that could be used to set off the fuel."[20] *Time* magazine claims bin Laden was frustrated in this effort and "settled on chemical weapons which are easier to manufacture."[21]

In regard to CBW, it is prudent to assume bin Laden's tannery in Sudan has legally purchased dual-use chemicals that allow production of chemical weapons as well as of leather. In the nuclear area, al Qaeda as early as 1993 drafted "plans to buy enriched uranium from the former Soviet Union to produce portable light nuclear explosive canisters to be used in terrorist operations."[22] Suggesting al Qaeda's interest in biological weapons, moreover, is Saudi journalist Jamal Khashogji's recollection of visiting Sudan in the early 1990s and hearing bin Laden "earnestly discussing the virtues of genetically engineered crops."[23] In all these efforts, bin Laden's goal was to get a CBRN weapon to use on a U.S. target. *Al-Watan Al-Arabi* has said bin Laden especially wants the capability of "manufacturing mobile weapons of mass destruction that could be used in terrorist operations and in confronting the United States in particular."[24]

Whatever progress bin Laden made in Sudan toward arming al Qaeda with CBRN weapons appears to have had Turabi's approval and was supported by the Khartoum factories of the Military Industrial Corporation (MIC) — where bin Laden had a private office — or other NIF-controlled facilities.[25] A Sudanese military engineer named Colonel Abd-al-Basit Hamza — who now builds military factories and once built roads for bin Laden's Al-Hijra Company[26] — reportedly manages a "group of companies . . . run by the NIF in cooperation with Iraq and bin Laden. The operation of this program is led by Iraqi scientists and technicians, led by Dr. Khalil Ibrahim Mubaruhah, and by Asian and foreign experts."[27] The *New Republic* quotes a Sudanese military defector as saying that "up to 60 Iraqi military experts rotate through Sudan every six months, and that some of these experts are involved in some kind of munitions development" at the MIC.[28] In addition, Sudanese oppositionists — not the most unbiased sources — claim Iraq's technicians are helping Sudan build chemical weapons at MIC facilities in Khartoum and, in return, Iraqi chemical weapons have been hidden by Sudan at the Yarmuk Military Manufacturing Complex in Sheggara, south of Khartoum.[29]

(I have left in place the foregoing paragraphs, and several paragraphs later in the book, because they accurately present the information my research uncovered when preparing the first edition of this book. The paragraphs represent the public record as I found it and, as such, they merit being available for other researchers to

evaluate. Now, however, I believe that my description and analysis of CBRN and other cooperation between al Qaeda and Saddam Hussein's Iraq in this section — and elsewhere in this book — is incorrect. My judgment is not based on publicly available information, but rather on an extensive review of the classified information pertinent to the subject located in the files of the Central Intelligence Agency. This material is not now, of course, available to the public; indeed, it seems likely that most of it will remain classified for many decades, and properly so to protect the Agency's sources and methods. I feel a bit like the historians of World War Two who had to go back and revise and correct their works decades after publication when the signal intercepts known as "ENIGMA" and "MAGIC" profoundly expanded their ability to understand, document, and analyze the wars against Germany and Japan. These historians were not wrong in their initial analysis; they used the best data then available. They did, however, have a professional obligation to factor the new information into their work, and they did so. On Iraq and al Qaeda I had a similar experience — better information came along after my first book was published.

(Given the restricted nature of the data that has changed my original analysis and judgment, I thought it best to describe in general terms the process by which I came to reverse my position on the issue. Readers will recall that before the invasion of Iraq in March 2003, the Department of Defense's analytic unit headed by Mr. Douglas Feith published a number of classified papers dealing with aspects of Iraq's activities that most negatively affected U.S. interests, ranging from Weapons of Mass Destruction to terrorism. Many of these papers appear to have been leaked to the media, causing a great deal of discussion over the points they purported to document, none more so than the description of "cooperation" between al Qaeda and Iraq on a variety of issues.

(Before moving to a specific discussion of the paper Mr. Feith's unit produced on the Iraq–al Qaeda relationship, a general comment on the quality of the analysis from Mr. Feith's unit is in order. While I do not claim to have read all of the unit's papers, those I did read struck me as rather amateurish. The bane of the professional intelligence officer's life is that data are available to support virtually any line of analysis one wants to present, or, more dangerous, any line of analysis politicians want to have delivered. Because of this situation, an intelligence officer, to be worth anything to his policy-making masters, must be able to discern between quality information — because it is well-sourced, documentary, electronically intercepted, and so forth — and information that has little of quality about it. The officer also must be willing to defy policy makers who are more concerned with analysis that will support his or her policy preference than with the quality of data that goes into the analysis. Writing intelligence analysis is, in short, a tough business, and most senior analysts have lost a promotion or two in their career because they refused to use information of inferior quality.

(The analysis of Iraq–al Qaeda cooperation that came from Mr. Feith's unit struck me as either being prepared by inexperienced analysts — those not yet comfortable in discerning quality from inferior information — or by solid analysts who

were ordered to produce analysis that would mesh with and support the decisions policy makers intended to make. I have no way of knowing which of the two factors were at play. I would argue, however, that it would be a stretch to describe the analysis from Mr. Feith's unit on Iraq and al Qaeda as a professional product. It certainly was not analysis on which decisions about peace and war should be made.

(When the Department of Defense found a strong Iraq–al Qaeda relationship, Director of Central Intelligence George Tenet — much to his credit — requested the CIA's bin Laden department to review all files that might show signs of the relationship described by Mr. Feith's unit. I must add that this is an issue to which CIA had always paid close attention, and the review ordered by Mr. Tenet was meant either to revalidate the Agency's previous conclusion that no such relationship existed or to discover that the Agency had missed or neglected data that supported the analysis produced by Mr. Feith's officers.

(For a number of reasons, I was available to perform the review of Agency files on Iraq and al Qaeda, and the chief of the bin Laden department handed me the assignment. I was delighted with the task, eager to begin, and sure that my research would support the analysis I had presented in Through Our Enemies' Eyes. For about four weeks in late 2002 and early 2003, I and several others were engaged full time in searching CIA files — seven days a week, often far more than eight hours a day. At the end of the effort, we had gone back ten years in the files and had reviewed nearly twenty thousand documents that amounted to well over fifty thousand pages of materials. I was both pleased and embarrassed by the results of the research. I was pleased because CIA's position was reaffirmed and the analysis of Mr. Feith's unit was discredited. There was no information that remotely supported the analysis that claimed there was a strong working relationship between Iraq and al Qaeda. I was embarrassed because this reality invalidated the analysis I had presented on the subject in my book.

(Lest readers think that the issue was left entirely to me and a few others, I must add that I was only the main researcher. The mountains of pertinent documents that were recovered and printed were turned over to the analysts of the CIA's Counterterrorist Center for final evaluation. As far as I know, they found what I found — no Iraq–al Qaeda relationship worthy of the name. It was with sharp surprise, therefore, when those of us who worked on the reevaluation of CIA data heard Secretary of State Colin Powell tell the UN Security Council that an effective Iraq–al Qaeda working relationship was in place.

(I have no explanation for how the research that was performed, and the analysis that was done on the basis of it, was shaped to yield Secretary Powell's assertion. I would add one more reality of the professional intelligence officer's life, however. The influence of even the best research and analysis depends at all times on the honesty, integrity, and toughness of those senior officers who are tasked to brief it to the president of the United States and his cabinet officers. A hard fact of analytic life is that the product that is written to assist the policy maker is not always the product that is delivered. Career ambitions and concerns, personal friendships that de-

velop between briefers and the president and his circle, and the certain knowledge of what those to be briefed want to hear are all factors that can skew the presentation of analysis at the most senior levels. I have no knowledge about what bottom line on the Iraq–al Qaeda relationship was presented by CIA briefers to the president and his cabinet, but I do know that Secretary Powell's statements did no reflect the reality we found in CIA files.

(How to rectify the discrepancy? Well, it will not be easy. During the presidency of George W. Bush, the director of Central Intelligence, George Tenet, appointed himself briefer-in-chief to the president. This was an unprecedented arrangement, as no previous DCI met daily with the president, nor was he always the primary briefer of the president when the two met. After Mr. Bush's inauguration, Mr. Tenet put himself squarely at the delivery end of the channel through which intelligence and analysis were delivered to the president and senior cabinet members. At day's end, therefore, Mr. Tenet perhaps is the only one who knows how the Iraq–al Qaeda analysis was garbled in the hour or so it took for him to carry it from CIA headquarters to the White House. Or, perhaps, if it was deliberately garbled before he left for the drive to the White House.)

Aid to NIF

Bin Laden's nearly five-year stay in Sudan also saw him support the NIF's consolidation of power, continue to expand the al Qaeda organization, and promote closer ties between it and like-minded Islamist groups. In Sudan, bin Laden was eager to assist Turabi and the NIF cement their hold on power, even to the extent, the media reports, of helping the NIF assassinate Sudanese opposition leaders. Militarily, bin Laden spent $2 million to construct military training camps; some reports say more than twenty camps were built for Arab Afghans brought from Afghanistan and Pakistan. The total number of Arab Afghans that bin Laden brought to Sudan is unknown, but Cairo's *Rose al-Yusuf* has reported that 380 Egyptian Arab Afghans arrived in Sudan in April–May 1993.[30] The training camps are reported to be located "throughout Sudan, not only near Khartoum and Port Sudan, but in the Damazin area of eastern Sudan and a base in the southern Equatoria Province, near the Ugandan border."[31] Bin Laden allowed NIF militia recruits to train in the camps and made fighters available to join NIF combat operations against John Garang's Christian rebels in southern Sudan.[32]

In early 1996 bin Laden negotiated a deal between the NIF and several Yemeni Islamist groups to create a "naval bridge" between Aden and Port Sudan; this pact formalized an ad hoc arrangement made during the Afghan jihad that was operating, according to *Al-Watan Al-Arabi,* when bin Laden's fighters tried to attack U.S. soldiers in Aden in December 1992. Bin Laden wanted to use the route to move al Qaeda fighters from Yemen to

Sudan to support the NIF and "ship the large supplies of weapons looted by [Islamic] religious extremists during the summer of 1994 war in Yemen." Several shiploads of weapons were moved to Port Sudan, but the bridge's status has been unclear since bin Laden left Sudan.[33] Financially, as previously noted, bin Laden contributed $50 million to the capitalization of the NIF-dominated al-Shimal bank, and, according to *Al-Watan Al-Arabi,* in late 1998 he had "$500 million . . . deposited in the Sudanese Central Bank to cover the Sudanese pound and Sudan's import ability." It is unclear if the latter amount came from bin Laden, his supporters, or both.[34]

To expand al Qaeda's strength and geographical reach, bin Laden brought with him to Sudan the most senior members of his organization, almost all of whom had fought at his side in the Afghan war. As noted, Abu Hajir appears to have run bin Laden's weapons procurement activities — conventional and unconventional — while managing Taba Investment Company and acting as financial chief for the al-Themar al-Mubaraka Fruit Company.[35] In addition, Wadih el-Hage returned from the United States to become bin Laden's private secretary.[36]

It appears that the overall financial administrator of bin Laden's Sudan-based endeavors, as well as the approving officer for the organization's expenditures overseas, was a Saudi national named Siddi Maddani al-Tayyib, aka Abu Fadl. Bin Laden, according to Abu Hajir, made Tayyib responsible for approving all expenditures over $1,000. Tayyib was married to bin Laden's niece and worked as director of the Taba Investment Company in Khartoum. Tayyib would later become a source of trouble for bin Laden when he surrendered, or was captured by, the Saudis in the late 1990s.[37] Although it is unclear when they arrived, bin Laden also brought his top military commanders, the Egyptians Abu Hafs al-Masri and Abu Ubaydah al-Banshiri, to Sudan. Both quickly became involved in resettling Arab Afghans, expanding al Qaeda's presence and military capabilities in East Africa, and, eventually, participating in or facilitating combat operations.[38] Also joining bin Laden in Sudan was the Gama'at's operations chief, Mustafa Hamza, who had known bin Laden in Afghanistan and who had earlier worked for him in an unknown capacity in Cairo.[39]

Expansion in East Africa

While running training camps and concentrating fighters in Sudan, bin Laden assigned Abu Ubaydah and Abu Hafs the job of building al Qaeda's East Africa infrastructure.[40] As early as 1992, Abu Ubaydah sent veteran Arab Afghans to Africa from Afghanistan, including, the Egyptian police say, alleged Dar es Salaam embassy bomber Mustafa Mahmud Said Ahmed.[41] Abu Ubaydah's work was responsible for "the strength of [bin Laden's] African network and the multiplicity of its cells," which was ap-

a meeting that was attended by the leaders of the religious extremist move-ments in Yemen."[60] Pretty dry stuff, but probably a fair description of the content of most visits. It is certainly in character for bin Laden to promote unity among Islamist groups and listen more than talk. Bin Laden did, how-ever, take advantage of his status as the world's best-known Arab Afghan to meet Islamist leaders, contribute to their activities, preach Muslim unity and anti-U.S. actions, and generally lay the groundwork for future cooperation and coordination. On balance, little military planning probably went on during these trips, although bin Laden's brother-in-law, Muhammad Jamal Khalifah, was active in that sort of activity—with Wali Khan and Ramzi Ahmed Yousef—in the Philippines during this time frame. Khalifah had been active in the Philippines since at least 1993, according to Manila's intelli-gence services, and worked with the Abu Sayyaf Group in "sowing terror-ism in Zamboanga, Sulu, and other parts of Mindanao."[61] Finally, as will be seen, Abu Ubaydah and Abu Hafs were busy expanding al Qaeda in Africa.

Maintenance of Afghanistan Connections

Before discussing the military operations al Qaeda and its allies con-ducted during bin Laden's Sudan interlude, it is worth looking at the con-nections bin Laden simultaneously maintained in Afghanistan. There is no indication that any of the bin Laden-sponsored camps in Afghanistan were shut down after he left for Khartoum. What seems to have happened, how-ever, was that the camps' military curriculum was expanded to make the training pertinent to combat situations like those in Afghanistan—that is, for rural insurgencies—as well as for Islamist fighters destined for venues where urban warfare would be on tap or where they would be infrastruc-ture builders, not warriors. Convicted Nairobi embassy bomber Mohammed Sadiq said he was trained at one of bin Laden's Afghan camps in the 1990s, receiving instruction "as a Stinger missile operator provided by an Arab instructor who had an impressive record of shooting down Soviet aircraft during the Afghan war." Sadiq added that bin Laden's camps "are the best in Afghanistan and have produced some of the best guerrillas,"[62] while Cairo's *Rose al-Yousef* has claimed that after the Soviets left, bin Laden added such topics as "how to make explosives, poisons, [and] secret acids for forg-ery" to the curriculum of his Afghan camps. As always, al Qaeda camps coupled military training with instruction in such "practical skills" as basic engineering, technical skills, farming, and vehicle driving and maintenance, each of which would benefit an insurgent no matter where in the Islamic world he went to fight or build infrastructure.[63] The high quality of training offered in bin Laden's Afghan camps was reaffirmed by the *New York Times* after it had examined materials seized in Afghanistan since October 2001. "The [captured] documentary trove punctures two myths," the *Times* explained in March 2002. "One was that the camps were turning out tens of thousands of suicide bombers. In fact, they were training soldiers for a war. The second was that the forces were disorganized and ragtag. They were, in reality, quite well disciplined."[64]

Perhaps the biggest change in camp curriculum was the addition of training to produce fighters capable of precision attacks in urban settings. Professor Magnus Ranstorp has written that bin Laden commands "battle-hardened Islamic revolutionaries [who] are highly skilled in urban guerrilla warfare tactics."[65] While this evaluation has become true, it was not the case during the Afghan jihad. One reason why the Soviets and Afghan Communists held on for thirteen years was that the insurgents lacked motivation for destructive urban warfare — because most had family in the cities, urban areas were heavily defended, and they wanted to preserve the little modern infrastructure Afghanistan possessed — and made a deliberate decision not to wage all-out war in the cities. Assassinations and kidnappings, however, were staged in Kabul, Kandahar, Herat, and Jalalabad.[66] In the 1990s, bin Laden's camps taught urban warfare skills, although he too told his fighters to avoid "harming the vital utilities and strategic wealth" of the Muslim world. The tactics taught to bin Laden's cadre will be apparent to those who recall the attacks on President Hosni Mubarak in Ethiopia in 1995; on tourists in Luxor in 1997; on sightseeing buses in Cairo, leisure boats plying the Nile; Egyptian police during the 1990s; and — more recently — the insurgent campaigns in Afghanistan and Iraq and the renewed attacks on tourists in Egypt. Now-imprisoned EIJ fighter Mohammed Attiyah described the training in the bin Laden-associated Badr camp near Khowst as including,

> the use of weapons inside cities. I also studied topography, military tactics, how to ambush patrols, and how to shoot with the left hand in case the right hand was hit. I was taught how to shoot while riding a motorcycle or in a speeding car and how to rescue a hostage from [a] kidnapper by blocking roads and pointing guns at the kidnappers. The daily program in the camp started after dawn prayers where we formed a circle to read the Koran, then we did physical exercises before breakfast. Then military training and lessons began, followed by noon prayers. After prayers, the training focused on attacking tourist buses. Barrels were placed in such a way to form the shape of a bus. Other barrels were put within to designate humans. The plan required the use of an open van. One person sat behind the wheel and another sat next to him and two others sat in the back. The vehicle had to get as near as possible to the bus. The two in the back would get off and one of them would throw a hand grenade on the bus. The other took up a position near the second door while his colleague went to the rear door.

Both of them would then open fire on the dummies and then withdraw to their vehicle and be driven away. Those in charge of the training told us: Just imagine that the bus passengers are Israeli or Jewish tourists. Practical training was preceded by theoretical training about the target area, the attack, and escape plans which required abandoning the vehicle used in the attack and getting into another one waiting at a predetermined place. We also trained in attacking tourist boats. A house was used for that purpose [as the target]. A van carrying three persons would get as close as possible to the boat. One of them would fire an RPG while the others covered him. There was also training in attacking police stations in a similar way."[67]

10

BIN LADEN BEGINS: INCITING AND WAGING JIHAD FROM SUDAN, 1992-1996

Tis true, but little or more are nothing to him that has the truth on his side; Though a host should encamp against me, said one, my heart shall not fear: Though war should rise against me, in this I will be confident. Besides, said he, I have read in some records, that one man has fought an army: And how many did Samson slay with the jaw-bone of an ass?

The Pilgrim's Progress, 1678

In late 1993 journalist Robert Fisk interviewed Osama bin Laden while bin Laden was directing the construction of the Khartoum-to-Port Sudan highway. One question Fisk asked bin Laden was if he was running military training camps in Sudan. Bin Laden indignantly answered Fisk, telling him the idea was "the rubbish of the media and the embassies. I am a construction engineer and an agriculturist. If I had training camps, I couldn't possibly do this job." Bin Laden was not candid.[1]

Between 1992 and bin Laden's return to Afghanistan, bin Laden, Abu Hafs al-Masri, Abu Ubaydah, and their subordinates were, in essence, continuing to build and expand a self-supporting international insurgent organization with which to attack U.S., Israeli, Christian (almost exclusively Catholic), Egyptian, and other pro-Western Muslim targets. As is known, however, bin Laden did not publicly declare jihad on the United States until his 1996 return to Afghanistan. In evaluating bin Laden's activities in the 1992–1996 period, a look will first be taken at bin Laden's premier military operations of the period: al Qaeda's attacks on U.S. forces attached to the UN's "Operation Restore Hope" in Yemen and Somalia. The latter al Qaeda operation used the East Africa network bin Laden had put in place in a relatively short time, and which would score more successes against the United States in 1998. The Somalia operations also showed the skill of bin Laden's fighters in terms of insurgent capabilities and their talent as trainers who are able to teach their skills to novice but eager-to-learn students. After the Somali discussion, the narrative will be broadened to assess bin Laden's overall "war effort" while he was based in Sudan.

Operations in Somalia and Yemen

When the UN announced in late 1992 that it would put a U.S.-led multinational force in Somalia, bin Laden quickly moved to damage U.S. units therein. His motivation was twofold. First, after the USSR's demise, the United States became bin Laden's top enemy, and so U.S. troops were a natural target; bin Laden has said that after the UN stated its plans, "the Muslim fighters headed for Somalia and another long battle, thinking that the Americans were like the Russians."[2] The second motivation was a shared belief among bin Laden, his lieutenants, and senior National Islamic Front (NIF) leaders that "the United States would use Somalia as a staging ground to attack Sudan."[3] In 1997, for example, bin Laden told the daily *Pakistan* that during the UN intervention, "the U.S. tried to make a base under the UN umbrella so that it could capture Sudan and Yemen."[4]

Bin Laden believes the UN is Washington's tool and that even in 1992 the United States—as the UN readied for Somalia—was using it to force a "broad-based" government on the Afghans that would deny them and Islam the fruits of victory. Al Qaeda's quickly formulated plan for Somalia had two stages: interdicting U.S. forces traveling to Somalia, and attacking the forces after they arrived. In both cases, al Qaeda would use Arab Afghans and local Islamists. Two Yemeni comrades of bin Laden's, Jamal al-Hindi and Tariq al-Fahdli—the latter fought with bin Laden at Jalalabad in 1989 and was wounded[5]—led a hastily improvised attack in Aden, while bin Laden's top military leaders, Abu Ubaydah and Abu Hafs al-Masri, were charged with running al Qaeda's anti-U.S. operations in Somalia. Although a bit tabloidish, John Miller was on the mark when he wrote in *Esquire* that "when the Marines landed [in Somalia] in the last days of 1992, bin Laden sent in his own soldiers, armed with AK-47s and rocket launchers. Soon, using the techniques they had perfected against the Russians, they were shooting down American helicopters."[6] Concurring, bin Laden has said, "the only non-Somali group that fought the Americans was the Arab Mujahedin brothers who had come from Afghanistan. . . . These were successful battles in which we inflicted big losses on the Americans. We used to hunt them down in Mogadishu."[7]

In Yemen, al Qaeda's attacks smacked of poor intelligence on the target and a lack of urban warfare skills. As UN forces assembled for Somalia, some U.S. military personnel transited Aden and occupied hotels for a few days. Al Qaeda focused on two hotels it believed the Americans used—the Gold Mohur and the Movenpick—and on 29 December 1992 detonated a bomb in the former. The bomb intended for the latter exploded prematurely in the hotel's parking lot. Overall, two tourists were killed and seven other people were wounded. Yemeni security arrested several men and found weapons and explosives in their truck in the Movenpick's parking lot.[8] Although no U.S. soldiers were in the hotels when the attacks occurred—a nearby hotel did billet U.S. soldiers—they have entered al Qaeda battle lore as total victories, because within days after the attacks, all U.S. soldiers left Yemen.[9]

In 1998 bin Laden summarized the standard version of the event. "The United States wanted to set up a military base for U.S. soldiers in Yemen so that it could send fresh troops to Somalia," bin Laden told the daily *Pakistan*. "The Arab mujahedin related to the Afghan jihad carried out two bomb explosions in Yemen to warn the United States, causing damage to some Americans staying in those hotels. The United States received our warning and gave up the idea of setting up its military bases in Yemen. This was the first al Qaeda victory scored against the Crusaders."[10]

Interestingly, the al Qaeda attacks on U.S. targets in Aden occurred when the Yemeni regime was trying to stop a series of bombings and assassinations by Islamists in several areas of the country. The results of the Yemenis' investigation of the attempted hotel bombings and the other violent incidents pointed directly at bin Laden and Zawahiri's Egyptian Islamic Jihad (EIJ). Even before the hotel attacks, for example, the Yemenis had detained twenty individuals who claimed to be from the "Osama Group" and the "Islamic Jihad Organization."[11] Although most Western terrorism experts identified the Yemeni Islamic Jihad, not bin Laden or Zawahiri, as the culprit for the hotel attacks, media reporting at the time—when put in the context of what since has been reported about bin Laden—strongly suggests the accuracy of his claim of responsibility. In mid-1999, for example, the media reported the Yemeni Islamic Jihad was formed and led in the 1980s by EIJ fighter Muhammed Ibrahim Sharaf. Contemporary reports also suggested bin Laden's involvement. "Security sources [in Yemen]," *Al-Sharq Al-Awsat* wrote,

> revealed that the "Islamic Jihad Organization" [involved in the violence in Yemen] has branches in other Arab countries, including Egypt, that its leadership is in Khartoum, and that it is financed by a prominent Arab businessman currently residing in Sudan. The sources pointed out that the Organization's branch in Yemen received their [*sic*] training in Afghanistan and Pakistan. . . . Investigations have revealed . . . that there is a strong link between the

military leadership of the Yemen branch and the main political and military organization in Khartoum.[12]

In Africa, bin Laden sent Abu Hafs al-Masri to Somalia to assess the prospects of success for the Arab Afghans he was deploying and to evaluate the ability of local Muslim tribesmen to absorb military training.[13] On his return, Abu Hafs apparently reported positively and the future Nairobi embassy bombers Mohammed Sadiq Odeh, Mohammed Sadiq Howaida, and Fazul Abdullah Mohammed were among those sent to Mogadishu to train fighters from Farah Aideed's group.[14] In total, bin Laden has said he sent 250 fighters to help Aideed and other Somali leaders fighting U.S.-led forces.[15] The *Washington Post* has reported that after his capture in August 1998, Odeh told police "that he helped to train Islamic militants in Somalia who opposed the UN peacekeeping mission there."[16] Islamabad's the *News* said another alleged Nairobi bomber, Mohammed Sadiq Howaida, told Pakistani police after his August 1998 arrest that he was one of "a select group of Arabs" sent in 1993 to help Aideed, and *Al-Hayah* has reported Abu Ubaydah himself commanded just such a group "in the fight against U.S. forces in Somalia."[17] In addition, journalist Mark Bowden in his brilliant book *Black Hawk Down* says, "Aideed's men received some expert guidance [on the use of rocket-propelled grenades] from Islamic soldiers smuggled in from Sudan, who had experience fighting Russian helicopters in Afghanistan. . . . Their fundamentalist advisers told them that the helicopter's tail rotor was its most vulnerable spot. So they learned to wait until it passed over, and to shoot up at it from behind." Bowden and others who have looked at the loss of two U.S. Black Hawk helicopters on 3 October 1993 report they were hit in the tail rotor by a rocket-propelled grenade.[18]

While it is not yet possible to definitively document the military activities and successes of al Qaeda and its Somali trainees, al Qaeda fighters Howaida and Ali Muhammed — both now in jail in the United States — have said bin Laden's forces were directly involved in downing a U.S. helicopter and in two attacks using land mines.[19] In 1997 bin Laden told Pakistani journalist Hamid Mirthat his fighters caught a helicopter pilot and "tied his legs, and dragged him through the streets," and when ABC correspondent John Miller interviewed bin Laden in May 1998, an unnamed bin Laden fighter told Miller "with a big grin" that he claimed credit for "slitting the throats of three American soldiers in Somalia."[20]

Whether these attacks were made by al Qaeda fighters, local al Qaeda-trained Somali tribals, or a combination of both — which seems likely, because Abu Ubaydah led combat missions against U.S. forces in Somalia — is of little consequence in terms of the extremely positive impact they had on bin Laden's organization, its allies, and its international reputation. Bin Laden told *Al-Quds Al-Arabi*, "U.S. soldiers showed their cowardice and feebleness during the Somali experiment," and has since cited the attack in rhetorically challenging the U.S. military to come after him. "The Americans are cowards," bin Laden said in August 1997, "and cannot confront me. If they even think of confronting me, I will teach them a lesson similar to the lesson they were taught a few years ago in Somalia."[21]

For bin Laden and his followers, the withdrawal of U.S. forces from Somalia meant, in John Miller's breezy phrase, "Another superpower humiliated. Another Bin Ladin victory. . . . [I]n Somalia, Bin Ladin had taken a swing at the biggest kid in the school yard and given him a black eye." [22] While it is difficult to know how the Muslim man-in-the-street saw the U.S. withdrawal, it is certain that the "street" saw the Soviet withdrawal from Afghanistan a landmark victory for the mujahedin and, more important, for Islam. Remarks by bin Laden, Abu Hafs al-Masri, and Mohammed Sadiq Howaida strongly suggest that al-Qaeda sees Somalia as another landmark victory. Howaida's rank in the organization was akin to that of a noncommissioned officer, and his remarks have something of a man-on-the-street quality.

Bin Laden: "The youth [al Qaeda fighters in Somalia] were surprised at the low morale of the American soldiers and realized more than before that the American soldier was a paper tiger and [would] after a few blows run in defeat. And America forgot all the hoopla and media propaganda . . . about being the world leader and the leader of the New World Order, and after a few blows they forget about this title and left, dragging their corpses and their shameful defeat. . . . With the blessed bullets of our brethren, Allah blunted their edge, destroyed their machination, and defeated their troops. Thus, the band of Christian allies broke up and the cloud of the world order disappeared. They ran away defeated like stray camels running to their resting place near a water hole, when they saw the war show its children [young fighters] and bare its teeth."[23]

Abu Hafs al-Masri: "If you could hear our brothers in Somalia, the children and the youth, describe how they were hounding the U.S. troops, you would laugh a great deal to hear how scared the U.S. soldiers were of Somalia children and how they thought death would inevitably come through them. After the Americans failed to control Somalia and found no one to blame for causing their defeat, they blamed us."[24]

Sadiq Howaida: "Usama Bin Ladin's biggest triumph was the eviction of the U.S. Army from Somalia and he took pride that he and his group stayed for one full year in Somalia and had, along with Farah Aideed, inflicted humiliation on the U.S. Army. We defeated the Soviet army in Afghanistan and the U.S. Army in Somalia. Is that a small success?"[25]

Worldwide Activities 1991–1996

In addition to high-profile attacks in Yemen and Somalia, a review of the 1992–1996 period shows bin Laden was involved in other facets of the worldwide anti-U.S. insurgency he is conducting and striving to incite others to join. The following time line covers the late-1991 through May 1996 period—the period of bin Laden's stay in Sudan—and clearly shows bin Laden and his organization were consistently active in the military arena, as were groups with which he was known to be in contact. Again, the following is not to say that bin Laden masterminded, ordered, or had foreknowledge of all the attacks. Neither is it to say bin Laden was funding or logistically supporting all the groups. It is simply to say that these activities fit squarely with the themes bin Laden has outlined; they are guerrilla attacks of the sort he wants to incite and they benefit his cause whether or not he was involved in them.

The following outline is not chronological, a fact that in itself shows the uniqueness of the bin Laden phenomenon. A chronological time line is simple to construct for attacks of Hizballah and the Abu Nidal Organization, groups that are in the traditional "terrorist" category; each has a hierarchical command structure and controls all attacks. It is impossible to build such a time line for bin Laden's organization, however, because al Qaeda has been more involved in supporting long-term Islamist insurgencies—over which it has little, if any, control. The following events should be read as a scorecard showing that bin Laden in this period succeeded in terms of the measures of success he, not the West, has established.

- 1991–1994: The Abu Sayyaf Group (ASG) in the Philippines carried out attacks financed by bin Laden's brother-in-law Muhammed Jamal Khalifah. The attacks included the December 1991 bombing of a Catholic Church in Jolo and the murder of Italian missionary priest Father Carceda. In the period, Catholic priests—Filipino and missionary—were favorite ASG targets. From 1991 to 1994, the ASG conducted 26 bombings, 21 kidnappings, 132 murders, and 28 firefights with Philippine forces.[26]
- 1992–1996: Bin Laden lieutenants Abu Ubaydah and Abu Hafs al-Masri led Arab Afghans and local Islamists in attacks on government forces in Eritrea, Uganda, and the Ogaden area of Ethiopia.[27]
- 1992–1994: Until his late-1994 death, Gama'at leader Anwar Shaban used bin Laden's money to "set up camps [in Bosnia] for the Islamic Group and Jihad Organization [EIJ] through which Arab and Egyptian strugglers flooded into the areas." Bin Laden also gave Muslim volunteers traveling to Bosnia "1,000 Saudi riyals as pocket money."[28]
- 27 January 1994: Arab Afghans killed British aid worker Paul

Goodall in Zenica, Bosnia.[29]

- 1992–1994: Bin Laden's brother-in-law Mohammed Jamal Khalifah funded, and perhaps directed, a Jordan-based Islamist group called "Mohammed's Army." This group staged a series of bombings in Jordan meant to "eradicate forbidden conduct by force" and, over time, to "topple the Hashemite Kingdom of Jordan." Twenty-five members of the group were tried in 1994, and eleven — including Khalifah in absentia — were sentenced to death. The U.S. government detained Khalifah in late 1994 and sent him to Jordan. A witness in the case recanted his testimony about Khalifah, and he was released and went to Saudi Arabia, where Saudi officials greeted him at the airport. Jordanian authorities later said bin Laden also funded the attacks of Mohammed's Army.[30]

- 1992–1995: Until the Dayton Accord ended the Bosnian war, bin Laden gave money to Fatih Hasanein, head of the Third World Relief Agency (TWRA), to buy weapons for Bosnian fighters and fund the recruitment and training of foreign Islamists.[31]

- 1994–1996: After Algeria's Armed Islamic Group (GIA) — to which bin Laden gave "seed money" and whose leaders are mostly Arab Afghans — published plans to eliminate Algeria's "Jews, Christians, and polytheists," the group began attacking non-Muslim foreigners, killing 114 people by late 1996. Catholic targets topped the GIA list: two priests and five nuns were killed from October 1994 to December 1995; seven monks were beheaded in May 1996; and the Bishop of Oran was assassinated in August 1996.[32]

- 24–27 December 1994: On 24 December four GIA fighters hijacked an Air France flight in Algiers and forced it to fly to Marseilles. In Marseilles, the hijackers killed three French passengers. After the murders, French security forces stormed the aircraft and killed the four GIA fighters. On 27 December, the GIA murdered four French priests in Algeria to retaliate for the death of its fighters in Marseilles.[33]

- 1991–1994: In Yemen, al Qaeda and the EIJ attacked two hotels in Aden where they mistakenly believed U.S. troops were billeted on their way to Somalia. Between 1991 and at least the end of 1992, bin Laden operatives also attacked Yemeni petroleum installations and assassinated Yemeni socialist party officials. Then, in 1993 and 1994, bin Laden sent al Qaeda fighters from Pakistan and Afghanistan — via Sudan — to fight the Yemeni Communists in the civil war that yielded a reunified Yemen.[34]

- 1993–1996: Bin Laden broadened his international involvement by supporting Islamists in Lebanon, Bosnia, Kashmir, Tajikistan, and Chechnya. Between 1993 and his death in May 1996, bin Laden's military chief, Abu Ubaydah, participated "in operations carried out by Islamists" in Tajikistan, Burma, Kashmir, Chechnya, Bosnia, and Libya.[35]

- January 1993–October 1994: Bin Laden's Arab Afghans and/or the Somali Islamists they trained attacked U.S. troops in Somalia.[36]

- 26 February 1993: Ramzi Yousef detonated a bomb in the underground garage of the World Trade Center in New York City, killing six people and wounding one thousand. Bin Laden said Yousef was "a Muslim who defended Islam from American aggression."[37]

- 7 and 13 December 1993: On 7 December ASG fighters threw hand grenades into Davao City's Catholic cathedral, killing 7 and wounding 130. On 13 December insurgents in Buluan, Maquindinao — probably ASG fighters — stopped a bus and executed nine passengers after identifying them as Christians.[38]

- 27 February 1994: In Zuk, Lebanon, Sunni Islamists bombed a Maronite Christian Church, killing nine and wounding sixty. The media speculated the attack was to deter a visit by Pope John Paul II. The Vatican canceled the visit soon after the attack.[39]

- 24 August 1994: North African Islamist fighters raided the Atlas-Sane Hotel in Marrakech, Morocco, killing two Spanish tourists and wounding two other people. The attackers also robbed the hotel's cashier. After the Islamists were caught, Moroccan authorities found the attackers' group had planned additional assaults in Fez, Casablanca, and Tangiers. Targets in the cities included uniformed policemen, a synagogue, tourist buses, and a beach used by European tourists for nude bathing.[40]

- 11 December 1994: A bomb put on a Philippines Air 747 by Ramzi Yousef exploded in flight between Manila and Tokyo. One person died and ten were wounded.[41]

- 1995: When the Dayton Accord was signed, bin Laden used the Islamic nongovernmental organization Human Concern International (HCI) — started with bin Laden's funds during the Afghan jihad — to move Islamist fighters from Bosnia. Some were resettled in Sudan.[42]

- January 1995: Plots to assassinate Pope John Paul II and President Bill Clinton were stopped in Manila, as were plans to bomb U.S. airliners flying the Pacific. The plots were devised by Wali Khan and Ramzi Yousef and supported by Khalifah.[43]

- 4 April 1995: The ASG raided Ipil in Zamboanga del Suro, killing fifty-three and wounding forty-five, mostly Catholics. It also burned 120 commercial and residential buildings, destroyed 25 vehicles, and robbed 4 banks.[44]

- 26 June 1995: The Egyptian Gama'at tried to assassinate President

Mubarak in Addis Ababa, Ethiopia. The attack was planned by Gama'at operations chief Mustafa Hamza, who at the time managed a bin Laden business in Khartoum.[45]

- 4–8 July 1995: Kashmir's Harakat-ul-Ansar — using the name "al-Faran" — kidnapped five Western hikers in Kashmir: a German, an American, two Britons, and a Norwegian; one escapes, the Norwegian is decapitated, the others are not found.[46]

- July–October 1995: Algeria's GIA staged nine bombings in France, most in Paris, which killed 9 and wounded 160. The media quoted the French Ministry of Interior as saying bin Laden funded the Paris attacks. Rashid Randa, leader of the attacks, is an Arab Afghan who had known bin Laden since the 1980s. *Time* magazine reported that after Randa's arrest, British police found records of wire transfers to him from bin Laden companies in Sudan. According to the director of the Algerian Judicial Police, Mohamed Isouli, bin Laden was a sponsor of Algeria's Islamists — GIA and the Islamic Salvation Front — and helped them "maintain a genuine network supplying arms and military equipment to the Algerian guerrillas." Isouli added that with "bin Laden's financial support," the Islamists have "active structures and networks abroad, responsible for propaganda, fund-raising, and setting up a logistical structure for the benefit of armed groups."[47]

- 20 September 1995: The Egyptian Gama'at detonated a car bomb near police headquarters in Rijeka, Croatia, killing one and wounding dozens. The Gama'at claims credit, saying the attack was in retaliation for the disappearance of Gama'at leader Talat Fuad Kassem, who had been detained by Zagreb police in September 1994.[48]

- 13 November 1995: Bin Laden associates detonated a car bomb near the U.S. Office of Program Management-Saudi Arabian National Guard (OPM-SANG), killing seven and wounding forty-two. Five of the dead were Americans. About the OPM-SANG bombers, bin Laden has said, "We describe those [attackers] as heroes and describe them as men. They have pulled down the disgrace and submissiveness off the forehead of their nation." Bin Laden and his aides see the attack as more evidence of U.S. weakness, given the post-attack reduction and reconcentration of U.S. troops in Saudi Arabia.[49]

- 19 November 1995: The EIJ used a car bomb to attack Egypt's embassy in Islamabad, killing sixteen and wounding sixty. Al Qaeda provided logistic support to the attackers and assisted their escape.[50]

- 16 April 1996: Ibn Khattab's force of Arab-Afghan/Chechen insurgents "attack[ed] and destroy[e]d" a Russian military convoy leaving Chechnya. The U.K.-based Islamic Observation Center cited a report from "Russian military sources" of 50 vehicles destroyed and 273 Russian soldiers killed.[51]

Again, the importance of this meandering, lengthy, but not comprehensive list is not that the line of responsibility for each attack leads to bin Laden; it does not. What is important is that the attacks fit the thematic parameters bin Laden has set for the "guerrilla" war he is waging and inciting against the Crusaders and "apostate" Muslim regimes. At a minimum, the attacks above suggest bin Laden's views and aspirations are shared by Islamists in many areas of the world, from Zuk, Lebanon, to Davao City in the Philippines. U.S. troops are attacked in Yemen and Somalia, for example, and the Egyptian government is attacked in Pakistan, Egypt, and Ethiopia. The Abu Sayyaf Group seeks Muslim dominance over the Catholic population of Mindanao, and attacks are staged in French cities. The World Trade Center in New York is bombed; Catholic and Christian churches and clergy are attacked in the Philippines, Somalia, Lebanon, Egypt, and Algeria; and funding, fighters, and weapons are supplied to Balkan Muslims fighting Catholic Croats and Orthodox Christian Serbs. A U.S. facility in Riyadh is car-bombed and plans are laid to kill President Bill Clinton and Pope John Paul II in Manila. All the events fit the pattern bin Laden has established for his war, all contribute to the same goal. In this context, by 1996 bin Laden's worldwide insurgency against the Crusaders was well under way.

As in all wars, both sides took casualties. Bin Laden, his allies, and his associates were no exception in the 1992–1996 period. In February 1994, Pakistan captured Ramzi Yousef and returned him to the United States; later in 1994, the Malaysians likewise caught and returned Wali Khan Amin Shah. In late 1994, Gama'at al-Islamiyya (IG) leader Anwar Shaban was ambushed and killed by security forces in Bosnia, and many Arab Afghans evacuated Bosnia after the Dayton Accord.

In addition, *Al-Sharq Al-Awsat* has reported that the Bosnian war cost bin Laden's allies a large loss of veteran fighters. Captured EIJ fighters have told Egyptian courts that in Bosnia "a large number of the Organization's [EIJ's] members" were uncovered. "Bosnia was an open field for the arrest of many Jihad and Islamic Group members when they tried to turn Bosnia into another Afghanistan in the heart of Europe and to move the phenomenon of Afghan Arabs to it." Attacks on the pope, President Clinton, and U.S. airliners were halted, and the attack on Mubarak in Addis Ababa was unsuccessful and almost all of the attackers were killed or captured. Egyptian security forces also stopped a second planned attack on Mubarak in Cairo in December 1995. Likewise, most of the team that executed the November 1995 attack on Egypt's embassy in Islamabad were killed or captured. Another senior Europe-based IG leader, Talat Fuad Kassem, disappeared while transiting Croatia in September 1995. It was later reported that bin Laden valued Kassem as highly as he has EIJ leader Zawahiri.[52]

Wins and losses, triumphs and disasters, these are the characteristics of all wars. But in a guerrilla war, as has been seen in Afghanistan, Kashmir, Vietnam, and elsewhere, if the guerrilla force survives, it is winning. And bin Laden's organization not only survived this four-year period, but also grew in size, reach, and capability; made new friends and allies; learned how to plan for, absorb, and survive the losses of war; and relocated to Afghanistan, an area more remote and less vulnerable than Sudan.

Return to Afghanistan

After he had spent five productive years in Sudan, several factors coalesced to cause bin Laden to go to Afghanistan for the third time since 1979. In the first instance, Sudan had heated up markedly in terms of earning the West's attention and enmity since bin Laden arrived in 1992. The NIF's open-door for Arabs — Arabs coming to Sudan in the bin Laden years needed no visas — made Khartoum a haven for Islamist insurgents and terrorists. By the middle of bin Laden's stay, the EIJ; the IG; HAMAS (Islamic Resistance Movement); the Palestine Islamic Jihad; the ANO; several Algerian, Libyan, and Tunisian groups; the Eritrean Islamic Jihad; groups of Ethiopian, Ugandan, and Somali Islamists; and Lebanese Hizballah — among others — were in Khartoum. The combination of hosting these Islamist fighters and bin Laden's presence, at least after it was clear he aided the attacks on Mubarak and OPM-SANG, led the United States to name Sudan a state sponsor of terrorism, an act followed by the imposition of U.S. and UN sanctions. These sanctions were one more strain on NIF leader al-Turabi's fledgling Islamic state, which already was fighting a protracted civil war with Sudanese Christians; fencing with Egypt over the attack on Mubarak, boundary demarcation, and access to Nile waters; suffering from a decaying economy; and being loudly criticized by the international community for abusing human rights and limiting freedom of worship. By early 1996, then, Sudan was becoming too hot for bin Laden, and bin Laden was another point of irritation between the West and Sudan that al-Turabi did not need.[53]

Two other factors also motivated bin Laden to leave Sudan. First, he was again a target for assassination; two attacks failed in early 1994. On 4 February Takfir al-Hijra fighters — a group that thinks bin Laden is not a strict enough Muslim — tried to kill bin Laden in the meeting hall next to his Khartoum home. The attack was defeated by bin Laden's bodyguard and Sudanese security. In the battle bin Laden and his eldest son Abdallah returned fire with AK-47s. "We used to meet [at my residence compound] with the brother guests at 1700 hours every evening," bin Laden told *Al-Quds Al-Arabi* in 1996.

On that day, and for a reason known to God, I was late. Then I heard a barrage of bullets fired on the guest [meeting?] room, which is detached from the house. Some bullets were [fired] at me. So I took my weapon and went to a position overlooking the house to investigate the matter. I gave my eldest son (Abdallah) a weapon and told him to take a position inside the house. I thought that an armed group had attacked the guards, and we prepared ourselves for a clash. But it was discovered that the attack was aimed directly at the guest room, which was stormed by three young men who opened fire at the guests, three of whom were seriously wounded. They opened fire on the place where I use to sit. One [guest] was hit in the abdomen, another in the thigh, and the third in the leg. The brothers clashed with them. There were Sudanese security forces near the house, so they clashed with them, killing two and wounding the third. Some of the brothers sustained minor injuries."[54]

A few weeks later, the Takfir attacked and killed worshippers at Friday prayers in the Al-Thawrah Mosque in the Omdurman section of Khartoum where bin Laden may have been present. Bin Laden says he was there during the attack, but media reports say he was not and that his absence may have saved his life.[55]

The final factor prompting bin Laden's departure from Sudan was the increasing discomfort of the Saudi regime and the al-Saud family with bin Laden's public criticism and defiance of them; Riyadh, along with the Qataris, had been a major benefactor of the Sudanese NIF even before it took power and did not look kindly on the NIF hosting bin Laden. After bin Laden left the kingdom in April 1991, Saudi authorities continued to act against him. In late 1991, for example, Riyadh revoked the passport he traveled on to Pakistan, announcing that Saudi intelligence had found that bin Laden was smuggling weapons to Yemen from the kingdom.[56] Then, at some point in 1992, according to the Associated Press, "Saudi Arabia froze his [bin Laden's] bank accounts" in the kingdom.

In addition, Mary Anne Weaver has reported in the *Atlantic Monthly* that the Saudis sent "hit teams" to Sudan in the 1991–1992 period to kill bin Laden, a point supported by the testimony in a U.S. court of an al Qaeda defector who was close to bin Laden in Sudan.[57] On 16 May 1993 Riyadh issued an arrest warrant for bin Laden "both because of his support for fundamentalist groups involved in terrorist operations in Algeria and Egypt and because of his ties with upstart religious circles [read: religious critics of the al-Sauds] that tried to establish an independent human rights organization in Saudi Arabia at the beginning of May [1993]."[58] Given the usual glacierlike movement of Saudi bureaucrats, the speed with which the warrant was issued after the start of the human rights campaign—no more than sixteen days—it is reasonable to assume the warrant was issued because of the latter, not the former.

By late 1994, ensuring that bin Laden did not reenter the kingdom was not sufficient for Saudi authorities. In September, Saudi security forces arrested some of the harshest religious critics of the al-Sauds. Included were Shaykh al-Awdah and Shaykh al-Hawali, two clerics whom bin Laden has long identified as his personal heroes and the rightful leaders of Islam's jihad against America.[59] When the clerics were arrested and "the State prevented the clerics from speaking," bin Laden has said he and his colleagues in Sudan "set up the advice committee [the London-based Advice and Reform Committee (ARC)] and began to reveal the truth and clarify matters [to the Saudi people], seeking reform and guidance for the nation, and reminding people of the long time our Ulema had spent working to reform [Saudi society] through good preaching."[60] Bin Laden told Abd al-Bari Atwan of *Al-Quds Al-Arabi* that ARC communiqués, issued from Sudan and London, were read by the Saudi people, and

> when the Saudi government discovered the great impact and effect of these statements, it transcended all its disagreements with the Sudanese regime, which had exerted great efforts to rectify its relations with the Riyadh government and to end the [Saudi] boycott [against Khartoum] but encountered a lack of response and arrogance [from Riyadh]. After [ARC] Statement No. 17—it was an open letter to the King on the occasion of the cabinet reshuffle—the Saudi Government contacted the Sudanese Government at the highest level, requesting [Saudi-Sudanese] reconciliation on the condition that Osama bin Laden and the sons of the two Holy Mosques accompanying him in Sudan were expelled and that they stopped [*sic*] issuing statements. The Sudanese Government at the highest level informed me of its difficult position and the scale of Saudi pressure. They [the Sudanese] asked me to stop issuing statements. On the day I was told to stop issuing statements I sought to find an alternative land capable of bearing the word of truth and we came to the land of Khorasan [Afghanistan] once again.[61]

While pressing the NIF to oust bin Laden, the Saudis simultaneously sent olive-branch-carrying envoys to Sudan to try to get bin Laden to reconcile with the al-Sauds and return home. These emissaries, bin Laden said, told him he could return to Saudi Arabia and receive "my identity card, passport, and money . . . if I say through the media that the King is a good Muslim." "I would like to state," bin Laden told ABC in late 1998, "that the Saudi government initiated contacts [with me] during the last period in

Sudan. They sent several delegations to enter into negotiations aimed at convincing me to keep silent on the unjust American occupation of the land of the two mosques." Among the envoys were bin Laden's mother and Bakr bin Laden, his eldest brother and family patriarch; bin Laden told Robert Fisk the al-Sauds "had offered his family 2 billion riyals ($535 million) if he abandons his 'holy war'" — a tactic like the al-Sauds' earlier offer of a $90 million construction contract to deflect bin Laden's focus from the Afghan jihad. As an unnamed acquaintance of bin Laden has said, "He is so kind and tender toward his kinsmen. But this has nothing to do with the formulation of his platform or decisions."[62] Bin Laden also discussed the issue with CNN, and you could almost picture bin Laden scratching his head and wondering why the Saudis just do not get it.

> They sent me my mother, my uncle, and my brothers in almost nine visits to Khartoum asking me to stop and return to Arabia to apologize to King Fahd. I apologized to my family kindly because I know they were driven by force to come to talk to me. This regime wants to create a problem between me and my family and in order to take some measures against them. But, with Allah's grace, this regime did not get his [*sic*] wish fulfilled. I refused to go back. They — my family — conveyed the Saudi government's message that if I don't go back, they'll freeze my assets, deprive me of my citizenship, my passport, and my Saudi I.D., and distort my picture in the Saudi and foreign media. They think that a Muslim may bargain on his religion. I said to them do whatever you may wish. It is with Allah's bounty, we refused to go back. We are living in dignity and for whom [*sic* — which?] we thank Allah. It is much better for us to live here under a tree here on these mountains than to live in palaces in the most sacred land of Allah, while being subjected to disgrace not worshiping Allah in the most sacred land on earth, where injustice is so widespread. There is no strength except in Allah.[63]

Bin Laden turned the emissaries down flat, thereby precipitating another Saudi move against him. Having issued an arrest warrant, Riyadh was now faced with the terrifying possibility that at some point someone would seize and return an unrepentant bin Laden to the kingdom, thereby making him a rallying point for internal dissidents. Cornered by a dilemma of their own making, the Saudis moved on 10 April 1994 to erase the problem by withdrawing bin Laden's nationality, a sort of a de-Saudification process. Officially, the interior ministry's decree said bin Laden's nationality was canceled because he engaged in "irresponsible acts which run counter to the Kingdom's interest and offend against its relations with sister countries, and for his failure to comply with instructions."[64] In traditional Saudi head-in-the-sand fashion, Riyadh tried to frame the bin Laden issue—he had not yet staged an attack in the kingdom—as the world's problem, not its own. After the November 1995 bombing of the OPM-SANG building, the Saudis moved to further refine this portrait to make it appear the confrontation was exclusively between bin Laden and the United States.

With pressures converging, bin Laden decided to leave Sudan by early May 1996. At the time, bin Laden was silent about his departure and by his silence allowed the NIF to appear responsive to Saudi concerns and, partially, to U.S. and UN demands that Sudan stop supporting terrorism.[65] The NIF did not claim that it deported bin Laden, but it did nothing at first to negate that impression. It appears that its silence on this score angered some pro-bin Laden NIF members in Sudan and abroad, a lesson the Taliban regime surely has taken to heart. In early 1997, for example, Sudan's information ministry said Sudan did not deport bin Laden and "the Afghan brothers" and that "Sheikh Osama and the Afghan brothers left Sudan of their own volition, knowing the pressures Sudan is facing and so that they can destroy the opportunity for the enemies of Islam and Sudan."[66] Later, in April 1997, NIF leader al-Turabi underscored that bin Laden decided to leave because he saw his presence "was at the root of much pressure exercised by Saudi Arabi and the United States on the government in Khartoum."[67]

The Arab media pretty much agreed with official Sudanese commentary, with Amman's *Sawt al-Mar'ah* saying that bin Laden left "voluntarily . . . [and] his departure from Khartoum had nothing to do with Washington's demands,"[68] and *Al-Watan Al-Arabi* simply asserting that bin Laden decided to leave Sudan "to reduce regional and international pressure on al-Turabi and to prevent further sanctions on Sudan." Long after his departure, bin Laden in May 1998 said he left the country because he "felt the government of Sudan could not afford to bear [U.S.] pressure any more."[69]

On balance, I believe bin Laden decided to leave Sudan on his own hook because of the assassination attempts, because he saw a need to ease international pressure on al-Turabi's new Islamic state, and because he had decided it was time to intensify his anti-U.S. guerrilla war from a redoubt that offered tremendous topographical advantages to the defender. Finally, bin Laden knew he had closer friendships of longer duration in Afghanistan and, for those friends, protecting guests was a matter of national pride, as well as an unavoidable tribal duty and religious obligation.

IV

WAR YEARS, 1996–2001

11

BIN LADEN RETURNS TO AFGHANISTAN: GETTING SETTLED AND POLITICKING

Now I saw in my dream, that by this time the Pilgrims were got over the enchanted ground, and entering into the country of Beulah, whose air was very sweet and pleasant, the Way lying directly through it, they solaced themselves there for a season. . . . In this country the sun shineth night and day; wherefore this was beyond the valley of the Shadow of Death, and also out of the reach of Giant Despair, neither from this place could they so much as see Doubting-Castle. Here they were within sight of the City they were going to; also here they met some of the inhabitants thereof: For in this land the Shining Ones commonly walk, because it is on the borders of Heaven.

The Lord of these mountains hath given us a Charge not to be forgetful of strangers, therefore the good of the place is even before you.

The Pilgrim's Progress, 1678

As always with bin Laden's travel, the details of his return to Afghanistan are fuzzy. He arrived sometime between mid-May and mid-June 1996, but the means and place of arrival are unclear. The media report him arriving by aircraft in Kabul, then going by car to Jalalabad, and then southeast to the Hadda farm compound of Hisbi Islami leader Yunis Khalis; by an aircraft to Peshawar and then by car to Khalis's farm; or by an assortment of other means that have him turning up variously at Khowst, Islamabad, Karachi, or Jalalabad.

Bin Laden became no easier to track after he arrived in Afghanistan, notwithstanding efforts by more than a few governments to keep him in their sights, literally and figuratively. While the mode and route of travel from Sudan are unclear, what is plainly apparent is that bin Laden had no shortage of friends in Afghanistan. He was allowed into the country and given an Afghan passport by Jamiat Islami party leader and then-prime minister Burhanuddin Rabbani — an acquaintance of his youth and father-in-law of legendary Afghan commander Ahmed Shah Masood — and the then-foreign minister Gulbuddin Hekmatyar, and was hosted on arrival by Khalis, thereby covering both sides of the country's historic Pashtun/non-Pashtun ethnic divide and ongoing civil war. Because of the reputation he earned during and after the Afghan jihad, bin Laden, like Kipling's Kim, was welcomed as "the little friend of all the world." "When he [bin Laden] arrived there," *Frontline* has noted, "the situation in Afghanistan was unsettled between the many factions, but he had very good relations with all the factions and all would protect him." An August 1998 statement by Hekmatyar, leader of his own Hisbi Islami group and then a senior member of Masood's anti-Taliban alliance, emphasized the accuracy of *Frontline*'s analysis. "Bin Laden has been in Afghanistan since the Afghan jihad era," Hekmatyar said. "Although he is now under Taliban protection, we believe that no one has the right to expel him from Afghan territory or to hand him over to any foreign party. The Afghan people will not accept such a thing."[1]

Even the Taliban's most dangerous Afghan foe, the late Northern Alliance chief Masood, demonstrated in 1998–1999 that he would not act against bin Laden, despite the aid bin Laden was giving the Taliban. In fall 1998, for example, Taliban media began accusing Masood of apostasy and trying to kill bin Laden. "Ahmed Shah Masood has decided to face two *Qiblahs*," Taliban radio declared, "and now in addition to Moscow, he also worships the United States." The broadcast claimed "the main focus of Masood's agenda and the U.S. is the martyring of our mujahid guest Osama bin Laden," and asked "[i]s Masood not aware that this action will hurt the feelings of a billion Muslims across the world." These accusations were too much for Masood, who had earlier said that bin Laden was the Afghan people's enemy and was harming "Islam's reputation"; he also had derided bin Laden's attacks in East Africa as too limited from the military perspective, saying "we cannot bring America down by these actions." Reversing himself, Masood now said charges that he was cooperating with the United States to kill bin Laden were "a slander started by the Taliban."[2]

More recently, Masood kept an eloquent silence on bin Laden in interviews linguistically accessible to Afghans, Pakistanis, or Arabs, while continuing to tease the Western governments on his leash by promising European correspondents to turn over bin Laden "as soon as circumstances allow me to do so" — a meaningless promise if ever one was made. By stressing the Afghan tradition of protecting guests and bin Laden's status as an Islamic hero, the Taliban put Masood in a corner. After decades of playing the West like a violin by shambling along in combat fatigues, wearing a wispy Dylan-like beard, and telling reporters in a world-weary French that "Victor Hugo is still the writer I prefer, but there is now little time to read," the Taliban forced Masood to present himself as the strict Islamist he always has been, and not the media-manufactured new-age Muslim who would rather have put flowers in the muzzles of Soviet AK-47s than make war in Allah's name.[3]

To digress for a moment, Masood's mystique is astonishingly pervasive in both its military and political manifestations, and much of it is based on his ability to con Western journalists and European politicians. Since 1996, Sebastian Junger wrote in early 2001, "the Taleban has fractured his [Masood's] alliance and cut its territory in half. Masood was confined to the mountainous northeast, which, although easily defensible, depended on, long tortuous supply lines to Tajikistan." Notwithstanding Junger's graphic description of Masood in extremis, and that fact that he now depends on support from Afghanistan's historic Russian, Iranian, and Indian enemies, there is an emerging view in the West — one that Junger inexplicably shares — that Masood can be the West's military tool for ending the bin Laden and Taliban problems. "To really put Mr. Bin Laden out of business," R. M. Gerecht another recent interviewer of Masood, argued in the *New York Times*, "America must shut down his operations in Afghanistan. . . . [I]t is not too late for America to play hardball. The Bush administration can give a small slice of the multibillion dollar counterterrorism budget to Mr. Masood. That might bring Mullah Omar down to earth." And when Masood finishes dispatching Omar and bin Laden, Washington can have him defang Saddam and democratize Beijing's bullyboys.[4]

Masood also continues to thrive on the political front. In March 2001, for example, journalists from London's *Sunday Times* visited him in Afghanistan and quoted him as saying that his alliance holds that "[Afghan] women should have the same rights as women in the rest of the world; the right to work, to go to school and vote." After talking to Masood, the journalists toured his area of control and found reality different from the commander's rhetoric. "Women must wear the *burqa* to cover the face," the reporters wrote, "just as they do under the Taleban. Few find the courage to work: the social taboo is too great. There have been no elections." Ignoring this snapshot of reality, a month later the European parliament invited Masood to give an address — in his "halting French" — before it in Strasbourg. Nicole Fontaine, the parliament's president, told *Agence France-Presse* that Masood was asked to speak because of his liberal views on democracy and women. He would explain the situation in his country, Fontaine said, where Masood opposes the Taliban ban on women "working outside [the home] and . . . from the educational system."

Met "with open arms," Masood's April 2001 visit to Strasbourg, Paris, and Brussels was a masterful exercise in deceiving those eager to be deceived. As always, Masood cut a striking figure, playing to European biases against Pakistan, militant Islam, the Taliban, and bin Laden, and telling the media things appropriate to his reputation as a liberal, erudite, and pro-Western insurgent commander. Masood told the Europeans that his forces "would work towards the return of democracy" in Afghanistan and that the Taliban "turned Afghan women into second class citizens." He claimed that he would stop these "insults to Afghan women [which are] unprecedented in our history"; eliminate religious fanaticism and use Islam "to serve the people and help them improve their material and spiritual lives"; and ensure the Taliban "criminals [are] tried by the international community."

After addressing issues vital in Europe but irrelevant in the Afghan context, Masood turned in an exquisite performance as the Masood the gullible Europeans love best: the war-weary and sensitive aesthete. "My primary objective is to remind the world of Afghanistan's great cultural and humanitarian heritage," Masood told the fawning and presumably damp-eyed media, "Afghanistan was the cradle for several cultures that go back thousands of years. A large number of great poets and philosophers who have been immortalized by their humanitarian teachings and love of beauty were born in our country. . . . Without the war I would have been an architect. That is what I was trained as. I wanted to build beautiful things in Afghanistan."

Having artfully manipulated his audiences, Masood pocketed wide, positive and reality-defying commentary. The Belgian foreign minister, for example, said that Masood's plan for his country "is in fact a republican model, with free elections" and that his "is a moderate Islamism, which of course recognizes the supremacy of free elections, human rights, [and] legal rights for men and women." Masood also received promises of increased financial aid from France and the European Union, and probably pledges of clandestine military assistance from his wishful-thinking European hosts. As he selected the latest Parisian materials for new *burqas* for his housebound wives and daughters, one can picture Masood smiling in delight at having again hoodwinked the West.[5]

Getting Settled

After arriving in Afghanistan, bin Laden began building or refurbishing facilities near Jalalabad for himself, his family, and his followers. The Afghan civil war was continuing and he wanted to get his family and staff out of harm's way. For example, Khalis's farm—a compound about 150 kilometers east of Kabul—is well known and close to Pakistan's border, and therefore did not give bin Laden much privacy from well-wishers and favor-askers, or security from those who meant him harm, a number that had presumably increased after the November 1995 attack on the Office of Program Management-Saudi Arabian National Guard (OPM-SANG) building and the June 1996 attack on a U.S. military residence in Dhahran. By late 1996, bin Laden had established bases at a place called Tora Bora, which had been a key base for Khalis's guerrilla forces during the Soviet war, and at a site known as Malawi in approximately the same area. Both were about twenty-five kilometers from Jalalabad.[6]

Despite these efforts to enhance security, there were several assassination attempts on bin Laden during the eight months he was in Nangarhar Province, including the assassination of engineer Mahmud, Hisbi Islami commander who had been charged by Khalis with helping bin Laden get securely settled. While media reports show that there may have been four or five attempts on bin Laden's life, the two attempts in March 1997 appear to be the ones that prompted him to leave for southern Afghanistan. Since bin Laden's arrival, Yunis Khalis had protected him; Khalis had a deal with the Taliban guaranteeing the safety of bin Laden's people and facilities in Nangarhar. Of the major Afghan party leaders, only Khalis built productive ties to the Taliban; this was, in equal parts, because Khalis, like the Taliban's leaders, is a Pashtun and a religious scholar; he was and is militarily and politically strong in Nangarhar, where the Taliban needed allies to take Jalalabad and Kabul; and because Taliban chief Mullah Omar was a Khalis commander in the jihad.[7]

Notwithstanding the agreement with Khalis, the Taliban's views about bin Laden were not clear until it took Jalalabad late in 1996. Then, *Frontline*'s unattributed biography says, bin Laden "was surprised when a delegation of Taliban came to meet him by order of Mullah Omar . . . with instructions to reassure him that he will have even better protection under the Taliban. The delegation expressed the Taliban honor of protecting someone like him who had sacrificed a lot for the sake of jihad." For a time, bin Laden held the chit, but after the March 1997 assassination attempts he used it, and in May 1997 he moved to the Taliban's headquarters in Kandahar.[8]

Taliban Decision to Host bin Laden

A pertinent question is why the Taliban decided to buy so much trouble from the West by hosting Osama bin Laden. The first two reasons are the most obvious and most often ignored by a secular and cynical West. As the Taliban delegation said when it visited bin Laden in late 1996, he had indeed "sacrificed a lot for the sake of [the Afghan] jihad." For the Taliban, *Frontline* has reported, bin Laden "is a saint. He is a symbol of sacrifice for the sake of jihad. They see him as a very rich Arab from the Holy Land [of

Saudi Arabia] who gave up his wealth and luxury to fight for the sake of his brother Muslims in Afghanistan."[9] Egyptian Islamic Jihad (EIJ) fighter Ibrahim al-Sayyid al-Najjar likewise recalls that during the jihad the mujahedin had "talked about [the] heroism and battles fought by the man [bin Laden] himself against the Soviet occupation."[10] Sa'd al-Faqih also captures the impression bin Laden left on his Afghan comrades in arms. "So he [bin Laden] was there," notes al-Faqih, "moving from Saudi Arabia with all those advantages to Afghanistan and donating himself. Donating his money. Donating his reputation. Donating his history and family relations to the jihad."[11]

The second factor is that the Taliban, like all Afghans but especially the Pashtuns, believe hospitality to a guest is a top-rank moral and Islamic responsibility and that they are obligated to protect a guest with their lives, even if he is tainted. As *Frontline* explained in its program on bin Laden, the Taliban "see themselves as performing a double duty here, an Islamic duty of protecting the distinguished person and a tribal duty of protecting a descent [sic — decent?] refugee. The latter is a big value in Afghanistan."[12] From the jihad years, bin Laden knew this Afghan trait, and likewise knew he could count on it. "He [bin Laden] knows for sure," Pakistan's the *News* explained, "that the Taliban, who are mostly Pashtoon and known for even sacrificing their lives while protecting their guests, would never hand him over to the Americans."[13]

Beyond the obligation to protect a guest, bin Laden's presence has over time appealed to other Pashtun character traits and, for that matter, character traits of most Afghans. Those familiar with the Afghan-Soviet war will recall the tenacity, endurance, stubbornness, fatalism, xenophobia, devoutness, and masculine pride Afghans take in their ability to absorb punishment and loss and still persevere to victory. The U.S.-led Western pressure to surrender bin Laden brought these characteristics to the fore. As a result, the once-simple issue of protecting an honored guest grew to an issue of national pride and dignity, and caused a decision to zestfully defy foreign pressure whatever the cost.

In the male-dominated Afghan culture infused with the attitude of settling differences man-to-man, Washington's pressure and especially the August 1998 U.S. cruise missile attack on Khowst earned the scorn of Afghans across the board. "Some Afghans were outraged that Washington had not challenged Mr. Bin Laden to a fair fight, and attacked without warning," reported the *Guardian*. The paper quoted one Afghan as saying that "If America wants to fight let them bring their forces here. It is not the act of a brave man to attack from the back."[14] Bin Laden had earlier set the stage for this reaction by saying, "I want the Americans to proceed toward Afghanistan, where all their misconceptions and illusions will be removed. I am sure, however, that the Americans will not come because they are cowards. They attack [with soldiers] only the unarmed and weaker peoples,"[15] and "God is the real superpower, so there is no need to be afraid of the U.S. We will die at the will of God, not at the will of the U.S."[16]

The missile strike also brought out the xenophobic stubbornness of the Afghan character, what bin Laden has described as the reality that "Afghans do not bargain away their respect despite severe opposition. They shelter mujhadein despite difficulties." The attack, Mullah Omar said, showed that foreigners were trying to take over the Taliban's "decision-making process . . . [and] they are not even ready to listen to our view point."[17] Omar concluded by declaring, "as a proud Muslim nation we will make our own decisions on the basis of the principles of Islam."[18]

Bin Laden also has deftly and truthfully appealed to the Afghans' perception of themselves as steadfast and pious Islamic rocks upon which infidel ships invariably founder. The United States, bin Laden told his hosts, is not attacking

> Usama, as there are thousands of Usamas in the Muslim world. Their real target is to eliminate the Islamic identity of Afghanistan. The United States should understand that Afghanistan cannot be intimidated. In the last century two of the world's super powers faced defeat here: first the British Empire and then the Soviet Union. Countries that do not take a lesson from history face destruction. Afghanistan is a land of self-respecting Muslims. It cannot be pressured, allured, or intimidated into submission. Personally, I am extremely grateful to the people of Afghanistan and the Taleban that they have allowed me to live here despite facing difficulties. They have entertained me as a guest and taken care of me. It is true that only the Afghans could take this burden. God blessed them with power and ability.[19]

Recognizing the centrality of these Afghan cultural and character traits, it is no surprise that in October 1998 Mullah Omar candidly told *Al-Hayah* that "if I expel bin Laden, it will be the end of me." Buttressing Mullah Omar's analysis, the Afghan paper *Hewad* indignantly noted it was absurd for the Americans to think bin Laden would be surrendered when "the mujahid Afghan nation tolerated every sort of hardship . . . and did not tilt even a hair breadth toward compromise in the struggle against the communist atheist ideology."[20]

Beyond the Afghans' attitude, however, Omar had solid and measurable reasons for not only tolerating but wanting bin Laden to stay in Afghanistan. The most obvious, but not the most important, was the money bin Laden contributed to the Taliban's coffers. It is clear that bin Laden paid for his keep in Afghanistan in the same way he did in Sudan; that is, by helping the Taliban consolidate power. Bin Laden's reputation, persuasiveness, and funds, for example, brought tangible benefit to the Taliban almost as soon as he relocated to Afghanistan. Just after his arrival, *Al-Quds Al-Arabi* has reported, bin Laden visited Hizbi Islami commander Jalaluddin Haqqani—whom he had fought alongside at Khowst late in the 1980s—and convinced him to put his military expertise and fighters into the service of the Taliban, thereby augmenting the professionalism of his own Arab Afghan cadre with Haqqani's leadership skills and veteran insurgents. Then, according to *Newsweek,* bin Laden provided cash that allowed the Taliban in 1996 to buy strategic defections among Masood's commanders "that stripped away Kabul's defenses" and facilitated its capture.[21]

Bin Laden also supplied his hosts "a number of specialized young people to help the Taliban in planning, management, and development of the new state." These professionals helped begin rebuilding the country's war-damaged infrastructure by supervising the building of roads, housing, and irrigation systems in southern and eastern Afghanistan, thereby providing jobs for Afghans and al Qaeda's fighters. It is likely too that these specialists applied modern agricultural methods to poppy cultivation and heroin production.[22] Also, as he did with the National Islamic Front (NIF) in Sudan, bin Laden signed agreements with the Taliban allowing him to start "large-scale businesses" in Afghanistan.[23] The first of these were agricultural projects that profited himself and his hosts. "Osama has managed to take various agricultural farms on lease in Jalalabad . . . and adjacent areas," Peshawar's *Frontier Post* has said. "He has been allowed to export fruit from these farms to the Gulf States, using Peshawar as the transit route. These farms mostly produced olive, lemon, orange and pomegranate. Especially olive, which is in great demand in the Gulf states."[24] If bin Laden was following the tack he used in Sudan, he made partners of many senior Taliban officials, thus giving them a chance to make a buck and another reason to let him stay in Afghanistan.

Bin Laden's Support for the Taliban

After returning to Afghanistan, bin Laden strengthened Mullah Omar's stature—publicly calling Mullah Omar "our chief," pledging loyalty to him as "legitimate ruler of the state of Afghanistan," and describing him as the "embodiment of Islamic respect"—and increased the Taliban's international credibility as an Islamist government. Bin Laden also praised the hospitality, piety, and Islamist purity of his Taliban hosts, and also showed respect for their religious scholars by consulting senior Afghan ulema. "The Taliban have established the rule of Allah in Afghanistan," bin Laden told the Muslim media, "the pious caliphate will start from Afghanistan." This constituted the expected, and in bin Laden's case genuine, politeness and gratitude from a guest, but it also served to paint Mullah Omar and his Taliban lieutenants further into a corner from which escape might well be suicidal. Through public and private words bin Laden established that a Taliban failure to protect him would amount to abandoning Islam and kowtowing to America. In this dual-pronged approach, bin Laden made use of what ABC's John Miller has described as a "public relations apparatus [that] is a sophisticated and complete network of agents and intermediaries."[25]

Bin Laden also repeatedly lectured all Muslims about their duty to help ensure the Taliban's survival. "As it is a religious obligation for every Muslim to support the mujahedin fighting for the freedom of the sacred places," bin Laden said in 1998, "similarly they are also obligated by their religion to support the Taliban government in Afghanistan, because by enforcing Shariat in Afghanistan the Taliban have established the system of God on God's land."[26] In 1999–2000, bin Laden explained the importance of the Taliban regime to the Muslim world and extolled his excellent relations with the regime.

> Any aggression by the United States today against Afghanistan would not be against Afghanistan in itself, but against the Afghanistan that hoists the banner of Islam in the Muslim world, the true, mujahed Islam, which fights for the sake of God. Praised be God our relationship with them [the Taliban] is very strong and deep. This is an ideological relationship, based on doctrine, and not on political or commercial positions. Many states tried to pressure the Taliban, using the carrot and the stick, but God Almighty has made them firm in their stand.
>
> Allah has blessed Afghanistan, the people of Afghanistan, after the crusaders have split it into five sectors to turn them against each other. They were able to unify the country under the Taliban and under the leadership of Amir Mu'imineen [commander of the faithful] Mulanna Omar. So today, Afghanistan is the only country in the world that has the Sharia. Therefore, it is compulsory upon all the Muslims all over the world to help Afghanistan. And to make hijra to this land, because it is from this land that we will dispatch our armies all over the world to smash all kuffar all over the world (and to spread al-Islam).[27]

Another step bin Laden took again had the politically astute impact of securing legitimate religious sanction for his February 1998 anti-U.S. fatwa, thereby reducing the chance of wavering among his Taliban hosts. *Frontline*'s unattributed biography says that bin Laden knew the senior Afghan ulema, or religious scholars, are the "driving force" in Taliban councils and acted to turn this to his advantage. According to the biography, bin Laden built a strong relationship with the Afghan ulema and "lobbied [them] specifically for the subject of American forces in the Arabian Peninsula." As a result, the Afghan ulema issued a May 1998 fatwa "sanctioning the use of all means to expel American forces from the Peninsula."[28] This fatwa gave bin Laden more leverage with the Taliban because it came from the body the Taliban consults to ensure its policies and actions track with Islamic law. And, again, it displayed bin Laden's respect for Islamic scholars by making sure that his future action had credible religious validation.[29]

The most important contributions bin Laden made to Mullah Omar and the Taliban, and the ones the Taliban most valued and could least do without, lay in the military and domestic political spheres. From mid-1996, bin Laden and his senior cadre took control of most of the non-Afghan mujahedin who remained in post-Soviet Afghanistan, as well as those near Peshawar; in fact, *Agence France-Presse* and *Al-Sharq Al-Awsat* have claimed the Taliban required bin Laden to control the fighters as a condition of safe haven in Afghanistan. In any event, the importance of bin Laden's veteran guerrilla fighters to the Taliban war effort has become apparent. As early as the summer of 1997, *Al-Hayah* attributed the slowing of the Northern Alliance's advance toward Kabul to the "stiffening" provided to Taliban forces by bin Laden's fighters. "It was the steadfastness of these fighters in the recent battles," *Al-Hayah* claimed "that halted the advance of the alliance opposed to the Taliban."[30]

Then slowly, over the next two years, bin Laden's forces, through their training activities, leadership, and combat performance, helped turn the tide of the war in the Taliban's favor. Late in 1997, *Al-Hayah* again noted, "the hundreds of Arab fighters associated with bin Laden . . . enabled the Taliban to stop the advance of the anti-Taliban Northern Alliance" north of Kabul.[31] Then, when the Taliban took the offensive in 1998, the *Boston Globe* reported, bin Laden "provided critical support. . . . He trained Taliban fighters and loaned his own personal army to fight along side the Taliban."[32] As the Taliban advanced against the Northern Alliance, the important role of bin Laden's guerrilla cadre was obvious. When the Taliban took Bamiyan Province in September 1998, for example, "Arab fighters loyal to bin Laden reportedly were seen in the front line."[33]

During the Taliban's partially successful summer 1999 offensive in northern Afghanistan, bin Laden's fighters played a spearhead role. At the start of the offensive, Ahme d Rashid wrote in the *Washington Times*, "a brigade of some 400 Arab Islamic militants from a dozen countries in the Middle East, under the control of wanted Saudi terrorist Osama bin Laden, have been moved from the barracks in Rishkor in Kabul and taken up positions along an eight-mile section of the front-line north of the city." In the summer 2000 campaign, moreover, bin Laden's veteran fighters played a pivotal role in the Taliban's capture of Masood's capital of Taloqan in Tahkar Province, as well as in other battles that by winter gave Mullah Omar control of 95 percent of Afghanistan.[34]

Bin Laden also tried to help Mullah Omar in the Byzantine world of Afghan politics. As noted, bin Laden involved himself deeply in trying to reconcile the Afghan resistance parties in the 1990–1991 period, and, while not successful, earned a reputation as an honest broker. After returning to Afghanistan, bin Laden tried to use his reputation and negotiating skills to draw to the Taliban the two major Pashtun leaders — Gulbuddin Hekmatyar and Abdur Rasul Sayyaf — of Masood's overwhelmingly non-Pashtun Northern Alliance. EIJ leader Zawahiri and retired Pakistani intelligence chief Lt. General Hamid Gul, both of whom worked with Hekmatyar and Sayyaf in the Afghan jihad, assisted bin Laden.[35]

Early in 1998, when the Taliban was preparing its spring offensive, bin Laden contacted Hekmatyar, then in exile in Iran, to try to reconcile him with the Taliban.[36] This try was unsuccessful, and bin Laden waited to make another until the Taliban scored some battlefield successes, which made Masood's senior Pashtun colleagues begin to worry about being caught on the wrong side of the fence if the Alliance was decisively defeated. In late 1998, then, bin Laden — in what the *Frontier Post* called an "unexpected move" — renewed his efforts to reconcile Sayyaf and Gulbuddin with the Taliban by sending emissaries to talk to the two Pashtun leaders. The substance of the envoys' talks with bin Laden's former comrades-in-arms is not known. That bin Laden's representatives were received warmly and given a hearing cannot be doubted, however, because "both Hekmatyar and Sayyaf have enjoyed a very close relation with Osama and the two leaders reportedly still had a soft corner for the Saudi dissident."[37]

In January 1999, bin Laden made his first visit to northern Afghanistan since returning from Sudan. His move into what had long been Masood's sphere of influence was made possible, according to *Al-Hayah*, because the area was "under the control of commanders affiliated with the Islamic Party which is led by Gulbuddin Hekmatyar and allied with the Taliban Movement."[38]

Taliban Denunciations of United States

Recognizing bin Laden's vital contributions to the Taliban, motivated by respect for bin Laden and the "respectable lot" of Arab Afghans, and faced by the probably catastrophic consequences of selling out the "great mujahid," Mullah Omar and his aides did the necessary and attacked the United States. In March 1999, Peshawar's *Frontier Post* reported Mullah Omar had written President Bill Clinton to warn of the dangers inherent in another U.S. attack on Afghanistan. "Any attack on Afghanistan will be construed as an attack on our Islamic faith," Omar wrote in terms precisely echoing bin Laden and reflecting Afghan character traits millennia old. "There is virtually nothing in Afghanistan to be destroyed," Omar continued. "You definitely cannot destroy our will, nor [do] we fear death. The only thing we have is our faith in the Almighty God and the Holy Koran. And definitely you would not be able to destroy that faith."[39] Omar's adviser Mowlawi Wakil Ahmed Mutawakil followed with more from bin Laden's script, damning the United States for its double standard in dealing with Muslims. Washington, Mutawakil said, has a standard for those it considers "human beings" and another it "applies to other peoples, especially Muslim peoples. It deals with them as though they are not human beings or even living creatures." Mutawakil summed up the Taliban's decision to stand by bin Laden come what may in *Al-Watan Al-Arabi*. Telling his interviewer "we will never turn him over, since this will turn the Islamic world against us," Mutawakil displayed quintessential Afghan pride, fatalism, and defiance. Mutawakil told the paper that

> Bin Laden lives in Afghanistan under the protection of a special [Taliban] security committee that supervises his residence and ensures his safety. . . . We believe that the continuous U.S. claims against Osama bin Laden are arousing reservations among many Muslims. And if the United States tried to abduct or assassinate him, the whole Islamic world would turn against it. What the U.S. administration cannot imagine is the strong reaction and rivers of blood which would flow if anything evil happens to this man. The United States does not realize that its interests in the whole world will be affected. . . . We do not control bin Laden or impose any ban on him. We provide him with protection and safety, because we know he is wanted. . . . He is not a prisoner. He has full freedom of movement but under Afghan protection.[40]

Mutawakil ended the interview by saying "we believe in what we are doing, although only God is perfect. We apply the teachings of Islam." When asked why the Taliban had not attacked U.S. interests after the 1998 attack and if they would do so if the United States attacked again, Mutawakil said, "We reserve the right to respond with the method and the time of our choice."[41]

Bin Laden's Overtures to Pakistan

As a fail-safe, bin Laden began a four-part policy toward Pakistan that saw him court the main elements of Pakistani society: the military, the politicians, the Islamic establishment, and the media. His goal was to ensure the Taliban's benefactors in then-prime minister Nawaz Sharif's regime did not cut support for, or acquiescence in, Mullah Omar's decision to host him. Bin Laden and his aides worked this plan — which continued after General

Pervez Musharraf and the military deposed Sharif in October 1999 — by publicly praising Pakistan and simultaneously reminding Pakistanis of the history of their often-arrogant treatment by America; by currying favor and purchasing influence in the Pakistani media; and by expanding support from Pakistan's religious elders and Islamist party leaders.

An excellent example of bin Laden singling out Pakistan for praise came after the country's May 1998 nuclear weapons test. In a statement published by *Al-Quds Al-Arabi*, bin Laden congratulated "Muslim" Pakistan at a historic moment, marking the "first time in the history of the Muslims" that they possessed nuclear weapons. "The explosions conducted by Pakistan over recent days have caused a disruption in the international balance and a change in the balance of conflicts," bin Laden said, "which the nations of atheism have been eager to prevent the Islamic nation and all its people from influencing." Saluting Pakistan's achievement, bin Laden stressed that Pakistan's leaders must "strengthen their nuclear power and demonstrate it with full strength," and told all Muslims "to support the jihad of the Pakistani people and the Muslim peoples afflicted by the Indian occupation [of Kashmir]."[42]

Bin Laden also used the test to portray Pakistan as being hurt by the U.S. double standard toward Muslims. "It is very strange," he told *Newsweek*, "if America has all the mass destruction weapons, that is nothing. If the Jewish state has the same weapons, it is OK. But if a Muslim state like Pakistan tries to defend itself against the Hindu hegemony in South Asia, everything should be done to prevent it from doing so." Just after bin Laden's praise and pledge of support — which he complemented by asserting the United States "has started conspiracies against Pakistan whereas it is covertly supporting India"[43] — the newspaper *Pakistan* cited bin Laden's increasing popularity with Pakistanis. In describing bin Laden's support for Pakistan and attacks on "U.S. tyranny," the paper said, with some hyperbole, that the "Pakistani ulema, taleba [religious students], and thousands of young people love Osama bin Laden and are eagerly waiting to sacrifice their lives if he calls. . . . Every Pakistani has accepted Osama bin Laden as his hero."[44]

Much of the favorable popular opinion arose naturally. The Islamization of Pakistan has been gradually accelerating since Moscow's Afghan misadventure began in 1979 and, indeed, has been in train since Lord Mountbatten scuttled the Raj in 1947. In January 2000, for example, the *Nation* warned that Pakistan's "ruling elite [is] gradually succumbing to the ideological onslaught of the conservative ulema, which started soon after the creation of Pakistan." In Pakistan's military forces, the most pivotal subset of Pakistani society, this process was fueled in the ranks and officer corps during General Zia ul-Haq's eleven-year rule (1977–1988) because of Zia's genuine personal piety, his Islamization of Pakistan's legal and economic systems, his official support for the Afghan and Kashmir jihads, and his close ties to Pakistan's religious parties. "Zia was an extremely modest man, and a genuinely religious one," Eric Margolis has written, "[and he] was a passionate Muslim who ardently believed what he said and truly thought of himself as a Muslim soldier, whose duty, as the Koran says, is to defend the Muslim community when it is attacked." Zia's support for the Afghan jihad, moreover, raised the level of religious commitment among military and civilian Pakistanis, increased the stature and power of the country's Islamic scholars, and permitted the unfettered entry of Islamist groups and nongovernmental organizations from across the Muslim world. From a ramshackle beachhead, these groups established a now virtually permanent presence in Pakistan that contributes to the militancy of Islam in Pakistan and rivals the government in the provision of basic social services.[45]

In this hospitable environment, bin Laden and his lieutenants have labored to win the media's favor and respect. After returning to Afghanistan, for example, bin Laden made himself available to Pakistani journalists far more regularly than to any others. In late 1998, bin Laden wrote to a Peshawar editor stressing the vital role of Muslim media in jihad. "We realize that successful journalistic work," bin Laden wrote, "is one of the most important weapons which our [Islamic] nation is armed in its current battle." The Islamic media, bin Laden said, must confront and defeat the West's use of "the largest media machine against us to erase the facts and spread lies in order to deceive our new generations in regard to the nature of the battle and to distract them from the secrets of power." Not willing to rely on moral suasion, there are reports that cash accompanies bin Laden's arguments. *Al-Hayah*, for example, has said bin Laden is "buying off" Pakistani journalists, authors, and publishers to ensure full and favorable media coverage.[46]

Bin Laden also might have used money to influence Pakistani politics. In this realm, former prime minister Benazir Bhutto — herself a reputed past master of corrupt practices — has accused deposed Prime Minister Sharif of using funds from bin Laden to try to defeat her government. Bhutto claimed that bin Laden sent Sharif money in the 1980s "to buy parliamentary deputies for an unsuccessful no-confidence vote to oust her as Pakistani prime minister." This claim was amplified in July 1999 when the Islamabad paper *Al-Akhbar* claimed, "before the elections in 1990, Osama bin Laden's friends and relatives gave Nawaz Sharif one billion rupees." While there is no definitive proof for the claims by Bhutto and *Al-Akhbar*, they are interesting. And it is true, at least from bin Laden's perspective, that Sharif "always played an exemplary role in the Afghan jihad," while Benazir trimmed and tacked as warranted by her political fortunes and the demands of her close American friends. Bin Laden also bitterly complained that Bhutto and her party prevented the Arab Afghans from fighting Indian forces in Kashmir after the Soviets left Afghanistan. "We wanted to go to Kashmir for a jihad after the Afghan jihad ended," bin Laden told Pakistani journalist Abu Shiraz in 1998, "but the People's Party Government in Pakistan did not allow us, but rather arrested a lot of our mujahid brothers from Peshawar and handed them over to the governments concerned on the instructions of the United States."[47] In addition, bin Laden has no use for the democratic system and it is safe to assume he had little use for the concept or reality of a female prime minister in a Muslim country.

With Pakistani public opinion already favorably disposed toward him, the 20 August 1998 U.S. attack on Khowst and the violation of Pakistani airspace it unavoidably entailed gave bin Laden's popularity and anti-U.S. sentiment in Pakistan a substantial and enduring boost. In its 21 August 1998 Lahore edition, for example, the *Nation* said, "a large cross-section of Lahoreites describe him [bin Laden] as a Muslim Hero of modern times. . . . But perhaps in the wake of strong [post–cruise missile strike] anti-American sentiments, which prevail more strongly in the masses, the general perception was that in Osama's taking up arms against the West, they see the resurgence of the era of the Sultan Salahud Din Ayubi [Saladin] who waged a holy war against evil forces."[48]

After touching base with the public and media, bin Laden next sought strategic depth in Pakistan by seeking support from the country's religious elders and most religiously motivated political leaders. The former seem to have been an easy sell, and bin Laden sent his number two, Mohammed Atef, to meet senior Islamic clerics in Muzafarabad, Peshawar, and Karachi to "coordinate positions . . . in the face of U.S. hegemony in the Islamic world."[49] Among the latter, bin Laden's allies in the Harakat al-Mujahedin (HUM) helpfully "decided to spread the 'message' of Osama bin Laden all over Pakistan."[50] The HUM's action was no surprise, because bin Laden had courted the group for years, visiting its senior leaders and exerting "a very powerful hold on the minds of the movement's members." Several HUM fighters had been killed in the 1998 U.S. missile strike on Khowst, where bin Laden has long supported HUM training camps. Bin Laden also sent cadre to join HUM forces in Kashmir, and violently denounced the U.S. government in 1997 when it placed the HUM — then known as the HUA — on its proscribed list of terrorist organizations. At that time, bin Laden said the U.S. action was expected because Americans always work "against an organization fighting for truth and justice." He damned the United States for failing to "see the dishonoring of thousands of Kashmiri Muslim women by Indian security forces," and asked the Muslim world to support the HUA because it "is a mujahid organization which played [a] commendable part in Afghanistan and in Kashmir [and] also is playing an important role in the [international] Islamic jihad." Because of the HUM's post-August 1998 efforts to spread bin Laden's message, according to the *News*, "independent authorities confirmed that audio-taped Arabic speeches of Osama bin Laden with their translation in Urdu and Pashto were being distributed from some mosques in all major cities of the country."[51]

Bin Laden's courting of Pakistan's religious establishment, which fathered the Taliban, had the benefit of keeping the Taliban and Pakistan's politicians on the straight and narrow regarding his residence in Afghanistan. Mullah Omar and many senior Taliban clerics received theological training in Pakistani religious schools, or madrassas, and Pakistan's senior Islamic scholars and jurists will not reject their successful offspring.[52] After the Taliban leaders decided to host and protect bin Laden, their Pakistani mentors could be counted on to keep them up to mark. For example, Shaykh Mufti Nizam al-Din, whom *Al-Quds Al-Arabi* has identified as "the most outstanding authority on the Prophet's sayings in Pakistan," bluntly warned Sharif's government that if it "or any other government helps the Americans against Shaykh Bin Laden, it will be necessary to call for a jihad against these governments and that Muslims should help to overthrow the rulers who help the Americans."[53] The leader of two Islamic universities in Pakistan that have produced at least 30 percent of the Taliban's leaders and thousands of its followers, Maulana Sami al-Haq, also underscored religious support for bin Laden. "For each of the thousands of Pakistani and Afghan Taliban studying in my two universities," Haq said, "Osama bin Laden is an ultimate hero. I can see that our youth are getting desperate to pay back the Americans in their own coin."[54] Finally, in July 1999, a panel of senior Pakistani religious scholars went to Kandahar to make "it clear to Supreme Leader Mullah Omar that [the] Taliban's cooperation with the United States against Osama would affect the Taliban's position."[55]

Musharraf Reverses, bin Laden and Omar Stay the Course

Since the 11 September 2001 attacks in the United States, Pakistani president Pervez Musharraf appears to have taken up permanent residence between the proverbial rock and a hard place. In an effort to avoid American ire and win Western aid for Pakistan's failing economy, Musharraf provided bases from which the U.S. military has attacked bin Laden and took an array of policy gambles that would have stunned the most experienced riverboat gambler. In fewer than ninety days, Musharraf reversed twenty-two years of Pakistani Afghan policy and helped to unseat the first genuinely pro-Pakistan government in Kabul since partition of the subcontinent. He next announced steps to begin backing Pakistan away from its historic support for the jihad in Kashmir, in essence, according to the daily the *Nation*, reversing "54 years of the Kashmir policy" and throwing the "Kashmiris and the Kashmir cause to the wolves."[56] Finally, Musharraf embarked on a program to reduce the political power and armaments of the country's religious parties and mandated changes that would moderate the content of the Islamic education presented by the vast, mujahedin-producing network of religious schools, or madrassas, in Pakistan.

With each of these steps, Musharraf struck at Islam — the core of Pakistan's national identity and the glue that binds its multiethnic society — and he has not yet earned an even remotely acceptable return on his investment. He has won some economic aid, but not enough to stop the economy's deterioration. He also has not been able to pry loose from the United States Pakistan's long bought-and-paid-for F-16s. Thus, his support for the U.S. war on terrorism has not won the expected large-scale benefits. His Afghan policy has been described as "earning Afghanistan's enmity" and nothing else. "With an enemy already to the east of us [India], but now one to the West also," Gauhar Humayun wrote in the *Nation* in November 2001, "Pakistan is the quintessential meat in the sandwich."[57] The goal of Musharraf's moves to tame militant Islam in Pakistan have received some positive domestic response, but they are increasingly opposed because they are being characterized as kowtowing to the Americans, who, the prestigious daily *Nawa-I-Waqt* argued, "will try to target the jihadi organizations and the religious seminaries in Pakistan by declaring them as terrorist camps."[58] Adding to Musharraf's troubles, New Delhi has befriended the new regime in Kabul — a historic Pakistani dread — and is trying to coerce Musharraf into placing more drastic and humiliating limits on Pakistan's Islamists and the Kashmiris by staging an unprecedented military mobilization that has the subcontinent on the brink of war.

Can Musharraf make his changes stick, bring the country's ardent, well-armed Islamists to heel, re-create an ally in Kabul, and avoid a war with India? Who knows? It is not even clear, given Musharraf's survival and minimal civil unrest in Pakistan, that his radical policy shifts are pinching those they are aimed at as severely as is believed in the West. What is clear, however, is that bin Laden, Mullah Omar, and the Taliban are betting Musharraf's policies are a stopgap that will fail and that he will end up backtracking or ousted. In a situation where bin Laden and Omar could rightly feel betrayed, they carefully have avoided condemning Pakistan for its actions and limited themselves to criticizing Musharraf in a nonthreatening manner. "We realize that Pakistan changed its Afghan policy under pressure from the U.S.," the Taliban minister of education said more in sorrow than anger. "But we didn't expect the Pakistani government to start a propaganda against the Taliban after remaining our friend for years."[59] Even the deposed Taliban leader sought only to shame Musharraf. "It is a matter of regret," Omar said of Musharraf's policies, "for those who have turned their backs on Islam and the proud history of their ancestors and turned their face toward the Americans."[60] Joining the Taliban to make sure no bridges to Pakistan are destroyed, bin Laden gently dismissed Musharraf — saying that he "disappointed us . . . and will receive punishment from God and the Pakistani people" — and asserted that the Islamization of Pakistan cannot be reversed and that he was sure Pakistanis remained on his side and the Taliban's.[61] He also reiterated that "Pakistan is the first line of defense of Islam in this region," and reassured Pakistanis that "we will not let the 'Pakistani land and its people' stand alone" if they are attacked.[62]

12

BIN LADEN IN AFGHANISTAN: TARGETING AMERICA AND EXPANDING AL QAEDA

There are cases which cannot be overdone by language, and this is one. There are persons, too, who see not the full extent of the evil which threatens them; they solace themselves with hopes that the enemy, if he succeed, will be merciful. It is the madness of folly to expect mercy from those who have refused to do justice; and even mercy, where conquest is the object, is only a trick of war; the cunning of the fox is as murderous as the violence of the wolf, and we ought to guard equally against them both.

Thomas Paine, *The American Crisis,* 23 December 1776

As they did when they were based in Sudan, bin Laden and his lieutenants worked from their Afghan headquarters to expand al Qaeda's international presence and to increase the range and lethality of its military capabilities. Central to this effort was bin Laden's struggle to reorient the targeting of his allies, especially the Gama'at and the Egyptian Islamic Jihad (EIJ). In the 1980s and most of the 1990s, the ambitions of Sunni Islamist insurgent and terrorist organizations were overwhelmingly aimed against individual nations. The Egyptian groups wanted to overthrow the Sadat and Mubarak regimes, the Algerians wanted to destroy the secular government in Algiers, the Afghans wanted their country back from the Soviet and Afghan Communists, the Moro Islamic Liberation Front (MILF) and Abu Sayyaf wanted

Mindanao for an independent Islamic homeland in the Philippines, and some of the Kashmiris wanted an independent nation, not an entity that would be folded into Pakistan. All the groups fought in the name of Allah, the Prophet Mohammed, and the Koran, but their goals were nation specific; they did not conceive or claim, at this stage, that they were fighting to restore the freedom and dignity of the ummah, the borderless worldwide Muslim community. That would come later, after the defeat of what the Koran described as the "near enemy."

Refocusing on America

Bin Laden has long opposed the Islamists' focus on defeating individual national governments and consistently has argued that for Muslims "geographical boundaries have no importance," adding that it is "incumbent on all Muslims to ignore these borders and boundaries, which the kuffar have laid down between Muslim lands, the Jews and the Christians, for the sole purpose of dividing us." In the context of these words, an "Arab intellectual" who claims to be a friend of bin Laden has said, "bin Laden himself comes from a generation that dreams of one Arab nation united by Islam. If he survives the next few years, he will be the most important example for the jihadist movement, equal to Khomeni. All revolutionary jihadist armies respect him."[1] In Afghanistan, then, after May 1996, bin Laden would prove he had moved past aiming for "an Arab nation united by Islam" and now aspired to unite the ummah and "remove Americans from all Muslim land." In late 1996 bin Laden told *Al-Quds Al-Arabi* that "I am not addressing the sons of the [Arabian] peninsula only; U.S. interests exist throughout the Islamic world."[2]

In reality, bin Laden started the framework for an international organization in the early 1980s when he began, as he told British journalist Robert Fisk, to move "not hundreds but thousands" of Muslim volunteers to fight in Afghanistan.[3] As noted, bin Laden built a unique, multiethnic organization that includes not just Arabs but Muslims from the world over. When forging this organization, bin Laden first addressed the Egyptian Gama'at al-Islamiyya (IG) and the Egyptian Islamic Jihad (EIJ), his most militarily proficient allies.

Bin Laden began pushing for the unification of the IG and the EIJ during the Afghan jihad. By mid-1996, the two groups were talking, but unity remained elusive, as it does today. At that point, bin Laden's efforts toward uniting the two organizations suffered a sharp blow when al Qaeda's military commander, Abu Ubaydah, drowned in Uganda's Lake Victoria. Abu Ubaydah had been bin Laden's agent for resolving the IG-EIJ conflict and was the author of the concept of a multiethnic "Islamic Army" with the united Egyptian groups at its core.[4]

Faced with each group's recalcitrance, and minus the solvent Abu Ubaydah brought to intra-Egyptian problems, bin Laden appears to have changed tack and to have tried to focus EIJ and IG attacks on U.S. interests, perhaps hoping that by doing so the groups would move closer together notwithstanding their divergent views on theology, leadership, and targets. According to EIJ leader al-Najjar, bin Laden put his point to the EIJ and IG leaders in a simple manner. "I myself heard bin Laden say," al-Najjar told Egyptian authorities, "that our main objective is limited to one state only, the United States, and involves waging a guerrilla war against all U.S. interests not only in the Arab region but also throughout the world, and that this operation on the whole would ultimately force the United States and those gravitating within its sphere to review their policies toward the Islamic groups."[5] Al-Najjar said bin Laden believed

The Jewish lobby controlled the United States and [this] was the reason for the weakness of Muslim peoples and governments and that removing this [American] hegemony must be a principal objective. Therefore, one of the front's primary objectives was to rid Arab and Islamic territories of U.S. hegemony by launching a guerrilla war targeting all U.S. interests, not only in Arab and Islamic countries, but worldwide. The purpose of these operations was to compel the United States and those who help it to review their policies on Arab and Islamic issues. This meant that the front's objective was to direct U.S. policy. Bin Laden also believes that the achievement of this objective, despite his weak resources and small forces compared to the Arab and Islamic resources and armies, will show the extent of these countries' weakness.[6]

Al-Najjar's description of bin Laden's U.S.-focused policy is seconded by Abd al-Bari Atwan of *Al-Quds Al-Arabi,* who interviewed bin Laden after he returned to Afghanistan. In June 1999 Atwan told Qatar's Al-Jazirah television

I felt that the man [bin Laden] had his own vision and special strategy. This strategy is based on his concept of the region. The first point in his strategy is that the U.S. administration or U.S. forces, which he considers occupation forces in the Gulf and the Arabian Peninsula, are a prelude to a comprehensive Israeli-Jewish hegemony over the region with the aim of looting its wealth and humiliating its Muslim people. One senses that this is the essence of his creed and strategy. Therefore, he believes that expelling the U.S. forces from the Arab world is a top priority. He believes that the regimes [in the Muslim world] should be reformed or, more cor-

rectly, changed. The regimes immune to reform should be changed.
. . . This is a summary of his strategy. Currently, he does not want
to fight the regimes. That is what he told me. He wants to fight the
Americans, who are protecting the regimes.[7]

Bin Laden pitched the America-first policy hardest and with most success to EIJ leader Zawahiri and his colleagues, particularly with EIJ military chief Muhammad Muhandis Zawahiri, Aiman's younger brother and a popular, influential figure in the group. Still, the elder Zawahiri faced stiff opposition from many in the EIJ over his intention to drop the group's historic Egypt-first orientation. "Some Jihad leaders," *Al-Hayah* reported, "objected to al-Zawahiri's insistence on cooperating with bin Laden, saying that that had caused the Jihad group to deviate from its main aim [establishing an Islamic state in Egypt through a military coup] and pushed the organization into battle with the United States, a battle whose results include the U.S. intelligence service's pursuit of the organization's elements over more than one state."[8]

That Zawahiri prevailed was verified by EIJ fighter al-Najjar. "He [al-Najjar] confirmed," *Al-Hayah* said in early 1999, "that these two [bin Laden and Zawahiri] are now cooperating to confront U.S. tyranny and injustice. . . . He [al-Najjar] said that he expects more operations against U.S. targets in the coming stage."[9] Another EIJ fighter, Nabil Nuaym, told an Egyptian court "operations against the officials and installations in Egypt would gradually decline until they disappear" because "experience has shown that action inside Egypt is extremely costly."[10] In July 1998 Zawahiri foreshadowed al-Najjar's confirmation of the EIJ's shift in focus using phrases echoing bin Laden. "America insists on humiliating the [Muslim] nation, robbing its resources, and imposing sanctions on it" the EIJ chief said. "Therefore the only choice that is available to the Muslim nation is to wage a holy war against America and Israel."[11]

The persuasiveness of bin Laden's worldview was strengthened by the more nuts-and-bolts arguments he made to Zawahiri. Bin Laden told Zawahiri, for example, that he believed "operations against Americans and Israelis would widen the scope for Islamists' actions," and that "announcing U.S. interests are the targets and then carrying out operations against them will boost Arab and Islamic morale." Bin Laden also told Zawahiri that attacks in Egypt were hurting the EIJ and making it less effective militarily. Al-Najjar has said bin Laden did this in strong terms because he had "reservations" about attacks in Egypt instead of against the United States and even showed "displeasure whenever Jihad members carried out operations inside Egypt." Bin Laden argued that attacks on Americans

were economically better, since any operation against an American or Israeli target would need only a few persons, while Jihad's operations inside Egypt required huge amounts of money to buy and smuggle weapons, shelter the perpetrators, and then smuggle [them] out of the country, and [the] care of their families in addition to taking care of the other families of other Islamists usually arrested by Egyptian authorities whenever one of the operations was carried out inside the country.[12]

For Zawahiri it was tough to deny bin Laden had the better of the argument, but, as will be seen, the cost of bin Laden's war in 1997–1998 was severe for al Qaeda and its allies in terms of disrupted cells and captured fighters. As a result, then, of bin Laden's urgings and the high financial and human costs of attacks in Egypt, Zawahiri concurred and after an EIJ fighter was killed in September 1998 resisting arrest in Tirana, Albania — in a police action the EIJ says was "run by U.S. intelligence" — the EIJ issued a statement that clearly displayed movement toward an "America First" orientation. Praising the courage of the slain fighter, the EIJ statement claimed the Americans had killed him because he "refused to yield to its [U.S.] arrogance and to keep silent about its aggression against his religion and nation." "We too have learned the lesson [from the fighter's death], praise be to God, Lord of the worlds," the statement said, and "we call on our Muslim brothers to learn the lesson with us; let us all fight this Crusader onslaught on Islam. . . . We consider the United States primarily responsible for all these crimes, and thus it has to bear the bulk of the retaliation."[13]

Bin Laden's success with the Gama'at has been much less complete. Although he has spent a decade trying to win the group's loyalty and promoting reconciliation with the EIJ, he has not enjoyed with the IG the "extremely special" relationship he has had with Zawahiri's group.[14] That said, bin Laden has continued cultivating the Gama'at. He has been, for example, a frequent and outspoken advocate of imprisoned IG spiritual leader Shaykh Rahman. "The imprisonment of Shaykh Omar is an attack on the Muslim religion and countries," bin Laden said. "He is a Muslim scholar well-known all over the Muslim world. He represents the kind of injustice that is adopted by the U.S. A baseless case was fabricated against him even though he is a blind old man. . . . He is now very badly treated and [is treated] in no way fit for an old man like him or any Muslim scholar."[15] Bin Laden also has been taking care of Shaykh Rahman's two eldest sons for several years, and suspected Nairobi embassy bomber Mohammed Sadiq Odeh has said that bin Laden "treats [Shaykh] Omar's sons as his own children."[16] He also has hosted such IG luminaries as Mohammed Shawqi Islambouli and senior IG leader Rifa'i Taha in Afghanistan and has long worked closely with current IG chief Mustafa Hamza.

These ties notwithstanding, most IG leaders remain determined to keep an arm's-length relationship with bin Laden. There are several reasons for this decision. First, the IG leaders still resent the EIJ's theologically justified refusal to accept Shaykh Rahman's leadership because he is blind; the EIJ made sure the anger would run long and deep by publishing a sixty-four-page anti-Rahman indictment titled "The Case for the Ineligibility of a Blind Man to Govern," which contained "arguments based on the Koran, the Prophet's teachings, and Islamic legal rulings." Second, the IG believes that bin Laden has given too much prominence to Zawahiri and the EIJ; the IG is larger and historically has been more militarily active in Egypt. Third, the IG suffered many fewer significant losses than the EIJ in the late 1990s and so felt less need to shelter under bin Laden's wing. Fourth, the IG's roots are more populist and rural than the EIJ's and its Egypt-centric focus — the IG has reasserted its belief that "the liberation of Jerusalem begins with the liberation of Cairo" — consequently is more durable.[17]

A final reason for bin Laden's not-fully successful wooing of the Gama'at lies in its internal disarray. Since 1997, the group has been embroiled in an internal battle between some overseas leaders and IG members known as the "historic leaders." The latter founded the group and/or participated in the attack on Sadat, have long been jailed in Egypt, and sparked the imbroglio with a 5 July 1997 call for a cease-fire in Egypt and abroad. Bin Laden, in the midst of the intra-Egyptian acrimony — Zawahiri's EIJ roundly condemned the IG's decision to stop fighting — caused by the cease-fire call, took advantage of an unexpectedly auspicious media environment to announce, on 23 February 1998, the founding of the "World Islamic Front against Jews and Crusaders." This media opportunity had surfaced because it appeared certain the United States and the United Kingdom would resume aerial attacks on Iraq because it was again blocking weapons of mass destruction (WMD) inspections. Although the strikes were not launched, bin Laden's fatwa designated the United States as the front's primary target, justifying this decision by citing "the Americans' continuing aggression against the Iraqi people, using the [Arabian] Peninsula as a staging base." The fatwa was signed by bin Laden, EIJ chief Zawahiri, Shaykh Mir Hamza of Pakistan's Jamaat Islami party, Fazul Rahman of the Jihad Movement in Bangladesh, and the IG's Taha. Later, when criticized by the IG's historic leaders, Taha claimed that he had signed for himself and not on behalf of the Gama'at.[18]

While not a stellar list of signatories aside from bin Laden and the Egyptians — Algerians, Somalis, Sudanese, Kashmiris, and Afghans are notably absent — the fatwa provided focus and, as bin Laden explained, would be "an umbrella to all organizations fighting the jihad against Jews and Crusaders." It also could be that bin Laden again was trying to moderate intra-Egyptian quarreling by focusing them on U.S. targets, to put America on the bull's-eye of all Islamists, and to create what *Al-Watan Al-Arabi* called "an organizational configuration" regularizing "past ad hoc cooperation among the groups."[19]

Islamist reaction to formation of the World Islamic Front sympathized with bin Laden's aims — particularly for attacking the United States — but displayed reluctance to sign on with bin Laden until more groups joined. It also exhibited a continuing preference for destroying national regimes before attacking the United States. From the United Kingdom, the Vanguards of Conquest, an EIJ faction, called the creation of the front "a step forward and in the right direction," but asked bin Laden to "expand its membership to include other tendencies on the scene . . . [and] all colors of the fundamentalist movement wishing to join such an alliance in the Arab and Islamic worlds."[20] In regard to the proper priority target for the front — either the United States or what Sa'd al-Faqih has called the "unjust governments in the region"[21] — several U.K.-based Sunni extremist leaders differed with bin Laden. The U.K.-based Al-Mujahroun leader and bin Laden advocate, Omar Bakri Mohammed, agreed that an "international army — Mohammed's Army" must be formed, but said it first should be used "to combat occupying governments."[22] Also from London, Shaykh Abu Hamzah al-Masri, the Egyptian leader of the Followers of the Sharia, said, "We all agree with bin Laden on the issue of hitting the Americans and their bases. But I differ with him over one issue, namely that it is the ruling regimes that must be fought first because they are the ones letting the Americans run amok in our countries and then a war of attrition on the Americans will follow the war on the regimes."[23]

Bin Laden also encountered resistance closer to home. The chief of Pakistan's hard-line Sunni party Lashkar-i-Tayyaba, Professor Hafiz Mohammed Saeed, simply told the editors of *Ausaf*, "The Holy Koran has set the itinerary for the holy war. It asks Muslims to start their holy war with those infidels who live nearby. Therefore, our first target should be India, according to the Holy Koran." More recently, Maulana Masood Azhar — the Harakat al-Mujahedin (HUM) leader freed in December 1999 in return for the release of a hijacked Air India aircraft — told cheering crowds in Pakistan that war against India is the first order of business. "I need mujahedin who can fight for the liberation of Kashmir," Azhar said in January 2000. "So marry for jihad, give birth for jihad and earn money only for jihad till the cruelty of America and India ends. But India first."[24]

Despite the lack of unanimous support among Islamist leaders for the World Front's U.S.-first focus, bin Laden did successfully alert the Muslim world to a new pole around which anti-American sentiment could rally. In addition, Zawahiri's allegiance to the front signaled bin Laden's success in getting the militarily proficient EIJ to refocus on the U.S. target.[25] EIJ fighter Ibrahim al-Najjar and other "Returnees from Albania" have said that at bin Laden's request, the Jihad's leaders "expanded the scope of their targets. They stopped limiting them to Egyptian and Arab figures and included the interests of the major powers, especially U.S. and French."[26] The expansion apparently was rapid and successful, because EIJ operatives would play roles in attacking the U.S. embassies in Nairobi and Dar es Salaam later in 1998.[27]

The primacy of U.S. targets, moreover, gave bin Laden yet another chance to make hay in terms of publicity. Captured bin Laden operative Said Salamah has told an Egyptian court that bin Laden believed that "targeting these countries' interests was bound to have massive media value, and [that] this would confirm the organization's capabilities, which some quarters had begun to doubt." Salamah also said the list of targeted U.S. interests was not limited to "blowing up installations" but now also "included the kidnapping of figures and hostages."[28] Salamah's claim of expanded targeting is supported by an August 1998 World Front communiqué that said the list of U.S. and Israel targets now includes plans to "bring down their aircraft; prevent the safe passage of their ships; orchestrate occupation of their embassies; [and] force the closure of American and Israeli companies and banks."[29]

Expanding al Qaeda's Reach

After creating the World Front, bin Laden and his lieutenants continued to expand al Qaeda's international reach. This expansion occurred in the organization's worldwide physical presence, its and bin Laden's reputation, and the degree of international awareness of the existence, activities, and goals of both. Where once bin Laden and al Qaeda had been on the scope of world governments in a general, media-driven way — bin Laden as *Time's* shadowy "Paladin of the Jihad" and the *Independent's* stealthy "Anti-Soviet Warrior"[30] — by mid-1999 bin Laden was counted among the top enemies of the United States, the West, Israel, and the Muslim regimes cooperating with them. By summer 1999, moreover, Osama bin Laden's name had been added to the FBI's internationally known "10 Most Wanted List" — a hybrid combination, one supposes, of a Bedouin Dillinger and a more ambitious, less precise Unabomber — and a former senior U.S. government counterterrorism official was bemoaning Washington's portrayal of bin Laden: "He's 10 feet tall, he's everywhere, he knows everything, he's got lots of money, and he can't be challenged."[31]

From mid-1996, bin Laden and his allies are reported to have established a "new" presence, or, alternatively, various national security authorities have discovered their presence, in countries in Africa, Asia, Europe, the Gulf, and East Asia. From late 1996, for example, the media reported that bin Laden's organization in Albania has contacts with Muslims in Fiji; that he "has his sights set on Kashmir" and is funding "three fundamentalist groups now well-entrenched in West Bengal"; that he sent an Iraqi operative named Hamoud Abaid al-Anezi to recruit Muslims in Melbourne, Australia, to "join a jihad . . . in Kosovo and Chechnya"; that he was sponsoring the paramilitary training of Malaysian Muslims in the Philippines; that he had a network of supporters in Mauritania; that he was active in Bangladesh and had established a cell in Jordan; and that he "is planning to turn Kuwait into a major center of extremist fundamentalists in the region."[32] As if this was not enough, bin Laden had associates in the United Kingdom who "concentrated their efforts on recruiting volunteers to fight in China . . . to support the Uighur Muslims who are being persecuted and oppressed by the Chinese government"; he was "planning a future reliance on Eritrean [Islamic] groups"; the alleged planner of the Nairobi embassy bombing was from the Comoro Islands, suggesting a presence in the Indian Ocean; retired Iraqi military officers trained bin Laden-related fighters in northern Nigeria and EIJ operatives collected information about and monitored "U.S. installations and interests" in that country; and he has sent "Egyptians, Saudis, Algerians, Tunisian, Sudanese, and Kuwaiti fundamentalists . . . to back the Kosovo Liberation Army."[33] As the ever-cheeky, but cleared-eyed John Miller has written, in today's world "wherever Muslims are in trouble, it seems, Usama Bin Ladin will be there, slaying enemies, real or perceived. A modern nightmare really — a big-screen villain, a free-lancer with the resources of a state, but without all the nasty obligations."[34]

Whether bin Laden did all the things noted above is unknowable, but some exaggeration is likely. He could not have been everywhere at once. That said, bin Laden did not receive much media ink until the first World Trade Center bombing in February 1993, and then only small amounts until al Qaeda bombed the Office of Program Management-Saudi Arabian National Guard (OPM-SANG) building in Riyadh in November 1995. Thus, bin Laden enjoyed nearly sixteen years of virtual anonymity in which he went about his business largely unnoticed and unimpeded. In addition, bin Laden and Zawahiri appear to have expanded al Qaeda not only to project power, but also to disperse assets, thereby making it more flexible and redundant and thus more difficult for its foes to strike a truly disabling blow. In July 1999 *Al-Sharq Al-Awsat* reported "the group is based on the idea of spreading the organization with the aim of scattering the Western and Arab intelligence services' activities. If one or more of these services scores some successes from time to time, the group's own infrastructure prepares it to resume its activities because it is capable of growing and multiplying." While the precise dimensions of al Qaeda's international organization are unclear, it is accurate to say that bin Laden expanded an already-substantial al Qaeda presence in Somalia and the Philippines. Both merit attention because they have been cited as likely emergency safe havens for bin Laden if he chooses, or is forced, to leave Afghanistan.[35]

Al Qaeda Expansion in Somalia

Africa has remained a high-interest locale for bin Laden since the 1994 withdrawal of UN and U.S. forces from Somalia, and his operatives have remained active there in — at least — Sudan, Somalia, Morocco, South Africa, Libya, Algeria, Mauritania, Nigeria, Madagascar, Uganda, Ethiopia, and Eritrea.[36] Given al Qaeda's August 1998 attacks in Kenya and Tanzania, bin Laden obviously has strong bases in each of those countries. Somalia, however, seems a case apart, and bin Laden expended sizable amounts of time, money, and manpower to expand there after he returned to Afghanistan. At his death in 1996, according to the U.K.-based journal *Al-Hawadith,* Abu Ubaydah left a strong al Qaeda presence in Africa, although the article exaggerates when it says he created a formal "federation of African fundamentalist groups, which rallied financially and organizationally around bin Laden's al Qaeda banner."[37] What seems fair to say is that Abu Ubaydah built a mature al Qaeda presence in Kenya, Tanzania, Sudan, and a growing infrastructure in Somalia. Bin Laden's still-functioning infrastructure in Sudan, for example, is now more than a decade old, and there is every chance that his organization in Kenya is still active — at least in the port of Mombassa — notwithstanding the September 1997 departure of Wadih el-Hage and the arrest of some cell members after the August 1998 bombing. Somalia, however, now seems the focus of al Qaeda's efforts in Africa.

In Somalia, the media have reported that anywhere from a few dozen to a few hundred of bin Laden's Arab Afghans remained in and around Mogadishu after UN and U.S. forces departed.[38] The stay-behinds' mission appears threefold. First, to consolidate and expand the Somali base al Qaeda built while attacking UN forces; second, to expand its liaison with armed Somali Islamist groups; and, third, to reach out from Somalia and build al Qaeda's organization elsewhere in Africa.[39]

To secure al Qaeda's Somali base, bin Laden's fighters focused on backing Farah Aideed's son Husyan and supporting al-Ittehad-i-Islami (AII), or the Islamic Unity Party.[40] The political chaos and physical devastation left in Somalia after the civil war and UN intervention made the groups eager for bin Laden's financial and military support as they compete for supremacy in Somalia.[41] Over the past several years, bin Laden's Somalia-based force reportedly has risen to between four hundred and two thousand fighters, and there are reports of senior bin Laden lieutenants — most frequently the IG's Mustafa Hamza — visiting the country to survey al Qaeda's progress in Africa and the needs of its Somali allies.[42] In May 1999, *Al-Sharq Al-Awsat* said al Qaeda was setting up a camp near the coastal town of Raas Kamboni and was installing sophisticated communications there.[43] In addition, bin Laden's fighters reportedly have built "structures and training camps in the region of Gedo, near the border between Somalia and Ethiopia," and possibly are trying to acquire and mine some of the abundant and mostly unexploited uranium deposits in northern Somalia.[44] Al Qaeda also appears to use Somalia as a base for dealing with the Eritrean Islamic Jihad, taking advantage of the unstable politics yielded by the 1998–1999 Great Lakes war to contact Islamists in central Africa, and supplying weapons to al Qaeda operatives in Kenya.[45]

In Somalia, al Qaeda now has close ties to the AII guerrilla organization and to an Islamist grouping called the United Front for the Liberation of Western Somalia (UF), consisting of the AII, the Western Somali Liberation Front, and the Somali Peoples' Liberation Front.[46] Al Qaeda provides unspecified support to the AII and in return trains some of its fighters in UF camps, which the West watches far less closely than those in Sudan, Yemen, and Afghanistan.[47] Formation of the UF began in late 1996 after the Ethiopian army made cross-border "preemptive strikes" on AII bases in Somalia. According to *Al-Awsat,* the August 1996 Ethiopian raids on the AII "almost broke its back"; the Ethiopians also claimed to have "apprehended . . . a number of 'Afghan Arabs' who were financed by Osama bin Laden" and who were serving with the AII. After this setback, the AII joined the two above-mentioned groups to form the UF, which was created "with the recommendation of Osama bin Laden," who also "facilitated the arrival of a group of his followers in southern Somalia and financed their purchase of sophisticated weapons" to assist the UF's organizational efforts. Bin Laden's aid, according to *Al-Awsat,* has been effective to the point where "the Islamic groups . . . have indeed regained their strength."[48] Bin Laden's support for the Somali Islamists has ensured three things: Al Qaeda has a force in being and a base for staging attacks in Africa; bin Laden has a potential personal safe haven there; and he has earned the enmity of the Eritrean and Ethiopian governments. Ethiopia, in particular, is bin Laden's foe, because al Qaeda has "carried out operations in Ethiopia, especially in its capital Addis Ababa."[49]

Al Qaeda Expansion in the Philippines

The Philippines has received steady attention from bin Laden since 1996, at least, in part, because the insurgency there is the only Muslim one that is directly fighting the ascendancy of what al Qaeda would classify as a crusading Catholic power. His forces have had a presence there since the late 1980s, largely through the charitable, business, and subversive activities of his brother-in-law, Mohammed Jamal Khalifah.[50] The Philippine media say bin Laden visited the islands several times, acquired investments there, and still "owns three businesses in the country."[51] Manila authorities have long been aware of bin Laden's activities in their country, recognizing that it has become "a refuge for Afghan Arabs who fled Afghanistan."[52] Even before bin Laden left Sudan, for example, the Filipinos accused him of "supporting the Abu Sayyaf Group (ASG)" through Khalifah's Manila-based business and charitable activities.[53] In 1995, moreover, the *Philippine Daily Inquirer* reported that Khalifah had been serving as ASG "operations officer" since 1992. Subsequently, the myriad terrorist planning activities of Ramzi

Yousef and Wali Khan in Manila have been linked to bin Laden and Khalifah.[54] Most recently, one of the convicted attackers of the U.S. embassy in Nairobi, Muhammed Sadiq, told Pakistani interrogators there is a "significant presence of Osama's followers in the Philippines . . . and that he [Sadiq] had been sent to the Philippines to 'oversee' some work."[55]

Since late 1998, the pace of al Qaeda-related activities in the Philippines has picked up. In September 1998, for example, Khalifah sent a close associate and fellow Saudi businessman named Hussain Mustafa to assess the needs and provide support to the Moro Islamic Liberation Front (MILF) at the group's Abu Bakr camp, then its main military base in Mindanao. Quoting unnamed Philippine military sources, the *Manila Times* said Mustafa delivered funds to the MILF that have been "used to set up an international satellite communications system" in the Abu Bakr camp, and to "set up the MILF web page in [*sic*] the Internet."[56] It is unclear how much of the communications equipment survived the 1999–2001 battles around the Abu Bakr camp, but the Internet site is still operating.

Also in 1998, the Manila media reported that the Philippine military was monitoring a new group called the "Salafiyah Fighters." According to the report, the military believed the group was founded by Khalifah, was staffed by Muslim fighters from the ASG, and was training Malaysians in its camps.[57] Then, in February 1999 *Agence France-Presse* reported that bin Laden was funding the delivery of "3,000 high-powered weapons" to the Moros. "The shipment to the MILF," the *AFP* correspondent said, "is believed to have been procured using money provided by Saudi dissident Osama bin Laden, who Manila has said was sending aid to accredited Islamic relief operations in the Philippines."[58]

The use of Islamic nongovernmental organizations (NGOs) for cover also suggests Khalifah's involvement. Interestingly, *Jane's Intelligence Review* noted in May 1998 that the MILF was short of weapons despite the ease with which ordnance can be smuggled into Mindanao. *Jane's* conjectured that the MILF might not have enough funds to purchase weapons, and it may well be that bin Laden has now rectified that problem. In March 2000, for example, the Philippine defense secretary told the media that the MILF had expanded its arsenal of firearms from three thousand in 1997 to more than eleven thousand currently. These press stories cut close to the bone, and MILF leader Hashim Salamat — who was schooled at Al-Ahzar in Cairo and trained in Afghan camps tied to bin Laden[59] — felt compelled to respond to the allegations.

At the MILF leader's press conference, the *Philippine Star* said, Salamat confirmed his group "received funds from bin Laden, but eventually decided that they could carry on their crusade without the aid." The *Star* said Salamat described bin Laden's aid as benign and, while not saying how much bin Laden money he was given, explained "[that] the funds were spent on building mosques, health centers, and schools in poor Muslim areas of Mindanao, and denied that any of the aid went to the purchase of firearms and ammunition." Salamat, of course, failed to say that bin Laden money spent on social welfare and religious activities freed other funds for MILF military activities.[60]

As in Somalia, bin Laden's involvement in Mindanao is meant to assist local Islamists and to afford al Qaeda a contingency safe haven. In a pinch, the island would be attractive to bin Laden as a large, geographically isolated, and easily defended stronghold. In addition, the Arab Afghans have a decade-old presence there, the island's Moro Islamist insurgent groups are strong and growing, and businesses and NGOs with ties to bin Laden and Khalifah are present in several locations in the Philippines. Mindanao's vast and porous coastline and its proximity to Indonesia and Malaysia, moreover, would ensure al Qaeda ease of access and egress, resupply, and contact with other Islamist fighters and supporters in the Far East.

Al Qaeda and the State Sponsors

There is no persuasive reporting or analysis showing that bin Laden and al Qaeda are dependent on any state for essential material or logistic support, although the ease with which al Qaeda operatives have moved internationally suggests some regimes have turned a blind eye to transiting fighters as a quid pro quo for not having attacks occur on their territory. That said, bin Laden has had to deal with several states designated by the United States as "state sponsors" of terrorism, or at least has had to recognize they share a hatred for the United States and Israel. Of the three state sponsors al Qaeda must factor into its planning and intentions—Sudan, Iran, and Iraq—ties to Sudan are the most developed, public, and understandable. Bin Laden left Sudan on good terms with NIF leader al-Turabi—although al-Turabi's political star has since declined—and media reports indicate several of his businesses continue operating profitably there; that al Qaeda, EIJ, and IG fighters still live in or transit Sudan; and that bin Laden remains a partner in the NIF's Al-Shimal Bank.[61]

While not holding identical views on applying Islam, al-Turabi and bin Laden share the identical anti-U.S. animosities; al-Turabi's 1995 warning to the Islamic world that the Crusades are not over and "the enemy is America . . . if we are challenged militarily, we will have to fight back" could as easily have come from bin Laden.[62] In a February 1998 letter to Sudanese president Umar Hassan Bashir—who was rumored to have forced bin Laden out of Sudan—bin Laden reaffirmed his support for him against "the international Christian crusade [which] is rushing madly against our country Sudan and against the heart of the Islamic world."[63]

Bin Laden has genuinely supported the NIF's efforts to expand the sway of Islam in the Horn of Africa, but his remarks in recent years also seem—like some he has made supporting the Taliban—to be meant to associate Sudan with al Qaeda and its goals. In September 1998, for example, bin Laden told a conference of religious scholars in Pakistan that the August 1998 U.S. cruise missile strikes were not aimed at him. "After all," bin Laden asked the scholars, "why did the United States carry out attacks on Afghanistan and Sudan? This is because the youths of these two countries are determined to implement Islam in their countries, and this is why the United States is against them."[64] Bin Laden later again said the U.S. attack on Sudan was not aimed at him. "The United States bombed it [the el-Shifa pharmaceutical plant in Khartoum] without the slightest proof," bin Laden explained, "because [President] Clinton wanted to hide his misdemeanors and resorted to massacring Muslims because in his eyes their blood is cheap." Finally, bin Laden has vehemently denounced Western support for the anti-NIF military operations of John Garang's primarily Christian guerrillas. In justifying the August 1998 East Africa bombings, for example, bin Laden said the United States was using its Nairobi embassy as a base to create "the gangs of [the] criminal Garang, in order to divide Sudan, to separate its south from its north, to block the efforts to implement God's law, and to kill and starve thousands of Muslim women, children, and old men. The [Garang-led] mutiny in Sudan has almost allowed the Westerners to control Sudan so that their forces are less than 280 kilometers from Mecca."[65]

Regarding Iraq, bin Laden, as noted, was in contact with Baghdad's intelligence service since at least 1994. (See p. 134.) He reportedly cooperated with it in the area of chemical-biological-radiological-nuclear (CBRN) weapons and may have trained some fighters in Iraq at camps run by Saddam's anti-Iran force, the Mujahedin e-Khalq (MEK). The first group of bin Laden's fighters is reported to have been sent to the MEK camps in June 1998; MEK cadre also were then providing technical and military training for Taliban forces and running the Taliban's anti-Iran propaganda. I, however, have found no record of bin Laden publicly saying anything that could be construed as supportive of Saddam before he returned to Afghanistan. Bin Laden had several anti-Saddam Iraqi Kurds fighting with his unit in the Afghan jihad—Abu Hajir, for example—and he clearly opposed Saddam in 1990–1991 and was ready to fight Iraq's forces.[66]

That said, since 1996 bin Laden has made public statements that benefit Saddam, focusing on what he describes as the U.S. intention to break the country's power and divide "Iraq into three" by maintaining UN sanctions.[67] "Is there any terrorism uglier or more brutal," bin Laden asked in May 1998, "than the killing by the United States of hundreds of thousands of women, children, and elderly people by sentencing them to death by starvation in Iraq?"[68] "When 60 Jews are killed inside Palestine," he told journalist Robert Fisk, "all the world gathers within 7 days [at Sharm al-Shaykh, Egypt] to criticize this action, while the death of 600,000 Iraqi children did not receive the same reaction. Killing those Iraqi children is a crusade against Islam. We, as Muslims, do not like the Iraqi regime, but we think the Iraqi people and their children are our brothers and we care about their future."[69] Bin Laden later asked ABC's John Miller "Is any shame left in America?" and add that "by the testimony of relief workers in Iraq, the American-led sanctions, [have] resulted in the death of more than one million Iraqi children."[70]

As for Iran, there is little evidence there has been cooperation between bin Laden and the clerics in Tehran, or with the latter's Lebanese Hizballah allies. That al Qaeda has a presence in Lebanon is almost certain; *Al-Watan Al-Arabi,* the U.S. Department of Justice, and other media sources have reported that "Arab Afghans" trained and funded by bin Laden are prominent in the Sunni guerrilla forces, which have attacked Christian churches in Lebanon, the Lebanese army in the country's north, and the Russian embassy in Beirut. "Many do not know," al-Muhajuroun leader Umar Bakri told the media, "that it was Osama bin Laden who supported the Muslims in Lebanon's latest events that were detonated by an armed Islamic movement in the mountain[s]."[71]

In addition, the contiguity of Iran, Afghanistan, and Pakistan suggests bin Laden's fighters have transited Iran on the way to or from Kandahar, Quetta, and Karachi. Aside from these rather elementary conclusions, there are reports that al Qaeda, EIJ, and IG fighters train in Hizballah's Al-Biqa Valley camps; that bin Laden, Iran, and Hizballah cooperated to attack U.S. forces in Dhahran, Saudi Arabia, in 1996; that Iran and Hizballah are cooperating with bin Laden, Sudan, and Iraq to acquire CBRN weapons; and the not-infrequent claims by media and academic experts that there "must" be close ties between bin Laden and Tehran.[72]

In the realm of ruminations, *Al-Watan Al-Arabi* interviewed a terrorism expert in spring 1997. The expert discussed the growth of bin Laden's organization and other armed Islamist groups. In bin Laden's case, the expert said, "the establishment of an active international army requires a country's support. Such a huge organization needs an intelligence service." Not considering that bin Laden saw this need and formed his own intelligence service, the expert asserts, "Iran is the only country that can sponsor an international Islamic extremist movement, because it has intelligence, logistical, and training facilities. It is practically the main country that supports Islamic extremist organizations in the world."[73]

To be fair, Iran, Hizballah, and bin Laden are past masters at operating over the horizon. The truth is that there is not much in the public domain that sheds light on the extent, nature, and substance of this trilateral relationship — if it exists. Given bin Laden's rigid Sunni faith, and after reviewing his utterances, there is no reason to think he has any affection or respect for the Shia, be they Iranian, Lebanese, Afghan, or other. Tehran must have noted bin Laden's silence during the 1998–2001 period, when his Taliban hosts merrily slaughtered Afghan Shias — and a few Iranian diplomats — after their forces took Shia areas in central and northern Afghanistan. *Frontline*'s unattributed biography of bin Laden has said "the trust between the two [bin Laden and Iran] is minimal but both have avoided criticizing each other publicly," and that judgment seems right.[74] Indeed, bin Laden has identified Hizballah's 1983 bombing of the U.S. Marine barracks in Beirut as a major U.S. defeat, one that proved that America's best forces "can run in less than 24 hours." The defeat of the Marines, bin Laden said, signaled "the decline of the American government and the weakness of the American soldier who is ready to wage cold wars and unprepared to fight long wars."[75]

On the Shia side of the ledger, it is hard to see a benefit Iran and Hizballah would derive from formal military cooperation with al Qaeda that they would not gain from standing on the sidelines and watching bin Laden damage, bedevil, and embarrass the United States and its allies. Iran and Hizballah suffer from a perennial, intractable, and potentially fatal problem — each has a fixed address. While cruise missiles are nearly useless against al Qaeda's dispersed forces, they are a strong deterrent against nation-states and terrorist groups whose infrastructure is concentrated in a single state. If Iran or Hizballah attack the United States, the U.S. military knows where they live and can, with impunity, destroy their government ministries, political headquarters, military bases, ports and airports, electrical grids, training facilities, petroleum facilities, and other vital assets.

Bin Laden, however, has no fixed address. When American military might comes calling the odds are bin Laden, like Muhammad Ali, will float like a Muslim butterfly and live to sting another day like the Prophet's bee. All this is to say that it is counterintuitive for Hizballah and Iran — and Sudan and Iraq, for that matter — to deliberately put their heads on the chopping block with al Qaeda when they derive the same benefit by doing nothing. Al Qaeda already has killed Americans, embarrassed Washington by forcing U.S. leaders into a war of words with a Saudi they cannot find, increased anti-Americanism among Muslims, caused the United States to spend $1.4 billion for security upgrades for its embassies and double its counterterrorism budget in five years, and put U.S. forces in Saudi Arabia into isolated desert cantonments at a prolonged and enervating state of alert. All this is in the interest of Hizballah and Iran and, to date, they have benefited at no cost to themselves.

There may well be other forms of cooperation among the three parties. But transit privileges, travel documents, help in weapons procurement, logistical support, temporary residence, and specialized training have never been activities that earned a U.S. military response. Iran and Hizballah know that even if this kind of aid to bin Laden became public knowledge, the odds are hugely against a U.S. retaliatory strike against them.

Finally, there is a geopolitical factor at play in the refusal of Iran and Hizballah to formally ally themselves with al Qaeda. Neither has a long-term interest in helping to make the Sunni Osama bin Laden the world's premier anti-American Muslim leader, an event that would ensure that the interests and ambitions of the Shias remain a small, hated, and heretical boil on the body politic of Islam, one that would be inevitably and lethally lanced by triumphant Sunnism. For Iran, and Hizballah, at this point, less is definitely more in terms of formal cooperation with al Qaeda.[76]

The Search for CBRN Weapons

After they returned to Afghanistan, bin Laden and his aides focused on acquiring CBRN weapons or components. Reports of bin Laden's success in this area may or may not be exaggerated, but Mohammed Mabruk — the EIJ's third senior leader and someone in a position to know — told an Egyptian court in spring 1999 that bin Laden's World Front already controlled chemical and biological weapons.[77] In June 1998 Stefan Leader essentially concurred with al-Najjar in *Jane's Intelligence Review*. "There is a good chance," Leader wrote, "that he [bin Laden] has acquired or fabricated a chemical agent or agents and may well be looking for a suitable opportunity to use such a weapon."[78]

There has been little exaggeration in the reporting about the prolonged efforts bin Laden and his organization have made to acquire this capability; bin Laden's own repeated public assertions in this regard validate this reporting. Bin Laden first charged his lieutenants to acquire these weapons while he was in Sudan from 1991 to 1996, and it is prudent to assume his involvement with the NIF's Military Industrial Corporation was in part an effort to produce CBRN weapons. It is clear bin Laden believes Muslims can successfully defend themselves against the "Crusaders and Jews" only when they have such weapons, and he stressed after Pakistan's nuclear tests that Muslim nations "should not be lax in possessing nuclear, chemical, and biological weapons."[79] Soon after Pakistan's tests, bin Laden said, "it is the duty of every Muslim to struggle for its [the United States'] annihilation," a choice of words suggesting that catastrophic damage of one kind or another must be inflicted on the Americans.[80] Then, in December 1998 bin Laden curtly dismissed the U.S. assertions that even an attempt to acquire CBRN weapons made terrorists of him and his followers. "This is not a charge to be leveled against anyone," bin Laden said. "Our nation [the ummah] is facing aggression and it has the right to possess what is necessary to defend itself."[81]

Early in 1999, bin Laden made the point more clearly when he was asked if his group possessed chemical and biological weapons. "Trying to obtain them is not a crime," bin Laden explained. "It is even a religious duty and it would be a sin for any Muslim to give up because our enemies have some. Do we have any weapons? Do we know how to use them? That is our business." There also is a hint of hurt pride in bin Laden's statements about CBRN weapons, a sentiment that bristles over the fact that the West allows Islam's foes to possess the weapons but works to keep them from Muslims simply because they are Muslims. "America insists on belittling the [Muslim] nation," Zawahiri told the press, "while Israel every day expands and builds its nuclear arsenal." As in so much of what bin Laden says, it is exceedingly difficult for Muslim regimes — even those bin Laden wants to destroy — to publicly condemn his position on CBRN weapons. On this issue, bin Laden and most Muslim governments are on the same side — as they are on such issues as Jerusalem, Western popular culture, sanctions on Iraq, and secularism — in that each sees a need for a Muslim capability matching Israel's. "The existence of an Israeli nuclear arsenal," argued the Saudi paper *Al-Jazirah* in early 2000, "makes the Arab states duty-bound to reconsider their position on acquiring weapons of mass destruction as long as Israel possesses many of these weapons."[82]

The work of bin Laden and al Qaeda in the CBRN arena has included attempts to hire Muslim and non-Muslim scientists who can assemble weapons, adapt them, and fabricate means of delivery.[83] There also have been attempts to buy components for CBRN weapons; to establish turnkey facilities in which the weapons can be developed, produced, and modified; and to purchase off-the-shelf weapons.[84] The broad range of these endeavors suggests al Qaeda would settle for what it could get and has not been seeking the perfect CBRN weapon. What al Qaeda wants, simply, is a tool to kill as many non-Muslims — Americans, Britons, Catholics, Jews, Christians generally, Israelis, and others — as possible in one stroke. It does not require symmetrical mushroom clouds or sophisticated intercontinental delivery systems, although it would take either. What al Qaeda wants is a high body count as soon as possible, and it will use whatever CBRN materials it gets in ways that will ensure the most corpses. As an Italian journalist has written, bin Laden has sought "toxins for poisoning water mains. Lethal gases for use against human beings. 'Fungi' for destroying harvests. These are the aims of the 'Jihad Front against Jews and Christians.'"[85]

Al Qaeda attempts to recruit scientists and technicians to help develop CBRN capability have focused on Muslims, but they also have included hiring non-Muslims in Eastern Europe and the former Soviet Union (FSU) — another example of bin Laden dealing with the devil to defeat a greater evil. Using Arab Afghans as recruiters, bin Laden arranged, according to Milan's *Corriere della Sera,* for seven Saudis and one Egyptian educated in pharmacy, medicine, and microbiology in Romania and Hungary to be trained in Afghanistan by "a number of Ukrainian experts (chemists and biologists)" in the areas of "poisons and toxins."

The training program includes the preparation of more sophisticated explosive devices and kits with toxins and chemical agents (such as sarin). There will be special courses on establishing "lethal biological cultures" using substances readily available on the commercial market or in university laboratories. Once they have completed their training, the millionaire terrorist [bin Laden] intends to send the militiamen back to their native countries or infiltrate them into Europe.[86]

For turnkey factories, CBRN components, and ready-to-use weapons, bin Laden and al Qaeda again turned first, but not exclusively, to Eastern Europe and the FSU. *Corriere della Sera* has reported bin Laden's representatives "bought three chemical and biological agent production laboratories in the former Yugoslavia in early May [1998]."[87] One lab is unaccounted for and another is in Kandahar Province. *Al-Watan Al-Arabi* reported bin Laden has "expressed his hope that Iraqi experts would assist this laboratory, like they did in Sudan," and John Miller wrote in *Esquire* that by late 1998 "12 Iraqi experts in chemical weapons" arrived to work in bin Laden's Afghan laboratories.[88] The third laboratory is reported to be in Zenica, Bosnia, a "village that the Muslim volunteers made their base during the war. A humanitarian organization connected with Osama's network has bought an old farm there and turned it into a 'research cluster.'"[89] In addition, the Italian magazine *Sette* claims bin Laden established "a well-equipped laboratory in Kandahar that produces poison and various lethal gases, which he bought as a complete unit from the Ukraine."[90] Other laboratory and production facilities available to bin Laden are reported in the Khowst and Jalalabad areas, and in the Khartoum suburb of Kubar. The latter facility is said to be a "new chemical and bacteriological factory" cooperatively built by Sudan, bin Laden, and Iraq, and may be one of several in Sudan. In January 1999, *Al-Watan Al-Arabi* reported that by late 1998, "Iraq, Sudan, and bin Laden were cooperating and coordinating in the field of chemical weapons. The reports say that several chemical factories were built in Sudan. They were financed by bin Laden and supervised by Iraqi experts."[91]

Bin Laden also made a broader international effort to acquire CBRN components and off-the-shelf weapons. Ukraine appears to be a place where bin Laden had luck in both areas, perhaps because al Qaeda had a presence there; senior Ukrainian security officials have said that "Members of foreign terrorist and illegal paramilitary organizations have been staying in our country permanently and quite legally." *Al-Hayah's* also said, "Bin Laden has established a network of contacts with influential figures in the [FSU] republics, especially Ukraine."[92] In addition to the labs bought in Ukraine, bin Laden's representatives are reported to have purchased and shipped to Afghanistan anthrax and plague viruses; insecticides; chemical weapons; and radioactive materials from Ukraine, Kazakhstan, and North Korea.[93]

The EIJ fighters captured in 1998 in the Balkans and Caucasus also have testified in Egypt that bin Laden's organization has obtained "germ and biological weapons by post at a cheap price." According to the fighters' published testimony, factories in Europe have provided E. coli and salmonella and factories in Southeast Asia have supplied "anthrax gas" and "other toxic gases." A Czech firm also agreed to sell "samples of the lethal butolinum germ at $7,500 a sample." According to *Al-Sharq Al-Arabi*, "it is possible to use a microscopic quantity of these viruses to kill hundreds of people by inhaling it or eating contaminated food."[94] Quoting "a prominent fundamentalist residing outside Egypt," *Al-Hayah* has reported bin Laden and Zawahiri plan "to distribute quantities of these [chemical and biological] weapons to the World Front in several states for use when necessary against U.S. and Israeli targets in the event of the failure to carry out operations against these targets through the use of explosives and conventional weapons."[95]

Bin Laden seems to have turned to off-the-shelf nuclear weaponry after failing to buy weapons-grade uranium because of scams or missed opportunities. He tried and failed to purchase uranium while living in Sudan and, by the time he returned to Afghanistan, appears have concluded it was too hard and expensive to build a bomb. He decided, therefore, to try to buy a complete tactical nuclear weapon, and, at the same time, to acquire sub-weapons-grade uranium. The latter, according to Milan's *Panorama*, to "poison the waters of some pro-U.S. state or, alternatively, to build a radioactive bomb."[96] In this regard, at least two troubling incidents have occurred. In November 1998, a Taliban-like group in Albania called Sefelizmn — perhaps a corruption of the Arabic term *Salifiya*, a twentieth-century Muslim reform movement urging a return to the principles of Muhammad and his immediate successors — was reported to be trying to buy radioactive waste from Albania's nuclear power plants. The group was said to have received funds from the Islamic nongovernmental organization Muwaffaq, which has been linked to bin Laden since he was in Sudan. Then, in March 2000, Uzbek customs officials on the border with Kazakhstan seized "10 lead-lined containers . . . filled with enough radio active material to make dozens of crude weapons, each capable of contaminating a large area for many years." The shipment contained strontium 90 and carried official Kazakh documents certifying it was not radioactive. The cargo was addressed to a firm in Quetta, Pakistan, which is a haven for Afghan narcotraffickers, heavily influenced by the Taliban, and, as Robert Kaplan wrote, "has increasingly become an Afghan city inside Pakistan." A former U.S. official said the contraband is "an ideal terror weapon, used in a city, and especially places like subways, to cause maximum harm. There is therefore a high possibility that [the seized consignment] was going to terrorist groups in Pakistan and that it might well have been for bin Laden."[97]

In pursuing tactical nuclear weapons, bin Laden has focused on the FSU states and has sought and received help from Iraq. While there is, and should be, doubt about whether bin Laden has acquired such weapons, there should be no doubt in any mind that he has been trying to acquire one and that al Qaeda would use it if the organization had it. Indeed, the reporting available on this aspect of bin Laden's activities has become more compelling over time. In October 1998, for example, *Al-Hayah* reported he had "acquired nuclear weapons from the Islamic republics of Central Asia set up after the collapse of the Soviet Union." The daily credited the information to "informed diplomatic sources in Asia," but the claim was sensational and not convincing. *Al-Watan Al-Arabi* ran a similar but even less specific story soon thereafter.[98]

In November 1998, the bin Laden-CBRN-weapons story started becoming more complex, detailed, and, to an extent, plausible. *Al-Watan Al-Arabi* published a long article in November 1998 claiming bin Laden had, in September 1998, "purchased nuclear warheads [that were] smuggled out of the former Soviet Union." *Al-Watan Al-Arabi* had reported in spring 1997 that bin Laden and Zawahiri were working with the Russian Mafia to "transfer [CBRN] weapons to Dubayy [*sic*]," and followed that article with another that included a warning from a leading French counterterrorism expert. This expert said the West must pay closer attention to "the cooperation between Islamic extremist movements and the Russian Mafia, which will in the future supply the latter [*sic* – former?] with biological and chemical weapons."[99] Now, in autumn 1998, the Paris-based Arabic daily reported this cooperation had secured for bin Laden not chemical and biological weapons, but rather twenty tactical nuclear warheads.[100]

The trail to the warheads, not surprisingly, began in Afghanistan. After the Soviet defeat, some Arab Afghans went to Chechnya to help Muslims there prepare to fight to evict Russian forces from the country. As the fighting evolved in Chechnya, *Al-Watan Al-Arabi* says, bin Laden "financed the 'jihad' against the Russians" and "sent groups of his supporters to fight alongside the Chechens." Over time, bin Laden's fighters built "wide ranging relations with some former [Chechen] officials and current rebels." Among the contacts, apparently, were members of the Chechen Mafia, an organization that "is highly placed among the most important Russian Mafia groups led by former senior officers in the KGB and Red Army." A September 1998 meeting near Grozny put "the final touches on 'the nuclear warheads deal.'"[101]

> According to reliable sources, the deal cost $30 million in cash from bin Laden's treasury and a "grant" of two tons of Afghan heroin that were donated by the Taliban. The heroin has been estimated to be worth $70 million. Some quarters say that bin Laden was ready

to pay "any price" not for nuclear technology, but [for] nuclear warheads ready for use and experts specialized in assembly, usage, and "conversion" if the need arises. Bin Laden underscored his interest in tactical nuclear weapons that can be carried in small suitcases. The Russians have hundreds of these weapons and bombs. . . . *Al-Watan al-Arabi* information confirms that these warheads — estimated at more than twenty in number in various sizes and strengths — have come from several republics and different arsenals in different areas, such as Ukraine, Kazakhstan, Turkmenistan, and even Russia. The information adds that five Muslim Turkmen nuclear experts later arrived near Khost [*sic*] where the warheads were stored in tunnels several hundred meters deep. . . . The information says that in the days of the former Soviet Union, the leader of this nuclear team worked on the center of the Iraqi Tammaz reactor before it was bombed in the 1980s. This nuclear expert is now in charge of preparing a nuclear laboratory in that secret base [in Afghanistan].[102]

The story has the ring of plausibility, perhaps even echoes of truth. We know for certain that bin Laden was seeking CBRN weapons; that his procurement agents have been unsuccessful and his chief procurer, Abu Hajer, is now in jail in Manhattan awaiting trial; that bin Laden, Zawahiri, and the Taliban have been supporting the Chechen Islamists against the Russians; that bin Laden has had large amounts of money of his own and from wealthy, dependable donors; that two tons of heroin is a tiny fraction of the tonnage that was produced in the Taliban's domain; that the international media are full of stories about the Russians and its allied mafias having access to nuclear weapons; that Russian general Aleksandr Lebed told the U.S. Congress and *60 Minutes* that Russia had lost "100 small nuclear bombs [that] could be put inside ordinary suitcases"; that during the Afghan war, bin Laden built a well-protected, sophisticated tunnel complex at Khowst, and perhaps at Jaji; and that Iraq and Sudan have been cooperating with bin Laden on CBRN weapon acquisition and development. On the last point, Milan's *Corriere della Sera* reported in late 1998 that Iraq's ambassador to Turkey and former intelligence chief, Faruk Hidjazi, met bin Laden in Kandahar on 21 December 1998.[103] The daily said Hidjazi offered bin Laden sanctuary in Iraq, stressing that Baghdad would not forget bin Laden's protests against U.S.-U.K. air attacks on Iraq.[104] Whether Hidjazi discussed CBRN issues with bin Laden is unknown, but it is interesting to note that *Al-Watan Al-Arabi* reported that in October 1998 the Iraqis "suggested to bin Laden to involve [in his search for CBRN weapons] elements from the Russian Mafia who were above suspicion. It was learned that these trusted elements were Red Army officers who established ties of friendship and trust with officers in the Iraqi army in the past when Iraqi army and intelligence officers used to go to the Soviet Union for training courses and Moscow sent its military specialists to Baghdad."[105]

In summer 1999, two U.S. news services reported U.S. government experts had concluded that bin Laden's effort to militarily strengthen al Qaeda after returning to Afghanistan had been successful. On 16 June 1999, ABC journalist John McWethy said, "Intelligence sources say there is mounting evidence [that] bin Laden's network has acquired ingredients for chemical or biological weapons through the countries that were once part of the Soviet Union." Then, on 6 August 1999, CBS reported, "U.S. intelligence sources say they have made a fundamental shift in their assessment of terrorist leader Osama bin Laden. Once confident that bin Laden only had enough resources to strike targets overseas, like the East Africa embassies that are still under repair, they now believe he has the money and people to strike in the continental United States as well." The same senior U.S. counterterrorism official who told *60 Minutes* in October 2000 that a CBRN attack is "100 percent" certain in the decade ahead, said matter-of-factly that when such an attack occurs "most of the people in the immediate zone [of the attack] will die."[106] These conclusions were given added gravity when it was discovered in late 2001 that several Pakistani nuclear scientists had worked with al Qaeda. In March 2002, the *Washington Post* reported that when one of these scientists, Bashiruddin Mahmood, met bin Laden, the latter hinted that the Uzbeck Islamists already had supplied al Qaeda with fissile material from the FSU. Bin Laden then asked Mahmood — who has a reputation as a strict and committed Islamist — "to help find other Pakistani scientists more versed in the mechanics of bomb-building."

13

BIN LADEN STANDS AT ARMAGEDDON AND BATTLES FOR HIS LORD

They tell us, sir, that we are weak — unable to cope with so formidable an adversary. But when shall we be stronger? Will it be the next week or the next year? Will it be when we are totally disarmed and when a British guard will be stationed in every house? Shall we gather strength by irresolution and inaction? Shall we acquire the means of effectual resistance by lying supinely on our backs and hugging the delusive phantom of hope, until our enemies have bound us hand and foot? Sir, we are not weak, if we make proper use of those means which the God of nature hath placed in our power.

Patrick Henry, 1775

This chapter's title is a play on Theodore Roosevelt's speech accepting the 1912 presidential nomination at the Progressive Party's "Bull Moose" convention in Chicago. It was chosen because there are ways in which bin Laden and TR are alike, an analogy planted in the author's mind by a question ABC's John Miller asked Osama bin Laden in May 1998.[1] Bin Laden and Roosevelt clearly shared black-and-white moralistic views of human and world affairs, discerned the active presence of evil in the world, believed they knew God's plan for how the world should work, were certain of what each individual's moral responsibilities entail, and warned their brethren of the shame and dishonor that attach to individuals and nations when duties are shirked. This single-minded attitude in both men, moreover, proved to be accompanied by a subtle, patient, practical, and innovative mind. In the face of blatant evildoing, TR clearly believed that war was absolutely preferable to a cowardly evasion of responsibility for the sake of safety and ease. Bin Laden manifests exactly the same attitude. He, for example, gave up his family's palatial estates and luxurious lifestyle for the Afghan deserts, caves, and mountains, risked his life in combat against the Soviets, and has preached an Islamist version of TR's "Strenuous Life," urging Muslims to struggle "by sacrificing their wealth and life as long as their holy places are not liberated from subjugation of Jews and Christians."[2]

On this track, an unnamed former confident of bin Laden told the Associated Press after the 1998 East Africa bombing that "Osama sees the world in very simplistic terms, as a struggle between Muslims on one side, and on the other, Jews and Christians bent on oppressing them. He will not rest until either the United States leaves Saudi Arabia or he dies trying to make it happen."[3] Both bin Laden and TR also aspired to make their nations great, powerful, and, from their own perspective, good, and likewise both personally determined to stay, as TR said, in "the arena" — no matter how battered and bloody they became — until the goal was attained or they were dead. While TR urged Americans to "fear God and take your own part," bin Laden can be said to be urging Muslims to "fear God and take God's part."

The two men, however, definitively part company in their respective approaches to war. TR always saw war in a somewhat idealized manner. Battles occurred between armies of trained men, prisoners of war were spared, civilians and property were respected and protected as much as possible, and the complete and arbitrary devastation of the enemy — military and civilian — was never the goal. TR, of course, died before the full reality of the Great War's carnage hit American society, but even the combat death of his youngest son, Quentin, in France in 1918 appears not to have fully eliminated his idealization of war.[4]

Bin Laden and his followers, in contrast, are learned in the history of the Crusades — where the slaughter of captured soldiers and noncombatants by Catholic fighters and Muslim mujahedin was commonplace — and are the products of the century of total war, where civilians and economic infrastructure have not only been targets, but have also been primary targets. Bin Laden clearly believes the twentieth century was characterized by a steady return to barbarism, and, more precisely, barbarism refined, modernized, and practiced by the Christian West, and especially by the United States, against Muslims in a high-tech replay of the murderous practices used by Catholic armies during three-plus centuries of Crusades. "As we have said," Bin Laden told journalist Jamal Ismail, "the recent events, whether the attack on Afghanistan or Sudan or Iraq . . . show that the law of the jungle, the law of cruise missiles from a distance by those cowards, is what governs the world today." Bin Laden is loath to accept this reality. He has claimed that the United States is responsible for setting the standard for large-scale civilian casualties and that to protect Islam and Muslims he will fight fire with fire. "American history does not distinguish between civilian and military, not even women and children," bin Laden told John Miller in 1998. "They [the Americans] are the ones who used [atomic] bombs against Nagasaki: Can these bombs distinguish between infants and military? America does not have a religion that will prevent it from destroying all people."[5]

In 1999 bin Laden specifically addressed the issue of large-scale civilian casualties — or "collateral damage" in the shamefully obfuscating parlance that dominates Western discourse — when he was asked by *Jeune Afrique* if he was troubled by the number of civilians killed or wounded in the Nairobi embassy bombing. "Imagine it was my own children [who] were taken hostage," bin Laden told the journal, "and that shielded by this human shield, Islam's enemies started to massacre Muslims. I would not hesitate, I would kill the assassins even if to do that I had to kill my children with my own hands. So one evil will have avoided an even greater evil. Sometimes, alas, the death of innocents is unavoidable. Islam allows that."[6]

Ironically, just as bin Laden is adopting a no-holds-barred style of warfare similar to that of American Civil War general William T. Sherman, the U.S. government is completing the abandonment of the Sherman model — even though America has never been defeated using that model — and is being consumed with a "zero-casualty" obsession that covers its own and enemy forces. The United States, the *Christian Science Monitor* has written, is becoming a "a paper tiger, one that bombs from long range, runs ineffective interventions, and invests heavily in fantastic but untested weapons systems." As al Qaeda seeks tools with which to conduct a military campaign more searing than Sherman's march through Georgia and the Carolinas, the *Monitor* notes, "U.S. officials are increasingly defining success by the [smallest possible] number of losses." Amplifying this hamstringing approach to war, U.S. military commanders in the field are further shackled by their political leaders' demands that they "also avoid excessive casualties to their adversaries' civilian populations."

As Pentagon planners strive to wage the casualty-free brand of war their political masters demand, they must defy reality and pretend that Sherman's method of war is no longer needed, that putting large numbers of combat boots on the ground and devastating civilian populations and property need no longer occur. In this context, how foreign, politically incorrect, and fear-producing would be the commonsense letter Sherman sent to General George H. Thomas — another great American master of war — just before the former left Atlanta with 65,000 sets of boot bound for Savannah and the sea. "I propose to demonstrate the vulnerability of the South," Sherman wrote, "and make its inhabitants feel that war and individual ruin are synonymous. . . . We are not only fighting hostile armies, but hostile peoples, and most make old and young, rich and poor, feel the hard hand of war." Sherman and Thomas understood this eternal truth, but their military descendants would blanche and cower if it was now spoken. For Americans, unfortunately, bin Laden and his military commander Mohammad Atef accept the reality and promise of Sherman's war-making method and will use it to make Americans "feel the hard hand of war."[7]

Adding to the irony, most Western commentators have not noted that America's military response to bin Laden closely resembles the attacks Western leaders term cowardly when used against Western interests. After al Qaeda's 1998 East Africa attacks, in which the group had fighters killed, wounded, and captured, the editors of the *Economist* dusted off the West's traditional bromide about terrorism. "However frequently it occurs," the esteemed journal prattled, "terrorism does not lose its ability to shock. Nor should it. It remains one of the most despicable of crimes, both because the killing and wounding of innocents is central to its purpose, and because its perpetrators can so easily do their work without having to confront their enemies before slinking off to safety." Given the self-sacrifice of al Qaeda's fighters, it is hard to see the engagements in Kenya and Tanzania as other than face-to-face confrontations, especially after al Qaeda's claim of responsibility immediately after the attack. The U.S. response to the attacks, however, more nearly approximates the *Economist*'s definition of "despicable" actions: a surprise attack with nearly eighty unmanned cruise missiles. This sort of hypocrisy has not been missed in the Muslim world. "[T]he Americans," the militant Egyptian propagandist Yasir al-Sirri mocked in 1999, "are always fighting from behind a wall or with long-range missiles out of concern for their sons, while the faithful do not fear death but seek it."[8]

It is in this context that bin Laden, between 1996 and 2001, incrementally increased the violence of his rhetoric and the destructiveness of his attacks on the United States. This six-year period saw bin Laden, his allies, and his associates score significant military victories, which in turn led to increased popularity for bin Laden and his cause in the Muslim world. At the same time, however, bin Laden's forces have endured an unprecedented series of defeats. Indeed, the number of blows he and his colleagues successfully have absorbed since 1996 should give pause to those who believe the strength, reach, and popularity of his organization have been exaggerated.

Of this ilk, for example, *U.S. News & World Report* remarked in late 1998 that bin Laden's al Qaeda "has been described in news accounts as an all-powerful, globe-spanning conspiracy worthy of a Tom Clancy thriller." The magazine concluded that the speed with which several of bin Laden's fighters were caught after the August 1998 attacks in East Africa "indicates that al Qaeda is not all it's cracked up to be," and quoted the U.S. Secret Service's former chief of counterterrorism as saying that "in the case of al

Qaeda, the tradecraft is not there, they don't have the support of a patron state's intelligence service."[9] But what was it if not superb tradecraft that allowed bin Laden to destroy two U.S. embassies 450 miles apart on the same day and at almost precisely the same moment—or, for that matter, the quantum growth in operational capability displayed in the near-simultaneous hijacking of four airliners and the ability to get three of the four to their targets? Lebanese Hizballah has never staged an attack that could even serve as the amateur opening act for these two al Qaeda operations, although most terrorism "experts" still are purveyors of the old-think mantra that a terrorist is only a serious threat to U.S. interests if he has a state sponsor, and, therefore, Iran-backed Hizballah is the only terrorist group to fear.[10] This, of course, ignores the fact that Hizballah has not attacked U.S. interests since 1991, and that bin Laden is waging an insurgency, not a terrorist campaign. Indeed, as Professor Magnus Ranstorp has said, "in the face of conventionally stronger enemies, bin Laden urges offensive guerrilla warfare (terrorism), for he and other Islamic activists appreciate that neither the U.S. nor Israel can politically afford high levels of military casualties, as previous events in Beirut, Somalia, and southern Lebanon have demonstrated."[11]

Events in bin Laden vs. Crusaders War 1996-2005

The following paragraphs sketch events in the "Bin Laden vs. Crusaders" war between May 1996 and 2005; as noted in the listing for the 1991-1996 period, the give-and-take of this war does not lend itself to a strict chronology.

In this revised edition, we have updated—for the reader's convenience—this chronology to cover the ongoing war through 1 October 2005. In the section dealing with al Qaeda's "victories," attacks are described that yielded dead and gutted tourists, demolished embassies, and ongoing—indeed, strengthening—Islamic insurgencies around the world. Western media and governments bemoan these attacks as "terrorism," and in this they are mistaken. Al Qaeda's victories, and those of its allies and supporters, are acts of war aimed at strategic objectives, motivated by faith, and conducted in a manner appropriate to the attackers' skills and resources. It is an arrogant and dangerous delusion to continue attaching the term "terrorism" to these events, because the term clouds the fact that much of the Muslim world deems itself under attack by U.S. foreign policy. These conscious acts of war will increase in lethality as skill levels rise and more sophisticated and deadly tools come to hand. Like the rose, war by any other name is still war.

- 25 June 1996: A truck loaded with explosives was detonated outside the U.S. military's Khubar Towers housing facility near Dhahran, Saudi Arabia, killing nineteen Americans and wounding some five hundred persons. While there appears to be no definitive proof of bin Laden's culpability, Saudi interior minister

Prince Nayif has said that "individuals motivated by bin Laden could have conducted the attack." Abd al-Bari Atwan of *Al-Quds Al-Arabi* has written that, in his interview with bin Laden, the latter spoke of the attacks on Khubar Towers and Office of Program Management-Saudi Arabian National Guard (OPM-SANG) and "expressed unusual sympathy with those who carried out the attack. He was very close to saying that they were from his supporters. He was close but did not say this. You sense pride in his eyes, that these real men, as he told me, were capable of implementing these two successful operations." Bin Laden said in late 1996 that "what happened in the Riyadh [OPM-SANG, November 1995] and al-Khubar blasts was praiseworthy terrorism because it was against thieves, not individuals but major states which went there [Saudi Arabia] to plunder the riches of the nation and to encroach on its greatest holy sites." He said the attacks were successful because they were "why the United States had to decide to reduce its forces in Saudi Arabia."[12]

- 18 September 1997: Gama'at al-Islamiyah (IG) fighters attacked a tour bus in front of a Cairo museum, killing nine German tourists and one Egyptian.[13]

- 17 November 1997: In the Gama'at's most lethal attack, its fighters killed fifty-eight foreign tourists and four Egyptians and wounded twenty-six other tourists at the Hatshepsut Temple near Luxor, Egypt. The IG attackers left leaflets — some carefully placed in the victim's gutted bodies — calling for the release of Gama'at spiritual leader Shaykh Rahman from his U.S. prison and saying they had intended to take hostages at Luxor to trade for the shaykh. Eyewitnesses reported, however, that the attackers took their time and systematically executed their victims. In June 2000, Gama'at military chief Rifa'i Taha told *Al-Sharq Al-Awsat* that the Luxor attackers were "a group inside the IG that was tasked with such actions . . . the Luxor incident was the IG's attempt to free its leaders, foremost of them Umar Abd-al-Rahman, Engineer Karam Zuhdi, Lieutenant Abbud al-Zummar and others." The attack severely damaged Egypt's tourist industry, one of its top foreign-exchange earners.[14]

- 22 December 1997: Led by bin Laden associate Ibn Khattab, a mixed Chechen–Arab Afghan force staged a nighttime raid on the cantonment of the Russian army's 136th Mechanized Brigade General Command about one hundred kilometers inside Russian territory. Dozens of military vehicles — tanks, trucks, and armored personnel carriers — were destroyed and some Russian servicemen were killed. A senior Afghan Arab, the Egyptian Abu Bakr Qaidah, was killed in the raid. As the insurgents withdrew to Chechnya, they lured pursuing Russian forces into an ambush where the Russians suffered more casualties and vehicle losses.[15]

- February 1998: A member of India's government said bin Laden "is responsible for the long night of explosions that shook Indian cities on the eve of legislative elections on 14 February 1998, resulting in more than 60 killed." The U.S. government noted that fifty people were killed and more than two hundred wounded, but it did not attribute the attacks to bin Laden.[16]

- 7 August 1998: Bin Laden's fighters attacked the U.S. embassies in Nairobi, Kenya, and Dar es Salaam, Tanzania, with car bombs within minutes of each other; 12 Americans died and 7 were wounded; 291 Africans were killed and nearly 5,100 were wounded. Bin Laden praised the attackers "who risked their lives to earn the pleasure of God, Praise and Glory be to Him," describing them as "real men, the true personification of the word men. They managed to rid the Islamic nation of disgrace. We highly respect them and hold them in the highest esteem." In late 2000 Egyptian Islamic Jihad (EIJ) fighter Ali Mohammed told a U.S. court he had surveilled and photographed the U.S. embassy in Nairobi at bin Laden's direction and that later "bin Laden looked at the picture of the American embassy and pointed to where a truck could go as a suicide bomber."[17]

- 16 December 1998: The Abu Sayyaf Group (ASG) bombed a shopping mall in Zamboanga, Philippines, wounding sixty Christians who were Christmas shopping.[18]

- December 1998: The bin Laden-linked "Islamic Aden-Abyan Army" kidnapped sixteen Westerners in Yemen. The Islamists executed three British citizens and one Australian when Yemeni forces tried to rescue the hostages.[19] A Yemeni official and Yemeni tribal sources claimed the kidnappers were "following bin Laden's lead" and the operation was "in response to a fatwa made by Osama bin Laden that sanctioned the killing of Westerners." In early 1999 the group's leader, Zayn-al-Abidin al-Muhdar, said the kidnappings were carried out "for the sake of Bin Laden."[20]

- 18–19 December 1998: Because of threats in bin Laden's statement supporting the "Iraqi people" during U.S. and U.K. air strikes on Iraq, "most American embassies in sub-Saharan Africa were ordered closed for two days." Thirty-eight embassies and three consulates were closed on 18–19 December 1999.[21]

- January–August 1999: Threats attributed to bin Laden, or U.S. government perceptions that bin Laden was about to attack, resulted in the temporary closing — twenty-four hours or more — of seventy U.S. embassies and consulates around the world. The State

Department's Diplomatic Security Service said this number marked "an all-time high," and Mary Anne Weaver marveled in the *New Yorker* that the closings showed that even without attacking "he [bin Laden] was holding the United States government hostage."[22]

- 16 February 1999: Uzbek authorities claimed bin Laden, Taliban leader Mullah Omar, and a "Jordanian citizen named Khattab, who lives in Chechnya," were responsible for "a series of bomb explosions" in Tashkent on 16 February. Media reports claimed one goal of the attacks was to assassinate Uzbek president Islam Karimov. According to Moscow's *Kommersant,* Karimov may have been targeted because he "is actively exploiting his image as an implacable warrior against fundamentalism and Wahabism to strengthen his ties to the West." Six bombs were detonated in Tashkent, killing 16 and wounding 128. The attackers are reported to belong to Tahir Yoldashev's Islamic Movement of Uzbekistan (IMU), which is trained and supported by bin Laden and the Taliban. Later, in August 1998, the IMU kidnapped four Japanese geologists working in Kryrgzstan. The geologists were released in October 1998 after a $3 million ransom was paid. The IMU fighters then withdrew after engaging Kyrgyz and Uzbek forces.[23]

- May–June 1999: Bin Laden-trained Kashmiri insurgents and members of bin Laden's Arab Afghan cadre participated in the Pakistani military's incursion into the Kargil area of Indian-held Kashmir. Indian military and police authorities claimed bin Laden was planning a bigger role in Kashmir, and the Indian media said Muslims in Kashmir increasingly were looking to bin Laden to "save them from India." Even before the Kargil operation, a reporter from London's *Sunday Times* quoted noncombatant Kashmiris as saying, "Our 'father' bin Laden has sent brothers from Afghanistan to wage jihad," and "Bin Laden is coming—he will purge the Indian army from Kashmir."[24]

- June 1999: The U.S. government temporarily closed its embassies in Senegal, Gambia, Liberia, Togo, Namibia, and Mauritania. U.K. embassies in Senegal, Gambia, Namibia, and Madagascar also were closed. U.S. officials said the closings were the result of bin Laden-related surveillance. Earlier in June, the State Department warned U.S. travelers "against terrorist threats that focused mainly on bin Laden."[25]

- July 1999: In a direct response to bin Laden's August 1998 attacks in East Africa, the U.S. Congress appropriated nearly $1.5 billion to strengthen the security of U.S. facilities overseas. Overall, in the years following bin Laden's 1996 Declaration of Jihad, the U.S. government's counterterrorism budget nearly doubled, from $5.7

billion in 1996 to $11.1 billion under the Clinton administration. The total budget was larger, the *Washington Post* wrote, because the $11.1 billion figure does not "include intelligence spending, which remains classified."[26]

- July 1999: The FBI suspended tourist tours of its headquarters. The suspension was based on "intelligence" showing bin Laden planned to attack the Hoover building.[27]

- July 1999: U.S. Secretary of Defense William Cohen canceled a trip to Albania "in part because of fears of a terrorist attack by followers of Osama bin Laden."[28]

- 6–14 August 1999: In a handwritten note to Reuters, the Aden-Abyan Islamic Army (AAIA) claimed responsibility for the 14 August 1999 bombing of a Yemeni military aircraft; seventeen Yemeni military officers were killed, including several senior Army officers. The AAIA also claimed credit for killing six people in a grenade attack on a Sana market on 6 August.[29]

- August 1999–April 2002: After entering Dagestan on 2 August 1999, a Chechen Islamist force—led by Ibn Khattab and veteran Arab Afghans—fought Russian forces in Chechnya and Dagestan. The insurgents also appeared responsible for three skilled car bombings that killed almost three hundred Russians on 4 September in Dagestan, and 8 and 13 September in Moscow. Increasingly, bin Laden and his allies viewed the Caucasus region as a pivotal battleground; bin Laden told Pakistani journalists "the mujahedin of Chechnya . . . were fighting for Islam and it was his moral responsibility to provide them with every kind of help," and other Muslim media said al Qaeda viewed "jihad against the Russians and Orthodox Christians, first in Kosovo and now in Chechnya, as a continuation of the great jihad the Arab Afghans waged to drive the Soviet Union from Afghanistan." In October 1999, Khattab said the "day Russia loses Dagestan, it will lose the whole of the Caucasus." He then echoed bin Laden on the killing of civilians, telling *Al-Watan Al-Arabi* the war "has been shifted to all Russian cities and would be directed against all Russians of all ages and ethnic backgrounds."[30]

- December 1999: The discovery by Jordanian authorities of plans by bin Laden's fighters to attack hotels and Christian holy sites in Jordan, and the U.S. Customs Service arrest of an Algerian smuggling explosives from Canada into Washington State, prompted travel warnings, intensified airport security, and caused the deployment of hundreds of Customs officers to the northern and southern U.S. borders. Citing a heightened bin Laden threat to crowds gathered for millennium celebrations, the U.S. State Department warned

Americans overseas to avoid large crowds. This warning — and the capture of the explosives-laden Algerian — caused widespread unease across the United States. The mayor of Seattle, for example, canceled his city's millennium celebrations, and the U.S. Congress began "pressuring Canada to tighten controls along the border between the two countries" after a U.S. Department of Justice official told the press that Washington is "concerned that Canada's laws do facilitate the entry into the United States of individuals who may pose a terrorist threat."[31]

- 24–31 December 1999: On 24 December, five Kashmiri insurgents hijacked an Air India flight carrying 155 passengers and crew and diverted it to Kandahar airport. The plane and passengers were released on 31 December after New Delhi agreed to release from prison senior HUM leader and Islamist scholar Masood Azhar — who had been jailed for more than six years — and two other veteran Kashmiri insurgents. Speaking in Pakistan after his release, Azhar said the hijacking was a great success. He said that "those who could hijack an Indian plane and get their people released could also rebuild the Babri Masjid [mosque] and get occupied Kashmir liberated." Taunting the Indians, Azhar asked "Where is your 1.3 million-man army? Where is your RAW [India's intelligence service]? Can they grab these five people who shattered your security system?" Azhar also hinted that bin Laden might have had a role in the hijacking when he called him "the world's greatest Holy warrior and asset of the Muslim world to be proud of."[32]

- 1–4 July 2000: Because of concerns about possible attacks by bin Laden-associated groups, the U.S. government canceled celebrations in Belgium and Jordan marking American independence day. The cancellation moved Jordanian officials to denounce the U.S. action as an attempt to force Jordan to support Washington's policy on the Arab-Israeli peace process by acting to hurt tourism and thereby Jordan's economy.[33]

- 2–3 July 2000: Chechen Islamist insurgents staged five attacks. According to Russian military sources, the attacks killed thirty-three, wounded eighty-four, and left six missing. The assaults included suicide attacks on "hard military tactics," suggesting that, as in Kashmir, leadership and tactics are passing to the hands of veteran Arab Afghans.[34]

- 8–22 August 2000: On 8 August, a bomb blast killed 12 Russians and wounded 108 near a highway underpass in Moscow's Pushkin Square. Russian authorities claimed the bombers were trained in "Chechen camps for saboteurs, where the subject of mines and explosives is taught by Osama bin Laden's instructors." On 22

August, a suicide bomber destroyed a café in Grozny, killing nine Russians and wounding twenty.[35]

- 12 October 2000: In Aden, Yemen, the U.S. destroyer *Cole* was nearly sunk by suicide bombers twenty days after bin Laden's deputy, Ayman Zawahiri, said, "Enough of words, it is time to take action against this iniquitous and faithless force [the U.S.] which has spread its troops through Egypt, Yemen, and Saudi Arabia." The attack left seventeen U.S. sailors dead and thirty-nine wounded. The *Cole* was in dry dock for a year and cost more than $250 million to repair. After the attack, President Clinton ordered all U.S. Navy ships in the Persian Gulf "to pull out of port and head to the relative safety of open waters." Concurrently, the U.S. Navy ordered its ships to stop using the Suez Canal for fear of additional attacks. In February 2001, bin Laden praised the *Cole* attack. The *Cole*, he said in a poem, "sails into the waves flanked by arrogance, haughtiness, and false power. To her doom she moves slowly. A dinghy awaits her riding the waves. In Aden, the young men stood up for holy war and destroyed a destroyer feared by the powerful." Hinting of more attacks, bin Laden said "your brothers in the East readied their mounts . . . and the battle camels are prepared to go."[36]

- 30 October–15 November 2000: Chechen Islamist insurgents carried out more than one hundred attacks against Russian forces in Chechnya. Nearly half of the attacks were in the cities of Grozny and Gudermes, which the Russians claimed to control. Even with the loss of two hundred soldiers per month, President Vladimir Putin has said that "it would be an unforgivable mistake to retreat and abandon the republic again."[37]

- 24–30 December 2000: Islamist insurgents in Indonesia and the Philippines staged anti-Christian attacks in eight Indonesian cities, Manila, and Jolo. The 24 December bombings in Indonesia were aimed at Christian churches holding Christmas Eve services, killing eighteen and wounding ninety-six. The Indonesian authorities said the attacks were to "a concerted attack on Christians as they celebrated Christmas." The casualty toll would have been higher, but authorities defused half the bombs that had been planted. The bombings in Manila on 30 December killed twenty-two and wounded about one hundred people; a Catholic priest was murdered in Jolo two days earlier.[38]

- 11 September 2001: In a surprise attack, al Qaeda fighters commandeered four U.S. commercial airliners and flew two into the World Trade Center and one into the Pentagon. The fourth crashed en route to its target. More than three thousand people were killed and the U.S. economy was disrupted. It has been estimated that by the end of 2003, the U.S. economy will lose 1.8 million jobs and estimates of total damage to the economy range from $100 billion to $300 billion — all attributable to the attacks. In addition, the U.S. military response to the attacks had cost $6.4 billion by late January 2002, and the planned budget for fiscal year 2003 showed increases of more than $65 billion for defense and homeland security. These human and financial losses, according to the *New York Times*, were inflicted by al Qaeda at the cost of nineteen dead fighters and about $300,000. The *New York Times* reports that the fighters brought about $40,000 into the country on their persons and about $240,000 was sent to them by wire transfers.[39]

- 7 October 2001–20 April 2002: Al Qaeda and, as far as can be determined, Osama bin Laden so far have survived the U.S. military offensive initiated against them on 7 October. This fact, bin Laden's repeated public statements promising even more damaging attacks on the United States, and multiple FBI warnings of imminent attacks inside the United States, have again reinforced bin Laden's stature as the most effective and potent anti-American force in the Muslim world.

- 7 October 2001: U.S. and UK air forces bombed Taliban bases in Afghanistan, starting the U.S.-led invasion and guerrilla war bin Laden long wanted.

- 1–15 December 2001: After two weeks of U.S. air bombardment of al Qaeda forces in the Tora Bora Mountains, the Northern Alliance failed to fully engage al Qaeda; bin Laden, al-Zawahiri, and most of their fighters escaped to Pakistan. Of this victory, bin Laden said, "If all the forces of world evil could not achieve their goals on a one square mile area against a small number of mujahideen . . . how can these evil forces triumph over the Muslim world?"[40]

- 23 January 2002: *Wall Street Journal* reporter Daniel Pearl was abducted in Karachi while going to interview Shaykh Sayyid Giliani, leader of Jamaat al-Fuqra, a group based in Pakistan and North America and tied to al Qaeda and Kashmiri guerrillas. Pearl was beheaded. His remains were found in May 2002.

- 27 February–2 March 2002: After Muslims burned cars of a passenger train in Godhra, in India's Gujarat State — killing fifty-eight Hindus, wounding forty — Hindu mobs rioted in Ahmedabad, killing more than two thousand, mostly Muslims. Reports claimed the Hindu government "turned a blind eye" to the killings and property destruction. Satellite television coverage of the riots again validated for Muslims bin Laden's contention that the West would not intervene to stop the killing of Muslims.

- 3–18 March 2002: A U.S. military offensive into the Shahi Kowt area of eastern Afghanistan ended in failure when most of al Qaeda's force escaped into Pakistan. The U.S. military's Afghan auxiliaries were again reluctant to fight. U.S. forces suffered eight killed and about one hundred wounded; many casualties came from an undetected al Qaeda ambush in the helicopter landing zone. Initial U.S. estimates claimed seven hundred to one thousand al Qaeda fighters were killed, but only a few dozen bodies were recovered.

- 17 March 2002: An attack on the Protestant International Church in Islamabad's diplomatic enclave killed five and wounded forty-six; two dead and nine wounded were Americans. The church was attended by foreign diplomats, their families, and other expatriates.
- 5 April 2002: Four thousand men in Sakaka in al-Jawf Province demonstrated against Riyadh's support for Israel and the United States. Five hundred Saudi riot police were sent to control the area.
- 11 April 2002: An al Qaeda fighter detonated a truck bomb at a synagogue on Tunisia's Djerba Island, killing fourteen German tourists and seven others. Al Qaeda's post-attack statement said, "The Jewish synagogue in Djerba village was targeted by one single person, the hero Nizar (Sayf-al-Din al-Tunisi). . . . It followed the same pattern and course of the blessed jihad in defense of our Islam's sacred places and in support for the jihad of our Muslim brothers in all parts of the world."[41]
- 17–18 April 2002: On 17 April, Chechen guerrillas killed six Russian soldiers in Noviye Atagi, a village ten miles southeast of Grozny. On 18 April, guerrillas detonated a mine in a roadway in Grozny, killing seventeen Russian servicemen.
- 8 May 2002: In Karachi, a car bomb was driven into a minibus carrying French naval technicians who were working for Pakistan's navy. Eleven French workers were killed, twelve wounded; two Pakistanis were killed and twelve wounded. Al Qaeda said that "the armed operation that targeted the French military technicians has come to show the weakness of this regime [Pakistan's] and prove that what the regime had built [has] started to crumble like a deck of cards."[42]
- 17 June 2002: A car bomb exploded outside the U.S. consulate in Karachi, killing eleven and wounding more than forty.
- 4 July 2002: Egyptian Hesham Mohamed Ali Hadayet killed two U.S. citizens at the El Al counter in Los Angeles airport. He was killed by El Al security.
- 13 July 2002: Grenades were thrown at an archaeological site near Manshera, Pakistan, wounding twelve, including seven Germans, one Austrian, and one Slovak.
- 5 August 2002: Islamists raided a Christian school for the children

of foreign aid workers northwest of Islamabad. Six staff members were killed.

- 10 August 2002: A Christian church in Taxila, Pakistan, was bombed. Five people were killed, including three nurses, and twenty-five were wounded.
- 19 August 2002: Chechen guerrillas shot down a Russian MI-26 helicopter using a STRELA surface-to-air missile, killing 118 and wounding twenty-nine.
- 27 August 2002: In Beijing, U.S. Deputy Secretary of State Richard Armitage announced U.S. support for Chinese military actions against Uighur separatists in western China, saying the United States agreed that the Uighurs had "committed acts of terrorism." In Washington, the State Department adds the East Turkistan Islamic Movement to its list of proscribed terrorist organizations.
- 6 October 2002: An al Qaeda suicide bomber sailed an explosives-laden boat into the 290,000 ton, French-owned tanker *Limburg* off Aden, Yemen. The tanker was carrying 397,000 barrels of Saudi crude to Malaysia. The attack was a warning to France, said al Qaeda's claim for the bombing, as well as to "the regime of treason and treachery in Yemen [that] did all it could . . . to hunt down, pursue, and arrest the Muslim mujahid youths in Yemen." The attack was the second success in al Qaeda's maritime jihad and was meant to "stop the theft of the Muslims' wealth [i.e., oil] for which nothing worth mentioning is paid."[43]
- 8 October 2002: Two Islamists killed a U.S. Marine and wounded another on Kuwait's Faylaka Island. Both Islamists were killed. Al Qaeda claimed the attack, saying it was "the correct, on-target attack at this stage," praised "the mujahedin Anas al-Kandari and Jasim Hajiri," and told "the Americans: your road to Iraq and the other countries of the Muslims will not be as easy as you imagine and hope."[44]
- 12 October 2002: Indonesia's al Qaeda-tied Jemaah Islamiya (JI) detonated a suicide car bomb at a Bali nightclub, killing more than two hundred, about half Australians. A JI fighter named Amorzi, who ran the attack, later said, "There's some pride in my heart. For the white people it serves them right. They know how to destroy religion by the most subtle ways through bars and gambling dens."[45]
- 23–26 October 2002: Chechen Islamists seized a theater in Moscow and held more than eight hundred people for fifty-eight hours before Russian forces retook the theater. More than forty Chechen guerrillas were killed, including several female fighters. At least 129 in the audience died from gas used by the security units before they stormed the theater. "As a goal it was an extremely daring

operation," al Qaeda said in congratulating the Chechens, ". . . the mujahideen have clearly demonstrated that they can strike at the enemy on its own turf whenever they want."[46]

- 28 October 2002: Two attackers—a Libyan and a Jordanian—killed U.S. diplomat Laurence Foley at his home in Amman, Jordan. Foley worked in the U.S. embassy. The attackers probably were from Jordanian Abu Musab al-Zarqawi's group, which is tied to al Qaeda and northern Iraq's Ansar al-Islam.

- 20 November 2002: President Bush supported Russia's handling of the October 2002 Chechen raid on a Moscow theater, stating Chechnya "is Russia's internal affair . . ." He equated Chechens with "the killers who came to America," said President Putin should "do what it takes to protect his people," and rejected those who "tried to blame Vladimir. They ought to blame the terrorists. They're the ones who caused the situation, not President Putin." Al Qaeda damned Washington and its allies for letting Russia "liquidate the Chechen issue through brutality."[47]

- 20 November 2002: American nurse Bonnie Penner Wetherall was killed at a Christian church in Sidon, Lebanon. Penner was an active proselytizer bent on converting young Muslims to Christianity. Penner had been warned to stop, and Shaykh Maher Mammoud of Sidon said that "the murder occurred within the context of widespread anger at America . . . we do not condemn [it]."[48]

- 20–23 November 2002: Muslims rioting in Kaduna, Nigeria, left 220 dead, fifteen hundred wounded, six thousand families homeless, and sixteen churches and nine mosques destroyed. Rioting was sparked by a reporter's "blasphemous" claim that, if alive, the Prophet might have wanted a wife from the women in the Miss World contest to be held in Kaduna. The event was moved to the U.K. Muslim leaders called it a "parade of nudity" and criticized the government for agreeing to host the Miss World contest during Ramadan.

- 21 November 2002: A Kuwaiti policeman wounded two U.S. soldiers after he stopped their car. The policeman fled to Saudi Arabia but was returned.

- 28 November 2002: Al Qaeda attacked Israeli interests in Mombasa, Kenya, using a suicide car bomb against the Israeli-owned Paradise Hotel and firing a surface-to-air missile at a Boeing 757 owned by an Israeli charter company. Twelve Kenyans and three Israelis were killed at the hotel, forty others were wounded. The missile missed the aircraft, which was carrying 261 Israelis. "The message here," *Al-Ansar* explained, "is to pursue the Zionist targets all over the world. . . ."[49]

- 27 December 2002: Ahmed Ali Jarallah killed Yemen's Socialist Party chief. When captured, Jarallah said he killed the man because he was a "secularist" and said: "I do not regret what I did because I am seeking paradise. I wish I had an atomic bomb that explodes and incinerates every secularist and renegade."[50]
- 27 December 2002: In Grozny, Chechen fighters drove car bombs into the headquarters of the Russian-backed regime and a communications center. More than sixty people were killed and more than a hundred were wounded.
- 30 December 2002: Islamist fighters from a group linked to al Qaeda attacked the Jiblah Hospital in southern Yemen, killing three American medical workers and wounding another. The hospital had been run for thirty-five years by Southern Baptist missionaries from the United States. Yemeni officials later said the facility was attacked because it was converting Muslims to Christianity.
- 21 January 2003: A U.S. military civilian contractor was killed and another wounded when their car was ambushed on a Kuwaiti highway near Qatar. The attacker was a Kuwaiti civil servant, Sami Mutairi. He fled to Saudi Arabia but was captured and returned by Saudi authorities. Mutairi told Kuwaiti officials the attack was meant as a "gift for Osama bin Laden."
- 16 February 2003: A group of thirty-two editors, representing the world's leading scientific journals, said they would delete details from studies they published if they might help terrorists build biological weapons. The editors said they would "censor scientific data" and admitted this could slow breakthroughs in basic science and engineering. Among the to-be-censored journals were *Science, Nature, The Lancet, The New England Journal of Medicine,* and the *Proceedings of the National Academy of Sciences.*
- 17 February 2003: Islamists ambushed and killed Dr. Hamid bin-Abd-al-Rhaman al-Wardi, the U.S. educated, deputy governor of Saudi Arabia's al-Jawf Province. Al-Wardi had been involving Saudi politicians in women's gatherings, and in doing so, according to the Islamist Web site *Ilaf,* had "angered the people of al-Jawf who are known for their hard-line attitude on matters of honor."[51]
- 20 February 2003: Robert Dent, a thirty-seven-year-old British Aerospace employee, was shot to death at a traffic light in Riyadh. Saudi police arrested Yemen-born Saudi national Saud ibn Ali ibn Nasser and suggested he was tied to al Qaeda.
- 21 February 2003: Envelopes containing cyanide were received by the U.S. embassy and the Australian and British high commissions in Wellington, New Zealand. The letter said: "Our purpose is to challenge the actions of the great Satan America and resist its imperialist ambitions in the Islamic world."[52]

- 28 February 2003: Islamists attacked Pakistani police guarding the U.S. consulate in Karachi, leaving two dead and five wounded. Pakistani officials claimed that "[t]he policemen were hate-targets because they were protecting Americans."[53]
- 18 March 2003: A Yemeni Islamist shot four Hunt Oil Company employees in the Al-Safir area of northern Yemen, killing an American, a Yemeni, and a Canadian. Another Canadian was wounded. The attacker then killed himself.
- 20 March 2003: The U.S.-led coalition invaded Iraq. "Bin Laden must be laughing in his grave or cave," Professor Gerges Fawaz wrote in the *Los Angeles Times*. ". . . [W]hat was unthinkable 18 months ago has happened. The U.S. has alienated those in the Islamic world who were its best hope." Al Qaeda applauded the war, rejoicing that with U.S. forces in Afghanistan, the Arabian Peninsula, and Iraq, "The enemy is now spread out, close at hand, and easy to target."[54]
- 25 March 2003: Two Saudi security officers were shot by drive-by gunmen at a roadblock in Sakaka, al-Jawf Province. One was killed, the other wounded.
- 11 April 2003: Ten al Qaeda fighters escaped a Yemeni high-security prison. All were suspects in the October 2000 bombing of the U.S. destroyer *Cole*; two of them were thought to have run the attack: Jamal al-Badawi and Fahd al-Qasa.
- 1 May–1 June 2003: Chechen insurgents attacked Russian forces using ambushes, land mines, and remotely detonated mines. In this period, thirty-two Russian military and security personnel were killed, eight were wounded, and twenty-nine trucks, cars, and armored vehicles were destroyed. Russian sappers, in addition, defused 120 explosive devices—including twenty-four land mines—between 26 May and 1 June.
- 12 May 2003: A two-story building housing officials of the Russian-backed Chechen government and of the Russian security services was destroyed in the town of Znamenskoye. The town was in an area of northern Chechnya that had been largely untouched by war. The insurgents drove a suicide truck bomb containing about a ton of TNT into the compound, killing fifty-nine and wounding 197.
- 12 May 2003: Al Qaeda suicide car bombs hit three expatriate compounds in Riyadh; bin Laden hinted at the attacks in late 2002, warning, "[The] people of the Peninsula . . . are facing difficult days ahead and very dangerous ordeals that Allah will test you with. . . ." Nearly simultaneous, the attacks killed thirty-four people—nine U.S. citizens—and wounded two hundred. The cars drove far into two compounds, suggesting that the guards helped. For Muslims,

the attacks had anti-Christian salience; the compounds were named by the Saudis — with their usual contempt for the West — for three Christian-conquered cities of Islamic Anadalusia, today's Spain.

- 16 May 2003: Fourteen Islamists in five teams attacked targets in Casablanca, Morocco, including a Spanish restaurant, a Jewish-owned Italian restaurant, a Jewish cemetery, a Kuwaiti-owned hotel, and a Jewish community center. The attacks were roughly simultaneous and used homemade explosives strapped to the attackers; fourteen of the fifteen fighters were killed. The attacks killed forty-six and wounded about one hundred. Moroccan police said the fighters belonged to local Islamist groups and had received fifty thousand dollars from al Qaeda to fund the operations.

- 5 June 2003: A female Chechen suicide bomber stopped and destroyed a bus near Russia's military airfield at Mozdok, North Ossetia. The attack killed twenty Russian air force personnel and wounded fifteen. Mozdok was the main north Caucasus air base for fixed- and rotary-wing aircraft flying combat missions in Chechnya.

- 7 June 2003: In Kabul, a taxi exploded next to a bus of German troops from the International Stabilization and Assistance Force. Four died; twenty-nine were wounded.

- 5 July 2003: Two female Chechen suicide bombers detonated themselves at a concert at Moscow's Tushino Airfield. Sixteen were killed and twenty wounded.

- 1 August 2003: Chechens detonated a suicide truck bomb at Russia's military hospital in Mozdok, killing fifty, wounding sixty-four, and destroying the hospital.

- 5 August 2003: A JI suicide bomber attacked the Marriott Hotel in Jakarta — a popular meeting place for Americans — killing ten and wounding 152. Indonesian police said casualties would have been worse, but the driver detonated the bomb prematurely. Imam Samudra, on trial for the 2002 Bali bombing, said: "I'm happy . . . Thanks to Allah . . . [The Marriott attack] was part of the war against America. The revenge on the suppressors of Muslims will continue."[55]

- 7 August 2003: A car bomb was detonated at the perimeter wall of Jordan's embassy compound in Baghdad, blowing a thirty-foot hole in the wall and damaging several buildings. The attack killed nineteen and wounded sixty-five. The al Qaeda-related group Ansar al-Islam was among the suspected perpetrators.

- 20 August 2003: A suicide truck bomb was driven into the UN's Baghdad headquarters in the Canal Hotel. The UN special representative for Iraq, Sergio Vieira de Mello, and twenty-two others were killed; more than a hundred were wounded. "This criminal, Sergio Vieira de Mello," al Qaeda wrote in claiming the attack, ". . . was the Crusader who carved up part of the land of Islam (East Timor)." [56]

- 25 August 2003: Two taxis packed with the military explosive RDX were detonated fifteen minutes apart in the Indian city of Mumbai, killing fifty-three and wounding more than 190. Indian police arrested four men they said belonged to the Kashmiri Lashkar-e Tayyiba—an ally of al Qaeda—and were tied to India's Student Islamic Movement. The Indians said the groups also detonated bombs in Mumbai in December 2002, killing seventeen and wounding 189, and speculated that both attacks were retaliation for anti-Muslim riots in Gujarat state in March 2002.

- September–October 2003: Egypt and Yemen released, respectively, 113 and one thousand Islamists from prison, the former group reportedly at the end of their sentences, the latter because they repented. Many of the Yemenis were tied to al Qaeda; all the Egyptians belonged to the Islamic Group. The releases mimicked the way some Arab regimes freed jailed Islamists early in the Afghan jihad if they would go to Afghanistan and join the mujahedin. If past is prologue, as Victor Hanson Davis wrote, the regimes might use the same device to "export them all to Iraq." [57]

- September–October 2003: Events undercut Pakistan president Musharraf's pro-U.S. policy. Israeli prime minister Sharon made an official visit to India, supported India on Kashmir, and sold India three Phalcon radar systems. The Phalcons would allow India to see far into Pakistan and, said *Jane's Defense Weekly*, "give India a big strategic advantage over Pakistan." The visit coincided with U.S. criticism of Musharraf for letting Kashmiri fighters enter India, and a joint U.S.–Indian Special Forces exercise in Indian Kashmir. Al Qaeda's al-Zawahiri cited the events, warning the arms deal and "[t]he visit by criminal Sharon . . . are only the tip of the iceberg. This U.S.–Jewish–Indian alliance is against Muslims." [58]

- 11 September 2003: The Salafist Group for Call and Combat (GSPC)—Algeria's main Islamist insurgents—declared allegiance to "the direction of Mullah Omar and the [al Qaeda] organization of Shaykh Usama Bin Ladin," as well as an intention to attack U.S. interests. The GSPC was long stubbornly Algeria-centric, and its decision to take al Qaeda's lead and give priority to anti-U.S. attacks was a major accomplishment for bin Laden.

- 11–13 September 2003: Two elderly Moroccan Jews were killed in Casablanca and Meknes, respectively. The police tied the attacks to the Salafia Jihadia group, which was linked to the 16 May 2003 Casablanca bombings.

- 7 October 2003: NATO announced it would deploy more troops to Afghanistan, and for the first time deploy them outside Kabul. The action appeared to Afghans as the spreading and lengthening of the Western occupation of their country.

- 26–27 October 2003: On 26 October, rockets hit Baghdad's Al-Rashid Hotel—headquarters of the U.S. occupation authority—killing one U.S. soldier and wounding seventeen people. On 27 October, the headquarters of the International Committee of the Red Cross and four Baghdad police stations were car-bombed in a period of forty-five minutes. A fifth police station was spared when the driver of another vehicle was shot. The attacks, which killed thirty-five and wounded 224, were attributed to foreign mujahedin.

- 9 November 2003: Al-Muhaya residential compound in Riyadh was bombed; eighteen were killed and more than two hundred wounded. Nearly all casualties were expatriate Muslims. Al Qaeda issued a statement denying responsibility for the attack.

- 12 November 2003: The headquarters of the Italian military police in al-Nasariyah, Iraq, was attacked with a truck bomb. Eighteen Italian military personnel and eleven Iraqis were killed. More than a hundred people were wounded.

- 15 November 2003: Two Jewish synagogues in Istanbul were attacked by suicide car bombs; twenty-three people were killed and 303 were wounded.

- 20 November 2003: The UK Consulate and HSBC Bank building in Istanbul were attacked with suicide car bombs, killing twenty-seven people and wounding at least 450. In Iraq, a remotely detonated bomb destroyed a Polish military vehicle but caused no casualties; earlier, on 6 November, a Polish officer had been killed by insurgents.

- 30 November 2003: Insurgents killed seven Spanish intelligence officers near Baghdad and two Japanese diplomats in Tikrit. Another Spanish intelligence officer had been killed in Baghdad on 9 October 2003. In March 2003, an al Qaeda associate had warned Spain not to go to Iraq. "The wound of the occupation of Andalusia [Spain] has not healed," Ahmed Rafat wrote, "and the decision of your government, which represents the old crusaders, to support the new crusade of U.S. Protestants is a real threat to the safety of every Spaniard. . . ."[59]

- 5 December 2003: A female Chechen suicide bomber detonated herself on an intercity commuter train in Russia's Stavropol region near Chechnya. At least forty-two people were killed, and more than one hundred were wounded.

- 14 and 25 December 2003: Pakistan president Musharraf survived two attempted assassinations near Islamabad. On 14 December a mine was detonated along his travel route; on 25 December his convoy was hit by two suicide car bombs.
- 27 December 2003: In Karbala, Iraq, Islamist fighters killed four Bulgarian soldiers and two Thai soldiers.
- 27 and 28 January 2004: Suicide car bombs in Kabul on successive days killed a Canadian and a UK soldier; three Canadian and four UK soldiers were wounded.
- 1 February 2004: In Iraq, Islamist insurgents detonated themselves in the Irbil headquarters of the two main Kurdish political parties, killing 110 and wounding almost 250.
- 6 February 2004: A Chechen suicide bomber detonated himself on the Moscow subway, killing thirty-nine people and wounding 134.
- 11 March 2004: In Madrid, al Qaeda detonated ten nearly simultaneous bombs in four packed commuter trains, killing 191 people and wounding more than twelve hundred. When claiming responsibility for the attack, al Qaeda described the operation as "part of a settlement of old accounts with Crusade[r] Spain, the ally of the United States in its war against Islam." Several days later, the conservative Spanish government was defeated in a general election, and the new socialist prime minister announced he would withdraw Spanish troops from Iraq.
- 15 March 2004: Iraqi mujahedin killed four Southern Baptist missionaries near Mosul, in northern Iraq. The attack brought to eight the number of Southern Baptist missionaries killed by Islamists around the world since 2003.
- 22 March 2004: Israel assassinated wheelchair-bound HAMAS leader Shaykh Ahmed Yasin as he left the mosque after prayers. Yasin was a loss to HAMAS and the Islamist movement generally, but his status as martyr would increase recruits for Islamist groups worldwide. The United States enhanced the benefit derived by Islamists from Yasin's murder by vetoing a UN resolution censuring the Israeli attack and reasserting Israel's "right to defend herself from terror."
- 28–31 March 2004: Multiple bombs were detonated by Islamist fighters in the Uzbek capital Tashkent over three days. The bombings and subsequent gunfights resulted in the death of thirty-three Islamists, seven of whom were women. Fourteen Uzbeks—including ten policemen—were killed and thirty-five were wounded. The Uzbek government suspected that the Islamic Movement of Uzbekistan was responsible for the attacks.
- 2 May 2004: Islamist fighters attacked a major Saudi/Exxon-Mobil

oil facility at Yanbu, 350 kilometers north of Jeddah. Five Westerners — two Americans, two Britons, and an Australian — and a Saudi were killed, and twenty-eight people were wounded. Three attackers were employees of the facility and used their passes to get the fourth attacker inside. All four were killed.[60]

- 29 May 2004: Islamist fighters attacked several oil company compounds in Yanbu. Twenty-two people were killed; nineteen were non-Saudis.[61]

- 9 September 2004: JI detonated a suicide car bomb near Australia's embassy in Jakarta, killing nine and wounding 173. The JI's postattack communiqué explained, "We decided to call Australia to account, which we consider one of the worst of God's enemies, and God's religion of Islam."[62]

- 7 October 2004: Islamist fighters detonated three bombs — one a suicide car bomb — at the Hilton Hotel in the Sinai resort town of Taba, Egypt, and two campsites in nearby Ras al-Shitan. Thirty-four people were killed, 173 were wounded. Many of the dead were foreigners, including thirteen Israeli tourists. Several groups claimed credit for the attack, including the Abdullah Azzam Brigades reportedly allied with al Qaeda.[63]

- 3 November 2004: Dutch-Moroccan Islamist Mohammad Bouyeri repeatedly shot and slit the throat of Dutch filmmaker Theo van Gogh, a well-known critic of Islam. Bouyeri, a youth counselor said to be a "studious and respectable young man," was arrested, and Dutch intelligence officials said he had "links to the international al-Qaeda network." Van Gogh's murder was followed by arson attacks against several Dutch mosques.[64]

- 6 December 2004: Al Qaeda fighters forcibly entered the U.S. Consulate's compound in Jeddah and attacked with small arms, killing nine and wounding ten. There were no American casualties. The raid was the first on a Western diplomatic mission in Saudi Arabia.[65]

- 19 March 2005: A suicide car bomb was detonated outside the British School's theater in Doha, Qatar. One Briton was killed, sixteen people were wounded. The attacker, Omar Ahmed Abdullah Ali, was an Egyptian who had been employed as an IT professional by the Qatar Petroleum Company since 1990. He was married with children. The attack was the first suicide bombing in Qatar and occurred two days after al Qaeda's leader in Saudi Arabia, Saleh al-Awfi, had called for attacks on Westerners in the Persian Gulf.[66]

- 7 April 2005: An Islamist suicide bomber riding a motorcycle detonated himself among tourists in Cairo's Khal al-Khalili bazaar. Two Frenchmen and one American were killed; twenty people were wounded. The attack was the first in Cairo in seven years.[67]

- April–June 2005: Several concurrent incidents suggested there was no slackening of Islamist militancy among the Saudi people and government. On 20 April, Saudi security forces arrested forty Pakistani Christians in a private home in Riyadh for holding prayers and practicing a religion other than Islam. On 23 April, Islamist candidates overwhelmingly won elections for 178 municipal councils, the first such elections in thirty years. The winners came from a "Golden List" of candidates endorsed and campaigned for by the government's religious establishment. By late May, the Saudi interior ministry claimed that religiously devote Saudi males were going to Iraq to fight U.S. forces; unofficial estimates are that fifteen hundred to twenty-five hundred Saudis are fighting in Iraq.[68]

- 25 April 2005: U.S. diplomats and intelligence officials told Congress that the number of "significant" terrorist attacks increased in 2004. Official statistics show there were 650 such attacks in 2004, compared with 174 in 2003. The 2003 figure had been a twenty-year high.[69]

- 26 April 2005: Syria's military completed withdrawing from Lebanon. The event opened Lebanese politics to increased factionalism among Shia, Sunni, and Christian parties. Without Syrian control, militant Sunnis would become major political players in the country. In Syria, the withdrawal was considered a humiliation. From Jordan, the exiled Syrian Muslim Brotherhood chief, Dr. Hassan Howiedy, warned that unless President al-Asad allowed Syria's Sunni Islamists greater freedom he would encounter a "great interior pressure, yet unrevealed, that will cause savage behavior — as happened in the past."[70]

- 30 April 2005: Two female Islamist fighters attacked a bus carrying Israeli tourists in Cairo just after the attackers' husband and brother attacked tourists near the Egyptian Museum. The latter died when his bomb exploded prematurely. Both women were killed; one shot the other and then herself. Nine people were wounded in the attacks; four were foreigners. This was the first attack by female fighters in Egypt, and the attackers were wearing burkas and were veiled. The Abdullah Azzam Brigades again claimed credit for the attacks.[71]

- 9 May 2005: *Newsweek* published a story describing the desecration of Korans by U.S. guards at Guantánamo Bay. The story sparked widespread anger and violent protests in the Muslim world. *Newsweek*'s later retraction was met with skepticism. The episode allowed Islamist writers to sharpen anti-Americanism that was already high because of Muslim resentment of prisoner treatment at Guantánamo Bay and Abu Ghraib prison in Iraq.[72]

- 13–14 May 2005: Islamists stormed a prison in the Uzbek city of Andijon to free twenty-three local businessmen who were jailed for being Islamic extremists. The storming led to large demonstrations and a violent confrontation with Uzbek security forces in which at least 750 demonstrators were killed. U.S. government criticisms of the Uzbek regime's handling of the demonstrations prompted Uzbek president Islam Karimov to evict U.S. forces from the Karshi Khanabad air base, a key facility for logistical support for multinational forces in Afghanistan.[73]

- 28 May 2005: Indonesia's JI appeared responsible for detonating several bombs in the market of the Christian town of Tentena on Sulawesi Island. The attack killed twenty-two and wounded fifty and was the first incident of interfaith conflict since a 2001 Muslim-Christian peace agreement.[74]

- 4 June 2005: GSPC attacked a Mauritanian military barracks in Linghet near the border with Algeria and Mali, killing fifteen soldiers and wounding thirteen. The GSPC's communiqué said the attack was to "avenge our brothers who have been imprisoned by the infidel [Mauritanian] regime." Abu Musab al-Zarqawi's al Qaeda in Iraq saluted the attack, "blessing the Algerian mujahedin operation against the enemies of God in Mauritania."[75]

- 7 July 2005: Islamist suicide attackers detonated four bombs in four separate locations in London's public transport system — one bus and three subway trains — killing fifty-six and wounding seven hundred. The attacks disrupted the first day of the annual G-8 Summit in Scotland. About a month before the attacks, British authorities lowered the alert level, concluding that "at present there is not a group with both the current intent and the capability to attack the UK." Bin Laden's deputy al-Zawahiri claimed credit for the attack.[76]

- 21 July 2005: Islamist attackers detonated four bombs in London's public transport system; as on 7 July, the bombs were in one bus and three subway trains. The detonators failed to set off the explosives, however. There were no casualties, and the four attackers are soon arrested. Although damage was minor, the attackers beat the Western world's best urban security services for the second time in two weeks.[77]

- 23 July 2005: Islamist fighters attacked the Egyptian resort town of Sharm al-Sheikh with two suicide car bombs and a satchel bomb, killing ninety and wounding 240. The resort had long been a priority target for bin Laden, who believed the several "peace conferences" held there were symbols of Arab regimes betraying the Palestinians to the United States and Israel. Al Qaeda also considered the resort an "Israeli" target; an estimated ten thousand Israeli tourists were in the resort's vicinity when the attacks occurred. The Abdullah Azzam Brigades, the al Qaeda organization in the Levant and Egypt, and the Tawid and Jihad Group in Egypt claimed credit for the attack. After the attack, Egyptian security forces conducted a prolonged operation to eliminate Islamists insurgents based in the Sinai Peninsula's mountainous northern region.[78]

- 3 August 2005: The Mauritanian military successfully overthrew the pro-U.S. regime of President Maaouya Ould Sid' Taya. Taya was a key ally of the U.S. antiterrorism campaign in West Africa who imprisoned Islamic militants from several West African countries. The new military regime soon released several hundred "political prisoners," including many Islamists jailed by Taya's regime.[79]

- 17 August 2005: The Indonesian government reduces the jail terms of JI's spiritual leader Abu Bakr Bashir and nineteen other Islamists who had been convicted of playing roles in the October 2002 Bali bombings.[80]

- 17 August 2005: More than three hundred crude time bombs are detonated within an hour in sixty-three of Bangladesh's sixty-four political districts, killing two and wounding 150. Public and government venues were the main targets. Leaflets were found at the attack sites claiming credit for the "Jamaat ul Mujahedin." The leaflets asserted that the attacks were aimed at the Dhaka regime and were also meant "to warn Bush and Blair to vacate Muslim countries or to [sic] facer [a] Muslim upsurge." Analysts described the attacks as emblematic of the "rising tide of Islamic militarism" in Bangladesh; the media reported that there were fifty-eight known Islamic militant groups operating in the country.[81]

- 19 August 2005: Islamists fired Katyusha rockets at two U.S. Navy ships in the harbor of Aqaba, Jordan; one landed in the Israeli city of Eilat. The rockets missed and the ships pulled out to sea. Abu Musab al-Zarqawi's al Qaeda organization in Iraq claimed the attack was a warning: "To the tyrant of Jordan [King Abdullah II] we say . . . the lions of God have stepped into Jordan and hold a grudge against you, so end the injustice exerted on our scholars in your prisons and abdicate." Zarqawi also warned that the world would see attacks "soon in Tel Aviv." The Aqaba attack was the first in what is likely to be an increasing flow of Islamist attacks into Jordan and Syria from Islamist insurgent bases in Iraq.[82]

- 27 August 2005: Under threat of deportation from the UK government, Saudi dissident Dr. Muhammed al-Massari closed his London-based Web site. The closure would be seen in the Arab world as Britain yielding to Saudi pressure and would reinforce bin Laden's claim that the West protected freedom of expression for "whites," but forbid it to Muslims.[83]

- 28 August 2005: Indian prime minister Manmohan Singh pledged to provide Afghan president Hamid Karzai "all possible assistance . . . to fight terrorism and rebuild." Singh's pledge — which implied an alliance between Karzai's nominally Islamic regime and polytheist India — would harden Pakistan's religious parties' determination to support the Taliban and al Qaeda against Karzai's regime and would increase the Pakistani military's already strong belief that India was trying to surround Pakistan by creating an anti-Pakistani state on the country's western border.[84]

- 29 August 2005: Saudi security forces battled five Iraqi Islamists in the industrial town of Jubail, east of Riyadh, killing one and capturing three. One infiltrator escaped. The Iraqis entered Saudi Arabia from Iraq to steal cars, apparently intending to take them to Iraq for military use. The Saudi interior ministry said this was the first such infiltration. The incident was the first in what was likely to be an increasing flow of Islamist insurgent infiltrators entering the Gulf states from bases in Iraq.[85]

- 30 August 2005: By this date, the U.S. Department of Defense was running extensive, military-assistance programs in Africa and Southeast Asia to train, equip, and advise indigenous conterterrorism forces. The programs were multiyear and slated to cost nearly a billion dollars. Even if effective, the programs contributed to bin Laden's efforts to, in his words, "spread out U.S. forces" and "bleed [America] to bankruptcy."[86]

- 12 September 2005: Israel's military completed its withdrawal from Gaza. Islamist militants worldwide saw the withdrawal as another step toward Israel's defeat, a step that followed victories in the concessions won in the Oslo negotiations, the Madrid conference, and the first and second Intifadahs, as well as from Israel's forced withdrawal from southern Lebanon.[87]

- 1 October 2005: Three JI suicide bombers detonated themselves in a nightclub-restaurant district in Bali, killing twenty-six and wounding more than one hundred.

While the destruction of two U.S. embassies in Africa, the crippling of the U.S. destroyer *Cole* in Yemen, and the attacks on the World Trade Center and the Pentagon dominated media reporting of bin Laden's 1996–2005 activities, the range of military, political, economic, and propaganda successes outlined above covered the patient Islamist insurgent chief's gamut of activities: fatalities, physical destruction, and acute embarrassment inflicted on the world's greatest power in East Africa, in Yemen, and within the United States itself; the intimidation of U.S. forces worldwide; the terrorizing of Christians in East Asia; the addition of a high-profile irritant to the usually amiable conduct of Canada-U.S. diplomatic relations; support to jihads in Uzbekistan, Kashmir, Chechnya, and the Philippines; and attacks on "atheist" regimes in Russia, Chechnya, and Dagestan, an "infidel" regime in India, and the "apostate" al-Saud regime and U.S. forces in Saudi Arabia.

Loss for Standing Governments

In addition to these positive results for the al Qaeda forces, the attacks yielded other benefits that could not but be dear to the heart of a mujahid who fought in Afghanistan. The Islamist insurgencies in which bin Laden has been involved are causing the targeted governments economic losses and diplomatic complications. Egypt, Israel, the Philippines, and Yemen, for example, have suffered declines in tourism that for each is a top foreign-exchange earner. Manila and New Delhi are losing servicemen regularly and each is reported to be spending up to $2.5 million per day to fight the Islamist insurgents; oil exploration and development have been slowed in several Indonesian provinces; Manila is coping with "investigations" of its treatment of Muslims by the United Nations, the Organization of the Islamic Conference, and the Vatican; and the Philippine economy has slowed, with Japanese bankers, the IMF, the World Bank, and the Asian Development Bank delaying investment disbursements because of the fighting in Mindanao.

These sorts of pressures put Manila, Jakarta, and New Delhi in the same intractable predicament the Soviet Union encountered during its occupation of Afghanistan. Moscow's attempt to staunch its human and economic bleeding by using indiscriminate military power to end the war backfired by sharply increasing diplomatic, human rights, and economic pressure on the Soviet Union to stop the war by giving up rather than by winning. Boxed in by this conundrum, the Soviets eventually gave up and went home, an option not available to the already-at-home governments in Manila, Jakarta, and New Delhi. The attacks noted above also have given bin Laden and his allies unprecedented recognition among Muslims and in the world as a whole.

Bin Laden's attacks and threats also humiliated America, always a top-priority goal for him. As described in this chapter's chronology, until October 2000 he had not attacked U.S. interests since August 1998 and yet he had U.S. authorities running from pillar to post in fear of the Arab Afghans. In this regard, an 8 March 2000 *Wall Street Journal* article, titled "Casting a Global Net, U.S. Security Forces Survive Terrorist Test," graphically depicted how the senior levels of the U.S. government were tied in knots for an entire month because they feared a bin Laden attack at New Year's 2000. This article is, incidentally, eloquent food for thought for those experts, scholars, and wise men who denigrate as "old-fashioned" the idea that a single individual's words and actions can have a substantial impact on history. This point was dramatically underscored when the director of Central Intelligence told Congress in February 2001 that bin Laden was the nation's "top national security threat."

Overall, bin Laden's 1996–2001 attempts to humble, humiliate, and defeat the United States came in violent and nonviolent forms, and, as the official Chinese newspaper *Renmin Ribao* said in August 1999, the nonviolent form on offer from "the Saudi with the heavy beard" produced a situation in which "the United States has totally lost its face and bearing as a big country." In terms familiar to his countrymen, U.S. terrorism expert Bruce Hoffman told the *Los Angeles Times* bin Laden resembles an Islamist P. T. Barnum: "He issues a threat and we react. He makes us jump." In terms of gauging the level of humiliation imposed on the United States by bin Laden, there is no better summary than Robert Fisk's description of the U.S. president's March 2000 arrival in Pakistan. "So fearful were they of [a bin Laden] 'terrorist' attack on their president," Fisk wrote, "that Clinton's personal jet turned up on the tarmac of Islamabad's military airport with a cargo of FBI men, while the most powerful man on earth slunk in later in an unmarked plane. For a man who was to read the riot act to [Pakistan chief executive] General Pervez Musharraf . . . it was a pathetic performance."[88]

Gains for Insurgencies

Special attention must be paid to the Islamist insurgencies in which bin Laden's cadre, funds, or inspiration play a part. While destroyed embassies in Africa, disemboweled tourists in Luxor, heavily listing naval combatants in Aden, and collapsed skyscrapers garner the lion's share of media coverage, the survival and, in most cases, the progress of the world's multiple ongoing Islamist insurgencies are likely the events that will have the most long-term positive effect for bin Laden's al Qaeda movement. As shown in Afghanistan, Kashmir, and Chechnya, the in-God's-name struggles are magnets for devoted Muslim youths, incubators that breed international connections and loyalties, and schools for inculcating military training, combat experience, and theology. By mid-2001, the balance sheet showed bin Laden was very much in the black vis-à-vis insurgencies.

The Philippines

The Philippine insurgency remains vibrant, with frequent heavy fighting between the Abu Sayyaf Group and Moro Islamic Liberation Front (MILF) and Manila's military since fall 1999. In November 1999, for example, fighting in North Catabato had displaced six thousand people from their villages, and the MILF's Afghanistan-trained leader, Hashim Salamat, confidently rebuffed Philippine defense minister Orlando Mercado's request for intensive peace negotiations. The MILF's leaders, Salamat said, "are not keen on accelerating the [peace] talks," and, in any event, the MILF would continue strengthening its military forces during the government's "peace venture." By early 2002, combat had increased to the point where Manila had asked for U.S. assistance and the United States had deployed a training force of 650 soldiers, 160 from the Special Forces. The presence of U.S. forces appears to be promoting cooperation among the Abu Sayyaf Group, the MILF, and other Muslim forces.[89]

Kashmir

The Islamist insurgents in Kashmir likewise were active, and they were directly assisted in summer 1999 by Pakistani forces. Together they staged an incursion into the Kargil area of Indian-held Kashmir, embarrassing the government in New Delhi and giving the plight of Kashmiri Muslims unprecedented worldwide media exposure. While the incursion was ultimately repelled by a combination of coercive U.S. pressure on Pakistani prime minister Nawaz Sharif—which led to the coup that toppled his government—and India's combined-arms operations, the Kargil incursion was a huge substantive success for Pakistan, the Kashmiri insurgents, and the Kashmiris' foreign supporters, particularly Osama bin Laden.

In terms of casualties, *Jane's Intelligence Review* has reported India's forces suffered nearly five hundred officers and men killed and about one thousand wounded in the two-month campaign, and that since the end of the Kargil campaign, attacks by Kashmiri insurgents on Indian soldiers and policemen in Kashmir have quadrupled the pre-Kargil rate. More important in the long run, according to an unidentified Indian army officer, is that the need to keep larger forces deployed in the area to prevent another Kargil "will bleed India financially" to the tune of more than $2 million per day. "India may have pushed back the Pakistani invasion [of Kargil]," the officer concluded, "but it has lost the battle as it frantically prepares for the formidable and hugely expensive task of permanently manning the LoC [Line of Control] to prevent further intrusions."[90]

Indian government, security, police, and military officials also have claimed that media coverage of the Kargil fighting stimulated a steady influx of Islamist fighters from Afghanistan, Burma, Bangladesh, Sudan, Pakistan, and elsewhere. The *Hindustan Times* wrote in late November 1999, for example, that Kashmiri guerrilla groups had been significantly strengthened by "foreign mercenaries whose presence has been noted in many areas of Kashmir," while the *Indian Express* claimed "about 3,500 foreign insurgents continue to stay put in Kashmir and are planning to step up their activities in [the Kashmiri capital] Srinigar to gain greater [international] focus on their presence." This development, the *Hindustan Times* argued, has given the insurgency in Kashmir "a more overt appeal to Islam."[91]

International media coverage of Kashmir was sharpened again at year's end in 1999, 2000, and 2001. In 1999, the hijacking of an India Air flight to Kandahar and New Delhi's decision to exchange three imprisoned Kashmiri insurgent leaders for the release of the aircraft yielded a propaganda coup for the Kashmiris. In December 2000, Kashmiri attacks between 22 and 25 December again produced physical damage and humiliating media coverage for India. On 22 December, the Pakistan-based Lashkar-e Toiba attacked the historic "Red Fort" in the heart of New Delhi. The attackers killed three and escaped after striking a blow against what the Indian media termed "the nation's most important symbol of invincibility." On 25 December, Kashmiri insurgents detonated a car bomb in the headquarters compound of India's 15th Corps in Srinigar, the capital of Kashmir. The attack killed eleven and wounded twenty-six.[92] On 13 December 2001, Kashmiri fighters — apparently from the Lashkar-i-Taiyibah — again humiliated the Indian government by launching a suicide attack on the parliament building in New Delhi. This attack on the "very soul of Indian democracy," in turn, sparked the largest-ever Indian military mobilization, leaving the subcontinent a hairsbreath from war.

Overall, the 1999–2001 period saw major gains for the Kashmir insurgency. "Just six months ago," Pamela Constable wrote in January 2000 in the *Washington Post,* "Indian authorities declared the local insurgent movement vanquished" but "today a newly revived rebel movement has Indian forces on the defensive." The revitalized insurgents are well armed, well trained, and well financed, courtesy of Pakistan, the Taliban, bin Laden, and wealthy Gulf Muslims, and are no longer "the hodge-podge of Kashmiri youths with rifles and grenades who once dreamed of driving Indian forces from this part of their homeland." A senior Indian military officer told *Al-Quds Al-Arabi* that "60 percent of the [insurgent] movement members in Kashmir are foreign mercenaries and Afghan mujahedin" — an exaggeration but indicative of the internationalization of the struggle — and the BBC's correspondent in Kashmir, Altaf Husayn, has said "the involvement of foreign fighters (meaning non-Kashmiris) in the conflict has completely changed the map of the separatist movement. At the beginning of the 1990s, the movement operated like an amateur body, but now it is more skillful and its fighters are more committed and loyal."[93]

Supporting Husayn's judgment, Constable reported that since November 1999 the insurgents have attacked half a dozen compounds defended by Indian security forces, and that several attacks used suicide car bombs, a heretofore-unknown tactic in Kashmir. These hard-target attacks suggest the Kashmiris have abandoned their previous preference for soft targets — Hindu civilians, off-duty servicemen, and so forth — and have validated the prediction of an Indian military officer about the impact of aid from bin Laden.[94]

"Bin Laden is funding a sophisticated fighting force," an Indian security officer told the media in August 1998. "This is not a riff-raff operation." In seeking foreign assistance to defeat this "sophisticated fighting force," the Indians have presented the Kashmiris and their supporters an enormous and unanticipated windfall by reaching out in a very public way to Israel's security and intelligence services for counterterrorism training; to Israel's military to modernize India's fighter aircraft and naval combatants; and to the Israeli government for a "nuclear relationship." It is hard to imagine a better gift from Allah to the Kashmiri Islamists and their foreign backers than a highly publicized intelligence, military, and nuclear "special relationship" between the Hindu hegemonists and the Zionist entity.[95]

Algeria

In Algeria, *Al-Sharq Al-Awsat* reported in mid-1999 that bin Laden was "financing and arming the Armed Islamic Group [GIA], [and] urging it not to join the truce declared by the Algerian Islamic Salvation Front." To sharpen the GIA's military efficiency, *Al-Sharq Al-Awsat* reported, bin Laden developed the group's international logistics infrastructure, a network that is "smuggling large quantities of weapons, ammunition, and funds into Algeria." By the end of 1999, the pace of attacks in Algeria by the GIA and the bin Laden-backed Salafist Group for Call and Combat (GSPC) — which has been called al Qaeda's arm in Algeria — was increasing, and the media was giving "more weight" to previous speculation that there is "a connection between Osama bin Laden and the surge of violence in Algeria." Algiers' *El-Watan* was warning that the "security situation had deteriorated in recent weeks," and *AFP* reported that more than seventy people were killed in the first week of Ramadan, which began in December 1999. In 2000 the Algerian insurgency claimed over twenty-five hundred deaths and saw the Islamists focus on hard targets — as have their Kashmiri brethren — "to weaken the military establishment and prove its incompetence," killing nearly five hundred officers in the process. As in the past, the month of Ramadan was bloody in 2000, with more than 250 deaths. In 2001, the insurgency claimed about two thousand lives.[96]

Indonesia

The pace and violence of Islamist guerrilla activity accelerated in Indonesia's overwhelmingly Muslim Aceh Province — known as the "verandah of Mecca" — where the Free Aceh Movement (GAM) has been fighting since the mid-1970s to create an independent Muslim state and where GAM leaders are now seeking international support for that goal. The Aceh fighters receive some weapons from supporters in the Indonesian military, a military-to-insurgents pipeline also seen in the Philippines and Kashmir, and funds are flowing to the insurgents from wealthy expatriate Acehnese businessmen in Malaysia and Thailand. In the first quarter of 2000, combat between the Islamists and the Indonesian military resulted in more than three hundred deaths, the suspension of petroleum exploration by Exxon-Oil, and the initiation of attacks by Christian militias on Muslim civilians similar to those contemporaneously occurring in the Philippines. As fighting intensified, the media reported bin Laden was sending support to the Acehnese, perhaps backing with actions the words he used in 1998 to applaud the Muslim people of Indonesia "where Suharto, a despot who has ruled 30 years, was overthrown." By mid-June 2000, Melbourne's *Age* reported growing regional concern that bin Laden is "funding Islamic groups in the Indonesian provinces of Aceh and Ambon." Finally, resentment still is simmering in Muslim Indonesians over the UN referendum that gave birth to an independent Christian state in East Timor. Anger over the vote seemed to foreshadow a revanchist Muslim insurgency, and the referendum itself is already causing trouble for New Delhi and Manila, because the Kashmiris and Moros have demanded identical UN referenda.[97]

Downside of al Qaeda's Battle Ledger, 1996–2005

Notwithstanding the successes just discussed, there is a substantial downside to al Qaeda for the period from 1996 through early October 2005. Likewise, the U.S.-led military offensive against the Taliban and al Qaeda has cost bin Laden the lives or services of several senior lieutenants and has denied the Islamists—at least temporarily—full freedom of movement in Afghanistan. Al Qaeda and its closest allies suffered substantial attrition in the period. Fighters were killed, captured, and jailed; cells and networks were disrupted and sometimes dismantled; large financial and human resources were spent on the Taliban's war effort and at least a half dozen Islamist insurgencies; and steady U.S. rhetoric about bin Laden presumably alerted security and police services worldwide, thereby making operational travel and procurement somewhat more difficult. Bin Laden and his allies have suffered telling setbacks, and—until the enormous amount of death and economic damage inflicted on the United States on 11 September 2001—the Crusaders had more physically battered the Islamists than the Islamists had battered the Crusaders.

- Spring 1997: Sidi al-Madani al-Tayyib, who is married to bin Laden's niece, was captured by or surrendered to Saudi authorities. Tayyib was bin Laden's chief financial officer in Sudan, and, as Abu Hajir noted, he approved all transactions over $1,000. Tayyib's admissions "severely harmed" bin Laden's organization and gave Saudi officials information on "all of his [bin Laden's] investments abroad and the names of several of the movement's members inside Saudi

Arabia." In 1997 Tayyib was pardoned "in return for exposing some of bin Laden's financial operations."[98]

- May 1996–March 1999: In this period, Saudi authorities "detained . . . a large number of jihad youth, including many followers and supporters of the Shaykh [bin Laden]. The authorities discovered that some of the detainees were on the verge of carrying out specific and targeted operations." In early 1999, for example, "300 companions and supporters of bin Laden" were arrested as they prepared to attack "U.S. soldiers in Saudi Arabia." Press reports said Saudi authorities had been lucky to stumble on nascent operations. Reports quoting official Saudi documents show "the existence of large numbers [of bin Laden followers] who have not and will not be rounded up or even have their locations, provisions, logistics, or plans and directives identified by Saudi authorities." Bin Laden gave an idea of al Qaeda's size in the kingdom in 1998, telling the daily *Pakistan* that "800 of his mujahids are under arrest [in Saudi Arabia] and he prays that may God bless them with shahadat martyrdom." Bin Laden said most arrests occurred near Mecca and that Saudi security forces had confiscated "a sizable quantity of arms used by our mujahedin, including seven rockets and Stinger missiles." He added, however, "what was captured was much less than what was not captured."[99]

- August 1997: Kenyan police and FBI agents raided bin Laden lieutenant Wadih el-Hage's home in Nairobi, seizing his personal papers and computer. U.S. authorities claimed, according to the *New York Times,* that El-Hage's records showed that he had met bin Laden in early 1997 and, when the raid occurred, was preparing "300 activists" for military activity. El-Hage left for the United States soon after the raid.[100]

- June 1998: Saudi authorities deported bin Laden financial aide Sa'id Sayyed Salamah to Egypt; Salamah is an Egyptian and an EIJ member. He had worked for bin Laden in Sudan and was an accountant for the bin Laden family company when he was arrested. The Saudis acted after noticing Salamah traveled frequently to Pakistan, Sudan, and Europe. He apparently "visited several countries, including some African countries, and carried funds belonging to 'The Base' organization [al Qaeda] in the countries he visited."[101]

- 20 August 1998: The United States attacked bin Laden-related targets in Afghanistan and Sudan with cruise missiles. The strikes caused casualties and varying degrees of damage to several training camps near Khowst. The U.S. attack also destroyed the El-Shifa pharmaceutical plant in Khartoum, which was reported to have been involved in bin Laden's efforts to manufacture chemical and biological weapons.[102]

- August 1998: Bulgarian authorities captured and deported to Egypt EIJ member Issam Abdel-Alim on the basis of an "American charge" and "after days of interrogation at the hands of Bulgarian and U.S. intelligence agents."[103]
- August 1998: Two alleged bombers of the U.S. embassy in Kenya were arrested and sent to the United States for arraignment: Mohammed Sadiq Odeh from Pakistan and Mohamed Rashed Daoud al-Owali from Kenya.[104]
- June–September 1998: Four EIJ-bin Laden fighters were arrested in Albania and sent to Egypt: Ahmad Ibrahim al-Najjar, Majed Mustafa, Mohamed Hassan, and Mohamed Huda. When caught, the four had "material indicating that they intended to bomb the American embassy in Tirana." All four had been working in the Tirana branch of the Kuwaiti Society for the Revival of the Islamic Heritage, an Islamic nongovernmental organization.[105]
- 10 September 1998: Al Qaeda weapons trainer Ali Muhammed was arrested in the United States. Muhammed is a former Egyptian army officer and a former noncommissioned officer in the U.S. Special Forces. Muhammed trained and fought in Afghanistan when on leave from the U.S. Army. He is a specialist in surveillance, obtaining false documents, and "trained Islamic militants in basic military techniques in the New York City area."[106]
- 16–24 September 1998: On 16 September German authorities arrested senior bin Laden lieutenant and chief weapons and communications procurer Mamdouh Mahmud Salim—aka Abu Hajir—in Munich, Germany. He was extradited to the United States on 20 December 1998. On 24 September Ugandan authorities detained twenty suspects, including two ringleaders, who are believed to have been planning to bomb the U.S. embassy in Kampala. The plot's leaders reportedly are tied to Osama bin Laden.[107]
- 23 September 1998: British authorities arrested seven Islamists, all "believed linked to the Saudi terrorist kingpin." Four have since been released, but the United States has requested the extradition of bin Laden's U.K.-based lieutenant Khalid Fawwaz, and senior EIJ members Ibrahim Husayn Eidarous and Adil Abd-al-Majid Abd-al-Bari. Fawwaz is a civil engineer and headed bin Laden's Advice and Reform Committee, which was founded in August 1994. Fawwaz earlier served as bin Laden's representative in Kenya and is believed, according to *Al-Majallah,* to have "issued direct orders to one of the cells belonging to Osama bin Laden in East Africa to carry out the operation in [August 1998]." By May 2000,

the United Kingdom had agreed to extradite Fawwaz, Eidarous, and al-Bari, and by late 2001, each had lost his appeal and was awaiting movement to the United States.[108]

- September 1998: Three EIJ members—two of them senior operatives—were deported from Baku, Azerbaijan, to Egypt: Ihab Abdullah Saqr, Isam al-Din Hafiz, and Ahmad Salamah Mabruk. Mabruk is the EIJ's number-three leader and was captured with "a computer disk listing 100 possible American and Israeli targets," and which gave the Egyptian government "a map of the stations where . . . leading members of al Jihad and al Qaeda were deployed." Saqr is an EIJ explosives expert and was involved in the November 1995 attack on Egypt's embassy in Pakistan.[109]
- 1–2 October 1998: Italian police arrested EIJ operative Ahmed Naji after he fled Albania. The Italian press said Naji "masterminded the failed attack on the U.S. embassy in Tirana."[110]
- 7 October 1998: Senior bin Laden lieutenant Wadih El-Hage was arrested and indicted in the United States. El-Hage was bin Laden's personal secretary in Sudan and ran al Qaeda operations in Kenya until September 1997. Among the charges against El-Hage was "providing false passports and other assistance to bin Laden loyalists who are suspected of attacking U.S. and UN forces in Somalia in 1993 and 1994." El-Hage also was providing false passports to bin Laden operatives traveling to the Caucasus. U.S. authorities reportedly seized computer diskettes from El-Hage's home in Texas that "held secrets of his [bin Laden's] front companies and dealings with businessmen."[111]
- 25 October 1998: EIJ-bin Laden fighter Salah Muhammad Umar Sa'id was killed in gunfight with Albanian police while resisting arrest. The press claimed Sa'id was part of the bin Laden team responsible for the aborted attack on the U.S. embassy in Tirana.[112]
- November 1998: South Africa deported three EIJ members to Egypt: Abd al-Munim Mutawaali Abu Sari, Tariq Mursi Wabbah, and Jamal Shuayb. The three had been collecting funds from South Africa's Muslims and sending the funds to the EIJ in Egypt.[113]
- December 1998: Kuwait deported to Egypt fifteen bin Laden- and EIJ-related Islamists. Three important EIJ members were in the group: Ahmad Hasan Badi, Majid Fahmi, and Muhammad Faraj. Several of the deportees worked for the Kuwaiti Society for the Revival of the Islamic Heritage. Materials seized from the group showed it sought to overthrow the Kuwaiti regime because it was allied with the United States against Iraq.[114]
- December 1998: Abdurajik Abubakr Janjalani, leader of the Filipino ASG, was killed in a clash with the Philippine military out-

side Isabel, the capital of Basilan Island.[115]

- 18 January 1999: French police arrested Ahmed Laidouni — age thirty and born in France to Algerian parents — because of his ties to bin Laden. Laidouni was charged with "criminal association with a terrorist enterprise." Laidouni fought with the Bosnian Muslims from 1992 to 1995 and was trained on weapons and explosives in Afghan camps. He told French authorities that bin Laden brother-in-law Muhammed Jamal Khalifah is still bin Laden's conduit to "Filipino fighters."[116]

- January 1999: Indian police arrested Bangladeshi Sayyid Abu-Nassir and three other men the Indians reported were connected to bin Laden. The Indian authorities claimed the four were planning to bomb the U.S. embassy in New Delhi and the U.S. consulates in Calcutta and Madras.[117]

- 30 January 1999: Bangladeshi security forces arrested two self-confessed bin Laden operatives: a South African named Ahmed Sadek and a Pakistani named Mohammed Sajid. The two were charged with attacking the country's leading secular poet, Shamsur Rahman. Security forces also identified five bank accounts used by bin Laden-linked Bangladeshi Islamists to fund religious schools used to recruit militant youths.[118]

- 8 January 1999: Albanian authorities arrested an ethnic Albanian named Maksi Ciciku for carrying out espionage activities for bin Laden. Ciciku owned a private security company in Tirana that he used, according to the Albanian press, to follow "the movements of the ambassador and the personnel of the U.S. embassy."[119]

- March 1999: Mauritanian authorities arrested six people and interrogated twenty others with suspected ties to bin Laden. Many of the individuals were traders and professionals, and the authorities thought they could throw "more light on what is referred to in Nouakchott as a section of the 'Mauritanian Afghans.'" One of those arrested, Mohamed Yahya Ould Saad, was part of an "underground network." He was in Afghanistan from 1993 until 1997, "where he is believed to have undergone training at a military camp set up by bin Laden. Others of those arrested also were thought to have spent time in Afghanistan."[120]

- 1 March 1999: French authorities arrested French citizen David Courtailler. He was trained in a bin Laden camp in Afghanistan in the 1997–1998 period.[121]

- October 1999: South African authorities captured Khalfan Khamis Mohammed, a suspected participant in the August 1998 bombing of the U.S. embassy in Tanzania. Khalfan was turned over to the FBI, indicted, and convicted.[122]

- October 1999: Yemeni authorities execute Abyan Islamic Army leader Zayn-al-Abidin al-Muhdar for the December 1998 kidnapping and murder of three U.K. and one Australian tourists. Al-Muhdar staged the kidnappings in bin Laden's name.[123]

- 12 November 1999: Albania deported a dual Albanian-Jordanian citizen named Abdul Latif Salah because it believed he was an EIJ member and "a man close to arch-terrorist bin Laden." Salah had lived in Tirana since 1992 and had ingratiated himself with all Albanian political parties. He worked with a variety of Islamic non-governmental organizations and helped build the EIJ network in Albania. Salah had accumulated substantial wealth through construction and other businesses.[124]

- 5 December 1999–3 January 2000: Actions by security services and plain bad luck aborted bin Laden's plan for multiple anti-U.S. attacks in what came to be known as the "Millennium Plot." Jordanian authorities arrested thirteen bin Laden operatives in Jordan — eleven Jordanians, an Iraqi, and an Algerian — who were preparing to attack hotels in Amman and Christian holy sites along the Jordan River during the New Year's period. The Islamists had been smuggling explosives into Jordan since at least early 1998. On 18 December Pakistan arrested and sent to Jordan a dual Jordanian-U.S. citizen named Khalil al-Deeq, who was controlling the group arrested in Jordan from his base in Peshawar. Al-Deeq had been a U.S. serviceman and previously was convicted and jailed for his role in a 1993 series of bombings in Jordan that were financed by bin Laden and Mohammed Jamal Khalifah. On 14 December U.S. Customs in Washington State arrested Algerian national Ahmed Ressam for smuggling explosives from Canada to the United States. Ressam was trained in one of bin Laden's Afghan camps, and was carrying a forged Canadian passport, fifty-four kilograms of nitroglycerin, and a number of "advanced detonators." Ressam and his associates in Canada are members of Algeria's Armed Islamic Group, but the *Wall Street Journal* quoted U.S. authorities as saying that Ressam and his colleagues may have been working for al Qaeda. On 3 January 2000, a boat laden with explosives sank before it could be detonated next to the U.S. destroyer *The Sullivans*, then refueling in Aden, Yemen.[125]

- March 2000: After raiding an Auckland home, New Zealand police arrested several Afghan refugees who had in their possession "a map of Sydney [Australia] with the nuclear reactor and its entry and exit points highlighted." The police also found "a virtual command center, complete with conference table and maps, and entries in a notebook outlining police security tactics, standards, and chains of command for the Auckland Commonwealth Games in 1990." The media reported the Afghans were tied to bin Laden and planned to attack the Lucas Heights nuclear reactor in Sydney during the 2000 Summer Olympics. The police also found that the Afghans were trafficking narcotics, smuggling aliens, and dealing in counterfeit passports and money.[126]

- June–August 2000: Israeli and Palestinian security services arrested twenty-three Islamists, some of whom the services claimed were linked to bin Laden. The services also seized six kilograms of TNT, some C-4 explosive, and remote control equipment. Israel claimed a Palestinian named Nabil Okal was the group's leader and that he was trained in bin Laden's Afghan camps and funded by HAMAS's (Islamic Resistance Movement) Shaykh Yasin. HAMAS rejected the latter allegation.[127]

- 7–29 July 2000: On 7 July Canadian police arrested Muhammed Mahjub, a senior leader of the Vanguards of Conquest, an EIJ faction. Mahjub was arrested because of his links to Egyptian Islamists and bin Laden. On 29 August Pakistani security officials arrested Abdel Rahman al-Kanadi for his role in the EIJ's 1995 bombing of Egypt's embassy in Pakistan. When arrested, al-Kanadi carried a Canadian passport and was chief of the nongovernmental organization Human Concern International's office in Peshawar. Mahjub and al-Kanadi are being held pending possible extradition to Egypt.[128]

- 18 September 2000: Jordan's security court convicted twenty-eight Islamists charged in the aborted December 1999 attacks on Jewish and Christian targets in Jordan. Six of the Islamists were acquitted, sixteen got fifteen-year sentences, and six were sentenced to death; four of the latter are at large. Of the twenty-eight men, twelve were tried in absentia.[129]

- 31 October–6 November 2000: Kuwaiti authorities arrested eleven Islamists on terrorism-related charges; two were Kuwaitis and officers in Kuwait's security services. Also seized were 133 kilograms of explosives, 5 hand grenades, and 1,450 detonators. The authorities said the group was tied to bin Laden and EIJ leader Zawahiri and was planning to use explosive-laden vehicles to attack U.S. military convoys in Kuwait. The group also was planning attacks on a U.S. military base in Kuwait and on individual Western personnel in their vehicles and residences.[130]

- November 2000: Yemeni authorities stopped an attack on a convoy carrying U.S. soldiers who were assisting in mine-clearing operations. The arrested men are reported to be associated with bin Laden and had details of the routes the convoy used.[131]

- 26 December 2000–4 April 2001: On 26 December German authorities raided a Frankfurt home and arrested four Algerian Islamists police say were connected to bin Laden. Also seized was $14,000 in cash, forged passports, computers and encrypted computer discs, rifles with telescopic sights, a machine gun, pistols with silencers, and "large quantities of chemicals for the production of explosives." The police also recovered a twelve-minute video of the Christmas fair in Strasbourg, France, which they speculated was a surveillance film of the group's target. In April 2001 Italian authorities used information seized in Frankfurt to arrest five bin Laden-associated Islamists near Milan, while the German police simultaneously arrested another Islamist in Bavaria. Bavaria's interior minister said the Islamist and those arrested earlier in Frankfurt were also tied to senior bin Laden lieutenant Abu Hajir, who had been arrested in Bavaria in September 1998 and extradited to the United States. The group arrested in April was reported to have been targeting the U.S. embassy in Rome and the 2001 G-8 Economic Summit in Genoa.[132]
- April 2001: On 7 April a U.S. court convicted Algerian Ahmed Ressam on terrorism charges, sentencing him to 130 years in prison. Ressam was arrested in December 1999 for smuggling explosives into the United States from Canada. Ressam was reported to have been part of bin Laden's plans for simultaneous New Year's attacks in Yemen, Jordan, and the United States. Earlier, in late March, Algerian authorities arrested Abdelmajid Dahoumane, who U.S. officials identified as Ressam's right-hand man. Dahoumane received explosives training in Afghanistan, and in the early 1990s he managed the office of the Islamic nongovernmental organization Al-Kifah in Zagreb, Croatia. Dahoumane will stand trial in Algeria.[133]
- 29 May 2001: Four al Qaeda fighters — Wadiha el-Hage, Mohammed Sadiq Odeh, Rashed Daoud al-Owali, and Khaffan Khamis Mohammed — were convicted in a U.S. court in New York of participating in the conspiracy that destroyed the U.S. embassies in Kenya and Tanzania in August 1998. Each will be imprisoned for life.[134]
- 11 September 2001: Nineteen al Qaeda fighters perished in the group's attack on the World Trade Center in New York City and the Pentagon in Washington, D.C.
- 9–24 December 2001: Singaporean authorities arrested fifteen members of a group called Jemmah Islamiyah. The authorities captured documents linking the group to al Qaeda and recovered forged documents, training manuals, and casing reports — some with

video — of targets in Singapore, including the U.S. and Israeli embassies, U.S. business interests, and naval installations used by ships of the U.S. Navy. The Jemmah Islamiyah's aim was to establish an organization in Singapore, Malaysia, Indonesia, and the Philippines, and like its Islamist counterparts elsewhere, its members "were mostly educated, productive members of society."[135]

- 20 December 2001: Senior Vanguards of Conquest leader and Zawahiri associate Ahmad Husayn Agizah was returned to Egypt by the Swedish government. Agizah faces a life sentence he received when tried in absentia in the "Returnees from Albania" trial.[136]

- 22 December 2001: Passengers aboard an American Airlines Paris–Miami flight subdued al Qaeda fighter Richard C. Reid before he could detonate explosives concealed in the heels of his shoes. The airliner was diverted to Boston, where the FBI later told a U.S. court that Reid had enough explosives in his shoes to puncture the fuselage of the aircraft and perhaps to have made it crash.[137]

- Since 7 October 2001: As a result of U.S.-led military attacks on Afghanistan, al Qaeda and the Taliban have lost their freedom of movement in Afghanistan and much military material. They have suffered several thousand deaths among their forces, and U.S. forces have detained about five hundred fighters. While difficult to gauge, al Qaeda's ability to attack U.S. targets outside Afghanistan appears relatively unimpaired, as only three important bin Laden lieutenants have been reported killed or captured: Mohammed Atef was killed in November 2001; Ibn-al-Shaykh al-Libi was captured in December 2001; and Abu Zubaydah was captured in March 2002. At least two senior EIJ leaders have also been killed. Anwar al-Sayyed Ahmad and Muhammed Salah — both members of the EIJ leadership council — were killed in Khowst in October 2001.[138]

- 9–24 December 2001: Singaporean police broke up a JI cell and arrested fifteen Islamists, fourteen Singaporeans, and one Malaysian. Thirteen of fifteen were JI members, and eight of those received physical and religious training in Malaysia and military training in Afghanistan. The cell was formed in 1997 and had planned six truck-bomb attacks against U.S., UK, Israeli, and Australian diplomatic and military targets, as well as against U.S.-owned businesses.

- 14 December 2001: U.S. Marines entered the Qandahar airport to establish the U.S.-led coalition's control of the Taliban's capital. The action ended the Afghan war's first battle, one that evicted the Taliban and al Qaeda from Afghan cities.

- 20–21 December 2001: Egyptian Islamic Jihad faction leaders Ahmad

Husayn Aghiza and Mohammed Sulayman al-Dharri were extradited from Sweden to Egypt. Aghiza took part in the 1995 bombing of Egypt's embassy in Pakistan.

- 19 March 2002: Ibn al-Khattab, leader of the Arab Afghans fighting in Chechnya, was killed by a letter contaminated with poison. The letter was made by Russian authorities and delivered to al-Khattab by a Chechen suborned by them. Al-Khattab also had fought in Tajik and Afghan jihads and was a folk hero among Islamists. A Saudi national, his true name was Salim Suwaylin.

- 28 March 2002: Al Qaeda ally Abu Zubaydah was captured in Faisalbad, Pakistan. A thirty-year-old Palestinian with Saudi citizenship, Zubaydah was a chief recruiter and ran an Afghan training camp. He was under a Jordanian death sentence for his part in al Qaeda's millennium plot to attack U.S. and Israeli targets.

- Late May 2002: Moroccan security arrested five al Qaeda fighters of Saudi nationality in Rabat and Casablanca for planning attacks on U.S. and UK warships in the Straits of Gibraltar. The Saudis had come to Morocco from Afghanistan after transiting Iran and Syria.

- 10 September 2002: Ramzi bin al-Shibh was arrested in Karachi. He was to be a pilot in the 11 September attacks but failed to get a U.S. visa.

- 12 September 2002: Al Qaeda's chief for northern and western Africa, a thirty-seven-year-old Yemeni named Emad Abdelwahid Ahmed Alwan, was killed by Algerian police in eastern Algeria. Alwan was al Qaeda's liaison to GSPC.

- 13–15 September 2002: The FBI arrested seven Yemen-born men in a suburb of Buffalo, New York, saying they were an al Qaeda "sleeper cell" and had received religious training in Pakistan and military training in Afghanistan.

- Late October 2002: United Arab Emirates (UAE) authorities arrested al Qaeda's Persian Gulf operations chief, Abdel-Rahim al-Nashiri. A Yemen-born Saudi citizen, al-Nashiri was charged with planning to destroy "vital economic targets" in the UAE. He also helped plan attacks on U.S. and UK warships in the Straits of Gibraltar, and ships of the U.S. Fifth Fleet in Bahrain. Al-Nashiri was an explosives specialist, fought in Afghanistan with bin Laden, and fought in Bosnia. He took part in al Qaeda's 1998 East Africa attacks, the attacks on the U.S. destroyers *The Sullivans* and *Cole*, and the attack on the French super tanker *Limburg*.

- 3 November 2002: CIA's unmanned "Predator" aircraft destroyed a vehicle, killing six al Qaeda members. Among the dead were al Qaeda's chief in Yemen, al-Qaed Sinan al-Harithi, and U.S.-citizen/

al Qaeda member Ahmed Hijazi. Afterward al Qaeda deputy leader al-Zawahiri said: "When Abu al-Harithi was killed by U.S. missiles in Yemen, it was a warning to us that the Israeli method of killing the mujahideen in Palestine has come to the Arab world."[139]

- 5–23 January 2003: British police arrested eight men — six Algerians, an Ethiopian, and a Moroccan — and one woman in London. They found equipment for a chemical laboratory and traces of the toxin ricin in one of the raided apartments. The British suspected the group might be tied to Algerian Islamists in France and the Islamist leader Abu Musab al-Zarqawi, who was allied with al Qaeda.

- 12–15 February 2003: Bahrain's National Security Agency arrested five al Qaeda–associated Bahrainis for plotting terrorist attacks. It also recovered four AK-47s, two handguns, ammunition, chemical "powders," and a bomb-making manual on a CD-ROM.

- 13 February 2003: Police in Quetta arrested Mohammed Abdul Rahman, son of jailed Gama'a al-Islamiyya's spiritual leader Shaykh Omar Abdul Rahman. Bin Laden had cared for him after his father's arrest in the United States.

- 24 February 2003: Kuwaiti police arrested three Kuwaiti nationals who were planning to attack U.S. military convoys in Kuwait. One had been in Afghanistan in 2001, and all three expressed support for bin Laden after their arrest.

- 1 March 2003: A car bomb killed EIJ leader Abd-al-Sattar al-Masri in Ayn al-Hilwah refugee camp in Lebanon. Al-Masri — true name Mohammed Abdel-Hamid Shanouha — was an explosives expert and an Afghan veteran. He was al Qaeda's leader in the camp and was killed by the Israelis or their proxies.

- 1 March 2003: Pakistani police arrested al Qaeda operations chief Khalid Shaykh Mohammed in an upscale section of Rawalpindi. They also seized his computer, cell phones, and documents. Mohammed designed the 11 September attacks, was involved in the East Africa and *Cole* bombings, and participated in Ramzi Ahmed Yousef's 1995 plot to destroy U.S. airliners flying Pacific routes.

- 1 March 2003: Pakistani police arrested al Qaeda financial officer Mustafa Ahmed al-Hisawai. Al-Hisawai funded the 11 September attackers via wire transfers.

- 15 March 2003: Pakistani authorities arrested Moroccan national Yasser al-Jazeri, who, according to U.S. officials, was a "trusted subordinate of Osama bin Laden." He was responsible for facilitating communications among al Qaeda leaders and was captured in a "posh" neighborhood in Lahore.

- 29 April 2003: In Karachi, Pakistani police arrested Tawfiq bin Attash and Amar al-Baluchi, Khalid Shaykh Mohammed's nephew. A Saudi citizen of Yemeni origin, bin Attash was a close friend of bin Laden, had fought with him in Afghanistan—where he lost a leg—and had run the attack on the U.S. destroyer *Cole*. Al-Baluchi was an al Qaeda financial officer and had sent nearly $120,000 to Mohammed Atta, the leader of the 11 September attacks.
- 6 May 2003: Saudi security raided an al Qaeda safe house in Riyadh near an expatriate housing compound. The Saudis captured no one but recovered more than eight hundred pounds of explosives, fifty-five hand grenades, dozens of assault rifles, other weapons, disguises, twenty-five hundred rounds of ammunition, and eighty-thousand dollars in cash. Some of the weapons were traced to stocks owned by the Saudi National Guard.
- 31 May 2003: Saudi police killed Yusuf bin Salih al-Ayiri, al Qaeda's senior propagandist, and captured his deputy Abdullah ibn Ibrahim Abdullah al-Shabrani. The shootout occurred near the town of Ha'il; two Saudi officers were killed and three wounded. Al-Ayiri ran al Qaeda's *Al-Neda* Web site and was said to be the group's "unknown soldier." The UK-based EIJ exile and specialist on Islamism Hani al-Saba'i said al-Ayiri provided Islamic guidance "for al Qaeda inside the Gulf region." al-Ayiri was a close friend of bin Laden and traveled on the same plane when al Qaeda's chief flew from Afghanistan to Sudan in 1991.[140]
- 12 June 2003: U.S. forces raided and destroyed a base for non-Iraqi mujahedin at Rawah, Iraq, about thirty miles from the Syrian border. The attack killed more than eighty foreign Muslims in Iraq to fight the U.S.-led occupation. Among the dead were Saudis, Yemenis, Syrians, Afghans, and Sudanese.
- 12 August 2003: Thai police arrested JI operations chief Nurjaman Ridwan Isamuddin—a.k.a. Hambali—in Ayuttahya, north of Bangkok. U.S. officials said he played an "important role" in the October 2002 Bali attack and was al Qaeda's "top strategist" in Southeast Asia. Before Thailand, Hambali lived in the Muslim community of Phnom Phenn, Cambodia, from September 2002 to March 2003. Hambali fought the Soviets in Afghanistan, worked in the 1990s with Khalid Shaykh Mohammed and Ramzi Yousef, and was one of the few non-Arabs in al Qaeda authorized to make independent decisions.
- 20 September 2003: Pakistani security arrested fifteen Asian Islamic seminary students in Karachi—two Malaysians, thirteen Indonesians—and charged them with being linked to JI.
- 25 November 2003: Yemeni authorities announced the arrest of

Abu-Asim al-Makki, a leading member of the al Qaeda organization in Yemen. The Yemenis also announced the earlier arrest of al Qaeda leader Hadi Dalqam.

- 15 and 23 January 2004: In Iraq, U.S. authorities captured al Qaeda operatives Husam al-Yemeni and Hasan Ghul. Ghul was known to have been a senior aide to 11 September planner Khalid Shaykh Mohammed.

- 15 March 2004: Saudi security forces killed two senior al Qaeda operatives — Khaled Ali Ali Haj and Ibrahim al-Mezeini — in Riyadh when they tried to run a roadblock. The dead Yemeni nationals had six grenades, two AK-47s, three 9mm pistols, and $137,000 in cash in their car.

- 31 March–2 April 2004: Ten Islamist fighters were arrested in Canada and Britain after a long police investigation; all were Pakistanis and naturalized Canadians or Britons. British police also seized eleven hundred pounds of fertilizer suitable for making a bomb. UK intelligence sources told the media that the eight men arrested in London were tied to al Qaeda members in Pakistan.

- 4 April 2004: Spanish police cornered six members of the al Qaeda cell that conducted the 11 March 2004 railway bombings in Madrid. The six fighters blew themselves up rather than be captured. The leader of the railway attack — the Tunisian Sarhane Abdelmajid Fakhet — was one of the dead. Police recovered twenty-two pounds of explosives identical to those used in the railway bombing.

- 22 April 2005: The Spanish government began the trial of the reputed al Qaeda leader in Spain, the Syria-born Imad Eddin Barakat Yarkas. Yarkas was charged with aiding the 9/11 hijackers, and he, *Al-Jazirah* journalist Taysir Alouni, and twenty-two others were charged with supporting al Qaeda.[141]

- 2 May 2005: Reputed al Qaeda third-in-command Abu Ashraf al-Libi (a.k.a. Dr. Taufeeq) was arrested by Pakistani security in Mardan, north of Peshawar. A longtime confident of bin Laden, al-Libi was said to have been in recent contact with the al Qaeda chief and had been serving as al Qaeda's chief of operations since the capture of Khalid Shaykh Mohammed. Washington said al-Libi's capture was a "critical victory" in the war on terrorism.[142]

- 5 June 2005: The library of al-Azhar University, the Muslim world's oldest, most respected school, became available on the Internet in an effort to "promote a moderate image if Islam" and offset the militant Islamists' use of only portions of religious texts. Eventually, 6 million pages of rare manuscripts and 37,000 books would be mounted on the site in facsimile and digitized copies.[143]

- 7 August 2005: Turkish police arrested Syria-born Luia Sakra in southeast Turkey as he tried to board a plane for Istanbul. Sakra was trained in Afghanistan as an explosives expert and was al Qaeda's chief in Turkey. He was said to have had preknowledge of the 9/11 attacks and to have played a key role in the November 2003 al Qaeda attacks in Istanbul. He recently cooperated with Abu Musab al-Zarqawi's forces in Iraq.[144]

- 27 September 2005: Spain's National Court convicts eighteen of twenty-four al Qaeda defendants, including Imad Eddin Barakat Yarkas, the group's reputed chief in Spain, and *Al-Jazirah* journalist Taysir Alouni. Yarkas received a twenty-seven-year sentence for participating in plans for the 9/11 attacks; Alouni was sentenced to seven years from supporting al Qaeda.[145]

Although not precisely quantifiable, it is unlikely that any Islamist group, or coalition of groups, has ever suffered such a series of setbacks in a comparable period. And matters might have been worse. In late 1997, police in Dagestan arrested EIJ leader Zawahiri and several other EIJ members, including Zawahiri's number two, Thirwat Shihata, as they crossed the border from Azerbaijan. Zawahiri and his colleagues spent several months in prison but were misidentified because they carried false documents and ultimately were freed when bin Laden sent an operative to purchase their release from his contacts among Dagestani officials. According to *Al-Watan Al-Arabi*, senior Dagestani officials had been planning to turn the group over to the United States.

In addition, the foregoing does not account for the human, financial, and material resources bin Laden and his allies have expended in Afghanistan and in the Islamic insurgencies they support. This amount of damage done to what the West defines as a "terrorist" group would have caused its demise, or at least its paralysis. This has not happened to bin Laden's organization, because of bin Laden's even-keel leadership style, al Qaeda's structure as an Islamist insurgent vice a terrorist organization and its resulting resilience and capacity for absorbing attrition, and the powerful motivation for devout Muslims—in both theological and historical terms—of the concept of a defensive jihad. In the wake of several severe losses in the 1996–1998 period, for example, bin Laden simply shrugged and told ABC in late 1998, "There are ups and downs in war. One day we win and one day we lose." In terms of structure, al Qaeda is like Lebanon's Hizballah, Sri Lanka's Tamil Tigers, and the Philippine's Moro Islamic Liberation Front, which are similarly resilient because they are insurgent organizations that have been trained to fight and have been bloodied, in the insurgencies they are waging against Israeli, Sri Lankan, and Philippine armed forces, just as bin Laden's fighters are gaining combat experience against guerrilla and conventional forces in Kashmir, the Philippines, Kosovo, Chechnya, Dagestan, Afghanistan, and Central Asia. As a result, Hizballah, the Tamils, and the Moros, like al Qaeda, always have a "ready reserve" to call on when fighters fall or are captured. Indeed, the fact that guerrilla organizations must have a deep bench to survive, helps to explain U.S. terrorism expert Bruce Hoffman's marveling in the *Los Angeles Times* over al Qaeda's "enormous replicating ability" despite being, as the *Washington Post* said, "constantly pressured and compromised." At the same time, al Qaeda's recuperative powers make the claim of a senior U.S. counterterrorism official "that we're picking it [bin Laden's organization] apart limb by limb. We're not done yet but we will be. . . . We've been winning for a few years now," sound like nothing so much as an arrogant ninny whistling past the graveyard.[146]

Not to be lost in the mix, moreover, is the simple but powerful fact that in Islam the prophet Muhammad "preached the legitimacy of war . . . [and] most orthodox Islamic jurists and theologians would place jihad very high on the scale of religious obligations." Thus, by articulately appealing to the concept of defensive jihad, bin Laden has tapped a force that amplifies the resiliency and durability of al Qaeda and other jihadist groups. The concept of jihad, Emmanuel Sivan has explained, is an essential element of Islam's "foundation myth."

> It is indeed in the sphere of motivation that one can detect jihad's major contribution to the historic Islamic experience of warfare. It has guaranteed for fourteen centuries that wars waged by Muslims against external enemies will almost always be perceived by meaningful segments of the [Islamic] polity as having a transcendental dimension closely interwoven with the "foundation myth" of the culture to which the society belongs.
>
> The motivational dimension of the jihad has not only a cognitive function, but an affective one as well. It ensures a sense of solidarity with one's own and, almost ineluctably, generates zeal, steadfastness, and readiness for self-sacrifice.[147]

Even with this demonstrated resiliency, the losses outlined are far from inconsequential. The loss of such senior leaders as Tayyib, Abu Hajir, Talat Fuad Qassim, Mabruk, Khalid Fawwaz, and al-Najjar, as well as talented operatives like Wadih el-Hage, Ibrahim Saqr, and Ibrahim Eidarous, is extremely debilitating and will be felt across the organization for years. Moreover, many of the Islamist fighters apprehended and taken to Egypt were members of the Egyptian Islamic Jihad, one of bin Laden's most important allies. Coming either from Zawahiri's group or the EIJ's Vanguards of Conquest (VOC) faction, these fighters ranged from foot soldiers to senior leaders. As U.K.-based EIJ leader Hani al-Siba'i has said, the EIJ "had the lion's share of the security chases, abductions, extraditions, imprisonment, military trials, and death." In addition to fighters deported to Egypt, Egypt's security and police forces—using the returnees' confessions, statements in court, and documents—have struck additional blows against the organizations in Egypt. Soon after the return of the EIJ operatives from Albania and the Caucuses, for example, Egyptian police arrested twenty-two VOC members in the northern al-Sarqiyah Governorate. Then, in late 1998, Egyptian authorities in al-Minuifiyah Province "arrested thirteen members of the [Egyptian Islamic] Jihad organization." The cell was tied to Albanian returnee al-Najjar, and information about it was disclosed by two of al-Najjar's fellow defendants. More recently, *Al-Sharq Al-Awsat* reported that the return to Egypt of three EIJ fighters from the UAE and Kuwait led to the arrest of "23 people suspected of setting up an illegal group in Cairo" with the advice of the EIJ returnees.[148] Parenthetically, these domestic arrests again illustrate the appeal of jihadist messages like bin Laden's to educated Muslims: all twenty-three were "professional people from Cairo's affluent Al-Ma'adi district." In terms of Egypt's internal stability, then, the domestic anti-jihadist operations made possible by information from the "Returnees from Albania" and other Islamist fighters captured abroad are more important than the apprehension of the overseas Egyptian Islamist leaders themselves.[149]

So severe were the EIJ's losses of senior leaders that in April 1999, *Al-Wasat* reported, the question being asked in Cairo was "What is left of the 'Jihad Organization'?" The journal's answer was that "Egyptian security services" had concluded that in 1998 the EIJ had "sustained massive losses among its elements and military cadres who belong to the al-Zawahiri generation." *Al-Sharq Al-Awsat* also said the Egyptian authorities' success against "the financial and armament sources abroad for the group's military elements inside the country . . . [had] reduced the fugitive leaders' opportunities for implementing their objectives inside Egypt." The services warned, however, that the EIJ "does not lack strong fighters, although its condition today can hardly be compared with what it was between 1981 and 1997."[150] In addition, *Al-Sharq Al-Awsat* reported in early 1999 that Zawahiri had not taken the setbacks sitting down. The daily said Zawahiri had "established a financial and administrative program for reviving the organization and issued responsibilities to its [EIJ's] station officers in Yemen, Albania, Azerbaijan, Sudan, and Afghanistan to assist the al-Jihad organization in Cairo in creating a new generation of zealous young fundamentalists." In Egypt, Zawahiri had an "extensive plan" to revive the EIJ "at the universities."[151]

Still, rebuilding takes times and money, and so Zawahiri appears to have made a virtue of necessity, joining bin Laden's World Front and later apparently merging the EIJ into al Qaeda and agreeing to make U.S. targets the top priority. That said, Zawahiri also had a solid EIJ-specific reason to attack Americans: the EIJ blamed the United States for the capture of some of its most senior operatives. At New Year's 1999, Zawahiri and the EIJ stood with a score to settle, one that had to be squared to maintain the group's pride and morale. Zawahiri and the EIJ expressed this motivation, as follows, in communiqués issued in late 1998 and early 1999.

- August 1998: When EIJ members were caught in Albania, the EIJ published a statement called "About the Extradition of Three of Our Brothers." "We are interested in briefly telling the Americans," the statement said, "that their message has been received and that the response, which we hope they will read carefully, is being [prepared], because we — with God's help — will write it in the language they understand."[152]

- November 1998: After an EIJ fighter was killed in a gunfight with Albanian police, the EIJ published a statement, titled "The Jihad Announces the Death of One of Its Heroes," which mixed the EIJ's eagerness for revenge with the goals of bin Laden's World Front. "We pledge to Almighty God," the statement said, "to take revenge against the enemies of this religion. . . . We remind them [the mujahedin] that this Muslim Mujahid was killed by the United States and its agents. . . . And revenge for him against the United States and its agents is the duty of every Muslim, because he [the dead EIJ fighter] followed the jihad path just for the sake of defending his nation, on whose Sharia, holy sites, land, and riches the United States has encroached."[153]

- February 1999: Citing Kuwait's repatriation of fifteen Islamists to Egypt in January 1999, an EIJ communiqué said, "We reiterate here that the United States should pay the price for all this: Blood for Blood and destruction for destruction. The United States and its agents are well aware of the Jihad Group, which will not give up retaliation even if a long time passes. . . . the Jihad Group is aware of the extent of U.S. cowardice and the fact that the so-called superpower is only a myth. The coming days have many things in store."[154]

In addition to solidifying the bin Laden-Zawahiri alliance, the actions of bin Laden's adversaries, especially U.S. actions, focused the Muslim world not on the inherent right of the United States to self-protection — even preemptively — but on what is widely perceived as Washington's double standard when dealing with Muslims. In this category, the U.S. cruise missile raids on Afghanistan and Sudan appear to have been the primary actions that swung Islamic opinion toward bin Laden in a way that was increasingly sympathetic, if not yet fully approving. In short, bin Laden's survival into the twenty-first century and defiant response appear to have transformed America's stealthy and impressive flexing of superpower muscle into a propaganda defeat. In April 1999, *Frontline*'s unattributed biography of bin Laden described the clarifying effect of the U.S. attacks for an Islamic world already prone to believe that the United States habitually maltreats Muslims.

> The American missiles then played a very strong role in sorting the controversy. After the American attack on Sudan and Afghanistan, it became almost shameful to criticize bin Laden. People inside Saudi Arabia and other Arab countries were full of anger toward America, and whoever could antagonize America would provide a fulfillment of their desire of discharging their anger. The American strike with the associated remarks by Clinton and American officials proved that bin Laden is a big challenge to America. In the mind of the average Arab and Muslim, bin Laden appeared as the man who could drive America so crazy that it started shooting haphazardly at unjustified targets. There was another factor that made people forget the scene of civilian casualties [in Nairobi and Dar es Salaam], the special nature of the Sudanese factory. Those who had reservations about the African bombings thought that this arrogance of the Americans is much worse than the embassy bombings. Their view was that while bin Laden and others can make [an] executive mistake because of their difficult circumstances, logistics, and communication, America is not suppose to do this mistake unless it is done on purpose.[155]

In the Islamic world, the image of the world's greatest power using its military might to chase one man who is acting at the behest of Allah and His Prophet, who loudly champions the rights of Muslims, and who is working to purify and secure Islam's holiest sites, strikes many Muslims as a demonstration of the resolve of the United States to punish any Muslim resisting its dictates. "He's [bin Laden] a man on the run, whose only friends are the Taliban," said Sahib Zada Khalid Jan Binuri, the head of Pakistan's most influential Islamic seminary. "How can he be a threat to the world's most powerful nation?"[156]

Others concluded that, although charges of U.S. persecution of Muslims were overdone, the attacks did increase bin Laden's stature in the Islamic world. "Many Muslims," wrote Yousef al-Khoei, "see the American strikes . . . as a huge arrogance of power. Muslims who carry out these attacks [the East Africa bombings] are the fringe. But those who applaud are the disenfranchised Muslims everywhere who see the double standard of the United States taking unilateral action against an Islamic nation. Now everyone who stands up to the U.S. becomes a hero."[157] It remains to be seen how much of a positive impact the ongoing U.S. military offensive in Afghanistan will have on al Qaeda and — if he has survived to this point — bin Laden. Much will depend on whether he can make America's military look impotent — at least in the eyes of Muslims — by staging another major attack on U.S. interests.

Beyond hard-to-measure perceptions, statistics too seem to confirm the impression among Muslims that Washington is gunning for Islam. "When some ask about the reasons for the increased feelings of hostility toward the United States," Cairo's *Al-Ahram* noted in September 1998,

> especially in the Arab and Islamic worlds — feelings that do not target America as a people as much as U.S. policy — a precise count of the U.S. military strikes in the last ten years show that they were only aimed against Arab or Islamic countries, wherein dealing with any emergency problems or incidents, Washington did not hesitate to use military force as an alternative to political effort. In such cases, Washington's patience quickly ran out and discipline through military force was the first response and remedy, without compunction or notice of innocent civilian victims. . . . Thousands of civilian Muslim victims [in Iraq, for example,] find no one to shed a tear for them, for in the eyes of Clinton and Blair, they are not worth the price of the missiles that decimated them.[158]

A retired U.S. intelligence officer made the same point more concisely. "It is not missed in Friday prayers [across the Islamic world]," he told *Frontline*, "that we sent $75 million worth of missiles flying against the two poorest Islamic countries in the world, Afghanistan and Sudan."[159] We have since repeated that lesson on a massive scale in Afghanistan.

V

NO END IN SIGHT

14

WHAT TO EXPECT FROM AL QAEDA

> Like the Old Testament warriors he admired and resembled,
> he yearned to carry the war into Babylon. He studied books on
> guerrilla warfare and slave revolts fascinated by the ability of
> small bands to hold off larger forces in mountainous terrain.
>
> Historian James MacPherson on John Brown
> (*Battle Cry of Freedom*, 1988)

In the wonderfully entertaining 1940 Warner Brothers' swashbuckler titled *The Sea Hawk*, Queen Elizabeth I, played by the inestimable Flora Robson, angrily convokes her courageous, dashing, and exceptionally handsome band of privateers — known collectively in the movie as "the Sea Hawks" — for having had the temerity to sink in the English Channel a Spanish galleon carrying the new ambassador of Spain to her court. With the recently rescued, and presumably still soggy, Spanish ambassador looking on, the queen addresses herself to Captain Geoffrey Thorpe — played by the equally inestimable Errol Flynn — who is the leader of the Sea Hawks, the queen's favorite, and the sinker of said galleon. "Do you imagine, Captain Thorpe, that we are at war with Spain?" the queen thunders. Thorpe, with due respect for his sovereign, responds firmly: "Madam, Spain is at war with the world." Flash ahead sixty years and a similar question posed by any national leader in Christendom might accurately earn the response: "Madam (or Sir), Osama bin Laden is at war with the Christian world."

The Sea Hawk, made in the second year of World War II by a film-maker eager for American intervention, was designed not only to entertain, but also to educate its audience about the threat posed by Hitler's Germany. The movie's depiction of the ruthless ambitions of Spain's Philip II and his dream that, before his death, he would gaze at a map that had ceased to be the world and was instead simply a map of Spain was a none-too-subtle reminder of Hitler's ongoing ransacking of Europe. If the exchanges above are reimagined to focus on Osama bin Laden, they would have little entertainment value, but their resulting unsubtle messages — that bin Laden has been at war with Christendom, and has longed to see a world map that is simply a map of the House of Islam — should be taken with deadly seriousness. Bin Laden has declared war on the United States, the leader of invading, barbarous Crusaders, and intends there to be a struggle to the death against the United States.

In early 1998 bin Laden warned the Muslim world that the Crusaders' "fleets are plowing the seas of Islam. They are besieging and blockading the people of the region as a whole with a total disregard for pledges or charters, and are violating the sacred sites and draining all the wealth."[1] Faced with this threat, bin Laden said, "the highest priority, after faith, is to repel the incursive enemy which corrupts religion and the world. . . . We are all servants of God, praise and glory be to Him, and He has prescribed for us killing and fighting." While "our battle with the Americans is larger than our battle with the Russians," bin Laden told ABC in May 1998, "we are sure of Allah's victory and our victory against the Americans and the Jews, as the Prophet promised, peace be upon Him. . . . The Muslim masses are moving towards liberating the Muslim worlds. Allah willing, we will win."[2]

United States as Priority Target

What should be expected as Osama bin Laden's al Qaeda forces continue to attack what bin Laden has termed Crusader interests and incite Muslims worldwide to do the same? First, as should be obvious, the United States will remain the jihad's priority target. "The United States itself," bin Laden has said, "is the biggest mischief maker, terrorist, and rogue in the world, and challenging its authority will be a good deed in Islam in every respect." U.S. policy in the Middle East and South Asia, if it remains even broadly consistent with the policy of recent decades, will provide a fertile environment for al Qaeda's efforts.

As Professor Magnus Ranstorp has noted, bin Laden's basic claim, that the United States is attacking the religion, sanctities, resources, children, and dignity of Islam, is a view increasingly held by Muslims around the world.[3] Mostly unquestioning support for Israel; economic sanctions on Iraq; the basing of U.S. and U.K. forces in Saudi Arabia; U.S. pressure on

Pakistan over nuclear, narcotics, terrorism, and return-to-democracy issues; U.S.-enabled destruction of the Taliban; and the well-documented U.S. propensity to use of force against Muslim targets will all be used by al Qaeda and other Islamists as clear examples of the U.S.-led Crusaders' contempt for Muslims and their survival.

It matters not a whit if bin Laden's anti-American accusations have not been entirely accurate, and it matters even less if U.S. policies can be defended as being in U.S. best interests. In this case, perception is everything and then some, and the strengthening Muslim perception that Washington is prosecuting a systematic and brutal anti-Islamic policy has stacked the deck in al Qaeda's favor. "Driving Islamic militants is a fear that the Christian West, abetted by the Jews, is bent on destroying and subjugating Islam," Richard Mackenzie explained in the *New Republic* in September 1998. "Sheikh Yusef al-Qaradawi, one of the world's most revered Islamic clerics, has written that 'we [the Muslim ummah] are being confronted by the unrelenting hostility—and infiltration—of secularism, communism, Zionism, and Christianity' and that Islam is the victim of a 'devilish alliance of Zionist, Christian, and atheist powers for a vicious and united campaign against Islam and Muslims.'" Bin Laden could not have said it better, and *Al-Quds Al-Arabi* has suggested al-Qaradawi—and implicitly bin Laden—has spoken for much of the Muslim world. "We thank God for granting this nation ulema like Shaykh Yusuf al-Qaradawi," the London daily wrote when al-Qaradawi reconfirmed that suicide operations are religiously permissible, "who always stand in the trench and back everything that that uplifts the nation's standing and restores its dignity and honor."[4]

In addition, Russia, the United States, and Israel could not have given more credence to al-Qaradawi's warning than they did by uniting to impose UN sanctions on Afghanistan in November 1999 and December 2000, and by the U.S.-led West failing to take similar action against Russia for its attacks on Muslim fighters and civilians in Chechnya—which Israel, India, and China also publicly said they "understood."[5] Needless to say, the membership of the U.S.-led coalition now waging war in Afghanistan again underscores the same perception.

Other Targets

The United States, however, will not be the only target of the forces bin Laden has incited. Those who take up jihad and attack any of the host of targets that fall under the catchall term "Crusaders" are, whether deliberately or not, pushing ahead bin Laden's agenda. As this is written, there are Islamist insurgencies under way against the rump Communist governments in Tajikistan, Uzbekistan, Chechnya, and Dagestan, as well as the threat of car bomb attacks in Moscow and other Russian cities. Likewise, Islamist insurgencies continue against the predominantly Catholic government in the Philippines, the secular government in Algiers, and the Hindu government in Kashmir. Islamist discontent and armed assertiveness are bubbling up in western China, parts of eastern India, Kyrgyzstan, Malaysia, Yemen, Indonesia, and the Horn of Africa. And it is prudent to assume the last sectarian bloodletting in Bosnia and Kosovo has not been seen. Over the horizon, but perhaps not too far over, are prospects for increasing Islamist militancy and violence in southern Thailand, southern Africa, East Asia, and North America. Beyond such emerging flashpoints, there are also bound to be unexpected Islam-related causes célèbres that redound to al Qaeda's favor.

Will the late-1999 UN mission to East Timor — which cinched the territory's independence — ultimately be seen as the agent by which Catholics stole land from the world's largest Muslim country? First Spain, then Palestine, now East Timor? In this vein, the Islamabad daily *News* already has contrasted the "criminal procrastination" of the United States in aiding Bosnian and Kosovar Muslims with its "rapid and robust response in [Catholic] East Timor."[6] Overall, al Qaeda's mission to incite jihad against the Crusaders will, for the foreseeable future, have a receptive audience, no shortage of recruits, and worldwide opportunities for violence.

In targeting the United States, al Qaeda will kill as many Americans as possible in as many attacks as it can carefully prepare and execute. Al Qaeda's attacks to date have shown increasing lethality and patient preparation. Its patience has been especially notable since 11 September 2001; it has not lashed out in response to heavy U.S. air attacks on its Afghan bases. Because bin Laden's organization views military actions as a means to change U.S. policy, the next attack is likely to be bigger than the September 2001 attacks. Al Qaeda clearly is building up to the point where it will use a chemical-biological-radiological-nuclear (CBRN) weapon, but whether it is ready to use one the next time out is an open question. Al Qaeda may well try one or more conventional attacks before moving on to the CBRN arena, especially after seeing the amount of death, destruction, and economic dislocation caused by the conventional attacks on New York and Washington. "Bin Laden believes that what we [the United States] consider to be terrorism," John Miller explained in February 1999, "is just the amount of violence needed to get the attention of the American people. His aim is to force us to consider whether continued support of Israel [or our presence in Saudi Arabia or the embargo on Iraq] is worth the bloodshed he promises." Given that the 11 September attacks produced no change on any of these fronts, al Qaeda likely will once again escalate the casualty-causing potential of its next attack, keep the attack focused on America, and attack only when planning is complete.[7] Bin Laden clearly believes that U.S., British, and other Western leaders cannot tolerate high casualties and — especially in America's case — repeated public humiliations from attacks to which effective military responses are not possible. "We will keep moving on the path of God and the Holy Prophet," bin Laden has written,

> In reality the infidel powers are not as dangerous as they look. Only our fear [Muslims's fear] makes them bigger. They are like an inflated balloon in front of which a needle looks inferior and minor, but this needle brings the balloon to its fate. The one who is afraid of God is not afraid of anyone, and no one can frighten him. But he who is not afraid of God is afraid of everyone. He is afraid of losing his life, money, luxury, and power. Islam attaches great importance to the fear of God.[8]

Jews and Israel

Israeli and Jewish interests also must be included high on the list of bin Laden's future targets. "[T]he legitimate duty [of Muslims] toward Palestine," bin Laden wrote in early 1995, "is jihad in God's name and the nation's [ummah's] incitement against the enemy until Palestine is completely liberated and returned to Islamic sovereignty. . . . I believe that this issue cannot be resolved except by taking account of the Islamic issue, uniting in solidarity to rescue it and fighting the Jews through an Islamic jihad until the land is returned to its people and until the scattered Jews [are] back to their own countries." Bin Laden referred to the Palestinian struggle seven times in his 1996 declaration of war on the United States, and then after the 1998 East Africa attacks, he told "the women of Palestine and its heroic children and patient old men . . . [d]o not worry. We have taken revenge for you on the American crusader criminal gang and, God willing, we will take revenge on their Jewish allies."[9]

It has been a mystery to me as to why al Qaeda has so far refrained from attacking a specifically Jewish or Israeli target, especially because bin Laden has long supported the Palestinians — though not Arafat and the PLO — and praised "the sons of Muslim Palestine and their blessed Intifadah" who "despite the scale of the catastrophe . . . [have become] the glimmer of hope [that] has become a reality and hopes that are kept alive through the martyrs' blood, and the bullets of those fighting for God's cause." Strategically speaking, a successful attack against a Jewish target in the name of alleviating what bin Laden describes as "the suffering of the Muslim people in Palestine who have been persecuted for more than a century" could have only a positive impact for al Qaeda in the Muslim world. Bin Laden has repeatedly praised Islamic Resistance Movement (HAMAS) fighters for their attacks: "I also view with great esteem our brother cubs in Palestine who are teaching the Jews lessons in faith and the pride of the faithful,"[10] and, theoretically, an anti-Israel attack by bin Laden would boost the morale of

HAMAS, other fighters, and the whole population of "occupied Palestine," as well as strike a blow against "the so-called Palestinian authority," or "Arafat regime," which is run by "those who sympathize with the infidels."

It may be, of course, that bin Laden has tried and failed to attack Jewish targets. Bin Laden and al Qaeda, in this regard, may be like Ayman Zawahiri and the Egyptian Islamic Jihad (EIJ). When Palestinian journalist Jamal Ismail in late 1998 asked Zawahiri "why we have not seen anything and heard very little about its [the EIJ's] operations against the Jews," Zawahiri simply replied, "we have tried operations against the Jews. However, the Most High God has ordained that we not complete them." The EIJ chief cited an aborted EIJ attack on Cairo's Khan al-Khalil market as an example, one that would have killed many Israeli tourists if successful. In this vein, the *Wall Street Journal* recently reported that al Qaeda fighter Richard C. Reid — who tried to down a U.S. airliner in December 2001 — scouted inside Israel in 2001 and found good targets for causing mass casualties but also found exceedingly tight security.[11]

A second positive result of a successful anti-Israeli attack producing heavy casualties or severe destruction would be to give al Qaeda the bona fides to be seen by Muslims as an active foe of Israel, and not, as it is now incorrectly perceived, as a largely rhetorical enemy. While bin Laden has railed against the reality that the "Al-Aqsa Mosque remains the prisoner of the Christian-Jewish Alliance"; decried "Zionist terrorism in Palestine, Lebanon, and elsewhere"; condemned "the state of the Jews that has a policy to destroy the future of these [Palestinian] children"; and anguished over the fact that "Jews are wreaking corruption in the Al-Aqsa Mosque, the site of the Prophet's ascension to heaven," he has not been known to have mounted an attack specifically designed to kill Jews.[12] This, if you will, is a credentials-acquiring loop one would assume al Qaeda would like to close, although, to be sure, it would sap some credibility from bin Laden's contention that the United States must be Islam's primary target.

After attacking Israel, bin Laden would have carved the four most vital notches in the stock of his well-used AK-47 — dead Russians, dead Americans, dead Hindus, and dead Jews. Such an attack also would settle a personal score: bin Laden has long intended to avenge the murder of his mentor Shaykh Azzam, whom he believes was assassinated by "Israel, with some of its Arab agents."[13] Finally, an anti-Israel attack would yield a strategic victory for al Qaeda by increasing the already-severe difficulty the United States has in eliciting significant help against bin Laden from Saudi Arabia and other Muslim states. While it would be tough at any time for a Muslim regime to turn over the heroic Mujahid of Islam to the Crusaders, it would be especially so once said heroic Mujahid struck a lethal blow against the "Zionist entity."

While an al Qaeda attack on an Israeli or Jewish target must be considered likely—since late September 2001, bin Laden said "punishment should reach Israel" and Zawahiri noted "al Qaeda's next target was Tel Aviv"—bin Laden has never shown that he is too worried about the Jews. That he hates Jews and Israel and wants both annihilated is clear, his position being that "every effort concentrated on . . . the Zionists will bring good, direct and positive results." But as in the case of secular or pro-Western Muslim regimes, bin Laden believes the "Zionists" are the creatures and an extension of the United States, and that without U.S. backing, they will fall like ripe fruit to Islam's forces. In this attitude, bin Laden shares a view of Israel that Professor Immanuel Wallerstein says is common among Islamists. Israel, Wallerstein has explained, "is regarded as primarily an outpost of the West, a settler state akin to the Crusader states of the Middle Ages" and, for bin Laden and his ilk "the recipe for resolution is the historical one: evict the Crusaders and their states whither." Although bin Laden believes the "Jewish lobby" is powerful in America and at times can "pull the ropes of politics in the United States" in the direction of "weakening Muslim peoples and governments,"[14] he is confident that U.S. backing alone permits Israel's survival. The entry of U.S. forces into Saudi Arabia in 1990, bin Laden wrote, "is a new disaster the Christians have inflicted [after] having already enabled the Jews to seize Jerusalem and the blessed land around it."[15] All told, bin Laden would certainly concur with the late-1999 claim by Amman's *Al-Sabil* that "the Jews would not [have] dared to Judaize and unify Jerusalem under the 'Israeli' flag were it not for U.S. support and encouragement."[16] For bin Laden, then, the key to destroying Israel, as it is for destroying the al-Sauds, Mubarak, and others, is to defeat the United States.

Britain and France

Of America's Western allies, Britain and France were atop bin Laden's hit list long before the two nations committed forces to the current Afghan war; indeed, bin Laden has said "the British were in the forefront, sometimes even ahead of the United States, in advocating siege, collective punishment, and sanctions against the Muslim peoples of Sudan, Iran, Libya, and Iraq." In 1996, for example, bin Laden told *Nida'ul Islam* that, with the United States, "Britain bears the greatest enmity toward the Islamic world," and in a June 2000 speech he detailed the United Kingdom's historic and contemporary transgressions. "The British are responsible for destroying the Caliphate system," bin Laden said. "They are the ones who created the Palestinian problem. They are the ones who created the Kashmiri problem. They are the ones who put the arms embargo on the Muslims of Bosnia so that two million Muslims were killed. They are the ones who are starving the Iraqi children. And they are continuously dropping bombs on these innocent Iraqi children."[17]

Adding to this litany of grievances, British forces remain based in Saudi Arabia, and, in the United Kingdom, the British government has earned bin Laden's ire by trying to close businesses owned by the country's leading Islamist organizations — including Al-Muhajaroun and the Followers of the Sharia — and to amend terrorism laws to make it easier to convict people speaking in a way that can be construed as part of a conspiracy to incite terrorism. In this context, British Muslim journalist Faisal Bodi described the law as specifically targeting Muslims. "At a stroke the new act has reshaped the landscape in which opposition groups can work," Bodi wrote in the *Guardian*. "It is now illegal to call for the violent overthrow of unelected, despotic governments in countries such as Algeria; to campaign for the liberation of occupied lands such as Kashmir and Palestine; or to engage in weapons training for purposes of freedom and self-determination. . . . You are now a threat to national security if you merely hold certain views or associations even if you don't follow them through." When the law took effect in early 2001, twenty-one groups — most Islamist — were named "terrorist organizations," and the law was accompanied by U.K. security services arresting several Islamists in London, actions that earned the scorn of Islamists, Muslim governments, and the Arab League. The U.K.-based, pro-bin Laden Islamist Omar Bakri, for example, said the law "is tantamount to a disdain for all Muslims acting to liberate their countries," while the official Saudi position was delivered by *Al-Watan*, which said the law shows "that the word Islam has come to be synonymous with terror."[18]

Also important, bin Laden stridently attacked the British government for arresting Khalid al-Fawwaz, one of his senior lieutenants and the chief of bin Laden's London-based Advice and Reformation Committee (ARC). The United Kingdom's arrest and readiness to extradite Fawwaz to the United States appear to have been the last straw for bin Laden vis-à-vis Britain. After the arrest, bin Laden said henceforth he would target British civilians. "The Committee vehemently denounces the British authorities actions [regarding Fawwaz]," the ARC communiqué said,

> the real motive behind which seems to be British Crusader hatred against Muslims and the appeasement of the Americans, which has become a distinctive feature of British foreign policy, as demonstrated by Britain's blind support of the hostile stands against Muslim peoples on more than one occasion. Britain's support of the U.S. aggression against Sudan and Afghanistan recently and the U.S. policy against the besieged Iraqi people is nothing but an indication of this orientation of this policy. Does Britain want to put itself in the same corner as the United States?[19]

France has been sitting squarely in bin Laden's sights since its participation in the war against Iraq. Beyond this offense, however, lies a more powerful animosity toward the French government based on its support for the Algerian government, harassment of Muslims living in France, reported cooperation with the United States and United Kingdom in hunting and capturing Islamists around the world, and military aid to Masood's Northern Alliance. In February 2000, French prime minister Lionel Jospin capped these offenses by labeling all Arab opponents of Israel as "terrorists." Bin Laden and his allies have long railed against the "French-made army in Algeria," which they claim in early 1992 "swooped down on the Algerian people's will and put the leaders of the [Islamic Salvation] Front in prison,"[20] as well as against what the *Los Angeles Times* has described as France's domestic "police and judicial war on armed Muslim extremism."[21] Bin Laden publicly has damned France for taking "the lead in supporting the military junta in Algeria" and for "persecuting and hounding over four million Muslims, mainly of North African origin living in France for generations, simply because they refuse to compromise their Islamic identity." In addition, according to bin Laden, French intelligence has joined U.K. and U.S. services to counter al Qaeda's operations by pursuing Algerian and Egyptian Islamists "inside and outside their [the services'] territories."[22] Finally, bin Laden and Mullah Omar have claimed that France delayed the Taliban's final victory by sending assistance to Masood, a belief strengthened by Masood's official visit to France in April 2001.

Taliban journals have blamed France—along with Iran, India, the United States, and Russia—for preventing the final "annihilation" of Alliance forces by sending Masood money, military advisers, trainers, and equipment, including Milan antitank missiles. Masood's Pansjher Valley base "is not a holiday destination," several Taliban journals have said, while demanding France and the others "stop this interference," whose only "objective is to create chaos in Afghanistan and to keep the war going." In October 2000 it became clear that al Qaeda had long been planning to attack French targets. In pleading guilty to terrorism charges before a U.S. court, EIJ and al Qaeda member Ali Mohammed testified that in 1994 bin Laden sent him to Djibouti to surveil several facilities, including French military bases and the U.S. embassy. Ali Mohammed also said that he had surveilled "French interests in Senegal in 1993 and France's embassy and cultural center in Nairobi in 1994."[23]

Possible Attack Sites

Bin Laden and his allies have demonstrated that they will attack in countries where their organizations have been hurt and against the organizations they hold responsible for inflicting the damage. Al Qaeda operates very much on an eye-for-an-eye basis; the pervasive common wisdom of the media's dated terrorism experts that terrorists will not attack in places where they acquire funds or have developed infrastructures should have been cast aside even before the 11 September 2001 attacks on the U.S. homeland. Bin Laden's cell in Nairobi, for example, was disrupted but not destroyed by Kenyan authorities and their allies in August–September 1997 and yet bin Laden destroyed the U.S. embassy there a year later, an action ensuring an even more determined effort to root out al Qaeda's Kenyan network.[24] Likewise, a cell in Tirana belonging to the EIJ, bin Laden's closest ally, was damaged but not eliminated in summer 1998 by the Albanian police and others, and shortly thereafter the Albanians just barely thwarted an EIJ attempt to car bomb the U.S. embassy in Tirana.

Thus, if past is prologue, there probably are bin Laden retaliatory attacks ready for such places as Germany, where Abu Hajir was arrested in September 1998, and subsequently extradited to the United States, and bin Laden-related Islamists were arrested in December 2000 and April 2001; in Kuwait and the United Arab Emirates, where EIJ cells were broken up in late 1998 and late 2000; in London, where authorities arrested seven EIJ and bin Laden operatives in September 1998 and where they have agreed to extradite to the United States bin Laden's lieutenant Khalid al-Fawwaz and two senior EIJ fighters, Ibrahim Eidarous and Yasir al-Sirri; in Baku, Azerbaijan, where an EIJ group was captured in October 1998; in South Africa, where authorities arrested three EIJ operatives in September 1998 and deported them to Egypt; in Mauritania, where police disrupted a bin Laden unit in March 1999; in Croatia, where senior Gama'at leader Talat Fuad Qassim disappeared in September 1995; in Jordan, where security forces broke up a bin Laden unit just before the millennium; and in Egypt, where many of the captured bin Laden-EIJ operatives have surfaced for trial and subsequent incarceration or execution. This recital, of course, does not mention the United States, Saudi Arabia, and Pakistan, where al Qaeda fighters, EIJ members, and/or prominent Muslim clerics supported by bin Laden are imprisoned. And none of the foregoing is to say bin Laden's planners will stop looking to hit soft American targets — in June 1999, for example, al Qaeda surveilled U.S. embassies in Ghana, Senegal, and Mozambique — or will not stage repeat attacks in Kenya, Tanzania, or New York to again humiliate the U.S. government.[25] It does say, however, that there is no chance al Qaeda will back away from attacking either hard targets or targets in sites important to al Qaeda for financial, logistical, or safe-haven reasons.

Another type of revenge attack high on al Qaeda's priority list will be actions to kill or kidnap American civilians or, especially, officials — diplomats, intelligence officers, and military personnel — at home and abroad. If there is a knee-jerk mantra common among Muslims, it is certainly that the U.S. intelligence service is everywhere, can do anything, and is the cause of most trouble in the Islamic world. Ubiquitous, omnipotent, and malignantly anti-Muslim, the U.S. service — for bin Laden and his lieutenants — has been the infidel world's quintessential instigator and string-puller that has been working to assassinate him; destroy Islamic governments, as in Sudan and Afghanistan; humiliate Muslims by desecrating Islamic holy places in Saudi Arabia and Jerusalem; and generally squash any Muslim individual or entity that has, in bin Laden's words, raised the banner of "there is no God but Allah, and Mohammed is the Prophet of Allah." From this mind-set, it is the smallest of steps to the conviction that U.S. intelligence is responsible for the multiple defeats suffered by bin Laden and the EIJ in the late 1990s. Indeed, bin Laden has said his attack in Nairobi was made in part because the U.S. embassy "housed the largest CIA center in the African Continent" and because it "had supervised the killing of at least 13,000 Somali civilians in the treacherous aggression against that Muslim country." More recently, a leading Pakistani Islamist journal reported that the "CIA has started an active strategy against the Islamic movements throughout the world" and that its top five goals are to prevent Muslim unity, identify all Islamists as terrorists, halt Pakistan's nuclear program and stop other Muslim states from developing such weapons, make false criminal charges against Islamists to impugn their character, and fund anti-Islamist organizations.[26] While in no need of strengthening, repeated leaks by anonymous "senior U.S. officials" eager to grab credit for any success against bin Laden have and will continue to validate the Islamists' view of the U.S. service. Notwithstanding that many captured bin Laden and EIJ operatives have been tried, jailed, and, at times, executed in Egypt, the CIA will be seen as the wizard behind the curtain making bad things happen to good Muslims.

There are two other factors that suggest al Qaeda will take revenge against U.S. civilians, intelligence officers, diplomats, and military personnel when it is in a position to do so. First, bin Laden has had, and presumably has valued, a sterling reputation for taking care of his al Qaeda fighters and their allies, as well as taking a tooth-for-a-tooth from their enemies. From caring for wounded and crippled Arab Afghans and their families during and after the anti-Soviet jihad, to evacuating the families of EIJ members captured in Albania in 1998, to destroying the U.S. embassy in Nairobi a year after his network was disrupted, bin Laden is well known to have been a reliable, protective leader.

It is clear that bin Laden and the Islamic world generally believe that Americans have played the major role in capturing al Qaeda and EIJ fighters and therefore that the onus is on bin Laden's movement to respond. It is not, for example, a coincidence that one of bin Laden's demands for ceasing hostilities after his August 1998 attacks was "an end to the war of eradication being waged by the United States with the aid of governments in its pay, against young Muslims under the pretext of fighting terrorism."[27] Robert Fisk also has reported the growing ire among Islamists and across the Muslim world over "the vicious intelligence conflict being played out between America and Muslim groups in the United States" and internationally in which "America's snatch squads . . . have abducted wanted men from Muslim countries—in past years, from Malaysia, Pakistan, Lebanon, and now Albania."[28] In this context, one of bin Laden's most valuable coins—a reputation for evening scores and going his foe one better — would be greatly debased if he fails to exact a pound of flesh from U.S. "snatch squads."

A second factor motivating bin Laden against this U.S. target set is the organizational imperative to respond to U.S. intelligence service attacks on the EIJ. U.S. actions are perceived by many in the group to be the result of Zawahiri's decision to attach the EIJ to bin Laden's World Front. Zawahiri had to face down internal critics who warned that joining bin Laden's World Front and refocusing EIJ attacks on U.S. rather than Egyptian targets would cause the United States and other Western security services to pursue and catch EIJ operatives outside Egypt. These predictions came to pass, and Zawahiri and the forces of bin Laden will certainly try to blunt the dissension-raising potential of the I-told-you-so'ers by making the U.S. diplomatic and intelligence services pay a price for their successes.

Captured EIJ fighters have made clear that bin Laden and Zawahiri are planning revenge against the U.S. intelligence service. In early 1999, for example, imprisoned EIJ operative Ibrahim al-Najjar said that "the Islamist organizations will react violently to the U.S. intelligence services' pursuit of fundamentalists." He also told an Egyptian court that bin Laden's World Front has expanded its target list to include kidnappings and hostage taking "so as to bargain with the ruling regimes and security services for the release of the detained members of the Islamic group or other pro-loyal groups." In this regard, the consensus of the EIJ's "Returnees from Albania" was that "U.S. and French interests" would be especially targeted because of their "pursuit of the organization's members inside and outside their territories." Even the EIJ's not-always-collegial coreligionists in the Gama'at al-Islamiyya (IG) have supported such attacks; current IG chief Mustafa Hamza said in 1996 that the Gama'at was even then considering kidnapping Americans and using them to "ransom" Shaykh Rahman.[29]

á In October 1999, Gama'at leader Rifai'i Taha urged action "to force the United States to curtail its policy of kidnapping leaders of the [Egyptian Islamic] Jihad movement and pursuing them on behalf of the Egyptian government or any other regime in the region." These sentiments were kept to the fore by what are seen in the Islamic world as the CIA-orchestrated late-1999 deportation of Islamists Abdul Latif Salah and Khalid al-Deeq to Jordan—from Albania and Pakistan, respectively—because of their ties to bin Laden and Washington's policy of "seeking to completely eliminate the Jihad group [EIJ]"; by the May 2000 British decision to extradite EIJ leaders Eidarous and al-Bari to America; and by the Lebanese government's May 2000 deportation to Cairo of an EIJ fighter named Jamal Tantawi, the leader of a bin

Laden unit in Lebanon. After Beirut's action, the Egyptian Islamists' attorney Muntasir al-Zayyat warned, "If the United States continues to lead the efforts to eradicate the Islamic movements and hunt down Islamic symbols" the result would be steady increases in "the feelings of hostility and hatred toward the United States which could result in reprisal actions." Needless to say, the U.S. capture in Afghanistan of several hundred al Qaeda and Taliban fighters, and their subsequent relocation to a detention camp in Guantánamo Bay, Cuba, will further fuel this sentiment and give al Qaeda another reason to go the 11 September 2001 attacks one better.[30]

Moreover, bin Laden's call on individual Muslims to defend Islam against U.S. aggression by killing Americans wherever possible raises the danger to U.S. civilians, intelligence officers, diplomats, and military personnel who are known, or easily identified, in their foreign communities. Clearly, overt U.S. government officers and their families in the United States would be even easier targets; in particular, the U.S.-based FBI officers and Department of Justice prosecutors who have caught, tried, and convicted EIJ and bin Laden fighters must be atop al Qaeda's hit list. In either scenario, a Muslim unconnected to but inspired by bin Laden and obligated by the Koran to defend Islam could act on his own to find and kill an American, therefore affording no opportunity to be detected and preempted. Bin Laden's strengthening international stature as a respected "man of the call"—an Islamic proselytizer—produces an unquantifiable threat to U.S. citizens. As Kamil Yusuf Husayn wrote in his book *Osama Bin Laden: Legend of the Century*, bin Laden's catalogue of potential operatives

> includes thousands of people not only concentrated in the countries we mentioned earlier [countries listed in the U.S. indictment of bin Laden], but within a much broader geographical domain. They look to Osama bin Laden as the source of inspiration or ideology on operational levels. Clearly, they have no organizational connection to him and do not maintain secret contacts with him. They view themselves as individuals committed to obey his general orders, particularly the fatwas issued by religious scholars at Bin Laden's request.[31]

Threat from bin Laden's Peers

Another largely undiscussed source of potential problems for the United States must be presumed to exist among those of bin Laden's peers who accompanied him to Afghanistan or separately made their way there to fight God's fight against the Soviets. The bin Laden family, of course, is not the only immensely wealthy nonroyal Saudi merchant, business, or banking family. The al-Olayans, al-Amoudis, Jamjoons, al-Rajhis, Kamels, bin

Mahfouzes, and other families are as large, as religiously committed, and nearly as wealthy as the bin Ladens. *Forbes Magazine* listed these families as billionaires in July 1999. The bin Mahfouz family is particularly interesting, because, like the bin Laden family, it has Yemeni origins and because the family patriarch, Khalid bin Mahfouz, is or was married to one of bin Laden's sisters. The bin Mahfouz family also holds a large share of the Saudi banking industry, and, as noted, has been tied to a U.K.-based Islamic charity accused of supporting bin Laden.[32]

Because bin Laden has been outspoken, confrontational, and militarily active, he has been the focus of media coverage that, in turn, has made the West see him as a solo Saladin whose organization would fall apart without him. While there is no gainsaying bin Laden's demise would disrupt his organization and perhaps paralyze the World Front, it is far from certain there is no one out there who could replace him. Beyond the strong and varied talents of his lieutenants, bin Laden's fame and success have created a shadow in which others of like pedigree may be operating anonymously and growing in ability. Bin Laden told ABC's John Miller that "During the days of the [Afghan] jihad, thousands of young men who were well off financially left the Arabian Peninsula and other areas and joined the fighting." While bin Laden said hundreds of Islamist youths died in Afghanistan and later in Chechnya and Bosnia, it is unlikely in the extreme that all these young men did their duty by dying in battle to please the regimes that happily packed them off to war.[33]

With or Without bin Laden and Our Allies

While it is unlikely that there are "hundreds" of individuals with bin Laden-like leadership capabilities — as a Taliban official once told journalist Ahmed Rashid — it certainly is true that the movement led by bin Laden will continue with or without him. As noted earlier, bin Laden's senior lieutenants are a talented and experienced group; there is no lack of military, political, theological, scientific, technical, or propaganda know-how in the inner circle. Moreover, because the Islamic movement that today is symbolized by al Qaeda is international in scope, there surely are talented Islamist leaders in areas of the world that have so far received little attention from the West — in East Asia, Africa, and Central Asia, for example.

If, then, bin Laden is killed or captured during the Afghan war, al Qaeda will survive. In the aftermath of his departure, al Qaeda's leaders are likely to pull in their horns a bit to protect the organization's structure as the new leader — probably Ayman al-Zawahiri — takes over and comes up to speed. Given al Qaeda's marked professionalism, it is unlikely that the new leadership would launch a series of ill-planned or inconsequential revenge attacks, although random attacks by grieving groups or individuals not under al

Qaeda's direct control must be anticipated. For al Qaeda, bin Laden's patient credo of "excellent preparation . . . for operations of a specific type that will make an impact on the enemy"[34] will prevail with or without his presence.

If bin Laden survives the present war, al Qaeda's operations are likely to continue to follow the long-established pattern of incrementally increasing lethality. Bin Laden announced this doctrine in 1996 when he said that though he believed the attacks on OPM-SANG and Dhahran had been "a sufficient signal for people of intelligence among American decision-makers," such was not the case, and therefore attacks of greater lethality were necessary.[35] Bin Laden intends to apply whatever level of destructiveness is necessary to force the United States to withdraw from Saudi Arabia, terminate aid to Israel, and end the embargo on Iraq.

In addition to the death and destruction the United States will suffer if bin Laden survives, Washington also is likely to find support for its anti-al Qaeda efforts withering over time. The longer the Afghan war continues, for example, the more difficult Pakistani president Musharraf will find it to support U.S. policy and military operations. He already is running out of fingers to put in the dike. Only an immediate economic renaissance in Pakistan or a massive infusion of U.S. arms to redress the military balance with India will prevent the undoing of Musharraf's unprecedented initiatives and the resurgence of the virulently anti-American forces he has sought to control, if not suppress. Elsewhere in the Islamic world, bin Laden's survival and continued attacks — as long as they focus on U.S. interests — will enhance his leadership appeal among Muslims and simultaneously erode the ability of Islamic states to support U.S. policy. Support from these states has been tepid since the latest Afghan war began, and, according to *Jane's Intelligence Review*, Egypt, Jordan, Sudan, Yemen, and Saudi Arabia "are taking the opportunity presented by the 'war on terrorism' to repress their opponents [Islamists and secularists alike] and delay reform" — actions that also will increase bin Laden's appeal.[36]

Support from Europe, perhaps with the exception of the United Kingdom, may decline more quickly than that from Muslim nations because the latter hate us for what we do — especially vis-à-vis Israel and Palestine — while the former hate us for our power and wealth in what amounts to a rather blatant racism. While bin Laden's 11 September 2001 attacks temporarily silenced Europe's anti-Americanism — what the writer William Shawcross describes as the "one racism that is tolerated . . . not just tolerated but often applauded"[37] — bin Laden's survival and the Afghan war's unexpected duration have prompted the steady reemergence of this sentiment. The movement of captured al Qaeda and Taliban fighters to detention camps at Guantánamo Bay, Cuba, prompted a massive and ferocious storm of anti-American abuse from Europe. From behind their banner of protecting human rights — always a sign Europe wants to avoid or disengage from doing hard but necessary things — media and/or government spokesmen in the United Kingdom, France, Germany, Italy, Spain, Ireland, and Canada assailed what the Paris daily *Le Figaro* called an effort by "the United States to avoid international legal constraints."[38] Two headlines from the British press suffice to show the Europeans' joy at finding a vehicle for distancing themselves from U.S. policy and their unbounded zest for abusing America: from London's *Guardian*, "We Will Not Tolerate the Abuse of War Prisoners; Guantanamo Could Be Where America and Europe Part Company," and from the same city's the *Independent*, "Spare Us Wild West Justice."[39] With friends like these . . .

With or without Osama bin Laden and with or without our allies, the clash of civilizations — Islam versus what-passes-for Christendom — appears to be as inevitable as it will be bloody. On this issue, bin Laden has again staked out a position that makes him largely immune from criticism in the Islamic world. While Muslim leaders and clerics will genuinely deplore attacks on Christians, bin Laden's description of Christians as rapacious Crusaders bent on converting or annihilating Muslims has the ring of historical truth — as noted, the Crusades are still a fresh memory and wound across the Islamic world — and is validated by CNN's real-time coverage of events that always seem to leave Muslims battered, bloodied, or dead at the hands of non-Muslims, particularly Christian and Jewish hands.

Historically, proselytizing and military force are seen by Muslims as integral parts of Western imperialism and as the main tools of the contemporary Christian West's approach to its relations with Islam; Professor Lewis has written, for example, that the term "imperialist," when used by contemporary Islamists, is often "given a distinctly religious significance, being used in association, and some times interchangeably with 'missionary.'" For many Muslims, Christian efforts to convert Muslims are "a systematic effort to erase their identity and turn them away from their faith." The Taliban's voice in Kabul, *Hewad*, for example, argued that "anyone who calls our people to Christianity embarks on an act against our Muslim nation, and which is considered an attack on our values."[40]

Christian proselytizing, when teamed with the provision of basic health and education services, is seen as a quiet and especially insidious form of imperialism that saps the Islamic world's future strength by converting its youths. In this context, it is understandable why bin Laden-associated Yemeni Islamists have twice bombed a nonprofit health clinic run by the only Christian church in Aden, the Christ Anglican Church. Many Islamic scholars, moreover, view Christian-sponsored humanitarian aid as a conscious effort to exploit the fact that low literacy rates mean that "not all Muslims are versed in religion" and so are vulnerable to persuasive missionaries.[41]

There is a perception in the Muslim world — which bin Laden has fed —

that the Christian West is always ready to use economic coercion and military force if proselytizing does not work, or does not work quickly. The latter is an intense irritant in the Islamic world and is, as Professor Samuel Huntington noted, grounded in fact: from 1980 to 1995 "the United States engaged in seventeen military operations in the Middle East, all of them directed at Muslims. No comparable pattern of U.S. military operations occurred against the people of any other civilization."[42] Tough economic sanctions have been simultaneously enforced by the West against several Muslim states. As noted, bin Laden has been outspoken in condemning the Crusaders' eagerness to put sanctions on Sudan, Iraq, and Libya; to tolerate prolonged military aggression against Muslim Bosnians, Somalis, Kashmiris, and Kosovars; and to conspire to divide Muslim states such as Afghanistan, Iraq, and Saudi Arabia. In voicing these views, bin Laden is more virulent than most Muslims, but he is not a lone voice. In denouncing any Muslim-Christian dialogue as "nothing but bait to lure us into renouncing our religion—a scheme to uproot Islam and Christianize the world," the Saudi journal *Al-Madinah* said in February 2000 that Pope John Paul II "seeks to lead the entire world to reach his dream of Christianizing the world by the third millennium."[43] Aligning the official Saudi position with bin Laden's claim that "Christian powers are busy in conspiracies against Muslims," *Al-Madinah* warned that if the pope could not force apostasy on Muslims by proselytizing, more aggressive measures would be forthcoming.

> The Christianization process was not exclusive to apostasy. It took the form of liquidation and uprooting as well. We saw proof to that in what happened since 1995. Battles with Muslim minorities developed into massacres to annihilate Muslims in India, Burma, the Philippines, and Somalia, as well as Bosnia-Herzegovina. The same thing is now happening in Chechnya and other places. It is a synchronized undertaking under the name of religion, although this kind of violence runs adversary to the spirit of Christ, may God's peace be upon him.[44]

Thus, with or without bin Laden, and whether or not the West accepts it, many Muslims appear to think a war against Islam is under way. Events of early 2002 reinforced this notion as U.S.-led forces fought in Afghanistan, Russian and Chinese troops battled Muslim insurgents, and Israel invaded the West Bank. "Misfortunes are befalling us one after another," bin Laden said. "[T]he Christian Crusade is . . . the fiercest battle. Muslims have never faced anything bigger than this."[45] Again, this is not to say bin Laden is correct, but the daily events Muslims watch on CNN, BBC, and Al-Jazirah make it hard for them to accept the West's contention that the war on terrorism is not a war on Islam. Perhaps Ayman Zawahiri best described the difficulties Muslims have in reconciling the contention with reality. "How can we forget," Zawahiri asked in late 2001,

> that the very name Israel—which is supported by the United States—is based on a religious belief. For Israel is one of the prophets of God, may God's peace and blessings be upon them. It [Israel] captures our land and kills our children and women on a religious basis, as they claim. It considers Jerusalem its eternal capital on a religious basis. It calls on the United States to transfer its capital [sic—embassy?] to Jerusalem on a religious basis. After all this, the United States claims that its campaign against jihad—which it terms terrorism—and in defense of Israel is not a religious war.[46]

15

SPRING 2002: WHERE ARE WE? WHERE ARE WE GOING?

Just as they are killing us, we have to kill them so there will be a balance of terror. This is the first time that the balance of terror has been close between the two parties, between Muslims and Americans in the modern age. We will do as they do. If they kill our women and innocent people, we will kill their women and innocent people until they stop.

Osama bin Laden, October 2001

They [bin Laden and al Qaeda] can no longer conceive a new operation in Afghanistan. . . . We have basically eviscerated their capacity to project power outside Afghanistan. They are now in a survival-only mode. . . . Unable to communicate with their global cells, the two [bin Laden and Zawahiri] constantly move from cave to brick hut to cave, their survival now the prime operational goal. . . . They [al Qaeda] are severely disrupted. About all they can do is hide out and not get caught. They are not in a position to conduct operations.

Unnamed U.S. officials and a retired
U.S. Army lieutenant general,
December 2001–January 2002[1]

As spring 2002 arrives, the quotations above present two starkly different views of reality. If bin Laden's reality is closer to fact—he says "God's relief and victory are coming soon"[2] — Americans can count on al Qaeda attacks that will surpass those of September 2001 in terms of death, destruction, and humiliation. If the current and retired U.S. officials are on the mark, bin Laden, al Qaeda, and Mullah Omar's Taliban are already little more than a painful and embarrassing memory. Some of America's experts, in fact, have adopted a triumphant tone, claiming that Islamic fundamentalism "has suffered a grievous blow"[3] and celebrating the dimensions of a U.S. victory that "didn't just wipe out the Taliban experiment to create the world's purest Islamic state. In a ripple effect, it is also rolling back the tide of political Islam in the religion's heartland, the Arabian Peninsula."[4] Perhaps we should cordon off Pennsylvania Avenue and erect bleachers for a victory parade. Perhaps we should despair.

Where Are We?

AL QAEDA AND THE TALIBAN: As this is written, Osama bin Laden apparently is alive and his forces remain largely intact. The losses al Qaeda has suffered since 7 October 2001 — outlined in chapter 13 — have been serious but not debilitating. The death of bin Laden's right-hand man, Abu Hafs al-Masri, hurts al Qaeda, but he has been succeeded by Muhammed Makkawi, a senior EIJ member and a former colonel in the Egyptian army's Special Forces. He was cashiered when it was discovered that he was helping to plot a coup against the government and planning to free fellow EIJ members from prison.[5] Makkawi may not yet have the personal rapport Abu Hafs had with bin Laden, but he brings far more pertinent military experience to the position. Al Qaeda also lost an unknown number of fighters to U.S.-led bombing, nearly five hundred more are in captivity, and presumably the group lost much military materiel to the bombing.[6] In addition, al Qaeda's freedom of movement inside Afghanistan and internationally has been constrained.

While these losses are not insignificant, there is no reason to believe that bin Laden's network has been defeated or, for that matter, is even more than moderately distracted. As argued earlier, al Qaeda is a veteran insurgent organization; it is large, disciplined, well trained, and resilient. It also is dispersed worldwide, and so most of the organization that is targeted against the United States and its allies has not been attacked or disrupted by the U.S. military. The loyalty of al Qaeda's leaders and foot soldiers remains rock solid — not a single defection has been reported in the media — and bin Laden himself has long since become accustomed to changing his location on a daily basis, if not more frequently. Overall, the impact of the U.S. military onslaught on al Qaeda has caused bin Laden's forces logistical disruptions, personal sorrow, and some uncomfortable nights in chilled caves; it has not, however, seriously eroded their ability to wage war.

Neither should too much be made of what many in the West have described as the Taliban's complete military and political collapse. It obviously is true that the Taliban has lost control of the major Afghan urban centers. With that loss, however, the Taliban also has been freed of the duty to feed, protect, and provide social, health, and administrative services to the urban populace. Having originated in the mid-1990s as a rural-based insurgency, the Taliban has been returned to its proper state of nature, courtesy of the U.S. military. The Taliban—and al Qaeda for that matter—has done what all of history's successful insurgent organizations have done to survive; they have abandoned the cities. "Unlike traditional armies," Lawrence Friedman recently reminded readers of the journal *Survival*, "guerrilla groups and terrorists do not expect to hold territory. They need time more than space, for it is their ability to endure while mounting regular attacks that enables them to grow while the enemy is drained of patience and credibility."[7] Many Muslim commentators and analysts have made this point; Abd-al-Bari Atwan in the United Kingdom.[8] and Humayun Akhtar in Pakistan,[9] for example. The latter also has raised the interesting point that no one in the West has accounted for the more than forty thousand soldiers the Taliban still had under arms when Kandahar fell. In the West, few have mirrored this line of analysis, although more notice should be taken of the views of Milton Bearden, a retired senior U.S. intelligence officer. In warning his countrymen not to count unhatched chickens, Bearden wrote the following in mid-November 2001:

> As a rule, set-piece battles for major urban centers are not the way of combat in Afghanistan, especially when a foreign element as prominent as U.S. air support in the current fighting is involved. Getting into Afghan cities, particularly for foreign armies, has always been pretty easy; it took the Soviets less than two weeks to take most of the cities. . . . The hard part always has been what comes next. . . . So to call the Taliban down for the count because a string of urban centers has fallen, while possibly true, would be needlessly pushing our luck.[10]

Bin Laden, Mullah Omar, and the Taliban also draw strength from several other factors. First, the interim government of Hamid Karzai is kept in power by foreign, Christian forces, has no Islamist credentials, and is dominated by Masood's senior lieutenants—Tajiks all. The interim regime therefore is transparently an artificial Western creation, made up of what a Pakistani commentator accurately has called a "minority jing bang lot of nationalities, and I dare say Martians too. Their government will be a mongrel of uncertain parentage and will not last." It also is devoid of any credible representation from the country's numerically and historically dominant Pashtun tribe.[11]

Rather than the interim government being a new beginning for Afghanistan, it is more likely to be a catalyst for steadily intensifying domestic strife. In an excellent and prescient essay in *Foreign Affairs,* Milton Bearden told his countrymen that not much stability could be expected from a Tajik-dominated regime. "On the contrary," Bearden argued, "the more likely consequences of a U.S. alliance with the late Masood's fighters would be the coalescing of Afghanistan's majority Pashtun tribes around their Taliban leaders and the rekindling of a brutal, general civil war that would continue until the United States simply gave up."[12]

The situation on the ground in Afghanistan also bodes well for a resurgence of the Taliban and their al Qaeda associates. Since the fall of Kandahar, multiple regional warlords—many of whom served as anti-Taliban proxies for the U.S.-led coalition[13]—have established control over personal fiefdoms across the country, creating "a land so perilous it can boggle the mind of anyone who has lived in peace."[14] The murder, bribery, kidnapping, and extortion that the Taliban had all but eliminated have again become commonplace. "I was born in a time of fighting," a female nursing student in Kandahar told the *Washington Post* in early 2002, "and I never saw stable conditions except with the Taliban. In the time of [religious] extremism, I could study safely. Now I can't."[15] As Afghanistan again descends into the barbarous, crime-ridden conditions that fostered the Taliban's rise to power in the 1990s, Mullah Omar and bin Laden—assuming they have survived—will bide their time until, as bin Laden's senior aide, Mahfouz Ould Walid, told Al-Jazirah television in November 2001, "The same conditions that helped the Taliban seize these cities in the past will enable the Taliban to recapture these cities in the near future, God willing."[16] As always, Afghans will take extremism over violence and instability every time.

AMERICA AND ITS ALLIES: As signaled by its premature triumphant tone, the United States seems to have learned little since 11 September 2001. As noted in an epigram above, we still lack respect for bin Laden, we still misidentify his organization as terrorist vice insurgent, and—most dangerously—we still manifest an aversion to military casualties so intense that we have overestimated the impact our air power and military technology have made on al Qaeda and the Taliban. We have shown our might, but we have not inflicted it with full effect, forgetting that, as Ralph Peters has written, "No display of might will change the essence . . . of the man driven by God."[17] Simply put, we have failed utterly to kill enough Taliban or al Qaeda fighters to make an impression on or deter them. "Americans might not like thinking about vengeance . . . but that isn't true of the denizens of the Middle East," Reuel Marc Gerecht brilliantly wrote in the *Weekly Standard.*

> The ability to inflict *intigam,* vengeance, is their essential element
> of power and dominion. If we do not scorch all those who gave aid

to al Qaeda, we will mercilessly belittle ourselves before men who have an acute sense of the jugular. . . .

The United States must have a [military] victory sooner, not later, in Afghanistan. Our enemies in the Middle East must see our dead seriousness about eradicating in Afghanistan and elsewhere in the Middle East those who have drawn American blood. If bin Laden, Mullah Omar, and their Taliban cohorts are still alive next spring, producing videocassettes trenchantly dissecting our weakness and the immorality of our Muslim "allies," then we will have hell to pay. No sane Muslim in the Middle East or elsewhere will then want to ally himself with the United States. No non-Muslim, either.[18]

The United States also continues to be hamstrung by the analyses of our "experts," as well as by the pervasiveness of our beliefs in the universality of our culture and values. The fixation of the former on state sponsors of terrorism, for example, continues to blind Americans to the reality of al Qaeda's military and logistics capabilities. While the World Trade Center and the Pentagon were still blazing, a former CIA director and his colleague told Americans that the nature of the attacks "point significantly to the involvement of state sponsorship"[19]; a prominent historian wrote that "it will become apparent" that the attacks could not have occurred "without the assistance of some governments"[20]; a usually insightful commentator erred and said that bin Laden "received critical assistance" from "Middle Eastern states"[21]; and — inevitably — a veteran journalist identified Lebanese Hizballah terrorist Imad Mugniyah as the leader of an Iraq-Iran-Hizballah-al Qaeda conspiracy to attack the World Trade Center.[22] One almost sensed that these writers felt that bin Laden and al Qaeda were an irritating distraction from the major goal of turning U.S. military power against Iran, Iraq, and other states sponsors. Sad as it is to say, it appears that al Qaeda will have to cause another mass of American dead before Americans can free themselves from the thrall of the incorrect boilerplate analysis of yesterday's experts.

The experts' disdain for bin Laden's capabilities also have caused them to urge the application of limited military power in Afghanistan to pave the way for democracy there and elsewhere in the Muslim world. The Afghan war, then, is an opportunity for social work of international scope, not an opportunity to destroy al Qaeda. The day after the U.S. attacks on Afghanistan began, Jim Hoagland wrote in the *Washington Post* that the administration must maintain a "steady, calculated, and merciful approach to the war," while Brian M. Jenkins had scolded U.S. leaders even earlier that "Our violence must be measured. . . . And American values must be preserved." Temperate military actions, for Hoagland, would allow the United States to get on with its true mission "to transform the shock of the waves of military strikes into a force for change in societies that have fundamentally given up on themselves and the world." Speaking in tones worthy of the lamentable Woodrow Wilson at his most absurd, Andrew Sullivan went even further into the deep end and explained to Americans that "We are not fighting for our country as such or for our flag. We are fighting for the universal principles of our Constitution—and the possibility of free religious faith it guarantees."[23] Imperial hubris, it seems, is alive, well, and ready to make our sons and daughters die in its name.

Tragically, many American experts have displayed simple laziness in their research and have fallen back on what a Jesuit professor of mine once termed "analysis by assertion." They have not, for example, read what bin Laden has written and said about Palestine since 1993 and so they glibly and incorrectly—as has been documented throughout this work—claim that "as longtime bin Laden watchers know he has never been especially concerned with the plight of the Palestinians," and that "bin Laden embraced the Palestinian cause only when his own future turned bleak."[24] They have ignored the very real accomplishments and popular acceptance of the Taliban government in Afghanistan—the documentation of which is full and easily accessible[25]—and have taken their lead from Mrs. Jay Leno and the Hollywood wives and equated the fall of Kabul with the liberation of Dachau, thereby obscuring for their countrymen the genuine possibility of a Taliban rebound.

The experts have again rushed to find final answers to the bin Laden threat by asserting that money is the source of his power and therefore the key to his defeat. Ed Blanche has written in *Jane's Intelligence Review*, for example, that "Bin Laden's popularity is due in large part to the millions of dollars he has spent from his personal fortune," and former U.S. government official W. F. Wechsler claims that bin Laden "derives much of his authority and influence from the money under his control."[26] Lost in this American-centric approach to understanding a problem foreign to their experience, analysts such as Jim Hoagland conclude that "finding and destroying the money trails to bin Laden is essential to finding and destroying the group," while another scholar asserts the way to defeat al Qaeda is to increase the staff and budget of something called the Office of Foreign Assets Control at the Treasury Department.[27] At this threat, bin Laden is surely shaking—from laughter.

Also indicative of how far America's experts are from understanding bin Laden is their analysis of the videotapes bin Laden has released, or U.S. forces have acquired, since 11 September 2001. This analysis painfully demonstrates their inability to get past appearances to substance. "Gone is that kind of jocular spirit," the *New York Times'* Judith Miller said about the videos. "He is gaunt, he is gray, and he is alone. And he is obviously very depressed." Concurring, Ambassador Phyllis Oakley said "the fact is this is a diminished man and a diminished organization."[28] Other experts remarked on the growing whiteness of bin Laden's beard, a possible injury to his arm, the kind of watch and ring he wears, and how much water he drinks while speaking. After the informal video of bin Laden discussing the 11 September attacks was broadcast by the U.S. government,[29] the experts ignored how and what bin Laden said—the intricate, professional planning of the attack and the dedication, skill, and bravery of the attackers—and instead decided that he was gleeful and gloating over the attacks, betraying his murderous character, and smugly proud of having tricked the attackers into undertaking a suicide mission. Because the experts continue to confuse bin Laden with a terrorist like Abu Nidal, they missed the awe in which he held the men who sacrificed their lives for their God, as well as his gentle, soft-spoken, and nonboastful manner. "Contrary to the expectation of the Americans," a late-December 2001 article on Sa'd al-Faqih's Web site insightfully noted,

> the tape will have reflected positively on Osama bin Laden who was shown in the footage to be relaxed in contrast to how he came across in [staged] interviews. As to the contention by the Americans that Osama bin Laden appeared to rejoice and gloat over the deaths of civilians, obviously the vast cultural divide had gotten in the way of the Americans' understanding of his feelings.[30]

Finally, most Americans—experts, officials, and civilians—have still not addressed the role of Islam in bin Laden's activities and message in a frank and analytic manner. While since September there has been more discussion of the role of religion in the war in which the United States is engaged, this discussion continues to occur within the confines of what a British journalist has described as the West's "suffocating atmosphere of multicultural political correctness." Bin Laden's supporters are said to "pray to the God of hate .. [and are] driven by pure hate and nihilism," their faith is decried as "terrorist fundamentalism," and they are demonized as "fiends ... [and] dedicated fanatics" who hate "with every fiber of their twisted soul."[31] While it is useful to hate the enemy you must kill, it is counterproductive to sail into a war armed with hatred but no understanding of your foe's worthiness, skill, or appeal. In bin Laden's case, hate and our unwillingness to talk frankly about Islam have blinded many Americans to the fact that bin Laden has been, in the words of Thomas L. Friedman, "a brilliant and dedicated foe."[32]

Instead of belaboring this point, I would suggest that the reader ponder the following words. They came in November 2001 from a senior member of the Muslim Brotherhood's branch in Jordan, a group with a worldwide presence that dwarfs al Qaeda's and which is nonviolent in its approach to promoting Islamism. Note in particular that the Brotherhood's disagreements with bin Laden are theological ones over his attitudes toward other Muslims and not toward his actions against the United States and the West.

We regard Bin laden as a Muslim person. He came from a wealthy class and had a lot of money he used to further a noble and honorable pursuit, namely jihad against the Communist Russian occupation of Afghanistan. He played a significant role in this endeavor. Bin Laden subscribes to a particular ideology. He is inclined to Salafi thought [emulation of early Muslims]. We do not doubt his Islamic commitment and loyalty to his religion. A certain line of thought that holds other Muslims as infidels — and this line of thought came from Egypt — tried to drive him toward a renunciation and repudiation form of ideology that we regard as foreign to our concepts. For this reason we oppose him on many of the issues that he adopted, including intellectual issues and efforts at religious interpretations. Still, we cannot say he is a traitor [to Islam], God forbid. He has sacrificed his future and social standing to go and live in the caves and mountains. Hence, his commitment to Islam is undoubted but we do not support many of his ideas or the way he expresses them. . . . What is demonstrably true in our view is that bin Laden performed a jihad role against the Russians and that he is now carrying out jihad against the Americans by defending Afghanistan, the oppressed Muslim country against which the United States is launching a war in which it uses its powerful weapons without reason or proof.[33]

Where Are We Going?

"Well, General, our goal was to get them [the Union army] out of Virginia and into the open. Now, they are in the open." So says Lt. General James Longstreet to Robert E. Lee in the great movie *Gettysburg*, as the two men discuss events at the close of the first day of that epic battle. These words encapsulate bin Laden's current position. He has long wanted U.S. ground forces "out in the open," and Abd-al-Bari Atwan is on the mark when he says "he [bin Laden] believes that attracting U.S. forces to Afghanistan was one of the aims he planned very well."[34] If bin Laden is alive, he must be doubly pleased that U.S. ground forces have deployed to the Philippines and may soon turn up in Somalia and Yemen. Bin Laden no longer has to rely solely on his urban fighters and now can bring to bear the guerrilla forces of al Qaeda, the Taliban, other veteran Afghan fighters led by Khalis, Sayyaf, Hekmatyar, and Haqqani, and other allies and associates in the just-mentioned nations.

With the promise of useful employment for all their fighters, and armed with a specific strategy and well-defined war aims, bin Laden's forces will proceed in their usual professional and patient manner. The United States, however, has yet to understand bin Laden or the dimensions of the threat his forces pose, and has neither a clear strategy nor a recognizable set of war aims. Are we out to smash al Qaeda once and for all, bring democracy and secularism to Afghanistan and then to the rest of the Islamic world, and make friends in the Muslim world and avoid offending the Europeans? Or are we warming up militarily for the main event against Iraq or Iran, or simply trying to intimidate al Qaeda and the Afghans—fat chance—while trying to make sure no American soldier gets killed? Are we after a mix of these or some as yet unstated goal? Until we figure what we face and what we want, our fortunes are likely to be as barren as those of the forces of bin Laden will be flush.

AL QAEDA: This organization's future course can be described with dispatch, because, as David Ignatius has written, bin Laden is "a distinctly modern man with a very clear strategy of attack."[35] Bin Laden's intent has been to defeat the United States by steadily increasing the number of casualties and level of economic damage caused by his attacks on U.S. interests. Al Qaeda will now complement those attacks with insurgent operations against U.S. forces deployed overseas. How will it recognize victory? Easy, by forcing drastic changes in U.S. foreign policy. Al Qaeda will judge Islam victorious when U.S. and British forces evacuate Saudi Arabia and the rest of the Arabian Peninsula, when the United States has terminated all aid to Israel, and when the U.S. and UN embargoes on Iraq are lifted. These attainments, bin Laden has believed, will lead inevitably to destruction of Israel and what bin Laden has called the regimes of "hypocrites" in Saudi Arabia, Egypt, Jordan, and elsewhere.[36] We in the United States and the West make a mistake when we argue, as has Thomas L. Friedman, that bin Laden's attacks are "not aimed at reversing any specific U.S. policy," or, as Steve Simon and Daniel Benjamin did in *Survival* in early 2002, that bin Laden has "no discrete set of negotiable political demands."[37] He clearly does have such demands and he has voiced them clearly and repeatedly. They are, in some ways, the same negotiating demands often used by the United States in its history; that is, unconditional surrender. We may not like them, we may not understand them, and we may not believe they are plausible or attainable, but there they are—and they are well understood and probably favored by most Muslims. On these three goals, bin Laden and his brethren worldwide pretty much have been unanimous; their differences have been over the means through which they are to be secured.

We can also expect bin Laden's network to exploit a historic opportunity, or rather an opportunity made great by historical considerations. "In his pronouncements bin Laden makes frequent references to history," Bernard Lewis reminded his readers in the *New Yorker* in November 2001.

> In current American usage, the phrase "that's history" is commonly used to dismiss something as unimportant, or no relevance to cur-

rent concerns, and, despite immense investment in the teaching and writing of history, the general level of historical knowledge in our society is abysmally low. The Muslim peoples, like everyone else in the world, are shaped by their history, but, unlike some others, they are keenly aware of it. . . . Middle Easterners' perceptions of history is nourished from the pulpit, and by the media, and, although it may be—indeed, often is—slanted and inaccurate, it is nevertheless vivid and powerfully resonant.[38]

Enter bin Laden, who always has been conscious of the content and rhythms of Islamic history, and who, as Reuel Marc Gerecht correctly noted, has been for most of a decade "tweaking the nerves of Islamic civilization, which has experienced 300 years of defeats by Western armies, but vividly remembers a millennium of triumphs over Christians and Jews."[39] Currently, the followers of bin Laden hold a stacked deck in terms of Islamic history. First, al Qaeda and its allies look like they are down and out. While it is crazy to think that al Qaeda welcomes every aspect of its current situation, it is one that can be turned to the organization's advantage because it has been sketched out in scripture. "In the holy Koran," senior al Qaeda member Mahfouz Ould Walid told Al-Jazirah television on 29 November 2001, "God Almighty has taught us that he always tries his prophets and puts them to the test. . . . We believe this group [al Qaeda] will be tried, will face harm, will lose fortunes and souls, and will face hunger and fear, but God will not abandon them."[40] In addition to the U.S.-led military attack on Afghanistan, Western demands for restricting the activities of Islamic charities and calls for "modernizing" the content of Islamic teaching also have the appearance of attacking two of the five pillars of Islam, charity and the word of God. Finally, the Muslim world's sense that Islam is being attacked on all sides by infidel armies is growing, as Russia, India, and China use the cover of America's Afghan war to beat the hell out of their Muslim minorities and Israel smashes the Palestinians.

Thus, the stage of Islamic history, if you will, is set for the forces of bin Laden. In addition, bin Laden has emerged for tens of millions of Muslims as the defender of Islam in the modern age, a man "with a clean record who can make a match for the Americans, can do them harm, and can inflict pain on them."[41] Again, the annals of Islamic history are replete with men of iron resolve and dauntless courage—heroic soldiers such as Nur-al-Din, Saladin, and, yes, the Prophet Muhammed—whose records are models to be honored and imitated. "It is worth remembering," Michael Scott Doran wrote in a brilliant essay in *Foreign Affairs* in early 2002, "that the rise of Islam represents a miraculous case of the triumph of the human will. With little more than their beliefs to gird them, the Prophet Muhammed and a small number of devoted followers started a movement that brought the most powerful empires of the day crashing to the ground."[42] In this context, if al Qaeda comes off the ropes and hits the United States with a blow that matches or exceeds those of 11 September 2001 — especially against the backdrop of Israel's recent invasion of the West Bank — it will not only humiliate and damage America, but it also will evoke for most Muslims, with spectacular clarity, some of the legendary come-from-behind military victories of the Prophet Muhammed and his early successors, such as those at the Battle of Badr (624), the Battle of the Trench (627), and the Battle of Yarmuk (636).[43]

THE UNITED STATES: "The Americans had lost the war even before they started it," Abd-al-Bari Atwan wrote in *Al-Quds Al-Arabi* on 29 October 2001, "because it is a preposterous, open-ended war of arrogance without specific goals." The statement is too harsh and premature, but, as already noted, dead on the mark regarding vague and jumbled goals. What is the right set of goals for the United States, and in what order should they be pursued? Those questions need to be answered by others far more intelligent and knowledgeable than I am. That said, my view, in the words of some of those others, is laid out below and is meant to answer the following questions: What is the goal? Who is the enemy? What is the means to victory? What is the bottom line?

> You ask: "What is our aim?" I can answer in one word: It is victory, victory at all costs, victory in spite of all terror, victory, however long and hard the road may be; for without victory there is no survival.
>
> Winston Churchill, May, 1940[44]

> And this is definitely a fight to the bitter end, which means first and foremost that we must eliminate Osama bin Laden. As long as he lives, we have lost the war against Islamic terrorism. He will never stop bombing us. His magnetism within militant Islamic circles is undeniable. He will never stop recruiting others to his cause. He has made a rag-tag outfit of Islamic militants, his terrorist umbrella organization al Qaeda, in just a few years, the most celebrated holy warriors in modern Islamic history.
>
> Reuel Marc Gerecht, September 2001[45]

> Westerners have learned, by harsh experience, that the proper response [when attacked by Islamic raiders] is not to take fright but to marshal their forces, to launch massive retaliation and to persist relentlessly until the raiders have either been eliminated or so cowed by the violence inflicted that they relapse into inactivity. . . . The world must learn again that the United States, when severely an-

tagonized, is to be feared; that it grinds its mortal enemies to powder as it did sixty years ago, that the widespread view in extremist
Islamic circles that it is cowardly, decadent, and easily intimidated
by the thought of casualties is false.

> Sir John Keegan, October 2001, and Conrad Black,
> January 2002[46]

The range of American policy options in the [Middle East]
region is reduced to two alternatives, both disagreeable: Get tough
or get out.

> Bernard Lewis, December 2001[47]

Epilogue: "That They May Go in and Look Their Redeemer in the Face with Joy"

> The boys take all after their father, and covet to tread in his steps. Yea, if they but see any place where the old Pilgrim has lain, or any print of his foot, it ministereith joy to their hearts, and they covet to lie or tread in the same.
>
> *The Pilgrim's Progress,* 1678

I believe that the ongoing confrontation between the forces led and inspired by Osama bin Laden and those led by the United States is fast moving toward the status of a clash of civilizations. And, increasingly, bin Laden's religion-based indictment of U.S. foreign policy and call for a defensive jihad are fueling — bin Laden would use the word inciting — the completion of the Muslim world's transit from moderation to militancy. I believe that the materials researched for this study and presented here suggest that violent clashes between the West and Islam will be a central feature of world affairs for the foreseeable future.

The pace and bloodiness of the conflict, while impossible to predict with precision, may be in large measure a function of future words and actions of bin Laden — or of whoever replaces him at the helm of the al Qaeda movement. If bin Laden soon dies or is killed, the acceleration and proliferation of Islamist militancy may moderate. If he lives and manages to reassemble and resettle the al Qaeda forces and if he has the great good fortune to have as his foil a relatively status quo U.S. policy toward the Muslim world, the pace, violence, and internationalization of the defensive jihad he calls for likely will grow. Even if bin Laden does not survive the U.S.-led operations in Afghanistan, the anti-Western activities and passions he has set loose most likely will continue as long as U.S. policy in the Muslim world is unchanged, al Qaeda's extensive network survives and functions, and the

—287

United States continues to apply only a fraction of its military power, and even that almost daintily.

After two decades of bin Laden's organizational and military activities, Americans are only just beginning to fully recognize what he is up to and the growing support his words and actions are garnering in the Muslim world. "Mr. Bin Laden has merely tapped into a powerful and growing wave of religiously motivated hatred of the West," two senior U.S. National Security Council officials recently wrote. Bin Laden's supporters — or "these terrorists," as the officials glibly call them — "are highly motivated, not by a cult of personality, but by a worldview in which they are the vanguard of a divinely ordained battle to liberate Muslim lands. . . . The terrorists allied with Mr. Bin Laden do not want a place at the table; they want to shatter the table."[1]

One can only hope Americans are beginning to understand that the concepts for which Osama bin Laden and his al Qaeda organization have been fighting, like those of John Bunyan's struggling pilgrim Christian, have stood and are standing the test of time. Like Christian, bin Laden has endured the wounds and losses of battle, the sorrow of leaving behind home and family, and the trials of difficult and dangerous travel. Also like Christian and Theodore Roosevelt, bin Laden and his al Qaeda movement have fallen, been bruised, bloodied, and battered in previous battles, and have stood up and returned to the fray, suffering for their faith in a calm and resolute manner, confident in winning that which they value most, God's approval and a place in paradise. "Although we may disagree with Osama about his ideological and political views," journalist Jamal Ismail has written in recognition of the esteem bin Laden has won among Muslims, "no member of our nation [the ummah] can ever place him among the enemies of the nation and its aspirations."[2]

Let the last words be John Bunyan's. In *The Pilgrim's Progress*, Mr. Sagacity is asked whether he has ever heard "what happen'd to a man some time ago in this Town, (whose name was Christian) that went on Pilgrimage up towards the higher Regions?" In response, Mr. Sagacity recalls the man everyone ridiculed and harried and replies affirmatively, explaining that there is growing interest in and admiration for Christian's efforts, and that the widening awareness of Christian's pilgrimage is inspiring others to emulate him. While far from a perfect analogy, Mr. Sagacity's remarks are a fair appraisal of the accumulating effect bin Laden is having in the Islamic world — especially among the young — since beginning his own still-unfinished pilgrimage to what Bunyan called the "Celestial City" more than two decades ago. "Hear of him!" Mr. Sagacity exclaimed,

> Ay: and I also heard of the molestations, troubles, wars, captivities, cries, groans, frights and fears that he met with and had in his Journey; besides, I must tell you, all our country rings of him; there are

but few houses that have heard of him and his doings, but have sought after, and got the Records of his Pilgrimage; yea, I think I may say, his hazardous Journey has got many well-wishers to his ways: For though when he was here, he was *Fool* in every man's mouth, yet now he is gone, he is highly commended of all; for, 'tis said, he lives bravely where he is: Yea, many of them that are resolved never to run his hazards, yet have their mouths water at his gains.[3]

Epilogue to the Revised Edition

It is to be regretted, I confess, that democratical states must always feel before they can see, it is this that makes their government slow, but the people will be right at last.

George Washington, 1787

The great mass of our citizens require only to understand matters rightly, to form right decisions.

George Washington, 1789

On his way to Washington to be inaugurated in the secession winter of 1861, Abraham Lincoln spoke to an audience in Indianapolis, Indiana, on 11 February and stressed the central role all loyal American citizens must play in preserving the Union. "In all the trying positions in which I will be placed," Lincoln said,

my reliance will be placed upon you and the people of the United States—and I wish you to remember now and forever, that it is your business and not mine; that if the union of these States and the liberties of this people, shall be lost, it is but little to any one man of fifty-two years of age, but a great deal to the thirty millions of people who inhabit these United States, and to their posterity in all coming time.[1]

It is well, I believe, to recall Lincoln's words and the heavy burden of responsibility they properly placed on the shoulders of Americans. As I edit this manuscript for the final time on 24 July 2005, America and its allies have taken a three-week pasting from al Qaeda and its allies, and this after Bush administration officials and Democratic leaders repeatedly have assured Americans that al Qaeda's "back is broken." On 7 July 2005, four simultaneous suicide attacks hit four separate locations in London's transportation system, killing 56 and wounding 700.[2] On 21 July, an identical series of explosions hit four different targets in the system, but either because of ineptness or intent, the attacks wounded only one person, while shutting down the system and causing widespread panic. After the second attack, Western politicians, officials, and media commentators crowed a bit about the "botched" and "amateurish attacks," but few noted that even after the 7 July attacks, which prompted an immense increase in deployed British security and police officers and the raising of the alert level to the highest, the attackers again completely surprised British authorities and put bombs precisely where they wanted to.[3] That 21 July was not a repeat of 7 July was the result of either bad tradecraft by the attackers or a deliberate intent to show Britons that they, and not the security forces, held the whip hand.

Then, on 22 July 2005, another group claiming ties to al Qaeda detonated several car bombs at luxury hotels and tourist-oriented markets at Sharm al-Sheikh, an upscale resort on Egypt's Red Sea coast and a longtime bête noire for bin Laden as the site of conferences in which Arab governments "sold out" the Palestinians to the United States and Israel. The attacks killed 88 and wounded more than 200. The casualties included Egyptian nationals and European tourists.[4] The attacks also struck a telling blow against the Egyptian economy, which in 2004 derived nearly 5 percent of its GNP — about $6 billion — from tourism. The tourism industry also is Egypt's primary earner of foreign exchange.[5]

Taken together, these three attacks, I think, again demonstrate the extraordinary focus of Osama bin Laden on the priorities he has set for al Qaeda, which — as I have explained in this book and *Imperial Hubris* — boil down to attacking the United States and its allies in ways that will increase the economic, human, and psychological costs to the point where America will disengage to the greatest extent possible from the Islamic world, and especially the Middle East. But how, one might ask, do three attacks outside America further al Qaeda's cause of defeating the United States? Simple. At the economic level, the three attacks have produced a knee-jerk reaction in the U.S. government to raise the nationwide security level, thereby deploying extra legions of police and security officials, all being paid at overtime rates. Ground transportation of all kinds has been subjected to increased security scrutiny, which slows human and freight travel and produces a drag on the economy. In addition, the bombings sparked a mindless, sophomoric, and bipartisan frenzy in the Congress as the distinguished representatives bloviate and stuff extra billions into the federal budget for grand-transportation security in what, ultimately, will be a vain effort to convince citizens that they are doing something effective to protect them and not just their political sinecures. Score one for bin Laden.

The three attacks also have scored a bulls-eye in damaging the confidence of Americans that their government can protect them. London is the best-policed city in the Western world, and the British Security Service (BSS, or MI5) is likewise that world's finest national-level security organization. Egypt is a police state and is protected by efficient and ruthless police services, whose activities are virtually unencumbered by civil-liberty or human-rights concerns. In each country, the Islamist attackers struck precisely where and when they wanted to. Neither the British nor the Egyptian police and security services had the slightest inkling that an attack was imminent; indeed, the U.K. government lowered its alert level just before the 7 July attacks.

What this means for America is clear: at home, the United States is virtually defenseless. The director of the FBI, Robert Mueller, has presided over a hundred-million-dollar failure to purchase a workable computer system for his officers. He also has publicly endorsed the belief of his senior lieutenants that knowledge of the Middle East and Islamic extremism is not essential for FBI officers working against al Qaeda. For breathtakingly obtuse perspectives that expose the limited perspective and brain power of the Mueller-backed senior FBI officers, try these on for size. In a sworn statement, Dale Watson, the FBI's counterterrorism chief from 2001 to 2003, said, "A bombing case is a bombing case. A crime scene in a bank robbery case is the same as a crime scene . . . across the board." He added the only thing an FBI officer needed to know to fight terrorism is "the attorney general's guidelines for counterterrorism and counterintelligence investigation." Gary Bald, one of Watson's successors, added that knowledge of Islam and the Middle East was not needed by FBI officers. "You need leadership," Bald said. "You don't need subject matter expertise. It is certainly not what I look for in selecting an official for a counterterrorism position." Today, the FBI remains what it was before 9/11, an organization of smart, dedicated men and women at the working level who are led—at least under Judge Freeh, Mr. Mueller, and their senior lieutenants—by incompetent and unreformable bureaucrats more interested in protecting the FBI's reputation than in protecting Americans.[6]

Adding to this disaster was the 15 July 2005 announcement by Michael Chertoff, secretary of the Department of Homeland Security (DHS), that he had ordered a "massive overhaul" of DHS's intelligence apparatus. This arm of DHS was "designed to be the [U.S.] government's chief center for analyzing information about terrorist threats," and was "the foundation of why the department was stood up."[7] Chertoff's announcement signals that four years after 9/11, the masters of U.S. domestic security are sprinting back to the drawing board. And as lethal coda to the foregoing, the Congress has, in a knowing and bipartisan manner, hamstrung U.S. law enforcement at all levels of government by its four-year failure to act to protect our borders and enforce immigration laws already on the books. As always, Congress can be counted on to be devoid of common sense and fail to do the minimum. Score two for bin Laden.

Finally, the West's reaction to the July 2005 attacks has reassured bin Laden and his allies that Washington and its allies continue to deliberately ignore their enemies' motivation and lie to their publics on that issue. In rhetorical responses as predictable as they are pathetic, Pavlovian Western leaders and pundits continued to assert that their countries are being attacked by Islamist militants because of "who we are and what we believe, not what we do in the Muslim world." British prime minister Tony Blair was first out of the box, singing that old, sweet song proclaiming, "we are confronting an evil ideology" and emphasizing his belief that the attackers distorted Islam, were relatively few in number, and were mere criminals. "It is not a clash of civilizations," Blair said.

> All civilised people, Muslim or other, feel revulsion at it. But it is a global struggle. It is a battle of ideas and hearts and minds, both within Islam and outside it. . . . This is the battle that must be won. A battle not just about terrorists' methods but their views. Not just their barbaric ideas but their barbaric acts. Not only about what they do but what they think, and the thinking they would impose on others. . . . In the end, it is by the power of argument, debate, true religious faith and true legitimate politics that we will defeat this threat.[8]

Blair's formula, as always, boils down to the idea that none of the Western threats to Islam perceived by Islamists, their millions of followers, and their tens of millions of sympathizers are legitimate, and that the West need change no policies toward the Muslim world. Victory, says Blair, lies in teaching Muslims that what the West wants is good for them, and that, to use his own phrase, Western thinking is what he and his allies will "impose on others" — read Muslims. The ardent multiculturalism-diversity monger Blair avoided noting that unchanged Western policies toward the Islamic world mean his brand of "imposing" must be done by bayonet, while simultaneously striving to make Her Majesty's subjects believe the Islamist threat can be erased simply by his media-soaked, nonstop round of consultation and kumbayah-ing with Muslim leaders in the U.K.

In a fascinating pairing of opposites, the socialist Blair was, after the 7 July attacks, joined by President George W. Bush and his neoconservative acolytes in an effort to prevent any erosion of the Big Lie that holds al Qaeda is attacking the West for what it is, not what it does. Like Blair, Mr. Bush is nothing if not consistent. He assured Americans "[t]he attack on London was an attack on the civilized world" and on that world's liberties and freedoms. The president took Blair's version of the Big Lie as his own. Standing against the onslaught of evildoers is, the president said, quoting Blair, "Our determination to defend our values and our way of life. . . . We will not yield. We will defend our freedom." On how to defend "our freedom," Mr. Bush was less coy than Blair, saying the thinking he would "impose on others" was the forced "spread of democracy . . . [which] will make the world more peaceful and America more secure."[9] The president adroitly refrained from saying he had launched America on a course mirroring that of his lamentable mentor Woodrow Wilson, one that would teach Muslims to elect good men via persuasive schooling by U.S. military forces.

Rallying to Blair and Bush were America's abyss-bound, Iraq-war-loving band of neoconservative pundits, with Victor Davis Hanson and Charles Krauthammer in the van of the pack. Mr. Hanson is among the foremost purveyors of the Big Lie that denies legitimacy — real or perceived — to the Islamists' statements regarding their motivation for fighting the United States and the West. "They are fighting us," Mr. Hanson asserted in the *Washington Times,* because of "the blind hatred instilled by militant Islam. . . . Americans and others in the West should not be surprised at the Islamists' determination to wage an all-out war because of who we are rather than what we do."[10] Joining Hanson's paean of praise to willful, suicidal neocon blindness, Mr. Krauthammer attributes the Islamists' motivation to "a sickness incubated within Arab/Islamic culture, a toxic combination of repression, corruption, intolerance, and fanaticism, fed by tyrannical governments eager to deflect popular anger from themselves onto the American infidel. [Note: Mr. Krauthammer here is referring to the police-state regimes coddled, funded, and protected by the United States and its allies for more than thirty years.] "[11]

In essence, Mssrs. Blair, Bush, Hanson, Krauthammer, and their like are telling Americans not to think for themselves. They claim to have the answer and to know the Muslim mind better than any Muslim. They also know their version of history is right, Islamic history is irrelevant, and America can set the world right by militarily smashing every Muslim political system or group that either does not accept a U.S.-style secular, capitalist democracy or threatens Israel. The later, oddly, always seems far more important to neoconservatives than protecting Americans and their interests. Finally, they also limit the extent of domestic debate by damning those who disagree with them about U.S. foreign policy as either — and Mssrs. Hanson and Krauthammer are masters of this nonpunishable form of hate speech — anti-Semites or America haters. Score a hat trick for bin Laden.

And this leads us back to where we started, to the insights of Abraham Lincoln. The only attribute I share with Mr. Lincoln is that I write this, as he wrote the passage quoted above, at the age of fifty-two years. And I must tell you that Lincoln's claim that the survival of the Union depended on its citizens' efforts is just as pertinent today as on the eve of civil war. In the past four years, I have learned that in America's war for survival against the forces bin Laden leads and symbolizes, one person counts for little in attacking the elite, bipartisan chanters of the Big Lie. From President Bush to Senator John Kerry, from Senator John McCain to President Bill Clinton, from the *New York Times* to the *Washington Times,* Americans have been indoctrinated with the same mantra: They hate us for what we are, not what we do. Trusting their leaders, Americans cannot see clearly that their country is drifting toward defeat in economic, human, lifestyle, and geopolitical terms.

To paraphrase Lincoln, protecting the Union is both your business and mine. And I am not asking you to accept what I have written as gospel. I do urge you, however, to entertain the possibility that our leaders are wrong — some knowingly so to the point of treason — and then proceed to read the words spoken and written by bin Laden and other Islamists. Reflect on those words, compare them to your leaders' assertions, and decide for yourselves where the truth lies. I have done so repeatedly for a decade and have concluded the truth lies in the enemy's mouth when he says the motivation for attacking America comes from a belief that U.S. policy threatens Islam's survival. This fact makes America's Islamist enemies infinitely more lethal, patient, and enduring than a foe who is motivated simply by hate for elections, R-rated movies, and gender equality.

The conclusion I urge you to consider is that America's leaders have for fifteen years and more deliberately underestimated the Islamist theat to the United States. They have spat out the rhetoric of warriors, but given our military and intelligence services rules of engagement that make them targets and allow the enemy to flourish. They have spent hundreds of billions of dollars for security and military force but proved moral cowards in the face of attack, more interested in currying international favor than in acting to protect you and your children. And each time America has been attacked, they have been faster to constrict civil liberties than to destroy the enemy. They have loudly called the enemy "gangster," "criminal," and "lunatic fringe" to avoid the politically incorrect and costly necessity of telling voters that Muslims deem U.S. foreign policy a threat to Islam, and that the Americans who died in East Africa, Aden, New York, Washington, Afghanistan, and Iraq are a mere down payment on the total human cost we will ultimately endure. Our leaders consistently have lied about, failed to preempt when the chance came, and appeased the enemy. They cannot be counted on to change for the better, or even for the truer.

And so it is up to us — you and I — to think for ourselves and decide how best to defend America. The elites in both parties have not done so, and will not do so unless and until we force them to act in our country's defense. "The dogmas of the quiet past, are inadequate to the stormy present," Lincoln told the Congress in December 1862. "The occasion is piled high with difficulty, and we must rise with the occasion. As our case is new, so we must think anew, and act anew. We must disenthrall ourselves, and then we shall save our country." I urge you, my fellow citizens, to heed Mr. Lincoln's advice; as he said, we "hold the power, and bear the responsibility." Destroy the thrall under which you are deceived by the tellers of the Big Lie. Read the plentiful and easily accessible evidence, think for yourselves, form an accurate understanding of the enemy, and then act to prevent our country's defeat, a defeat which would mean today what it would have meant in 1862, that we have been content to "meanly lose, the last best hope of earth."[12]

Appendix:
"We Are Not Ashamed of Our Jihad": Bin Laden's Growth as an Islamic Leader and Hero After 1996

> He was a fighter and a purifier such as was long overdue. We had felt in our hearts to expect one such as he; it had somehow been foretold.
>
> Franklin Sanborn on John Brown, 1859

> Yet I have a commandment to resist sin, to overcome evil, to fight the good fight of Faith: And I pray, with whom should I fight this good fight if not with Giant Despair? I will therefore attempt the taking away of his life, and the Demolishing of Doubting-Castle. Then said, he, who will go with me.
>
> *The Pilgrim's Progress*, 1678

> I love the man who can smile in trouble, that can gather strength from distress and grow brave by reflection. 'Tis the business of little minds to shrink, but he whose heart is firm and whose conscience approves his conduct will pursue his principles unto death.
>
> Thomas Paine, December 1776

Osama bin Laden. Is he a devout Muslim, murderous nut cake, avenging messiah, media celebrity, heroic warrior, gullible rich-man's son, religious fakir, evolving political leader, or a megalomaniac "who wants to take over the world," as President Husni Mubarak once described him?

The West has pretty much decided that bin Laden is a serious threat, but only because he is a trigger-happy nut, psychopath, or violence-prone

−299

youngster who never grew up. Frank Smyth and Jason Vest have written in *Newsday* that bin Laden is "neither a mainstream Muslim nor a paragon of sanity" and quoted a U.S. government psychologist's assessment that bin Laden is a "malignant narcissist" who views people as objects to be killed or protected.[1] In the same article, Sam Husseini, former spokesman of the Arab-American Anti-Discrimination Committee said bin Laden is "definitely a fringe character."[2] A former senior U.S. counterterrorism official has said bin Laden is "a symbol where you get to rebel against your parents and make a statement, but it hasn't translated yet into people being willing to take up arms . . . and incur the possible threat of retaliation."[3] The same former official has said bin Laden is "not a very effective leader, he's not a very effective organizer. He certainly has the passion, but he hasn't the ability to rally and mobilize and really create a movement that becomes, if you will, a trans-Islamic political movement."[4] And academe has chimed in with its judgment that bin Laden's "tactical alliances with other 'like-minded' mainstream, as well as radical Islamic groups . . . may have more to do with Bin Ladin's generous financial contributions than with anything else."[5]

In addition to these facile judgments, others have atypically emanated from usually excellent, insightful writers. These individuals inexplicably lose their objectivity and pontificate about those not intelligent enough to acknowledge the universal applicability of the West's secular values. The superb and courageous Australian journalist Richard Mackenzie — who, with Edward Jiradet, may have been the best Western journalists covering the Afghan jihad — fell prey to this trap twice in a short article in *The New Republic*.[6] "Islamic fundamentalism," Mackenzie writes, "represents a minority that would impose religious doctrine from an earlier historical era." Then, he claims, "the vast majority of Muslims worldwide do not support violence. They deserve leaders who will unequivocally condemn the extremist wing of militant Islamic theology."[7] One wonders how Mackenzie gained access to the collected views of "the vast majority of Muslims worldwide."

Paul Fregosi, Simon Reeve, and Peter Bergen echo Mackenzie's mantra. In his book *Jihad in the West: Muslim Conquests from the 7th to the 21st Centuries,* Fregosi asserts, without describing the basis of his judgment, that "[m]any modern-day Muslims condemn this new fanatical Jihad even more strongly then to Westerners. The Jihad of today is for them a political Jihad with no connection to the religious Jihads of the past. They do not recognize themselves in this new Jihad, nor the preachings of their Prophet." Following suit are Simon Reeve who, in his fine book *The New Jackals,* maintains "[t]here are more than one billion followers of the Prophet Muhammad on the planet, and the vast majority want global harmony and reconciliation between different religious groups," and the outstanding journalist Peter Bergen, who told CNN in May 2001 that "in the end, you know, 99.9 percent of Muslims reject the kind of violence . . . that he's [bin Laden] proposing."[8]

The question that arises is why such demonstrably courageous and thoughtful men would make categorical statements based on largely unscientific data and without taking seriously bin Laden's words? Reading elsewhere in Mackenzie's article, however, it becomes clear that his calculations — and those of Fregosi, Reeve, Bergen, and others — are solidly based on the well-honed tradition of Western arrogance and assumed intellectual superiority, one that has become, I think, so deeply engrained in Western consciousness that it is the lens through which we see all other cultures and with which we try to explain what we deem their shortcomings and failures. "Yet unlike Christianity and Judaism," Mackenzie explains, "Islam has yet to undergo a reformation of enlightenment — and that allows some clerics to claim religious justification for violence."[9] *In short, Muslims have not followed the globally suitable and ultimately inevitable secular model for societal development laid down by the West: Ignore your faith and history, follow our lead, and you will be fine; that is, just like us. This notwithstanding the fact our reformation brought a hundred years of devastating religious war, and the enlightenment fueled the horrors of the French and Bolshevik revolutions. This position also begs important questions: Could bin Laden be the catalyzing agent of an incipient Islamic reformation? Could the monarchical and dictatorial police states of the Islamic world be prompting bin Laden's actions, just as the absolute monarchy called the Roman Catholic Church spurred the Lutherite reformers of our Reformation? Could U.S. and Western economic, political, and military support for those police states be preventing some form of Islamic reformation?*

Anyway, from the commentary above, which is a small sampling of a mass of similar analysis, one could easily assume that Osama bin Laden is only an aberrant flash in the pan. Today, after all, a person who decides to make himself a megacelebrity begins by saying or doing something splashy and exploits modern communication technologies to broadcast those words or deeds far and wide. The fifteen minutes of Warholian fame are not hard to come by. To secure such fame, declaring war on the United States and destroying two U.S. embassies would certainly do for starters. And bin Laden has made sure his message has been widely disseminated by hosting in Afghanistan *Al-Quds Al-Arabi* editor in chief Abd-al-Bari Atwan; numerous pro-Islamist Pakistani reporters; Western journalists, like Peter Arnett, Peter Bergen, and Robert Fisk, who oppose U.S. foreign policy in the Muslim world; and correspondents from such major networks as ABC, CNN, and Al-Jazirah, the latter a Qatar-based, Arabic-version of CNN.

Bin Laden's deftness with reporters has led some commentators to conclude that he is mainly a vacuous media manipulator, not unlike many major Western politicians. *U.S. News & World Report* led the way in this regard. Before the East Africa bombings, the *Report* reminded its readers, bin Laden's "group was almost unknown in the West. Since then . . . al-Qaidah is said to be flush with cash and to control operatives in two dozen countries who have had a hand in everything from the 1993 World Trade Center bombing to an attempt to kill the pope,"[10] On the same tack, an unnamed London-based security consultant told *The Observer*, "I just don't think a guy in a cave in Afghanistan can send off e-mails over a satellite phone ordering mass destruction anywhere in the world. Real life is not like James Bond movies. It is just not that easy to hold the world ransom."[11] In October 1998, the *Washington Post* added to the chorus by noting "that some critics have questioned the image of Bin Ladin as a master puppeteer with marionettes distributed around the world."[12] The *Post* quoted a counterterrorism expert as saying that "Bin Ladin's a pretty ambitious guy, but there is a danger in making him look like the Soviet military at the height of its power."[13]

Standing by his lonesome amid the media's rush to find an easy and — in terms of contemporary Western culture — understandable and politically acceptable answer, Professor Magnus Ranstorp in the *Journal of Conflict and Terrorism* notes that bin Laden is both a substantive leader and knowledgeable about the media's power.[14] Bin Laden's decision to send statements to *Al-Quds Al-Arabi*, Ranstorp argues, "is a calculated decision to maximize both [*sic*] the distribution of his message among broader segments of the Muslim community, as London is positioned as the unrivaled worldwide distribution node because of the presence and publishing activities of various Islamic movements." In his use of propaganda, bin Laden has taken a lesson from Islamic history and the medieval Muslim leaders who fought the Crusaders. Amin Malouf, for example, has written that the Muslim military leader Nur-al-Din "understood the invaluable role of psychological mobilization, and therefore built a genuine propaganda apparatus . . . with the mission of winning the active sympathy of the people and thereby forcing the leaders of the Arab world to flock to his banner."

Bin Laden's media behavior mirrors Nur-al-Din's and, as Issam Darraz suggested nearly a decade ago, the Saudi had learned the lesson that in addition to "intensive military training [for Islamic youths] . . . there is a need for the psychological and spiritual mobilization of young individuals who are joining the Muslim struggle." To date, bin Laden has beaten the West hands down in the contest for the hearts and minds of young Muslims. This does not mean all Muslims agree with and support bin Laden, but it is to say that his views are gaining ground in the Islamic world, and America's efforts to defame him are either falling on deaf ears or counterproductive. If U.S. policy makers want to understand bin Laden's heroic stature in the Muslim world, says Professor Eshan Ahari of the U.S. Joint Forces Staff College, they need only take a "stroll through the bazaars in Karachi, Lahore, and Peshawar, where bin Laden's picture is prominently displayed as the 'great mujahid' (religious fighter)."[15]

Sadly, Manstorp and Ahari are spitting into the wind. The West has judged bin Laden a nut cake, a charter member of the Muslim lunatic fringe, and a master media manipulator who has parlayed that talent into international celebrity. On the surface, it is hard to argue with these authorities, most of whom have covered Islamic insurgencies, interviewed bin Laden, or gone into combat with Arab Afghans. Still, much Western commentary is trite, amounts to analysis by assertion, and is underpinned by the Western elites' determination to denigrate as deviant or fanatical any individual or group that demands God's word be the basis for how life is lived. Though an uncomfortable fact, the bin Laden that emerges from a thorough review of the pertinent literature is more the Islamic hero and leader than the media-savvy charlatan.

Where does bin Laden's reputation and stature come from? Does it derive from the intense media coverage of the 1998 East Africa and 2000 Aden attacks and the existence of "an Islamic world desperately short of genuine heroes"?[16] Is bin Laden just another Gucci guerrilla who in the Afghan jihad was, a former senior U.S. intelligence officer claims, "more of a fund-raiser and organizer than a fighter"? Or is he, as argued by Pakistani journalist Raziud Din Sayed, "the symbol of the Islamic ideal of life. He is the continuity of the revealed idea of holy war. He is not a terrorist. He is a hero and a holy warrior."[17]

To answer the question, the place to start is with bin Laden's activities during the Afghans' war against the Soviets and Afghan communists. In that war, bin Laden spent his own fortune to support the mujahedin and used his family's connections to harvest other funds for the insurgents. He also worked tirelessly to mend rifts among Afghan factions and between other Islamist groups. Most important, bin Laden repeatedly risked his life while laboring as a combat engineer worker and fighting as an insurgent commander. That bin Laden's military prowess and activities have been exaggerated is certain; *Frontline*'s biography of bin Laden claims he was in "5 major battles" and "hundreds of small operations and exchanges of fire." This glitzy gloss, however, does not detract from the fact that his behavior in combat earned him a reputation for personal courage. "He will not show a flicker [of fear] even if a bomb exploded near him," *Frontline* noted,[18] and senior al Qaeda member Khalid al-Fawwaz has said bin Laden is "a very brave man."[19] Perhaps the best testimony to the legitimacy of bin Laden's combat record is that it only has been challenged by U.S. and Western "experts" and not by Afghans who fought alongside him or know his record.[20]

Bin Laden's personality also fits the heroic model in Islamic history, one which is not prone to making heroes of men who are brazen, boisterous, boastful, and notoriety seeking. Nur-al-Din and Saladin, the two greatest Muslim military leaders during the era of the Crusades, have been described, respectively, as "a pious, reserved and just man, one who kept his word, and was thoroughly devoted to the jihad against the enemies of Islam," and as a man whose greatness lay a modesty "which made him so different from the monarchs of the time; he was humble with the humble, even after he became the most powerful of the powerful." Western and Muslim journalists, after interviewing bin Laden, have written descriptions substantially similar to those just quoted, showing bin Laden squarely in historic model of Islamic hero "where modesty in appearance and behavior is considered a cardinal virtue."

On the Western side, Associated Press writers have described bin Laden as "a soft-spoken, modest but charismatic man, infused with the serenity of the deeply devout."[21] ABC's John Miller found bin Laden "calm, fixed and steady" in the chaotic surroundings of their interview, and said that he spoke with a voice "soft and slightly high, with a raspy quality that gave it texture and the sound of an old uncle giving good advice."[22] On the Muslim side, *Frontline's* unattributed biography says bin Laden has a "dominating personality" despite being shy, and that "he speaks very little and looks serious most of the time. He would appear with a soft smile but would seldom laugh. His followers see a lot of aura on him and show him great voluntary respect."[23] A senior Algerian Islamist has recalled that during the Afghan jihad bin Laden "ate very little. Slept very little. [He was] Very generous. He'd give you his clothes. He'd give you his money. . . . When you sit with Usama, you don't want to leave the meeting. You wish to continue talking to him because he is very calm, very fluent." Bin Laden also is renowned for his eagerness to share the common lot and common danger; when with his fighters bin Laden "very frequently cooks with them and serves them . . . [he] is always anxious to embrace death. His innocent children are Mujahid."

As a point of comparison for Americans, the admiration and affection of al Qaeda fighters for bin Laden is reminiscent of the esteem the soldiers of William T. Sherman held for their commander. "His men loved him [Sherman] for the informality of his leadership and his refusal to stand on ceremony," Stephen E. Bower has written.

> His clothing was as informal as the rest of him. At times it was easy to mistake him for the private he would just as soon talk with as one of his officers. He commanded one of the most powerful armies in the world, but he became "Uncle Billy" to many of his soldiers. [Just as bin Laden is known to his men as "Abu Abdallah."] He was one of the boys who just happened to be in charge. He made few attempts to cut himself out of the crowd, and he seemed to use his authority only when it mattered most, and when it best served the interest of his men, his armies, and their appointed mission. His common manner and his deference to the egalitarian nature of his armies endeared him to all his soldiers. [Just as bin Laden's behavior is congruent with the intensely egalitarian nature of Is-

lam.] His men admired him for his and their success, but also because he did not break his connection with them and flaunt it. It was a part of Sherman that enabled him to command, as he put it, "the souls of his men, as well as their bodies and legs." . . . What his men saw in him, was what he saw in them, enforcing at all times the notion that his soldiers were Americans rather than citizens of particular states or regions of the country. [Just as bin Laden tells his fighters that they are all members of a single Islamic nation, not simply Saudis, Afghans, Filipinos, etc.][24]

Bin Laden's humility is often displayed in downplaying his personal part in the Afghan jihad. "Yes I fought there," bin Laden told Robert Fisk in late 1993, "but my fellow Muslims did much more than I. Many of them died and I am still alive." And the Egyptian journalist Issam Darraz has written that during the jihad he pursued bin Laden "for a full year from Peshawar to the battle fronts to make him talk. He assured me he was convinced of the importance of the media in serving Islamic causes. But he was not convinced of talking about his role or his jihad."

Saudi dissident Sa'd al-Faqih and *Al-Quds Al-Arabi*'s Abd-al-Bari Atwan also have produced similar portraits of bin Laden's personality.

al-Faqih: "Well in his desert life, he's very humble. And people who work with him or live with him like him a lot. Because he is having the two characters [*sic* — characteristics?] for people to be liked. The charisma, the aura on the one side. And also the humbleness and being simple and being generous and soft on the other side. . . . [T]he people who have lived with him very closely, they told me that you are taken by his personality. And you are forced to have a strong affection toward him. And respect."[25]

Atwan: "I found him to be a man who is very modest in nature. He believes in every word he says. He does not lie, he does not exaggerate. He does not complement anyone. He does not even try to hide anything. He expresses everything he feels. He is very enigmatic. His voice is calm and well-mannered. I spent a whole day with him and truly sensed his charm, his refined manners, and his true modesty, not exaggerated or with fake modesty."[26]

Also within the model of Islamic hero is bin Laden's aggressive and confrontational approach on the issue of overriding importance to most Muslims, namely, Islam. Just as there are mantras Westerners repeat about the Islamic world, the primary mantra repeated to Western audiences by Muslims is that Islam is a religion that informs and shapes all aspects of the believer's life: personal, marital, familial, social, and religious, as well as in the realms of domestic politics, military affairs, and international relations. God's words and the Prophet's sayings and traditions, Christendom is told, guide and govern a Muslim's life. "We [Muslims] are a nation and have a long history," bin Laden told CNN's Peter Arnett in May 1997. "We are now in the 15th century of this great religion, the complete and comprehensive methodology have [*sic* — has?] clarified the dealing between an individual and another, the duties of the believer toward God, and the relationship between the Muslim country and other countries in time of peace and in time of war."[27]

While bin Laden's version of the mantra may not apply to all Muslims — many rich Gulf Arabs appear exceptions — the words do seem valid in regard to the Islamic world's working poor; that is, most of the world's Muslims. Bin Laden's Muslim interviewers have found him mesmerizing on this issue. Pakistani journalist Qari Hashimi, for example, said "his [bin Laden's] love for Islam, his grief over the decline of the Muslim Ummah, his love for Muslim sacred places, and his hatred for Jews and Christians are exceptional."[28] In late 1998, a correspondent from Karachi's *Newsline* also saw bin Laden's confrontational demeanor. The daily reported that bin Laden displayed "deep emotion whenever he mentioned the names of Islam's holy places [which are] currently under 'American and Israeli occupation'."[29] In these words, the interviewer wrote, "one could feel the zeal and the strength emanating from the man."[30] Pakistan's *News* also described the "choked voice" in which bin Laden excoriated the West for stationing "infidel" soldiers on the Arabian Peninsula.[31] "This is the first time," bin Laden said, "after prophet hood was bestowed on our Holy Prophet (Peace Be Upon Him) that infidels are in control of this holy land."[32]

It is one thing to assert bin Laden is respected and supported by large numbers of the world's Muslims, but it is quite another to prove that statement, much less to quantify it. Since there are few reliable polls in the Islamic world, and occasions for exit polling are rare, reliance must be placed mainly on anecdotal evidence and the testimony of those who have met, interviewed, fought alongside, or studied bin Laden.

The less-than-scientific data shows that the shy, gracious, quiet, and yet religiously confrontational bin Laden, who has fought, suffered, and spent in God's way, is increasingly seen as a Muslim leader and hero. After the August 1998 U.S. retaliatory attacks on Sudan and Afghanistan, for example, protestors in Palestine called bin Laden "the beloved of God"; in Pakistan, "Usama the lion"; and in Afghanistan, "the soldier of Islam."[33] On the same line, Abd-al-Bari Atwan said that after his interview of bin Laden was published "he received calls from countless young men from the Middle East, Europe, and America wanting to know how they could find bin Laden to join his fighters."[34] A similar vote of confidence in bin Laden occurred in terms of donations. In July 1999, the Associated Press reported bin Laden "received millions of dollars from Saudi and Gulf businessmen to reinvigorate his campaign against the United States."[35] AP's sources said the donations came from "devout Muslims" after Washington offered a $5 million reward for bin Laden and may have totaled $50 million.[36]

There are also telling anecdotes on what might be called the more homey side of the stature-of-bin-Laden ledger. In Pakistan's oldest and largest religious school, for example, "a poster of Mr. Bin Laden hangs. . . . He is smiling, holding an automatic rifle. The poster calls him a holy warrior."[37] The school's headmaster explains that "Usama is a hero. Every young man wants to be like him." In addition, Pakistan's most famous actress has announced that she is making a film that will star her son—the country's current Errol Flynn—and "highlight the achievements of that famous hero of Islam, Usama Bin Ladin. The entire world will see Usama's character presented realistically and will see the facts in their true light . . . the film will give a full response to the propaganda against him.[38]

Elsewhere in Pakistan, the media have reported that each day "hundreds of couples" give their male babies the first name "Usama."[39] Bin Laden is said to be pleased by this practice but "modestly adds that they are not doing it for me but to honor of Osama bin Zaid, the Prophet's companion,"[40] adding that "martyrdom is my passion because my martyrdom would lead to the birth of thousands of Usamas."[41] The Pakistani media also reports that people have "displayed his [bin Laden's] picture at their shops, and drivers have put his pictures in the back of his vehicles." Photographers, too, are selling thousands of his pictures, vehicles are often labeled "Usama's express," vendors are selling T-shirts emblazoned with his photo like "hot cakes," and new businesses frequently make use of his name, as in the "Usama Poultry Farm" in Chakadara, the "Usama Medical Store" in Swat, and the "Usama Bakers" in Uch.[42] Popular support for bin Laden has been seen in Afghanistan. In summer 1999, Pakistan's *News* reported tribal elders near Jalalabad openly backed the Saudi, claiming "Bin Ladin had earned the enmity of all infidels on account of his strong Islamic beliefs," and asserting "no sacrifice would be big enough in an effort to protect Usama Bin Ladin and even Afghan girls would do so in case of need."

More recently, John F. Burns, in an excellent series of analytic articles from Yemen in the *New York Times,* found surging support for bin Laden after al Qaeda attacked the U.S. destroyer *Cole.* The attack yielded, Burns wrote, "a ground swell of backing, especially among the young, for Mr. Bin Ladin. His name is scrawled on walls and plastered on magazine covers; tapes of his speeches sell in the bazaars, making him an icon Arab leaders cannot ignore." Similar post-*Cole* events occurred in Pakistan where counterfeited *Nike* T-shirts bearing bin Laden's photograph and the phrase "The Great Mujahid of Islam" appeared on shop shelves alongside calendars labeled "Look Out America, Usama Is Coming."[43]

Another key indicator of bin Laden's leadership stature is found in statements by his fighters. Passed by word of mouth, stories about bin Laden's reliability and concern for his men help explain the intense loyalty he receives from al Qaeda's rank and file. From the start of the Afghan jihad, for example, the "soft spoken" bin Laden focused on caring for wounded mujahedin and their families. Early in that war, Mary Anne Weaver wrote in the *New Yorker,* bin Laden visited the hospitals treating wounded insurgents and "went from bed to bed dispensing cashews and English chocolates and carefully noting each man's name and address. Weeks later the man's family would receive a generous check." Then, when non-Afghan Muslim mujahedin could not return to their countries of origin after the Red Army's defeat, bin Laden made arrangements — presumably through his family's business networks — "to secure the arrival and entry of Afghan Arabs into European, Asian, and African countries and to arrange political asylum for some of them and residence for others after the Afghan war was over."[44]

Captured Egyptian Islamic Jihad leader Ahmad Ibrahim al-Najjar also has recounted bin Laden's actions after the EIJ's November 1995 attack on Egypt's embassy in Islamabad. "Usama Bin Ladin had offered to bring them [the surviving attackers] to Afghanistan, provide them with accommodations and secure their safety," al-Najjar said.[45] "Bin Laden [also] earmarked $100 per month to be paid to regular [EIJ] members as well as to each family of those detained in Egypt."[46] In testimony before an Egyptian court, Mohammad Atta, another EIJ fighter, explained that "Bin Ladin paid for his wife's medical care in Saudi Arabia, and frequently covered medical bills of Islamic militants as an unidentified Saudi hospital."[47]

Other media articles also show bin Laden caring for his own after successful U.S. counterterrorism operations. After al-Najjar was captured in Tirana, Albania, in late summer 1998, a senior Albanian intelligence officer told the media that two weeks later "a man came from Egypt, armed with five airline tickets, in order to take the Islamic activist's wife and three children to Afghanistan."[48] Alleged Nairobi embassy bomber Mohammad Sadiq also has said "Usama takes care of his men like a father."[49] According to Sadiq, he "received prompt payments in U.S. dollars on all his foreign visits" for al Qaeda, and his "family in Nairobi had been receiving regular payments from an unidentified visitor."[50] As the above-mentioned Albanian intelligence official said, "Bin Ladin is not noted for leaving his followers in the lurch."[51]

Western and Muslim commentators likewise see bin Laden as an emerging Islamic leader and hero, although there is no unanimity on what part of bin Laden's stature results from his talents and how much stems from the fact that, as former Pakistani intelligence chief Lt. General Hamid Gul has said, he is "a darling throughout the Islamic movement because he has become a symbol of defiance."[52] The *Economist*'s editors claim that "his [bin Laden's] words are striking a chord on the Saudi street" when he talks about U.S. support for Israel's "expansionist policies" and the "deaths of thousands of Iraqi children" caused by U.S.-backed UN sanctions.[53] Saudi dissident al-Faqih argued in mid-1998 that Washington is dangerously wrong to think bin Laden is simply a terrorist who does not speak for a sizable portion of Muslims when he attacks U.S. double standards.[54] "The formation of the current U.S. Government and the domination of the Zionist lobby over it makes it impossible to expect any improvement in the behavior of the U.S. government," al-Faqih wrote. "From the statements made by U.S. officials, one notes that there is no grasp of the issue; there is no sense that grave errors are being made and that the enmity of Muslims is being courted against the United States. There is deep dream about U.S. greatness, excluding any readiness to understand what is going on in the Islamic world."[55] Shaykh Omar Abd al-Rahman's aid Ahmed Sattar sharpened al-Faqih's point, insisting bin Laden is not America's major enemy but rather one of that enemy's leaders.

> The American government has one enemy . . . the Islamic movement all over the world, whether it's armed struggle or peaceful. . . . Now, the people, especially in the Arab and Islamic world, look at you [the United States] the same way that they looked at the British and French occupation forces in the mid-30s and 40s. You are an empire that will do anything to oppress people outside the United States. . . . [Attacks like those in East Africa] are not going to end. Until you take a hard and good look at your policies in the Islamic world and the Muslim world. As long as you are supporting dictators like Mubarak. . . .[56]

The romance surrounding bin Laden's words and deeds also have enhanced his international stature—as Hamid Gul said, bin Laden is now the "quintessence of defiance" to the United States.[57] "The Americans can block all roads," bin Laden said in 1998 when asked if he feared capture by U.S. forces, "but they cannot stop the ways of Allah. We are in the ninth year of our struggle and I am still alive."[58] Other media stories have added to the romance of such statements. "Planning strategy in damp caves infested with scorpion and rats," the Associated Press reported in August 1998, "bin Ladin maintained a disciplined lifestyle, waking up before dawn for prayers, then eating a simple breakfast of cheese and bread. Now he has emerged from the obscurity of caves to dominate the front pages. . . ."[59] Early in 1999, *Newsweek* piped in along the same line. "In the Islamic world," said the weekly, "hiding . . . in some remote mountain fastness, Usama Bin Ladin has been transformed . . . into a 'legend and a myth'."[60] The *Economist* worried that "Mr. Bin Ladin . . . commands an increasing fascination for ordinary

Arabs,"[61] and prominent Palestinian journalist Sa'id Aburish told *Frontline*, "I think to some people he is already a folk hero. . . . I think you have a fellow there in Afghanistan sort of hiding away from the only superpower in the world. He has become somewhat of a Robin Hood . . . sort of a romantic revolutionary in the middle of nowhere. What do you have to do to avoid capture by the United States or be killed by the United States. You have to have something special to do that."[62]

Even media coverage of bin Laden's reputed poor health strengthens his image as a patient and stoic individual, implacably defiant in the face of adversity. Issam Darraz, in his study of bin Laden in the Afghan jihad, wrote that bin Laden fought the infidels although he "suffered from extremely low blood pressure which, at times, debilitated him, compelled him to lie on the floor for long hours, and once required him to receive "medical solutions" while under Soviet artillery fire.[63] In May 1998, Islamabad's *News* described bin Laden's arrival at Khowst in similar heroic terms. "[H]e was tall, frail and walked with the help of a stick," the paper told its readers, "The rigorous lifestyle and punishing discipline that the billionaire Saudi has imposed on himself has already taken its toll but he remains defiant as ever."[64]

After the East Africa bombings, Karachi-based *Newsline* noted that "although he walked slowly with the help of a stick, as if suffering from back pain . . . bin Ladin nonetheless cut a distinctive figure."[65] From London, *The Times* and *Al-Quds Al-Arabi* painted a portrait of a sickly but supremely confident man, carrying on in spite of pain. "He suffers from back pain and walks with a stick," *The Times* noted. "He is skinny; a long black beard flows from his sunken cheeks and he is unprepossessing, except when he talks of his 'holy mission' in a passionate flow of Arabic. . . . He spoke softly, he seemed shy." *Al-Quds Al-Arabi*'s Abd-al-Bari Atwan reported that bin Laden "is tall, slightly built but not weak. . . . He is very modest, nice to be with, his voice is low but can be heard. He smiles all the time. His smile reflects reassurance and reduces the distance between him and his guests. . . ." Even infidel journalists have made the same points. "Bin Ladin never raises his voice," ABC's John Miller said in 1999, "and to listen to his untranslated answers, one could imagine that he was talking about something that did not concern him much."[66]

Pertinent experience, substantive expertise, and personal charisma feed into a leader's development; charisma alone is often enough to create a celebrity. Participating in a momentous event can also push an individual toward leadership. In bin Laden's life, there have been several such events: the Afghan jihad and the first Gulf War, for example. Bin Laden's performance in each was an important contributor to his development as a leader. His stature also has been enhanced by matching words and deeds; as the *Washington Post* reminded its readers after the 1998 East Africa attacks, "we [Americans] fail to grasp that such atrocities appear heroic to hundreds of millions of people who resent or hate or fear us."

Ironically, however, the event that greatly accelerated the growth of bin Laden's stature was the 20 August 1998 U.S. cruise-missile raids on Sudan and Afghanistan. The East Africa bombings strengthened bin Laden's reputation for honesty — attack promised, attack delivered — but the failure of U.S. retaliation made him *the* hero of Islam. As the *Economist*'s editors wrote, bin Laden "has survived — by the grace of God, as he put it — a devastating attack on his Afghan base by the world's only superpower. Just as Iraq's Saddam Hussein has been able to pop-up from the rubble of cruise missile attacks with his regime intact, Mr. bin Laden's survival enhances his stature. Almost overnight, everyone in the region wants to know who he is and what he stands for." The U.S. attack also silenced Muslim leaders generally supportive of U.S. antiterrorism policies. While bin Laden "may appear a sinister fanatic to the West," Cambridge University's Akbar S. Ahmed argued the missile strikes hurt America among pro-Western Muslim elites. The strikes raised support for bin Laden in the Muslim world's Islamist-dominated "favalas, bazaars, and villages," he wrote, making it politically unwise for Muslim elites to condemn bin Laden. Muslim leaders favoring dialogue with the West and religious tolerance "suddenly [were] under pressure to keep quiet and lie low."[67]

U.S. retaliation also validated bin Laden as the foremost champion of the Islamic struggle against what has been variously termed American: oppression, racism, hatred of Islam, double standards, barbarity, crusading, and support for the Zionist entity. "Bin Ladin survived. And in the teeming cities of the Islamic world, among the hundreds of thousands of young men, disaffected equally by the godless, arrogant nations of the West and their own weak, corrupt states, his legend grew," explained U.K.-based Islamist Omar Bakri Muhammed to *Newsweek*.[68] "Americans cannot imagine how much strength Americans have injected into Bin Ladin's position," Sa'd al-Faqih told *Frontline*, "[a]nd then Clinton standing in a press conference and talking about Bin Ladin as a superpower against America. . . . That's the best gift [that] can be given to Bin Ladin. Or from Bill Clinton to Bin Ladin."[69] To the recipients of his organization's newsletter, al-Faqih went into greater detail on this point.

> the [U.S. air] strike would fulfill two objectives dear to both Bin Ladin and the Jihad groups. The first objective is that the strike would show them as a real and great opponent of the United States. This was realized by the fact that Bin Ladin was named by the U.S. president, the defense minister [sic], and other officials. The second objective would be the mobilization of Islamic public opinion at large, and Arab public opinion in particular, against the United States. . . . The recent [U.S.] strike was nothing but a response to a trap set by Bin Ladin and his group. The way the strike was pre-

sented by U.S. officials and its justification before the information media greatly served Bin Ladin and the Jihad groups, because it showed Bin Ladin as a genuine, strong, and credible opponent of the United States.[70]

Bin Laden's steady, defiant reaction to the U.S. strikes also enhanced his stature. Less than an hour after cruise missiles hit Khowst, an al Qaeda spokesman told *Al-Quds Al-Arabi* that bin Laden was safe and that "the battle had not yet started. The response will be with actions not words."[71] The *Wall Street Journal* worried that the U.S. raid might not be a deterrent because "Mr. Bin Ladin and his Afghan followers . . . grew up on a constant diet of Soviet mines, bombs, and missiles."[72] A month later, bin Laden verified the *Journal*'s surmise by telling Abd-al-Bari Atwan that he "was safe and well, and also that he will answer Mr. Clinton with deeds and action."[73] Calm, dignified, and threatening, bin Laden told the Islamic world al Qaeda was not deterred, would attack at a time and place of its choosing, and would not engage in a tit-for-tat response. Muslims knew bin Laden was at the helm, Sa'd al-Faqih said, "and he's the man that can meet the expectations of many Muslims for a man who can irritate and drive America crazy. That is — the only man who did it was bin Ladin. And he forced Clinton to stand up and mention his name three times." In this context, one can imagine the boost bin Laden's stature received in February 2001 when Director of Central Intelligence George Tenet said al Qaeda was America's "most immediate and serious transnational threat."[74]

A final way to assess bin Laden's growing stature and grassroots popularity is to look at how Muslim governments and the media they control responded after the East Africa episode. For the most part, the response of these entities has been a nearly complete silence. "Although few Saudis and other Gulf Arabs supported the bombing of American embassies in East Africa," the *Economist* wrote, "most were appalled by America's reaction."[75] After the U.S. raids, the *New York Times* focused on the "backdrop of near silence from so many Arab governments, including most of those that . . . [endorsed] the joint declaration [at Sharm al-Sheikh, Egypt, in 1996] in which all vowed to work together in battling terrorism around the world."[76] The Muslim regimes apparently decided that bin Laden's support on the "street" was too great to condemn "the great Mujahid of Islam." On *Frontline*, Ahmed Sattar said the U.S. missile raid posed a huge problem for America's friends in the Muslim world. "Last year," Sattar mused, "if you asked the average man on the street in downtown Cairo . . . who is the son of [Muhammed] Bin Ladin, he would not have been known. Now, ask a five or six year old, who's Usama Bin ladin, they'll tell you exactly who is Usama Bin Ladin. He is our hero. This is how he is going to put it to you."[77] As always, *Al-Quds Al-Arabi* put the bottom line most cogently the day after the U.S. raids.

These U.S. strikes will not get rid of Usama Bin Ladin or the Afghan Arabs fighting under his banner who were rejected by their own countries and by the United States itself after they fought the Soviet forces together. Instead, it will reaffirm these peoples' excuse, justify their hostility toward the United States in the eyes of millions of Arab and Islamic youths, and will embarrass the moderate Arab and Islamic regimes which have forged alliances with successive U.S. governments and fought terrorism with them.[78]

Overall, the years between 1996 and 2001 saw the rise and solidification of bin Laden's status as an Islamic leader and hero. The years ahead, moreover, hold ample room for more growth not only on the basis of what he says and does—and anti-Crusader attacks of greater lethality are certain—but because the international political environment could not be better prepared for the advent of a charismatic, talented, and militarily proficient Muslim leader. Nor could the Islamic world be in more of a need for a credible and heroic leader, and on this score, the amount of grist for bin Laden's mill is almost unlimited, given the maintenance of civilian-killing sanctions on Iraq; the ongoing confrontation between Iraq and Anglo-U.S. air power; the manifest bankruptcy of the Middle East peace process; the start of the second Intifadah; the murderous Russian attacks on Chechen civilians; the continued basing of U.S. forces on the Arabian Peninsula; the destabilizing impact of the ongoing jihads in Kashmir, Central Asia, the Caucasus, the Horn of Africa, and the Balkans; the Taliban's struggle for primacy in Afghanistan; the U.S.-Russia-sponsored UN sanctions on the Taliban for hosting bin Laden; and America's unstinting and unquestioning support for Israel.

For many Americans, what have been described above as opportunities for bin Laden will seem counterintuitive. The United States, after all, is supporting a Palestinian state, trying to defeat the tyrannical Saddam, and protecting the Prophet's homeland. In this vein, Bernard Lewis has written that "the statement [bin Laden's 1998 fatwa]—is a magnificent piece of eloquent, at times even poetic prose [that] reveals a version of history that most Westerners will find unfamiliar. Bin Ladin's grievances are not quite many would expect."[79] Lewis notes that America's "crimes"—occupying Saudi Arabia, unwavering support for Israel, and killing Iraqi civilians—amount, for bin Laden, "to a clear declaration of war by the Americans against God, the Prophet, and Muslims."[80] Professor Manstorp also noted the salience in the Muslim world of these and other issues specified by bin Laden as examples of the Crusaders' attacks on Islam. "The content of Bin Ladin's fatwa,"

Ranstorp wrote, "is neither revolutionary nor unique, as it encapsulates broad sentiments in the Islamic world, especially that of Islam being on the defensive against foreign forces and modernization. . . . [A]lthough the 'Bin Ladin phenomenon' can be seen as a novelty when viewed in isolation, it nonetheless arguably represents the unfolding ethnopolitical and religious forces in the greater Middle East."

If Lewis and Ranstorp are correct — and they surely are — it is more than likely that Osama bin Laden's growth as a major leader in the Islamic world has just begun, as has that world's approval for his military approach to dealing with the West. On this line, Dr. Iffat S. Malik has noted the irony of a situation in which "there are indications that just as bin Ladin has become the 'public face' of Islamic militancy for the West, so too has he for the Muslim world. The West could be inadvertently converting what was a genuinely diverse, fragmented phenomenon into — under Bin Ladin's leadership — the green monolith it claims it is."[81]

Note on Sources

As one trained as a professional historian specializing in the diplomatic history of the British Empire, I am accustomed to having mounds of private and public documents at my disposal. While costly travel to one archive or another is often required, as is now and then dickering with a relative for access to a great-uncle's previously unused papers, the most difficult aspects of my research usually is dealing with the volume of documents and, once in a while, deciphering faded or nearly illegible handwriting. Primary sources are available in quantity and are exploitable if one expends time and industry. As a result, with adequate brains, effort, prose, and an esoteric topic, an author in the field of British imperial history can write a credible book. He or she can even dream of that rapturous review in a learned journal that concludes: "In sum, this brilliantly researched and elegantly written work may well be the definitive book on the subject for this generation."

Undertake a study of Osama bin Laden, however, and the pleasant, primary-source-rich world of the professional historian flies out the window and said historian finds himself harrowingly ensnarled in material that is overwhelmingly secondary, translated with varying degrees of accuracy, and sensationalized or embellished by the need to sell copies or by the sloth of those doing insufficient research. In addition, the Internet-era author can never be sure that he has consulted all sources or even a fair cross-section of sources. My uncertainty in this regard was geometrically increased by the flood of writing about bin Laden that appeared after 11 September 2001. Researching material running the gamut from the brilliant scholar of Islam Bernard Lewis, to conspiracy-mongering "terrorist experts," to sensationalist Pakistani tabloids leaves me absolutely confident my work on this topic will not remotely approach the status of a definitive book. Abundant satisfaction, in fact, will accrue if this study provides a fairly comprehensive and accurate description, and some understanding, of Osama bin Laden, of what he has been up to, and of why he was up to it. I also hope that this study will be a baseline for those better versed in Islamic politics, history, and theology to produce more sophisticated and enduring studies.

Still, for a historian there is at least one supreme bright side to researching bin Laden. It has been my great good fortune to find that bin Laden is the only so-called Islamic terrorist who has given the world a detailed explanation of what he is doing and why he is doing it. Bin Laden has spoken at length about his mission in interviews given to Muslim and Western journalists. This series of interviews and published statements gives the historian a set of detailed primary-source documents; according to a leading analyst of Islamism, bin Laden "evokes the prophetic tradition" and has produced "a written corpus of work that is likely to motivate the faithful for years to come. . . . And his ideas will survive martyrdom."[1] Bin Laden's intentions and goals are grounded in his reading of the Koran, the Prophet's sayings and practices, and the interpretations of classical and contemporary Islamic scholars and jurists. Bin Laden has spoken in simple, precise prose that allows the non-Muslim to understand the religious duties and requirements he believes compel his activities. In my view, bin Laden wants Muslims and Islam's foes to understand what he is concerned about and acting against. Bin Laden's own words help to sort, weigh, and assess the mass of reporting, and I, educated in a tradition where even secondary imperial functionaries merit two-volume biographies, have allowed bin Laden to speak for himself as often and fully as possible.

The secondary material about bin Laden, his beliefs and intentions, and his organization, allies, and associates is voluminous but of uneven quality. The U.S. and European media are of modest value. While they have produced a large number of articles, their coverage is sporadic, their understanding of bin Laden is minimal, and their attempt to educate their publics about him and the threat he poses is virtually nonexistent. The Western media, however, are invaluable as a source of facts — dates, times, places, names, types of weapons, chasers. Reading the Western media on bin Laden is like reading the police blotter; they pay close attention to the who, what, when, and where, but the why takes the hindmost, if it takes anything at all. The Western media, therefore, are of great assistance in providing names, dates, places, quotes from Western government officials and documents, and so forth, much more so than the Islamic media.

There are exceptions to this fairly barren Western journalistic landscape of which the following, in my view, are most significant. ABC's John Miller, in his *Esquire* article and televised interview with bin Laden, has given Americans a sense of the man and a strong analysis of what bin Laden believes and intends to do, and Miller has done so in direct, brash, and clear prose. The *Independent*'s Robert Fisk — a consistently harsh critic of U.S. foreign policy in the Islamic world — has done several interviews with and articles about bin Laden and has provided extremely useful insights into the man and his growing influence in the Muslim world. Fisk also has been fair-minded in presenting to his English-speaking audience a persuasive explanation of the issues he believes are fueling the Muslim world's anger toward the United States and its allies, and why that anger has created a receptive environment for bin Laden. The *Wall Street Journal,* which provided steady, thoughtful reporting on the Afghan jihad and always sought to assess its impact on overall U.S. foreign policy, has done good, if so far limited, work on bin Laden.

The *Journal* has explained that bin Laden is not just another terrorist, but rather an Islamist leader who poses multiple dilemmas for the U.S. government. As during the Afghan war, the *Journal* is trying to educate its readers about bin Laden's importance in the larger context of U.S. relations with the Muslim world, as well as to the fact that not all the world sees bin Laden as a terrorist. "Many [world] leaders," the *Journal* said in August 1999, "see Mr. Bin Laden as the core of an impassioned Islamic insurgency that threatens their own status quo." More recently, the *New York Times'* John F. Burns has written an excellent series about the attack on the USS *Cole* in Yemen and, as important, about the depth of pro-Islamist and pro-bin Laden sentiment in that strategically located country, and for more than a year Reuel Marc Gerecht has produced in the *Weekly Standard* a stream of thoughtful articles about Osama bin Laden, Afghanistan, and militant Sunni Islam. In what largely has been superficial coverage of bin Laden by the West's electronic media, two fine exceptions stand out: John Miller's ABC interview of bin Laden and an episode of the Public Broadcasting Service's program *Frontline* titled "The Terrorist and the State." *Frontline* also published a wonderfully useful, though woefully edited, compendium of background pieces and interviews done for the episode. This work is a primary source and is a laudable effort to educate Americans about the many dimensions of the bin Laden issue.[2]

The media in the Muslim world have provided the context and education missing in the Western media, though their reporting is at times tainted by government sponsorship, virulent anti-Americanism, sensationalism, and conspiracy theories. Still, the Islamic media — in Europe and around the world — have taken the position that it is important to listen to and understand what bin Laden and his allies are saying and doing, and to understand how those words and actions are being received on the Muslim "street." In a sense, the Islamic media are simply saying that these people — bin Laden and other leading Islamists — say what they mean, mean what they say, and intend to act on their beliefs in a concerted and patient fashion until the United States fundamentally alters its foreign policy toward the Islamic world. Muslims apparently have not yet accepted the Western notion that no political leader ever says what he or — rarely — she means, and that he or she will be consistent only while consistency serves personal or political goals.

As a result, the Islamic media provides extensive space to simply reporting, without analytical dissection and uninformed speculation, what bin Laden says and how his words influence Muslims. It also has produced many cogent editorial and op-ed pieces explaining why U.S. policy toward the Muslim world is giving bin Laden's statements, actions, and goals increasing emotional, religious, and intellectual appeal.

At this point, I, since I speak only English, must take a moment to thank and salute the men and women of the U.S. government's Foreign Broadcast Information Service (FBIS). If the present work serves at all to help Americans understand the threat bin Laden poses to their country, it will be due in large measure to the painstaking and tireless efforts of FBIS officers to ensure that their countrymen are informed. Words are powerful weapons, and it is FBIS's genius that it reliably identifies, translates, and publishes the words Americans need to read to protect their nation, homes, and kin.

On balance, the Islamic media's taste for what the West terms sensationalizing and conspiracy mongering is less than meets the eye. Based on my research, it is apparent that the Islamic media's correspondents and editors work harder, dig deeper, and think more than most of their Western counterparts. This is not to say that the Islamic media do not suffer from sensationalized conspiracy theories, but they probably are no more prone to those faults than their Western colleagues.

Pakistani journalist Jamal Ismail caught two themes — bin Laden's importance in the Muslim world and the West's denigration of Muslim journalism — in the London newspaper *Al-Zaman* in summer 2000. When asked why he had not sold his December 1998 interview of bin Laden to the Western media, Ismail answered,

> I said that I would rather have Al-Jazirah [Satellite Channel Television in Qatar] broadcast the interview first in Arabic to Arab viewers [and] then to the world to fulfill the right of the Arab and world viewers to hear the views of this man [bin Laden]. The world has heard many charges against this man, but had not heard his views about these charges. The world had also heard and saw many programs about him, but had not heard or seen him speak directly in these programs to explain his objectives. I told them [the managers of Al-Jazirah] that this would make the world understand that the question of press scoops was not a monopoly of the Western media. This would show that we [Muslim journalists] are more daring than they are and more courageous than their journalists in enduring the hardships of searching for the truth and the news.[3]

In addition to Jamal Ismail, there are several journalists and editors in the Islamic media who stand out for the time, effort, and thought they have put into trying to understand and explain bin Laden. A 1991 book by the Egyptian journalist Issam Darraz, *Osama Bin Laden Recounts Arab Al-Ansar Lion's Lair Battles in Afghanistan,* is essential for understanding bin Laden's activities in Afghanistan, the wide ring of his associates there, and the effect the Afghans' culture and victory have had on bin Laden's thinking and worldview. Several other Muslim journalists also have excelled in telling the world about why bin Laden thinks and acts as he does, about the nature, structure, and capabilities of his organization, and about the role of his closest allies, especially the Egyptian Islamists. Topping this list are Muhammad Salah of the London-based *Al-Hayah*; Ahmad Muwaffaq Zaydan, also of *Al-Hayah* and a perceptive analyst of the enduring impact of the Afghan war on the Muslim world; Rahimullah Yusufzai of Pakistan's the *News* and Hamid Mir of the same country's *Ausaf* ; and Sa'id al-Qaysi of the Paris-based *Al-Watan Al-Arabi.* Several of *Al-Watan Al-Arabi*'s reporters also have done interesting work in the opaque world of bin Laden's finances and his search for weapons of mass destruction. Reporting on these two aspects of the bin Laden issue has been simultaneously the most desired, sensational, ridiculed, and least verifiable.

In addition, the editor in chief of the prestigious U.K.-based daily *Al-Quds Al-Arabi,* Abd-al-Bari Atwan, has provided insightful and provocative commentary on bin Laden, his effect on Muslims, and on what both mean for relations between Christendom and Islam. Atwan also conducted one of the first interviews of bin Laden in Afghanistan, and it is still one of the best. Finally, numerous insightful but usually unsigned editorials and op-ed pieces in the Muslim media — from London to Amman to Karachi — have sounded a similar refrain; namely, the Islamic world, at all societal levels, is fed up with what it views as a U.S.-led Western/Christian attack on the Muslim world's religion, people, dignity, and economic resources. Many of the pieces urge the West to recognize that these grievances have created a warm welcome for bin Laden's inciting words, as well as a growing tolerance for his use of force.

The body of work on bin Laden by Western academics and political analysts was not extensive before 11 September 2001. Head and shoulders above the rest stands an essay in the November–December 1998 issue of *Foreign Affairs* by Professor Bernard Lewis titled "License to Kill: Osama Bin Laden's Declaration of Jihad." In the essay, Professor Lewis seeks not to demonize bin Laden but to explain what he has said and why what he has said — especially about the Islamic holy places in Saudi Arabia — is influencing the Muslim world. Aside from this essay, there are slim pickings in the groves of academe. Scottish professor Magnus Ranstorp has produced in *Studies in Conflict and Terrorism* an insightful article that dissects bin Laden's fatwa, but this article misses the point that bin Laden has never claimed to be a "religious" scholar or leader. Dr. Michael Dunn, in *Middle East Policy,* has published an essay that is a glib regurgitation of the invalid mantra: "Bin Laden is important because of his money and the way to defeat bin Laden is deny him his money." The two pre-September 2001 book-length studies of bin Laden were written by Yossef Bodansky[4] and Simon Reeve.[5] The Bodansky book — titled *Bin Laden: The Man Who Declared War on America* — appears to draw on many of the materials used in the present study, although Mr. Bodansky's refusal to cite sources in order to protect his "sources and methods" makes his book of little use as a basis for further investigation. The information he uses, moreover, is shaped to fit the author's thesis that there is an Iranian-Syrian-Iraqi "terrorist international" that is out to destroy America and Israel, and that bin Laden is mainly a cog, albeit an important cog, in that state-sponsored organization. I share Bodansky's belief that bin Laden has been a greater threat than has so far been recognized, but I believe bin Laden has posed this threat because he was motivated by ideas and had no need or desire to associate with state sponsors.

In contrast, Simon Reeve's book — titled *The New Jackals: Ramzi Yousef, Osama Bin Laden, and the Future of Terrorism* — presents data he gathered on Yousef and bin Laden in a straightforward manner without spinning conspiracy theories. Reeve had excellent access to senior FBI officials who dealt with Yousef and have been tracking bin Laden. Reeve's portrait of Yousef is well done, graphically portraying Yousef's genius for disguise, organization, leadership, and designing unique explosive devices. As important, Reeve painstakingly describes the worldwide Sunni community in which Yousef moved at will and undetected until he was undone by his own cockiness. Traveling unnoticed, and finding hubs of support in North America, the Middle and East Asia, South Asia, Europe, and North Africa, Yousef used the same Sunni Islamist milieu that supports bin Laden's leadership and activities, and that in part explains bin Laden's success. Reeve's discussion of bin Laden is not as complete as that of Yousef, but his bottom line is accurate. "His [bin Laden's] influence within the Muslim world cannot be underestimated," argues Reeve. "Even among moderate Muslims bin Laden is viewed with grudging respect as a man prepared to stand up to the arrogance of the world's only remaining superpower."[6]

Since 11 September 2001, a book and several essays have appeared that make strong contributions to our understanding of bin Laden and his international impact. Peter L. Bergen's book, *Holy War, Inc.*, shows signs of rushed publication but presents useful discussions of bin Laden's personality and beliefs; his roots and strength in Yemen; and the influence of Shaykh Abdullah Azzam on the jihad movement. I think that Bergen underestimates the depth of bin Laden's hatred for American culture and the breadth of his appeal among the world's Muslims, but these are points for further research and debate. Bergen writes with wit and provides a point of departure for those intending to study Afghanistan. Describing travel in Afghanistan,

Bergen notes the trips always took longer than expected. "Like all estimates about time in Afghanistan," Bergen wisely advises, "the more pessimistic are proved accurate."[7]

Among a mass of newspaper and periodical literature, Robert Fisk, Reuel Marc Gerecht, Adb-al-Bari Atwan, Ahmad Muwaffaq Zaydan, and Muhammed Salah have continued producing thought-provoking analysis. Gerecht's essay "The Gospel According to Osama Bin Laden" is especially useful — and ominous. Four essays by others have, in particular, broken new ground and advanced our understanding of bin Laden and the historical, cultural, and religious contexts in which he is acting: Bernard Lewis's "The Revolt of Islam"; Michael Scott Doran's "Somebody Else's Civil War"; Milt Bearden's "Afghanistan, Graveyard of Empires"; and Daniel Pipes's "God and Mammon: Does Poverty Cause Militant Islam?" The latter essay will, I hope, prompt a discussion that will start to undermine the tenet of U.S. foreign policy that decrees that poverty and unemployment cause terrorism, and thereby make room for an effort to understand the overwhelming centrality of religion in all of bin Laden's activities.

It also was my good fortune to discover an essay by Ralph Peters that I earlier missed. Peters's 1999 essay in *Parameters,* "Our Old New Enemies," brilliantly encapsulates the dilemma facing America and really should be the first piece read by those charged with confronting bin Laden and his ilk. "We maintain a cordon sanitaire around military operations," Peters warned,

> ignoring the frightening effect of belief on our enemy's will and persistence. We accept the CNN reality of "mad mullahs" and intoxicated masses, yet we do not consider belief a noteworthy factor when assessing our combat opponents. . . . We shy away from manifestations of faith, suspecting them or ignoring them, or, at best, analyzing them in the dehydrated language of the sociologist. But if we want to understand the warriors of the world and the fury that drives them, we had better open our minds to the power of belief.[8]

Notes

Preface to the Second Edition

1. Hilaire Belloc, *The Great Heresies* (Rockford, IL: Tan Books and Publishers, Inc., 1991), 73–76.

Preface

1. "Transcript of Osama bin Laden Video Tape," CNN Web site, accessed 13 December 2001.
2. James Risen, "Al Qaeda Still Able to Strike U.S., Head of CIA Says," *New York Times,* 7 February 2002, 1.
3. Mark Helprin, "We Beat Hitler. We Can Vanquish This Foe, Too," *Wall Street Journal,* 12 September 2001.

Acknowledgments

1. Mark Helprin, "Statesmanship and Its Betrayal: The Definition of a Politician," *Vital Speeches of the Day* 64, no. 20 (1 August 1998).
2. Ibid.

Introduction

1. Abu Shiraz, "May 1998 Interview with Bin Laden Reported," *Pakistan,* 20 February 1999. (Interview was conducted in May 1998 but was not then published.)
2. Ronald Steel, "Blowback. Terrorism and the U.S. Role in the Middle East," *New Republic,* 28 July 1996.
3. Robert Fisk, "As My Grocer Said: Thank You Mr. Clinton for the Fine Words . . . ," *Independent,* 22 August 1998, 3.
4. Interview of Undersecretary of State Thomas Pickering, *Frontline,* April 1999.

5. Hamid Mir, "Interview of Osama Bin Laden," *Pakistan,* 18 March 1997.

6. Muhammed Salah, "Bin Laden Front Falls Back and Egyptian Groups Undertake the Mission," *Al-Wasat Magazine,* 11–17 January 1999, 14–15.

7. "Laden Declares Jihad against U.S. Forces," *News,* 28 May 1998.

8. "Egypt's Jihad Asked by Bin Laden to Turn Guns on U.S.," *Agence France-Presse* (hereafter *AFP*), 24 February 1999.

9. Kamal Azfar, "Bin Laden Warns of 'Full Fledged' Action against U.S.," *Ausaf,* 9 January 1999, 1, 4.

10. John Miller, "Greetings America: My Name Is Osama Bin Laden. Now That I Have Your Attention . . . A Conversation with the Most Dangerous Man in the World," *Esquire* (Internet version) (February 1999).

11. Abd-al-Bari Atwan, "Bush War and What Will Follow," *Al-Quds Al-Arabi,* 8 October 2001.

12. "First War of the Century: Statement by Al Qaeda Leader Osama Bin Laden," *Al-Jizarah Satellite Channel Television,* 27 December 2001.

Chapter 1

1. James Turner Johnson, *The Holy War Idea in Western and Islamic Traditions* (University Park: Pennsylvania State University, 1997), 19.

2. Ibid., 15, 32, and 133.

3. Thomas Luxon, "John Bunyan in Context (Review)," *Journal of Religion* 78, no. 1 (January 1998): 121.

4. Ken Chowder, "The Father of American Terrorism," *American Heritage* 51, no. 1 (February 2000): 81.

5. David W. Blight, "John Brown's Triumphant Failure," *The American Prospect* 11, no. 9 (13 March 2000): 44.

6. Emory M. Thomas, *The Confederate Nation, 1861–1865* (New York: Harper and Row, 1979), 3.

7. G. A. Fine, "John Brown's Body: Elites, Heroic Embodiment, and the Legitimization of Political Violence," *Social Problems* 46, no. 22 (1999).

8. "Osama Says Taliban Rejected US Billions for Arrest," *Ausaf,* 28 December 1998, 1, 7.

9. Henry Mayer, *All on Fire: William Lloyd Garrison and the Abolition of Slavery* (New York: St. Martin's Press, 1998), 495, 500.

10. James McPherson, *Battle Cry of Freedom* (New York: Oxford University Press, 1988), 210; David W. Blight, "John Brown's Triumphant Failure," *The American Prospect* 11, no. 9 (13 March 2000): 40.

11. The edition of Bunyan's classic work used in this study is John Bunyan, *The Pilgrim's Progress* (Uhrichsville, OH: Barbour Publishing Co., 1988), 303.

12. Ibid., 82, 128.

13. Ibid., 36, 37.

14. Ibid., 284.

15. Fine, "John Brown's Body."

16. Bunyan, *The Pilgrim's Progress,* 301.

17. John L. Esposito, *The Islamic Threat. Myth or Reality?* 3d ed. (New York: Oxford University Press, 1999), 279; "Double Standard of the United States,"

Nawa-i-Waqt (Editorial), 13 August 1999, 6.

18. McPherson, *Battle Cry of Freedom,* 203.

19. Thomas Jefferson, *Declaration of Independence.*

20. William J. Bennet, ed., *Our Sacred Honor: Words of Advice from the Founders in Stories, Letters, Poems, and Speeches* (New York: Simon & Schuster, 1997), 34–35.

21. Esposito, *The Islamic Threat,* 278.

22. Fine, "John Brown's Body."

23. Ikram Sehgel, "Osama Bin Laden Syndrome: Freedom Fighter or Terrorist," *The Nation* (Lahore edition; Internet version), 29 August 1998.

24. Issam Darraz, *Osama Bin Laden Recounts Arab al-Ansar Lions' Lair (Masadah) Battles in Afghanistan* (Cairo: no publisher, 1991).

25. Qari Naved Masood Hashmi, "Osama Bin Laden—A Man as Strong as a Rock," *Pakistan,* 10 June 1998, 10.

26. "Declaration of Jihad against the United States," *Al-Islah,* 2 September 1996, 1.

27. "Bin Laden's Statement: Circumstances and Implications," *Al-Islah,* 2 September 1996, 1, 2.

28. Bennet, *Our Sacred Honor,* 34–35.

29. Fine, "John Brown's Body."

30. "Declaration of Jihad," *Al-Islah*; Magnus Ranstorp, "Interpreting the Broader Context and Meaning of Bin Laden's Fatwa," *Studies in Conflict and Terrorism* 21, no. 4 (1998): 325.

31. Esposito, *The Islamic Threat,* 280.

32. Paul Glad et al., eds., *The Process of American History. Volume 1: Early America* (Englewood Cliffs, NJ: Prentice-Hall, 1969), 211; Nelson F. Adkins, ed., *Paine. Common Sense and Other Political Writings* (Indianapolis, IN.: Bobbs-Merrill, 1953), 55–56.

Chapter 2

1. Miller, "Greetings America: My Name Is Osama Bin Laden. Now That I Have Your Attention"; Robin Fox, "Fatal Attraction: War and Human Nature," *National Interest* 51 (Winter 1992/93): 11–20.

2. Fox, "Fatal Attraction"; Mark Helprin, "Defense of the Realm," *Wall Street Journal* (Op-Ed, Internet version), 1 August 2000.

3. "Washington: Progress in Investigation into Destroyer Blast in Aden," *Al-Hayah,* 19 October 2000, 1.

4. Ibid.

5. "The Century's First War: Speech by Osama Bin Laden," Al-Jazirah Satellite Channel Television, 3 November 2001.

6. Williamson Murray, "Clausewitz Out, Computer In: Military Culture and Technological Hubris." *National Interest* 48 (Summer 1997).

7. Anatol Lieven, "Nasty Little Wars," *The National Interest* 62 (Winter 2000/01): 66.

8. Bruce B. Auster, "An Inside Look at Terror Inc.," *U.S. News & World Report,* 19 October 1998.

9. Michael Collins Dunn, "Osama Bin Laden: The Nature of the Challenge," *Middle East Policy* 6, no. 2 (October 1998): 24, 28.

10. "The Terrorist and the State," *Frontline Online,* April 1999, interview with Larry C. Johnson.

11. Amy E. Wisgerhop, "International Non-state Terrorism and the Translate Paradigm," *Low Intensity Conflict and Law Enforcement* 8, no. 2 (Summer 1999): 60–61.

12. Marie Colvin, "The New Face of World Terrorism," London *Sunday Times* (Internet version), 30 August 1998.

13. David Gardner, "U.S. Bombing: Moslem Allies Fear Backlash from 'Afghan Arabs,'" FT.com, 21 August 1998.

14. "Report on the Threat to Arab Countries by Terrorist Bin Laden," *Sawt al-Mar'ah,* 31 March 1998.

15. "Declaration of Jihad against the Americans," *Al-Islah.*

16. "Text of the World Front's Statement Urging Jihad against Jews and Crusaders," *Al-Quds Al-Arabi,* 23 February 1998, 3.

17. "Caveman Terrorist Spooks the West," *Observer,* 3 January 1998.

18. "Letter from Kandahar," Associated Press, 16 March 1998; "World Front for Fighting the Jews and the Crusaders, Statement No. 4,"; "World Front for Fighting the Jews and the Crusaders, Statement No. 4," *Al-Hayah.*

19. Egyptian Islamic Jihad, "A Bulletin Issued by the Media Office of the Jihad Group-Egypt, No. 43," 10 December 1998.

20. "Today's New Cult Hero," *Economist* (Editorial), 29 August–4 September 1998.

21. Azfar, "Bin Laden Warns of 'Full Fledged' Action against U.S."

22. Ralph Peters, "We Don't Have the Stomach for This Kind of Fight," *Washington Post* (Op-Ed), 30 August 1998, C-1, C-8.

23. Mary Anne Weaver, "The Real Bin Laden," *New Yorker* (24 January 2000): 32; Jim Hoagland, "Turncoat Terrorists," *Washington Post,* 16 January 2000, B-7; Milt Bearden, "A Terrorist's Long Shadow," *New York Times* (Op-Ed), 22 December 1999, A-31; Brian M. Jenkins, "This Time Is Different," *San Diego Union Tribune,* 16 September 2001.

24. Walter T. Vollman, "Letter from Afghanistan: Across the Divide," *New Yorker,* 15 May 2000.

25. Radek Sikorski, *Dust of the Saints. A Journey to Herat in Time of War* (London: Chatto and Windus, 1989); Robert D. Kaplan, *Soldiers of God: With the Mujahedin in Afghanistan* (Boston: Houghton Mifflin, 1990); Eric S. Margolis, *War at the Top of the World: The Struggle for Afghanistan, Kashmir, and Tibet* (New York: Routledge, 2000), 18.

26. Samuel P. Huntington, *The Clash of Civilizations and the Remaking of World Order* (New York: Touchstone, 1997).

27. Richard E. Rubenstein and Jarle Crocker, "Challenging Huntington," *Foreign Policy* 94 (Fall 1994): 128.

28. Gertrude Himmelfarb, "A Dark and Bloody Crossroads," *The National Interest* 32 (Summer 1993): 53.

29. David Welch, "The 'Clash of Civilizations' as an Argument and as a Phenomenon," *Security Studies* 6, no. 4 (Summer 1997): 216; Fouad Ajami, "The

Summoning, 'But They Will Not Hearken,'" *Foreign Affairs* 72, no. 4 (September/October 1993): 7; Pierre Haussner, "Huntington's Clash: 1. Morally Objectionable, Politically Dangerous," *The National Interest* 46 (Winter 1996/97): 63.

30. Mark Huband, *Warriors of the Prophet: The Struggle for Islam* (Boulder, CO: Westview Press, 1999), 138.

31. Mahmood Monshipouri, "The West's Modern Encounter with Islam: From Discourse to Reality," *Journal of Church and State* (Internet version) 40, no. 1 (Winter 1998).

32. Wang Gungwu, "Huntington's Clash: II: A Machiavelli for Our Times," *The National Interest* 46 (Winter 1996/97): 71.

33. "Sermon of Shaykh Yusuf al-Qaradawi," Qatar Television, 11 January 2002.

34. John Kelsay, *Islam and War: A Study in Comparative Ethics* (Louisville, KY: Westminster/John Knox Press, 1993), 103.

35. "Transcript of Bin Laden's October [2001] Interview," CNN.com, accessed 5 February 2002.

Chapter 3

1. Scott Macleod, "The Paladin of the Jihad," *Time*, 6 May 1996, 51–52.

2. Michael Grunwald, "Africa Blast Suspects to Stand Trial in the U.S.," *Washington Post*, 28 August 1998, A-1, A-20.

3. Lee Michael Katz, "Financial Records Lifting Veil on Bin Laden Network," *USA Today*, 1 October 1998.

4. Faiza Saleh Amba, "Saudi Militant's Wish: To Die Fighting America," Associated Press, 30 August 1998.

5. Paul R. Pillar, *Terrorism and U.S. Foreign Policy* (Washington, DC: Brookings Institution Press, 2002), 93.

6. "U.S. Aid for Ahmed Shah Masood against Osama," *Jang* (Editorial), 29 December 1998, 10.

7. "Unattributed Biography of Osama bin Laden," *Frontline Online*, April 1999.

8. Brig. (ret'd) M. Abdul Hafiz, "Growing Legend of Osama Bin Laden," *Frontier Post*, 25 August 1999, 6.

9. "Bin Laden's Statement: Circumstances and Implications," *Al-Islah*, 2 September 1996.

10. Fisk, "As My Grocer Said," 3.

11. Bernard Lewis, "License to Kill: Osama Bin Laden's Declaration of Jihad," *Foreign Affairs* 77, no. 6 (November/December 1998): 18–19.

12. Dunn, "Osama Bin Laden: The Nature of the Challenge," 28.

13. "Expel the Mushkireen from the Arabian Peninsula," *Abdullah Azzam Home Page*, 7 August 1997; *Al-Quds Al-Arabi*, 27 November 1996; U.S. State Department, "Fact Sheet on Osama Bin Laden," 14 August 1996; "Report on Bin Laden's Activities, Wealth," *Al-Watan Al-Arabi*, 4 September 1998, 23–28.

14. Auster, "An Inside Look at Terror Inc."; "Interview with Sa'd al-Faqih," *Frontline Online*, April 1999; "Collapse of BCCI Shorts Bin Laden," UPI, 1 March 2001.

15. Alan Feuer, "Jihad, Inc.: The Bin Laden Network of Companies Exporting Terror," *New York Times*, 13 February 2001, C-17.

16. Fayzah al-Sab, "Yemeni Ties with U.S., Bin Laden," *Al-Watan Al-Arabi*, 12 June 1998, 5.

17. "Security Report, Bin Laden Has Weapons Worth $51 Million," *Al-Sharq Al-Awsat*, 30 July 1999, 2.

18. "Interview with Roland Jaquard, Monitor of International Terrorism," *Al-Watan Al-Arabi*, 11 April 1997; "Bin Laden Allowed to Conduct Business in Afghanistan," *Frontier Post*, 28 December 1998, 1.

19. "Bin Laden Took Advantage of the Situation of the Egyptian Jihad and Islamic Group Organizations to Impose His Control on Them and Form a World Front for 'Liberating the Holy Places,'" *Al-Sharq Al-Awsat*, 20 April 1999, 3.

20. "Interview with Roland Jacquard."

21. "Report on Bin Laden's Activities, Wealth," *Al-Watan Al-Arabi*; Muhammad al-Shafai, "Curry Restaurants, Car Dealerships, and Mobile Phone Shops Are the New Fronts for Fundamentalists That They Depend on for Their Activities in Britain," *Al-Sharq Al-Awsat*, 22 January 2000, 3; Nadiah Mahdid, "Britain Closes Down a Fundamentalist's 'Front Company' and the Muhajiroun Organization Rushes to Open Another One," *Al-Sharq Al-Awsat*, 28 January 2000, 3; "Bin Laden Took Advantage," *Al-Sharq Al-Awsat*.

22. "Unattributed Biography of Bin Laden," *Frontline Online*.

23. "Secrets of the Worldwide Campaign Chasing Osama Bin Laden: From Afghanistan to Sudan to Somalia: The Terrorist Who Baffled the World Intelligence Services," *Al-Watan Al-Arabi*, 16 February 1996; Sa'id al-Qubaysi, "Kuwait, UAE Banks Said Tied to Bin Laden," *Al-Watan Al-Arabi*, 31 December 1999, 22, 24; Barry Schweid, "Senior Officials Quietly Join Probe of Terrorism Support," Associated Press, 8 July 1998; "Press Report Links Bin Laden to Tirana Banks, Companies," ATA, 6 September 1998.

24. James Risen and Benjamin Weiser, "U.S. Officials Say Aid for Terrorists Came through Two Persian Gulf Countries," *New York Times*, 8 July 1999, A-8.

25. John Kentner, "Bombings in East Africa: The Suspect," *New York Times*, 14 August 1998.

26. "'The United States Should Search Itself': Exclusive Interview with Osama Bin Laden," *Ummat*, 28 September 2001, 1, 7.

27. "Report on Bin Laden's Activities, Wealth," *Al-Watan Al-Arabi*.

28. John Mintz, "Bin Laden's Finances Are a Moving Target: Penetrating Empire Could Take Years," *Washington Post*, 28 August 1998.

29. "Interview with Sa'd al-Faqih," *Frontline Online*.

30. Vladimir Yemelyarenko, "Ahmed Shah Mas'ud: Afghan War Will End in Pakistan," *Izvestiya*, 2 December 2000.

31. Khalid Duran, "Cairo: A Torrent of Frightening Disclosures — Holy Terror as the Vanguard of Globalization," *World and I* 15, no. 11 (November 2000): 300.

32. "Interview with Sa'id Aburish," *Frontline Online*, April 1999.

33. Austere, "An Inside Look at Terror Inc."; Tim Weiner, "Missile Strikes against Bin Laden Won Him Esteem in Muslim Lands, U.S. Officials Say," *New York Times*, 8 February 1999, A-13.

34. Jack Kelley, "Saudi Money Aiding Terrorist Bin Laden," *USA Today*, 29 October 1999, 1; "Saudi Executives Give Funds to Bin Laden," Reuters, 29 October 1999.

35. "Heroin Funds Bin Laden's War against the West," *Washington Times,* 30 November 1998, A-13.

36. Salah Nasrawi, "Osama Bin Laden Reportedly Receiving Millions in Donations," Associated Press, 6 July 1999.

37. Weiner, "Missile Strikes against Bin Laden Won Him Esteem."

38. Ranstorp, "Interpreting the Broader Context and Meaning of Bin Laden's Fatwa," 325–26.

39. Renaud Girard, "On Osama Bin Laden's Trail," *Le Figaro,* 30 September 1998, 6.

40. Muhammad al-Shafai, "Muhajiroun Movement Leader Confirms Legal Loopholes Were Exploited to Send Fundamentalists for Military Training in the United States. Omar Bakri: Islamic Movement's Sons Learned Guerrilla Warfare and How to Make Explosives in the Missouri, Michigan, and Virginia Camps," *Al-Sharq Al-Awsat,* 30 May 2000, 3; "Scotland Yard Questions Arab Fundamentalist Advocating Assassination of British Prime Minister," *Al-Sharq Al-Awsat,* 14 December 2000; Dalip Singh and James Clark, "Britons Take War Holidays in Kashmir," *Sunday Times* (Internet version), 21 January 2001.

41. "Report on Bin Laden's Activities, Wealth," *Al-Watan Al-Arabi.*

42. "Mindanao Cops Have Photos of Saudi Tycoon," *Philippine Daily Inquirer* (Internet version), 25 August 1998; Rose Miranda, "Philippine Military Monitoring NGOs Used by Bin Laden to Send Support to MILF," *Abante* (Internet version), 23 June 2000; "Philippine Military Intelligence Chief Says Bin Laden Gave $3 Million to the MILF," GMA-7 Television, 19 June 2000; Paolo Romero, "Further on Bin Laden Aid to MILF; Mindanao Rehabilitation Fund Explained," *Philippine Star* (Internet version), 20 June 2000.

43. "Heroin Funds Bin Laden's War against the West," *Washington Times;* Jason Burke, "Bin Laden's Opium War," *Observer* (Internet version), 29 November 1998.

44. Soumya Gosh, "Laden to Talibanize Kashmir with Heroin Money," *Pioneer,* 21 October 1999, 5; Muhammed Salah et al., "Moscow: Bin Laden Has 'Links' with Chechen Narcotics Dealers," *Al-Hayah* (Internet version), 18 September 1999, 1, 6; Muhammad Khalaf, "Shamil Basayev: A Terrorist or a National Hero?" *Al-Sharq Al-Awsat,* 5 January 2000, 10; Salah Najm and Isam al-Ayyash, "Report Views Bin Laden Operations, Counterterrorism Efforts," *Al-Hawadith,* 26 January 2001.

45. Mintz, "Bin Laden's Finances Are a Moving Target"; "Report on Bin Laden's Activities, Wealth," *Al-Watan Al-Arabi;* William Hall, "Output in Afghanistan Doubles," *Financial Times,* 31 January 2000, 2.

46. Salah Najm, "Osama bin Laden, the Destruction of the Base," Al-Jazirah Space Channel Television, 10 June 1999 (This interview was conducted in December 1998 but not broadcast or published until the following June); Gosh, "Laden to Talibanize Kashmir with Heroin Money"; Barbara Crossette, "Afghan Heroin Feeds Addiction in Region, UN Reports," *New York Times,* 1 March 2000, A-6.

47. Shekhar Gupta et al., "India's Most Wanted Family," *India Today,* 15 April 1993, 40–41, 49, 51.

48. "Complicity of Dawood Ibrahim Confirmed," *Sunday Observer,* 4 April

1993, 5; "Three Pakistani-based Dons behind Delhi Bomb Blasts," All India Radio Network, 18 June 1996.

49. Gupta et al., "India's Most Wanted Family"; Riyad Alam-al-Din, "Cash Couriers Linked to Bin Laden," *Al-Watan Al-Arabi*, 4 February 2000.

Chapter 4

1. Bernard Lewis, "The Roots of Muslim Rage," *Atlantic Monthly* (September 1990); Abd-al-Bari Atwan, "Interview with Saudi Oppositionist Osama Bin Laden," *Al-Quds Al-Arabi*, 27 November 1996, 5; "Interview (Written) of Osama Bin Laden," *Ghazi Magazine*, 20–27 August 2000.

2. "Declaration of Jihad against the Americans," *Al-Islah*.

3. "Transcript of Bin Laden's October [2001] Interview," CNN.com, accessed 5 February 2002.

4. Amin Malouf, *The Crusades through Arab Eyes* (New York: Shocken Books, 1984), 29, 51–52.

5. Ranstorp, "Interpreting the Broader Context and Meaning of Bin Laden's Fatwa," 325; Najm, "The Destruction of the Base."

6. See "World Front for Fighting the Jews and the Crusaders, Statement No. 4." *Al-Hayah*; "*Nida'ul Islam* Exclusive Interview with Osama Bin Laden: Of Jihad and Terror, the New Powder Keg in the Middle East," *Nida'ul Islam* (Internet version), 15 (October/November 1996); John Miller, "Exclusive Interview with Osama Bin Laden," abcnews.com, 28 May 1998.

7. "Usama Bin Ladin, Letter from Qandahar," Associated Press, 16 March 1998.

8. See Robert Fisk, "U.S. Airstrikes: Bin Laden Will Take His Revenge," *Independent*, 21 August 1998, 1, 2; Peter Arnett, "Osama Bin Laden: The Interview." *CNN/TIME IMPACT: Holy Terror* (Internet version), 11 May 1997.

9. Najm, "The Destruction of the Base"; "'I Am Not Afraid of Death.' Osama Bin Laden Talks about the Embassy Bombings, the Strikes on Iraq, and His War on America." NEWSWEEK.com, 4 January 1999.

10. "World Front for Fighting the Jews and the Crusaders, Statement No. 4," *Al-Hayah*.

11. Bruce James, "Middle East: Arab Veterans of the Afghan War — Trained Forces in Waiting," *Jane's Intelligence Review* 7, no. 4 (April 1995): 175–79; Emmanuel Sivan, "The Holy War Tradition in Islam," *Orbis* 42, no. 2 (Spring 1998).

12. "Declaration of Jihad against the Americans," *Al-Islah*; Mir, "Interview with Osama Bin Laden"; Abd-al-Bari Atwan, "America's Harvest of Blood," *Al-Quds Al-Arabi*, 10 August 1998, 1.

13. Atwan, "American's Harvest of Blood," 1.

14. "World Front for Fighting the Jews and the Crusaders, Statement No. 4," *Al-Hayah*; Rahimullah Yusufzai, "World's Most Wanted Terrorist: An Interview with Osama Bin Laden," abcnews.com, 28 December 1998; Bakhit Ullah Jan Hasrat, "Osama Bin Laden Denounces U.S.-Sponsored 'World Order,'" *Pakistan*, 9 January 2000, 1.

15. "Speech by Osama Bin Laden," Al-Jazirah Satellite Television, 7 October 2001.

16. "Declaration of Jihad against Americans," *Al-Islah*; "Bin Laden's Statement: Circumstances and Implications," *Al-Islah*; "Osama Bin Laden, Letter from Kandahar," Associated Press; Robert Fisk, "Arab Rebel Leader Warns British: 'Get Out of the Gulf,'" *Independent*, 10 July 1996; Yusufzai, "World's Most Wanted Terrorist"; Advice and Reformation Committee, "Communiqué No. 19: The Saudi Regime and the Recurrent Tragedies of the Pilgrims," 16 April 1997.

17. "World's Most Wanted Terrorist: An Interview with Osama Bin Laden," abcnews.com.

18. Arnett, "Osama Bin Laden: The Interview"; "Declaration of Jihad against the Americans," *Al-Islah*; Fisk, "Arab Rebel Leader Warns British: 'Get Out of the Gulf.'"

19. Atwan, "Interview with Saudi Oppositionist Osama Bin Laden"; Advice and Reformation Committee, "Communiqué No. 19."

20. Arnett, "Osama Bin Laden: The Interview."

21. Atwan, "Interview with Saudi Oppositionist Osama Bin Laden"; Mir, "Interview with Osama Bin Laden"; Arnett, "Osama Bin Laden: The Interview"; Atwan, "America's Harvest of Blood"; Mubarak al-Mubarak, "The Difficulty of Admission to Universities and the Domination of the Security Obsession: Severe Crisis Facing Saudi Arabia, Necessitating Speedy Reforms," *Al-Quds Al-Arabi*, 30 August 2000, 18.

22. Arnett, "Osama Bin Laden: The Interview."

23. Mir, "Interview of Osama Bin Laden."

24. Miller, "Exclusive Interview with Osama Bin Laden."

25. Yusufzai. "World's Most Wanted Terrorist."

26. Najm, "The Destruction of the Base."

27. Mir, "Interview with Osama Bin Laden"; Ghulam Mohammad Khalid, "The U.S. Agenda and the Islamic Revolution," *Jasarat* (Internet version), 10 October 1999.

28. Al-Abd al-Karim and Ahmad al-Nur al-Nur, "Interview with Saudi Businessman Osama Bin Laden," *Al-Quds Al-Arabi*, 9 March 1994, 4.

29. "Declaration of Jihad against the Americans," *Al-Islah*.

30. "Osama Bin Laden: Letter from Kandahar," Associated Press.

31. Lewis, "License to Kill."

32. "Life and Religion," Al-Jazirah Satellite Channel, 22 April 2001.

33. John Kelsay, "Islam and the Distinction between Combatants and Noncombatants," in *Cross, Crescent, and Sword. The Justification and Limitation of War in Western and Islamic Tradition*, ed. James Turner Johnson and John Kelsay (New York: Greenwood Press, 1990), 200; Kelsay, *Islam and War*, 97.

34. "Text of the World Front's Statement Urging Jihad against Jews and Crusaders," *Al-Quds Al-Arabi*.

35. Ibid.; Johnson, *The Holy War Idea in Western and Islamic Traditions*, 156, 158, 160.

36. Khaled Abou el-Fadl, "Holy War versus Jihad (Review)," *Ethics and International Affairs* 14 (2000): 133–40.

37. Ranstorp. "Interpreting the Broader Context and Meaning of Bin Laden's Fatwa."

38. Huband, *Warriors of the Prophet*, 49.

39. "Declaration of Jihad against the Americans" *Al-Islah.*

40. Ahmed Khalid, "Report Notes U.S. Attempt to Arrest Osama Bin Laden," *Friday Times,* 30 July–5 August 1999, 3; Alberto Gaino, "Ndrangheta Arms for Terrorists," *La Stampa,* 27 November 1999, 32; Riyad Alam-al-Din, "Report Details Plan to Hunt Bin Laden Too," *Albania,* 11 March 2001, 2; Rose Tamay et al., "'High-Powered' Firearms Flood Abu Sayyaf Camp," *Philpino Star Ngayon* (Internet version), 23 August 2000.

41. Yusufzai, "World's Most Wanted Terrorist."

42. Johnson, *The Holy War Idea in Western and Islamic Traditions,* 115–16, 122; Muhammad Abu-Khudayr, "Shaykh Yasin to *Al-Ra'y Al-Amm:* Spilling of All Israeli Blood Is Lawful," *Al-Ra'y Al-Amm* (Internet version), 20 December 2000.

43. Johnson, *The Holy War Idea in Western and Islamic Traditions,* 122, ix, 185.

44. "Declaration of Jihad against the Americans," *Al-Islah.*

45. Ibid.

46. Atwan, "Interview with Saudi Oppositionist Osama Bin Laden."

47. "Text of the World Front's Statement Urging Jihad against Jews and Crusaders," *Al-Quds Al-Arabi.*

48. Atwan, "Interview with Saudi Oppositionist Osama Bin Laden."

49. "Excerpts from Ayman al-Zawahiri's book *Knights under the Prophet's Banner,*" *Al-Hayah,* December 2001, serialized in twelve parts.

50. Robert Gwyn, "Dispatches," Channel 4 Television Network, 20 February 1997.

51. "Text of the World Front's Statement Urging Jihad against Jews and Crusaders," *Al-Quds Al-Arabi.*

52. "Bin Laden Urges Jihad and Expulsion of U.S. Forces from Gulf, Praises Prince Talal Bin-Abd al-Aziz's Recent Statement," *Al-Quds Al-Arabi,* 23 March 1998, 4; "Osama Interview: Not Up to Him to Call for Holy War," *Takbeer,* 5–12 August 1990, 22; "Osama Urges Muslims to Help Afghans, Wage Jihad," *Nation* (Lahore Edition; Internet version), 10 April 2001; Kathy Gannon, "Bin Laden Tells Youth to Train for 'Holy Wars,'" *San Diego Union-Tribune,* 12 April 2001.

53. Mark Bowden, "Tracking Bin Laden 1 Yr. since the Bombing," *Philadelphia Inquirer,* 8 August 1998, A-2.

54. Jamal Ismail, "Al-Jazeerah, Bin Laden, and I," *Al-Zaman,* July 2000.

55. Miller, "Exclusive Interview with Osama Bin Laden"; Darraz, *Osama Bin Laden Recounts.*

56. "Interview with Sa'id Aburish"; Mary Anne Weaver, *Portrait of Egypt: A Journey through the World of Militant Islam* (New York: Farrar, Straus and Giroux, 1999), 261.

57. "Declaration of Jihad against the Americans," *Al-Islah.*

58. Ibid.; "Bin Laden Warns against U.S. Plan to Eliminate Afghan Arabs," *Al-Quds Al-Arabi,* 15 April 1998, 1; Najm, "The Destruction of the Base."

59. "Declaration of Jihad against the Americans" *Al-Islah.*

60. Milt Bearden, "Making Osama Bin Laden's Day," *New York Times* (Op-Ed), 13 August 1998, A-19.

61. Dunn, "Osama Bin Laden: The Nature of the Challenge"; Jason Burke and Harinder Baweja, "Target . . . India," *India Today,* 4 October 1999, 54; Mufid

Abd-al-Rahim, "*Al-Watan* Report on Osama Bin Laden," *Al-Watan Al-Arabi*, 26 March 1999, 20–23.

62. Atwan, "Interview with Saudi Oppositionist Osama Bin Laden"; Jamal Mahmud Ismail, "Bin Laden Urges Attacks against U.S., UK Interests," *Al-Sharq Al-Awsat* (Internet version), 25 December 1998.

63. Najm, "The Destruction of the Base."

64. Steven Emerson, "Abdullah Azzam, The Man before Osama Bin Laden," *Journal of Counterterrorism and Security International* 5, no. 3 (Fall 1998): 27.

65. Najm, "The Destruction of the Base"; Ismail, "Al-Jazeerah, Bin Laden, and I."

66. "Osama Bin Laden, Letter from Kandahar," Associated Press.

67. Najm, "The Destruction of the Base."

68. Rahimullah, "World's Most Wanted Terrorist."

69. Miller, "Exclusive Interview with Osama Bin Laden."

70. Ibid.; Shaykh Kamal Khatib, "Osama and Shamil in the Confrontation of the Drunk and the Philanderer," *Sawt al-Haqq wa al-Hurriyah*, 5 November 1999, 4.

71. Al-Abd al-Karim and Ahmad al-Nur al-Nur, "Interview with Saudi Businessman Osama Bin Laden," *Al-Quds Al-Arabi*, 9 March 1994.

72. Tariq Seed, "Bin Laden Calls for Holy War against Jews, Christians," *Pakistan Observer* (Internet version), 2 September 2000.

73. "From Noor ud Din Zangi to Osama Bin Laden," *Ausaf*, 4 March 2001, 4.

74. Malouf, *The Crusades through Arab Eyes*, 1, 66; "The Will of Abdullah Azzam, Who Is Poor to His Lord," Azzam Publications Web site at http://panther.netmania.co.uk, April 1986; Palestinian Information Center (Internet version), 7 November 1999.

75. "Declaration of Jihad against the Americans" *Al-Islah*, 2 September 1996.

76. Abdul Sattar, "Osama Urges Ummah to Continue Jihad," *News* (Internet version), 7 May 2001.

77. Atwan, "Interview with Saudi Oppositionist Osama Bin Laden": "MIRA Bulletin No. 253," *Movement for Islamic Reform in Arabia* (Internet version), 19 February 2001.

78. "Osama Bin Laden, Letter from Kandahar," Associated Press.

79. Ibid.; Mir, "Interview with Osama Bin Laden"; Huband, *Warriors of the Prophet*, 103; Eric S. Margolis, *War at the Top of the World. The Struggle for Afghanistan, Kashmir, and Tibet* (New York: Routledge, 2000), 94; Ahmad Muwaffaq Zaydan, "Bin Laden Thanks God for U.S. Destroyer Bombing," *Al-Hayah* (Internet version), 4 November 2000, 1, 6.

80. "Interview (Written) of Osama Bin Laden," *Ghazi Magazine*; Ejaz Haider, "Pakistan and Hezb's 'Surprise Move,'" *Friday Times* (Internet version), 28 July–3 August 2000; Lt. Gen. (ret'd) Javid Nasir, "The Cease-fire Implications," *Nation* (Lahore edition, Internet version), 1 August 2000; "A Tightrope Walk," *Times of India* (Editorial; Internet version), 1 August 2000; "Hizbul Mujahedin Ceasefire Angers Compatriots in Afghanistan," *AFP*, 24 July 2000; Manoj Joshi, "Indian Home Ministry Welcomes Announcement of Cease-fire by Hizbal Mujahedin," *Times of India* (Internet version), 25 July 2000.

81. "World Front for Fighting the Jews and the Crusaders, Statement No. 4," *Al-Hayah*.

82. "Osama Bin Laden, Letter from Kandahar," Associated Press.

83. "New Offer for Bin Laden," *Al-Islah*, 3 March 1997, 1.

84. Raymond Close, "Hard Target: We Cannot Defeat Terrorism with Bombs and Bombast," *Washington Post* (Op-Ed), 30 August 1998, C-1, C-5.

85. Yusufzai, "World's Most Wanted Terrorist."

86. Najm, "The Destruction of the Base."

87. "World Front for Fighting the Jews and the Crusaders, Statement No. 4," *Al-Hayah*.

88. Mark Macaskill et al., "Straw's Dilemma: The Home Secretary Has Been Called to Act after Bakri Wrote Bin Laden Supporting Terrorism," *Sunday Times* (Internet version), 5 September 1999.

89. Ibid.; Kelsay, "Islam and the Distinction between Combatants and Noncombatants," 201, 205; Kelsay, *Islam and War*, 65.

90. "Life and Religion," 22 April 2001.

Chapter 5

1. "Osama Bin Laden, Letter from Kandahar," Associated Press.

2. Miller, "Exclusive Interview with Osama Bin Laden."

3. *"Nida'ul Islam* Exclusive Interview with Osama Bin Laden," *Nida'ul Islam*; "The Will of Abdullah Azzam," Azzam Publications Web site.

4. Atwan, "Interview with Saudi Oppositionist Osama Bin Laden."

5. Dunn, "Osama Bin Laden: The Nature of the Challenge," 24–25.

6. Ranstorp. "Interpreting the Broader Context and Meaning of Bin Laden's Fatwa," 324; Kelsay, *Islam and War*, 95–97; Johnson, *The Holy War Idea in Western and Islamic Traditions*, 71, 115.

7. *"Nida'ul Islam* Exclusive Interview with Osama Bin Laden," *Nida'ul Islam*; "Interview (Written) of Osama Bin Laden," *Ghazi Magazine*.

8. Atwan, "Interview with Saudi Oppositionist Osama Bin Laden."

9. Ibid.; Cherif Quazani, "The Bin Laden Mystery: An Investigation into the Man Who Has Defied America," *Jeune Afrique*, 7 September 1998, 54–57; Johnson, *The Holy War Idea in Western and Islamic Traditions*, 62; Wa'el al-Ibrushi, "Interview with Abu Hamzah al-Masri," *Rose al-Yusuf*, 28 October 2000, 56.

10. Khalid Khalil Asaad, *Osama Bin Laden: The Whole Story*, trans. Ahmed M. Ibrahim, n.p./n.d., 24.

11. Ranstorp, "Interpreting the Broader Context and Meaning of Bin Laden's Fatwa."

12. Robert Fisk, "Muslim Leader Warns of New Assault on U.S. Forces," *Independent*, 22 March 1997, 1.

13. Yusufzai, "World's Most Wanted Terrorist."

14. Shiraz. "May 1998 Interview with Bin Laden Reported," 10.

15. "Declaration of Jihad against the Americans," *Al-Islah*.

16. Duran, "Cairo: A Torrent of Frightening Disclosures."

17. "I Am Not Afraid of Death," NEWSWEEK.com.

18. Lieven, "Nasty Little Wars," 69.

19. Ranstorp, "Interpreting the Broader Context and Meaning of Bin Laden's Fatwa"; Atwan, "Interview with Saudi Oppositionist Osama Bin Laden."

20. David Leppard et al., "The Global Terrorist," *Sunday Times* (Internet version), 7 February 1999; "Battalion Churns out Disinformation," *Rossiyskaya Gazeta,* 2 November 1999, 1; Abdallah Ould Mohamedi, "Interview with Mohamedu Ould Slahi," *Al-Sharq Al-Awast,* 22 February 2000, 3; Kathy Gannon, "Suspected Terrorists Enjoy Taliban's Protection," *Washington Times,* 11 March 2000, A-8; Nabil Sharif-al-Din, "The Afghanistan of the Caucasus: Bin Laden and Ibn-al-Khattab in Dagestan," *Al-Ahram Al-Arabi,* 9 October 1999, 32; "Commander of the Foreign Mujahedin in the Caucasus," Islamic Observation Center Web site (Internet version), 10 September 1999; "Unattributed Biography of Bin Laden," *Frontline Online*; Carlotta Gall and Thomas de Waal, *Chechnya. Calamity in the Caucasus* (New York: New York University Press, 1998), 108; Lieven, "Nasty Little Wars"; Carla Power, "Chasing a Man, Fixing a Nation," *Newsweek International,* 29 January 2001, 60; Najm and Al-Ayyash, "Report Views Bin Laden Operations, Counterterrorism Efforts."

21. Monshipouri, "The West's Modern Encounter with Islam."

Chapter 6

1. "Closer Look: Portraits of Osama Bin Laden," *Time Daily* (Internet version), 31 March 1999.

2. "Unattributed Biography of Bin Laden," *Frontline Online*; Lally Weymouth et al., "Pieces of the Puzzle," *Newsweek,* 18 December 2000, 48; John F. Burns, "Yemenis Say Saudi Man Is Top Suspect in *Cole* Attack," *New York Times,* 13 December 2000; John F. Burns, "Remote Yemen May Be Key to Terrorist's Past and Future," *New York Times,* 5 November 2000, A-1.

3. Al-Karim and Al-Nur, "Interview with Saudi Businessman Osama Bin Laden"; "Declaration of Jihad against the Americans," *Al-Islah.*

4. Khalid al-Hammadi, "Yemeni Tribes Condemn the Hunt for Bin Laden," *Al-Quds Al-Arabi,* 6 November 1999, 1.

5. Jane Mayer, "The House of Bin Laden," *New Yorker* (12 November 2001): 54–56, 61–65.

6. "Unattributed Biography of Bin Laden," *Frontline Online.*

7. Najm, "The Destruction of the Base"; Bin Laden group Web site, http://www.saudi-binLaden-group.com (this Web site has disappeared from the Internet).

8. "Bin Laden Family Businesses Scrutinized for Ties to Terrorism," *Le Monde* (Internet version), 23 September 2001.

9. Bin Laden group Web site, http://www.saudi-binLaden-group.com; John K. Cooley, *Unholy Wars: Afghanistan, America, and International Terrorism* (London: Pluto Press, 1999), 188.

10. Ranstorp, "Interpreting the Broader Context and Meaning of Bin Laden's Fatwa," 325; "Unattributed Biography of Bin Laden," *Frontline Online*; Macleod, "Paladin of the Jihad"; Mouna Naim, "Osama Bin Laden, the Banker of the Jihad," *Le Monde,* 11 April 1997.

11. "Unattributed Biography of Bin Laden," *Frontline Online.*

12. Ibid.; Macleod, "Paladin of the Jihad"; Najm, "The Destruction of the Base"; Abu Shiraz, "May 1998 Interview with Bin Laden Reported," *Pakistan,* 20 February 1999.

13. "Unattributed Biography of Bin Laden," *Frontline Online.*

14. Ibid.; *Dunn and Bradstreet,* 1999.

15. Ibid.; Mir, "Interview with Osama Bin Laden," 1, 7.

16. "Unattributed Biography of Bin Laden," *Frontline Online;* Naim, "Osama Bin Laden, the Banker of the Jihad"; Said K. Aburish, *The Rise, Corruption and Coming Fall of the House of Saud* (New York: St. Martin's Press, 1994), 200.

17. Jamal Kashoggi, "Interview with Prince Turki al-Faisal," *Arab News* (Internet version), 4–9 November 2001.

18. Burns, "Remote Yemen May Be Key to Terrorist's Past and Future," A-1.

19. Christopher Dickey et al., "Making a Symbol of Terror," *Newsweek,* 1 March 1998, 40–43; "Closer Look. Portraits of Osama Bin Laden," *Time Daily;* Weaver, "The Real Bin Laden"; Ouazani, "The Bin Laden Mystery," 54–57.

20. Michael Slackman, "Bin Laden's Family Ties Bind and Bedevil a Syrian Clan," *Los Angeles Times,* 13 November 2001; "Statement by Mother of Osama Bin Laden," *Arab News* (Internet version), 9 December 2001; Dr. Khalid Muhammad Batarfi, "Denying She Is Angry with Him, Saying She Prays to Guide Him on the Right Path, Mother of Osama Bin Laden Says: I Do Not Agree with My Son," *Al-Madinah,* 8 December 2001, 1.

21. Ouazani, "The Bin Laden Mystery"; Cooley, *Unholy Wars,* 117; "Biography of Osama Bin Laden," Islamic Observation Center (Internet version), 22 April 2000.

22. Mir, "Interview with Osama Bin Laden."

23. Dickey, "Making a Symbol of Terror."

24. Najm, "The Destruction of the Base."

25. Kiyohito Kokita and Yuji Moronaga, "Terrorist Asks Writer to Compile a Biography — Testimony of Pakistanis Who Have Met Bin Laden," *AERA,* 8 October 2001, 16–18.

26. Bassam al-Umash, "The Mentality of Osama Bin Laden," *Al Ra'y,* 16 August 1999, 30; Mir, "Interview with Osama Bin Laden"; Timothy R. Furnish, "Bin Laden: The Man Who Would Be Mahdi," *Middle East Quarterly* 9, no. 2 (Spring 2002): 56.

27. Mir, "Interview with Osama Bin Laden"; "Interview (Written) of Osama Bin Laden," *Ghazi Magazine.*

28. "A Strange Sudanese," *Le Point,* 12 March 1994.

29. Rahimullah Yusufzai, "In the Way of Allah," *Pakistan* (Internet version), 15 June 1998.

30. "Interview with Sa'd al-Faqih," *Frontline Online.*

31. "Unattributed Biography of Bin Laden," *Frontline Online;* "Bin Laden Full of Praise for Attack on USS *Cole* at Son's Wedding," *AFP,* 1 March 2001. "Today's Harvest," Al-Jizarah Satellite Channel Television, 28 February 2001.

32. "Interview (Written) of Osama Bin Laden," *Ghazi Magazine.*

33. NEWSWEEK.com, 4 January 1999; "Interview (Written) of Osama Bin Laden," *Ghazi Magazine.*

34. Atwan, "Interview with Saudi Oppositionist Osama Bin Laden."

35. "Interview with Sa'd al-Faqih," *Frontline Online*; Rahimullah Yusufzai, "From the Horse's Mouth," *News* (Internet version), 27 August 1998; Edward Giradet, "A Brush with Laden on the Jihad Front Line," *Christian Science Monitor*, 31 August 1998, 19; Ian Henderson, "Interview with Peter Bergen," *Yemen Observer* (Internet version), 9 December 2000.

36. Jason Burke, "The Making of the World's Most Wanted Man," *The Observer* (Internet version), 28 October 2001.

37. Mir, "Interview with Osama Bin Laden"; Dickey, "Making a Symbol of Terror"; Najm, "The Destruction of the Base"; "Closer Look: Portraits of Osama Bin Laden," *Time Daily*; "Khartoum: Secrets of the Rift between al-Turabi and Bin Laden," *Al-Watan Al-Arabi*, 29 December 1995, 30–32; Amir Tahiri, "Interview with Unidentified Algerian Senior Counterterrorism Officer," *Al-Sharq Al-Awsat*, 4 November 1997, 16.

38. Weaver, *Portrait of Egypt*, 261; Huband, *Warriors of the Prophet*, 2.

39. Albert Hourani, *A History of the Arab People* (Cambridge, MA: Harvard University Press, 1991), xix, 228; John L. Esposito, ed., *The Oxford History of Islam* (New York: Oxford University Press, 1999), 300, 675; Malik H. Iftikhar, "Islamic Discourse on Jihad, War and Violence," *Journal of South Asian and Middle Eastern Studies* 21, no. 4 (Summer 1998): 66.

40. Adnan Musallam, "Sayyid Qutb's View of Islam, Society and Militancy," *Journal of South Asian and Middle Eastern Studies* 22, no. 1 (Fall 1998): 64–87.

41. "Interview with Sa'd al-Faqih," *Frontline Online*; Emerson, "Abdullah Azzam, The Man before Osama Bin Laden," 27; Asaad, *Osama Bin Laden: The Whole Story*, 75.

42. "Interview with Sa'd al-Faqih, *Frontline Online*; Dickey, "Making a Symbol of Terror"; Najm, "The Destruction of the Base."

43. "The World Number One Wanted Bin Laden: The Ally Who Became Enemy," *Al-Majallah*, 5 September 1998; "Unattributed Biography of Bin Laden," *Frontline Online*; Frank Smyth, "Culture Shock: Bin Laden, Khartoum, and the War against the West," *Jane's Intelligence Review* 10, no. 10 (October 1998): 22–25.

44. Macleod, "Paladin of the Jihad."

45. "Closer Look: Portraits of Osama Bin Laden," *Time Daily*.

46. "Unattributed Biography of Bin Laden," *Frontline Online*; Ouazani, "The Bin Laden Mystery"; "Biography of Osama Bin Laden," Islamic Observation Center.

47. "The World Number One Wanted Bin Laden," *Al-Majallah*.

48. "Unattributed Biography of Bin Laden," *Frontline Online*.

49. Ibid.; Ouazani, "The Bin Laden Mystery"; "Biography of Osama Bin Laden," Islamic Observation Center.

50. "Unattributed Biography of Bin Laden," *Frontline Online*; Dickey, "Making a Symbol of Terror."

51. Najm, "The Destruction of the Base"; James, "Middle East: Arab Veterans of the Afghan War"; "Unattributed Biography of Bin Laden," *Frontline Online*.

52. Amba, "Saudi Militant's Wish: To Die Fighting America."

53. Ibid.; "The Opposition," *Jane's Intelligence Review* 8, no. 12 (December 1996).

54. Najm, "The Destruction of the Base"; James, "Middle East: Arab Veterans of the Afghan War"; "Unattributed Biography of Bin Laden," *Frontline Online*; Kamil Yusuf Husayn, "Osama Bin Laden: Legend of the Century," *Al-Bayan* (serialized book), 24–30 November and 1–3 and 5–14 December 1999; "The Most Wanted Terrorist in the World," *Paris Match,* 3 May 2001, 26–28.

55. Jamal Kashoffi, "Interview with Prince Turki al-Faisal," *Arab News* (Internet version), 4–9 November 2000.

Chapter 7

1. Mary Anne Weaver, "Blowback," *Atlantic Monthly* (May 1996): 24–28, 36.

2. "Declaration of Jihad against the Americans," *Al-Islah.*

3. Ranstorp, "Interpreting the Broader Context and Meaning of Bin Laden's Fatwa."

4. Miller, "Greetings America: My Name Is Osama Bin Laden."

5. Al-Karim and al-Nur, "Interview with Saudi Businessman Osama Bin Laden."

6. Darraz, *Osama Bin Laden Recounts*; Weaver, "The Real Bin Laden."

7. Macleod, "Paladin of the Jihad."

8. Najm, "The Destruction of the Base."

9. Darraz, *Osama Bin Laden Recounts*; Robert Fisk, "Anti-Soviet Warrior Puts His Army on the Road to Peace," *Financial Times,* 6 December 1993, 10.

10. "Get Personal," *New Republic,* 14 and 21 September 1998, 11–12.

11. "Interview with Milt Bearden," *Frontline Online,* April 1999.

12. Robin Wright, "Saudi Dissident a Prime Suspect in Blast," *Los Angeles Times,* 14 August 1998; Weaver, "The Real Bin Laden"; Lisa Anderson and Stephen J. Hedges, "Terror Web Pulled into Daylight," *Chicago Tribune,* 11 February 2001, 1.

13. "Interview with Larry C. Johnson," *Frontline Online,* April 1999.

14. "Unattributed Biography of Bin Laden," *Frontline Online*; "Interview with Larry C. Johnson," *Frontline Online*; "Osama Bin Laden Sends Message to anti-U.S. Conference," *Al-Akhbar,* 12 September 1998.

15. Fisk, "Anti-Soviet Warrior Puts His Army on the Road to Peace,"

16. Ahmed Rashid, *Taliban: Militant Islam, Oil and Fundamentalism in Central Asia* (New Haven, CT: Yale University Press, 2000); Darraz, *Osama Bin Laden Recounts.*

17. "Unattributed Biography of Bin Laden," *Frontline Online*; Ouazani, "The Bin Laden Mystery."

18. For bin Laden's early ties to these leaders, see Weaver, "Blowback"; "Unattributed Biography of Bin Laden," *Frontline Online*; "Has the Countdown Begun in the Adventure of Osama Bin Laden?" *Al-Watan Al-Arabi,* 15 May 1997; Colum Lynch, "Taliban Hoping for a Way to Bid Adieu to Bin Laden," *Boston Globe,* 21 October 1998; "The World Number One Wanted Bin Laden: The Ally Who Became Enemy," *Al-Majallah.*

19. Weaver, "Blowback."

20. Khamran Khan, "Osama's Narrow Escape, Camp Hits Reported," *News,* 22 August 1998, 1, 8. For a sampling of articles discussing bin Laden's ties

to a wide variety of Islamic militant groups, see "Secrets of the Worldwide Campaign Chasing Osama Bin Laden," *Al-Watan Al-Arabi*; Anthony Hyman, "Arab Involvement in the Afghan War," *Beirut Review* (Spring 1994): 73–89; Tim Weiner, "Blowback from the Afghan Battlefield," *New York Times Magazine*, 13 March 1994; Darraz, *Osama Bin Laden Recounts*; Anthony Davis, "Foreign Combatants in Afghanistan," *Jane's Intelligence Review* 5, no. 7 (July 1993): 327–31.

21. Isam al-Ayyash and Salah Najm, "Behind the Scenes of the American Strike against Bin Laden's Secret Cells; Balkan and Afghan Rings Plot against U.S. Interests," *Al-Hawadith*, 13 November 1998, 34–38.

22. Fisk, "Anti-Soviet Warrior Puts His Army on the Road to Peace"; "A Strange Sudanese," *Le Point*; Sa'id al-Qaysi, "U.S.-Yemen-Bin Laden Relations," *Al-Watan Al-Arabi*, 15 January 1999, 24–26.

23. Hamdi Rizq et al., "Osama Bin Laden, a Millionaire Financially Supporting Terrorism in Egypt and Saudi Arabia," *Rose al-Yusuf*, 17 May 1993, 6–10; Asaad, *Osama Bin Laden. The Whole Story*, 20.

24. Khan, "Osama's Narrow Escape, Camp Hits Reported"; "Interview with Sa'd al Faqih," *Frontline Online*; "The World Number One Wanted Bin Laden: The Ally Who Became Enemy," *Al-Majallah*.

25. Hamdi Rizq, "Jihad Unilaterally Won Over Bin Laden, While the Group Was Content with Financial Support," *Al-Wasat Magazine*, 31 August–6 September 1998, 26–27; "CIA Report on Bin Laden's Filipino Links," *Al-Sharq Al-Awsat* (Internet version), 22 May 1999.

26. Muhammed Salah, "A Record of Jihad Years from Ayn Shams to Tirana," *Al-Wasat Magazine*, 1–7 March 1999, 30, 31; Muhammed Salah, "Secret of the Relationship between al-Zawahiri and Bin Laden: The Jihad Leader Turned Bin Laden into a Mujahid," *Al-Wasat Magazine*, 8–14 March 1999, 30, 31.

27. Darraz, *Osama Bin Laden Recounts*; Miller, "Exclusive Interview with Osama Bin Laden"; "Kingdom Sends SR170m Supplies to Kosovars," *Arab News*, 26 June 1999; Ismail Khan, "Government Orders Arabs Expelled in Crackdown," *News*, 10 April 1993, 1; Rizq et al., "Osama Bin Laden, a Millionaire Financially Supporting Terrorism in Egypt and Saudi Arabia"; Najm, "The Destruction of the Base"; "Peshawar, Which Exports Terrorism to the World," *Al-Musawwar* no. 3754 (9 April 1993); James M. Dorsey et al., "Evidence Gap Slows Bid to Freeze Funds," *Wall Street Journal*, 30 November 2001, A12.

28. "Islamist Leader Bin Laden Urges Muslims to Kill Britons," *AFP*, 25 December 1998; Raymond Bonner, "Seeking Bombs? No, Wife, Arab Suspect Tells FBI," *New York Times*, 5 December 1998, A-4.

29. Benjamin Weiser, "U.S. Says It Can Tie Bin Laden to Embassy Bombings," *New York Times*, 8 October 1998, A-3; Jamal Mahmud Ismail, "Abu Hafs al-Masri: I Had Nothing to Do with What Happened to the Americans in Kenya," *Al-Sharq Al-Awsat*, 6 January 1999, 4; Karl Vick, "Assault on a U.S. Embassy: A Plot Both Wide and Deep," *Washington Post*, 23 November 1998, A-1.

30. Al-Ayyash and Najm, "Behind the Scenes of the American Strike against Bin Laden's Secret Cells; Balkan and Afghan Rings Plot against U.S. Interests"; Salah, "Secret of the Relationship between al-Zawahiri and Bin Laden"; Muhammed Salahiz, "Leader of 'Afghan Arabs' Killed in African State," *Al-Hayah*, 11 June 1996, 11; Muhammed Salah, "Ali al-Rashidi: The Egyptian

Policeman Who Paved the Way for 'Afghan Arabs' in Africa and Prepared Them to Take Revenge against the Americans," *Al-Hayah,* 30 September 1998, 1, 6; Khalid Duran, "Holy World War," *Gazeta Wyborcza,* 11–12 September 1999; Duran, "Cairo: A Torrent of Frightening Disclosures."

31. Muhammed Salah, "Egypt Supplies United States with Information about 'Abu Hafs,'" *Al-Hayah,* 6 December 1998, 5; Rahimullah Yusufzai, "Their Last Sanctuary," *News,* 26 January 1999; Salah, "Secret of the Relationship between al-Zawahiri and Bin Laden."

32. Darraz, *Osama Bin Laden Recounts*; "Secrets of Worldwide Campaign Chasing Osama Bin Laden," *Al-Watan Al-Arabi*; "Press Report on Presence of Osama Bin Laden and 'Afghan Arabs' in Yemen," *Al-Watan Al-Arabi,* 27 December 1996; Asaad, *Osama Bin Laden: The Whole Story,* 20; John F. Burns, "Yemen Links to Bin Laden Gnaw at FBI on *Cole* Inquiry," *New York Times,* 26 November 2000, A-1.

33. Ismail Khan, "Alleged Egyptian Terrorist Comments on Plot against Mubarak," *News,* 9 May 1996.

34. Various interviews with *Frontline Online,* April 1999; Miller, "Greetings America: My Name Is Osama Bin Laden"; Arnett, "Osama Bin Laden: The Interview."

35. Darraz, *Osama Bin Laden Recounts*; Fisk, "Muslim Leader Warns of New Assault on U.S. Forces."

36. Ibid.; Anthony Davis, "Targeting Bin Laden: The War on Terror Threatens Pakistan," *Asiaweek,* 4 September 1998; for summaries of the battle at Zhawar Khili, see Mohammed Yousef and Mark Adkins, *Bear Trap: Afghanistan's Untold Story* (Lahore, Pakistan: Jang Publishers Press, 1992), 166–73, and Mark Urban, *War in Afghanistan,* 2d ed. (New York: St. Martin's Press, 1990), 191–95.

37. "The World Number One Wanted Bin Laden: The Ally Who Became Enemy," *Al-Majallah.*

38. SAUDI-BINLADIN-GROUP.com

39. Darraz, *Osama Bin Laden Recounts*; "Philippine Military Says MILF Force Decimated," *Abante* (Internet version), 11 May 2000.

40. Macleod, "The Paladin of the Jihad." For accounts of the final battle for Khowst, see Bruce Richardson, "Khost Busters: Mujahedin Forces (Finally) Kick Puppets from Provincial Capital," *Soldier of Fortune* (November 1991): 60–65, 73; Ahmed Rashid, "The Khost Story," *Herald,* April 1991, 41–43; Salamat Ali, "Bargaining Chip," *Far Eastern Economic Review,* 18 April 1991, 21; Kesava Menon, "Fall of Khost," *Frontline,* 27 April 1991, 85–87.

41. "America's No. 1 Target: Osama Bin Laden," *Guardian* (Internet version), 26 August 1998.

42. Darraz, *Osama Bin Laden Recounts.*

43. Macleod, "The Paladin of the Jihad"; Kenneth R. Timmerman, "This Man Wants You Dead," *Reader's Digest* (July 1998): 50–57.

44. Miller, "Greetings America: My Name Is Osama Bin Laden."

45. Darraz, *Osama Bin Laden Recounts*; Fisk, "Anti-Soviet Warrior Puts His Army on the Road to Peace"; Rizq et al., "Osama Bin Laden, a Millionaire Financially Supporting Terrorism in Egypt and Saudi Arabia"; Jamal Khashuqji, "Al Qaeda Organization: Huge Aims without Programs or Cells," *Al-Hayah,* 12 October 1998, 6.

46. Khashuqji, "Al Qaeda Organization"; Al-Karim and al-Nur, "Interview with Saudi Businessman Osama Bin Laden."

47. Darraz, *Osama Bin Laden Recounts.*

48. "Secrets of the Worldwide Campaign Chasing Osama Bin Laden," *Al-Watan Al-Arabi*; "Confessions from the Last Leader of the Jihad Organization," *Rose al-Yusuf*, 24 February 1997; Najm, "The Destruction of the Base"; Darraz, *Osama Bin Laden Recounts.*

49. Darraz, *Osama Bin Laden Recounts.*

50. Ibid.

51. Ibid.; Hyman, "Arab Involvement in the Afghan War."

52. Pamela Constable and Khan Khamran, "U.S. Strike Is Blow to Pakistan's Rulers; Islamic Ire Upsets Shaky Balance," *Washington Post*, 21 August 1998, A-15.

53. Darraz, *Osama Bin Laden Recounts.*

54. Ibid.

55. Ibid.

56. Macleod, "The Paladin of the Jihad."

57. Darraz, *Osama Bin Laden Recounts.*

58. Khashuqji, "Al Qaeda Organization"; Emerson, "Abdallah Azzam: The Man before Osama Bin Laden"; Al-Ayyash and Salah, "Behind the Scenes of the American Strike against Bin Laden's Secret Cells"; Stephen Engelbert et al., "One Man and a Global Web of Violence," *New York Times*, 14 January 2001, A-1.

59. Darraz, *Osama Bin Laden Recounts.*

60. Najm, "The Destruction of the Base."

61. Ibid.

62. Darraz, *Osama Bin Laden Recounts.*

63. Ibid.

64. Abu Ubaydah's support for building an "Islamic Army" capable of fighting across the world is noted in al-Ayyash and Najm, "Behind the Scenes of the American Strike against Bin Laden's Secret Cells."

65. Khashuqji, "Al Qaeda Organization."

66. "Interview with Milt Bearden."

67. "Interview with Abdul Sattar."

68. Graham Fuller, "The Threat of Jihad," CNN/TIME IMPACT (Internet version), 7 April 1997.

69. Yousef and Adkins, *Bear Trap.*

70. Darraz, *Osama Bin Laden Recounts.*

71. Ahmad Muwaffaq Zaydan, "Bin Laden Fortifies His Position at Jalalabad and Will Respond with SAM and Stinger Missiles," *Al-Wasat Magazine*, 21 February 1999, 16, 17.

72. Darraz, *Osama Bin Laden Recounts.*

73. Dickey, "Making a Symbol of Terror."

74. Darraz, *Osama Bin Laden Recounts.*

75. Ibid.

76. Ibid.

77. Miller, "Greetings America: My Name Is Osama Bin Laden."

78. Tariq Masud, "The Arabs and Islam: The Troubled Search for Legiti-

macy," *Daedalus* 128, no. 2 (Spring 1999); "Avoiding Madeleine's Mine," *News* (Internet version), 2 February 2001; Huband, *Warriors of the Prophet*; Arnett, "Osama Bin Laden: The Interview."

79. Margolis, *War at the Top of the World.*

80. Mir, "Interview of Osama Bin Laden"; Fisk, "Anti-Soviet Warrior Puts His Army on the Road to Peace."

81. "Unattributed Biography of Bin Laden," *Frontline Online.*

82. Najm, "The Destruction of the Base."

83. Hyman, "Arab Involvement in the Afghan War"; Margolis, *War at the Top of the World.*

84. Timmerman, "This Man Wants You Dead."

85. Darraz, *Osama Bin Laden Recounts.*

86. Mahmud Sadiq, "Cairo Combats Islamists Overseas," *Al-Watan Al-Arabi,* 28 May 1999, 4–6; Weiner, "Blowback from the Afghan Battlefield," 52–55; Davis, "Foreign Combatants in Afghanistan," 327–31; Xavier Raufer, "Investigation into Terrorist Multinational," *VSD,* 3–9 September 1998, 16–23.

Chapter 8

1. Margolis, *War at the Top of the World,* 90.

2. Masud, "The Arabs and Islam."

3. "Interview with Sa'd al-Faqih," *Frontline Online*; Sanobar Shermatova, "Islamic Sword-Bearer," *Moskovskiyo Novosti* 4 (31 January 1999), 14.

4. Ibid.

5. "Interview with Milt Bearden," *Frontline Online.*

6. Fisk, "Anti-Soviet Warrior Puts His Army on the Road to Peace."

7. "Unattributed Biography of Bin Laden," *Frontline Online.*

8. "Expel the Mushikireen from the Arabian Peninsula," *Abdullah Azzam* Internet home page.

9. Fisk, "Anti-Soviet Warrior Puts His Army on the Road to Peace."

10. "Expel the Mushikireen from the Arabian Peninsula," *Abdullah Azzam* Internet home page.

11. "Unattributed Biography of Bin Laden," *Frontline Online*; "*Nida'ul Islam* Exclusive Interview with Osama Bin Laden: Of Jihad and Terror, the New Powder Keg in the Middle East," *Nida'ul Islam*; Burns, "Yemen Links to Bin Laden Gnaw at FBI on *Cole* Inquiry."

12. Sue Lackey, "Yemen: Unlikely Key to Western Security," *Jane's Intelligence Review* 11, no. 7 (July 1999), 24–29; Fisk, "Anti-Soviet Warrior Puts His Army on the Road to Peace."

13. Atwan, "Interview with Saudi Oppositionist Osama Bin Laden."

14. "Expel the Mushkireen from the Arabian Peninsula," *Abdullah Azzam* Internet home page; Raufer, "Investigation into Terrorist Multinational"; Frank Smyth and Jason Vest, "One Man's Private Jihad," *Village Voice,* 25 August 1998.

15. Amba, "Saudi Militant's Wish: To Die Fighting America."

16. Michael Georgy, "Saudi Dissident Bin Laden Seen as a Serious Threat," Reuters, 25 February 1997.

17. "Interview with Sa'id Aburish," *Frontline Online*; Rashid, *Taliban, Mili-*

tant Islam, Oil and Fundamentalism in Central Asia, 133.

18. Georgy, "Saudi Dissident Bin Laden Seen as a Serious Threat."

19. "Interview with Sa'ad al-Faqih, *Frontline Online;* Nawaf E. Obaid, "The Power of Saudi Arabi's Islamic Leader," *Middle East Quarterly* 6, no. 3 (September 1999): 51–58.

20. Ibid.

21. Timmerman, "This Man Wants You Dead."

22. Amba, "Saudi Militant's Wish: To Die Fighting America."

23. "Interview with Sa'd al-Faqih," *Frontline Online.*

24. Wright, "Saudi Dissident a Prime Suspect in Blast."

25. Tariq Masud, "Desert Storm," *New Republic,* 28 December 1998.

26. Wright, "Saudi Dissident a Prime Suspect in Blast"; "Osama Bin Laden, Letter from Kandahar," Associated Press.

27. Bernard Lewis, *Foreign Affairs,* November/December 1998, 15–16.

28. "Interview with Sa'd al-Faqih," *Frontline Online;* Fisk, "Muslim Leader Warns of New Assaults on U.S. Forces."

29. "Americans Are Paper Tigers," *Der Spiegel,* 17 August 1998.

30. Ibid.; "*Nida'ul Islam* Exclusive Interview with Osama Bin Laden," *Nida'ul Islam;* Advice and Reformation Committee, "Communiqué No. 19: The Saudi Regime and the Recurrent Tragedies of the Pilgrims"; "MIRA Bulletin No. 253," *Movement for Islamic Reform in Arabia.*

31. "Americans Are Paper Tigers," *Der Spiegel.*

32. Ibid.

33. "Unattributed Biography of Bin Laden," *Frontline Online;* "Biography of Osama Bin Laden," Islamic Observation Center.

34. "Biography of Osama Bin Laden," Islamic Observation Center; Obaid, "The Power of Saudi Arabi's Islamic Leaders."

35. Fisk, "Muslim Leader Warns of New Assaults on U.S. Forces."

36. "*Nida'ul Islam* Exclusive Interview with Osama Bin Laden," *Nida'ul Islam;* Ahmed al-Huni, "If Faysal Were Alive," *Al-Arab Al-Alamiyah,* 31 October 2000, 1.

37. "Declaration of Jihad against the Americans," *Al-Islah.*

38. Ibid.; "Unattributed Biography of Bin Laden," *Frontline Online.*

39. "Biography of Osama Bin Laden," Islamic Observation Center; "Interview with Sa'd al-Faqih," *Frontline Online;* Dickey, "Making a Symbol of Terror"; Atwan, "Interview with Saudi Oppositionist Osama Bin Laden."

Chapter 9

1. Fisk, "Arab Rebel Leader Warns British: 'Get Out of the Gulf.'"

2. "Unattributed Biography of Osama Bin Laden," *Frontline Online.*

3. Salamat Ali, "Cause and Effect," *Far Eastern Economic Review,* 23 May 1991, 24.

4. "Unattributed Biography of Osama Bin Laden," *Frontline Online.*

5. Najm, "The Destruction of the Base."

6. Ikram Sehgel, "Osama Bin Laden Syndrome: Freedom Fighter or Terrorist?" *Nation* (Lahore edition, Internet version), 29 August 1998; "Unattributed Biography of Osama Bin Laden," *Frontline Online.*

7. "Interview with Sa'd al-Faqih," *Frontline Online*; Cooley, *Unholy Wars*, 222; Yusufzai, "World's Most Wanted Terrorist"; Raufer, "Investigation into Terrorist Multinational."

8. "Secrets of the Worldwide Campaign Chasing Osama Bin Laden," *Al-Watan Al-Arabi.*

9. Al-Karim and al-Nur, "Interview with Saudi Businessman Osama Bin Laden," 4.

10. "Secrets of the Worldwide Campaign Chasing Osama Bin Laden," *Al-Watan Al-Arabi.*

11. U.S. State Department, "Fact Sheet on Osama Bin Laden"; Macleod, "The Paladin of the Jihad"; Paul Hoi, "Bin Laden, the Moneyman behind International Terrorism," *Berlinske Tidende,* 9 September 1998, 8; Feuer, "Jihad, Inc.: The Bin Laden Network of Companies Exporting Terror"; "Part One of a Series of Reports on Bin Laden's Life in Sudan," *Al-Quds Al-Arabi* (Internet version), 24 November 2001, 13.

12. Feuer, "Jihad, Inc.: The Bin Laden Network of Companies Exporting Terror"; Shermatova, "Islamic Sword-Bearer."

13. James Bennet, "U.S. Cruise Missiles Strike Sudan and Afghan Targets Tied to Terrorist Network," *New York Times,* 21 August 1998; "Sudan Financier Monopolizes Exports," *African Economic Digest,* 29 August 1994; Samia Nakul, "Sudan and West at Odds over Terrorism Charges," Reuters, 5 July 1995.

14. Fisk, "Anti-Soviet Warrior Puts His Army on the Road to Peace."

15. "Unattributed Biography of Osama Bin Laden," *Frontline Online.*

16. Rizq, "Jihad Unilaterally Won Over Bin Laden, While the Group Was Content with Financial Support"; Mark Bowden, *Black Hawk Down. A Study of Modern War* (New York: Atlantic Monthly Press, 1999), 110.

17. Leppard et al., "The Global Terrorist."

18. Bennet, "U.S. Cruise Missiles Strike Sudan and Afghan Targets Tied to Terrorist Network"; Tim Weiner and James Risen, "Long Running Dispute on Sudan Marked Counterattack Plans," *New York Times News Service,* 21 September 1998.

19. Guido Olimpio, "Saddam's Latest Challenge: Refuge for Osama Bin Laden," *Corriere della Sera* (Internet version), 17 September 1998; Guido Olimpio, "A Secret Pact with Bin Laden, the Terror Shaykh," *Corriere della Sera* (Internet version), 28 December 1998, 7.

20. Douglas Waller, "Inside the Hunt for Osama," *Time,* 21 December 1998, 32; Paul Mann, "Bin Laden Linked to Nuclear Effort," *Aviation Week and Space Technology,* 12 October 1998, 58.

21. Waller, "Inside the Hunt for Osama."

22. Mufid Abd-al-Rahim, "Bin Laden's New York Activities," *Al-Watan Al-Arabi,* 20 November 1998, 18–22.

23. Dickey, "Making a Symbol of Terror."

24. Abd-al-Rahim, "Bin Laden's New York Activities."

25. "Report on Bin Laden's Activities, Wealth," *Al-Watan Al-Arabi,* 23–28.

26. Daniel Pearl, "In Sudanese Bombing, 'Evidence' Depends on Who Is Viewing It," *Wall Street Journal,* 28 October 1998.

27. "Report on Bin Laden's Activities, Wealth," *Al-Watan Al-Arabi.*

28. Steven Emerson, "Unholy War," *New Republic,* 14 and 21 September 1998, 22–23.

29. Frank Smyth, "Culture Shock," 22–25.

30. "Secrets of the Worldwide Campaign Chasing Osama Bin Laden," *Al-Watan Al-Arabi;* Rizq et al., "Osama Bin Laden, a Millionaire Financially Supporting Terrorism in Egypt and Saudi Arabia."

31. "Bin Laden Trained Ugandans," *New Vision,* 1 September 1998, 1; Feuer, "Jihad, Inc.: The Bin Laden Network of Companies Exporting Terror."

32. Adil al-Jawjari, "'Terrorist' Bin Laden Returns to Yemen," *Al-Watan Al-Arabi,* 20 March 1998, 32–34.

33. Ibid.; Lufti Shatarah and Hammid Munsir, "Twenty Jihad Organization Members Arrested in Yemen," *Al-Sharq Al-Awsat,* 28 December 1992, 1, 4.

34. "Report on Bin Laden's Activities, Wealth," *Al-Watan Al-Arabi.*

35. "Murky Information from Source 'CS-1,'" *Der Spiegel,* 19 October 1998; Bonner, "Seeking Bombs? No, Wife, Arab Suspect Tells FBI," A-4.

36. Weiser, "U.S. Says It Can Tie Bin Laden to Embassy Bombings"; John J. Goldman, "Accused Was Businessman, Not Terrorist, Lawyer Says," *Los Angeles Times,* 4 May 2001.

37. Bonner, "Seeking Bombs? No, Wife, Arab Suspect Tells FBI"; "Saudi Arabia Denies Citizen Told U.S. of New York Bomb Plot," AP-Dow Jones, 3 August 1997; "Weekly Says Bin Laden Financial Manager to Testify," *AFP,* 8 December 1998.

38. David S. Cloud, "U.S. Officials Charge Bin Laden and Aide with Conspiracy in Embassy Bombings," *Wall Street Journal,* 5 November 1998, A-6; Al-Ayyash and Najm, "Behind the Scenes of the American Strike against Bin Laden's Secret Cells."

39. "Secrets of the Worldwide Campaign Chasing Osama Bin Laden," *Al-Watan Al-Arabi.*

40. Salahiz, "Leader of 'Afghan Arabs' Killed in African State"; Al-Ayyash and Najm, "Behind the Scenes of the American Strike against Bin Laden's Secret Cells."

41. Hamoud Mounassar and Mohammed Attar, "Yemen Hostages Recover from Horrific Slaughter for Four Friends," *AFP,* 30 December 1998.

42. Al-Ayyash and Najm, "Behind the Scenes of the American Strike against Bin Laden's Secret Cells."

43. Al-Qaysi, "U.S.-Yemen-Bin Laden Relations," 24–26.

44. "Americans Are Paper Tigers." *Der Spiegel;* Al-Qaysi, "U.S.-Yemen-Bin Laden Relations"; Vick, "Assault on a U.S. Embassy: A Plot Both Wide and Deep"; Al-Ayyash and Najm, "Behind the Scenes of the American Strike against Bin Laden's Secret Cells."

45. Leppard et al., "The Global Terrorist."

46. Al-Jawjari, "'Terrorist' Bin Laden Returns to Yemen."

47. Leppard et al., "The Global Terrorist."

48. Weiser, "U.S. Says It Can Tie Bin Laden to Embassy Bombings"; Vick, "Assault on a U.S. Embassy: A Plot Both Wide and Deep"; "The Saudi Islamic

Opposition 'Advice and Reform Commission' Headed by Shaykh Osama Bin Laden Has Announced the Opening of an Office in London," *Al-Quds Al-Arabi*, 8 August 1994, 1.

49. Vick, "Assault on a U.S. Embassy: A Plot Both Wide and Deep"

50. Al-Ayyash and Najm, "Behind the Scenes of the American Strike against Bin Laden's Secret Cells."

51. Bonner, "Seeking Bombs? No, Wife, Arab Suspect Tells FBI."

52. Michael Grunwald, "Bombing Suspect Alleges He Was Bullied into Confession," *Washington Post*, 4 September 1998, A-1, A-9; Leppard et al., "The Global Terrorist."

53. "Bin Laden Took Advantage of the Situation," *Al-Sharq Al-Awsat*, 3.

54. Al-Ayyash and Najm, "Behind the Scenes of the American Strike against Bin Laden's Secret Cells."

55. "Press Report on Presence of Osama Bin Laden and 'Afghan Arabs' in Yemen," *Al-Watan Al-Arabi*.

56. Rizq, "Jihad Unilaterally Won Over Bin Laden, While the Group Was Content with Financial Support," 26–27.

57. Jeff Gerth and Judith Miller, "Terror Money: A Special Report; Funds for Terrorists Traced to Persons, Gulf Businesses," *New York Times*, 14 August 1996; Cathy Canares and Cynthia D. Balana, "Spy Chief Claims Info on Bin Laden in Mindanao," *Philippine Daily Inquirer* (Internet version), 25 August 1998; "CIA Report on Bin Laden's Filipino Links," *Al-Sharq Al-Awsat*; Al-Jawjari, "'Terrorist' Bin Laden Returns to Yemen"; "el. Ma.," "Osama Bin Laden in Tirana Offices," *Gazeta Shqiptare*, 4 November 1998, 12; "Al-Alfi Claims Qatari Connection to Egyptian Militants," *Al-Ahram Weekly*, 13 January 1998; "Secrets of the Worldwide Campaign Chasing Osama Bin Laden," *Al-Watan Al-Arabi*.

58. Gamal Essam al-Din, "El-Alfi Claims Doha Connection," *Al-Ahram Weekly*, 8 January 1998, 3.

59. "Osama Bin Laden: Muslims Who Live in Europe Are Kafirs," *Rose al-Yusuf*, 9 December 1996.

60. Al-Jawjari, "'Terrorist' Bin Laden Returns to Yemen."

61. Cynthia D. Balana, "Is the U.S. Central Intelligence Agency Involved in the Terroristic Activities Here of the Abu Sayyaf," *Philippine Daily Inquirer*, 18 April 1995, 1, 11.

62. "Unattributed Biography of Osama Bin Laden," *Frontline Online*.

63. "Confessions from the Last Leader of the Jihad Organization," *Rose al-Yusuf*; "Eyewitness View of Bin Laden's Camps," *Terrorism and Security Monitor* (September 1998).

64. "A Revealing Trove in Afghanistan," *New York Times* (Editorial), 19 March 2002.

65. Ranstorp, "Interpreting the Broader Context and Meaning of Bin Laden's Fatwa."

66. For short discussions of the nature of urban warfare during the Afghan jihad, see Scott R. McMichael, *Stumbling Bear: Soviet Military Performance in Afghanistan* (London: Brassey's, 1991), 34, 59, and Yousef and Adkin, *Bear Trap*, 142–57.

67. Salah, "Secret of the Relationship between al-Zawahiri and Bin Laden."

Chapter 10

1. Fisk, "Anti-Soviet Warrior Puts His Army on the Road to Peace."

2. Miller, "Greetings America: My Name Is Osama Bin Laden."

3. Mark Matthews, "Bombing Probe Slowly Traces Tortuous Path of Terrorism," *Baltimore Sun*, 18 October 1998, A-1.

4. Mir, "Interview of Osama Bin Laden."

5. Darraz, *Osama Bin Laden Recounts.*

6. Miller, "Greetings America: My Name Is Osama Bin Laden."

7. Atwan, "Interview with Saudi Oppositionist Osama Bin Laden."

8. "Secrets of the Worldwide Campaign Chasing Osama Bin Laden," *Al-Watan Al-Arabi*; "A Strange Sudanese," *Le Point*; James Risen, "Bin Laden Was Target of U.S. Raid Plans since Spring," *New York Times* Web site, 6 September 1998; Radio Monte Carlo, 30 December 1992.

9. U.S. State Department, "Patterns of Global Terrorism, 1992," Washington, DC, April 1993, 20.

10. Shiraz, "May 1998 Interview with Osama Bin Laden."

11. Shatarah and Munsir, "Twenty Jihad Organization Members Arrested in Yemen," 1, 4.

12. Ibid.; "Report on Egyptian Fundamentalists," *Al-Sharq Al-Awsat*, 18 July 1999, 6; "Press Report on Presence of Osama Bin Laden and 'Afghan Arabs' in Yemen," *Al-Watan Al-Arabi.*

13. Cloud, "U.S. Officials Charge Bin Laden and Aide with Conspiracy in Embassy Bombings," A-6.

14. Michael Grunwald, "4 Followers of Bin Laden Indicted in Plot to Kill Americans," *Washington Post*, 8 October 1998.

15. Mir, "Interview of Osama Bin Laden."

16. Grunwald, "4 Followers of Bin Laden Indicted in Plot to Kill Americans."

17. Khan, "Osama's Narrow Escape, Camp Hits Reported."

18. Bowden, *Black Hawk Down.*

19. Khan, "Osama's Narrow Escape, Camp Hits Reported"; Benjamin Weiser, "Papers Shed Light on Informer's Role in Terror Inquiry," *New York Times*, 23 December 2000, A-26.

20. Miller, "Greetings America: My Name Is Osama Bin Laden."

21. "Bin Laden Urges Jihad and Expulsion of U.S. Forces from Gulf," *Al-Quds Al-Arabi*; "Bin Laden Warns CIA against Attempts to Arrest Him," *Al Majd*, 4 August 1997, 1.

22. Mir, "Interview of Osama Bin Laden"; Miller, "Greetings America: My Name Is Osama Bin Laden."

23. Ibid.

24. Ismail, "Abu Hafs al-Masri: I had Nothing to Do with What Happened to the Americans in Kenya."

25. Khamran Khan, "Palestinian Unveils Osama's International War against U.S.; Bombing Suspect Says His Men Hit Targets from Somalia to the Philippines," *News*, 19 August 1998; "Osama Bin Laden, Letter from Kandahar," Associated Press.

26. James Bruce, "Middle East: Arab Veterans of the Afghan War—Trained

Forces in Waiting," *Jane's Defense Weekly,* 1 April 1995; Raymond Burgos, "Mindanao Cops Have Photos of Saudi Tycoon," *Philippine Daily Inquirer* (Internet version), 25 August 1998; "RP Tightens Security on Terrorist Target," *Philippine Daily Inquirer* (Internet version), 25 August 1998; "Philippine Forces on Alert after Killing of Muslim Extremist Leader," *AFP,* 19 December 1998; Andrew Phillips and Barry Came, "The Prime Suspect," *Mclean's,* 24 January 2000, 27.

27. Salahiz, "Leader of 'Afghan Arabs' Killed in African State."

28. Rizq, "Jihad Unilaterally Won Over Bin Laden."

29. Julian Bolger, "Vengeful Islamic Guerrillas Threaten British Troops Bound for Bosnia," *Guardian,* 28 November 1995, 2.

30. Bruce, "Middle East: Arab Veterans of the Afghan War — Trained Forces in Waiting"; U.S. State Department, "Patterns of Global Terrorism, 1994," 17–18; "Reports on the Escape of Fundamentalists to Iraq for Fear of Being Arrested. Jordan Government Source: The Afghan Arabs to Washington Is Premature," *Al-Quds Al-Arabi,* 20 December 1999, 7; "Bombing Suspects' Organizations, Ties Detailed," *Al-Bilad,* 4 May 1994, 5; "Fresh Arrests among Jordanian Afghans," *Al-Bilad,* 4 May, 1994, 4; "Indictment for January Bombing Case Details Plans, Tactics," *Al-Dustur,* 8 July 1994, 5.

31. Georgi Milkov, "How the Top Terrorist Is Extending His Tentacles into Bulgaria," *Chasa,* 21 March 1999, 7; John Pomfret, "Bosnian Officials Involved in Arms Trade Tied to Radical States," *Washington Post,* 22 September 1996, A-26.

32. U.S. State Department, "Patterns of Global Terrorism, 1994," 15; U.S. State Department, "Patterns of Global Terrorism, 1995," 17–18; Engelbert et al., "One Man and a Global Web of Violence."

33. U.S. State Department, "Patterns of Global Terrorism, 1994," 31.

34. "A Strange Sudanese," *Le Point*; "Secrets of the Worldwide Campaign Chasing Osama Bin Laden," *Al-Watan Al-Arabi,* MENA, 31 December 1992.

35. Pomfret, "Bosnian Officials Involved in Arms Trade Tied to Radical States"; Salahiz, "Leader of 'Afghan Arabs' Killed in African State"; Bennet, "U.S. Cruise Missiles Strike Sudan and Afghan Targets Tied to Terrorist Network."

36. Bennet, "U.S. Cruise Missiles Strike Sudan and Afghan Targets Tied to Terrorist Network."

37. U.S. State Department, "Patterns of Global Terrorism, 1993," 28; Miller, "Exclusive Interview with Osama Bin Laden."

38. U.S. State Department, "Patterns of Global Terrorism, 1993," 6.

39. U.S. State Department, "Patterns of Global Terrorism, 1994," 18.

40. "Fez Court Examines Man Charged with Marrakech Hotel Attack," MAP Television, 24 September 1994; "Investigation Launched into Killing of Tourists," RTM Television Network, 24 August 1994; Serge Raffy, "Terrorism; Revelations on the Marrakech Slaughter; How the Islamists Recruit in France," *Le Nouvel Observateur* (October 1994), 40–44; Jean-Loup Reverier et al., "Islamic Killers: Leads, Networks," *Le Point,* 26 August 1995, 24–31.

41. "Philippine Forces on Alert after Killing of Muslim Extremist Leader," *AFP.*

42. "Secrets of the Worldwide Campaign Chasing Osama Bin Laden," *Al-Watan Al-Arabi.*

43. Bennet, "U.S. Cruise Missiles Strike Sudan and Afghan Targets Tied to Terrorist Network"; Risen, "Bin Laden Was Target of U.S. Raid Plans since Spring"; Ali Mu'in, "European Security Organs Get Ready to Dismantle Bin Laden's Network," *Al-Zaman,* 28 August 1998, 1.

44. U.S. State Department, "Patterns of Global Terrorism, 1994," 4.

45. International Policy Institute for Counterterrorism (Internet), 26 July 1998; Khalid Sharaf-al-Din, "Surprises from the Trial of the Largest International Terrorist Group in Egypt," *Al-Sharq Al-Awsat,* 6 March 1999, 5; "'Confessions' of Mubarak Plot Suspects," *Al-Watan Al-Arabi,* 21 June 1996.

46. Adrian Levy and Kathy Scott-Clark, "Bin Laden's Mercenaries Gather for Kashmir's Jihad," *Sunday Times* (Internet version), 4 October 1998; Roger Howard, "Wrath of Islam: The HUA Analyzed," *Jane's Intelligence Review* 9, no. 10 (October 1997): 466–68.

47. "Secrets of the Worldwide Campaign Chasing Osama Bin Laden," *Al-Watan Al-Arabi;* "French Sources: Bin Laden Financed All Operations in French Cities Last Year," *Al-Ahram,* 4 January 1996; Andreu Mansera, "Algiers Accuses the Saudi Millionaire Bin Laden of Paying GIA Terrorists," *El Pais* (Internet version), 8 October 1998; Macleod, "The Paladin of the Jihad"; Herve Brusini, "Police Believe GIA Orchestrator of Paris Attacks Identified," France-2 Television Network, 26 December 1995.

48. U.S. State Department, "Patterns of Global Terrorism, 1994," 9; Igor Alborghetti, "The Time Bomb in Rijeka," *Globus,* 3 October 1995, 2–4; Muhammed Salah and Kamil al-Tawil, "Egyptian 'Group' Threatens to 'Retaliate' against Croatia," *Al-Hayah,* 23 September 1996, 1, 6; Muhammed Salah, "Vanguards of Conquest Threaten Croatia with Revenge if It Extradites al-Qasimi," *Al-Hayah,* 25 September 1995, 1, 6; Muhammed Salah, "Islamic Group: Al-Qasimi Still in Croatia; His Extradition to Egypt Would Not Pass without Retaliation," *Al-Hayah,* 26 September 1999, 1, 6.

49. U.S. State Department, "Patterns of Global Terrorism, 1995," 22, 38; Macleod, "The Paladin of Jihad"; Arnett, "Osama Bin Laden: The Interview."

50. MENA, 28 December 1996; "Press Report on Presence of Osama Bin Laden and 'Afghan Arabs' in Yemen," *Al-Watan Al-Arabi.*

51. Islamic Observation Center Web site, 10 September 1999; Gall and de Waal, *Chechnya, Calamity in the Caucasus,* 308.

52. Sharaf-al-Din, "Surprises from the Trial of the Largest International Terrorist Group in Egypt"; Mahmud al-Hadari, "Al-Jihad Foiled Attempt on Mubarak Motorcade Detailed," *Al-Ahali,* 20 December 1995, 1, 4; Nabil Abu-Sayt, "Report on Egypt Islamic Jihad," *Al-Sharq Al-Awsat,* 6 February 2000, 6.

53. "Press Report on Presence of Osama Bin Laden and 'Afghan Arabs' in Yemen," *Al-Watan Al-Arabi;* Smyth, "Culture Shock."

54. Atwan, "Interview with Saudi Oppositionist Osama Bin Laden."

55. Ibid.; Edward Shirley, "The Etiquette of Killing Mr. Bin Laden," *Wall Street Journal* (Op-Ed), 27 August 1998; "Sudan: Two Suspects in February Attack on Mosque Confess on Television," BBC Monitoring Service, 14 March 1994.

56. Macleod, "The Paladin of Jihad."

57. "Interview with Sa'd al-Faqih," *Frontline Online;* Weaver, "Blowback"; Colum Lynch, "Plan to Kill Bin Laden Described in Court," *Washington Post,* 21

February 2001, A-19; Benjamin Weiser, "Plot to Kill Bin Laden Disclosed," *New York Times,* 21 February 2001.

58. "Unattributed Biography of Osama Bin Laden," *Frontline Online.*

59. "Prisons: The Dwelling of Our Scholars," *Nida'ul Islam* 21 (December 1997/January 1998).

60. Atwan, "Interview with Saudi Oppositionist Osama Bin Laden."

61. Ibid.

62. Ibid.; Yusufzai, "World's Most Wanted Terrorist"; Robert Fisk, "Talks with Osama Bin Laden: How an Afghan 'Freedom Fighter' Became 'America's Public Enemy Number One,'" *Nation* 267, no. 8 (21 September 1998); "Bin Laden Begins the Struggle," *Al Sha'b* (Internet version), 15 September 2001.

63. Arnett, "Osama Bin Laden: The Interview."

64. "Bin Laden's Shadowy Empire," *Indigo Publications Intelligence Newsletter,* 28 November 1996; Naim, "Osama Bin Laden, the Banker of the Jihad."

65. Sudan was placed on the U.S. government's list of state sponsors of terrorism in August 1993. U.S. State Department, "Patterns of Global Terrorism, 1993," 25; Naim, "Osama Bin Laden, the Banker of the Jihad."

66. "An Interview with the Secretary of the Sudanese Information Ministry," *Nida'ul Islam* (Internet version), 17 (February/March 1997).

67. Naim, "Osama Bin Laden, the Banker of the Jihad."

68. "Report on the Threat to Arab Countries by Terrorist Bin Laden," *Sawt al-Mar'ah.*

69. Shiraz, "May 1998 Interview with Bin Laden Reported."

Chapter 11

1. Ismail Khan, "'Muslim Extremist Financier' Reportedly Arrives," *News,* 11 July 1996, 12; "Has the Countdown Begun in the Adventure of Osama Bin Laden?" *Al-Watan Al-Arabi;* "Sanctions against Afghanistan: UN Must Refrain from Acting as a U.S. Appendage," *Al-Akhbar,* 18 October 1999, 6; Jabir al-Harmi, "Interview with Gulbuddin Hekmatyar," *Al-Ittihad,* 29 August 1999, 11; "Unattributed Biography of Osama Bin Laden," *Frontline Online.*

2. Voice of Radio Shariah Network, 2 January 1999; "Afghan Opposition Leader Says Bin Laden Harms Islam," Associated Press, 28 October 1998.

3. Rory McCarthy, "Taleban's Superior Forces Threaten Foe's Supply Route," *Washington Times,* 16 December 2000, A-8; Raffaelo Ciriello, "I Will Give You Bin Laden, He Is Only a Terrorist," *Famiglia Christiana,* 4 March 2001, 68–69.

4. Sebastian Junger, "The Lion in Winter," *National Geographic Adventure* (March-April 2001): 90; James Warren, "Same Battle, New Foe," *Chicago Tribune,* 2 March 2001; Reuel Marc Gerecht, "Taking Sides in Afghanistan," *New York Times* (Op-Ed), 8 March 2001.

5. Esther Oxford and Khuja Buhawadin, *The Sunday Times* (Internet version), 25 March 2001; Steven Coates, "EU Invitation to Masood Will Infuriate Taliban, Pakistan: Analysts," *AFP,* 2 April 2001; "Afghan Military Commander Masood Received at French National Assembly," *AFP,* 4 April 2001; Marc Delpho, "We Will Keep Fighting," *Le Seoir,* 5 April 2001; J.-P. P., "Masood, the Paris Appeal," *Liberation* (Internet version), 5 April 2001; Amir Taheri, "A Lion in

Paris," *Al-Sharq Al-Awsat,* 5 April 2001, 5; "Belgium Foreign Minister Says Masood Better Alternative for Afghanistan," RTBF La Premiere Radio, 7 April 2001; Adrien Jaulmes, "Masood Gets Support from European Parliament," *Le Figaro,* 6 April 2001, 3.

6. Tim McGirk, "The Taliban Allows a Top 'Sponsor' to Stay in Afghanistan," *Time,* 16 December 1997; "Bin Laden Hiding at Taliban Military Base," *AFP,* 17 February 1997; "Taliban Ask Bin Laden to Halt Anti-Saudi Activities," *Nation,* 27 March 1997, 1, 11; Julian West, "Western Spies Find Bin Laden in Afghanistan," *Sunday Telegraph* (Internet version), 21 March 1999.

7. "Has the Countdown Begun in the Adventure of Osama Bin Laden?" *Al-Watan Al-Arabi;* Sarhardi Zia, "Assassination Attempt on Osama Bin Laden Foiled in Afghanistan," *Muslimedia International* (Internet version), 1 May 1997; Jihad Salah, "Story of Attempt to Assassinate Bin Laden in Jalalabad," *Al-Watan Al-Arabi,* 18 April 1997; Dilip Hiro, "The 'Afghan Arabs' — America Turns on Its Creation," *Middle East International* 582 (4 September 1998): 17–19.

8. "Unattributed Biography of Osama Bin Laden," *Frontline Online;* Sarhadi Zia, "Assassination Attempt on Osama Bin Laden Foiled in Afghanistan," *Muslimmedia International* (Internet version), 1 May 1997; "Saudi Sought in Bombings Moves to Afghan Militia Capital," *Washington Post,* 11 April 1997; Ahmad Muwaffaq Zaydan, "Bin Laden in Kandahar to Keep Him Away from Media, and 'Out of Concern for His Safety,'" *Al-Hayah,* 8 April 1997, 1, 6.

9. "Unattributed Biography of Osama Bin Laden," *Frontline Online.*

10. Salah, "Secret of the Relationship between al-Zawahiri and Bin Laden," 30, 31.

11. "Interview with Sa'd al-Faqih," *Frontline Online.*

12. "Unattributed Biography of Osama Bin Laden," *Frontline Online;* "Interview with Sa'd al-Faqih," *Frontline Online.*

13. Rahimullah Yusufzai, "A Cult Hero Is Born," *News* (Internet version), 1 September 1998.

14. "America's No. 1 Target: Osama Bin Laden," *Guardian.*

15. Hamid Mir, "Osama Bin Laden Dares U.S. Commandos to Come to Afghanistan," *Pakistan,* 6 July 1997, 1, 7.

16. "Osama Says Taliban Rejected Billions for Arrest," *Ausaf,* 1, 7.

17. "Bin Laden's Poem," *Ausaf,* 3 March 2001, 1, 7; "Taliban Chief Criticizes Outside Pressure on Afghan Issue," *AFP,* 23 September 1998.

18. "Taliban Chief Criticizes Outside Pressure on Afghan Issue," *AFP.*

19. Zaydan, "Bin Laden Fortifies His Position at Jalalabad and Will Respond with SAM and Stinger Missiles"; "Interview (Written) of Osama Bin Laden," *Ghazi Magazine.*

20. Zaydan, "Bin Laden Fortifies His Position at Jalalabad and Will Respond with SAM and Stinger Missiles."

21. Ibid.; "Interview (Written) of Osama Bin Laden," *Ghazi Magazine.*

22. Ahmad Muwaffaq Zaydan and Turki al-Dahkil, "New U.S. Strike Expected because of Bin Laden," *Al-Hayah,* 21 October 1998, 1; "Afghanistan Is a Free and Nonaligned Country," *Hewad* (Editorial), 17 July 1999, 1. 2.

23. "Taliban Will Not Hand Over Bin Laden for the Following Reasons," *Al-Quds Al-Arabi* (Editorial), 17 November 1999, 19; Steven Levine et al., "Help-

ing Hand," *Newsweek*, 13 October 1997, 22.

24. "Biography of Osama Bin Laden," Islamic Observation Center; "Laden to Divert Iranian River to Afghanistan," *Nation*, 22 July 1997, 1.

25. Mir, "Interview of Osama Bin Laden"; Miller, "Greetings America: My Name Is Osama Bin Laden."

26. "Bin Laden Says Ties with Taliban 'Ideological,'" *Al-Jazirah*, 13 February 1999.

27. "Osama Speaks on Hijrah and the Islamic State," *Al-Jihaad Newsletter* (Supporters of Shahriah Web site), 4 (22 June 2000); "Unattributed Biography of Osama Bin Laden," *Frontline Online*.

28. "Unattributed Biography of Osama Bin Laden," *Frontline Online*.

29. Najm, "The Destruction of the Base."

30. Ahmed Sadiq, "Interview with Taliban Official Spokesman Wakil Ahmed Muttawakil," *Al-Watan Al-Arabi*, 23 July 1999, 20–22; "Bin Laden Took Advantage of the Situation," *Al-Sharq Al-Awsat*; Ahmad Muwaffaq Zaydan, "350 of Bin Laden's Men Fighting North of Kabul," *Al-Hayah*, 14 July 1997, 1, 6.

31. Zaydan, "350 of Bin Laden's Men Fighting North of Kabul."

32. Lynch, "Taliban Hoping for a Way to Bid Adieu to Bin Laden."

33. "Bin Laden Building New Bases in the Khandahar Area," *Sunday Telegraph* (Internet version), 4 October 1998.

34. Ahmed Rashid, "Taliban Prepares for 'Decisive' Attack with Help of Militants," *Washington Times*, 22 July 1999, A-13; "Back to the Taliban — Taliban Are Again Proving Afghanistan Pundits Wrong," *News* (Editorial; Internet version), 26 September 2000.

35. Iftikhar Mishwani, "India and Israel Helping Northern Alliance, an Exclusive Interview with Afghanistan's Information Minister, Mullah Amir Khan Motaqi," *Pakistan*, 30 August 1999, 9, 11; Sajjad Tarakzai, "Taliban, Hizb-e Islami Hold Talks in Peshawar, Both Groups Agree for Reconciliation," *Jang*, 8 May 2001, 1, 7.

36. Ahmad Muwaffaq Zaydan, "Bin Laden Mediates with Afghan Opposition to Stop Imminent Offensive against Taliban," *Al-Hayah*, 13 March 1998, 8.

37. Aimal Khan, "Osama Said Mediating between Hekmatyar, Sayyaf," *Frontier Post*, 29 December 1998, 1, 7.

38. Ahmad Muwaffaq Zaydan, "Field Commanders Threaten Taliban They Will Withdraw if Taliban Extradite Bin Laden," *Al-Hayah*, 22 January 2001, 1, 6.

39. Jamal Mahmud Ismail, "Mullah Omar's Advisers Tell *Al-Sharaq Al-Awsat*: Taliban Considers U.S. Reward for Bin Laden's Arrest a Terrorist Action," *Al-Sharq Al-Awsat*, 23 July 1999, 5.

40. Mahmud Sadiq, "Interview with Taliban Official Spokesman Wakil Ahman Mutawakil," *Al-Watan Al-Arabi*, 23 July 1999, 20–22.

41. Ibid.; "Taliban, JUI Threaten AmCits, Any Country Supporting Attacks," *Khabrain*, 2 November 2000, 3, 11; Tahir Khalil, "Afghan Foreign Minister Promised 'Crushing Reply' if U.S. Attacks," *Jang*, 27 October 2000, 7, 8.

42. "Bin Laden Congratulates Pakistan on Its Possession of Nuclear Weapon," *Al-Quds Al-Arabi*, 1 June 1998, 2; Shiraz, "May 1998 Interview with Bin Laden Reported."

43. Yusufzai, "World's Most Wanted Terrorist"; "Osama Says Taliban

Rejected US Billions for Arrest," *Ausaf.*

44. Qari Naved Masood Hashimi, "Osama Bin Laden—A Man as Strong as a Rock," *Pakistan,* 10 June 1998, 10.

45. Ahmad Aziz-ud-Din, "Jehadi Organizations and the Nation-State," *Nation* (Lahore edition, Internet version), 10 February 2000; Zahid Hussain, "In the Shadow of Terrorism," *Newsline,* 1–29 February 2000, 16–19, 21, 29; Margolis, *War at the Top of the World,* 39, 43.

46. Bin Laden's letter is quoted in Ahmad Muwaffaq Zaydan, "Bin Laden's Gifts Enable Him to Infiltrate Pakistani Media," *Al-Hayah,* 12 November 1998, 6.

47. Raja Ashgar, "Bin Laden Sparks Pakistan Duel," METIMES.com, 98–136; "Bin Laden Gave Sharif One Billion Rupees," *Al-Akhbar,* 19 July 1999, 7, 8; Shiraz, "May 1998 Interview with Bin Laden Reported," 20; "Bin Laden Pens Letter in Support of Kashmir Jihad," *Wahdat,* 8 June 1999, 1, 5.

48. "Hero of Modern Times," *Nation* (Lahore edition, Internet version), 21 August 1998.

49. Ismail, "Abu Hafs al-Masri: I had Nothing to Do with What Happened to the Americans in Kenya," 4.

50. Khamran Khan, "Bin Laden Loyalists Seek Revenge on U.S.," *News* (Internet version), 7 March 1999.

51. Ibid.; Khan, "Osama's Narrow Escape, Camp Hits Reported"; Mahmud Zafar, "Osama Backs Harakatul Ansar against U.S.," *Jang,* 20 October 1997, 7, 8; Hashimi, "Osama Bin Laden—A Man as Strong as a Rock," 10.

52. For a discussion of the deep and cohesive ties between Pakistan and the Taliban, see Adam Garfinckle, "Afghanistanding," *Orbis* 43, no. 3 (Summer 1999): 412–13.

53. "U.S. Reportedly Asks Taliban for Bin Laden," *Al-Quds Al-Arabi* (Internet version), 11–12 March 1998.

54. Khan, "Bin Laden Loyalists Seek Revenge on U.S."; Muzami Jaleel, "The Taliban Connection," *Indian Express* (Internet version), 2 June 2000; Jeffrey Goldberg, "The Education of a Holy Warrior," *New York Times Magazine,* 25 June 2000.

55. "Staff Increase in Pakistan Mission Linked to Bin Laden," *Ausaf,* 27 July 1999, 1, 7; William T. Vollman, "Letter from Afghanistan: Across the Divide," *New Yorker* (15 May 2000).

56. M. A. Niazi, "Compromising Kashmir," *Nation* (Lahore edition, Internet version), 28 December 2001.

57. Humayun Gauhar, "Dare to Win," *Nation* (Lahore edition, Internet version), 4 November 2001.

58. "The Hasty Decision to Cooperate with the United States," *Nawa-I-Waqt,* 17 September 2001, 6.

59. Rahimullah Yusufzai, "Taliban Hurt by Musharraf's Statement," *News* (Internet version), 6 October 2001.

60. "Statement from Taliban Leader Mullah Omar in Khadahar," Afghan Islamic News Press Agency, 13 October 2001.

61. Hamid Mir, "U.S. Using Chemical Weapons—Osama Bin Laden," *Ausaf,* 10 November 2001, 1, 7; "Letter by Osama Bin Laden to the Pakistani People," Al-Jazirah Satellite Channel Television, 24 September 2001.

62. "'The U.S. Should Look for Attackers within Itself': Exclusive Interview with Osama Bin Laden," *Ummat,* 28 September 2001, 1, 7.

Chapter 12

1. "The Real Threat to American Interests in Saudi Arabia," MediaGen (U.K.) Ltd. (Internet), 21 February 1997; Shiraz, "May 1998 Interview with Bin Laden Reported"; "Osama Speaks on Hijrah and the Islamic State," *Al-Jihaad Newsletter.*

2. Atwan, "Interview with Saudi Oppositionist Osama Bin Laden."

3. Fisk, "Anti-Soviet Warrior Puts His Army on the Road to Peace."

4. "Osama Bin Laden's Terrorist Plan in Yemen, Egypt, and Gulf," *Al Watan Al-Arabi,* 27 December 1996; Al-Ayyash and Najm, "Behind the Scenes of the American Strike against Bin Laden's Secret Cells."

5. "Bin Laden Took Advantage of the Situation," *Al-Sharq Al-Awsat;* Hisham Mubarak, "The Battle between the Blind Man and the Captive," *Rose al-Yusuf,* 24 August 1992, 22–24.

6. Salah, "Secret of the Relationship between al-Zawahiri and Bin Laden," 30, 31; Al-Ibrushi, "Interview with Abu Hamzah al-Masri," 16–17.

7. Najm, "The Destruction of the Base."

8. Muhammed Salah, "Cairo: 'Returnees from Albania' Case Is Biggest Blow to Jihad Groups," *Al-Hayah,* 20 April 1999, 3.

9. Muhammed Salah, "The Main Defendant Confirms the Islamists' Determination to Retaliate against United States," *Al-Hayah,* 5 February 1999, 5.

10. Salah, "Cairo: 'Returnees from Albania' Case Is Biggest Blow to Jihad Groups," 3.

11. "Militant Leader Urges Holy War on U.S., Israel," *Al-Rai Al-Amm,* 9 July 1998.

12. Salah, "Secret of the Relationship between al-Zawahiri and Bin Laden."

13. "Jihad Group Threatens to Take Revenge against United States," *Al-Quds Al-Arabi,* 2 November 1998, 8.

14. "Fundamentalists Emphasize that al-Islambouli Did Not Accompany Bin Laden," *Al-Hayah,* 26 February 1999, 6.

15. Arnett, "Osama Bin Laden: The Interview."

16. Khamran Khan, "Palestinian Unveils Osama's International War against U.S., *News."*

17. Sa'id al-Qaysi, "Bin Laden's New 'Islamic Front,'" *Al-Watan Al-Arabi,* 6 June 1998, 26–27; Mubarak, "The Battle between the Blind Man and the Captive," 22–24.

18. "Text of World Front's Statement Urging Jihad against Jews and Crusaders," *Al-Quds Al-Arabi.*

19. Al-Qaysi, "Bin Laden's New 'Islamic Front.'"

20. Muhammed al-Shifai'i, "Egyptian 'Armed Vanguards of Conquest' Calls on 'Islamic Front' to Expand Membership," *Al-Sharq Al-Awsat,* 26 February 1998, 4.

21. "Interview with Sa'd al-Faqih," *Frontline Online.*

22. Timmerman, "This Man Wants You Dead."

23. Wa'el al-Ibrushi, "Afghanistan's Extremists Disclose the Secrets of the Financier of Terrorism: Bin Laden Was Made by U.S. Intelligence," *Rose al-Yusuf,* 24 August 1998, 16–17.

24. Wajid Abassi, "Interview with Lashkar-I-Tayyaba Chief, Professor Hafiz Muhammed Saeed," *Ausaf,* 3 January 2000, 11, 12; Owais Tohid, "Azhar Calls for Jihad against India First, Then U.S.," *AFP,* 6 January 2000.

25. Al-Qaysi, "Bin Laden's New 'Islamic Front.'"

26. Sharaf-al-Din, "Surprises from the Trial of the Largest International Terrorist Group in Egypt," 5; John F. Burns, "Yemen on Delicate Path in Bin Laden Hunt," *New York Times,* 15 December 2000.

27. "Jailed Egyptian Islamist Warns of Anti-U.S. Attacks," *AFP,* 6 March 1999; "Jihad, Bin Laden Involved in Bombing of U.S. Embassies," *Al-Sharq Al-Awsat* (Internet version), 2 May 1999.

28. Sharaf-al-Din, "Surprises from the Trial of the Largest International Terrorist Group in Egypt."

29. Nick Hopkins et al., "U.S. on Terrorist Alert as Revenge Targets Named," *Sydney Morning Herald* (Internet version), 24 August 1998.

30. Macleod, "The Paladin of the Jihad"; Fisk, "Anti-Soviet Warrior Puts His Army on the Road to Peace."

31. "Interview with Larry C. Johnson," *Frontline Online.*

32. "Fiji Police Searching for Suspects with Terrorists Links," Internet Fiji Live, 4 May 1999; Levy and Scott-Clark, "Bin Laden's Mercenaries Gather for Kashmir's Jihad"; "Australians Being Recruited for Bin Laden Jihad," *AFP,* 29 April 1999; Peter Chen, "Osama Said Recruiting Muslims in Melbourne for Jihad," Taiwan Central News Agency (Internet version), 30 April 1999; Maki Pulido, "Military Monitoring New Philippine Terrorist Group," GMA-7 Radio-Television Arts Network, 27 October 1998; "World; Africa: Suspect Bin Laden Associate Arrested," BBC Online Network, 5 March 1999; "Suspected Bin Laden Supporters Held in Mauritania," *AFP,* 5 March 1999; "Mauritania Holds Man with Suspected Bin Laden Link," Reuters, 4 March 1999; Bob Drogin and Tracy Wilkinson, "Bin Laden Followers Indicted over Alleged Terrorist Plot," *Los Angeles Times,* 29 March 2000, A-3; "Duo Cites Bin Laden in Bangladesh Attack," *Washington Times,* 30 January 1999, A-9; "Secrets of Meetings between Iranians and Fundamentalists," *Al-Watan Al-Arabi,* 7 March 1997.

33. "Will Bin Laden End Up in China? Taliban Makes Afghan Arabs Wage Jihad in Xinjiang," *Al-Watan Al-Arabi,* 23 May 1997; "Osama Bin Laden's Terrorist Plan in Yemen, Egypt, and Gulf," *Al Watan Al-Arabi*; "Nairobi Bombing Suspect Eludes FBI," Reuters, 17 September 1998; "Jihad, Bin Laden Involved in Bombing of U.S. Embassies," *Al-Sharq Al-Awsat*; Muhammad al-Shafa'i, "Britain's Fundamentalist Movements Open Training Camps for Their Members in the United States and Others in Northern Nigeria," *Al-Sharq Al-Awsat,* 4 July 2000, 3; Peter Foster and Maurice Weaver, "Young Britons Heed Call to Arms for Holy War," *Daily Telegraph* (Internet version), 29 December 2000; Miroslav Lazanski, "The American Seed," *Veernje,* 6 December 1998, 6.

34. Miller, "Greetings America: My Name Is Osama Bin Laden."

35. "Sources View Options on Bin Laden's Whereabouts," *Al-Ittihad* (Internet version), 17 February 1999; "Americans Are Paper Tigers," *Der Spiegel.*

36. "Bin Laden Trained Ugandans," *New Vision*, 1.

37. Al-Ayyash and Najm, "Behind the Scenes of the American Strike."

38. For example, see "Osama Bin Laden's Terrorist Plan in Yemen, Egypt, and Gulf," *Al Watan Al-Arabi*.

39. "Americans Are Paper Tigers," *Der Spiegel*.

40. "Osama Bin Laden's Terrorist Plan in Yemen, Egypt, and Gulf," *Al-Watan Al-Arabi*; "Information on Bin Laden's Plans to Set Up Base in Somalia," *Al-Sharq Al-Awsat* (Internet version), 1 May 1999.

41. Al-Ayyash and Najm, "Behind the Scenes of the American Strike."

42. "Osama Bin Laden's Terrorist Plan in Yemen, Egypt, and Gulf," *Al Watan Al-Arabi*.

43. "Information on Bin Laden's Plans to Set Up Base in Somalia," *Al-Sharq Al-Awsat*.

44. Maurizio Molinari, "Bin Laden Has Bases in Somalia," *Le Stampa*, 19 June 1999, 10; "Israelis Invading 'Somaliland': Strategic Location, Natural Wealth, and Uranium," *Al-Wasat*, 2 April 2001, 16–19.

45. Al-Ayyash and Najm, "Behind the Scenes of the American Strike"; Benjamin Weiser, "Prosecutors Portray the Strands of a Bin Laden Web of Terror," *New York Times*, 23 January 2000, A-4.

46. Yusef Khazim, "Islamists Regroup Their Forces after Ethiopian Preemptive Strikes," *Al-Wasat Magazine*, 17–23 May 1999, 30–33.

47. Sa'id al-Qaysi, "Report on U.S. Embassy Bombing Probe," *Al-Watan Al-Arabi*, 30 October 1998, 26, 27.

48. Khazim, "Islamists Regroup Their Forces after Ethiopian Preemptive Strikes."

49. Weiser, "Prosecutors Portray the Strands of a Bin Laden Web of Terror"; Molinari, "Bin Laden Has Bases in Somalia."

50. Aremio Enracia Jr., "Khalifah Denies Links with Bin Laden," *Philippine Daily Inquirer* (Internet version), 21 December 1998.

51. "CIA Report on Bin Laden's Filipino Links," *Al-Sharq Al-Awsat*; Gerth and Miller, "Terror Money: A Special Report; Funds for Terrorists Traced to Persons, Gulf Businesses"; Canares and Balana, "Spy Chief Claims Info on Bin Laden in Mindanao."

52. Weaver, "Blowback"; "Secrets of the Worldwide Campaign Chasing Osama Bin Laden," *Al-Watan Al-Arabi*; "CIA Report on Bin Laden's Filipino Links," *Al-Sharq Al-Awsat*; "Taliban Expelling Arab Muslim Fundamentalists: Egypt," *AFP*, 27 December 1996.

53. Michael Sadim, "Bin Laden Said to Be Giving Military Aid to MILF," *Manila Times* (Internet version), 13 February 1999; Weaver, "Blowback"; Burgos, "Mindanao Cops Have Photos of Saudi Tycoon."

54. Risen, "Bin Laden Was Target of U.S. Raid Plans since Spring"; Mu'in, "European Security Organs Get Ready to Dismantle Bin Laden's Network"; Jerry Esplanada, "Four Suspected Foreign Financiers of Abu Sayyaf Identified," *Philippine Daily Inquirer*, 22 April 1995, 18.

55. Khan, "Palestinian Unveils Osama's International War against U.S."

56. Sadim, "Bin Laden Said to Be Giving Military Aid to MILF."

57. Pulido, "Military Monitoring New Philippine Terrorist Group."

58. "Philippine Muslim Rebels Await Afghan Arms Shipment," *AFP*, 21 February 1999.

59. Anthony Davis, "Islamic Guerrillas Threaten the Fragile Peace of Mindanao," *Jane's Intelligence Review* 10, no. 5 (May 1998): 30–35; N. P. Aquino and M. S. Villamor, "Filipino DefSec Reports on Arms Buildup by MILF," *Business World* (Internet version), 14 March 2000.

60. "Philippines' MILF Reveals Bin Laden Link," *Philippine Star* (Internet version), 10 February 1999.

61. Bennet, "U.S. Cruise Missiles Strike Sudan and Afghan Targets Tied to Terrorist Network": "U.S. Has Long Blamed Sudan for Harboring Terrorists," Associated Press, 20 August 1998; Alan Sipress, "Sudan, N. Korea Cited for Gains on Terrorism," *Washington Post*, 1 May 2000, A-8.

62. Louise Tunbridge, "Islam Crusade Warning for U.S. 'Enemy,'" *Daily Telegraph*, 15 August 1995, 8.

63. "Rebels Say Attack on Juba Imminent," *Al-Quds Al-Arabi*, 16 February 1998, 1.

64. "Osama Bin Laden Sends Message to Anti-U.S. Conference," *Al-Akhbar*, 7, 8.

65. "Islamist Leader Bin Laden Urges Muslims to Kill Britons," *AFP*; "World Front for Fighting the Jews and the Crusaders, Statement No. 4," *Al-Hayah*.

66. Olimpio, "Saddam's Latest Challenge"; "Story of Cooperation between Iraq and Both Taliban and Bin Laden; It Started before Operation Desert Fox," *Al-Majallah*, 10–16 January 1999, 25; Ahmad Muwaffaq Zaydan, "Amid Conflicting Reports on Expansion of His Current Contacts and Scarcity of His Resources, Washington Is Pursuing Bin Laden's Network in India in Anticipation of a New Strike by Him," *Al-Hayah*, 22 January 1998, 6; Timmerman, "This Man Wants You Dead"; "Unattributed Biography of Osama Bin Laden," *Frontline Online*.

67. Yusufzai, "World's Most Wanted Terrorist."

68. "Bin Laden: Afghanistan's Inclusion on U.S. 'Terrorism List' Is 'Certificate of Good Conduct' for Taliban," *Al-Quds Al-Arabi*, 18 May 1998, 3.

69. Fisk, "Arab Rebel Leader Warns the British: 'Get Out of the Gulf.'"

70. Miller, "Greetings America: My Name Is Osama Bin Laden."

71. "Secrets of the Worldwide Campaign Chasing Osama Bin Laden," *Al-Watan Al-Arabi*; Michael Grunwald, "Bin Laden Associate Indicted for Perjury," *Washington Post*, 22 September 1998, A-12; Nicholas Blanford, "Rebels from 'Islamist Internationale'?" *Daily Star* (Internet version), 3 January 2000; "Afghans and Algerians in North Lebanon Battles," *Al-Sharq Al-Awsat* (Internet version), 3 January 2000; Subhi Yaghi, "Bin Laden Said Funding Islamists Fighting Lebanese Army," *Al-Nahar* (Internet version), 5 January 2000; Ahmad Khalid, "Lebanese Islamists Link to Bin Laden Probed," *Al-Shira'*, 17 January 2000, 23–25; "Al-Murr: No Bases for Bin Laden or the 'Afghans' in Lebanon," *Al-Sharq Al-Awsat*, 26 January 2000, 5; Muhammed Salah-al-Din, "The Phenomenon of Profiting from Terrorism," *Al-Madinah*, 25 January 2000, 2; Wa'el al-Ibrashi, "Story of the Two Most Famous Egyptian Prisoners in London, the Faxed Fingerprint that Proved Connection between Egyptian Lawyer and Bin Laden, Umar Bakri on Differences with Bin Laden on Sectarianism and Fatwa to Kill American

Women and Children," *Rose Al-Yusuf,* 4 November 2000, 34–36; Sa'id al-Qaysi, "Bin Laden Reportedly Setting Up Camp in Lebanon," *Al-Watan Al-Arabi,* 18 August 2000, 16, 17.

72. "Osama Says Taliban Rejected US Billions for Arrest," *Ausaf,* 1, 7; Milt Bearden and Larry Johnson, "A Glimpse at the Alliances of Terror," *New York Times* (Op-Ed), 7 November 2000; Chris Kozlow, "The Bombing of Khobar Towers: Who Did It? And Who Funded It?" *Jane's Intelligence Review* 9, no. 12 (December 1997); Abd-al-Rahim, "Bin Laden's New York Activities," 18–22; "Report on the Threat to Arab Countries by Terrorist Bin Laden," *Sawt al-Mar'ah.*

73. "Interview with Roland Jaquard, Monitor of International Terrorism," *Al-Watan Al-Arabi.*

74. "Unattributed Biography of Osama Bin Laden," *Frontline Online.*

75. "Declaration of Jihad against the Americans," *Al-Islah*; Miller, "Exclusive Interview with Osama Bin Laden," "Osama Bin Laden, Letter from Kandahar."

76. Philip Shenon, "House Votes $1.4 Billion for Embassy Security," *New York Times,* 22 July 1999, A-9; "Report on Bin Laden's Activities, Wealth," *Al-Watan Al-Arabi,* 23-28.

77. Muhammed Salah, "Fundamentalist Source: Bin Laden Front Purchased Chemical Weapons from Eastern Europe," *Al-Hayah,* 20 April 1999, 1.

78. Stefan Leader, "Osama Bin Laden and the Terrorist Search for WMD," *Jane's Intelligence Review* 11, no. 6 (June 1999): 34–37.

79. "Bin Laden Congratulates Pakistan on Its Possession of Nuclear Weapon," *Al-Quds Al-Arabi,* 2.

80. Azeem Siddiqui, "Interview with Osama Bin Laden Reported," *Al-Akhbar,* 31 March 1998, 1, 8.

81. Ismail, "Bin Laden Urges Attacks against U.S., UK Interests."

82. Francois Soudan, "Thus Spoke Osama Bin Laden," *Jeune Afrique,* 8–26 January 1999, 20–21; "No Lack of Candidates for Embassy Bombings," Reuters, 7 August 1998; "What Does Israel's Acknowledgment of Possessing Nuclear Weapons Mean?" *Al-Jazirah* (Editorial), 21 January 2000, 3.

83. Guido Olimpio, "Islamic Cell Preparing Chemical Warfare, Toxins, Gases against West," *Corriere della Sera,* 8 July 1998, 8.

84. For example, see Ibid.; Guido Olimpio, "In Osama's Lair," *Sette Magazine,* 3 September 1998; Mann, "Bin Laden Linked to Nuclear Effort," 58; Ahmad Muwaffaw Zaydan and Shafiq al-Asadi, "Information about Nuclear Weapon for Bin Laden from Central Asia," *Al-Hayah,* 6 October 1998, 1, 6.

85. Olimpio, "Islamic Cell Preparing Chemical Warfare, Toxins, Gases against West"; Timmerman, "This Man Wants You Dead."

86. Olimpio, "Islamic Cell Preparing Chemical Warfare, Toxins, Gases against West."

87. Ibid.

88. Riyad Alam-al-Din, "Iraq, Bin Laden Ties Examined," *Al-Watan Al-Arabi,* 1 January 1999, 16–18; Miller, "Greetings America: My Name Is Osama Bin Laden."

89. Olimpio, "Islamic Cell Preparing Chemical Warfare, Toxins, Gases against West."

90. Olimpio, "In Osama's Lair."

91. John McWethy, "Osama Bin Laden Plans Attacks on United States," *ABC World News Tonight*, 16 June 1999; "U.S. Intelligence Cites Iraqi Ties to Sudan Plant," Associated Press, 25 August 1998; Alam-al-Din, "Iraq, Bin Laden Ties Examined."

92. Olimpio, "Islamic Cell Preparing Chemical Warfare, Toxins, Gases against West"; Svitlana Bulaneko, "Yuriy Volodymyrovych Zemlyanskyy Wave of Terrorism Awaits World in Third Millennium, " *Segodnya,* 9 February 2000, 14, 15 (Zemlyanskyy is deputy head of the Ukrainian State Security Service); Gannon, "Suspected Terrorists Enjoy Taliban Protection"; Paul Daley, "Report Says UBL-Linked Groups Possess 'Deadly' Anthrax and Plague Viruses," *Age* (Internet version), 4 June 2000.

93. Zaydan and al-Asadi, "Information about Nuclear Weapon for Bin Laden from Central Asia."

94. Sharaf-al-Din, "Surprises from the Trial of the Largest International Terrorist Group in Egypt."

95. Salah, "Fundamentalist Source: Bin Laden Front Purchased Chemical Weapons from Eastern Europe."

96. Auster, "An Inside Look at Terror Inc"; Waller, "Inside the Hunt for Osama," 32; Pino Buongiorno et al., "Alarm over Russia: All Clinton's and Blair's Next Moves," *Milan Panorama* (Internet version), 14 May 1998.

97. "el. Ma.," "Osama Bin Laden in Tirana Offices," 12; Robert D. Kaplan, "The Lawless Frontier," *Atlantic Monthly* (September 2000): 66; Julian West, "Atomic Haul Raises Fears of Bin Laden Terror Bomb," *Sunday Telegraph* (Internet version), 23 April 2000.

98. Zaydan and Al-Asadi, "Information about Nuclear Weapon for Bin Laden from Central Asia"; Abd-al-Rahim, "Bin Laden's New York Activities."

99. Riyad Alam-al-Din, "Report Links Bin Laden, Nuclear Weapons," *Al-Watan Al-Arabi,* 13 November 1998; Riyad Alam-al-Din, "Major Terrorist Plot against Dubai Revealed," *Al-Watan Al-Arabi,* 10 April 1998, 30, 31; "Interview with Roland Jaquard, Monitor of International Terrorism," *Al-Watan Al-Arabi.*

100. Alam-al-Din, "Report Links Bin Laden, Nuclear Weapons."

101. Ibid.

102. Ibid.

103. Olimpio, "A Secret Pact with Bin Laden, the Terror Shaykh," 7; Nabil Abu-Sutayt, "International Intelligence Conference Draws Up Three Scenarios for Chemical, Biological, and Nuclear Terrorist Attacks in the Middle East," *Al-Sharq Al-Awsat,* 11 November 1999, 3.

104. Guido Olimpio, "Osama Bin Laden Disappears from Kabul, and Baghdad Pops Up in the Terror Shaykh's New Travels," *Corriere della Sera,* 14 February 1999, 10.

105. Alam-al-Din, "Report Links Bin Laden, Nuclear Weapons"; Najm and Al-Ayyash, "Report Views Bin Laden Operations, Counterterrorism Efforts."

106. McWethy, "Osama Bin Laden Plans Attack on United States"; "Bin Laden Threatens Terrorism Hit in U.S.," *CBS Evening News,* 6 August 1999; Burke and Baweja, "Target . . . India"; Leslie Stahl, "Interview with Richard Clarke," *Federal News Service,* 24 October 2000; Peter Baker, "Pakistani Scientist Who Met

Bin Laden Failed Polygraphs, Renewing Suspicions," *Washington Post,* 3 March 2002, 1.

Chapter 13

1. Miller, "Exclusive Interview with Osama Bin Laden."

2. Mufti Jamil Khan, "Bin Laden: Expel Jews, Christians from Holy Places," *Jang,* 18 November 1998, 1, 7.

3. Amba, "Saudi Militant's Wish: To Die Fighting America."

4. Edward T. Renehan Jr., *The Lion's Pride. Theodore Roosevelt and His Family in Peace and War* (New York: Oxford University Press, 1998), xii, 289.

5. Miller, "Greetings America: My Name Is Osama Bin Laden."

6. Soudan, "Thus Spoke Osama Bin Laden"; "Strange Fatwas from Government Ulema," *Al-Quds Al-Arabi,* 24 April 2001, 19; Ismail, "Al-Jazeerah, Bin Laden, and I."

7. Justin Brown, "Risks of Waging Only Risk-Free Wars," *Christian Science Monitor,* 24 May 2000; Brooks D. Simpson and Jean V. Berlin, eds. *Sherman's Civil War: Selected Correspondence of William T. Sherman, 1960–1865* (Chapel Hill: University of North Carolina Press, 1999, 730; Wiley Sword, *Southern Invincibility: A History of the Confederate Heart* (New York: St. Martin's Griffin, 1999), 309.

8. "Punish and Be Damned," Economist.com (Editorial), 28 August 1998; Muhammed Salah, "Bin Laden Front Falls Back and Egyptian Groups Undertake the Mission," *Al-Wasat Magazine,* 11–17 January 1999, 14–15; Charles J. Dick, "Conflict Spills into the 21st Century," *Jane's Intelligence Review* 12, no. 12 (December 2000).

9. Auster, "An Inside Look at Terror Inc."

10. For example, see "Interview with Roland Jaquard, Monitor of International Terrorism," *Al-Watan Al-Arabi.*

11. Ranstorp, "Interpreting the Broader Context and Meaning of Bin Laden's Fatwa."

12. U.S. State Department, "Patterns of Global Terrorism, 1997," 21; U.S. State Department, "Patterns of Global Terrorism, 1998," 27; Kozlow, "The Bombing of Khobar Towers: Who Did It? And Who Funded It?"; Atwan, "Interview with Saudi Oppositionist Osama Bin Laden"; Najm, "The Destruction of the Base"; Shiraz, "May 1998 Interview with Bin Laden Reported."

13. U.S. State Department, "Patterns of Global Terrorism, 1997," 48.

14. Ibid., 25, 51.

15. Islamic Observation Center Web site, 10 September 1999; Adam Geibel, "Khattab's Audacious Raid (22 December 1997): Prelude to the Second Chechen War," *Central Asia Survey* 19, no. 3–4 (September/December 2000): 341–43.

16. Al-Ayyash and Najm, "Behind the Scenes of the American Strike against Bin Laden's Secret Cells"; U.S. State Department, "Patterns of Global Terrorism, 1998," 10.

17. U.S. State Department, "Patterns of Global Terrorism, 1998," 6–7; Yusufzai, "World's Most Wanted Terrorist"; Benjamin Weiser, "Bin Laden Linked to Embassy Blast by an Ex-Soldier," *New York Times,* 21 October 2000, 1.

18. "Philippine Forces on Alert after Killing of Muslim Extremist Leader,"

AFP; "Many Shoppers Hurt in Southern Philippines Bomb Attack," *AFP*, 16 December 1998; U.S. State Department, "Patterns of Global Terrorism, 1998," 11.

19. Mounassar and Attar, "Yemen Hostages Recover from Horrific Slaughter for Four Friends."

20. Khalid al-Hammadi, "Kidnapping Said the Result of Bin Laden Fatwa," *Al-Quds Al-Arabi*, 30 December 1998, 1; U.S. State Department, "Patterns of Global Terrorism, 1998," 23, 55; Kamil al-Tawil, "U.S. Investigators Reportedly Focusing on Bin Laden's Role," *Al-Hayah* (Internet version), 20 January 1999.

21. Phil Kuntz and Hugh Pope, "U.S. Officials, Fearing Retaliation, Close 38 Embassies in Africa," *Wall Street Journal*, 18 December 1998; "U.S. Temporarily Closes Six Embassies in Africa," Reuters, 24 June 1999.

22. David Briscoe, "Americans Are Warned against Terrorist Threats," Associated Press, 6 August 1999; Ben N. Venzke, "A Year after Embassy Bombings, The Threat of Terrorism Settles In," *Boston Globe*, 8 August 1999, E-1.

23. "Uzbekistan Accuses Taliban Leader and Bin Laden Attempting to Assassinate Its President," *Al-Sharq Al-Awsat*, 8 March 1999; Gulfira Gayeva, "Bin Laden Suspected of Organizing Tashkent Explosions," *Kommersant*, 3 March 1999, 4; Ahmed Rashid, "Afghanistan: Heart of Darkness," *Far East Economic Review*, 5 August 1999; Khashim Ibragimov, "Frightening Face of Extremism. Ramified Network of Islamic Terrorists Threaten CIS Countries," *Nevavisimaya Gazeta*, 3 February 2000, 5; "So There Will Be War in the Spring," *Delo No*, 1 March 2000, 4.

24. Levy and Scott-Clark, "Bin Laden's Mercenaries Gather for Kashmir's Jihad"; Ravi Bhatia, "Indian Agencies Keen on the Whereabouts of Bin Laden," *The Times of India* (Internet version), 6 July 1999.

25. James Rupert, "U.S. and Britain Close 10 Embassies in Africa," *Washington Post*, 26 June 1999, A-13; "U.S. Temporarily Closes Six Embassies in Africa," Reuters.

26. Shenon, "House Votes $1.4 Billion for Embassy Security," A-9; Michael Dobbs, "An Obscure Chief in U.S. War on Terror," *Washington Post*, 2 April 2000, A-1.

27. David Stout, "Citing Threats, FBI Suspends Public Tours of HQS," *New York Times*, 24 July 1999, A-4; Niles Lathan, "Bin Laden's Lemmings May Target Big Apple," *New York Post*, 5 August 1999.

28. Philip Shenon, "Fear of Attack Cancels Cohen's Trip to Albania," *New York Times*, 17 July 1999, A-4; Lathan, "Bin Laden's Lemmings May Target Big Apple."

29. "Islamists Claim Responsibility for Yemeni Air Crash," *Arab Daily*, 17 August 1998, 8.

30. "Four Gulf Fundamentalists Killed in Dagestan Battles," *Al-Sharq Al-Awsat*, 27 August 1999, 7; "Bin Laden Said to Fund Terrorism School in Chechnya," RIA News Service, 24 August 1999; Nurani, "Terrorist No. 1 Osama Bin Laden Is Funding Islamic Militants," *Zerkala*, 19 August 1999, 4; "UBL Urges Mujahedin to 'Arrest' Clinton, Shoot U.S. Commandos," *Pakistan*, 12 September 1999, 8, 11; Khalaf, "Shamil Basayev: A Terrorist or a National Hero?"

31. Said Hattar, "Pakistan Hands Over 14th Terror Suspect to Jordan," *Jordan Times* (Internet version), 18 December 1999; Ismail Khan, "Pakistan Hands

Over Bin Laden Aide to Jordan," *News,* 18 December 1999, 1, 8; Ahmed Muwaffaq Zaydan, "Pakistan Delivers to Jordan an Islamist Holding U.S. Citizenship," *Al-Hayah* (Internet version), 8 January 2000; "Canada to Propose Joint Anti-Terrorist Measures with U.S.," *AFP,* 29 January 2000; Ben Barber, "Justice Blames Canada for Terrorist's Entry," *Washington Times,* 21 December 1999, A-1.

32. Sarmad Azim, "Who Is Maulana Masood Azhar?" *Pakistan–Sunday Magazine,* 2 January 2000, 5, 21; "Azhar Urges Pakistanis to Wage Holy War against India," *News* (Internet version), 8 January 2000.

33. "Fear of Terrorism Prevents Festivities in Brussels," *Da Standaard,* 1 July 2000, 6; Musallom Ulaymat, "As Part of the Chain of Pressure on Jordan to Agree to Settlement Demands, U.S. Embassy Spreads Word about Existence of Terrorism in Jordan and Sets Up Barricades on Embassy Walls," *Shihan,* 8–14 July 2000, 5; "Senior Officials and Ministers are 'Angry' with Washington," *Al-Quds Al-Arabi,* 4 July 2000, 4.

34. Dodge Billingsley, "Chechen Rebels Hone Tactics for Long Haul," *Jane's Intelligence Review* 13, no. 2 (February 2001).

35. Igor Trifonov, "12 Killed, 108 Injured by 8 Aug Bomb Blast in Moscow," ITAR-TASS, 15 August 2000; "Moscow Blast Death Toll Rises to 12," Moscow NTV, 14 August 2000; Vladimir Yarov, "Fiendishly Precise Calculations. Terrorists Use Simple Bomb to Maximum," *Segodnya,* 10 August 2000, 3; "Chechen Suicide Bomber Blows Up Café in Grozny, Kills Nine Russians," Kavkaz-Tsenter News Agency (Internet version), 22 August 2000.

36. Robin Wright and Bob Drogin, "New Chapter in Terrorism May Have Begun," *Los Angeles Times,* 13 October 2000, 1; Ahmad Muhammad Zaydan, "Appearing at a Rally in Afghanistan to Support the Leader of the Islamic Group, Bin Laden, al-Zawahiri, and Rifa'i Taha Pledge to Set Umar Abd-al-Rahman Free," *Al-Hayah* (Internet version), 23 September 2000, 6; Rahimullah Yusufzai, "Taliban Arab Sources Say Video Telecast on Qatar TV was Fabricated," *News* (Internet version), 25 September 2000; Steve Goldstein, "Many Suspects in Ship Blast," *Philadelphia Enquirer,* 13 October 2000, 1; Robin Allen, "Middle East: Gulf States Show Growing Public Hostility to U.S. Presence," *Financial Times* (Internet version), 21 November 2000; John F. Burns and Steven Lee Myers, "Blast Kills Sailors on U.S. Ship in Yemen," *New York Times,* 13 October 2000, 1; Tarek Issawi, "Bin Laden Applauds *Cole* Attack," *Washington Post,* 2 March 2001, A-16; Ahmad Muwaffaq Zaydan, "Celebrated His Son's Marriage in Presence of Family Members. Bin Laden Hints at Indirect Role in the Bombing of Destroyer USS *Cole*," *Al-Hayah,* 1 March 2001, 1, 6; "Bin Laden Full of Praise for Attack on USS *Cole* at Son's Wedding," AFP.

37. Mark Galeotti, "No Respite in Chechen War," *Jane's Intelligence Review* 13, no. 2 (February 2001); Billingsley, "Chechen Rebels Hone Tactics for Long Haul."

38. "News Flash," *Philippine Star* (Internet version), 28 December 2000; "Latest News." *Jakarta Post* (Internet version), 26 December 2000; "At Least 15 People Killed in Christmas Eve Bombings across Indonesia," *Jakarta Post* (Internet version) 25 December 2000; Anthony Davis, "Southeast Asia Bombings Betray Islamic Links," *Jane's Intelligence Review* 13, no. 2 (February 2001).

39. "Attacks Are Estimated to Cost Nation 1.8 Million Jobs," *New York*

Times, 13 January 2002; Fareed Zakaria, "What's Next? — The New Rules of Engagement," *Newsweek,* 31 December 2001–7 January 2002, 91; Tony Capaccio, "Afghan War, Defense Cost $6.4 Bln since Sept. 11, Pentagon Says," Bloomberg.com, 22 January 2002; Bill Miller, "$37.7 Billion for Homeland Defense Is a Start, Says Bush," *Washington Post,* 25 January 2002, 15; Kurt Eichenwald, "Terror Money Hard to Block Officials Find," *New York Times,* 10 December 2001, A1.

40. "Message to Our Brothers in Iraq by Usama Bin Ladin, Leader of [the] al-Qaida Organization," Al-Jazirah Space Channel Television, 11 February 2003.

41. "Statement from Qaeda al-Jihad," *Al-Neda* (Internet), 27 April 2002.

42. "You Fight Fire with Fire," *Al-Ansar* (Internet), 14 May 2002.

43. Abu-Ubayd al-Qurashi, "America's Nightmares," *Al-Ansar* (Internet), 13 February 2002; and Salim al-Makki, "Believers Exact Sweet Revenge in Mukalla, Faylaka, and Bali," *Al-Neda* (Internet), 14 October 2002.

44. "Statement of al-Qaida Organization on the Faylaka Operation," *al-Qal'ah* (Internet), 18 October 2002.

45. "Bali Bombing Suspect Proud of Attack," *Washington Times,* 13 June 2003, 19.

46. Abu-Ubayd al-Qurashi, "The Moscow Theater Operation," *Al-Ansar* (Internet), 6 November 2002; and Fred Weir, "Shifting Tactics in Chechnya," *Christian Science Monitor,* 30 December 2002, 1.

47. "U.S. President Says Chechnya 'Internal Affair,'" *Interfax,* 21 November 2002; "A Separate War," *New Republic,* 2 December 2002, 7; and al-Qurashi, "Moscow Theater Operation."

48. M. Zaatari, "No Leads Yet in Probe of Murder in Sidon; American Woman Had Been Warned to Stop Proselytizing," *The Daily Star* (Internet version), 25 November 2002.

49. Abu-Ubayd al-Hilali, "Mombasa and the Fulfillment of the Promise," *Al-Ansar* (Internet), 5 December 2002.

50. Ian Fisher, "Recent Attacks in Yemen Seen as Sign of Large Terror Cell," *New York Times,* 3 January 2003; and Faysal Mukarram, "Sanaa: More Signs of Two Killers' Links to al Qaeda . . ." *Al-Hayat,* 3 January 2003, 1, 6.

51. "Deputy Amir of Al-Jawf Province in Northern Saudi Arabia Assassinated," *Ilaf* (Internet), 17 February 2003.

52. "Cyanide Sent to Three Missions in New Zealand," *Radio Australia,* 25 February 2003; and "New Zealand Police Release Text of Cyanide Threat Letter," *AFP,* 26 February 2003.

53. Erik Eckholm, "Pakistani Guards Shot Dead at U.S. Office," *New York Times,* 1 March 2003; and Ashraf Khan, "Gunman Kills 2 Police Guards Outside U.S. Consulate in Pakistan," *AFP,* 28 February 2003.

54. Fawaz Gerges, "Muslims Called to Jihad," *Los Angeles Times,* 26 March 2003; and Abu-Ayman al-Hilali, "The Fall of the Iraqi Regime and the Beginning of the Nation's Rise, Part 1," *Al-Ansar* (Internet), 17 April 2003.

55. Christine T. Tjandraningsih and Rudy Madanir, "Jakarta Blast Was against U.S.: Bali Bombing Suspect," *Kyodo World Service,* 6 August 2003.

56. "Statement of the Abu Hafs al-Masri Brigades," *Quds Press* (Internet version), 25 August 2003.

57. Victor Hanson Davis, "Hoping We Fail," *National Review Online*, 28 August 2003.

58. "Audio Recording of Ayman al-Zawahiri," *Al-Arabiyah Televsion*, 28 September 2003.

59. Ahmed Rafat, "The Spanish Will Not Be Safe Even in Their Homes," *Tiempo de Hoy*, 24 March 2003.

60. "Westerners Killed in Saudi Arabia," BBC News, http://newsvote. bbc.co.uk, 2 May 2004; James Cox, "Saudi Fields Are Vital to World's Oil Supply," *USA Today*, 10 May 2004; and Abdullah al-Shiri, "Explosions Rock Central Riyadh," Associated Press, 30 December 2005.

61. al-Shiri, "Explosions Rock Central Riyadh."

62. "Islamist Group Appears to Claim Jakarta Blast," Associated Press, 10 September 2004.

63. "Egypt Police in Gun Battles with Bomb Suspects," CNN News, www.CNN.com, 24 August 2005; John Vause and Ben Wedeman, "Death Toll Rises in Egypt Tourist Bombings," CNN News, www.CNN.com, 9 October 2004; and Sarah el Deeb, "83 Die in Car Bombs in Egyptian Resort," *Chicago Tribune*, 23 July 2005.

64. Craig S. Smith, "Dutch Look for Qaeda Link after Killing of Filmmaker," *New York Times*, 8 November 2004, A10; and "Dutch Muslim Community Targeted after Murder of Filmmaker," *AFP*, 8 November 2004.

65. Laith Abou-Raghab, "Bombers Strike Saudi Capital," Reuters, 29 December 2004; Roger Harrison, et al., "U.S. Consulate Attacked," *Arab News* (Internet version), 7 December 2004; and "U.S. on Guard in Saudi Arabia," CBS News, www.CBSnews.com, 7 December 2004.

66. "Egyptian Identified as Qatar Bomber," Associated Press, 21 March 2005; "Qatar Looks for Qaeda Link in Theater Suicide Bomb," Reuters, 20 March 2005; Odai Sirri, "New Lead in Qatar Bombing," Reuters, 21 March 2005; and "The Advent of Terrorism in Qatar," www.Forbes.com, 25 March 2005.

67. "Egypt Bomb Attacks Kill at Least 75, Wound 120 (Update 5)," Bloomberg.com, 22 July 2005; and "4 Yanks Hurt amid Cairo Terror Carnage," www.nypost.com, 8 April 2005.

68. "Saudis Arrest 40 Christians for Praying," Reuters, 22 April 2005; Steve Coll, "Islamic Activists Sweep Council Elections," *Washington Post*, 24 April 2005, A17; "Saudi Soldier's Journey to Death in Iraq," Reuters, 20 March 2005; and "Saudi Arabia Braces Itself for Return of Jihadists from Iraq," *AFP*, 1 June 2005.

69. Arshad Mohammed, "World Terror Attacks Tripled in 2004 by U.S. Count," www.washingtonpost.com, 26 April 2005.

70. "Key Events after al-Hariri's Killing," *AFP*, 30 August 2005; and Lucy Ashton, "Syria's Retreat from Lebanon Emboldens Opposition," *Financial Times*, 6 May 2005.

71. "Group Claims Responsibility in Cairo Bombing," *AFP*, 30 April 2005; "An Alarming First for Egypt, Women Turn to Militancy," *AFP*, 3 May 2005; and "200 Held after Cairo Attacks," www.CNN.com, 1 May 2005.

72. *Newsweek*, 9 May 2005 and 23 May 2005.

73. C. J. Chivers, "Survivors and Toe Tags Clues to Uzbek's Uprising," *New York Times*, 23 May 2005; Bagila Bukharbayeva, "Soldiers Fire on Crowd in

Day of Clashes in Uzbekistan," Associated Press, 13 May 2005; Andrew Stoehlin, "Uzbekistan: The Andijon Uprising," International Crisis Group, http://www.crisisgroup.org, 25 May 2005; "Death Toll Soars in Uzbekistan," CBS News, www.cbsnews.com, 16 May 2005; and "Central Asia: Weekly News Wrap," http://www.irinnews.org, 6 September 2005.

74. Chris Brummitt, "Indonesia Christians Bury Their Dead," Associated Press, 29 May 2005; Beawiharta and Nuri Sybil, "Indonesia Blasts Have Qaeda Similarities," Reuters, 29 May 2005; and Dean Yates, "Criticism Grows of Indonesia Security after Blasts," Reuters, 31 May 2005.

75. Sofiane Ait-Iflis, "Terrorist Attack in Mauritania: Salafist Group for Call and Combat Claims Responsibility," *Le Soir d'Algerie*, 8 June 2005; "A Statement by al-Qaida Organization [in Iraq]," www.jihad-algerie.com, 16 June 2005; and Ibrahim Sylla, "Mauritania Blames al-Qaeda Ally for Deadly Raid," Reuters, 5 June 2005.

76. Elaine Sciloino and Dale Van Natta Jr., "British Intelligence Downgraded Terror Threat before Attacks," *San Francisco Chronicle* (Internet version), 19 July 2005.

77. "Police Hold Four July 21 Bombers," BBC News, http://news.bbc.co.uk, 30 July 2005.

78. Deeb, "83 Die in Car Bomb Blasts at Egyptian Resort"; "Egypt Bomb Attacks Kill at Least 75, Wound 120 (Update 5)"; "Deaths in Sinai Sweep, Sharm Attacks Linked," www.gulftimes.com, 29 August 2005; and Michael Slackman and Mona al-Naggar, "Egypt Sends Huge Force to Terrorist Hunt," *New York Times*, 30 August 2005.

79. Nick Tattersall, "Mauritania Shows Risks in U.S. Strategy in Africa," Reuters, 18 August 2005.

80. Achmad Sukarsono, "Indonesia Cuts Jail Term for Bashir," Reuters, 17 August 2005.

81. "Serial Blasts Rock Country," http://nation.ittefaq.com, 17 August 2005; David Montero, "Quiet Bangladesh Woken by Bombs," *Christian Science Monitor*, 18 August 2005; and Mamun ar-Rashid, "Countless Militant Networks Like Spider's Net," *Dainik Janakantha*, 19 July 2005, 1, 11.

82. Claude Salhani, "The Aqaba Attack," http://www.khaleejtimes.com, 26 August 2005; Jamal Halaby, "Al-Zarqawi: Claims Jordan al-Qaida Attack," Associated Press, 24 August 2005; Megan K. Stack, "Militants' Rockets Miss 2 U.S. Navy Warships," *Los Angeles Times*, 20 August 2005; "Al-Qaida Affiliated Group Claims al-Aqabah, Eilat Rocket Attacks," *AFP*, 19 August 2005.

83. "Saudi Dissident Shuts Down Site," BBC News, http://newsvote.BBC.co.uk, 27 August 2005.

84. "India Offers Kabul Help to Fight Terrorism," PTI News Agency, 28 August 2005; and Yousuf Azimy, "Karzai Says Better India-Pakistan Ties Vital," Reuters, 28 August 2005.

85. Joe Avancena, et al., "Hunt for Escaped Gunmen; One of 5 Iraqi Infiltrators Dead," *Saudi Gazette* (Internet version), 31 August 2005; "Saudi Security Forces Arrest Iraqi Infiltrators in Jubayl," Saudi Press Agency, 20 August 2005; and "Saudi Forces Clash with Gunmen in Industrial City," Reuters, 29 August 2005.

86. Edward Harris, "U.S. Boosts Anti-terror Efforts in Africa," Associated Press, 25 May 2005; Donna Mills, "New Counterterrorism Initiative to Focus on Saharan Africa," http://www.defenselink.mil, 16 May 2005; "U.S. Offers to Help Bangladesh Combat Terrorism," Reuters, 18 April 2005; "U.S. Launches Training in Gulf of Guinea," Associated Press, 29 June 2005; and Jim Kouri, "Terrorism: U.S. Training South East Asian Security Forces," http://www.lincolntribune.com, 27 August 2005.

87. Jeffrey Heller, "Israeli Troops Ready to Role out of Gaza," http://www.swissinfo.html, 10 September 2005.

88. Li Nun, "Uneasy Days — Terrorist Activities Frighten U.S. Personnel Overseas," *Renmin Ribao*, 13 August 1999; Williamson Murray, "The Emerging Strategic Environment: An Historian's Thoughts," *Strategic Review* 27, no. 1 (Winter 1999): 34; Robert Fisk, "Clinton Gives Coup Leader an Easy Ride; He Was Expected to Read the Riot Act to Pakistan's Dictator, but He Only Offered Cliches," *Independent on Sunday* (Internet version), 26 March 2000; Charles Babington and Pamela Constable, "Clinton Aided by Decoys, Urges Peace on Pakistan," *Washington Post*, 26 March 2000, A-1, A-22; Bill Drogin, "U.S. Details Threats Linked to Clinton Trip," *Los Angeles Times*, 23 March 2000, 1.

89. John Unson et al., "Mercado Urges MILF Not to Postpone Talks with Manila," *Philippine Star* (Internet version), 29 November 1999; Steve Vogel, "Special Forces Sent to Philippines Fight," *Washington Post*, 16 January 2002, 1; Eric Schmitt, "U.S.-Philippine Command May Signal War's Next Phase," *New York Times*, 16 January 2002, 1.

90. Rahul Bedi, "Paying to Keep the High Ground," *Jane's Intelligence Review* 11, no. 10 (October 1999): 27–31.

91. Prem Shankar Jha, "Failure in Kashmir," *Hindustan Times* (Internet version), 17 December 1999; Mohammed Ayoub, "South Asia's Dangers and U.S. Foreign Policy," *Orbis* 45, no. 1 (Winter 2001); "Intelligence Services on Fresh Militant Attacks in Kashmir," *Hindustan Times* (Internet version), 29 November 1999.

92. Aasha Khosha, "Report: Kashmir Militants Plan to Step Up Activities," *Indian Express* (Internet version), 21 November 1999; Samiullah Qureshi, "Freedom Fighters' Operations against Indian Government," Radio Pakistan, 25 December 2000; "A Serious Breach," *Pioneer* (Editorial), 25 December 2000, 6; "Lashkar Up to Red Fort," *Hindustan* (editorial), 25 December 2000, 6; "Unready Citadel," *Telegraph* (Editorial), 25 December 2000, 6; "Kashmir Car Bomb Explosion; 11 Killed, 26 Injured," *Deccan Herald* (Internet version), 26 December 2000; "The Heart Stopped," *Asian Age* (Editorial), 14 December 2001, 12; "Time to (En)Act," *Pioneer* (Editorial), 14 December 2001, 6; B. Narayanan, "Terrorist Attack on Parliament House," All India Radio Home News Service, 14 December 2001.

93. Pamela Constable, "India on the Defensive," *Washington Post*, 16 January 2000, A-29, A-33; M. K. Narayanan, "The Iron Grip Tightens Yet Again," *Asian Age*, 15 November 1999, 12; Levy and Scott-Clark, "Bin Laden's Mercenaries Gather for Kashmir's Jihad"; Parna Panjeri, "Bin Laden Tied to Kashmir Islamic Movement," *Al-Quds Al-Arabi*, 24 March 1999, 4.

94. Constable, "India on the Defensive."

95. "Security Report, Bin Laden Has Weapons Worth $51 Million, 20 Foreign Bases, and 80 Front Companies," *Al-Sharq Al-Awsat*, 2; Margolis, *War at the Top of the World*, 109; "Indian Minister again Calls for Nuke Ties with Israel," *Middle East Newsline* (Internet version), 15 June 2000; Seema Mustafa, "India Seen Moving away from Arab World towards Israel," *Asian Age*, 16 June 2000, 1, 2; Robert Marquand, "New Faces Join Fray in Kashmir," *Christian Science Monitor*, 2 May 2000, 1.

96. "Security Report, Bin Laden Has Weapons Worth $51 Million, "*Al-Sharq Al-Awsat*, 2; SB, "Terrorism: The Psychological War," *El-Watan* (Internet version), 16 November 1999; "Algeria: 'Around 70' Killed since Beginning of Ramadan," AFP, 17 December 1999; "CIA Director Says Casio Watch Is the Hallmark of Every One of Osama Bin Laden's Operations," *Al-Hadith*, 27 December 1999, 5; Anis Rahmani, "Strife within Fundamentalist Groups," *Al-Mustaqillah* (Internet version), 31 August 1999, 1, 8; "Bin Laden Advised Algeria's Radical GIA," Reuters, 15 February 1999; Rachid B., "The Outcome of the Year 2000," *El-Youm* (Internet version), 31 December 2000; "Five Members of One Family Murdered," *El-Youm* (Internet version), 21 December 2000; Na'ilah B., "The Security Situation: Bullets Don't Fast and the Groups Fail to Repent," *El-Youm* (Internet version), 7 December 2000, 1, 3; Hassane Zerrouky, "Thousands of People Killed in 2000 — The Forgotten of the Concord," *Le Matin* (Internet version), 10 January 2001; "330 Killed during Ramadan in Algeria," *Washington Report on Middle East Affairs* 20, no. 2, (March 2001): 40.

97. "TNI to Verify Reported Arms Sales to Aceh Separatists," *Jakarta Post* (Internet version), 4 March 2000; "Jakarta Police Uncover Network Selling Arms to Gam," *Kompas* (Internet version), 3 March 2000; "Exxon-Oil Has Temporarily Halted Exploration and Administrative Activities in Aceh Due to Rising Concerns over Security," *Jakarta Post* (Internet version), 7 June 2000; "TNI Reinforcements Deploy to Paso to Repel Christian Attacks," *Republika* (Internet version), 7 June 2000; "Interview: Conversation with Terror," *Time*, 11 January 1999; "TNI Chief Warns against Growing Separatism in Aceh," Radio Republik Indonesia, 23 November 1999; Rajiv Chandrasekaran, "A War of Vengeance," *Washington Post*, 19 June 2000, A-1; Bertil Lintner, "Centrifugal Forces Stir Indonesia," *Jane's Intelligence Review* 12, no. 6 (June 2000); Marian Trinidad, "MILF Chief Calls for UN-Supervised Referendum," *Manila Times* (Internet version), 23 March 2000; Hamid Mir, "Spate of Conspiracies," *Ausaf*, 29 September 1999, 2; Mark Galeotti, "Costs of the Chechen War," *Jane's Intelligence Review* 12, no. 4 (April 2000): 8–9; Michael Orr, "Russia's Chechen War: Second Time Lucky," *Jane's Defense Weekly* 33 (8 March 2000): 32–36.

98. Amba, "Saudi Militant's Wish: To Die Fighting America"; "U.S. Reportedly Asks Taliban for Bin Laden," *Al-Quds Al-Arabi*; "Bin Laden and His Followers Preparing to Move to Yemen Mountains," *Al-Quds Al-Arabi*, 9 March 1998, 1; "Saudi Arabia Denies Citizen Told U.S. of New York Bomb Plot," AP-Dow Jones; "Aide to Terrorist Bin Laden Helped Bombing Investigators," Associated Press, 4 August 1997; "Weekly Says Bin Laden Financial Manager to Testify, "*AFP*.

99. "Over 300 Bin Laden Companions Arrested in Saudi Arabia," *Ausaf*, 26 March 1999, 1, 7; "Will Bin Laden Strike within Weeks?" *Al-Islah Weekly*, June

1998; Shiraz, "May 1998 Interview with Bin Laden Reported."

100. David S. Cloud, "Can a Tire Repairman from Texas Be the Key to Solving a Terror Plot?" *Wall Street Journal,* 22 October 1998; and Weiser, "Prosecutors Portray the Strands of a Bin Laden Web of Terror," A-1.

101. "Egypt Holds Alleged Plotters of Anti-U.S. Strike," Reuters, 25 June 1998; Alam-al-Din, "Report Links Bin Laden, Nuclear Weapons," 5; "Citing Confession Made by 'Albania' Case Defendant," *Al-Quds Al-Arabi,* 19 February 1999, 1.

102. Pearl, "In Sudanese Bombing, 'Evidence' Depends on Who Is Viewing It"; Yusufzai, "World's Most Wanted Terrorist."

103. Robin Wright, "Far Reaching Bin Laden Probe Pays Off," *Los Angeles Times,* 28 August 1998, A-1, Muhammed Salah, "An Islamic Organization Affirms Bulgaria Handed Over to Egypt a Jihad Organization Member," *Al-Hayah,* 25 August 1998, 5.

104. Grunwald, "Africa Blast Suspects to Stand Trial in the U.S.," A-1, A-20.

105. "Two Egyptians Connected with Fundamentalist Groups Arrested," *AFP,* 29 June 1998; Bennet, "U.S. Cruise Missiles Strike Sudan and Afghan Targets Tied to Terrorist Network"; Esmat Saleheddin, "Islamists Say Albania Extradited Militants to Egypt," Reuters, 2 August 1998; Muhammed Salah, "'Returnees from Albania Case' Aimed at Eliminating Jihad Group," *Al-Hayah,* 15 December 1998, 5.

106. Benjamin Weiser and James Risen, "The Masking of a Militant: A Special Report," *New York Times,* 1 December 1998, A-1.

107. William Droziak, "Bin Laden Aide Denies Link to Embassy Bombing," *Washington Post,* 21 September 1998, A-22; Girard, "On Osama Bin Laden's Trail," 6; "Massive Retaliation Feared," *Munich Focus,* 21 September 1998, 11; U.S. State Department, "Patterns of Global Terrorism, 1998," p. 16; Grunwald, "Africa Blast Suspects to Stand Trial in the U.S."; and Bonner, "Seeking Bombs? No, Wife, Arab Suspect Tells FBI," A-4.

108. Girard, "On Osama Bin Laden's Trail"; "Seven Arrested in London Linked to Bin Laden," London Press Association, 23 September 1998; Muhammed Al-Shafai'i, "UK Court to Review the Detention of Alleged Bin Laden Aide," *Al-Sharq Al-Awsat,* 29 October 1998, 1; Samir al-Mubarak, "Report on Islamic Movements in Britain," *Al-Watan Al-Arabi,* 12 December 1997, 4–8; Rahimi Afridi, "Islamic Affairs: Report on Fundamentalist 'War' on West in Gulf," *Al-Watan Al-Arabi,* 19 July 1996, 16–18; Muhammed Salah, "In Response to British Ruling to Extradite Two Egyptian Fundamentalists to the United States, Al-Zayyat Warns of Reprisal Operations against U.S. Interests," *Al-Hayah,* 5 May 2000, 5; Larry Neumeister, "Two Egyptians Held in London Added to Embassy Bombing Indictment," Associated Press, 9 May 2000.

109. Waller, "Inside the Hunt for Osama"; Muhammed Salah, "Interrogation of al-Zawahiri's Deputy Revealed the Jihad and Al Qaeda Secrets," *Al-Hayah,* 18 March 1999, 5; Bolger and Black, "The Western Nightmare: Saddam and Bin Laden Versus the World"; "71 Egyptian 'Terrorists' Referred to Military Court," *Al-Sharq Al-Awsat,* 7 July 1999, 2; Muhammad al-Shafai, "Egypt's Military Judiciary to Try Soon the Returnees from Azerbaijan, South Africa, and Kuwait Case Involving 77 Fundamentalists," *Al-Sharq Al-Awsat,* 12 August 1999,

4; "Excerpts from Muntasir al-Zayyat's 'Ayman al-Zawahiri as I Knew Him,'" *Al-Hayah,* 13 January 2002, 15.

110. Lodovico Poletto, "Wanted Terrorist Escapes Dragnet," *La Stampa* (Internet version), 5 October 1998; 'L. pol.,' "We Know Nothing about These Weapons," *La Stampa,* 6 October 1998, 1, 6.

111. Cloud, "Can a Tire Repairman from Texas Be the Key to Solving a Terror Plot?"; Weiser, "U.S. Says It Can Tie Bin Laden to Embassy Bombings," A-3; Benjamin Weiser, "U.S. May Ask Death Penalty in Bombings," *New York Times,* 9 October 1998, A-10; Weiser, "Prosecutors Portray the Strands of a Bin Laden Web of Terror"; Riyad Alam-al-Din, "Cash Couriers Linked to Bin Laden," *Al-Watan Al-Arabi,* 4 February 2000, 18–20.

112. "Egyptian Linked to Bin Laden Commits Suicide," Radio Tirana Network, 25 October 1998; Nur-al-Din Salih, "Campaign in Albania and Bosnia to Track Down Fundamentalist Networks," *Al-Sharq Al-Awsat,* 27 October 1998, 1; "Report by *Al-Quds Al-Arabi* Bureau in Tirana, Albania," *Al-Quds Al-Arabi,* 26 October 1998, 1; al-Ayyash and Najm, "Behind the Scenes of the American Strike against Bin Laden's Secret Cells"; "Jihad Group Threatens to Take Revenge against the United States," *Al-Quds Al-Arabi,* 8.

113. Muhammed al-Shifai'i, "The Vanguards of Conquest Case Will Be Referred to Egypt's Military Judiciary," *Al-Sharq Al-Awsat,* 28 May 1999, 4; Salih, "Campaign in Albania and Bosnia to Track Down Fundamentalist Networks"; "71 Egyptian 'Terrorists' Referred to Military Court," *Al-Sharq Al-Awsat;* al-Shifai'i, "Egypt's Military Judiciary to Try Soon the Returnees from Azerbaijan, South Africa, and Kuwait Case Involving 77 Fundamentalists," *Al-Sharq Al-Awsat;* Hamdi Marzuq, "Egypt Discovers by Accident the Organization 'Returnees from Africa'; Three Members of the Jihad Organization Collected Contributions in South Africa," *Al-Wasat Magazine,* 30 November–6 December 1998, 28–29.

114. Sadiq, "Cairo Combats Islamists Overseas"; "Kuwait: Fundamentalists' Families Deported; Measures to Contain Bin Laden Network," *Al-Quds Al-Arabi,* 24 February 1999, 1; "Egypt's Military Judiciary to Try Soon the Returnees from Azerbaijan, South Africa, and Kuwait Case Involving 77 Fundamentalists," *Al-Sharq Al-Awsat.*

115. U.S. State Department, "Patterns of Global Terrorism, 1998," 60; "Philippine Forces on Alert after Killing of Muslim Extremist Leader," *AFP.*

116. Susan Bell, "French Charge Friend of Terrorist Leader," *Times* (Internet version), 16 February 1999; "CIA Report on Bin Laden's Filipino Links," *Al-Sharq Al-Awsat.*

117. Zaydan, "Amid Conflicting Reports," 6.

118. "Duo Cites Bin Laden in Bangladesh Attack," *Washington Times,* A-9; Kenneth J. Cooper, "Bangladesh: Bin Laden's Next Target? Militant Seen Aiding New Islamic Force," *Washington Post,* 19 February 1999, A-17; Kamal Azfar, "Bangladesh Arrests Two Osama Aides, to Extradite to U.S.," *Ausaf,* 25 November 1998; "Bangladesh Police Identify Bank Accounts of Muslim Extremists," *AFP,* 29 January 1999.

119. Artan Hoxha, "These Are Ciciku's Dubious Alternatives," *Gazeta Shqiptare,* 17 August 1999, 7; Bledar Zaganjori, "Spies of U.S. Embassy Discov-

ered," *Gazeta Shqiptare,* 9 January 1999, 24; "Albanian Held for Spying on U.S. Ambassador," Reuters, 10 January 1999.

120. Abdullah Ould Mohameddi, "Mauritanians Pursue Afghan Organization, Inquire about Link with Bin Laden," *Al-Sharq Al-Awsat,* 12 March 1999, 1; "Mauritania Holds Man with Suspected Bin Laden Link," Reuters; "Suspected Bin Laden Supporters Held in Mauritania," *AFP.*

121. "Arrested Frenchman Thought to Be in Bin Laden Network," *AFP,* 3 March 1999.

122. Jimmy Seepe, "RSA, Tanzania in 'Bitter Row' over Bomber Handover to U.S.," *Sowetan,* 14 October, 1999, 1; "RSA Confirms Talks with Tanzania on Bomb Suspect," SAfm Radio Network, 14 October 1999; "Man Charged in Bombing of U.S. Embassy in Africa," *New York Times,* 9 October 1999, A-4.

123. Jadd al-Hajj, "'Bin Laden Specter' Overshadows Preparations for Opening of Olympic Games in Sydney," *Al-Hayah,* 4 July 2000, 6; Scott Inglis, "Refugee Hits Back at Terror Claims," *New Zealand Herald* (Internet version), 29 August 2000; "Further on New Zealand Police Announcing Plot to Target Sydney Reactor," *AFP,* 26 August 2000; "New Zealand Minister Praises Police for Uncovering Sydney Olympics Plot," Radio New Zealand International, 26 August 2000; and "Australian Government Urged to Shut Down Reactor after Terrorist Plot Uncovered," *Sydney Morning Herald* (Internet version), 26 August 2000.

124. Arieh O'Sullivan, "Bin Laden Ring Planned Mass Terror Campaign," *Jerusalem Post,* 22 August 2000; Hugh Dellios, "Israelis See Bin Laden's Hand Creeping into Gaza Strip," *Chicago Tribune,* 4 September 2000, 1.

125. Muhammed Salah, "Canada: Egyptian Fundamentalist Questioned over Links with Osama Bin Laden," *Al-Hayah,* 7 July 2000, 1, 6; "Report on the Threat to Arab Countries by Terrorist Bin Laden," *Sawt al-Mar'ah,* 3; Imtiaz Hussain "Pakistan Arrests Afghan NGO's Chief for 'Links' with Terrorist Groups," *Frontier Post* (Internet version), 29 July 2000.

126. Rahimullah Yusufzai, "No Reaction from Bin Laden to Death Penalty for His Men in Jordan," *News,* 19 September 2000, 1, 9; "Jordan Dooms 6 Extremists Tied to Plot by Bin Laden," *International Herald Tribune,* 19 September 2000.

127. "Abyan Islamic Army Leader Executed," *Al-Jazirah,* 17 October 1999.

128. "CIA Arrests Bin Laden Aide in Albania; Sanctions on Taliban Begin; Violent Demonstrations in Kabul," *Al-Hayah,* 15 November 1999, 1, 6; "Jordanian Expelled from Albania," *Jordan Times,* 15 November 1999, 3; Anila Prifti, "Bin Laden's Agent: Friend of Gjinushi and Berisha," *Koha Jone,* 14 November 1999, 5; Anila Prifti, "Bin Laden's Man: 'I Will Sue Albania,'" *Koha Jone,* 18 November 1999, 7; Tolga Sardon, "Istanbul Is Bin Laden's Bridge," *Milliyet* (Internet version), 17 December 1999.

129. Zaydan, "Pakistan Delivers to Jordan an Islamist Holding U.S. Citizenship," 1, 6; Bassam Baddarin, "United States Recruits Arab Intelligence Services in an All-Out Campaign against Bin Laden Aides," *Al-Quds Al-Arabi,* 18–19 December 1999, 1; Riyad Alam-al-Din and Ahmed Taysir, "Emergency U.S. Meeting on Bin Laden," *Al-Watan Al-Arabi,* 31 December 1999, 16–19; Hattar, "Pakistan Hands Over 14th Terror Suspect to Jordan"; Khan, "Pakistan Hands Over Bin Laden Aide to Jordan," 1, 8; John-Thor Dahlburg, "Some See U.S. as

Terrorists' Next Big Target," *Los Angeles Times,* 13 January 2000, A-1; "Reports on the Escape of Fundamentalists to Iraq," *Al-Quds Al-Arabi,* 7; David S. Cloud and Christopher Chipello, "Ressam Spent Time in Terrorist Camps Linked to Saudi Dissident Bin Laden," *Wall Street Journal,* 21 January 2000, A-20; Steven Lee Meyers, "Failed Plan to Bomb a U.S. Ship Reported," *New York Times,* 10 November 2000, A-7; Charles Aldinger, "Yemen Is Told of an Earlier Plot against a U.S. Ship," *Washington Post,* 10 November 2000, A-1; Abd-al-Salam Tahir and Steven Lee Myers, "Suspect in *Cole* Attack Reportedly Says Another U.S. Ship Was Targeted in January," *Al-Sharq Al-Awsat* (Internet version), 11 November 2000; Ahmed al-Haj, "At Least Three other Anti-U.S. Plots Foiled before *Cole,*" Associated Press, 11 November 2000.

130. "Kuwait Announces Arrest of Terrorist Groups; Explosives Seized," Kuwait Satellite Television Channel, 9 November 2000; "Two More Arrested in Kuwaiti Bomb Plots," *Washington Post,* 13 November 2000, A-20; "Explosives for Attacks on U.S. Targets Found," *Los Angeles Times,* 12 November 2000, A-4; Muhammed al-Shafai and al-Sa'd Shammari, "Kuwait Arrests 11 Fundamentalists, Among Them Two Police Officers, to Preempt Possible Attacks on U.S. Targets. One of Bin Laden's Aides Left the Country before His Arrest and the Detainees Include Yemenis, Syrians, and Egyptians," *Al-Sharq Al-Awsat,* 8 November 2000, 3; Hamud al-Jasir, "Two Kuwait Youths Arrested in the 'Terrorist Network' Case. Qatar Extradites to Kuwait an 'Explosives Expert' from an Arab Maghreb Country," *Al-Hayah,* 13 November 2000, 1, 6; "An Urgent Request to All Human Rights Organizations and Bodies: Kuwaiti Authorities Arrested a Group of Islamists and the Arrests Campaign Is Continuing," Islamic Observation Center (Internet version), 8 November 2000.

131. Al-Haj, "At Least Three Other Anti-U.S. Plots Failed before Cole."

132. Georg Mascolo, "Holy Warriors against Europe," *Der Spiegel* (Internet version), 24 February 2001; Dipesh Gadher, "MI5 Locates 'Bin Laden's London Base,'" *Sunday Times,* 4 March 2001; Judith Miller and Sarah Lyrell, "Hunting Bin Laden's Allies, U.S. Extends Net to Europe," *New York Times,* 21 February 2001, A-1; Alessandra Stanley, "Italy and Germany Arrest 6 Islamists in Failed 2000 Bomb Plot," *New York Times,* 6 April 2000; M. A. Calabro, "They Wanted to Kidnap a Top American Businessman," *Corriere della Sera,* 4 April 2001, 15; Pascal Ceaux, "DST Suspects Islamist Militants of Having Prepared Attacks in France," *Le Monde* (Internet version), 24 March 2001; Wolfgang Krach and Georg Mascolo, "Highly Alarmed," *Der Spiegel,* 9 April 2001, 22–24.

133. Thomas L. Lueck, "Algerian Is Found Guilty in Plot to Bomb Sites in the U.S.," *New York Times,* 7 April 2001; Muhammad Muqaddam, "Millennium Explosions: *Al-Hayah* Reveals Details of Arrest of Wanted Algerian," *Al-Hayah,* 28 March 2001, 1, 6; Muhammad Muqaddam, "Algeria Will Not Object to Informing Americans of Dahoumane's Replies to Questions on His Role in 'Millennium Plot,'" *Al-Hayah,* 30 March 2001, 6; Hassan Haider Diab, "The Americans Are Offering Five Million Dollars for the Humanitarians from Zagreb," *Vecernji List,* 18 April 2001, 15.

134. "The Embassy Bombing Verdicts," *New York Times* (Editorial), 30 May 2001; "A Verdict against Terrorism," *Washington Post* (Editorial), 30 May 2001, 18; Vernon Loeb and Alan Sipress, "Terrorist Verdicts Add to Message," *New*

York Times, 30 May 2001, 6; Peter Bergen, "The Bin Laden Trial: What Did We Learn," *Studies in Conflict and Terrorism* 24, no. 6 (2001): 429–34.

135. Leslie Lopez, "Asian Militants with Alleged Al Qaeda Ties Are Accused of Plotting against Embassies," *Wall Street Journal,* 7 January 2002; Barry Wain, "Allegations of Terror Targets in Singapore Rattle Region," *Wall Street Journal,* 8 January 2002; "Implications of Singapore Militants," *Utasan Malaysia* (Internet version), 20 January 2002; Dana Dillon and Paola Pasicolan, "Beware the Jihad in Southeast Asia," *Wall Street Journal,* 17 January 2002.

136. Muhammed Salah, "Sweden Extradited the Vanguards of Conquest Leader to Egypt," *Al-Hayah,* 20 December 2001, 4; Wa'il Al-Ibashi, "Ajizah, the Funky Islamist," *Rose al-Yusuf,* 22 December 2001, 76; Abduh Zaynah, "Al-Zayyat Fears Missing Date for Submitting Ujayzah's Appeal and Renotifies Egypt's Military Prosecutor," *Al-Sharq Al-Awasat,* 12 January 2002, 7.

137. Pamela Ferdinand, "No Bail for Bomb Case Suspect," *Washington Post,* 29 December 2001, 6; Alan Cullison and Andrew Higgins, "How Al Qaeda Scouted Attacks in Israel and Egypt," *Wall Street Journal,* 16 January 2002, A1.

138. E. A. Torriero and Michael Martinez, "Al Qaeda Architect's Influence Raises Fear," *Chicago Tribune,* 18 November 2001; "*Al-Sharq Al-Awsat* Visits Abu Hafs Al-Masri's Home; His Family Emphasizes He Is Alive; Refuses to Accept Condolences," *Al-Sharq Al-Awsat,* 30 November 2001, 6; Muhammad al-Shafai, "Arab Afghans Confirm Capture of Bin Laden's Aide Ibn-al-shaykh Al-Libi, Al-Sharq Sab'i," *Al-Sharq Al-Awsat,* 28 January 2002, 3; Ahmed Rashid, "Pakistan Raids Hideouts to Lose 'Safehaven' Tag," *Daily Telegraph,* 3 April 2002; Walter Pincus, "Seized Materials May Help Thwart Future Attacks," *Washington Post,* 3 April 2002, 14.

139. Ayman Zawahiri. *Loyalty and Enmity: An Inherited Doctrine and a Lost Reality.* London: No Publisher, December 2002, n.p.

140. "Militant Killed by Police Had Bin Ladin Letter," *Arab News* (Internet version), 4 June 2003.

141. Daniel Trotta, "Al-Qaeda Suspects Go on Trial in Spain," Reuters, 22 April 2005.

142. Paul Haven, "Pakistan Will Deport al-Qaeda Suspect," Associated Press, 31 May 2005; Aamer Ahmed Khan, "Profile: Abu Fraj al-Libi," BBC News, http://newsvote.bbc.co.uk; and Katherine Schraeder, "Classic Spy Work Leads to al-Qaeda Arrest," Associated Press, 4 May 2005.

143. Summer Said, "Prestigious Cairo Library Goes Online," *Arab News,* 5 June 2005.

144. Holger Stark, "Syrian Had Inside Knowledge of 9/11 and London Bombings," *Spiegel Online,* http://service.spiegel.de, 24 August 2005; Levent Korkut and Aysegul Usta, "Present at Execution of Turkish Truck Driver in Iraq," *Hurriyet* (Internet version), 12 August 2005; "Sakra Remanded in Custody," *NTV Online* (Internet), 12 August 2005; and "Turkey Detains Key al-Qaeda Figure," *Daily Telegraph,* 11 August 2005.

145. Leslie Crawford, "Madrid Court Sentences al Qaeda Suspect to 27 Years in Jail," *Financial Times,* 27 September 2005; and Jennifer Green, "Sept. 11 Figure Is Convicted in Spain," *Washington Post,* 27 September 2005, A-16.

146. Auster, "An Inside Look at Terror Inc."; Vernon Loeb, "Bin Laden

Still Seen as a Threat," *Washington Post,* 29 August 1999, A-3; Muhammed Salah, "Egyptian Fundamentalists Insist Zawahiri Is in Jalalabad," *Al-Hayah,* 21 March 1999, 5; Sa'd al-Qaysi, "Search for Jihad Movement's al-Zawahiri," *Al-Watan Al-Arabi,* 23 April 1999, 26–27; Yusufzai, "World's Most Wanted Terrorist"; Asaad, *Osama Bin Laden: The Whole Story,* 85; Stahl, "Interview with Richard Clarke."

147. Emmanuel Sivan, "The Holy War Tradition in Islam," *Orbis* 42, no. 2 (Spring 1988).

148. Muhammed Salah, "Egyptian Fundamentalist Reveals to *Al-Hayah*: Al-Zawahiri's Resignation Came Too Late. He Left Jihad Exhausted," *Al-Hayah,* 9 February 2000, 1, 6; "The Vanguards of Conquest Case Will Be Referred to Egypt's Military Judiciary," *Al-Sharq Al-Awsat*; Muhammed Salah, "Egypt: Arrest of 13 Members of the Jihad Organization," *Al-Hayah,* 25 November 1998, 5; Muhammed al-Shafi'i, "London Fundamentalists: Kuwait and the UAE Handed Over New Elements to Egypt," *Al-Sharq al-Awsat,* 7 June 2000; Fawaz A. Gerges, "The End of the Islamic Insurgency in Egypt? Costs and Prospects," *Middle East Journal,* 54, no. 4, (Autumn 2000): 592.

149. Saleh, "Egypt: Arrest of 13 Members of the Jihad Organization," 5; al-Shafi'i, "London Fundamentalists: Kuwait and the UAE Handed Over New Elements to Egypt."

150. Hamdi Rizq, "Would al-Zawahiri Fall into the Trap of Global Security? Confessions by 'Returnees from Albania' Signal the Demise of the Egyptian 'Jihad Organization,'" *Al-Wasat Magazine,* 19–25 April 1999, 32, 33; Nabil Abu-Sutayt, "Egypt's Security Services View War of Faxes as Evidence of the Isolation of Fundamentalist Leaders Abroad. Al-Zawahiri Attracted Al-Islambouli to His Side and Rifai'i Acts as Islamic Group's Leader," *Al-Sharq Al-Awsat,* 4 December 1999, 6.

151. Muhammed Al-Shafai, "Leaders of World Fundamentalist Movements to Gather at Conference in London Friday to Discuss West's Arrogance," *Al-Sharq Al-Awsat,* 22 February 1999, 5.

152. Muhammed Salah, "Jihad Group Vows to Take Revenge against the United States," *Al-Hayah,* 6 August 1998, 6.

153. "Jihad Group Threatens to Take Revenge against United States," *Al-Quds Al-Arabi,* 8.

154. "Egyptian Jihad Group Pledges Revenge on Kuwait," *Al-Quds Al-Arabi,* 6–7 February 1999, 1.

155. "Unattributed Biography of Osama Bin Laden," *Frontline Online.*

156. Marion Lloyd, "Where Bin Laden Is Beloved, Anti-U.S. Calls Mount," *Boston Globe,* 25 July 1999.

157. Colvin, "The New Face of World Terrorism."

158. Ahmed Salamah Salamah, "Types of Terrorism," *Al-Ahram,* 1 September 1998, 1.

159. "Interview with Milt Bearden," *Frontline Online.*

Chapter 14

1. "Rebels Say Attack on Juba Imminent," *Al-Quds Al-Arabi.*

2. "*Nida'ul Islam* Exclusive Interview with Osama Bin Laden, *Nida'ul Is-*

lam"; Miller, "Exclusive Interview with Osama Bin Laden."

3. Ranstorp, "Interpreting the Broader Context and Meaning of Bin Laden's Fatwa," 326–27.

4. Richard Mackenzie, "The Succession," *New Republic,* 14 and 21 September 1998.

5. "Russia Hails India's Position against Terrorism," Moscow RIA, 28 February 2000.

6. "Fanning the Flames," *News* (Editorial, Internet version), 2 October 1999.

7. Miller, "Greetings America: My Name is Osama Bin Laden."

8. Ibid.

9. *Al-Quds Al-Arabi,* 3 January 1995; "World Front for Fighting the Jews and the Crusaders, Statement No. 4." *Al-Hayah*; Muhammed Salah, "Canada: An Egyptian 'Planning' to Blow Up the Israeli Embassy Arrested," *Al-Hayah,* 8 March 2000, 1, 6.

10. Atwan, "Interview with Saudi Oppositionist Osama Bin Laden"; Najm, "The Destruction of the Base"; Muhammed Salah, "World Islamic Front Backs Intifadah of Palestine's Sons," *Al-Hayah,* 4 March 1998, 4.

11. Yusufzai, "World's Most Wanted Terrorist"; Fisk, "Arab Rebel Leader Warns the British: 'Get Out of the Gulf,'" 14; Al-Karim and al-Nur, "Interview with Saudi Businessman Osama Bin Laden," 4; "Interview of Rifa'i Taha," Islamic Observation Center (Internet version), 19 June 2000; "Interview with Ayman al-Zawahiri," in "Al-Jazeera, Bin Laden, and I," ed. Jamal Ismail, *Al-Zaman* (July 2000); Cullison and Higgins, "How Al Qaeda Scouted Attack Sites in Israel and Egypt," A1.

12. "Rebels Say Attack on Juba Imminent," *Al-Quds Al-Arabi*; "Bin Laden: Afghanistan's Inclusion on U.S. 'Terrorism List' Is 'Certificate of Good Conduct' for Taliban," *Al-Quds Al-Arabi,* 3; Miller, "Greetings America: My Name Is Osama Bin Laden"; "Declaration of Jihad against the Americans," *Al-Islah.*

13. Najm, "The Destruction of the Base."

14. "'The U.S. Should Search for Attackers inside Itself,'" *Ummat*; Rasheed Javed, "U.S. Will Treat Pakistan, Saudi Arabia, and Iran Very Harshly," *Jang,* 20 November 2001, 1, 7; "The Real Threat to American Interests in Saudi Arabia," MediaGen (U.K.) Ltd.; "Egypt's Jihad Asked by Bin Laden to Turn Guns on U.S.," *AFP*; Immanuel Wallerstein, "Islam, the West, and the World," *Journal of Islamic Studies* 10, no. 2 (May 1999).

15. "Letter from Kandahar," Associated Press.

16. Ibrahim Zayd al-Kilani, "Osama Bin Laden, the Eagle of Islam," *Al-Sabil,* 21 October 1999, 20.

17. "*Nida'ul Islam* Exclusive Interview with Osama Bin Laden, *Nida'ul Islam*"; "Osama Speaks on Hijra and the Islamic State," *Al-Jihaad Newsletter.*

18. "Observer," "Bin Laden: Dissident Turns Pan-Islamist," *Muslim,* 15 March 1997, 1, 11; Khalid Sharaf-al-Din, "Egypt: The Death Sentences against Jihad Leaders Will Be Dropped When They Are Arrested and Tried in Prison," *Al-Sharq Al-Awsat,* 23 April 1993, 3; al-Shafai'i, "Curry Restaurants, Car Dealerships, and Mobile Phones Shops"; Mahdid, "Britain Closes Down a Fundamentalist's 'Front Company,'" 3; Faisal Bodi, "Draco Would Be Proud: The New Terrorism Act Will Have Far-Reaching Consequences for Liberty Both

in Britain and Abroad," *Guardian* (Op-Ed; Internet version), 16 August 2000; Muhammad al-Shafai'i, "London Faces Crisis because of Terrorist Groups List," *Al-Sharq Al-Awsat*, 2 March 2001, 3; "Bizarre Classification," *Al-Watan* (Internet version), 2 March 2001.

19. Bolger and Black, "The Western Nightmare"; "In Statement from Khandahar, Where Bin Laden Is Based, Advice and Reform Committee Warns Britain, Demands al-Fawwaz's Immediate Release," *Al-Quds Al-Arabi*, 1 October 98.

20. Muhammad al-Shafai, "Egyptian 'Islamic Group' Leader Calls for 'Stepping Up Hostile Strategy' against United States," *Al-Sharq Al-Awsat*, 13 October 1999, 2.

21. Dahlburg, "Some See U.S. as Terrorists' Next Big Target."

22. "Observer," "Bin Laden: Dissident Turns Pan-Islamist"; "Surprises from the Trial of the Largest International Terrorist Group in Egypt," *Al-Sharq Al-Awsat*.

23. "No Need to Explain What Is Clear," *Sangar* (Op-Ed), 20 October 1999, 4; "Russians and Iranians in Panjsher," *Hewad* (Editorial), 2 October 1999, 1, 2; Samar Assad, "French Premier Takes Heat for Calling Arabs Terrorists," *Philadelphia Enquirer*, 28 February 2000, A-2; "Excerpts from Guilty Plea in Terrorist Case," *New York Times*, 21 October 2000, A-14.

24. Cloud, "U.S. Officials Charge Bin Laden and Aide with Conspiracy in Embassy Bombings."

25. McWethy, "Osama Bin Laden Plans Attacks on United States"; Hassan Haidar Diab, "We Shall Set Croatia on Fire with Car-Bombs," *Vecernji List*, 31 October 2000, 84; Bruno Lopandic, "Who Killed Abu-Tala'at: Foreign Agents of HVO?" *Slododna Dalmacija*, 2 November 2000, 2; D. Miljus and Hassan Haidar Diab, "Police Introduce Special Protective Measures because of Terrorist Threats," *Vecernji List*, 2 November 2000, 3; Mascolo, "Holy Warriors against Europe."

26. Yusufzai, "World's Most Wanted Terrorist"; al-Qaysi, "Report on U.S. Embassy Bombing Probe"; "Conspiracy against Muslim Ummah," *Quarterly Ziaul Islam*, 1 October–31 December 2000, 6–10.

27. "Group Claiming Anti-U.S. Bombings Spell Out Demands," *AFP*, 10 August 1998.

28. Robert Fisk, "The Saudi Connection," *Independent*, 9 August 1998, 19.

29. Salah, "The Main Defendant Confirms the Islamists' Determination to Retaliate against United States," 5; Sharaf-al-Din, "Surprises from the Trial of the Largest International Terrorist Group in Egypt," p. 5; Ahmad Muwaffaq Zaydan, "Interview with Mustafa Hamza," *Al-Hayah*, 21 April 1996.

30. Muhammed Al-Shafai'i, "Egyptian 'Islamic Group' Leader Calls for 'Stepping Up Hostile Strategy' against United States," *Al-Sharq Al-Awsat*, 13 October 1999, 2; Hattar, "Pakistan Hands Over 14th Terror Suspect to Jordan"; Salah, "In Response to British Ruling to Extradite Two Egyptian Fundamentalists to the United States, Al-Zayyat Warns of Reprisal Operations against U.S. Interests"; Yousef Diab, "Military Court to Try 'Terrorists,'" *Daily Star* (Internet version), 13 May 2000; "Lebanese Legal and Political Quarters Surprised by Extradition of 'Bin Laden' Group Leader to Egypt before His Trial," *Al-Sharq Al-Awsat* (Internet version), 14 May 2000.

31. Kamil Yusuf Husayn, *Osama Bin Laden: Legend of the Century* (Dubai:

Al-Bayan, 1999).

32. Juliette Rossant, "Billionaires," *Forbes Magazine,* 5 July 1999, 194; Pearl, "In Sudanese Bombing, 'Evidence' Depends on Who Is Viewing It"; "Report on Saudi Billionaire Financing Bin Laden: Saudi Billionaires from Hadhramout Are Living in Tension after the Tragedy of Khalid Bin Mahfuz and His Sudden Fall," *Al-Quds Al-Arabi,* 13 December 1999, 1.

33. Miller, "Exclusive Interview with Osama Bin Laden."

34. Abd-al-Bari Atwan, "Guns and Fried Eggs in a Mountain Cave," *Sunday Times* (Internet version), 16 September 2001.

35. Ibid.

36. Ed Blanche, "Arabs Crack Down on Islamists," *Jane's Intelligence Review* 14, no. 3 (March 2002).

37. William Shawcross, "Stop This Racism," *Guardian* (Internet version), 17 September 2001.

38. Alexandrine Bouilhet, "War on Al Qaeda: Choice of American Base in Cuba Enables the United States to Avoid International Legal Constraints: Guantanamo, Prison for Special Justice," *Le Figaro,* 18 January 2002, 2.

39. Hugo Young, "We Will Not Tolerate the Abuse of Prisoners of War; Guantanamo Could Be Where Europe and America Part Company," *Guardian* (Internet version), 17 January 2002; "Spare Us Wild West Justice," *Independent on Sunday* (Editorial; Internet version), 13 January 2002.

40. Abd-al Wahid al-Hamid, "Islamic Philanthropic Organizations — Lessons to Be Learned," *Al-Riyad,* 2 February 2000, 17; Lewis, "The Roots of Muslim Rage"; "Conversion to Christianity in Islamic society Is against the UN Charter," *Hewad* (Editorial), 13 January 2001, 1, 2.

41. Muhammad Aurangzeb Awan, "Islamic Seminar Discusses Shamzai's Fatwa," *Ausaf,* 27 August 1999, 11.

42. Huntington, *The Clash of Civilizations and the Remaking of World Order,* 217.

43. Suhaylah Zayn-al-Abidin Hammad, "The Christian-Muslim Dialogue Fraud," *Al-Madinah,* 7 February 2000, 7.

44. Muhammad Salah, "Mullah Omar, Bin Laden, and al-Zawahiri Are Alive and Eulogize Shaykh Badni. First Announcement That the Jihad Leader Has Become Al-Qaida Leader's Deputy," *Al Hayah,* 19 February 2002, 7; "Transcript of Bin Laden's October [2001] Interview," CNN.com, accessed 5 February 2002.

45. "Statement Read by Ayman al-Zawahiri," Al-Jazirah Satellite Channel Television, 9 November 2001.

46. Ibid.

Chapter 15

1. Rowan Scarborough, "Al Qaeda Now in 'Survival Only Mode,'" *Washington Times,* 3 December 2001, 1; Ronesh Ratnesar, "What's Become of Al Qaeda," *Times,* 12 January 2002, 38.

2. "Transcript of Bin Laden's October [2001] Interview," CNN.com.

3. Charles Krauthammer, "Only in Their Dreams," *Time,* 24 December 2001.

4. Yaroslav Trofimov, "As a Taliban Regime Falls inside Afghanistan, So Do Islamic Convictions outside Its Borders," *Wall Street Journal,* 31 December 2001.

5. Robin Wright, "Invisible War on Terrorism Accelerates Worldwide," *Los Angeles Times,* 7 January 2002; Greg Jaffe et al., "Prisoners Lack Rank to Assist U.S.' Search: Warlord Lied about Surrender, Official Says," *Wall Street Journal,* 10 January 2001.

6. "Profile of Mohammed Makkawi—New Military Commander of Al Qaeda," *Al-Sharq Al-Awsat,* 27 November 2001; Karim Subhi, "Profile of a Terrorist," *Rose al-Yusuf,* 1 December 2001, 20–21.

7. Lawrence Friedman, "The Third World War?" *Survival* 43, no. 4 (Winter 2001), 67.

8. Atwan, "Bush War and What Will Follow," 1.

9. Humayun Akhtar, "What Happens If Osama Is Not Caught?" *Nation* (Lahore edition, Internet version), 27 December 2001.

10. Milt Bearden, "As the War Turns," *Los Angeles Times,* 18 November 2001.

11. Humayun Gauhar, "Trust the USA? But Can We Trust Ourselves?" *Nation* (Lahore edition, Internet version), 7 October 2001.

12. Milt Bearden, "Afghanistan, Graveyard of Empires," *Foreign Affairs* 80, no. 6 (November/December 2001).

13. Ahmed Rashid, "Afghan Warlords Return to Their Old Ways after Helping to Oust Taliban with U.S. Aid," *Wall Street Journal,* 16 January 2002.

14. Eric Slater, "Rule of the Gun on the Rise after Ouster of the Taliban," *Los Angeles Times,* 13 January 2002, 1.

15. Pamela Constable, "In Kandahar, Some Mourn the End of Taliban Rule," *Washington Post,* 16 January 2002, 16.

16. Yusuf Al-Shuli, "Interview with Mahfouz Ould Walid," Al-Jazirah Satellite Television, 29 November 2001.

17. Ralph Peters, "Our Old New Enemies," *Parameters* 29 no. 2 (Summer 1999), 31.

18. Reuel Marc Gerecht, "Pakistan's Taliban Problem," *Weekly Standard,* 5 November 2001.

19. R. James Woolsey and Mansoor Ijaz, "Revenge Is a Dish Best Served Cold," *Los Angeles Times,* 12 September 2001.

20. Robert Kagan, "We Must Fight This War," *Washington Post,* 12 September 2001, 31.

21. Reuel Marc Gerecht, "Bin Laden, Beware," *Weekly Standard,* 24 September 2001.

22. Kenneth Timmerman, "Likely Mastermind of Tower Attacks," *Insight Magazine,* 31 December 2001.

23. Jim Hoagland, "Mortal Combat," *Washington Post,* 8 October 2001, 23; Brian Michael Jenkins, "This Time It Is Different," *San Diego Union-Tribune,* 16 September 2001; George Melloan, "Facing Up to the Task of Fighting a Shadow War," *Wall Street Journal,* 18 September 2001; Jim Hoagland, "Forcing the Choice," *Washington Post,* 10 October 2001, 23; Andrew Sullivan, "This Is a Religious War," *New York Times Magazine,* 7 October 2001, 44.

24. Peter Beinart, "Front Lines," *New Republic,* 1 October 2001, 8; Victor Davis Hanson, "The Longest War," *American Heritage* 53, no. 1 (January/February 2002): 36.

25. Michael Rubin, "Afghanistan: As Bad as Its Reputation?" *Middle East Quarterly* 3, no. 3 (September 2000): 55–56; Vollman, "Letter from Afghanistan," 58–59, 61–64, 66–73; Robert Marquand, "Neighbors Warming Up to Taliban," *Christian Science Monitor,* 5 October 2000; Zahid Rashd, "Clash of Civilization and Culture," *Pakistan,* 25 November 2001, 4; Jan Abid Ullah, "A Lesson from the Taliban Saga," *Pakistan Observer* (Internet version), 23 December 2001; Luke Harding, "Analysis: A Slide into Chaos," *Guardian* (Internet version), 10 December 2001; Peter Bergen, *Holy War, Inc. Inside the Secret World of Osama bin Laden* (New York: Free Press, 2001), 14–15.

26. Ed Blanche, "The Egyptians around Bin Laden," *Jane's Intelligence Review* 13, no. 12 (December 2001); William F. Wechsler, "Follow the Money," *Foreign Affairs* 80, no. 4 (July/August 2001): 40.

27. Jim Hoagland, "Dry Up the Money Trail," *Washington Post,* 30 September 2001; Paul L. Fitzgerald, "Tightening the Screws," *National Interest* 66 (Winter 2001/02): 76.

28. "Osama Bin Laden and the Al Qaeda Network," *PBS NewsHour* (transcript), 27 December 2001.

29. "Transcript of Osama Bin Laden Video Tape," CNN.com, accessed 13 December 2001.

30. "The Events of the Week," Movement for Islamic Reform on the Arabian Peninsula (Internet site), accessed 21 December 2001.

31. Daniel Johnson, "Bin Laden Is Winning the Battle in Britain," *Daily Telegraph* (Internet version), 28 December 2001; Thomas L. Friedman, "Smoking or Non-Smoking," *New York Times,* 14 September 2001; Yasushi Funatsu, "Interview with Historian Paul Johnson," Kyodo, 19 January 2002; David Hackworth, "Level of Combat," *Washington Times,* 29 September 2001.

32. Thomas L. Friedman, "World War III," *New York Times,* 13 September 2001.

33. "Interview with the Comptroller General of the Muslim Brotherhood in Jordan, Abd-al-Majid al-Dunaybat," *Al-Wasat,* 12 November 2001, 26.

34. Abd-al-Bari Atwan, "Bin Laden Still in Afghanistan Getting Ready for War of Attrition against the United States," *Al-Quds Al-Arabi,* 29–30 September 2001, 1.

35. David Ignatius. "The Psyche of Bin Laden," *Washington Post,* 28 October 2001, B7.

36. "Speech by Osama Bin Laden," Al-Jazirah TV.

37. Friedman, "Smoking or Non-Smoking"; Steve Simon and Daniel Benjamin, "The Terror," *Survival* 43, no. 4 (Winter 2001): 5.

38. Bernard Lewis, "The Revolt of Islam," *New Yorker* (19 November 2001): 50–51.

39. Gerecht, "Bin Laden Beware."

40. Al-Shuli, "Interview with Mahfouz Ould Walid."

41. "The Events of the Week," Movement for Islamic Reform on the Arabian Peninsula.

42. Michael Scott Doran, "Somebody Else's Civil War," *Foreign Affairs* 81, no. 1 (January/February 2002): 22.

43. John Bagot Glubb, *The Great Arab Conquests* (New York: Barnes and Noble Books, 1995), 65–68, 70–71, 84–86, 176–80.

44. Frederick Talbott, *Churchill on Courage* (Nashville, TN.: Thomas Nelson Publishers, 1996).

45. Gerecht, "Bin Laden, Beware."

46. Sir John Keegan, "In This War of Civilizations, the West Will Prevail," *Daily Telegraph* (Internet version), 8 October 2001; Conrad Black, "What Victory Means," *National Interest* 66 (Winter 2001/02): 156.

47. Bernard Lewis, "Did You Say 'American Imperialism'? Power, Weakness, and Choices in the Middle East," *National Review* 53, no. 24 (17 December 2001).

Epilogue

1. Daniel Benjamin and Steven Simon, "The New Face of Terrorism," *New York Times* (Op-Ed), 4 January 2000, A-23; "The United States and Russia Should Not Invite the Wrath of the Muslims of the World," *Ausaf*, 4 June 2000, 10.

2. Ismail, "Al-Jazeera Bin Laden and I."

3. Bunyan, *The Pilgrim's Progress*, 170.

Epilogue to the Revised Edition

1. Quoted in Ronald C. White Jr., *The Eloquent President. A Portrait of Lincoln through His Own Words* (New York: Random House, 2005), 30–31.

2. Paul Majendie, "Police Confident of Al Qaeda Link to London Bombs," Reuters (Internet), 15 July 2005; Sciloino and Natta, "British Intelligence Downgraded Terror Threat before Attacks."

3. Katherine Baldwin, "Police Hunting London Bombers Shoot Man in Station," Reuters (Internet), 22 July 2005; "Al Qaeda-Linked Group Claims Responsibility for Latest bombings," Associated Press (Internet), 22 July 2005.

4. Tom Perry, "Blasts Kill 83 in Egyptian Red Sea Resort," Reuters (Internet), 23 July 2005; Deeb, "83 Die in Car Bombs in Egyptian Resort"; Maggie Michael, "Al Qaeda-Linked Group Claims Egypt Attack," Associated Press, 23 July 2005.

5. "Egypt Bomb Attacks Kill at Least 75, Wound 120." Bloomberg.com, 23 July 2005.

6. Mark Sherwood, "Mueller: Cost of FBI Cyber Upgrade Unknown," Associated Press, 24 May 2005; John Solomon, "FBI Didn't Seek to Hire Terrorism Experts," *San Francisco Chronicle* (Internet version), 19 June 2005; John Solomon, "FBI Chief Won't Mandate Terror Expertise," *San Francisco Chronicle*, 20 June 2005.

7. Lara Jakes Jordan, "Homeland Security Faces Massive Overhaul," *Seattle Post-Intelligencer*, 17 June 2005.

8. "Blair Calls for Battle against Evil Ideology." Reuters, 16 July 2005; Robert Barr, "No One Hurt in Coordinated London Blasts." Associated Press, 21 July 2005.

9. President George W. Bush, "Fighting a Global War on Terrorism, Quantico, Virginia, 11 July 2005," http://www.WhiteHouse.gov

10. Victor Davis Hanson, "Enough Is Enough," *Washington Times* (Internet version), 22 July 2005; Bush, "Fighting a Global War on Terrorism"; "And Then They Came After Us," http://www.nationalreviewonline.com, 22 July 2005.

11. Charles Krauthammer, "Why That's Ridiculous," *Time* (Internet version), 23 July 2005.

12. Abraham Lincoln, "Annual Message to Congress, December 1, 1862," in *Abraham Lincoln, Volume II: Speeches and Writings, 1859–1865*, ed. Don E. Fehrenbacher, 414–15 (New York: The Library of America, 1989).

Appendix

1. Weaver, "Blowback"; Smyth and Vest, "One Man's Private Jihad."
2. Ibid.
3. "Interview with Larry Johnson," *Frontline Online.*
4. Ibid.
5. Ranstorp, "Interpreting the Broader Context and Meaning of Bin Laden's Fatwa," 323.
6. Mackenzie, "The Succession," 23–27.
7. Ibid.
8. Ibid.; Paul Fregosi, *Jihad in the West. Muslim Conquest from the 7th to the 21st Centuries* (Amherst, NY: Prometheus Books, 1996), 17–18; Reeve, *The New Jackals*, 232; "Terrorism and Osama Bin Laden." *CNN Burden of Proof* (Transcript), 17 May 2001.
9. Mackenzie, "The Succession."
10. Auster, "An Inside Look at Terror Inc."
11. "Caveman Terrorist Spooks the West," *Observer.*
12. Grunwald, "4 Followers of Bin Laden Indicted in Plot to Kill Americans."
13. Ibid.
14. Ranstorp, "Interpreting the Broader Context and Meaning of Bin Laden's Fatwa," 323.
15. Ibid.; Malouf, *The Crusades through Arab Eyes*, 143; Darraz, *Osama Bin Laden Recounts*; M. Esham Ahari, "Transnational Terrorism, Pakistan, and the United States," *Strategic Review* 29, no. 1 (Winter 2001), 14.
16. Yusufzai, "A Cult Hero Is Born."
17. "Interview with Milt Bearden," *Frontline Online*; Raziud Din Syed, "Osama Bin Laden—A Terrorist or the Continuity of the Islamic Idea of Life?" *Jasarat*, 4 January 2000, 4.
18. "Unattributed Biography of Bin Laden," *Frontline Online.*
19. David et al., "The Global Terrorist."
20. Fisk, "Anti-Soviet Warrior Puts His Army on the Road to Peace."
21. Amba, "Saudi Militant's Wish"; Malouf, *The Crusades through Arab Eyes*, 143, 177–178; Margolis, *War at the Top of the World*, 39.
22. Miller, "Greetings America: My Name Is Osama Bin Laden."
23. "Unattributed Biography of Bin Laden," *Frontline Online*; Darraz, *Osama Bin Laden Recounts.*

24. Hashimi, "Osama Bin Laden─A Man as Strong as a Rock"; Engelbert et al., "One Man and a Global Web of Violence, A-1; Stephen E. Bower, "Theology of the Battlefield: William Tecumseh Sherman and the U.S. Civil War," *Journal of Military History* 64, no. 4 (October 2000): 1014–15.

25. "Interview with Sa'd al-Faqih," *Frontline Online.*

26. Najm, "Osama Bin Laden, the Destruction of the Base."

27. Arnett, "Osama Bin Laden: The Interview."

28. Hashimi, "Osama Bin Laden─A Man as Strong as a Rock."

29. Rahimullah Yusufzai, "Myth and Man." *Newsline* (September 1998): 42, 43.

30. Ibid.

31. "Laden Declares Jihad against U.S. Forces," *News.*

32. Ibid.

33. Yusufzai, "Myth and Man."

34. Colvin, "The New Faces of World Terrorism."

35. Nasrawi, "Osama Bin Laden Reportedly Receiving Millions in Donations."

36. Ibid.

37. Weiner, "Long Running Dispute on Sudan Marked Counterattack Plans."

38. Ibid.; "Pakistani to Star in Movie on Bin Laden's 'Achievements'," *Pakistan,* 6 May 2000, 5.

39. Soudan, "Thus Spoke Osama Bin Laden," 20–21.

40. Ibid.; Daley, "Report Says UBL-Linked Groups Possess 'Deadly' Anthrax and Plague Viruses."

41. "Osama Says Taliban Rejected US Billions for Arrest," *Ausaf,* 1, 7.

42. Khan, "Bin Laden Loyalists Seek Revenge on U.S."; "Bin Laden T-Shirts Selling Like Hot Cakes," *Khabrain,* 27 April 2000, 3, 10; "Babies, Businesses Named after Osama Bin Laden," *Pakistan,* 8 July 1999, 2, 6.

43. "UBL Popularity Increased 'Manifold' in Northwest Pakistan," *Wahdat,* 23 July 1999. 1, 5; Kathy Gannon, "Trademark Pirates Glorify Terror Suspect on Fake Nike T-Shirts," Associated Press, 12 December 2000; Ahmed Rashid, "The Bloody Trail of the World's Most Wanted Terrorist," *London Daily Telegraph,* 21 December 2000.

44. Salah, "Secret of the Relationship between al-Zawahiri and Bin Laden," 30, 31; Weaver, "The Real Bin Laden."

45. MENA, 28 December 1996.

46. Muhammed al-Bahnasani, "Witnesses Reveal the Role of Bin Laden and Al-Zawahiri in Leading and Financing the Jihad Organization," *Al-Akhbar,* 22 February 1999, 16.

47. "Security Official Says Bin Laden Bankrolled Egypt's Jihad," AFP, 15 February 1999.

48. Girard, "On Osama Bin Laden's Trail," 6.

49. Khan, "Bin Laden Loyalists Seek Revenge on U.S."

50. Ibid.

51. Girard, "On Osama Bin Laden's Trail," 6.

52. "America's No. 1 Target: Osama Bin Laden." *Guardian* (Internet version).

53. "Today's New Cult Hero." *Economist* (Editorial).

54. Sa'd al-Faqih, "Saudi Oppositionist on U.S. Strikes on Sudan and Afghanistan," *Movement for Islamic Reform in Arabia* (Internet version), 28 August 1998.

55. "Interview with Sa'd al-Faqih," *Frontline Online*.

56. "Interview with Ahmed Sattar," *Frontline Online*, April 1999.

57. "America's No. 1 Target: Osama Bin Laden." *Guardian* (Internet version).

58. "Laden Creates New Front against U.S., Israel," *News*, 28 May 1998, 12.

59. Ambah, "Saudi Militant's Wish."

60. Dickey, "Making a Symbol of Terror."

61. "Today's New Cult Hero." *Economist* (Editorial).

62. "Interview with Sa'id Aburish," *Frontline Online*.

63. Darraz, *Osama Bin Laden Recounts*.

64. "Laden Declares Jihad against U.S. Forces." *News*.

65. Yusufzai, "Myth and Man," 42, 43.

66. Christopher Thomas, "Holy War Run from Ruined Afghan Hideout," The-Times.com, 21 August 1998; Atwan, "Interview with Saudi Oppositionish Osama Bin Laden." Miller, "Greetings America: My Name Is Osama Bin Laden."

67. "Today's New Cult Hero." *Economist* (Editorial); Close, "Hard Target: We Cannot Defeat Terrorism with Bombs and Bombast"; Akbar S. Ahmed, "Islam's Crossroads," *History Today* 49, no. 6 (June 1999): 24.

68. Dickey, "Making a Symbol of Terror."

69. "Interview with Sa'd al-Faqih," *Frontline Online*.

70. Al-Faqih, "Saudi Oppositionist on U.S. Strikes on Sudan and Afghanistan."

71. "Bin Laden Said to Warn Clinton of More Attacks," Reuters, 21 August 1998.

72. Shirley, "The Etiquette of Killing Mr. Bin Laden."

73. "Interview with Sa'd al-Faqih," *Frontline Online*.

74. "Today's New Cult Hero." *Economist* (Editorial); Walter Pincus and Vernon Loeb, "Bin Laden Called Top Terrorist Threat," *Washington Post*, 8 February 2001, A-16; Robert Burns, "CIA Chief Calls Bin Laden Biggest Threat to U.S. Security," Associated Press, 7 February 2001.

75. "Today's New Cult Hero." *Economist* (Editorial).

76. Douglas Jehl, "Muslims Voice Fury over U.S. Strikes," *New York Times* News Service, 22 August 1998; Tariq Warsi, *Nawa-I Waqt*, 30 December 1998, 9.

77. "Interview with Ahmed Sattar," *Frontline Online*.

78. Abd-al-Bari Atwan, "A More Dangerous U.S. Terrorism," *Al-Quds Al-Arabi*, 21 August 1998, 1.

79. Lewis, "License to Kill," 14–15.

80. Ibid.

81. Ranstorp, "Interpreting the Broader Context and Meaning of Bin Laden's Fatwa," 326–27; Dr. Iffat S. Malik, "Obsessed with Osama," *News* (Internet version), 19 April 2000.

Notes on Sources

1. Reuel Marc Gerecht, "The Gospel According to Osama Bin Laden," *Atlantic Monthly* (January 2002): 46–47.

2. Neil King Jr. "Instead of Big Strikes, U.S.'s Terrorism Battle Focuses on

Harassing Would-be Troublemakers," *Wall Street Journal*, 4 August 1999, A-24.

3. Ismail, "Al-Jazeerah, Bin Laden, and I."

4. Yossef Bodansky, *Bin Laden: The Man Who Declared War on America* (Rocklin, CA: Forum, 1999), xxiii, 439.

5. Simon Reeve, *The New Jackals: Ramzi Yousef, Osama Bin Laden, and the New Terrorism* (Boston: Northeastern University Press, 1999).

6. Ibid.

7. Bergen, *Holy War, Inc.*, 53.

8. Peters, "Our Old New Enemies," 28–30.

Glossary

1. Bergen, *Holy War, Inc.*, 53.

2. Arthur Jones, "Memory of Crusades Live on in Today's War: Conflict Continues Centuries of Clashes between Christian and Muslim Civilizations," *National Catholic Reporter* 38, no. 1 (26 October 2001).

3. "First War of the Century," Al-Jazirah TV; Hamid Mir, "The Attack on Maulana Samiul Haq," "The Attack on Maulana Samiul Haq." *Ausaf*, 1; Javed Quereshi and Shahid Riaz, "Afghanistan to Become the Graveyard of American Troops: Interview of Maulavi Jalaluddin Haqqani," *Pakistan*, 22 October 2001, 9.

4. Atwan, "Bin Laden Still in Afghanistan," 1.

5. Muhammed al-Shafai, "Interview with Hani al-Saba'i," *Al-Sharq Al-Awsat*, 28 January 2002, 3; "Excerpts from Muntasir al-Zayyat's 'Ayman al-Zawahiri as I Knew Him,'" *Al-Hayah*, 10 January 2002, 15; Magdi Allam, "The Fundamentalist Challenge Will Swing into Action Again; A New Levy of Suicide Bombers Is Ready," *La Republica*, 22 November 2001, 15.

Glossary

Osama bin Laden's movement operates across the globe and is involved with numerous personalities, organizations, and ethnic groups. The following navigational aid is meant to assist the reader of this book in maintaining focus.

Afghan Jihad: The war that began with the Soviet Union's invasion of Afghanistan in December 1979 and ended with the Red Army's defeat and withdrawal in February 1989.

Arab Afghans: The term originally used to describe the non-Afghan Muslims who fought alongside the Afghan insurgents in the 1979–1989 jihad. This group included not only Arabs, but also Muslims from virtually every country in the world with a Muslim population. Estimates of the total number of Afghan Arabs are all over the map, ranging from 5,000 to 100,000. Since the Soviet withdrawal in 1989, a steady flow of non-Afghan Muslims — still known as Arab Afghans — was trained at camps in Afghanistan, and these fighters are now reported to be fighting in the Philippines, Kashmir, Chechnya, Uzbekistan, Indonesia, Bangladesh, Sudan, western China, the Balkans, and eastern and southern Africa. Osama bin Laden is the most well-known Arab Afghan.

Atwan, Abd-al-Bari: Editor in chief of the prestigious and influential U.K.-based Arabic daily *Al-Quds Al-Arabi*. He has interviewed bin Laden on several occasions and maintains an editorial policy sympathetic to bin Laden's aspirations and goals. He has written insightfully about bin Laden's impact across the Islamic world.

Azzam, Shaykh Abdullah: Revered Palestinian Islamic scholar and a distinguished member of the Muslim Brotherhood, Azzam established mechanisms for bringing non-Afghan Muslims to Afghanistan to fight the Soviets. He believed the Afghan war would give Muslims the chance to reinvigorate the concept of jihad across the Islamic world. An eloquent and fiery speaker, Azzam inspired a generation of Islamists and his work —

Azzam's *The Verses of the Merciful* has been highly praised by Osama bin Laden—continue to instruct and incite young Muslims. Bin Laden was devoted to Shaykh Azzam and believed he was the most important non-Afghan figure of the Afghan jihad. Azzam likewise admired bin Laden and the two men worked together on many projects to assist the Afghan fighters and to create enthusiasm for jihad in the Muslim world. Azzam and two of his sons were murdered in Pakistan in late 1989. Azzam's slogan, "Jihad and the rifle alone: no negotiations, no conferences, no dialogues," encapsulates the mindset he passed to bin Laden.[1]

Al-Banshiri, Abu Ubaydah: Abu Ubaydah's real name was Ali-Amin al-Rashidi. He was an Egyptian national, a former Egyptian security officer, and left Egypt in 1983 for Afghanistan. He was a senior member of the Egyptian Islamic Jihad (EIJ), was a talented combat commander of Osama bin Laden's forces during the Afghan jihad, and served for a time as a senior commander for Ahmed Shah Masood's forces in northern Afghanistan, thereby establishing the link between bin Laden and Masood. Also a man of ideas, Abu Ubaydah worked to unite the EIJ and the Gama'at Al-lslamiyah (IG) into a single Islamist force and apparently helped conceive the plan for organizing and training a professional, multiethnic "Islamic Army" that could be deployed around the world to support Muslim insurgencies. During the Afghan jihad, he became bin Laden's top military commander and later led attacks on U.S. forces in Somalia. In May 1996, Abu Ubaydah drowned in Uganda's Lake Victoria.

Bin Laden, Bakr: Osama bin Laden's eldest brother and the current chief of the multibillion-dollar Saudi Bin Laden Group of companies. He is a confidant of the Saudi royal family.

Bin Laden, Muhammed: Osama bin Laden's father. Muhammed was a devout, puritanical Muslim and a brilliant businessman. He was born in Yemen and emigrated to Saudi Arabia in the late 1920s, where he started the construction company that formed the core of today's multibillion-dollar Saudi Bin Laden Group. Muhammed established close personal and business ties to the Saudi royal family, and his company became and remains the "king's contractor."

Bin Laden, Osama: Born in 1957, he is the youngest son of Muhammed bin Laden. Educated at King, Abdul Azziz University, he fought in the Afghan jihad and organized the al Qaeda group to assist armed Muslim insurgents around the world. Following the precedent set by the medieval Muslim military leader Saladin, bin Laden declared a defensive jihad against what he called the Crusaders—predominately Christian Western countries led by the United States—in the summer of 1996.

Crusades: Military campaigns by Catholic European forces meant to reclaim the Holy Land from Muslim control. The concept of the crusade was sanctioned by Pope Urban II in 1085, and between 1096 and roughly 1300 there were eight crusades focused on the Holy Land. Many Crusaders shared a view of their efforts that today is held by bin Laden and his associates. As Arthur Jones has written in the *National Catholic Reporter*, the Catholic knights saw themselves traveling a "novom salutis genus" —a new path to heaven.[2] In the Muslim world, the crusades were and are viewed as Christian military offensives meant to expand Christendom's domain and eliminate Islam. Osama bin Laden's description of the United States as leader of the "Crusaders" is evocative and resonates with Muslims who associate the term with the history of bloody Catholic aggression against Islam.

Darraz, Issam: An Egyptian journalist who on occasion traveled with Osama bin Laden during the final years of the Afghan jihad. His 1991 book, *Osama Bin Laden Recounts Arab Al-Ansar Lion's Lair (Masadah) Battles in Afghanistan,* is the fullest study of bin Laden's combat experience during the war.

Egyptian Islamic Jihad (EIJ, or Al-Jihad): A relatively small group that evolved from the Islamist movement in Egypt's universities in the late 1960s. Because of its limited size, the EIJ, unlike the IG, has stressed the need for clandestinity and quick decision making. Many EIJ members initially belonged to the IG but formed their own organization in part because of their unwillingness to accept Shaykh Rahman as their leader. The dissenters believed that the Koran forbid leadership being given to a blind man. In Egypt, the EIJ primarily has operated in the cities and has specialized in precision attacks such as assassination attempts on Egyptian cabinet ministers. Outside Egypt, the group has a strong presence in the Balkans, the Persian Gulf, Yemen, the United Kingdom, Pakistan, Western Europe, and Afghanistan. During the Afghan jihad, the EIJ also developed a cadre of excellent insurgent commanders, and these fighters have since participated in multiple Muslim insurgencies and in attacks on the United States. The EIJ is closely allied with Osama bin Laden's al Qaeda; indeed, the line between the two organizations has long been barely visible and there are reports that the two groups have merged. Some senior EIJ leaders declared a cease-fire in 2000.

Al-Faqih, Sa'd: A leading Saudi dissident living in exile in London. Al-Faqih heads the U.K.-based anti-al-Saud organization Movement for Islamic Reform in Arabia (MIRA), which publishes literature and propaganda attacking the Saudi royal family for its corruption, venality, political repressiveness, and un-Islamic practices. Al-Faqih generally supports Osama bin Laden.

Fatwa: A binding religious ruling made on the basis of Islamic law by a qualified Islamic scholar or jurist.

Al-Gama'at Al-Islamiyah (IG, Islamic Group, or Gama'at): Egypt's largest Islamist group, the IG evolved from the Islamist movement in Egypt's universities and has been active since the late 1960s. It is strongest in Cairo, Alexandria, and the country's southern provinces. The IG has attacked

Egypt's Coptic Christians, Egyptian police, military, and security officials, and foreign tourists inside Egypt. It has a worldwide presence, and especially is strong in Western Europe, North and South America, the Persian Gulf countries, Yemen, the Balkans and Caucasus, eastern and southern Africa, Afghanistan, Pakistan, and the Philippines. The IG has a large cadre of veteran insurgent fighters who have fought in Afghanistan, Central Asia, Chechnya, Kashmir, Sudan, and Bosnia. Generally, the IG's attacks are meant to cause large numbers of casualties, although its well-planned but unsuccessful 1995 attack on President Husni Mubarak in Ethiopia shows it can operate with precision. The Gam'at's imprisoned leaders declared a cease-fire in 1997, a call that has caused debilitating and seemingly endless public debate, bickering, and name-calling among the multitude that identify themselves as "IG leaders."

Hadhramaut: The mountainous Yemeni province that runs along the country's Arabian Sea coastline. The province is the ancestral home of Osama bin Laden's family. He enjoys strong support in the province.

Hamza, Mustafa: Trained as an agricultural engineer, Hamza spent the years between 1981 and 1987 in jail in Egypt for his role in the assassination of President Anwar al-Sadat. In 1989 he went to Afghanistan and received insurgent training. He worked for Osama bin Laden there and in Sudan, and was so employed in Khartoum when he engineered the Gama'at's June 1995 attempt to assassinate President Mubarak in Ethiopia. The failure prompted his removal as the IG's operations chief and he returned to Afghanistan. Rehabilitated in the late 1990s, Hamza is now the IG's senior leader outside Egypt. He avoids the media, appears to be the Gama'at member who is closest to bin Laden, and is deputy military commander of the World Islamic Front.

Haqqani, Jalaluddin: A major Afghan insurgent commander and Pashtun tribal leader in the Khowst area during and since the Afghan jihad. He welcomed non-Afghan Muslim fighters to his training camps in Paktia Province and has remunerative ties to wealthy Gulf Arabs. Haqqani has had a long and close relationship with Osama bin Laden, the Pakistani military, and the Taliban movement. Haqqani was educated and teaches at the Dar-ul-Uloom, an influential Islamic seminary near Peshawar. Many Taliban leaders graduated from the school, and at one time, Haqqani was the Taliban's minister of tribal affairs. Bin Laden has described Haqqani as a "hero struggler" and as "one of the most prominent former commanders of the jihad against the Soviet Union, who has rejected the U.S. occupation of Afghanistan." Haqqani himself has said that Soviet troops were tough and brave fighters, but "on the contrary, the Americans are very voluptuous and faint-hearted."[3]

Hekmatyar, Gulbuddin: An Afghan Pashtun, Hekmatyar has led a faction of the Hisbi Islami party since early in the Afghan jihad. A staunch

Islamist and an exceptionally talented political opportunist, Hekmatyar commanded effective fighting forces during the jihad, but he was a consistently disruptive factor in any plans for politically uniting the Afghan resistance. He was and is a favorite of Pakistan's intelligence service. Hekmatyar's devoutness and political talents have turned the nifty and unusual trick of simultaneously attracting funding and other assistance from both Iran and Saudi Arabia. Hekmatyar has long had close ties to Osama bin Laden. He outspokenly supported the Taliban's identification of bin Laden as a "Great Mujahid" and a protected guest of the Afghan people, and backed Mullah Omar's refusal to deport bin Laden.

Ibn Taymiyah, Taqial-din: A revered medieval Islamic theologian and jurist, Taymiyah was educated in Damascus, taught there and in Cairo, and believed that Islam had replaced Judaism and Christianity. He is the author of the famous anti-Christian religious tract, *The Correct Answer to Those Who Have Changed the Religion of Christ.* Taymiyah argued that jihad is the personal responsibility of each Muslim when Islam is attacked. Taymiyah's teachings inspired the puritanical eighteenth-century Wahabi movement in what today is Saudi Arabia. Osama bin Laden is a devoted follower and strong advocate of Taymiyah's teachings and literal interpretations of the Koran.

Interservices Intelligence Directorates (ISID): Pakistan's premier intelligence organization, and the agency that managed the program of dispensing international military and financial assistance to the Afghan insurgents during the 1979–1989 jihad. ISID has had ties to Osama bin Laden, Sayyaf, Haqqani, and Hekmatyar since the early 1980s, and with the Taliban since its inception. ISID remains the Pakistani government's action arm in Afghanistan and Kashmir.

Jihad: Often translated as "Holy War," the word is more accurately rendered "striving in the cause of God." The term is divided into two categories: the greater jihad is the individual's struggle against evil and temptation; the lesser jihad is the armed defense of Islam against aggression.

Julaidan, Wail: A Saudi national who abandoned graduate studies in the United States to serve as Osama bin Laden's logistics chief during the Afghan jihad. Julaidan also represented bin Laden's interests among Islamic nongovernmental organizations during the war, and since 1989 has been active in organizing and directing Islamic nongovernmental organizations in the Middle East, South Asia, and the Balkans. He resides in Saudi Arabia.

Kandahar: The main province of southern Afghanistan. The city of the same name is the province's capital and was the major stronghold and administrative center of the Taliban movement.

Khalifah, Muhammed Jamal: A Saudi national and Osama bin Laden's brother-in-law, Khalifah is a successful businessman and entrepreneur, and has long been associated with running Islamic nongovernmental organizations (NGOs), particularly in the Philippines. He is reported to have used

NGOs to fund and orchestrate insurgent and/or terrorist attacks in the Philippines and Jordan. He resides in Saudi Arabia.

Khowst: The capital of Paktia Province in eastern Afghanistan, adjacent to the country's border with Pakistan. The area around the city was the scene of extensive combat throughout most of the Afghan jihad. It also housed multiple insurgent training camps, including some run or sponsored by Osama bin Laden.

Maktab Al-Khidimat (MAK, or Services Bureau): An Islamic nongovernmental organization formed in the mid-1980s by Shaykh Abdullah Azzam and Osama bin Laden. The MAK helped Afghan refugees, but primarily assisted the travel, training, and deployment of non-Afghan Muslim volunteers to fight in the Afghan jihad. The MAK is the model on which a host of other Islamic NGOs have been based. The MAK appears to have first developed the modus operandi of delivering humanitarian aid that provided relief to refugees, while affording legitimate local documentation to fighters posing as relief workers and hiding the simultaneous delivery of ordnance and funds to Islamist insurgents.

Masood, Ahmed Shah: An ethnic Tajik and the most famous commander of the Afghan jihad, Masood had been the military commander of the anti-Taliban Northern Alliance until he was killed by suicide attackers on 9 September 2001. A brilliant strategist and tactician, Masood held off the Soviets in northern Afghanistan with force and cease-fires until the much more numerous and better-armed Pashtun insurgents in southern and eastern Afghanistan defeated the Red Army and its Afghan Communist allies. Masood also was a master media manipulator and kept a number of prominent Western correspondents on his leash for more than twenty years. Masood consistently misled these journalists — and some U.S. and European politicians — to believe that he was a pro-Western Muslim who would install democracy, diversity, and feminist policies in Afghanistan. His assassination appears to have been planned and executed by al Qaeda.[4]

Al-Masri, Abu Hafs: Abu Hafs's real name is Subhi Abu-Sita (aka Mohammed Atef). He is an Egyptian national, a former Cairo police official, and a senior member of the EIJ. Abu Hafs was a prominent combat commander during the Afghan jihad, planned attacks on U.S. forces in Somalia, and succeeded Abu Ubaydah as Osama bin Laden's top military commander. He most recently was bin Laden's right-hand man and appears to have run al Qaeda's day-to-day activities. Abu Hafs appears to have been killed by U.S. bombing in Afghanistan in late 2001.

Movement for Islamic Reform in Arabia (MIRA): The U.K.-based Saudi opposition organization that is headed by Sa'd al-Faqih. MIRA provides a base for Saudi dissidents of all stripes, publishes scholarly and propaganda pieces criticizing the Saudi royal family, and generally has supported Osama bin Laden.

Mujahid: Most often translated as "Holy Warrior," the term describes a Muslim who takes part in jihad. The collective term is mujahedin.

Northern Alliance: The Taliban's major armed opposition in Afghanistan, the Northern Alliance was led by Masood and is primarily made up of ethnic Tajiks, with a smattering of Uzbeks, Pashtuns, and Hazara Shias. By early 2001, the loyalty of the Alliance's major Pashtun leaders—Abdur Rasul Sayyaf and Gulbuddin Hekmatyar—was wavering under inducements from the overwhelmingly Pashtun Taliban movement and their mutual friend Osama bin Laden. The Alliance is strongest in northeastern Afghanistan, and has grown increasingly odious to many Afghans by accepting aid from the country's most-hated historical enemies: Iran, Russia, and India. The Alliance, led by Masood's senior lieutenants, now forms the core of the Afghan Interim Administration, an unrepresentative regime dominated by Afghan minority groups and tainted by its lack of Islamic credentials, lack of credible majority representation, and economic and military dependence on foreign powers.

Omar, Mullah Muhammed: An insurgent commander during the Afghan jihad, Mullah Omar was educated in Pakistan's religious schools and was the supreme leader of the Taliban movement. Omar is close to Osama bin Laden, and the latter pledged his loyalty to Mullah Omar as "the Prince of the Faithful." Omar also is close to the Saudi clerical establishment, having been taught by Pakistani scholars trained in the Wahabi tradition in the kingdom's universities.

Peshawar: The capital of Pakistan's Northwest Frontier Province. The city was host to much of the Afghan Islamist insurgents' logistical and political activities during the Afghan jihad. It also served as a transit point through which non-Afghan Muslim volunteers entered Afghanistan to fight the Soviets. Peshawar also served as the home base for many of the Islamic nongovernmental organizations that supported the Afghans during their jihad.

Al Qaeda (The Base): Formed about 1988 by Osama bin Laden and Abu Ubaydah al-Banshiri around a core of bin Laden's longtime lieutenants and Egyptian Islamists, al Qaeda was meant to be a multiethnic Sunni Islamist insurgent organization that would last beyond the end of the Afghan jihad. Al Qaeda's primary missions are to militarily assist Muslim insurgents fighting infidel regimes across the Islamic world, and to attack U.S. targets. Al Qaeda has performed in exactly this manner. It has supported Muslim insurgents in Kashmir, Central Asia, the Philippines, the Horn of Africa, and the Balkans, and has attacked U.S. interests in Yemen, Somalia, Saudi Arabia, Kenya, Tanzania, and the United States. Al Qaeda is reported to have representatives in more than sixty countries.

Al-Qaradawi, Muhammed Yusuf: A respected Egyptian Islamist scholar who is now living in exile in Qatar, al-Qaradawi is a senior leader of the Muslim Brotherhood and reaches a broad audience across the Muslim world through his presentations on Qatar's Al-Jazirah Satellite Channel television. Al-Qaradawi has issued a widely accepted religious decree declaring that martyrdom — suicide — attacks are permissible under the tenets of Sunni Islam. Until this decree, many Sunni scholars — unlike Shia scholars — maintained these attacks violated the Koran's prohibition against suicide. Al-Qaradawi's pronouncement and its subsequent wide acceptance among Islamic scholars have implicitly validated attacks by Osama bin Laden, the Islamic Resistance Movement (HAMAS), the EIJ, various Kashmiri and Chechen insurgent groups, and other Islamist organizations in religious terms.

Qutb, Sayid: A much-revered Egyptian Islamic scholar, Qutb was the theoretician of the Muslim Brotherhood until he was jailed and then executed by President Gamal Abdel Nasser's regime. Qutb's most famous and influential work is titled *Signposts along the Road.* In it, he damned Western and Christian civilization and urged jihad "against the enemies of Islam." Osama bin Laden has been much influenced by Qutb's teachings.

Rahman, Shaykh Omar Abdul: Now imprisoned for life in the United States for terrorism-related crimes, Shaykh Rahman — also known as the Blind Shaykh — remains the spiritual leader of the Egyptian Gama'at. An al-Azhar-trained Islamic scholar, Shaykh Rahman visited Afghanistan during the jihad and met Osama bin Laden there. Since the shaykh's arrest and conviction, bin Laden has been outspoken in calling for Rahman's freedom and for attacks on the United States to force his release. Currently, bin Laden cares for Shaykh Rahman's two eldest sons and is reported to treat them as his own children. Since 2000, Shaykh Rahman has issued statements from his U.S. prison that track with bin Laden's goals. He has, for example, called for Muslims to "kill Jews wherever they find them" and has told Muslims that jihad to liberate Palestine is the duty of each Muslim and that any "Muslim who can do this duty and fails to do it is a sinner who deserves God's wrath." Rahman also has withdrawn his personal support for the IG's cease-fire.

Saudi Bin Laden Group: The multibillion-dollar Bin Laden group of companies, currently headed by Bakr bin Laden. Among other interests, the group is involved in construction, infrastructure development, light manufacturing, and telecommunications. The group's businesses are active in the Middle East, southern Africa, Central Asia, the Far East, Europe, North America, and South Asia. The group employed about 35,000 people in 1999.

Sayyaf, Abdur Rasul: An Afghan, Sayyaf was educated at al-Azhar University in Cairo and became a member of the Muslim Brotherhood. During and since the Afghan jihad, Sayyaf has led the Islamic Union for the Liberation of Afghanistan and switched back and forth between the two sides of the post-Soviet Afghan civil war — the Taliban and Ahmed Shah Masood's Northern Alliance. Sayyaf's staunch Wahabi beliefs and excellent

classical Arabic have made him a favorite among Persian Gulf elites, especially the Saudi royal and upper classes. Since the early 1980s, the Saudis
have delivered substantial funding and ordnance to Sayyaf. He has had a
productive twenty-year relationship with Osama bin Laden.

Shaheed: A Muslim who loses his life while "striving in the cause of
God." Such a person is looked on as a martyr.

Taliban Movement: Many of the Taliban's leaders left Afghanistan
for Pakistan as children after the Soviet invasion or were born in Afghan
refugee camps there. They were educated in Pakistani religious schools — or
madrassas — by scholars trained mostly in Saudi universities. The Taliban
established its base in Kandahar and expanded across Afghanistan, taking
Kabul in 1996. By mid-2001, the Taliban controlled 90 to 95 percent of Afghanistan, had ended banditry and restored order in much of the country,
and was making diplomatic headway with Russia, France, China, the United
Kingdom, Germany, and several of its Central Asian neighbors. Although
reviled by the West as violent medieval madmen, the Taliban teamed its
imposition of strict Islamic law with a slow process of rebuilding and modernizing Afghanistan's war-ravaged infrastructure, especially in the areas
of hydroelectric development, telecommunications, light manufacturing,
road building, and irrigation — the first three in partnership with China, the
latter two with bin Laden. By late 2001, U.S. military attacks had driven the
Taliban from power, and it had dispersed its forces in eastern and southern
Afghanistan from where it is likely to begin a guerrilla war against the new
UN-backed government in Kabul.

Al-Turabi, Hasan: Founder and leader of Sudan's National Islamic
Front, and for much of the 1990s the de facto ruler of Sudan. Al-Turabi readily
hosted Osama bin Laden when he left Afghanistan in 1991 and allowed bin
Laden to resettle in Sudan with veteran Arab Afghans from Afghanistan
and later Bosnia.

World Islamic Front for Fighting Jews and Christians (World Front):
Formed by Osama bin Laden in February 1998 and intended to serve as an
umbrella organization under which Islamist groups can coalesce, communicate, and begin to cooperate. Bin Laden is the World Front's chief, EIJ leader
Ayman Zawahiri is his deputy and the Front's military commander, and
senior Gama'at leader Mustafa Hamza is Zawahiri's military deputy.

Yasin, Shaykh Ahmed: An Islamic scholar and the spiritual leader of
the main Palestinian Islamist resistance group HAMAS, Yasin has identified all Israelis — military and civilian — as legitimate military targets.

Al-Zawahiri, Ayman: An Egyptian national born in 1951, al-Zawahiri
is the eldest son of a prominent Egyptian family and a medical doctor. He
joined the Egyptian Islamist movement while at university and spent three
years in prison for being a member of the Egyptian Islamic Jihad. On release, he left Egypt about 1983 and traveled first to Saudi Arabia and then

Afghanistan. After becoming EIJ leader, he developed a close and enduring relationship with Osama bin Laden. While Afghanistan was his base for the past nearly twenty years, al-Zawahiri has traveled to Yemen, Western Europe, the Balkans, the Caucasus, Pakistan, the United States, and Sudan. In 1998 he became bin Laden's deputy in the World Islamic Front. Close associates have described al-Zawahiri as a quiet, shy, and intelligent man who shows little emotion and listens more than speaks. He is said to enjoy making decisions and is calm and focused under pressure.[5]

Al-Zayyat, Muntasir: A prominent Egyptian lawyer who specializes in defending captured Egyptian Islamist fighters, al-Zayyat frequently makes himself available for press interviews and therein provides a good deal of context about the current status of the Egyptian Islamist groups, their leaders, and their policies. He has been insightful about bin Laden's rise as an Islamist leader.

Bibliography

Books

Aburish, Said K. *The Rise, Corruption and Coming Fall of the House of Saud.* New York: St. Martin's Press, 1994.

Adkins, Nelson. F., ed. *Paine. Common Sense and Other Political Writings.* Indianapolis: Bobbs-Merrill, 1953.

Asaad, Khalid Khalil. *Osama Bin Laden: The Whole Story.* Translated by Ahmed M. Ibrahim. No publisher/date.

Bennet, William J., ed. *Our Sacred Honor: Words of Advice from the Founders in Stories, Letters, Poems, and Speeches.* New York: Simon & Schuster, 1997.

Bergen, Peter. *Holy War, Inc.: Inside the Secret World of Osama bin Laden.* New York: Free Press, 2001.

Bodansky, Yossef. *Bin Laden: The Man Who Declared War on America.* Rocklin, CA: Forum, 1999.

Bowden, Mark. *Black Hawk Down: A Study of Modern War.* New York: Atlantic Monthly Press, 1999.

Bunyan, John. *The Pilgrim's Progress.* Uhrichsville, OH: Barbour Publishing Co., 1988.

Cooley, John K. *Unholy Wars: Afghanistan, America, and International Terrorism.* London: Pluto Press, 1999.

Darraz, Issam. *Osama Bin Laden Recounts Arab al-Ansar Lions' Lair (Masdah) Battles in Afghanistan.* Cairo: no publisher, 1991.

Esposito, John L. *The Islamic Threat: Myth or Reality?* 3d ed. New York: Oxford University Press, 1999.

— — —, ed. *The Oxford History of Islam.* New York: Oxford University Press, 1999.

Gall, Carlotta, and Thomas de Waal. *Chechnya: Calamity in the Caucasus.* New York: New York University Press, 1998.

Glad., Paul et al., eds. *The Process of American History. Volume 1: Early America.* Englewood Cliffs, NJ: Prentice-Hall, 1969.

Glubb, John Bagot. *The Great Arab Conquests.* New York: Barnes and Noble Books, 1995.

Hourani, Albert. *A History of the Arab People.* Cambridge, MA: Harvard University Press, 1991.

Huband, Mark. *Warriors of the Prophet: The Struggle for Islam.* Boulder, CO: Westview Press, 1999.

Huntington, Samuel P. *The Clash of Civilizations and the Remaking of World Order.* New York: Touchstone, 1997.

Husayn, Kamil Yusuf. *Osama Bin Laden: Legend of the Century.* Dubai: *Al-Bayan,* 1999. This book was serialized in *Al-Bayan* on 24–30 November and 1–3 and 5–14 December 1999.

Johnson, James Turner. *The Holy War Idea in Western and Islamic Traditions.* University Park: Pennsylvania State University, 1997.

Johnson, James Turner, and John Kelsay, eds. *Cross, Crescent, and Sword: The Justification and Limitation of War in Western and Islamic Tradition.* New York: Greenwood Press, 1990.

Kaplan, Robert D. *Soldiers of God. With the Mujahedin Afghanistan.* Boston: Houghton Mifflin, 1990.

Kelsay, John. *Islam and War: A Study in Comparative Ethics.* Louisville, KY: Westminster/John Knox Press, 1993.

Lincoln, Abraham. "Annual Message to Congress, December 1, 1862." In *Abraham Lincoln, Volume II: Speeches and Writings, 1859–1865,* edited by Don E. Fehrenbacher, 414–15. New York: The Library of America, 1989.

Malouf, Amin. *The Crusades through Arab Eyes.* New York: Shocken Books, 1984.

Margolis, Eric S. *War at the Top of the World: The Struggle for Afghanistan, Kashmir, and Tibet.* New York: Routledge, 2000.

Mayer, Henry. *All on Fire: William Lloyd Garrison and the Abolition of Slavery.* New York: St. Martin's Press, 1998.

McMichael, Scott R. *Stumbling Bear: Soviet Military Performance in Afghanistan.* London: Brassey's, 1991.

McPherson, James. *Battle Cry of Freedom.* New York: Oxford University Press, 1988.

Pillar, Paul R. *Terrorism and U.S. Foreign Policy.* Washington, DC: Brookings Institution Press, 2002.

Rashid, Ahmed. *Taliban: Militant Islam, Oil and Fundamentalism in Central Asia.* New Haven, CT: Yale University Press, 2000.

Reeve, Simon. *The New Jackals: Ramzi Yousef, Osama Bin Laden, and the New Terrorism.* Boston: Northeastern University Press, 1999.

Renehan, Edward T. Jr. *The Lion's Pride: Theodore Roosevelt and His Family in Peace and War.* New York: Oxford University Press, 1998.

Sikorski, Radek. *Dust of the Saints. A Journey to Herat in Time of War.* London: Chatto and Windus, 1989.

Simpson, Brooks D., and Jean V. Berlin, eds. *Sherman's Civil War. Selected Correspondence of William T. Sherman, 1960–1865.* Chapel Hill: University of North Carolina Press, 1999.

Sword, Wiley. *Southern Invincibility. A History of the Confederate Heart.* New York: St. Martin's Griffin, 1999.

Talbott, Frederick. *Churchill on Courage.* Nashville, TN: Thomas Nelson Publishers, 1996.

Thomas, Emory M. *The Confederate Nation, 1861–1865*. New York: Harper and Row, 1979.

Urban, Mark. *War in Afghanistan*. 2d ed. New York: St. Martin's Press, 1990.

Weaver, Mary Anne, *Portrait of Egypt: A Journey through the World of Militant Islam*. New York: Farrar, Straus & Giroux, 1999.

White, Ronald C. Jr. *The Eloquent President. A Portrait of Lincoln through His Own Words*. New York: Random House, 2005.

Yousef, Mohammed, and Mark Adkins. *Bear Trap: Afghanistan's Untold Story*. Lahore, Pakistan: Jang Publishers Press, 1992.

Zawahiri, Ayman. *Loyalty and Enmity: An Inherited Doctrine and a Lost Reality*. London: No Publisher, December 2002.

Articles and Documents

Abassi, Wajid. "Interview with Lashkar-I-Tayyaba Chief, Professor Hafiz Muhammed Saeed." *Ausaf*, 3 January 2000.

Abd-al-Rahim, Mufid. "*Al-Watan* Report on Osama Bin Laden." *Al-Watan Al-Arabi*, 26 March 1999.

— — —. "Bin Laden's New York Activities." *Al-Watan Al-Arabi*, 20 November 1998.

Abid Ullah, Jan. "A Lesson from the Taliban Saga." *Pakistan Observer* (Internet version), 23 December 2001.

Abou-Raghab, Laith. "Bombers Strike Saudi Capital." Reuters, 29 December 2004.

Abu-Khudayr, Muhammad. "Shaykh Yasin to *Al-Ra'y Al-Amm*: Spilling of All Israeli Blood Is Lawful," *Al-Ra'y Al-Amm* (Internet version), 20 December 2000.

Abu-Sutayt, Nabil. "Report on Egypt Islamic Jihad." *Al-Sharq Al-Awsat*, 6 February 2000.

— — —. "Egypt's Security Services View War of Faxes as Evidence of the Isolation of Fundamentalist Leaders Abroad. Al-Zawahiri Attracted Al-Islambouli to His Side and Rifai'i Acts as Islamic Group's Leader." *Al-Sharq Al-Awsat*, 4 December 1999.

— — —. "International Intelligence Conference Draws Up Three Scenarios for Chemical, Biological, and Nuclear Terrorist Attacks in the Middle East." *Al-Sharq Al-Awsat*, 11 November 1999.

"Abyan Islamic Army Leader Executed." *Al-Jazirah*, 17 October 1999.

"The Advent of Terrorism in Qatar." www.Forbes.com, 25 March 2005. Advice and Reformation Committee. "Communiqué No. 19: The Saudi Regime and the Recurrent Tragedies of the Pilgrims." 16 April 1997.

"Afghanistan Is a Free and Nonaligned Country." *Hewad* (Editorial), 17 July 1999.

"Afghan Military Commander Masood Received at French National Assembly." *AFP*, 2 April 2001.

"Afghan Opposition Leader Says Bin Laden Harms Islam." Associated Press, 28 October 1998.

"Afghans and Algerians in North Lebanon Battles." *Al-Sharq Al-Awsat* (Internet version), 3 January 2000.

Afridi, Rahimi. "Islamic Affairs: Report on Fundamentalist 'War' on West in Gulf." *Al-Watan Al-Arabi,* 19 July 1996.

Ahmad, Aziz-ud-Din. "Jehadi Organizations and the Nation-State." *Nation* (Lahore edition; Internet version), 10 February 2000.

"Aide to Terrorist Bin Laden Helped Bombing Investigators." Associated Press, 4 August 1997.

Ait-Iflis, Sofiane. "Terrorist Attack in Mauritania: Salafist Group for Call and Combat Claims Responsibility." *Le Soir d'Algerie,* 8 June 2005.

Ajami, Fouad. "The Summoning, 'But They Will Not Hearken.'" *Foreign Affairs* 72, no. 4 (September/October 1993).

Akhtar, Humayun. "What Happens If Osama Is Not Caught?" *Nation* (Lahore edition, Internet version), 27 December 2001.

Alam-al-Din, Riyad. "Cash Couriers Linked to Bin Laden." *Al-Watan Al-Arabi,* 4 February 2000.

– – –. "Iraq, Bin Laden Ties Examined." *Al-Watan Al-Arabi,* 1 January 1999, 16–18.

– – –. "Major Terrorist Plot against Dubai Revealed." *Al-Watan Al-Arabi,* 10 April 1998.

– – –. "Report Details Plan to Hunt Bin Laden Too." *Al-Watan Al-Arabi,* 11 March 2001.

– – –. "Report Links Bin Laden, Nuclear Weapons." *Al-Watan Al-Arabi,* 13 November 1998.

Alam-al-Din, Riyad, and Ahmed Taysir. "Emergency U.S. Meeting on Bin Laden." *Al-Watan Al-Arabi,* 31 December 1999.

"Albanian Held for Spying on U.S. Ambassador." Reuters, 10 January 1999.

Alborghetti, Igor. "The Time Bomb in Rijeka." *Globus,* 3 October 1995.

Aldinger, Charles. "Yemen Is Told of an Earlier Plot against a U.S. Ship." *Washington Post,* 10 November 2000.

"Al-Alfi Claims Qatari Connection to Egyptian Militants." *Al-Ahram Weekly,* 13 January 1998.

"An Alarming First for Egypt, Women Turn to Militancy." *AFP,* 3 May 2005.

"Algeria: 'Around 70' Killed since Beginning of Ramadan." *AFP,* 17 December 1999.

Ali, Salamat. "Bargaining Chip." *Far Eastern Economic Review,* 18 April 1991.

– – –. "Causes and Effect." *Far Eastern Economic Review,* 23 May 1991, 24.

Allam, Magdi. "The Fundamentalist Challenge Will Swing into Action Again; A New Levy of Suicide Bombers Is Ready." *La Republica,* 22 November 2001.

Allen, Robin. "Middle East: Gulf States Show Growing Public Hostility to U.S. Presence," *Financial Times* (Internet version), 21 November 2000.

"Al Qaeda-Linked Group Claims Responsibility for Latest Bombings." Associated Press (Internet), 22 July 2005.

Amba, Faiza Saleh. "Saudi Militant's Wish: To Die Fighting America." Associated Press, 30 August 1998.

"Americans Are Paper Tigers." *Der Spiegel.* 17 August 1998.

"America's No. 1 Target: Osama Bin Laden." *Guardian* (Internet version), 26 August 1998.

Anderson, Lisa, and Stephen J. Hedges. "Terror Web Pulled into Daylight." *Chicago Tribune,* 11 February 2001.

"And Then They Came After Us." http://www.nationalreviewonline.com, 22 July 2005.

"An Urgent Request to All Human Rights Organizations and Bodies: Kuwaiti Authorities Arrested a Group of Islamists and the Arrests Campaign Is Continuing." Islamic Observation Center (Internet version), 8 November 2000.

Aquino, N. P., and M. S. Villamor. "Filipino DefSec Reports on Arms Buildup by MILF." *Business World* (Internet version), 14 March 2000.

Arnett, Peter. "Osama Bin Laden: The Interview." *CNN/TIME IMPACT: Holy Terror* (Internet version), 11 May 1997.

"Arrested Frenchman Thought to Be in Bin Laden Network." *AFP*, 3 March 1999.

Ashgar, Raja. "Bin Laden Sparks Pakistan Duel." METIMES.com, 98–136.

Ashton, Lucy. "Syria's Retreat from Lebanon Emboldens Opposition." *Financial Times*, 6 May 2005.

Assad, Samar. "French Premier Takes Heat for Calling Arabs Terrorists." *Philadelphia Enquirer,* 28 February 2000.

"At Least 15 People Killed in Christmas Eve Bombings across Indonesia." *Jakarta Post* (Internet version) 25 December 2000.

"Attacks Are Estimated to Cost Nation 1.8 Million Jobs." *New York Times,* 13 January 2002.

Atwan, Abd-al-Bari. "America's Harvest of Blood." *Al-Quds Al-Arabi,* 10 August 1998.

———. "Bin Laden Still in Afghanistan Getting Ready for War of Attrition against the United States." *Al-Quds Al-Arabi* (Internet version), 29–30 September 2001.

———. "Bush War and What Will Follow." *Al-Quds Al-Arabi,* 8 October 2001.

———. "Guns and Fried Eggs in a Mountain Cave." *Sunday Times* (Internet version), 16 September 2001.

———. "Interview with Saudi Oppositionist Osama Bin Laden." *Al-Quds Al-Arabi,* 27 November 1996.

———. "A More Dangerous U.S. Terrorism." *Al-Quds Al-Arabi,* 21 August 1998.

"Audio Recording of Ayman al-Zawahiri." *Al-Arabiyah Televsion*, 28 September 2003.

Auster, Bruce B. "An Inside Look at Terror Inc." *U.S. News & World Report,* 19 October 1998.

"Australian Government Urged to Shut Down Reactor after Terrorist Plot Uncovered." *Sydney Morning Herald* (Internet version), 26 August 2000.

"Australians Being Recruited for Bin Laden Jihad." *AFP*, 29 April 1999.

Avancena, Joe, et al. "Hunt for Escaped Gunmen; One of 5 Iraqi Infiltrators Dead." *Saudi Gazette* (Internet version), 31 August 2005.

"Avoiding Madeleine's Mine." *News* (Internet version), 2 February 2001.

Awan, Muhammad Aurangzeb. "Islamic Seminar Discusses Shamzai's Fatwa." *Ausaf,* 27 August 1999.

Ayoub, Mohammed. "South Asia's Dangers and U.S. Foreign Policy." *Orbis* 45, no. 1 (Winter 2001).

Al-Ayyash, Isam, and Salah Najm. "Behind the Scenes of the American Strike against Bin Laden's Secret Cells; Balkan and Afghan Rings Plot against U.S. Interests." *Al-Hawadith,* 13 November 1998.

Azfar, Kamal. "Bangladesh Arrests Two Osama Aides, to Extradite to U.S." *Ausaf,* 25 November 1998.

– – –. "Bin Laden Warns of 'Full Fledged' Action against U.S." *Ausaf,* 9 January 1999.

"Azhar Urges Pakistanis to Wage Holy War against India." *News* (Internet version), 8 January 2000.

Azim, Sarmad. "Who Is Maulana Masood Azhar?" *Pakistan–Sunday Magazine,* 2 January 2000.

Azimy, Yousuf. "Karzai Says Better India-Pakistan Ties Vital." Reuters, 28 August 2005.

Aziz-ud-Din, Ahmad. "Jehadi Organizations and the Nation-State." *Nation* (Lahore edition, Internet version), 10 February 2000.

Azzam, Abdullah. "The Man before Osama Bin Laden." *Journal of Counterterrorism and Security International* 5, no. 3 (Fall 1998).

B., Na'ilah. "The Security Situation: Bullets Don't Fast and the Groups Fail to Repent." *El-Youm* (Internet version), 7 December 2000.

B., Rachid. "The Outcome of the Year 2000." *El-Youm* (Internet version), 31 December 2000.

"Babies, Businesses Named after Osama Bin Laden." *Pakistan,* 8 July 1999, 2, 6.

Babington, Charles, and Pamela Constable. "Clinton Aided by Decoys, Urges Peace on Pakistan." *Washington Post,* 26 March 2000.

"Back to the Taliban — Taliban Are Again Proving Afghanistan Pundits Wrong." *News* (Editorial, Internet version), 26 September 2000.

Baddarin, Bassam. "United States Recruits Arab Intelligence Services in an All-Out Campaign against Bin Laden Aides." *Al-Quds Al-Arabi,* 18–19 December 1999.

Al-Bahnasani, Muhammed. "Witnesses Reveal the Role of Bin Laden and Al-Zawahiri in Leading and Financing the Jihad Organization." *Al-Akhbar,* 22 February 1999.

Baker, Peter. "Pakistani Scientist Who Met Bin Laden Failed Polygraph, Renewing Suspicions." *Washington Post,* 3 March 2001.

Balana, Cynthia D. "Is the U.S. Central Intelligence Agency Involved in the Terroristic Activities Here of the Abu Sayyaf." *Philippine Daily Inquirer,* 18 April 1995.

Baldwin, Katherine. "Police Hunting London Bombers Shoot Man in Station." Reuters (Internet), 22 July 2005.

"Bali Bombing Suspect Proud of Attack." *Washington Times,* 13 June 2003, 19.

"Bangladesh Police Identify Bank Accounts of Muslim Extremists." *AFP,* 29 January 1999.

Barber, Ben. "Justice Blames Canada for Terrorist's Entry." *Washington Times,* 21 December 1999.

Barr, Robert. "No One Hurt in Coordinated London Blasts." Associated Press, 21 July 2005.

Batarfi, Dr. Khalid Muhammad. "Denying She Is Angry with Him, Saying She Prays to Guide Him on the Right Path, Mother of Osama Bin Laden Says: I Do Not Agree with My Son." *Al-Madinah,* 8 December 2001, 1.

"Battalion Churns out Disinformation." *Rossiyskaya Gazeta,* 2 November 1999.

Bearden, Milt. "Afghanistan, Graveyard of Empires." *Foreign Affairs* 80, no. 6 (November/December 2001).

— — —. "As the War Turns." *Los Angeles Times,* 18 November 2001.

— — —. "Making Osama Bin Laden's Day." *New York Times* (Op-Ed), 13 August 1998.

— — —. "A Terrorist's Long Shadow." *New York Times* (Op-Ed), 22 December 1999.

Bearden, Milt, and Larry Johnson. "A Glimpse at the Alliances of Terror." *New York Times* (Op-Ed), 7 November 2000.

Beawiharta and Nuri Sybil. "Indonesia Blasts Have Qaeda Similarities." Reuters, 29 May 2005.

Bedi, Rahul. "Paying to Keep the High Ground." *Jane's Intelligence Review* 11, no. 10 (October 1999): 27–31.

Beinart, Peter. "Front Lines." *New Republic,* 1 October 2001.

"Belgian Foreign Minister Says Masood Better Alternative for Afghanistan," RTBF La Premier Radio, 7 April 2001.

Bell, Susan. "French Charge Friend of Terrorist Leader." *Times* (Internet version), 16 February 1999.

Benjamin, Daniel, and Steven Simon. "The New Face of Terrorism." *New York Times* (Op-Ed), 4 January 2000.

Bennet, James. "U.S. Cruise Missiles Strike Sudan and Afghan Targets Tied to Terrorist Network." *New York Times,* 21 August 1998.

Bergen, Peter. "The Bin Laden Trial: What Did We Learn." *Studies in Conflict and Terrorism* 24, no. 6 (2001): 429–34.

Bhatia, Ravi. "Indian Agencies Keen on the Whereabouts of Bin Laden." *The Times of India* (Internet version), 6 July 1999.

Billingsley, Dodge. "Chechen Rebels Hone Tactics for Long Haul." *Jane's Intelligence Review* 13, no. 2 (February 2001).

"Bin Laden Advised Algeria's Radical GIA." Reuters, 15 February 1999.

"Bin Laden: Afghanistan's Inclusion on U.S. 'Terrorism List' Is 'Certificate of Good Conduct' for Taliban." *Al-Quds Al-Arabi,* 18 May 1998.

"Bin Laden Allowed to Conduct Business in Afghanistan." *Frontier Post,* 28 December 1998.

"Bin Laden and His Followers Preparing to Move to Yemen Mountains." *Al-Quds Al-Arabi,* 9 March 1998.

"Bin Laden Begins the Struggle." *Al Sha'b* (Internet version), 15 September 2001.

"Bin Laden Building New Bases in the Khandahar Area." *Sunday Telegraph* (Internet version), 4 October 1998.

"Bin Laden Congratulates Pakistan on Its Possession of Nuclear Weapon." *Al-Quds Al-Arabi,* 1 June 1998.

"Bin Laden Family Businesses Scrutinized for Ties to Terrorism." *Le Monde* (Internet version), 23 September 2001.

"Bin Laden Full of Praise for Attack on USS *Cole* at Son's Wedding." *AFP*, 1 March 2001.

"Bin Laden Gave Sharif One Billion Rupees." *Al-Akhbar*, 19 July 1999.

Bin Laden group Web site, http://www.saudi-binLaden-group.com (no longer on Internet).

"Bin Laden Hiding at Taliban Military Base." *AFP*, 17 February 1997.

"Bin Laden Pens Letter in Support of Kashmir Jihad." *Wahdat*, 8 June 1999.

"Bin Laden Said to Fund Terrorism School in Chechnya." RIA News Service, 24 August 1999.

"Bin Laden Said to Warn Clinton of More Attacks." Reuters, 21 August 1998.

"Bin Laden Says Ties with Taliban 'Ideological.'" *Al-Jazirah*, 13 February 1999.

"Bin Laden's Hand Suspected behind India Plane Hijacking." *Pioneer*, 25 December 1999.

"Bin Laden's Poem." *Ausaf*, 3 March 2001.

"Bin Laden's Shadowy Empire." *Indigo Publications Intelligence Newsletter*, 28 November 1996.

"Bin Laden's Statement: Circumstances and Implications." *Al-Islah*, 2 September 1996.

"Bin Laden Threatens Terrorism Hit in U.S." *CBS Evening News*, 6 August 1999.

"Bin Laden Took Advantage of the Situation of the Egyptian Jihad and Islamic Group Organizations to Impose His Control on Them and Form a World Front for 'Liberating the Holy Places.'" *Al-Sharq Al-Awsat*, 20 April 1999.

"Bin Laden Trained Ugandans." *New Vision*, 1 September 1998.

"Bin Laden T-Shirts Selling Like Hot Cakes." *Khabrain*, 27 April 2000, 3, 10

"Bin Laden Urges Jihad and Expulsion of U.S. Forces from Gulf, Praises Prince Talal Bin-Abd al-Aziz's Recent Statement." *Al-Quds Al-Arabi*, 23 March 1998.

"Bin Laden Warns against U.S. Plan to Eliminate Afghan Arabs." *Al-Quds Al-Arabi*, 15 April 1998.

"Bin Laden Warns CIA against Attempts to Arrest Him." *Al Majd*, 4 August 1997.

"Biography of Osama Bin Laden." Islamic Observation Center (Internet version), 22 April 2000.

"Bizarre Classification." *Al-Watan* (Internet version), 2 March 2001.

Black, Conrad. "What Victory Means." *National Interest* 66 (Winter 2001/02).

"Blair Calls for Battle against Evil Ideology." Reuters. 16 July 2005.

Blanche, Ed. "Arabs Crack Down on Islamists." *Jane's Intelligence Review* 14, no. 3 (March 2002).

— — —. "The Egyptians around Bin Laden." *Jane's Intelligence Review* 13, no. 12 (December 2001).

Blanford, Nicholas. "Rebels from 'Islamist Internationale'?" *Daily Star* (Internet version), 3 January 2000.

Blight, David W. "John Brown's Triumphant Failure." *The American Prospect* 11, no. 9 (13 March 2000): 4.

Bodi Faisal. "Draco Would Be Proud: The New Terrorism Act Will Have Far-Reaching Consequences for Liberty Both in Britain and Abroad." *Guardian* (Op-Ed; Internet version), 16 August 2000.

Bolger, Julian. "Vengeful Islamic Guerrillas Threaten British Troops Bound for Bosnia." *Guardian,* 28 November 1995.

Bolger, Julian, and Ian Black. "The Western Nightmare: Saddam and Bin Laden Versus the World." *Guardian* (Internet version), 6 February 1999.

"Bombing Suspects' Organizations, Ties Detailed." *Al-Bilad,* 4 May 1994.

Bonner, Raymond. "Seeking Bombs? No, Wife, Arab Suspect Tells FBI." *New York Times,* 5 December 1998.

Bouilhet, Alexandrine. "War on Al Qaeda: Choice of American Base in Cuba Enables the United States to Avoid International Legal Constraints: Guantanamo, Prison for Special Justice." *Le Figaro,* 18 January 2002.

Bowden, Mark. "Tracking Bin Laden 1 Yr. Since the Bombing," *Philadelphia Enquirer,* 8 August 1998.

Bower, Stephen E. "Theology of the Battlefield: William Tecumseh Sherman and the U.S. Civil War." *Journal of Military History* 64, no. 4 (October 2000): 1014–15.

Briscoe, David. "Americans Are Warned against Terrorist Threats." Associated Press, 6 August 1999.

Brown, Justin. "Risks of Waging Only Risk-Free Wars," *Christian Science Monitor,* 24 May 2000.

Bruce, James. "Middle East: Arab Veterans of the Afghan War—Trained Forces in Waiting." *Jane's Defense Weekly,* 1 April 1995.

Brummitt, Chris. "Indonesia Christians Bury Their Dead." Associated Press, 29 May 2005.

Brusini, Herve. "Police Believe GIA Orchestrator of Paris Attacks Identified." France-2 Television Network, 26 December 1995.

Bukharbayeva, Bagila. "Soldiers Fire on Crowd in Day of Clashes in Uzbekistan." Associated Press, 13 May 2005.

Bulaneko, Svitlana. "Yuriy Volodymyrovych Zemlyanskyy [deputy head of the Ukrainian State Security Service]: Wave of Terrorism Awaits World in Third Millennium." *Segodnya,* 9 February 2000.

Buongiorno, Pino, et al. "Alarm over Russia: All Clinton's and Blair's Next Moves." *Milan Panorama* (Internet version), 14 May 1998.

Burgos, Raymond. "Mindanao Cops Have Photos of Saudi Tycoon." *Philippine Daily Inquirer* (Internet version), 25 August 1998.

Burke, Jason. "Bin Laden's Opium War." *Observer* (Internet version), 29 November 1998.

— — —. "The Making of the World's Most Wanted Man." *The Observer* (Internet version), 28 October 2001.

Burke, Jason, and Harinder Baweja. "Target . . . India." *India Today,* 4 October 1999.

Burns, John F. "Remote Yemen May Be Key to Terrorist's Past and Future." *New York Times,* 5 November 2000.

— — —. "Yemenis Say Saudi Man Is Top Suspect in *Cole* Attack." *New York Times,* 13 December 2000.

— — —. "Yemen Links to Bin Laden Gnaw at FBI on *Cole* Inquiry." *New York Times*, 26 November 2000.

— — —. "Yemen on Delicate Path in Bin Laden Hunt." *New York Times*, 15 December 2000.

Burns, John F., and Steven Lee Myers. "Blast Kills Sailors on U.S. Ship in Yemen." *New York Times*, 13 October 2000.

Burns, Robert. "CIA Chief Calls Bin Laden Biggest Threat to U.S. Security." Associated Press, 7 February 2001.

Bush, President George W. "Fighting a Global War on Terrorism, Quantico, Virginia, 11 July 2005." http://www.WhiteHouse.gov

Calabro, M. A. "They Wanted to Kidnap a Top American Businessman." *Corriere della Sera*, 4 April 2001.

"Canada to Propose Joint Anti-Terrorist Measures with U.S." *AFP*, 29 January 2000.

Canares, Cathy, and Cynthia D. Balana. "Spy Chief Claims Info on Bin Laden in Mindanao." *Philippine Daily Inquirer* (Internet version), 25 August 1998.

Capaccio, Tony. "Afghan War, Defense Cost $6.4 Bln since Sept. 11, Pentagon Says." Bloomberg.com, 22 January 2002.

"Caveman Terrorist Spooks the West." *Observer*, 3 January 1998.

Ceaux, Pascal. "DST Suspects Islamist Militants of Having Prepared Attacks in France." *Le Monde* (Internet version), 24 March 2001.

"Central Asia: Weekly News Wrap." http://www.irinnews.org, 6 September 2005.

"The Century's First War: Speech by Osama Bin Laden." Al-Jazirah Satellite Channel Television, 3 November 2001.

Chandrasekaran, Rajiv. "A War of Vengeance." *Washington Post*, 19 June 2000.

"Chechen Suicide Bomber Blows Up Café in Grozny, Kills Nine Russians." Kavkaz-Tsenter News Agency (Internet version), 22 August 2000.

Chen, Peter. "Osama Said Recruiting Muslims in Melbourne for Jihad." Taiwan Central News Agency (Internet version), 30 April 1999.

Chivers, C. J. "Survivors and Toe Tags Clues to Uzbek's Uprising." *New York Times*, 23 May 2005.

Chowder, Ken. "The Father of American Terrorism." *American Heritage* 51, no. 1 (February 2000): 81.

"CIA Arrests Bin Laden Aide in Albania; Sanctions on Taliban Begin; Violent Demonstrations in Kabul." *Al-Hayah*, 15 November 1999.

"CIA Director Says Casio Watch Is the Hallmark of Every One of Osama Bin Laden's Operations." *Al-Hadith*, 27 December 1999.

"CIA Report on Bin Laden's Filipino Links." *Al-Sharq Al-Awsat* (Internet version), 22 May 1999.

Ciriello, Raffaelo. "I Will Give You Bin Laden, He Is Only a Terrorist." *Famiglia Christiana*, 4 March 2001.

"Citing Confession Made by 'Albania' Case Defendant." *Al-Quds Al-Arabi*, 19 February 1999.

Close, Raymond. "Hard Target: We Cannot Defeat Terrorism with Bombs and Bombast." *Washington Post* (Op-Ed), 30 August 1998.

"Closer Look. Portraits of Osama Bin Laden." *Time Daily* (Internet version), 31 March 1999.

Cloud, David S. "Can a Tire Repairman from Texas Be the Key to Solving a Terror Plot?" *Wall Street Journal,* 22 October 1998.

— — —. "U.S. Officials Charge Bin Laden and Aide with Conspiracy in Embassy Bombings." *Wall Street Journal,* 5 November 1998.

Cloud, David S., and Christopher Chipello. "Ressam Spent Time in Terrorist Camps Linked to Saudi Dissident Bin Laden." *Wall Street Journal,* 21 January 2000.

Coates, Stephen. "EU Invitation to Masood Will Infuriate Taliban, Pakistan: Analysts." AFP, 4 April 2001.

Coll, Steve. "Islamic Activists Sweep Council Elections." *Washington Post,* 24 April 2005, A17.

"Collapse of BCCI Shorts Bin Laden." UPI, 1 March 2001.

Colvin, Marie. "The New Face of World Terrorism." London *Sunday Times* (Internet version), 30 August 1998.

"Commander of the Foreign Mujahedin in the Caucasus." Islamic Observation Center Web site (Internet version), 10 September 1999.

"Complicity of Dawood Ibrahim Confirmed." *Sunday Observer,* 4 April 1993.

"Confessions from the Last Leader of the Jihad Organization." *Rose al-Yusuf,* 24 February 1997.

"'Confessions' of Mubarak Plot Suspects." *Al-Watan Al-Arabi,* 21 June 1996.

"Conspiracy against Muslim Ummah." *Quarterly Ziaul Islam,* 1 October–31 December 2000.

Constable, Pamela. "India on the Defensive." *Washington Post,* 16 January 2000.

— — —. "In Kandahar, Some Mourn the End of Taliban Rule." *Washington Post,* 16 January 2002.

Constable, Pamela, and Khan Khamran, "U.S. Strike Is Blow to Pakistan's Rulers," *Washington Post,* 21 August 1908.

"Conversion to Christianity in Islamic Society Is against the UN Charter." *Hewad* (Editorial), 13 January 2001.

Cooper, Kenneth J. "Bangladesh: Bin Laden's Next Target? Militant Seen Aiding New Islamic Force." *Washington Post,* 19 February 1999.

Cox, James. "Saudi Fields Are Vital to World's Oil Supply." *USA Today,* 10 May 2004.

Crossette, Barbara. "Afghan Heroin Feeds Addiction in Region, UN Reports." *New York Times,* 1 March 2000.

Cullison, Alan, and Andrew Higgins. "How Al Qaeda Scouted Attacks in Israel and Egypt." *Wall Street Journal,* 16 January 2002.

"Cyanide Sent to Three Missions in New Zealand." *Radio Australia,* 25 February 2003.

Dahlburg, John-Thor. "Some See U.S. as Terrorists' Next Big Target." *Los Angeles Times,* 13 January 2000.

Daley, Paul. "Report Says UBL-Linked Groups Possess 'Deadly' Anthrax and Plague Viruses." *Age* (Internet version), 4 June 2000.

Davis, Anthony. "Foreign Combatants in Afghanistan." *Jane's Intelligence Review* 5, no. 7 (July 1993): 327–31.

— — —. "Islamic Guerrillas Threaten the Fragile Peace of Mindanao." *Jane's Intelligence Review* 10, no. 5 (May 1998): 30–35.

— — —. "Southeast Asia Bombings Betray Islamic Links." *Jane's Intelligence Review* 13, no. 2 (February 2001).

— — —. "Targeting Bin Laden: The War on Terror Threatens Pakistan." *Asiaweek*, 4 September 1998.

Davis, Victor Hanson. "Hoping We Fail." *National Review Online*, 28 August 2003.

"Death Toll Soars in Uzbekistan." CBS News, www.cbsnews.com, 16 May 2005.

"Deaths in Sinai Sweep, Sharm Attacks Linked." www.gulftimes.com, 29 August 2005.

"Declaration of Jihad against the United States," *Al-Islah*, 2 September 1996.

el Deeb, Sarah. "83 Die in Car Bombs in Egyptian Resort." *Chicago Tribune* (Internet version), 23 July 2005.

Dellios, Hugh. "Israelis See Bin Laden's Hand Creeping into Gaza Strip." *Chicago Tribune*, 4 September 2000.

Delpho, Marc. "We Will Keep fighting." *Le Soir*, 5 April 2001.

"Deputy Amir of Al-Jawf Province in Northern Saudi Arabia Assassinated." *Ilaf* (Internet), 17 February 2003.

Diab, Hassan Haider. "The Americans Are Offering Five Million Dollars for the Humanitarians from Zagreb." *Vecernji List*, 18 April 2001.

— — —. "We Shall Set Croatia on Fire with Car-Bombs," *Vecernji List*, 31 October 2000.

Diab, Yousef. "Military Court to Try 'Terrorists.'" *Daily Star* (Internet version), 13 May 2000.

Dick, Charles J. "Conflict Spills into the 21st Century." *Jane's Intelligence Review* 12, no. 12 (December 2000).

Dickey, Christopher, et al. "Making a Symbol of Terror." *Newsweek*, 1 March 1998.

Dillon, Dana, and Paolo Pasicolan. "Beware the Jihad in Southeast Asia." *Wall Street Journal*, 17 January 2002.

Dobbs, Michael. "An Obscure Chief in U.S. War on Terror." *Washington Post*, 2 April 2000.

Doran, Michael Scott. "Somebody Else's Civil War." *Foreign Affairs* 81, no. 2 (January/February 2002).

Dorsey, James M., et al. "Evidence Gap Slows Bid to Freeze Funds." *Wall Street Journal*, 30 November 2001.

"Double Standard of the United States." *Nawa-i-Waqt* (Editorial), 13 August 1999.

Drogin, Bob. "U.S. Details Threats Linked to Clinton Trip." *Los Angeles Times*, 23 March 2000.

Drogin, Bob, and Tracy Wilkinson. "Bin Laden Followers Indicted over Alleged Terrorist Plot." *Los Angeles Times*, 29 March 2000.

Droziak, William. "Bin Laden Aide Denies Link to Embassy Bombing." *Washington Post*, 21 September 1998.

"Duo Cites Bin Laden in Bangladesh Attack." *Washington Times*, 30 January 1999.

Dunn, Michael Collins. "Osama Bin Laden: The Nature of the Challenge." *Middle East Policy* 6, no. 2 (October 1998): 23–28.

Duran, Khalid. "Cairo: A Torrent of Frightening Disclosures—Holy Terror as the Vanguard of Globalization." *World and I* (Internet version) 15, no. 11 (November 2000).

— — —. "Holy World War." *Gazeta Wyborcza*, 11–12 September 1999.

"Dutch Muslim Community Targeted after Murder of Filmmaker," *AFP*, 8 November 2004.

Eckholm, Erik. "Pakistani Guards Shot Dead at U.S. Office." *New York Times*, 1 March 2003.

"Egypt Bomb Attacks Kill at Least 75, Wound 120." Bloomberg.com, 23 July 2005.

"Egypt Bomb Attacks Kill at Least 75, Wound 120 (Update 5)." Bloomberg.com, 22 July 2005.

"Egypt Holds Alleged Plotters of Anti-U.S. Strike." Reuters, 25 June 1998.

"Egypt Police in Gun Battles with Bomb Suspects," CNN News, www.CNN.com, 24 August 2005.

"Egyptian Identified as Qatar Bomber." Associated Press, 21 March 2005.

Egyptian Islamic Jihad. "A Bulletin Issued by the Media Office of the Jihad Group-Egypt, No. 43," 10 December 1998.

"Egyptian Jihad Group Pledges Revenge on Kuwait." *Al-Quds Al-Arabi*, 6–7 February 1999, 1.

"Egyptian Linked to Bin Laden Commits Suicide." Radio Tirana Network, 25 October 1998.

"Egypt's Jihad Asked by Bin Laden to Turn Guns on U.S." *AFP*, 24 February 1999.

Eichenwald, Kurt. "Terror Money Hard to Block Officials Find." *New York Times*, 10 December 2001.

"el. Ma.," "Osama Bin Laden in Tirana Offices." *Gazeta Shqiptare*, 4 November 1998.

"The Embassy Bombing Verdicts." *New York Times* (Editorial), 30 May 2001.

Emerson, Steven. "Abdallah Azzam: The Man before Osama Bin Laden." *Journal of Counterterrorism and Security International* 5, no. 3 (Fall 1998).

— — —. "Unholy War." *New Republic*, 14 and 21 September 1998.

Engelbert, Stephen, et al. "One Man and a Global Web of Violence." *New York Times*, 14 January 2001.

Enracia, Aremio Jr. "Khalifah Denies Links with Bin Laden." *Philippine Daily Inquirer* (Internet version), 21 December 1998.

Esplanada, Jerry. "Four Suspected Foreign Financiers of Abu Sayyaf Identified." *Philippine Daily Inquirer*, 22 April 1995.

Essam al-Din, Gamal. "El-Alfi Claims Doha Connection." *Al-Ahram Weekly*, 8 January 1998.

"The Events of the Week." Movement for Islamic Reform on the Arabian Peninsula (Internet site), 21 December 2001.

"Excerpts from Ayman al-Zawahiri's book 'Knights Under the Prophet's Banner.'" *Al-Hayah*, December 2001; serialized in twelve parts.

"Excerpts from Guilty Plea in Terrorist Case." *New York Times*, 21

October 2000.

"Excerpts from Muntasir al-Zayyat's 'Ayman al-Zawahiri as I Knew Him.'" *Al-Hayah.* 10 January 2002.

"Expel the Mushkireen from the Arabian Peninsula." *Abdullah Azzam Home Page,* 7 August 1997.

"Explosives for Attacks on U.S. Targets Found." *Los Angeles Times,* 12 November 2000.

"Exxon-Oil Has Temporarily Halted Exploration and Administrative Activities in Aceh Due to Rising Concerns over Security." *Jakarta Post* (Internet version), 7 June 2000.

"Eyewitness View of Bin Laden's Camps." *Terrorism and Security Monitor* (September 1998).

El-Fadl, Khaled Abou. "Holy War versus Jihad (Review)." *Ethics and International Affairs* 14 (2000): 133–40.

"Fanning the Flames." *News* (Editorial, Internet version), 2 October 1999.

Al-Faqih, Sa'd. "Saudi Oppositionist on U.S. Strikes on Sudan and Afghanistan." *Movement for Islamic Reform in Arabia* (Internet version), 28 August 1998.

"Fear of Terrorism Prevents Festivities in Brussels." *Da Standaard,* 1 July 2000.

Ferdinand, Pamela. "No Bail for Bomb Case Suspect." *Washington Post,* 29 December 2001.

Feuer, Alan. "Jihad, Inc.: The Bin Laden Network of Companies Exporting Terror." *New York Times,* 13 February 2001.

"Fez Court Examines Man Charged with Marrakech Hotel Attack." MAP Television, 24 September 1994.

"Fiji Police Searching for Suspects with Terrorists Links." Internet Fiji Live, 4 May 1999.

Fine, G. A. "John Brown's Body: Elites, Heroic Embodiment, and the Legitimization of Political Violence." *Social Problems* 46, no. 22 (1999).

"First War of the Century: Statement by Al Qaeda Leader Osama Bin Laden." Al-Jazirah Satellite Channel Television, 27 December 2001.

Fisher, Ian. "Recent Attacks in Yemen Seen as Sign of Large Terror Cell." *New York Times,* 3 January 2003

Fisk, Robert. "Anti-Soviet Warrior Puts His Army on the Road to Peace." *Financial Times,* 6 December 1993.

– – –. "Arab Rebel Leader Warns the British: 'Get Out of the Gulf.'" *Independent,* 10 July 1996.

– – –. "As My Grocer Said: Thank You Mr. Clinton for the Fine Words . . .", *Independent,* 22 August 1998.

– – –. "Clinton Gives Coup Leader an Easy Ride; He Was Expected to Read the Riot Act to Pakistan's Dictator, but He Only Offered Cliches." *Independent on Sunday* (Internet version), 26 March 2000.

– – –. "Intelligence That Barely Deserves the Name," *Independent* (Internet version), 24 November 2000.

– – –. "Muslim Leader Warns of New Assault on U.S. Forces." *Independent,* 22 March 1997.

– – –. "The Saudi Connection." *Independent,* 9 August 1998.

— — —. "Talks with Osama Bin Laden: How an Afghan 'Freedom Fighter' Became 'America's Public Enemy Number One.'" *Nation* 267, no. 8 (21 September 1998).

— — —. "U.S. Airstrikes: Bin Laden Will Take His Revenge." *Independent,* 21 August 1988.

Fitzgerald, Paul L. "Tightening the Screws." *National Interest* 66 (Winter 2001/02).

"Five Members of One Family Murdered." *El-Youm* (Internet version), 21 December 2000.

Foster, Peter, and Maurice Weaver. "Young Britons Heed Call to Arms for Holy War." *Daily Telegraph* (Internet version), 29 December 2000.

"Four Gulf Fundamentalists Killed in Dagestan Battles." *Al-Sharq Al-Awsat,* 27 August 1999.

"4 Yanks Hurt amid Cairo Terror Carnage." www.nypost.com, 8 April 2005.

Fox, Robin. "Fatal Attraction. War and Human Nature." *National Interest* 51 (Winter 1992/93).

Fregosi, Paul. *Jihad in the West. Muslim Conquest from the 7th to the 21st Centuries.* Amherst, NY: Prometheus Books, 1996.

"French Sources: Bin Laden Financed All Operations in French Cities Last Year." *Al-Ahram,* 4 January 1996.

"Fresh Arrests among Jordanian Afghans." *Al-Bilad,* 4 May, 1994.

Friedman, Lawrence. "The Third World War?" *Survival* 43, no. 4 (Winter 2001).

Friedman, Thomas L. "Smoking or Non-Smoking." *New York Times,* 14 September 2001.

— — —. "World War III." *New York Times,* 13 September 2001.

"From Noor ud Din Zangi to Osama Bin Laden." *Ausaf,* 4 March 2001.

Fuller, Graham. "The Threat of Jihad." CNN/Time Impact (Internet version), 7 April 1997.

Funatsu, Yasushi. "Interview with Historian Paul Johnson." Kyodo, 19 January 2002.

"Fundamentalists Emphasize That al-Islambouli Did Not Accompany Bin Laden." *Al-Hayah,* 26 February 1999.

Furnish, Timothy R. "Bin Laden: The Man Who Would Be Mahdi." *Middle East Quarterly* 9, no. 2 (Spring 2002).

"Further on New Zealand Police Announcing Plot to Target Sydney Reactor." *AFP,* 26 August 2000.

Gadher, Dipesh. "MI5 Locates 'Bin Laden's London Base.'" *Sunday Times,* 4 March 2001.

Gaino, Alberto. "Ndrangheta Arms for Terrorists," *La Stampa,* 27 November 1999.

Galeotti, Mark. "Costs of the Chechen War." *Jane's Intelligence Review* 12, no. 4 (April 2000): 8–9.

— — —. "No Respite in Chechen War." *Jane's Intelligence Review* 13, no. 2, (February, 2001).

Gannon, Kathy, "Trademark Pirates Glorify Terror Suspect on Fake Nike T-Shirts." Associated Press, 12 December 2000.

Gannon, Kelly. "Bin Laden Tells Youth to Train for 'Holy Wars.'" *San Diego Union-Tribune,* 12 April 2001.

— — —. "Suspected Terrorists Enjoy Taliban's Protection." *Washington Times,* 11 March 2000.

Gardner, David. "U.S. Bombing: Moslem Allies Fear Backlash from 'Afghan Arabs.'" FT.com, 21 August 1998.

Garfinckle, Adam. "Afghanistanding." *Orbis* 43, no. 3 (Summer 1999): 412-13.

Gauhar, Humayun. "Dare to Win." *Nation* (Lahore edition, Internet version), 4 November 2001.

— — —. "Trust the USA? But Can We Trust Ourselves?" *Nation* (Lahore edition, Internet version), 7 October 2001.

Gayeva, Gulfira. "Bin Laden Suspected of Organizing Tashkent Explosions." *Kommersant,* 3 March 1999.

Geibel, Adam. "Khattab's Audacious Raid (22 December 1997): Prelude to the Second Chechen War." *Central Asia Survey* 19, no. 3-4 (September–December 2000): 341-43.

Georgy, Michael. "Saudi Dissident Bin Laden Seen as a Serious Threat." Reuters, 25 February 1997.

Gerecht, Reuel Marc. "Bin Laden Beware." *Weekly Standard,* 24 September 2001.

— — —. "The Gospel According to Osama Bin Laden." *Atlantic Monthly* (January 2002): 46-47.

— — —. "Pakistan's Taliban Problem." *Weekly Standard,* 5 November 2001.

— — —. "Taking Sides in Afghanistan," *New York Times* (Op-Ed), 8 March 2001.

Gerges, Fawaz A. "The End of the Islamic Insurgency in Egypt? Costs and Prospects." *Middle East Journal* 54, no. 4, (Autumn 2000): 592.

— — —. "Muslims Called to Jihad." *Los Angeles Times,* 26 March 2003.

Gerth, Jeff, and Judith Miller. "Terror Money: A Special Report; Funds for Terrorists Traced to Persons, Gulf Businesses." *New York Times,* 14 August 1996.

"Get Personal." *New Republic,* 14 and 21 September 1998.

Giradet, Edward. "A Brush with Laden on the Jihad Front Line." *Christian Science Monitor,* 31 August 1998.

Girard, Renaud. "On Osama Bin Laden's Trail." *Le Figaro,* 30 September 1998.

Goldberg, Jeffrey. "The Education of a Holy Warrior." *New York Times Magazine,* 25 June 2000.

Goldman, John J. "Accused Was Businessman, Not Terrorist, Lawyer Says." *Los Angeles Times,* 4 May 2001.

Goldstein, Steve. "Many Suspects in Ship Blast." *Philadelphia Enquirer,* 13 October 2000.

Gosh, Soumya. "Laden to Talibanize Kashmir with Heroin Money." *Pioneer,* 21 October 1999.

"Group Claiming Anti-U.S. Bombings Spell Out Demands." *AFP,* 10 August 1998.

"Group Claims Responsibility in Cairo Bombing." *AFP,* 30 April 2005.

Grunwald, Michael. "Africa Blast Suspects to Stand Trial in the U.S." *Washington Post,* 28 August 1998.

— — —. "Bin Laden Associate Indicted for Perjury." *Washington Post,* 22 September 1998.

— — —. "Bombing Suspect Alleges He Was Bullied into Confession." *Washington Post*, 4 September 1998.

— — —. "4 Followers of Bin Laden Indicted in Plot to Kill Americans." *Washington Post*, 8 October 1998.

Gupta, Shekhar, et al. "India's Most Wanted Family." *India Today*, 15 April 1993.

Gwyn, Robert. "Dispatches." Channel 4 Television Network, 20 February 1997.

Hackworth, David. "Level of Combat." *Washington Times*, 29 September 2001.

Al-Hadari, Mahmud. "Al-Jihad Foiled Attempt on Mubarak Motorcade Detailed." *Al-Ahali*, 20 December 1995.

Hafiz, Brig. (ret'd) M. Abdul. "Growing Legend of Osama Bin Laden." *Frontier Post*, 25 August 1999.

Haider, Ejaz. "Pakistan and Hezb's 'Surprise Move.'" *Friday Times* (Internet version), 28 July–3 August 2000.

Al-Haj, Ahmed. "At Least Three Other Anti-U.S. Plots Foiled before *Cole*." Associated Press, 11 November 2000.

Al-Hajj, Jadd. "'Bin Laden Specter' Overshadows Preparations for Opening of Olympic Games in Sydney." *Al-Hayah*, 4 July 2000.

Halaby, Jamal. "Al-Zarqawi: Claims Jordan al-Qaida Attack." Associated Press, 24 August 2005.

Hall, William. "Output in Afghanistan Doubles." *Financial Times*, 31 January 2000.

Al-Hamid, Abd-al Wahid. "Islamic Philanthropic Organizations—Lessons to Be Learned." *Al-Riyad*, 2 February 2000.

Hammad, Suhaylah Zayn-al-Abidin. "The Christian-Muslim Dialogue Fraud." *Al-Madinah*, 7 February 2000.

Al-Hammadi, Khalid. "Yemeni Tribes Condemn the Hunt for Bin Laden." *Al-Quds Al-Arabi*, 6 November 1999.

— — —. "Kidnapping Said the Result of Bin Laden Fatwa." *Al-Quds Al-Arabi*, 30 December 1998.

Hanson, Victor Davis. "Enough Is Enough." *Washington Times* (Internet version), 22 July 2005.

— — —. "The Longest War." *American Heritage* 53, no. 1 (January/February 2002).

Harding, Luke. "Analysis: A Slide into Chaos." *Guardian* (Internet version), 10 December 2001.

Al-Harmi, Jabir. "Interview with Gulbuddin Hekmatyar." *Al-Ittihad*, 29 August 1999.

Harris, Edward. "U.S. Boosts Anti-terror Efforts in Africa." Associated Press, 25 May 2005.

Harrison, Roger, et al. "U.S. Consulate Attacked." *Arab News* (Internet version), 7 December 2004.

Hashimi, Qari Naved Masood. "Osama Bin Laden—A Man as Strong as a Rock." *Pakistan*, 10 June 1998.

Hasrat, Bakhit Ullah Jan. "Osama Bin Laden Denounces U.S.-Sponsored 'World Order.'" *Pakistan*, 9 January 2000.

"Has the Countdown Begun in the Adventure of Osama Bin Laden?" *Al-Watan Al-Arabi*, 15 May 1997.

"The Hasty Decision to Cooperate with the United States." *Nawa-I-Waqt*, 17 September 2001.

Hattar, Said. "Pakistan Hands Over 14th Terror Suspect to Jordan." *Jordan Times* (Internet version), 18 December 1999.

Haussner, Pierre. "Huntington's Clash: 1. Morally Objectionable, Politically Dangerous." *The National Interest* 46 (Winter 1996/97).

Haven, Paul. "Pakistan Will Deport al-Qaeda Suspect." Associated Press, 31 May 2005.

"The Heart Stopped." *Asian Age* (Editorial), 14 December 2001.

Heller, Jeffrey. "Israeli Troops Ready to Role out of Gaza." http://www.swissinfo.html, 10 September 2005.

Helprin, Mark. "Defense of the Realm." *Wall Street Journal* (Op-Ed, Internet version), 1 August 2000.

Henderson, Ian. "Interview with Peter Bergen." *Yemen Observer* (Internet version), 9 December 2000.

"Hero of Modern Times." *Nation* (Lahore edition, Internet version), 21 August 1998.

"Heroin Funds Bin Laden's War against the West." *Washington Times*, 30 November 1998.

al-Hilali, Abu-Ayman. "The Fall of the Iraqi Regime and the Beginning of the Nation's Rise, Part 1." *Al-Ansar* (Internet), 17 April 2003.

— — —. "Mombasa and the Fulfillment of the Promise." *Al-Ansar* (Internet), 5 December 2002.

Himmelfarb, Gertrude. "A Dark and Bloody Crossroads." *The National Interest* 32 (Summer 1993).

Hiro, Dilip. "The 'Afghan Arabs' — America Turns on Its Creation." *Middle East International* 582 (4 September 1998): 17–19.

"Hizbul Mujahedin Ceasefire Angers Compatriots in Afghanistan." *AFP*, 24 July 2000.

Hoagland, Jim. "Dry Up the Money Trail." *Washington Post*, 30 September 2001.

— — —. "Forcing the Choice." *Washington Post*, 10 October 2001.

— — —. "Mortal Combat." *Washington Post*, 8 October 2001.

— — —. "Turncoat Terrorists." *Washington Post*, 16 January 2000.

Hoi, Paul. "Bin Laden, the Moneyman behind International Terrorism." *Berlinske Tidende*, 9 September 1998.

Hopkins, Nick, et al. "U.S. on Terrorist Alert as Revenge Targets Named." *Sydney Morning Herald* (Internet version), 24 August 1998.

Howard, Roger. "Wrath of Islam: The HUA Analyzed." *Jane's Intelligence Review* 9, no. 10 (October 1997): 466–68.

Hoxha, Artan. "These Are Ciciku's Dubious Alternatives." *Gazeta Shqiptare*, 17 August 1999.

Humayun Gauhar. "Dare to Win." *Nation* (Lahore edition, Internet version), 4 November 2001.

Al-Huni, Ahmed. "If Faysal Were Alive." *Al-Arab Al-Alamiyah*, 31 October 2000.

Husayn, Kamil Yusuf. "Osama Bin Laden: Legend of the Century." *Al-*

Bayan (serialized book), 24–30 November and 1–3 and 5–14 December, 1999.

Hussain, Imtiaz. "Pakistan Arrests Afghan NGO's Chief for 'Links' with Terrorist Groups." *Frontier Post* (Internet version), 29 July 2000.

Hussain, Zahid. "In the Shadow of Terrorism." *Newsline,* 1–29 February 2000.

Hyman, Anthony. "Arab Involvement in the Afghan War." *Beirut Review* (Spring 1994): 73–89.

"I Am Not Afraid of Death: Osama Bin Laden Talks about the Embassy Bombings, the Strikes on Iraq, and His War on America." NEWSWEEK.com, 4 January 1999.

Ibragimov, Khahim. "Frightening Face of Extremism. Ramified Network of Islamic Terrorists Threaten CIS Countries." *Nevavisimaya Gazeta,* 3 February 2000.

Al-Ibrashi, Wa'el. "Afghanistan's Extremists Disclose the Secrets of the Financier of Terrorism: Bin Laden Was Made by U.S. Intelligence." *Rose al-Yusuf,* 24 August 1998.

— — —. "Ajizah, the Funky Islamist." *Rose al-Yusuf,* 22 December 2001.

— — —. "Interview with Abu Hamzah al-Masri." *Rose al-Yusuf,* 28 October 2000.

— — —. "Story of the Two Most Famous Egyptian Prisoners in London, the Faxed Fingerprint that Proved Connection between Egyptian Lawyer and Bin Laden, Umar Bakri on Differences with Bin Laden on Sectarianism and Fatwa to Kill American Women and Children." *Rose Al-Yusuf,* 4 November 2000, 34–36.

Iftikhar, Malik H. "Islamic Discourse on Jihad, War and Violence." *Journal of South Asian and Middle Eastern Studies* 21, no. 4 (Summer 1998).

Ignatius, David. "Interview with Abu Hamzah al-Masri." *Rose al-Yusuf,* 28 October 2000.

— — —. "The Psyche of Bin Laden." *Washington Post,* 28 October 2001, B7.

— — —. "Story of the Two Most Famous Egyptian Prisoners in London, the Faxed Fingerprint that Proved Connection between Egyptian Lawyer and Bin Laden, Umar Bakri on Differences with Bin Laden on Sectarianism and Fatwa to Kill American Women and Children." *Rose Al-Yusuf,* 4 November 2000.

"Implications of Singapore Militants." *Utasan Malaysia* (Internet version), 10 January 2002.

"India Offers Kabul Help to Fight Terrorism." PTI News Agency, 28 August 2005.

"Indian Minister again Calls for Nuke Ties with Israel." *Middle East Newsline* (Internet version), 15 June 2000.

"Indian Terrorist for Hire in Nepal Election." *Gujarat Samachar,* 31 March 1999.

"Indictment for January Bombing Case Details Plans, Tactics." *Al-Dustur,* 8 July 1994.

"Information on Bin Laden's Plans to Set Up Base in Somalia." *Al-Sharq Al-Awsat* (Internet version), 1 May 1999.

Inglis, Scott. "Refugee Hits Back at Terror Claims." *New Zealand Herald* (Internet version), 29 August 2000.

"In Statement from Khandahar, Where Bin Laden Is Based, Advice and Reform Committee Warns Britain, Demands al-Fawwaz's Immediate Release." *Al-Quds Al-Arabi,* 1 October 1998.

"Intelligence Services on Fresh Militant Attacks in Kashmir." *Hindustan Times* (Internet version), 29 November 1999.

"Interview: Conversation with Terror." *Time,* 11 January 1999.

"Interview of Rifa'i Taha." Islamic Observation Center (Internet version), 19 June 2000.

Interview of Undersecretary of State Thomas Pickering. *Frontline,* April 1999.

"Interview with Ahmed Sattar." *Frontline Online,* April 1999.

"Interview with Ayman al-Zawahiri." In "Al-Jazeera, Bin Ladin, and I," edited by Jamal Ismail, *Al-Zaman* (July 2000).

"Interview with Larry C. Johnson." *Frontline Online,* April 1999.

"Interview with Milt Bearden." *Frontline Online,* April 1999.

"Interview with Roland Jaquard, Monitor of International Terrorism." *Al-Watan Al-Arabi,* 11 April 1997.

"Interview with Sa'd al-Faqih." *Frontline Online,* April 1999.

"Interview with Sa'id Aburish." *Frontline Online,* April 1999.

"Interview with the Comptroller General of the Muslim Brotherhood in Jordan, Abd-al-Majid al-Dunaybat." *Al-Wasat,* 12 November 2001.

"An Interview with the Secretary of the Sudanese Information Ministry." *Nida'ul Islam* (Internet version) 17 (February/March 1997).

"Interview (Written) of Osama Bin Laden." *Ghazi Magazine,* 20–27 August 2000.

"Investigation Launched into Killing of Tourists." RTM Television Network, 24 August 1994.

"Islamist Group Appears to Claim Jakarta Blast," Associated Press, 10 September 2004.

"Islamist Leader Bin Laden Urges Muslims to Kill Britons." *AFP,* 25 December 1998.

"Islamists Claim Responsibility for Yemeni Air Crash." *Arab Daily,* 17 August 1998.

Ismail, Jamal Mahmud. "Abu Hafs al-Masri: I Had Nothing to Do with What Happened to the Americans in Kenya." *Al-Sharq Al-Awsat,* 6 January 1999.

– – –. "Bin Laden Urges Attacks against U.S., UK Interests." *Al-Sharq Al-Awsat* (Internet version), 25 December 1998.

– – –. "Al-Jazeerah, Bin Laden, and I." *Al-Zaman* (serialized book), July 2000.

– – –. "Mullah Omar's Advisers Tell *Al-Sharaq Al-Awsat:* Taliban Considers U.S. Reward for Bin Laden's Arrest a Terrorist Action." *Al-Sharq Al-Awsat,* 23 July 1999.

"Israelis Invading 'Somaliland': Strategic Location, Natural Wealth, and Uranium." *Al-Wasat,* 2 April 2001.

Issawi, Tarek. "Bin Laden Applauds *Cole* Attack." *Washington Post,* 2 March 2001.

Jaffe, Greg, et al. "Prisoners Lack Rank to Assist U.S.' Search: Warlord Lied about Surrender, Official Says." *Wall Street Journal,* 10 January 2001.

"Jailed Egyptian Islamist Warns of Anti-U.S. Attacks." *AFP,* 6 March 1999.

"Jakarta Police Uncover Network Selling Arms to Gam." *Kompas* (Internet version), 3 March 2000.

Jaleel, Muzami. "The Taliban Connection." *Indian Express* (Internet version), 2 June 2000.

James, Bruce. "Middle East: Arab Veterans of the Afghan War—Trained Forces in Waiting." *Jane's Defense Weekly* 7, no. 4 (April 1995): 175–79.

Al-Jasir, Hamud. "Two Kuwait Youths Arrested in the 'Terrorist Network' Case. Qatar Extradites to Kuwait an 'Explosives Expert' from an Arab Maghreb Country." *Al-Hayah,* 13 November 2000.

Jaulmes, Adrien. "Masood Gets Support from European Parliament." *Le Figaro,* 6 April 2001.

Javed, Rasheed. "U.S. Will Treat Pakistan, Saudi Arabia, and Iran Very Harshly." *Jang,* 20 November 2001.

Al-Jawjari, Adil. "'Terrorist' Bin Laden Returns to Yemen." *Al-Watan Al-Arabi,* 20 March 1998.

Jefferson, Thomas. *Declaration of Independence.*

Jehl, Douglas. "Muslims Voice Fury over U.S. Strikes." *New York Times* News Service, 22 August 1998.

Jenkins, Brian Michael. "This Time Is Different." *San Diego Union-Tribune,* 16 September 2001.

Jha, Prem Shankar. "Failure in Kashmir." *Hindustan Times* (Internet version), 17 December 1999.

"Jihad, Bin Laden Involved in Bombing of U.S. Embassies." *Al-Sharq Al-Awsat* (Internet version), 2 May 1999.

"Jihad Group Threatens to Take Revenge against United States." *Al-Quds Al-Arabi,* 2 November 1998.

Johnson, Daniel. "Bin Laden Is Winning the Battle in Britain." *Daily Telegraph* (Internet version), 28 December 2001.

Jones, Arthur. "Memory of Crusades Live on in Today's War: Conflict Continues Centuries of Clashes between Christian and Muslim Civilizations." *National Catholic Reporter* 38, no. 1 (26 October 2001).

"Jordan Dooms 6 Extremists Tied to Plot by Bin Laden." *International Herald Tribune,* 19 September 2000.

Jordan, Lara Jakes. "Homeland Security Faces Massive Overhaul." *Seattle Post-Intelligencer,* 2005.

"Jordanian Expelled from Albania." *Jordan Times,* 15 November 1999.

Joshi, Manoj. "Indian Home Ministry Welcomes Announcement of Cease-fire by Hizbal Mujahedin." *Times of India* (Internet version), 25 July 2000.

J.-P. P. "Masood, the Paris Appeal." *Liberation* (Internet version), 5 April 2001.

Jungers, Sebastian. "The Lion in Winter." *National Geographic Adventure,* March-April 2001.

Kagan, Robert. "We Must Fight This War." *Washington Post,* 12 September 2001.

Kaplan, Robert D. "The Lawless Frontier." *Atlantic Monthly* (September 2000): 66.

Al-Karim, Al-Abd, and Ahmad al-Nur al-Nur. "Interview with Saudi Businessman Osama Bin Laden." *Al-Quds Al-Arabi,* 9 March 1994.

"Kashmir Car Bomb Explosion; 11 Killed, 26 Injured." *Deccan Herald* (Internet version), 26 December 2000.

Kashoggi, Jamal. "Interview with Prince Turki al-Faisal." *Arab News* (Internet version), 4–9 November 2001.

Katz, Lee Michael. "Financial Records Lifting Veil on Bin Laden Network." *USA Today*, 1 October 1998.

Keegan, Sir John. "In This War of Civilizations, the West Will Prevail." *Daily Telegraph* (Internet version), 8 October 2001.

Kelley, Jack. "Saudi Money Aiding Terrorist Bin Laden." *USA Today*, 29 October 1999.

Kelsay, John. "Islam and the Distinction between Combatants and Non-combatants. The Justification and Limitation of War in Western and Islamic Tradition." In *Cross, Crescent and Sword,* edited by James Turner Johnson and John Kelsay, 200. New York: Greenwood Press, 1990.

Kentner, John. "Bombings in East Africa: The Suspect." *New York Times,* 14 August 1998.

"Key Events after al-Hariri's Killing." *AFP,* 30 August 2005.

Khan, Ashraf. "Gunman Kills 2 Police Guards Outside U.S. Consulate in Pakistan," *AFP,* 28 February 2003.

Khalaf, Muhammad. "Shamil Basayev: A Terrorist or a National Hero?" *Al-Sharq Al-Awsat,* 5 January 2000.

Khalid, Ahmed. "Lebanese Islamists Link to Bin Laden Probed." *Al-Shira',* 17 January 2000.

— — —. "Report Notes U.S. Attempt to Arrest Osama Bin Laden." *Friday Times,* 30 July–5 August 1999.

Khalid, Ghulam Mohammad. "The U.S. Agenda and the Islamic Revolution." *Jasarat* (Internet version), 10 October 1999.

Khalil, Tahir. "Afghan Foreign Minister Promised 'Crushing Reply' if U.S. Attacks." *Jang,* 27 October 2000.

Khan, Aamer Ahmed. "Profile: Abu Fraj al-Libi," BBC News, http://newsvote.bbc.co.uk.

Khan, Aimal. "Osama Said Mediating between Hekmatyar, Sayyaf." *Frontier Post,* 29 December 1998.

Khan, Ismail. "Alleged Egyptian Terrorist Comments on Plot against Mubarak." *News,* 9 May 1996.

— — —. "Government Orders Arabs Expelled in Crackdown." *News,* 10 April 1993.

— — —. "'Muslim Extremist Financier' Reportedly Arrives." *News,* 11 July 1996.

— — —. "Pakistan Hands Over Bin Laden Aide to Jordan." *News,* 18 December 1999.

Khan, Joseph. "House Votes to Combat Sale of Diamonds for War." *New York Times,* 29 November 2001.

Khan, Khamran. "Bin Laden Loyalists Seek Revenge on U.S." *News* (Internet version), 7 March 1999.

— — —. "Palestinian Unveils Osama's International War against U.S.; Bombing Suspect Says His Men Hit Targets from Somalia to the Philippines." *News,* 19 August 1998.

— — —. "Osama's Narrow Escape, Camp Hits Reported." *News,* 22 August 1998.

Khan, Mufti Jamil. "Bin Laden: Expel Jews, Christians from Holy Places." *Jang,* 18 November 1998.

"Khartoum: Secrets of the Rift between al-Turabi and Bin Laden." *Al-Watan Al-Arabi,* 29 December 1995.

Khashuqji, Jamal. "Al Qaeda Organization: Huge Aims without Programs or Cells." *Al-Hayah,* 12 October 1998.

Khatib, Shaykh Kamal. "Osama and Shamil in the Confrontation of the Drunk and the Philanderer." *Sawt al-Haqq wa at-Hurriyah,* 5 November 1999.

Khazim, Yusef. "Islamists Regroup Their Forces after Ethiopian Preemptive Strikes." *Al-Wasat Magazine,* 17–23 May 1999.

Khosha, Aasha. "Report: Kashmir Militants Plan to Step Up Activities." *Indian Express* (Internet version), 21 November 1999.

Al-Kilani, Ibrahim Zayd. "Osama Bin Laden, the Eagle of Islam." *Al-Sabil,* 21 October 1999.

King, Neil Jr. "Instead of Big Strikes, U.S.'s Terrorism Battle Focuses on Harassing Would-be Troublemakers." *Wall Street Journal,* 4 August 1999.

"Kingdom Sends SR170m Supplies to Kosovars." *Arab News,* 26 June 1999.

Kitfield, James. "Osama's Learning Curve." *National Journal,* 10 November 2001.

Kokita, Kiyohito, and Yuji Moronaga. "Terrorist Asks Writer to Compile a Biography—Testimony of Pakistanis Who Have Met Bin Laden." *AERA,* 8 October 2001.

Korkut, Levent, and Aysegul Usta. "Present at Execution of Turkish Truck Driver in Iraq." *Hurriyet* (Internet version), 12 August 2005

Kozlow, Chris. "The Bombing of Khobar Towers: Who Did It? And Who Funded It?" *Jane's Intelligence Review* 9, no. 12 (December 1997).

Krach, Wolfgang, and Georg Mascolo. "Highly Alarmed." *Der Spiegel,* 9 April 2001, 22–24.

Krauthammer, Charles. "Only in Their Dreams." *Time,* 24 December 2001.

– – –. "Why That's Ridiculous." *Time* (Internet version), 23 July 2005.

Kouri, Jim. "Terrorism: U.S. Training South East Asian Security Forces." http://www.lincolntribune.com, 27 August 2005.

Kuntz, Phil, and Hugh Pope. "U.S. Officials, Fearing Retaliation, Close 38 Embassies in Africa." *Wall Street Journal,* 18 December 1998.

"Kuwait Announces Arrest of Terrorist Groups; Explosives Seized." Kuwait Satellite Television Channel, 9 November 2000.

"Kuwait: Fundamentalists' Families Deported; Measures to Contain Bin Laden Network." *Al-Quds Al-Arabi,* 24 February 1999.

"L. pol." "We Know Nothing about These Weapons." *La Stampa,* 6 October 1998.

Lackey, Sue. "Yemen: Unlikely Key to Western Security." *Jane's Intelligence Review* 11, no. 7 (July 1999).

"Laden Creates New Front against U.S., Israel." *News,* 28 May 1998.

"Laden Declares Jihad against U.S. Forces." *News,* 28 May 1998.

"Laden to Divert Iranian River to Afghanistan." *Nation,* 22 July 1997.

"Lashkar Up to Red Fort." *Hindustan* (Editorial), 25 December 2000.

"Latest News." *Jakarta Post* (Internet version), 26 December 2000.

Lathan, Niles. "Bin Laden's Lemmings May Target Big Apple." *New York Post,* 5 August 1999.

Lazanski, Miroslav. "The American Seed." *Veernje,* 6 December 1998.

Leader, Stefan. "Osama Bin Laden and the Terrorist Search for WMD." *Jane's Intelligence Review* 11, no. 6 (June 1999): 34–37.

"Lebanese Legal and Political Quarters Surprised by Extradition of 'Bin Laden' Group Leader to Egypt before His Trial." *Al-Sharq Al-Awsat* (Internet version), 14 May 2000.

Leppard, David, et al. "The Global Terrorist." *Sunday Times* (Internet version), 7 February 1999.

"Letter by Osama Bin Laden to the Pakistani People." Al-Jazirah Satellite Channel Television, 24 September 2001.

Levine, Steven, et al. "Helping Hand." *Newsweek,* 13 October 1997.

Levy, Adrian, and Kathy Scott-Clark. "Bin Laden's Mercenaries Gather for Kashmir's Jihad." *Sunday Times* (Internet version), 4 October 1998.

Lewis, Bernard. "Did You Say 'American Imperialism'? Power, Weakness, and Choices in the Middle East." *National Review* 53, no. 24 (17 December 2001).

— — —. "License to Kill: Osama Bin Laden's Declaration of Jihad." *Foreign Affairs* 77, no. 6 (November/December 1998): 14–19.

— — —. "The Revolt of Islam." *New Yorker* (19 November 2001): 50–63.

— — —. "The Roots of Muslim Rage." *Atlantic Monthly* (Internet edition) (September 1990).

Lieven, Anatol. "Nasty Little Wars." *The National Interest* 62 (Winter 2000/01): 65–76.

"Life and Religion." Al-Jazirah Satellite Channel, 22 April 2001.

Lintner, Bertil. "Centrifugal Forces Stir Indonesia." *Jane's Intelligence Review* 12, no. 6 (June 2000).

Li Nun. "Uneasy Days—Terrorist Activities Frighten U.S. Personnel Overseas." *Renmin Ribao,* 13 August 1999.

Lloyd, Marion. "Where Bin Laden Is Beloved, Anti-U.S. Calls Mount." *Boston Globe,* 25 July 1999.

Loeb, Vernon. "Bin Ladin Still Seen as a Threat." *Washington Post,* 29 August 1999.

Loeb, Vernon, and Alan Sipress. "Terrorist Verdicts Add to Message." *New York Times,* 30 May 2001.

Lopandic, Bruno. "Who Killed Abu-Tala'at: Foreign Agents of HVO?" *Slododna Dalmacija,* 2 November 2000.

Lopez, Leslie. "Asian Militants with Alleged Al Qaeda Ties Are Accused of Plotting against Embassies." *Wall Street Journal,* 7 January 2002.

Lueck, Thomas L. "Algerian Is Found Guilty in Plot to Bomb Sites in the U.S." *New York Times,* 7 April 2001.

Luxon, Thomas. "John Bunyan in Context (Review)." *Journal of Religion* 78, no. 1 (January 1998): 121–22.

Lynch, Colum. "Plan to Kill Bin Laden Described in Court." *Washington Post,* 21 February 2001.

— — —. "Taliban Hoping for a Way to Bid Adieu to Bin Laden." *Boston Globe,* 21 October 1998.

Macaskill, Mark, et al. "Straw's Dilemma: The Home Secretary Has Been Called to Act after Bakri Wrote Bin Laden Supporting Terrorism." *Sunday Times* (Internet version), 5 September 1999.

Mackenzie, Richard. "The Succession." *New Republic,* 14 and 21 September 1998.

Macleod, Scott. "The Paladin of the Jihad." *Time,* 6 May 1996, 51–52.

"Mad Laden." *Lokasatta* (Editorial), 21 September 1999.

Mahdid, Nadhiah. "Britain Closes Down a Fundamentalist's 'Front Company' and the Muhajiroun Organization Rushes to Open Another One." *Al-Sharq Al-Awsat,* 28 January 2000.

al-Makki, Salim. "Believers Exact Sweet Revenge in Mukalla, Faylaka, and Bali." *Al-Neda* (Internet), 14 October 2002.

Malik, Dr. Iffat S. "Obsessed with Osama." *News* (Internet version), 19 April 2000.

"Man Charged in Bombing of U.S. Embassy in Africa." *New York Times,* 9 October 1999.

Mann, Paul. "Bin Laden Linked to Nuclear Effort." *Aviation Week and Space Technology,* 12 October 1998.

Mansera, Andreu. "Algiers Accuses the Saudi Millionaire Bin Laden of Paying GIA Terrorists." *El Pais* (Internet version), 8 October 1998.

"Many Shoppers Hurt in Southern Philippines Bomb Attack." *AFP,* 16 December 1998.

Marquand, Robert. "Neighbors Warming Up to Taliban." *Christian Science Monitor,* 5 October 2000.

— — —. "New Faces Join Fray in Kashmir." *Christian Science Monitor,* 2 May 2000.

Marzuq, Hamdi. "Egypt Discovers by Accident the Organization 'Returnees from Africa'; Three Members of the Jihad Organization Collected Contributions in South Africa." *Al-Wasat Magazine,* 30 November–6 December 1998.

Mascolo, Georg. "Holy Warriors against Europe." *Der Spiegel* (Internet version), 24 February 2001.

"Massive Retaliation Feared." *Munich Focus,* 21 September 1998.

Masud, Tariq. "The Arabs and Islam: The Troubled Search for Legitimacy." *Daedalus* 128, no. 2 (Spring 1999).

— — —. "Desert Storm." *New Republic,* 28 December 1998.

Matthews, Mark. "Bombing Probe Slowly Traces Tortuous Path of Terrorism." *Baltimore Sun,* 18 October 1998.

"Mauritania Holds Man with Suspected Bin Laden Link." Reuters, 4 March 1999.

Mayer, Jane. "The House of Bin Laden." *New Yorker* (12 November 2001).

McCarthy, Rory. "Taleban's Superior Forces Threaten Foe's Supply Route." *Washington Times,* 6 December 2000.

McGirk, Tim. "The Taliban Allows a Top 'Sponsor' to Stay in Afghanistan." *Time,* 16 December 1997.

McWethy, John. "Osama Bin Laden Plans Attacks on United States." *ABC World News Tonight,* 16 June 1999.

Melloan, George. "Facing Up to the Task of Fighting a Shadow War."

Wall Street Journal, 18 September 2001.

Menon, Kesava. "Fall of Khost." *Frontline,* 27 April 1991.

"Message from Osama bin-Muhammad bin-Laden to His Muslim Brothers in the Whole World and Especially in the Arabian Peninsula. Declaration of Jihad against the Americans Occupying the Land of the Two Holy Mosques: Expel the Heretics from the Arabian Peninsula." *Al-Islah* 2 (September 1996).

"Message to Our Brothers in Iraq by Usama Bin Ladin, Leader of [the] al-Qaida Organization." Al-Jazirah Space Channel Television, 11 February 2003.

Meyers, Steven Lee. "Failed Plan to Bomb a U.S. Ship Reported." *New York Times,* 10 November 2000.

Michael, Maggie. "Al Qaeda-Linked Group Claims Egypt Attack." Associated Press, 23 July 2005.

"Militant Killed by Police Had Bin Ladin Letter." *Arab News* (Internet version), 4 June 2003.

"Militant Leader Urges Holy War on U.S., Israel." *Al-Rai Al-Amm,* 9 July 1998.

Miljus, D., and Hassan Haidar Diab. "Police Introduce Special Protective Measures because of Terrorist Threats." *Vecernji List,* 2 November 2000.

Milkov, George. "How the Top Terrorist Is Extending His Tentacles into Bulgaria." *Chasa,* 21 March 1999.

Miller, Bill. "$37.7 Billion for Homeland Defense Is a Start, Says Bush." *Washington Post,* 25 January 2002.

Miller, John. "Exclusive Interview with Osama Bin Laden: Talking with Terror's Banker." abcnews.com, 28 May 1998.

— — —. "Greetings America: My Name Is Osama Bin Laden. Now That I Have Your Attention . . . A Conversation with the Most Dangerous Man in the World." *Esquire* (Internet version) (February 1999).

Miller, Judith, and Sarah Lyrell. "Hunting Bin Laden's Allies, U.S. Extends Net to Europe." *New York Times,* 21 February 2001.

Mills, Donna. "New Counterterrorism Initiative to Focus on Saharan Africa," http://www.defenselink.mil, 16 May 2005.

"Mindanao Cops Have Photos of Saudi Tycoon." *Philippine Daily Inquirer* (Internet version), 25 August 1998.

Mintz, John. "Bin Laden's Finances Are a Moving Target: Penetrating Empire Could Take Years." *Washington Post,* 28 August 1998.

Mir, Hamid. "The Attack on Maulana Samiul Haq." *Ausaf,* 20 October 2001.

— — —. "Interview of Osama Bin Laden." *Pakistan,* 18 March 1997.

— — —. "Osama Bin Laden Dares U.S. Commandos to Come to Afghanistan." *Pakistan,* 6 July 1997.

— — —. "Spate of Conspiracies." *Ausaf,* 29 September 1999.

— — —. "U.S. Using Chemical Weapons—Osama Bin Laden." *Ausaf,* 10 November 2001.

"MIRA Bulletin No. 253." *Movement for Islamic Reform in Arabia* (Internet version), 19 February 2001.

Miranda, Rose. "Philippine Military Monitoring NGOs Used by Bin Laden to Send Support to MILF." *Abante* (Internet version), 23 June 2000.

Mishwani, Iftikhar. "India and Israel Helping Northern Alliance, an Exclusive Interview with Afghanistan's Information Minister, Mullah Amir Khan Motaqi." *Pakistan,* 30 August 1999.

Mohamedi, Abdallah Ould. "Interview with Mohamedu Ould Slahi." *Al-Sharq Al-Awast,* 22 February 2000.

— — —. "Mauritanians Pursue Afghan Organization, Inquire about Link with Bin Laden." *Al-Sharq Al-Awsat,* 12 March 1999.

Mohammed, Arshad. "World Terror Attacks Tripled in 2004 by U.S. Count," www.washingtonpost.com, 26 April 2005.

Molinari, Maurizio. "Bin Laden Has Bases in Somalia." *Le Stampa,* 19 June 1999.

Monshipouri, Mahmood. "The West's Modern Encounter with Islam: From Discourse to Reality." *Journal of Church and State* 40, no. 1 (Winter 1998): 25–56.

Montero, David. "Quiet Bangladesh Woken by Bombs." *Christian Science Monitor,* 18 August 2005.

"Moscow Blast Death Toll Rises to 12." Moscow NTV, 14 August 2000.

"The Most Wanted Terrorist in the World." *Paris Match,* 3 May 2001.

Mounassar, Hamoud, and Mohammed Attar. "Yemen Hostages Recover from Horrific Slaughter for Four Friends." *AFP,* 30 December 1998.

Mubarak, Hisham. "The Battle between the Blind Man and the Captive." *Rose al-Yusuf,* 24 August 1992.

Al-Mubarak, Mubarak. "The Difficulty of Admission to Universities and the Domination of the Security Obsession: Severe Crisis Facing Saudi Arabia, Necessitating Speedy Reforms." *Al-Quds Al-Arabi,* 30 August 2000.

Al-Mubarak, Samir. "Report on Islamic Movements in Britain." *Al-Watan Al-Arabi,* 12 December 1997.

Mu'in, Ali. "European Security Organs Get Ready to Dismantle Bin Laden's Network." *Al-Zaman,* 28 August 1998.

Mujendie, Paul. "Police Confident of Al Qaeda Link to London Bombs." Reuters (Internet), 15 July 2005.

Mukarram, Faysal. "Sanaa: More Signs of Two Killers' Links to al Qaeda . . ." *Al-Hayat,* 3 January 2003, 1, 6.

"Mumbai Police Nab Four Persons Dealing with Fake Currency." *Indian Express* (Internet version), 3 July 1999.

Muqaddam, Muhammad. "Algeria Will Not Object to Informing Americans of Dahoumane's Replies to Questions on His Role in 'Millennium Plot.'" *Al-Hayah,* 30 March 2001.

— — —. "Millennium Explosions: *Al-Hayah* Reveals Details of Arrest of Wanted Algerian." *Al-Hayah,* 28 March 2001.

"Murky Information from Source 'CS-1.'" *Der Spiegel,* 19 October 1998.

"Al-Murr: No Bases for Bin Laden or the 'Afghans' in Lebanon." *Al-Sharq Al-Awsat,* 26 January 2000.

Murray, Williamson. "Clausewitz Out, Computer In: Military Culture and Technological Hubris." *National Interest* 48 (Summer 1997).

— — —. "The Emerging Strategic Environment: An Historian's Thoughts." *Strategic Review* 27, no. 1 (Winter 1999): 34.

Musallam, Adnan. "Sayyid Qutb's View of Islam, Society and Militancy."

Journal of South Asian and Middle Eastern Studies 22, no. 1 (Fall 1998): 64–87.

Mustafa, Seema. "India Seen Moving Away from Arab World towards Israel." *Asian Age,* 16 June 2000.

Naim, Mouna. "Osama Bin Laden, the Banker of the Jihad." *Le Monde,* 11 April 1997.

"Nairobi Bombing Suspect Eludes FBI." Reuters, 17 September 1998.

Najm, Salah. "Osama Bin Laden, the Destruction of the Base," Al-Jazirah Satellite Television, 10 June 1999.

Najm, Salah, and Isam al-Ayyash. "Report Views Bin Laden Operations, Counterterrorism Efforts." *Al-Hawadith,* 26 January 2001.

Narayanan, B. "Terrorist Attack on Parliament House." All India Radio Home News Service, 14 December 2001.

Narayanan, M. K. "The Iron Grip Tightens Yet Again." *Asian Age,* 15 November 1999.

Nasir, Lt. Gen. (ret'd) Javid. "The Cease-fire Implications." *Nation* (Lahore edition, Internet version), 1 August 2000.

Nasrawi, Salah. "Osama Bin Laden Reportedly Receiving Millions in Donations." Associated Press, 6 July 1999.

Neumeister, Larry. "Two Egyptians Held in London Added to Embassy Bombing Indictment." Associated Press, 9 May 2000.

"New Offer for Bin Laden." *Al-Islah,* 3 March 1997.

"News Flash." *Philippine Star* (Internet version), 28 December 2000.

"New Zealand Minister Praises Police for Uncovering Sydney Olympics Plot." Radio New Zealand International, 26 August 2000.

"New Zealand Police Release Text of Cyanide Threat Letter." *AFP,* 26 February 2003.

Niazi, M. A. "Compromising Kashmir." *Nation* (Lahore edition, Internet version), 28 December 2001.

"*Nida'ul Islam* Exclusive Interview with Osama Bin Laden: Of Jihad and Terror, the New Powder Keg in the Middle East." *Nida'ul Islam* (Internet version), 15 (October/November 1996).

"No Lack of Candidates for Embassy Bombings." Reuters, 7 August 1998.

"No Need to Explain What Is Clear." *Sangar* (Op-Ed), 20 October 1999.

Nurani, "Terrorist No. 1 Osama Bin Laden Is Funding Islamic Militants." *Zerkala,* 19 August 1999.

Obaid, Nawaf E. "The Power of Saudi Arabi's Islamic Leader." *Middle East Quarterly* 6, no. 3 (September 1999).

"Observer." "Bin Laden: Dissident Turns Pan-Islamist." *Muslim,* 15 March 1997.

Olimpio, Guido. "In Osama's Lair." *Sette Magazine,* 3 September 1998.

— — —. "Islamic Cell Preparing Chemical Warfare, Toxins, Gases against West." *Corriere della Sera,* 8 July 1998.

— — —. "Osama Bin Laden Disappears from Kabul, and Baghdad Pops Up in the Terror Shaykh's New Travels." *Corriere della Sera,* 14 February 1999.

— — —. "Saddam's Latest Challenge: Refuge for Osama Bin Laden." *Corriere della Sera* (Internet version), 17 September 1998.

— — —. "A Secret Pact with Bin Laden, the Terror Shaykh." *Corriere della Sera* (Internet version), 28 December 1998.

"The Opposition." *Jane's Intelligence Review* 8, no. 12 (December 1996).

Orr, Michael. "Russia's Chechen War: Second Time Lucky." *Jane's Defense Weekly* 33 (8 March 2000): 32–36.

"Osama Bin Laden and the Al Qaeda Network." *PBS NewsHour* (transcript), 27 December 2001.

"Osama Bin Laden, Letter from Kandahar." Associated Press, 16 March 1998.

"Osama Bin Laden: Muslims Who Live in Europe Are Kafirs." *Rose al-Yusuf,* 9 December 1996.

"Osama Bin Laden Sends Message to anti-U.S. Conference." *Al-Akhbar,* 12 September 1998.

"Osama Bin Laden's Terrorist Plan in Yemen, Egypt, and Gulf." *Al Watan Al-Arabi,* 27 December 1996.

"Osama Interview: Not Up to Him to Call for Holy War." *Takbeer,* 5–12 August 1990.

"Osama Says Taliban Rejected US Billions for Arrest." *Ausaf,* 28 December 1998.

"Osama Speaks on Hijra and the Islamic State." *Al-Jihaad Newsletter* (Followers of Shariah Web site) 4 (22 June 2000).

"Osama Urges Muslims to Help Afghans, Wage Jihad." *Nation* (Lahore edition, Internet version), 10 April 2001.

O'Sullivan, Arieh. "Bin Laden Ring Planned Mass Terror Campaign." *Jerusalem Post,* 22 August 2000.

Ouazani, Cherif. "The Bin Laden Mystery: An Investigation into the Man Who Has Defied America." *Jeune Afrique,* 7 September 1998.

"Over 300 Bin Laden Companions Arrested in Saudi Arabia." *Ausaf,* 26 March 1999.

Oxford, Esther, and Buhawadin Khuja. *The Sunday Times* (Internet version), 25 March 2001.

"Pakistani to Star in Movie on Bin Laden's 'Achievements.'" *Pakistan,* 6 May 2000, 5.

Panjeri, Parna. "Bin Laden Tied to Kashmir Islamic Movement." *Al-Quds Al-Arabi,* 24 March 1999.

"Part One of a Series of Reports on Bin Laden's Life in Sudan." *Al-Quds Al-Arabi* (Internet version), 24 November 2001.

Pearl, Daniel. "In Sudanese Bombing, 'Evidence' Depends on Who Is Viewing It." *Wall Street Journal,* 28 October 1998.

Perry, Tom. "Blast Kills 83 in Egyptian Red Sea Resort." Reuters (Internet), 23 July 2005.

"Peshawar, Which Exports Terrorism to the World." *Al-Musawwar* no. 3754 (9 April 1993).

Peters, Ralph. "Our Old New Enemies." *Parameters* 29 no. 2 (Summer 1999).

— — —. "We Don't Have the Stomach for This Kind of Fight." *Washington Post* (Op-Ed), 30 August 1998.

"Philippine Forces on Alert after Killing of Muslim Extremist Leader." *AFP,* 19 December 1998.

"Philippine Military Intelligence Chief Says Bin Laden Gave $3 Million to the MILF." GMA-7 Television, 19 June 2000.

"Philippine Military Says MILF Force Decimated." *Abante* (Internet version), 11 May 2000.

"Philippine Muslim Rebels Await Afghan Arms Shipment." *AFP*, 21 February 1999.

"Philippines' MILF Reveals Bin Laden Link." *Philippine Star* (Internet version), 10 February 1999.

Phillips, Andrew, and Barry Came. "The Prime Suspect." *Mclean's*, 24 January 2000.

Pincus, Walter. "Seized Materials May Help Thwart Future Attacks." *Washington Post*, 3 April 2002.

Pincus, Walter, and Vernon Loeb. "Bin Laden Called Top Terrorist Threat." *Washington Post*, 8 February 2001.

Pipes, Daniel. "God and Mammon: Does Poverty Cause Militant Islam?" *National Interest* 66 (Winter 2001/02): 14–21.

Poletto, Lodovico. "Wanted Terrorist Escapes Dragnet." *La Stampa* (Internet version), 5 October 1998.

"Police Hold Four July 21 Bombers." BBC News, http://news.bbc.co.uk, 30 July 2005.

Pomfret, John. "Bosnian Officials Involved in Arms Trade Tied to Radical States." *Washington Post*, 22 September 1996.

Power, Carla. "Chasing a Man, Fixing a Nation." *Newsweek International*, 29 January 2001.

"Press Report Links Bin Laden to Tirana Banks, Companies." ATA, 6 September 1998.

"Press Report on Presence of Osama Bin Laden and 'Afghan Arabs' in Yemen." *Al-Watan Al-Arabi*, 27 December 1996.

Prifti, Anila. "Bin Laden's Agent: Friend of Gjinushi and Berisha." *Koha Jone*, 14 November 1999.

———. "Bin Laden's Man: 'I Will Sue Albania.'" *Koha Jone*, 18 November 1999.

"Prisons: The Dwelling of Our Scholars." *Nida'ul Islam* 21 (December 1997/January 1998).

"Profile of Mohammed Makkawi—New Military Commander of Al Qaeda." *Al-Sharq Al-Awsat*, 27 November 2001.

Pulido, Maki. "Military Monitoring New Philippine Terrorist Group." GMA-7 Radio-Television Arts Network, 27 October 1998.

"Punish and Be Damned." Economist.com (Editorial), 28 August 1998.

"Al-Qaida Affiliated Group Claims al-Aqabah, Eilat Rocket Attacks." *AFP*, 19 August 2005.

"Qatar Looks for Qaeda Link in Theater Suicide Bomb." Reuters, 20 March 2005.

Al-Qaysi, Sa'id. "Bin Laden Reportedly Setting Up Camp in Lebanon." *Al-Watan Al-Arabi*, 18 August 2000.

———. "Bin Laden's New 'Islamic Front.'" *Al-Watan Al-Arabi*, 6 June 1998.

———. "Report on U.S. Embassy Bombing Probe." *Al-Watan Al-Arabi*, 30 October 1998.

———. "Search for Jihad Movement's al-Zawahiri." *Al-Watan Al-Arabi*, 23 April 1999.

— — —. "U.S.-Yemen-Bin Laden Relations." *Al-Watan Al-Arabi*, 15 January 1999.

Al-Qubaysi, Sa'id. "Kuwait, UAE Banks Said Tied to Bin Laden." *Al-Watan Al-Arabi*, 31 December 1999.

Quereshi, Javed, and Shahid Riaz. "Afghanistan to Become the Graveyard of American Troops: Interview of Maulavi Jalaluddin Haqqani." *Pakistan*, 22 October 2001.

al-Qurashi, Abu-Ubayd. "America's Nightmares." *Al-Ansar* (Internet), 13 February 2002.

— — —. "The Moscow Theater Operation." *Al-Ansar* (Internet), 6 November 2002.

Qureshi, Samiullah. "Freedom Fighters' Operations against Indian Government." Radio Pakistan, 25 December 2000.

Raffy, Serge. "Terrorism; Revelations on the Marrakech Slaughter; How the Islamists Recruit in France." *Le Nouvel Observateur* (October 1994).

Rahmani, Anis. "Strife within Fundamentalist Groups." *Al-Mustaqillah* (Internet version), 31 August 1999.

Rafat, Ahmed. "The Spanish Will Not Be Safe Even in Their Homes." *Tiempo de Hoy*, 24 March 2003.

Ranstorp, Magnus. "Interpreting the Broader Context and Meaning of Bin Laden's Fatwa." *Studies in Conflict and Terrorism* 21, no. 4 (1998).

Rashid, Ahmed. "Afghanistan: Heart of Darkness." *Far East Economic Review*, 5 August 1999.

— — —. "Afghan Warlords Return to Their Old Ways after Helping to Oust Taliban with U.S. Aid." *Wall Street Journal*, 16 January 2002.

— — —. "The Bloody Trail of the World's Most Wanted Terrorist." *London Daily Telegraph*, 21 December 2000.

— — —. "The Khost Story." *Herald*, April 1991, 41–43.

— — —. "Pakistan Raids Hideouts to Lose 'Safehaven' Tag." *Daily Telegraph*, 3 April 2002.

— — —. "Taliban Prepares for 'Decisive' Attack with Help of Militants." *Washington Times*, 22 July 1999.

ar-Rashid, Mamun. "Countless Militant Networks Like Spider's Net." *Dainik Janakantha*, 19 July 2005, 1, 11.

Rashid, Zahid. "Clash of Civilization and Culture." *Pakistan*, 25 November 2001.

Ratnesar, Ronesh. "What's Become of Al Qaeda." *Time*, 12 January 2002.

Raufer, Xavier. "Investigation into Terrorist Multinational." *VSD*, 3–9 September 1998.

"The Real Threat to American Interests in Saudi Arabia." MediaGen (U.K.) Ltd. (Internet), 21 February 1997.

"Rebels Say Attack on Juba Imminent." *Al-Quds Al-Arabi*, 16 February 1998.

"Report by *Al-Quds Al-Arabi* Bureau in Tirana, Albania." *Al-Quds Al-Arabi*, 26 October 1998.

"Report on Bin Laden's Activities, Wealth." *Al-Watan Al-Arabi*, 4 September 1998.

"Report on Egyptian Fundamentalists." *Al-Sharq Al-Awsat*, 18 July 1999.

"Report on Saudi Billionaire Financing Bin Ladin: Saudi Billionaires from Hadhramout Are Living in Tension after the Tragedy of Khalid Bin Mahfuz and His Sudden Fall." *Al-Quds Al-Arabi*, 13 December 1999.

"Report on the Threat to Arab Countries by Terrorist Bin Laden." *Sawt al-Mar'ah*, 31 March 1998.

"Reports on the Escape of Fundamentalists to Iraq for Fear of Being Arrested. Jordan Government Source. The Afghan Arabs to Washington Is Premature." *Al-Quds Al-Arabi*, 20 December 1999.

"'Returnees from Albania Case' Aimed at Eliminating Jihad Group." *Al-Hayah*, 15 December 1998.

"A Revealing Trove in Afghanistan." *New York Times*, 19 March 2002.

Reverier, Jean-Loup, et al. "Islamic Killers: Leads, Networks." *Le Point*, 26 August 1995.

Richardson, Bruce. "Khost Busters. Mujahedin Forces (Finally) Kick Puppets from Provincial Capital." *Soldier of Fortune* (November 1991): 60–65, 73.

Risen, James. "Al Qaeda Still Able to Strike U.S., Head of CIA Says." *New York Times*, 7 February 2002.

— — —. "Bin Laden Was Target of U.S. Raid Plans since Spring." *New York Times* Web site, 6 September 1998.

Risen, James, and Benjamin Weiser. "U.S. Officials Say Aid for Terrorists Came through Two Persian Gulf Countries." *New York Times*, 8 July 1999.

Rizq, Hamdi. "Jihad Unilaterally Won Over Bin Laden, While the Group was Content with Financial Support." *Al-Wasat Magazine*, 31 August–6 September 1998.

— — —. "Would al-Zawahiri Fall into the Trap of Global Security? Confessions by 'Returnees from Albania' Signal the Demise of the Egyptian 'Jihad Organization.'" *Al-Wasat Magazine*, 19–25 April 1999.

Rizq, Hamdi, et al. "Osama Bin Laden, a Millionaire Financially Supporting Terrorism in Egypt and Saudi Arabia." *Rose al-Yusuf*, 17 May 1993.

Romero, Paolo. "Further on Bin Laden Aid to MILF; Mindanao Rehabilitation Fund Explained." *Philippine Star* (Internet version), 20 June 2000.

Roox, Gilbert. "UN Expert Johan Peleman Discusses Africa's Black Holes — How Clean Is My Diamond." *De Standaard* (Internet version), 5 January 2002.

Rossant, Juliette. "Billionaires." *Forbes Magazine*, 5 July 1999.

"RP Tightens Security on Terrorist Target," *Philippine Daily Inquirer* (Internet version), 25 August 1998.

"RSA Confirms Talks with Tanzania on Bomb Suspect." SAfm Radio Network, 14 October 1999.

Rubenstein, Richard E., and Jarle Crocker. "Challenging Huntington." *Foreign Policy* 94 (Fall 1994): 113–28.

Rubin, Elizabeth. "Prep School." *New Yorker* (17 December 2001).

Rubin, Michael. "Afghanistan: As Bad as Its Reputation?" *Middle East Quarterly* 3, no. 3 (September 2000).

Rupert, James. "U.S. and Britain Close 10 Embassies in Africa." *Washington Post*, 26 June 1999.

"Russia Hails India's Position against Terrorism." Moscow RIA, 28 February 2000.

"Russians and Iranians in Panjsher." *Hewad* (Editorial), 2 October 1999.

Al-Sab, Fayzah. "Yemeni Ties with U.S., Bin Laden." *Al-Watan Al-Arabi,* 12 June 1998.

Sadim, Michael. "Bin Laden Said to Be Giving Military Aid to MILF." *Manila Times* (Internet version), 13 February 1999.

Sadiq, Ahmed. "Interview with Taliban Official Spokesman Wakil Ahmed Muttawakil." *Al-Watan Al-Arabi,* 23 July 1999.

Sadiq, Mahmud. "Cairo Combats Islamists Overseas." *Al-Watan Al-Arabi,* 28 May 1999.

Said, Summer. "Prestigious Cairo Library Goes Online." *Arab News,* 5 June 2005.

"Sakra Remanded in Custody," *NTV Online* (Internet), 12 August 2005.

Salah, Jihad. "Story of Attempt to Assassinate Bin Laden in Jalalabad." *Al-Watan Al-Arabi,* 18 April 1997.

Salah, Muhammed. "Ali al-Rashidi: The Egyptian Policeman Who Paved the Way for 'Afghan Arabs' in Africa and Prepared Them to Take Revenge against the Americans." *Al-Hayah,* 30 September 1998.

— — —. "Bin Laden Front Falls Back and Egyptian Groups Undertake the Mission." *Al-Wasat Magazine,* 11–17 January 1999.

— — —. "Cairo: 'Returnees from Albania' Case Is Biggest Blow to Jihad Groups." *Al-Hayah,* 20 April 1999.

— — —. "Canada: An Egyptian 'Planning' to Blow Up the Israeli Embassy Arrested." *Al-Hayah,* 8 March 2000.

— — —. "Canada: Egyptian Fundamentalist Questioned over Links with Osama Bin Laden." *Al-Hayah,* 7 July 2000.

— — —. "Egypt: Arrest of 13 Members of the Jihad Organization." *Al-Hayah,* 25 November 1998.

— — —. "Egyptian Fundamentalist Reveals to *Al-Hayah*: Al-Zawahiri's Resignation Came Too Late. He Left Jihad Exhausted." *Al-Hayah,* 9 February 2000.

— — —. "Egyptian Fundamentalists Insist Zawahiri Is in Jalalabad." *Al-Hayah,* 21 March 1999.

— — —. "Egypt Supplies United States with Information about 'Abu Hafs.'" *Al-Hayah,* 6 December 1998.

— — —. "Fundamentalist Source: Bin Laden Front Purchased Chemical Weapons from Eastern Europe." *Al-Hayah,* 20 April 1999.

— — —. "In Response to British Ruling to Extradite Two Egyptian Fundamentalists to the United States, Al-Zayyat Warns of Reprisal Operations against U.S. Interests." *Al-Hayah,* 5 May 2000.

— — —. "Interrogation of al-Zawahiri's Deputy Revealed the Jihad and Al Qaeda Secrets." *Al-Hayah,* 18 March 1999.

— — —. "Islamic Group: Al-Qasimi Still in Croatia; His Extradition to Egypt Would Not Pass without Retaliation." *Al-Hayah,* 26 September 1999.

— — —. "An Islamic Organization Affirms Bulgaria Handed Over to Egypt a Jihad Organization Member." *Al-Hayah,* 25 August 1998.

— — —. "Jihad Group Vows to Take Revenge against the United States." *Al-Hayah,* 6 August 1998.

— — —. "The Main Defendant Confirms the Islamists' Determination to Retaliate against United States." *Al-Hayah,* 5 February 1999.

— — —. "Mullah Omar, Bin Laden, and al-Zawahiri Are Alive and Eulogize Shaykh Badni. First Announcement That the Jihad Leader Has Become Al-Qaida Leader's Deputy." *Al Hayah,* 19 February 2002.

— — —. "A Record of Jihad Years from Ayn Shams to Tirana." *Al-Wasat Magazine,* 1–7 March 1999.

— — —. "'Returnees from Albania Case' Aimed at Eliminating Jihad Group." *Al-Hayah,* 15 December 1998.

— — —. "Secret of the Relationship between al-Zawahiri and Bin Laden: The Jihad Leader Turned Bin Laden into a Mujahid." *Al-Wasat Magazine,* 8–14 March 1999.

— — —. "Sweden Extradited the Vanguards of Conquest Leader to Egypt." *Al-Hayah,* 20 December 2001.

— — —. "Vanguards of Conquest Threaten Croatia with Revenge if It Extradites al-Qasimi." *Al-Hayah,* 25 September 1995.

— — —. "World Islamic Front Backs Intifadah of Palestine's Sons." *Al-Hayah,* 4 March 1998.

Salah, Muhammed, and Kamil al-Tawil. "Egyptian 'Group' Threatens to 'Retaliate' against Croatia." *Al-Hayah,* 23 September 1996.

Salah, Muhammed, et al. "Moscow: Bin Laden Has 'Links' with Chechen Narcotics Dealers." *Al-Hayah* (Internet version), 18 September 1999.

Salah-al-Din, Muhammed. "The Phenomenon of Profiting from Terrorism." *Al-Madinah,* 25 January 2000.

Salahiz, Muhammed. "Leader of 'Afghan Arabs' Killed in African State." *Al-Hayah,* 11 June 1996.

Salamah, Ahmed Salamah. "Types of Terrorism." *Al-Ahram,* 1 September 1998.

Saleheddin, Esmat. "Islamists Say Albania Extradited Militants to Egypt." Reuters, 2 August 1998.

Salhani, Claude. "The Aqaba Attack." http:// www.khaleejtimes.com, 26 August 2005.

Salih, Nur-al-Din. "Campaign in Albania and Bosnia to Track Down Fundamentalist Networks." *Al-Sharq Al-Awsat,* 27 October 1998.

"Sanctions against Afghanistan: UN Must Refrain from Acting as a U.S. Appendage." *Al-Akhbar,* 18 October 1999.

Sardon, Tolga. "Istanbul Is Bin Laden's Bridge." *Milliyet* (Internet version), 17 December 1999.

Sattar, Abdul. "Osama Urges Ummah to Continue Jihad." *News* (Internet version), 7 May 2001.

"Saudi Arabia Braces Itself for Return of Jihadists from Iraq." *AFP,* 1 June 2005.

"Saudi Arabia Denies Citizen Told U.S. of New York Bomb Plot." AP-Dow Jones, 3 August 1997.

"Saudi Dissident Shuts Down Site." BBC News, http:// newsvote.BBC.co.uk, 27 August 2005.

"Saudi Executives Give Funds to Bin Laden." Reuters, 29 October 1999.

"Saudi Forces Clash with Gunmen in Industrial City." Reuters, 29 August 2005.

"The Saudi Islamic Opposition 'Advice and Reform Commission' Headed by Shaykh Osama Bin Laden Has Announced the Opening of an Office in London." *Al-Qaeda Al-Arabi,* 8 August 1994.

"Saudi Security Forces Arrest Iraqi Infiltrators in Jubayl." Saudi Press Agency, 20 August 2005.

"Saudi Soldier's Journey to Death in Iraq." Reuters, 20 March 2005.

"Saudi Sought in Bombings Moves to Afghan Militia Capital." *Washington Post,* 11 April 1997.

"Saudis Arrest 40 Christians for Praying." Reuters, 22 April 2005.

SB. "Terrorism: The Psychological War." *El-Watan* (Internet version), 16 November 1999.

Scarborough, Rowan. "Al Qaeda Now in 'Survival Only Mode.'" *Washington Times,* 3 December 2001.

Schmitt, Eric. "U.S.-Philippine Command May Signal War's Next Phase." *New York Times,* 16 January 2002.

Schraeder, Katherine. "Classic Spy Work Leads to al-Qaeda Arrest." Associated Press, 4 May 2005.

Schweid, Barry. "Senior Officials Quietly Join Probe of Terrorism Support." Associated Press, 8 July 1998.

Sciloino, Elaine, and Don Van Natta Jr. "British Intelligence Downgraded Terror Threat before Attacks." *San Francisco Chronicle* (Internet version), 19 July 2005.

"Scotland Yard Questions Arab Fundamentalist Advocating Assassination of British Prime Minister." *Al-Sharq Al-Awsat,* 14 December 2000.

"Secrets of Meetings between Iranians and Fundamentalists." *Al-Watan Al-Arabi,* 7 March 1997.

"Secrets of the Worldwide Campaign Chasing Osama Bin Laden: From Afghanistan to Sudan to Somalia: The Terrorist Who Baffled the World Intelligence Services." *Al-Watan Al-Arabi,* 16 February 1996.

"Security Report, Bin Laden Has Weapons Worth $51 Million, 20 Foreign Bases, and 80 Front Companies." *Al-Sharq Al-Awsat,* 30 July 1999.

Seed, Tariq. "Bin Laden Calls for Holy War against Jews, Christians." *Pakistan Observer* (Internet version), 2 September 2000.

Seepe, Jimmy. "RSA, Tanzania in 'Bitter Row' over Bomber Handover to U.S." *Sowetan,* 14 October, 1999.

Sehgel, Ikram. "Osama Bin Laden Syndrome: Freedom Fighter or Terrorist?" *Nation* (Lahore edition, Internet version), 29 August 1998.

"Senior Officials and Ministers Are 'Angry' with Washington." *Al-Quds Al-Arabi,* 4 July 2000.

"A Separate War." *New Republic,* 2 December 2002, 7.

"Serial Blasts Rock Country." http://nation.ittefaq.com, 17 August 2005.

"A Serious Breach." *Pioneer* (Editorial), 25 December 2000.

"Sermon of Shaykh Yusuf al-Qaradawi." Qatar Television, 11 January 2002.

"Seven Arrested in London Linked to Bin Laden." London Press Association, 23 September 1998.

"71 Egyptian 'Terrorists' Referred to Military Court." *Al-Sharq Al-Awsat,* 7 July 1999.

Al-Shifai'i, Muhammed. "Arab Afghans Confirm Capture of Bin Laden's Aide Ibn-al-Shaykh Al-Libi, Al-Sharq Sab'i." *Al-Sharq Al-Awsat,* 28 January 2002.

— — —. "Britain's Fundamentalist Movements Open Training Camps for Their Members in the United States and Others in Northern Nigeria." *Al-Sharq Al-Awsat,* 4 July 2000.

— — —. "Curry Restaurants, Car Dealerships, and Mobile Phone Shops Are the New Fronts for Fundamentalists That They Depend on for Their Activities in Britain." *Al-Sharq Al-Awsat,* 22 January 2000.

— — —. "Egyptian 'Armed Vanguards of Conquest' Calls on 'Islamic Front' to Expand Membership." *Al-Sharq Al-Awsat,* 26 February 1998.

— — —. "Egyptian 'Islamic Group' Leader Calls for 'Stepping Up Hostile Strategy' against United States." *Al-Sharq Al-Awsat,* 13 October 1999.

— — —. "Egypt's Military Judiciary to Try Soon the Returnees from Azerbaijan, South Africa, and Kuwait Case Involving 77 Fundamentalists." *Al-Sharq Al-Awsat,* 12 August 1999.

— — —. "Interview with Hani al-Saba'i." *Al-Sharq Al-Awsat.* 28 January 2002.

— — —. "Leaders of World Fundamentalist Movements to Gather at Conference in London Friday to Discuss West's Arrogance." *Al-Sharq Al-Awsat,* 22 February 1999.

— — —. "London Faces Crisis because of Terrorist Groups List." *Al-Sharq Al-Awsat,* 2 March 2001.

— — —. "London Fundamentalists: Kuwait and the UAE Handed Over New Elements to Egypt." *Al-Sharq al-Awsat,* 7 June 2000.

— — —. "Muhajiroun Movement Leader Confirms Legal Loopholes Were Exploited to Send Fundamentalists for Military Training in the United States. Omar Bakri: Islamic Movement's Sons Learned Guerrilla Warfare and How to Make Explosives in the Missouri, Michigan, and Virginia Camps." *Al-Sharq Al-Awsat,* 30 May 2000.

— — —. "UK Court to Review the Detention of Alleged Bin Laden Aide." *Al-Sharq Al-Awsat,* 29 October 1998.

— — —. "The Vanguards of Conquest Case Will Be Referred to Egypt's Military Judiciary." *Al-Sharq Al-Awsat,* 28 May 1999.

Al-Shafai, Muhammad, and al-Sa'd Shammari, "Kuwait Arrests 11 Fundamentalists, Among Them Two Police Officers, to Preempt Possible Attacks on U.S. Targets. One of Bin Ladin's Aides Left the Country before His Arrest and the Detainees Include Yemenis, Syrians, and Egyptians." *Al-Sharq Al-Awsat,* 8 November 2000.

Sharaf-al-Din, Khalid. "Egypt: The Death Sentences against Jihad Leaders Will Be Dropped When They Are Arrested and Tried in Prison." *Al-Sharq Al-Awsat,* 23 April 1993.

— — —. "Surprises from the Trial of the Largest International Terrorist Group in Egypt." *Al-Sharq Al-Awsat,* 6 March 1999.

Sharif-al-Din, Nabil. "The Afghanistan of the Caucasus: Bin Laden and Ibn-al-Khattab in Dagestan." *Al-Ahram Al-Arabi,* 9 October 1999.

Sharma, Rajeev. "Cracking the Conspiracy." *Sunday,* 24 April 1993.

"*Al-Sharq Al-Awsat* Visits Abu Hafs Al-Masri's Home; His Family Emphasizes He Is Alive; Refuses to Accept Condolences." *Al-Sharq Al-Awsat,* 30 November 2001.

Shatarah, Lufti, and Hammid Munsir. "Twenty Jihad Organization Members Arrested in Yemen." *Al-Sharq Al-Awsat,* 28 December 1992.

Shawcross, William. "Stop This Racism." *Guardian* (Internet version), 17 September 2001.

Shenon, Philip. "Fear of Attack Cancels Cohen's Trip to Albania." *New York Times,* 17 July 1999.

— — —. "House Votes $1.4 Billion for Embassy Security." *New York Times,* 22 July 1999.

Shermatova, Sanobar. "Islamic Sword-Bearer." *Moskovskiyo Novosti* 4 (31 January 1999).

Sherwood, Mark. "Mueller: Cost of FBI Cyber Upgrade Unknown." Associated Press, 24 May 2005.

Shiraz, Abu. "May 1998 Interview with Bin Laden Reported." *Pakistan,* 20 February 1999.

al-Shiri, Abdullah. "Explosions Rock Central Riyadh," Associated Press, 30 December 2005.

Shirley, Edward. "The Etiquette of Killing Mr. Bin Laden." *Wall Street Journal* (Op-Ed), 27 August 1998.

Al-Shuli, Yusuf. "Interview with Mahfouz Ould Walid." Al-Jazirah Satellite Television, 29 November 2001.

Siddiqui, Azeem. "Interview with Osama Bin Laden Reported." *Al-Akhbar,* 31 March 1998.

Simon, Steve, and Daniel Benjamin. "The Terror." *Survival* 43, no. 4 (Winter 2001).

Singh, Dalip, and James Clark. "Britons Take War Holidays in Kashmir." *Sunday Times* (Internet version), 21 January 2001.

Sipress, Alan. "Sudan, N. Korea Cited for Gains on Terrorism." *Washington Post,* 1 May 2000.

Sirri, Odai. "New Lead in Qatar Bombing." Reuters, 21 March 2005

Sivan, Emmanuel. "The Holy War Tradition in Islam." *Orbis* 42, no. 2 (Spring 1998).

Slackman, Michael. "Bin Laden's Family Ties Bind and Bedevil a Syrian Clan." *Los Angeles Times,* 13 November 2001.

Slackman, Michael, and Mona al-Naggar. "Egypt Sends Huge Force to Terrorist Hunt." *New York Times,* 30 August 2005.

Slater, Eric. "Rule of the Gun on the Rise after Ouster of the Taliban." *Los Angeles Times,* 13 January 2002.

Smith, Craig S. "Dutch Look for Qaeda Link after Killing of Filmmaker." *New York Times,* 8 November 2004, A10.

Smyth, Frank. "Culture Shock: Bin Laden, Khartoum, and the War against the West." *Jane's Intelligence Review* 10, no. 10 (October 1998): 22–25.

Smyth, Frank, and Jason Vest. "One Man's Private Jihad." *Village Voice,* 25 August 1998.

Solomon, John. "FBI Chief Won't Mandate Terror Expertise." *San Francisco Chronicle,* 20 June 2005.

— — —. "FBI Didn't Seek to Hire Terrorism Experts." *San Francisco Chronicle* (Internet version), 19 June 2005.

"So There Will Be War in the Spring." *Delo No,* 1 March 2000.

Soudan, Francois. "Thus Spoke Osama Bin Laden." *Jeune Afrique,* 8–26 January 1999.

"Sources View Options on Bin Laden's Whereabouts." *Al-Ittihad* (Internet version), 17 February 1999.

"Spare Us Wild West Justice." *Independent on Sunday* (Editorial, Internet version), 13 January 2002.

"Speech by Osama Bin Laden." Al-Jazirah Satellite Television, 7 October 2001.

"Staff Increase in Pakistan Mission Linked to Bin Laden." *Ausaf,* 27 July 1999.

Stack, Megan K. "Militants' Rockets Miss 2 U.S. Navy Warships." *Los Angeles Times,* 20 August 2005.

Stahl, Leslie. "Interview with Richard Clarke." *Federal News Service,* 24 October 2000.

Stanley, Alessandra. "Italy and Germany Arrest 6 Islamists in Failed 2000 Bomb Plot." *New York Times,* 6 April 2000.

Stark, Holger. "Syrian Had Inside Knowledge of 9/11 and London Bombings." *Spiegel Online,* http://service.spiegel.de, 24 August 2005.

"A Statement by al-Qaida Organization [in Iraq]." www.jihad-algerie.com, 16 June 2005.

"Statement by Mother of Osama Bin Laden." *Arab News* (Internet version), 9 December 2001.

"Statement from Qaeda al-Jihad." *Al-Neda* (Internet), 27 April 2002.

"Statement from Taliban Leader Mullah Omar in Khandahar." Afghan Islamic News Press Agency, 13 October 2001.

"Statement of al-Qaida Organization on the Faylaka Operation." *al-Qal'ah* (Internet), 18 October 2002.

"Statement of the Abu Hafs al-Masri Brigades." *Quds Press* (Internet version), 25 August 2003.

"Statement Read by Ayman al-Zawahiri." Al-Jazirah Satellite Channel Television, 9 November 2001.

Steel, Ronald. "Blowback: Terrorism and the U.S. Role in the Middle East." *New Republic,* 28 July 1996.

Stern, Jessica. "Pakistan's Jihad Culture." *Foreign Affairs* 79, no. 6 (November/December 2000).

Stoehlin, Andrew. "Uzbekistan: The Andijon Uprising." International Crisis Group, http://www.crisisgroup.org, 25 May 2005.

"Story of Cooperation between Iraq and Both Taliban and Bin Laden; It Started before Operation Desert Fox." *Al-Majallah,* 10–16 January 1999.

Stout, David. "Citing Threats, FBI Suspends Public Tours of HQS." *New York Times,* 24 July 1999.

"Strange Fatwas from Government Ulema." *Al-Quds Al-Arabi,* 24 April 2001.

"A Strange Sudanese." *Le Point,* 12 March 1994.

Subhi, Karim. "Profile of a Terrorist." *Rose al-Yusuf,* 1 December 2001, 20–21.

"Sudan: Two Suspects in February Attack on Mosque Confess on Television." BBC Monitoring Service, 14 March 1994.

Sukarsono, Achmad. "Indonesia Cuts Jail Term for Bashir." Reuters, 17 August 2005.

Sullivan, Andrew. "This Is a Religious War." *New York Times Magazine,* 7 October 2001.

"Suspected Bin Laden Supporters Held in Mauritania." *AFP,* 5 March 1999.

Syed, Raziud Din. "Osama Bin Laden—A Terrorist or the Continuity of the Islamic Idea of Life?" *Jasarat,* 4 January 2000.

Sylla, Ibrahim. "Mauritania Blames al-Qaeda Ally for Deadly Raid." Reuters, 5 June 2005.

Tahir, Abd-al-Salam, and Steven Lee Myers. "Suspect in *Cole* Attack Reportedly Says Another U.S. Ship Was Targeted in January." *Al-Sharq Al-Awsat* (Internet version), 11 November 2000.

Tahiri, Amir. "A Lion in Paris." *Al-Sarq Al-Awsat,* 5 April 2001.

———. "Interview with Unidentified Algerian Senior Counterterrorism Officer." *Al-Sharq Al-Awsat,* 4 November 1997.

"Taliban Ask Bin Laden to Halt Anti-Saudi Activities." *Nation,* 27 March 1997.

"Taliban Chief Criticizes Outside Pressure on Afghan Issue." *AFP,* 23 September 1998.

"Taliban Expelling Arab Muslim Fundamentalists: Egypt." *AFP,* 27 December 1996.

"Taliban, JUI Threaten AmCits, Any Country Supporting Attacks." *Khabrain,* 2 November 2000.

"Taliban Will Not Hand Over Bin Laden for the Following Reasons." *Al-Quds Al-Arabi* (Editorial), 17 November 1999.

Tamay, Rose, et al. "'High-Powered' Firearms Flood Abu Sayyaf Camp." *Philpino Star Ngayon* (Internet version), 23 August 2000.

Tarakzai, Sajjad. "Taliban, Hizb-e Islami Hold Talks in Peshawar, Both Groups Agree for Reconciliation." *Jang,* 8 May 2001.

Tattersall, Nick. "Mauritania Shows Risks in U.S. Strategy in Africa." Reuters, 18 August 2005.

Al-Tawil, Kamil. "U.S. Investigators Reportedly Focusing on Bin Laden's Role." *Al-Hayah* (Internet version), 20 January 1999.

"Terrorism and Osama Bin Laden." *CNN Burden of Proof* (Transcript), 17 May 2001.

"The Terrorist and the State." *Frontline Online,* April 1999.

"Text of the World Front's Statement Urging Jihad against Jews and Crusaders." *Al-Quds Al-Arabi,* 23 February 1998.

Thomas, Christopher. "Holy War Run from Ruined Afghan Hideout." The-Times.com, 21 August 1998.

"330 Killed during Ramadan in Algeria." *Washington Report on Middle East Affairs* 20, no. 2, (March 2001): 40.

"Three Pakistani-based Dons Behind Delhi Bomb Blasts." All India Radio Network, 18 June 1996.

"A Tightrope Walk." *Times of India* (Editorial, Internet version), 1 August 2000.

Timmerman, Kenneth. "Likely Mastermind of Tower Attacks." *Insight Magazine,* 31 December 2001.

———. "Sudan Financier Monopolizes Exports." African Economic Digest, 29 August 1994.

———. "Time to (En)Act." *Pioneer* (Editorial), 14 December 2001.

— — —. "This Man Wants You Dead." *Reader's Digest* (July 1998): 50–57.

Tjandraningsih, Christine T., and Rudy Madanir. "Jakarta Blast Was against U.S.: Bali Bombing Suspect." *Kyodo World Service*, 6 August 2003.

"TNI Chief Warns against Growing Separatism in Aceh," Radio Republik Indonesia, 23 November 1999.

"TNI Reinforcements Deploy to Paso to Repel Christian Attacks." *Republika* (Internet version), 7 June 2000.

"TNI to Verify Reported Arms Sales to Aceh Separatists." *Jakarta Post* (Internet version), 4 March 2000.

"Today's Harvest." Al-Jazirah Space Channel Television, 28 February 2001.

"Today's New Cult Hero." *Economist* (Editorial), 29 August–4 September 1998.

Tohid, Owais. "Azhar Calls for Jihad against India First, Then U.S." *AFP*, 6 January 2000.

Torriero, E. A., and Michael Martinez. "Al Qaeda Architect's Influence Raises Fear." *Chicago Tribune*, 18 November 2001.

"Transcript of Bin Laden's October [2001] Interview." CNN.com, accessed 5 February 2002.

"Transcript of Osama Bin Laden Video Tape." CNN.com, accessed 13 December 2001.

Trifonov, Igor. "12 Killed, 108 Injured by 8 Aug Bomb Blast in Moscow." ITAR-TASS, 15 August 2000.

Trinidad, Marian. "MILF Chief Calls for UN-Supervised Referendum." *Manila Times* (Internet version), 23 March 2000.

Trofimov, Yaroslav. "As a Taliban Regime Falls inside Afghanistan, So Do Islamic Convictions outside Its Borders." *Wall Street Journal*, 31 December 2001.

Trotta, Daniel. "Al-Qaeda Suspects Go on Trial in Spain." Reuters, 22 April 2005.

Tunbridge, Louise. "Islam Crusade Warning for U.S. 'Enemy.'" *Daily Telegraph*, 15 August 1995.

"Turkey Detains Key al-Qaeda Figure." *Daily Telegraph*, 11 August 2005.

"Two Egyptians Connected with Fundamentalist Groups Arrested." *AFP*, 29 June 1998.

"200 Held after Cairo Attacks." www.CNN.com, 1 May 2005.

"Two More Arrested in Kuwaiti Bomb Plots." *Washington Post*, 13 November 2000.

"UBL Popularity Increased 'Manifold' in Northwest Pakistan." *Wahdat*, 23 July 1999. 1, 5.

"UBL Urges Mujahedin to 'Arrest' Clinton, Shoot U.S. Commandos." *Pakistan*, 12 September 1999.

Ulaymat, Musallom. "As Part of the Chain of Pressure on Jordan to Agree to Settlement Demands, U.S. Embassy Spreads Word about Existence of Terrorism in Jordan and Sets Up Barricades on Embassy Walls." *Shihan*, 8–14 July 2000.

Al-Umash, Bassam. "The Mentality of Osama Bin Laden." *Al Ra'y*, 16 August 1999.

"Unattributed Biography of Osama Bin Laden." *Frontline Online*, April 1999.

"The United States and Russia Should Not Invite the Wrath of the Muslims of the World." *Ausaf,* 4 June 2000.

"'The United States Should Search within Itself': Exclusive Interview with Osama Bin Laden." *Ummat,* 28 September 2001.

"Unready Citadel." *Telegraph* (Editorial), 25 December 2000.

Unson, John, et al. "Mercado Urges MILF Not to Postpone Talks with Manila." *Philippine Star* (Internet version), 29 November 1999.

"U.S. Aid for Ahmed Shah Masood against Osama." *Jang* (Editorial), 29 December 1998.

"U.S. Has Long Blamed Sudan for Harboring Terrorists." Associated Press, 20 August 1998.

"U.S. Intelligence Cites Iraqi Ties to Sudan Plant." Associated Press, 25 August 1998.

"U.S. Launches Training in Gulf of Guinea." Associated Press, 29 June 2005.

"U.S. Offers to Help Bangladesh Combat Terrorism." Reuters, 18 April 2005.

"U.S. on Guard in Saudi Arabia." CBS News, www.CBSnews.com, 7 December 2004.

"U.S. President Says Chechnya 'Internal Affair.'" *Interfax,* 21 November 2002.

"U.S. Reportedly Asks Taliban for Bin Laden." *Al-Quds Al-Arabi* (Internet version), 11–12 March 1998.

U.S. State Department. "Fact Sheet on Osama Bin Laden." 14 August 1996.

– – –. "Patterns of Global Terrorism, 1992." Washington, DC, April 1993.

– – –. "Patterns of Global Terrorism, 1993." Washington, DC, April 1994.

– – –. "Patterns of Global Terrorism, 1994." Washington, DC, April 1995.

– – –. "Patterns of Global Terrorism, 1995." Washington, DC, April 1996.

– – –. "Patterns of Global Terrorism, 1997." Washington, DC, April 1998.

– – –. "Patterns of Global Terrorism, 1998." Washington, DC, April 1999.

"U.S. Temporarily Closes Six Embassies in Africa." Reuters, 24 June 1999.

"Uzbekistan Accuses Taliban Leader and Bin Laden Attempting to Assassinate Its President." *Al-Sharq Al-Awsat,* 8 March 1999.

Vause, John, and Ben Wedeman. "Death Toll Rises in Egypt Tourist Bombings." CNN News, www.CNN.com, 9 October 2004.

Venzke, Ben N. "A Year after Embassy Bombings, the Threat of Terrorism Settles In." *Boston Globe,* 8 August 1999.

"A Verdict against Terrorism." *Washington Post* (Editorial), 30 May 2001, 18.

Vick, Karl. "Assault on a U.S. Embassy: A Plot Both Wide and Deep." *Washington Post,* 23 November 1998.

Vogel, Steve. "Special Forces Sent to Philippines Fight." *Washington Post,* 16 January 2002.

Vollman, William T. "Letter from Afghanistan: Across the Divide." *New Yorker* (15 May 2000).

Wain, Barry. "Allegations of Terror Targets in Singapore Rattle Region." *Wall Street Journal,* 8 January 2002.

Waller, Douglas. "Inside the Hunt for Osama." *Time,* 21 December 1998.

Wallerstein, Immanuel. "Islam, the West, and the World." *Journal of Islamic Studies* 10, no. 2 (May 1999): 109–25.

Wang Gungwu. "Huntington's Clash: II: A Machiavelli for Our Times." *The National Interest* 46 (Winter 1996/97): 69–73.

Wang, James. "Same Battle, New Foe." *Chicago Tribune,* 2 March 2001.

Warsi, Tariq. *Nawa-I Waqt,* 30 December 1998.

"Washington: Progress in Investigation into Destroyer Blast in Aden." *Al-Hayah,* 19 October 2000.

Weaver, Mary Anne. "Blowback," *Atlantic Monthly* (May 1996): 24–28, 36.

— — — "The Real Bin Laden." *New Yorker* (24 January 2000): 32–38.

Wechsler, William F. "Follow the Money." *Foreign Affairs* 80, no. 4 (July/August 2001).

"Weekly Says Bin Laden Financial Manager to Testify." *AFP,* 8 December 1998.

Weiner, Tim. "Blowback from the Afghan Battlefield." *New York Times Magazine,* 13 March 1994.

— — —. "Missile Strikes against Bin Laden Won Him Esteem in Muslim Lands, U.S. Officials Say." *New York Times,* 8 February 1999.

Weiner, Tim, and James Risen. "Long Running Dispute on Sudan Marked Counterattack Plans." *New York Times News Service,* 21 September 1998.

Weir, Fred. "Shifting Tactics in Chechnya." *Christian Science Monitor,* 30 December 2002, 1.

Weiser, Benjamin. "Bin Laden Linked to Embassy Blast by an Ex-Soldier." *New York Times,* 21 October 2000.

— — —. "Papers Shed Light on Informer's Role in Terror Inquiry." *New York Times,* 23 December 2000.

— — —. "Plot to Kill Bin Laden Disclosed." *New York Times,* 21 February 2001.

— — —. "Prosecutors Portray the Strands of a Bin Laden Web of Terror." *New York Times,* 23 January 2000.

— — —. "U.S. May Ask Death Penalty in Bombings." *New York Times,* 9 October 1998.

— — —. "U.S. Says It Can Tie Bin Laden to Embassy Bombings." *New York Times,* 8 October 1998.

Weiser, Benjamin, and James Risen. "The Masking of a Militant: A Special Report." *New York Times,* 1 December 1998.

Welch, David. "The 'Clash of Civilizations' as an Argument and as a Phenomenon." *Security Studies* 6, no. 4 (Summer 1997).

West, Julian. "Atomic Haul Raises Fears of Bin Laden Terror Bomb." *Sunday Telegraph* (Internet version), 23 April 2000.

— — —. "Western Spies Find Bin Laden in Afghanistan." *Sunday Telegraph* (Internet version), 21 March 1999.

"Westerners Killed in Saudi Arabia." BBC News, http://newsvote.bbc.co.uk, 2 May 2004.

Weymouth, Lally, et al. "Pieces of the Puzzle." *Newsweek,* 18 December 2000.

"What Does Israel's Acknowledgment of Possessing Nuclear Weapons Mean?" Al-Jazirah (Editorial), 21 January 2000.

"Will Bin Laden End Up in China? Taliban Makes Afghan Arabs Wage Jihad in Xinjiang." *Al-Watan Al-Arabi,* 23 May 1997.

"Will Bin Laden Strike within Weeks?" *Al-Islah Weekly,* June 1998.

"The Will of Abdullah Azzam, Who Is Poor to His Lord." Azzam Publications Web site at http://panther.netmania.co.uk, April 1986.

Wisgerhop, Amy E. "International Non-state Terrorism and the Translate Paradigm." *Low Intensity Conflict and Law Enforcement* 8, no. 2 (Summer 1999): 58–80.

Woolsey, R. James, and Mansoor Ijaz. "Revenge Is a Dish Best Served Cold." *Los Angeles Times,* 12 September 2001.

"World; Africa: Suspect Bin Laden Associate Arrested." BBC Online Network, 5 March 1999.

"World Front for Fighting the Jews and the Crusaders, Statement No. 4." *Al-Hayah,* 19 August 1998.

"The World Number One Wanted Bin Laden: The Ally Who Became Enemy." *Al-Majallah,* 5 September 1998.

Wright, Robin. "Far Reaching Bin Laden Probe Pays Off." *Los Angeles Times,* 28 August 1998.

— — —. "Invisible War on Terrorism Accelerates Worldwide." *Los Angeles Times,* 7 January 2002.

— — —. "Saudi Dissident a Prime Suspect in Blast." *Los Angeles Times,* 14 August 1998.

Wright, Robin, and Bob Drogin. "New Chapter in Terrorism May Have Begun." *Los Angeles Times,* 13 October 2000.

Yaghi, Subhi. "Bin Laden Said Funding Islamists Fighting Lebanese Army." *Al-Nahar* (Internet version), 5 January 2000.

Yarov, Vladimir. "Fiendishly Precise Calculations. Terrorists Use Simple Bomb to Maximum." *Segodnya,* 10 August 2000.

Yates, Dean. "Criticism Grows of Indonesia Security after Blasts." Reuters, 31 May 2005.

Yemelyarenko, Vladimir. "Ahmed Shah Mas'ud: Afghan War Will End in Pakistan." *Izvestiya,* 2 December 2000.

"You Fight Fire with Fire." *Al-Ansar* (Internet), 14 May 2002.

Young, Hugo. "We Will Not Tolerate the Abuse of Prisoners of War; Guantanamo Could Be Where Europe and America Part Company." *Guardian* (Internet version), 17 January 2002.

Yusufzai, Rahimullah. "A Cult Hero Is Born." *News* (Internet version), 1 September 1998.

— — —. "From the Horse's Mouth." *News* (Internet version), 27 August 1998.

— — —. "In the Way of Allah." *Pakistan* (Internet version), 15 June 1998.

— — —. :Man and Myth." *Newsline* (September 1998).

— — —. "No Reaction from Bin Laden to Death Penalty for His Men in Jordan." *News,* 19 September 2000.

— — —. "Taliban Arab Sources Say Video Telecast on Qatar TV was Fabricated." *News* (Internet version), 25 September 2000.

— — —. "Taliban Hurt by Musharraf's Statement." *News* (Internet version), 6 October 2001.

— — —. "Their Last Sanctuary," *News,* 26 January 1999.

— — —. "World's Most Wanted Terrorist: An Interview with Osama Bin Laden." abcnews.com, 28 December 1998.

Zaatari, M. "No Leads Yet in Probe of Murder in Sidon; American Woman Had Been Warned to Stop Proselytizing." *The Daily Star* (Internet version), 25 November 2002.

Zafar, Mahmud. "Osama Backs Harakatul Ansar against U.S." *Jang,* 20 October 1997.

Zaganjori, Bledar. "Spies of U.S. Embassy Discovered." *Gazeta Shqiptare,* 9 January 1999.

Zakaria, Fareed. "What's Next? — The New Rules of Engagement." *Newsweek,* 31 December 2001–7 January 2002.

Zaydan, Ahmad Muwaffaq. "Amid Conflicting Reports on Expansion of His Current Contacts and Scarcity of His Resources, Washington Is Pursuing Bin Laden's Network in India in Anticipation of a New Strike by Him." *Al-Hayah,* 22 January 1998.

— — —. "Appearing at a Rally in Afghanistan to Support the Leader of the Islamic Group, Bin Laden, al-Zawahiri, and Rifa'i Taha Pledge to Set Umar Abd-al-Rahman Free." *Al-Hayah* (Internet version), 23 September 2000.

— — —. "Bin Laden Fortifies His Position at Jalalabad and Will Respond with SAM and Stinger Missiles." *Al-Wasat Magazine,* 21 February 1999.

— — —. "Bin Laden in Kandahar to Keep Him Away from Media, and 'Out of Concern for His Safety.'" *Al-Hayah,* 8 April 1997.

— — —. "Bin Laden Mediates with Afghan Opposition to Stop Imminent Offensive against Taliban." *Al-Hayah,* 13 March 1998.

— — —. "Bin Laden's Gifts Enable Him to Infiltrate Pakistani Media." *Al-Hayah,* 12 November 1998.

— — —. "Bin Laden Thanks God for U.S. Destroyer Bombing." *Al-Hayah* (Internet version), 4 November 2000.

— — —. "Celebrated His Son's Marriage in Presence of Family Members. Bin Laden Hints at Indirect Role in the Bombing of Destroyer USS *Cole.*" *Al-Hayah,* 1 March 2001.

— — —. "Field Commanders Threaten Taliban They Will Withdraw if Taliban Extradite Bin Laden." *Al-Hayah,* 22 January 2001.

— — —. "Interview with Mustafa Hamza." *Al-Hayah,* 21 April 1996.

— — —. "Pakistan Delivers to Jordan an Islamist Holding U.S. Citizenship." *Al-Hayah* (Internet version), 8 January 2000.

— — —. "350 of Bin Laden's Men Fighting North of Kabul." *Al-Hayah,* 14 July 1997.

Zaydan, Ahmad Muwaffaq, and Turki al-Dahkil. "New U.S. Strike Expected because of Bin Laden." *Al-Hayah,* 21 October 1998.

Zaydan, Ahmad Muwaffaq, and Shafiq al-Asadi. "Information about Nuclear Weapon for Bin Laden from Central Asia." *Al-Hayah,* 6 October 1998.

Zaynah, Abduh. "Al-Zayyat Fears Missing Date for Submitting Ujayzah's Appeal and Renotifies Egypt's Military Prosecutor." *Al-Sharq Al-Awasat,* 12 January 2002.

Zerrouky, Hassane. "Thousands of People Killed in 2000 — The Forgotten of the Concord." *Le Matin* (Internet version), 10 January 2001.

Zia, Sarhardi. "Assassination Attempt on Osama Bin Laden Foiled in Afghanistan. *Muslimedia International* (Internet version), 1 May 1997.

Index

Note on Arabic names: The prefix "al-" has
been retained but ignored for purpose of
alphabetization. "Bin" is treated as a
primary element and appears under B.

Afghanistan. *See also* mujahedin
  Arab Afghan fighters, 110–13, 114–17
  as battlefield for radical groups, 119–21,
    278
  character of Afghans, 23–24, 168–69
  government of, 53–54, 277–78
  jihad, 26, 97–101, 113–17
  reaction to Soviet invasion, 119–21
  Soviet withdrawal from, 110–11, 113
Africa. *See* East Africa
Algeria, 235, 260
Arab Afghan fighters, 110–13, 114–17
Arab-only training camps, 106–10
Atef, Mohammed, 80–81, 102, 177, 244
Azzam, Shaykh Abdullah
  admiration for bin Laden, 109
  bin Laden's admiration for, 109
  death of, 78, 262
  duty of every Muslim, 68, 76
  influence of, 66, 78, 93
  Makhtab al-Khidimat (MAK) founding,
    41, 106
  parting ways with bin Laden, 109

Basayev, Shamil, 67–68
bin Laden, Bakr, 88
bin Laden, Mahrous, 95
bin Laden, Muhammed, 85, 86–88, 94
bin Laden, Osama. *See also* al Qaeda; jihad
  against U.S. and allies

Afghan jihad, lessons from, 97–98, 114–
  17
Afghan jihad activities, 97–101, 303, 305,
  308
Afghanistan, return to, 163–64
Afghanistan activities, 129, 130–31, 155,
  166–67
analogous to historical figures, 5–14,
  205–6, 288–89
anti-American sentiments, 46–50, 94–95
assassination attempts, 156–59, 167
character and personality, 3, 75–81, 105,
  114, 303–5
as cult hero, 25
early years of, 88–89, 93, 94
education of, 79–80, 89, 91–93
family of, 90–91
family origins, 85–86
finances
  bank use, 37–38
  donations to, 38–41
  Islamic NGOs, 40–42
  narcotic trafficking, 43–44
  personal fortune, 31, 35–38
  sources of funding, 31–32, 35
health of, 310
history, understanding of, 46–49, 283–84
influence of, 9, 10–11, 34–35
influence of father on, 88–90
leadership team
  Afghan jihad connections, 101–3
  education of, 80–81
marriages of, 93–94
media's portrait of, xix–xx, 299–303,
  316–21

Pakistan, departure for, 128
philosophy of, 3, 205–6, 316–17
popularity of, 121–23, 127, 164, 303–14
reaction to U.S. troops, 123–27
relationship with mother, 88–89
religious philosophy, 19, 305–6
research on, 315–21
Saudi Arabia, return to, 119, 121–28
sponsorship of, 22–23
Sudan, departure from, 155–59
Sudan activities, 129–30, 132–38
travels, international, 140–41
understanding, obstacles to, 17–30
U.S.-focused policy, 182–88, 231–32, 258–59
violence use by, 7
war with Christendom, 257–58
warfare philosophy, 206–9, 282
bin Mahfouz family, 270
biological weapons, 72–74, 133–34, 197–203, 260
Bosnia, 48, 154, 260
Britain, 263–64, 292, 293, 294–95
Brown, John, 5–7, 9, 11
Bunyan, John, 5, 7–9, 11, 288

casualties
civilian, 207
Egypt, 292
Kashmir, 233
military, 207, 209, 260, 278
Muslims as, 59–60, 71, 73–74
CBRN (chemical, biological, radiological, or nuclear) weapons, 72–74, 133–34, 197–203, 260
chemical weapons, 72–74, 133–34, 197–203, 260
Christian proselytizing, 272–73
civilizations, clash of, 27–29, 272–74, 287
Cole (U.S. destroyer), 7, 85, 215
Crusaders, 4, 24, 46–50, 56, 272
Crusaders war, 209–31
cults, 25

East Africa
al Qaeda expansion, 138–40
embassy bombings, 24, 25, 59, 208–9, 211, 212–13, 311
Egypt, 292
Egyptian Islamic Jihad (EIJ), 181, 182–86, 250–52, 262, 266, 268–69
experts, 20–23, 279–81

al-Fahdli, Tariq, 102–3, 146
France, 263, 264–65

Gama'at al-Islamiyya (IG), 181, 182–86

El-Hage, Wadih, 81, 102, 138, 139–40, 190, 237, 239, 243
HAMAS (Islamic Resistance Movement), 50, 225, 242, 261–62
Hamza, Mustafa, 80, 103, 138, 153, 185, 190
Henry, Patrick, 5, 10
Hizballah, 20, 21, 195–97, 209
Human Concern International (HCI), 42, 152

Ibrahim, Annis, 44
Ibrahim, Dawood, 44
imperial hubris, 25–30
Indonesia, 235–36
insurgencies, 269–70. *See also specific groups*
Iran, 195–97
Iraq, 123–28, 134–37, 194–95
Islam. *See also* Muslims
democracy movement, 114
encompassing nature of, 305–6
history of, 283–85
superiority of, 19
war against, xxi–xxii, 54–57, 272–74
Islamic nongovernmental organizations (NGOs), 40–42, 152, 238
Islamic Resistance Movement (HAMAS), 50, 225, 242, 261–62
Israel, 20, 50, 261–63, 274

Jefferson, Thomas, 5, 9–10
jihad against U.S. and allies
declaration of, 4, 11–13, 46–47, 145
goals of, 4
themes of
betrayal within Muslim world, 50–54
cooperation to attain goals, 57–60
duty of every Muslim, 60–62, 68–71, 76, 80, 269
enemies, 4, 46–50
incitement by bin Laden, 65–68, 75–76
self-defense, 54–57, 72–74
weapons, choices of, 71–74
youth, obligation of, 61–65
jihads
types of, 55
Western perception of, 4–5
Julaidan, Wa'il, 101

Kashmir, 212, 233-35
Kosovo, 48, 260
Kuwait, 123-28

Lebanon, 48, 195
Lincoln, Abraham, 291, 295-97

Makhtab al-Khidimat (MAK), 41-42, 106
martyrdom, 6-7, 33, 68
Masood, Ahmed Shah, 164-66
money, power of, 32-35, 280
Moro Islamic Liberation Front (MILF), 42,
   100, 104, 192-93, 232-33, 249-50
mujahedin. *See also* Afghanistan
   bin Laden assistance to, 103-5
   confidence of, 23, 115
   U.S. aid to, 26, 53-54, 115-16
Musharraf, Pervez, 175, 178-80, 271
Muslim Brotherhood, 92, 281-82
Muslims. *See also* Islam
   as casualties, 59-60, 71, 73-74
   duty to participate in jihad, 60-62, 68-
   71, 76, 80, 269
   foreign policy of U.S., 19-20, 29-30
   media's portrait of, 300-301
   Muslim media's portrait of bin Laden,
   317-19
   patience of, 79-80
   treatment of, by U.S., 252-54
   U.S. education of, 42
Muwaffaq Foundation, 42, 200

narcotic trafficking, 42-44
National Islamic Front (NIF), 129, 132, 137-
   38
nuclear weapons, 72-74, 133-34, 197-203,
   260

oil and natural resources, 51, 52-53
Omar, Mullah Muhammed, 167, 169-74,
   278

Paine, Thomas, 5, 13-14
Pakistan, 174-80
Palestine, 20, 48, 261-62. *See also* HAMAS
Pentagon, 215, 243
Philippines, 191-93, 232-33, 260
Pilgrim's Progress (Bunyan), 8-9, 288-89

al Qaeda. *See also* bin Laden, Osama
   activities, worldwide, 150-55
   attack sites, possible, 265-69, 283-85
   Egyptian Islamic Jihad (EIJ) merger, 252

expansion of, 181-82, 188-89
   in East Africa, 138-40
   Philippines, 191-93
   Somalia, 189-91
formation of, 110
gains for, 209-31, 232-36
Iraq, cooperation with, 134-37
leadership of, 270-71, 287-88
losses and setbacks for, 236-51, 276
losses for targeted governments, 231-32
patience of, 23-25
religious characteristics, 20-21
sponsorship of, 193-97
support for, 137-38, 145, 276
targets of, 259-61
   Britain, 263-64, 292
   Egypt, 292
   France, 263, 264-65
   Israel, 261-63
   United States, 94-95, 182-88, 231-32,
   258-59, 260-61, 271-72, 287-88,
   292-94
Qutb, Mohammed, 92-93

radiological weapons, 72-74, 133-34, 197-
   203, 260
Rahman, Shaykh Omar Abdul, 97, 185-86,
   210
al-Rashidi, Ali-Amin, 102
religion, 19-20
   civilizations, clash of, 27-29, 272-74, 287
   fanaticism, 32-33
Roosevelt, Theodore, 205-6

Salim, Mamdouh Mahmoud, 80-81, 101-2,
   238
al-Saud family
   betrayal of Islamic beliefs, 50-53
   indictments against, 11-12
   relationship with bin Laden family, 87-
   88, 91, 95-96
Saudi Arabia
   betrayal of Islamic beliefs, 50-53, 69
   bin Laden assassination attempts, 156-
   59
   financial support for bin Laden, 39-40
Saudi Bin Laden Group, 85, 86-87, 95
Sea Hawk, 257-58
Services Office, 41, 106
Somalia, 48, 146, 148-49, 152, 189-91
Sudan, 193-94

Taliban movement

activity of, 26
aid from bin Laden, 164, 169–73
denunciation of U.S., 173–74
hosting of bin Laden, 167–70
losses and setbacks for, 277
narcotic trafficking, 42–44
warfare philosophy, 277, 278
Tammiyah, Taqi al-Din Ibn, 92
terrorism
jihads versus, 4–5
states sponsorship of, 21–22
support for networks, 22–23
terrorist, xix–xx
terrorist chiefs, 22–23
training camps
Arab-only camps, 106–7
establishment of, 105–7, 145
funding of, 101, 106, 137
goals of, 106
location of, 137
military curriculum, 141–43

United States
American Revolution, 9–10
attributes of Americans, xix–xxi, 17–18
foreign policy, 19–20, 29–30, 258–59
goals of, 285–86
jihad against (*See* jihad against U.S. and allies)
Muslims, treatment of, 252–54
patience of, 17, 25
response to al Qaeda forces, xxii–xxiii, 278–80, 282–83, 292–95, 311–12
responsibility of Americans, 291, 295–97
support for policies of, 271–72
as target of Islamic groups, 182–88, 231–32
understanding of bin Laden and al Qaeda, xix–xxi, 3–5, 275–76, 278–81, 294–95, 296

Wali Khan Amin Shah, 101, 154
war
Crusaders war, 209–31
against Islam, xxi–xxii, 54–57, 272–74
as obsolete, 18
warfare philosophy of bin Laden, 206–9, 282
warfare philosophy of Taliban, 277, 278
weapons
chemical, biological, radiological, or nuclear (CBRN) weapons, 72–74, 133–34, 197–203, 260

choices of, 71–74
World Islamic Front, 186–88
World Trade Center, 59, 152, 215, 243

Yasin, Shaykh Ahmad, 59, 68, 225
Yemen, 85–86, 122, 137–38, 146, 147–48, 151
Yousef, Ramzi Ahmed, xxii, 81, 152, 154, 320

al-Zawahiri, Ayman, 61–62, 80, 147, 184–86, 187, 215, 249, 251–52, 262–63, 268, 270, 274

About the Author

Bestselling author Michael Scheuer is the former head of the CIA's Bin Laden Unit and has two decades of experience in national security issues related to Afghanistan and South Asia. After resigning from the agency in November 2004, he revealed his authorship of *Imperial Hubris* (Brassey's, Inc., 2004) and *Through Our Enemies' Eyes*, both originally published under the byline "Anonymous." Scheuer has been featured extensively on television, including *Sixty Minutes*, and has been the focus of print media worldwide. He is an adjunct professor of security studies at Georgetown University and a regular contributor to the Jamestown Foundation's *Terrorism Focus* (www.jamestown.org/terrorism). He lives in the Washington, D.C., area.